W9-AYV-895

COMMUNITY PSYCHOLOGY

COMMUNITY PSYCHOLOGY

Values, Research, and Action

by
JULIAN RAPPAPORT

University of Illinois,
Urbana-Champaign

HOLT, RINEHART AND WINSTON
New York   Chicago   San Francisco   Atlanta
Dallas   Montreal   Toronto   London   Sydney

For my father, Louis Joseph Rappaport,
who would have enjoyed knowing that
his memory rests on library shelves;
and for the women he would have loved—
Arlene, Loren, Amy, Joan—and my mother.

Library of Congress Cataloging in Publication Data

Rappaport, Julian.
   Community psychology.

   Bibliography: p. 411
   Includes index.
   1. Community psychology.   I. Title.
RA790.5.R38   362.2 '04 '2   76-55422
ISBN 0-03-006441-4

Copyright © 1977 by Holt, Rinehart and Winston
All rights reserved
Printed in the United States of America
   8 9 0 038 9 8 7 6 5 4 3 2

ACKNOWLEDGMENTS

For permission to reprint from copyrighted materials the author is indebted to the following:

ABT Associates, Inc. for Table 2 in *Pre-trial services: An evaluation of policy related research,* 1974, by J. Mullen. Published by ABT Associates, Inc., under contract NSF-C813 with the Division of Social Systems and Human Resources of the National Science Foundation.

Aldine Publishing Company for Table 2.1, Figures 12.1, 12.2, and 12.3 reprinted by permission from *Community life for the mentally ill* (Chicago: Aldine Publishing Company); by G. W. Fairweather, D. H. Sanders, D. L. Cressler, & H. Maynard. Reprinted by permission from G. W. Fairweather, D. H. Sanders, D. L. Cressler, & H. Maynard. Copyright © 1969 by Aldine Publishing Company.

American Association for the Advancement of Science for Table 1 from ''On being sane in insane places,'' in *Science,* Vol. 179, Jan., 1973, by D. Rosenhan. Copyright 1973 by the American Association for the Advancement of Science.

American Medical Association for Tables 2, 3, and 4 from the *Archives of General Psychiatry,* 1973, *29,* 508 and 510. Copyright 1973, American Medical Association.

American Psychological Association for permission to reprint Figure 1 from *Journal of Personality and Social Psychology,* 1965, *1,* 589–595, by A. Bandura. Copyright 1965 by the American Psychological Association; Figure 1 from *Journal of Comparative and Physiological Psychology,* 1962, *55,* 801–807, by D. Krech, M. R. Rosenzweig, and S. Bennet. Copyright 1962 by the American Psychological Association; Figure 1 from *Journal of Consulting and Clinical Psychology,* 1974, *42,* 471–481, by G. R. Patterson. Copyright 1974 by the American Psychological Association; Table 1 from *Professional Psychology,* 1974, *5,* 42–50, by J. Rappaport and J. M. Chinsky. Copyright 1974 by the American Psychological Association; Figure 1 from *Journal of*

Consulting and Clinical Psychology, 1973, *40*, 99–107, by J. Rappaport, T. Gross, and C. Lepper. Copyright 1973 by the American Psychological Association. Excerpts from "Community psychology, networks, and Mr. Everyman," *American Psychologist,* 1976, *31*, 327–328, by S. B. Sarason. Copyright 1976 by the American Psychological Association; Figure 1 from *Psychological Review,* 1973, *80*, 520, by M. Sashkin, W. C. Morris, and L. Horst. Copyright 1973 by the American Psychological Association; Table 3 from *Journal of Personality and Social Psychology,* 1969, *13*, 278–288, by A. Wicker. Copyright 1969 by the American Psychological Association. All reprinted by permission.

Basic Books for Figure 9-1, "The problem of lower-class culture and poverty-war strategy," Chapter 9, by Lee Rainwater, in *On understanding poverty,* edited by D. P. Moynihan, © 1968, 1969 by the American Academy of Arts and Sciences, Basic Books, Inc., Publishers, New York.

Brunner/Mazel for permission to reprint excerpts from *Disadvantaged child 3: Compensatory education: A national debate,* by J. Hellmuth (Ed.), New York, Brunner/Mazel, 1970.

Columbia University Press for Tables 1 and 2 from J. Rothman, *Social work practice,* 1968, copyright © National Conference on Social Welfare, Columbus, Ohio. New York: Columbia University Press, 1968, pp. 24–25, by permission of the publisher.

Consulting Psychologists Press for Table 2, reproduced by special permission from *The Social Climate Scales: An overview,* by Rudolf H. Moos, Ph.D., copyright 1974, published by the Consulting Psychologists Press.

Field Newspaper Syndicate for permission to reprint an editorial cartoon by John Fischetti. Courtesy of Field Newspaper Syndicate.

Harper & Row, for permission to reprint excerpts from pp. 63, 273–274, in *The manufacture of madness,* by Thomas S. Szasz, M.D. Copyright © 1970 by Thomas S. Szasz, Trustee. Reprinted by permission of Harper & Row, Publishers, Inc.

Johns Hopkins University Press for tables from *Preschool programs for the disadvantaged,* by J. C. Stanley. Copyright © 1972 by the Johns Hopkins University Press; for excerpts from *The right to be different,* by N. Kittrie. Copyright © 1971 by the Johns Hopkins University Press.

Jossey-Bass Publishers for Table 1 from *Social adjustment of young children,* by G. Spivack and M. B. Sure. Copyright © 1974 by Jossey-Bass Publishers.

National Association of Social Workers for Figure 1 from "Child advocacy in the justice system," by W. S. Davidson II and C. A. Rapp. Reprinted with permission of the National Association of Social Workers, from *Social Work,* Vol. 21. No. 3 (May 1976), p. 228.

NTL Institute for Table 1 from "Training police in family crisis intervention," in *The Journal of Applied Behavioral Science,* Vol. 9, No. 1, p. 77, by J. M. Driscoll, R. G. Meyer, and C. F. Schanie. Copyright, NTL Institute, 1973. Reprinted by special permission.

Pergamon Press, Inc. for Table 1 from J. Monahan, *Community Mental Health and the Criminal Justice System.* Copyright © 1976 by Pergamon Press Ltd.

Plenum Publishing Corporation for Table 1 from "The nonprofessional as a psychotherapeutic agent," in *American Journal of Community Psychology,* 1974, *2*, #1, 61–77, by A. E. Karlsruher; for Figure 1 from "The educational pyramid applied to a university setting," in *American Journal of Community Psychology,* 1974, *2*, by J. Rappaport.

Random House, Inc., for excerpts from *Rules for radicals,* by S. D. Alinsky. Copyright © 1972; for excerpts from *Blaming the victim,* by W. Ryan. Copyright © 1972.

Society for the Experimental Analysis of Behavior for Figure 1 from "Modification of social withdrawal through symbolic modeling," in *Journal of Applied Behavior Analysis,* 1969, *2*, by R. D. O'Connor. Copyright 1969.

University of Chicago Press, for excerpts from *The structure of scientific revolutions,* by T. Kuhn. Copyright © 1970 by the University of Chicago Press.

University Park Press for Tables 1 and 4, from *Crisis intervention in the community* by R. K. McGee. Copyright © 1974 University Park Press, Baltimore.

John Wiley & Sons, Inc. for Table 8.11 from *Prison treatment and parole survival* by G. Kassenbaum, D. Ward, & D. Wilner. Copyright © 1971 by John Wiley & Sons, Inc.; for Table 1 from *Community organization and social planning* by R. Perlman and A. Gurin. Copyright © 1972 by John Wiley & Sons, Inc.

Once upon a time there were two brothers who went searching for their identity. They had heard about the scarecrow, the tin man, and the lion who, with a wizard's help, had found themselves. One brother followed the yellow brick road, but the other wandered off the path. When the first brother reached the Wizard, he asked for the ability to establish himself in his own eyes and in those of others.

The Wizard responded, "You already have that ability. All you need are these bricks to build yourself a house, and this paint to write your name upon it for all to see. Then both you and all the world will know who you are."

"You know," he went on, "you remind me of three visitors who came to Oz some years ago. They already had intelligence, courage, and sensitivity, but lacked the means to let themselves and others know about it. So I let them have the physical resources and confidence to make these obvious, and soon everyone acknowledged them."

"What about my brother?" asked the young man. "Will he ever find himself? He has wandered off the yellow brick road, which we all know is the path to Oz."

Thoughtfully the Wizard replied, "There are many paths to Oz. Your brother also has the ability, but he is lacking only someone to tell him he has it, and the means to put it to use. Some will tell him that because he does not have the means he lacks the ability, and they will say that only if he follows their ways and behaves as they wish will he ever obtain the means. Beware of people who speak such benevolence, for that is what the wicked witches and warlocks want us to believe. They have fooled those who offer such help, and even they do not know of the evil results of their apparent benevolence. In the name of good they keep people weak and expecting to fail. Go now and tell your brother, and those who would help him, the truth. Share with him your bricks and paint, but let him build a house of his own."

PREFACE

Belying its placement at the beginning of the text, a preface is often submitted after a book is completed. This affords the author an opportunity to reflect on the manuscript and to comment to his readers. In my case, it has allowed me to understand that this book ends where community psychology should begin. I hope it will be read with this in mind. I offer no panaceas, only the hope that whatever your current status—student, professor, or practicing professional—you will consider the possibility that what seems logical and generates agreement from colleagues and peers is not necessarily "truth." Agreement is often based on shared but unexamined assumptions. I hope that this book will help you to examine some of your assumptions and bring to light some other possibilities. I have tried to draw on a wide range of available information and to bring it together in a conceptually coherent fashion that does not ignore values, research, or action. This book is intended to provide a framework for new directions as well as a framework for continual reexamination and change, rather than to be a reification of "programs."

When I began to write this book, I expected to show how much we already know about the proper directions for dealing with many social problems in education, mental health, and criminal justice. I wanted to show how helpful psychology and social science could be in contributing to a just and humane society. In researching, writing, and thinking out these issues, I became increasingly surprised to discover that many of the problems to which I was addressing myself were ironically and inadvertently created by the so-called helping systems themselves—the institutions and organizations developed by well-meaning scientists and professionals. I found that as providers of "solutions" to social problems, we often create more problems than we solve. This was something I had thought about off and on in my own work, but never really faced until I had to put it all together. It became necessary for me to take a "metaperspective," in which I stepped back from the original concerns and looked more closely at the values and goals of social scientists (both my own and others') as well as the paradigms or models through which we have viewed the issues as we have provided conceptions, data, and programs to create "social good." Once I stepped back and examined my own assumptions nondefensively, my understanding was aided by seeing community psychology as a *search for new paradigms,* a phrase which I hope will become clear to those who read this book.

In saying that the book ends where community psychology should begin, what I am suggesting is that after viewing the current state of affairs in the content areas covered by this volume, I am convinced of several things. Short of rewriting the book in the preface, some of these things are: (1) Professionals and social scientists have often substituted credentials for understanding, and a desire to control for a desire to serve. This observation requires an analysis of issues such as power and powerlessness, cultural relativity, legitimacy of authority, and the conflict between individual liberty and social good. (2) If social scientists and professionals are to be more than agents of social control, maintainers of the status quo, and rationalizers of the current social order, we will need to turn toward a *collaboration* with local community people in their natural environments. (3) Of equal, perhaps even greater, importance than any bit of empirical information, method of analysis, or intervention, are the implicit assumptions we make about people and society, and the values which guide our work in subtle ways. (4) The assumption that we can create a perfect society is an illusion that must be understood as such. The moral of the story of the tower of Babel, in which God tells humanity that heaven on earth (the utopian society) is impossible to achieve, is as true today as it was when the story was written. Social change is a process, not an end-product. (5) Community psychology must avoid professionalization and reification if it is to represent more than another special interest group. (6) In the future, community psychology will need to study, experience, and understand what is missing from this volume: the communities and naturally occurring helping systems that evolve in families, neighborhoods, and social networks in which people find meaning in life and a psychological sense of community. By understanding these systems we may be able to do more to provide alternatives for those who do not "fit in" than by trying to force such people into the existing limited options developed under professional control.

For those who wonder about the "level" of this book, my own experience has been to teach its contents to both graduate and undergraduate students, and to discuss it in seminars with colleagues. I have found that the issues raised are both understandable and meaningful to each of them. It is not so much the case that everyone has agreed with my analysis as that the issues raised are easy to recognize as crucial to the future of a community psychology.

Much of this book belongs to two people to whom I have been closest for my entire adult life. The first is my wife Arlene, who spent hour after hour listening to me read through notes and helping to clarify my often "fuzzy" writing. Without her devotion this book could not have been written. She not only helped me to think it through, but protected me from the daily temptations of family and friends. To her I am forever grateful, not just for her contribution to this book, but for her love and companionship.

The second person to whom this book belongs is my friend and colleague, Edward Seidman. So many of his thoughts are intertwined with my own that it is only his modesty that prevents this from being a co-authored volume. Ed has not only influenced the content of this work, but throughout its preparation he willingly assumed more than his share of our mutual responsibilities as co-principal investigators on a large and long-term research project.

I am also grateful for what I have learned from my colleagues, Thom Moore and Stephen Golding, and from several former and present students, particularly William Davidson, Ronald Roesch, Melvin Wilson, Jean Ann Linney, Phil Berck, Tod Gross, and Judy Kramer, as well as Ellen Becker, who probably does not even realize how much she influenced me. I am thankful to a great many other students whom I have had the privilege of learning from at the University of Illinois. In addition, several community people have taught me a great deal, the most important of whom are Alonzo Mitchell, a man whose talents have constantly left me in awe, and Ronald Simkins, a friend whose gifts are valued by all who know him, and who helped me to complete this manuscript when I was not sure that I would.

Although I am primarily responsible for what is presented here, I would also like to thank Richard Price of the University of Michigan, and both Marian MacDonald and Jerome L. Singer, two reviewers who have saved me much embarrassment by providing comments on the original manuscript, as well as Kathleen Nevils of Holt, Rinehart and Winston for shepherding it through its final stages.

Most of the typing as well as many helpful editorial suggestions came from the efforts of Linda Reaville and Yuki Llewellyn. I am grateful for their talents and for the help in indexing and referencing provided by Guy Desaulniers and Nance Leonard.

The largest portion of this book was written while I was on a sabbatical leave from the University of Illinois. To the University and to the ancient Jewish tradition of the sabbatical, which decrees that every seventh year the fields are to be left untilled, I am grateful. I am also grateful to the foresight of James McKeen Cattell and to the trustees of the Cattell Fund for the sabbatical award, which enabled me to take the time to write this book. I hope I have justified their confidence in me.

December 1976   *J. R.*
San Diego, Ca. and
Champaign, Ill.

CONTENTS

I

WHAT IS COMMUNITY PSYCHOLOGY AND WHERE DOES IT COME FROM?

Community 1. a social group of any size whose members reside in a specific locality, share government, and have a common cultural and historical heritage. 2. a social group sharing common characteristics or interests and perceived or perceiving itself as distinct in some respect from the larger society within which it exists (usually prec. by *the*): the business community; the community of scholars. 3. *Eccles.* a group of men or women leading a common life according to a rule. 4. *Ecol.* an assemblage of plant and animal populations occupying a given area. 5. joint possession, enjoyment, liability, etc.: community of property. 6. similar interests. 7. *the community,* the public; society: We must consider the needs of the community.

—*Random House Dictionary of the English Language*

What Is Community Psychology?

Community and psychology—brought together these two words form an almost paradoxical phrase. Community refers to a social group; psychology refers to the individual. Community psychology is by definition involved in the classic conflict between individuals and social groups. Men and women appear to thrive in social groups, but when the group becomes large and single-minded, taking under its authority many different people, there is a tendency to discourage individual differences. Will Durant, writing about the origins of the state, observed that "Every state begins in compulsion; but the habits of obedience become the content of conscience, and soon every citizen thrills with loyalty to the flag" (Durant, 1954, p. 24). More generally, the same may be said for the effects of socialization. But what of the person who does not fit in? What of the marginal people who are not socialized to the norm? What of the minority and cultural subgroups of society? What of those who are different, for whatever reason, be it by choice or as a function of social process? The usual view of such people is that they are abnormal in the negative sense, and

suffer from some sort of personal weakness or deficit.

Explanations for social deviance have differed from time to time. Currently, difference is sometimes viewed as inherent in the person's biological makeup, sometimes as a function of learned beliefs and behaviors, sometimes a result of current environmental forces. Regardless of the suspected etiology, often, as in the "helping professions," our aim has been to adjust marginal people to the norm. Community psychology is, in part, an attempt to find other alternatives for dealing with deviance from societal-based norms. What is sought is an approach that avoids labeling differences as necessarily negative or as requiring social control. Community psychology viewed in this way is an attempt to support every person's right to be different without risk of suffering material and psychological sanctions.

Can individual liberty be reconciled with the legitimate concerns of the larger community? Can a large society maintain respect for individual differences and at the same time provide a social systems network that makes the re-

1

sources for health, education, and welfare available to all its citizens? The underlying assumption for a community psychology is that such questions can be answered in the affirmative. It does not follow that community psychology alone can accomplish this, but it does follow that community psychology can be consistent with this aim, and therefore can be a part of its accomplishment. This is the optimism of community psychology.

Implied in the above paragraphs is the view that *if people have a right to be different, then they also have a right to be the same*. Being the same requires access to the resources of the society in which one lives. It follows then that community psychology is concerned with the right of all people to obtain the material, educational, and psychological resources available in their society. In this regard community psychology is a kind of reform movement within the larger field of applied psychology, and its adherents have advocated more equitable distribution of the resources that psychology and the "helping professionals" control. Once again, the reforms are not a panacea for all the inequities of society, but they are aimed in a direction that is consistent with the view of man and society presented above.

Community psychology has many formal definitions. Some of them are presented in this book. None of them are completely satisfactory. Because community psychology emerged out of a concern with the mental health problems of society which had most recently been viewed as almost totally intrapsychic, many definitions now emphasize a new concern with environmental factors as contributing to problems in living, or mental health.[1] As we shall see when we review the conceptions and applications of recent years, concerns which simply focus on "mental health" are now too limited as an accurate description of the activities of community

psychologists. Likewise, an emphasis on environmental factors as a defining aspect of community psychology is simply too general to be useful. Such an emphasis is characteristic of much of modern psychology.

In this book the views of many different writers will be presented, but there is one theme that will emerge. This theme is actually a perspective rather than a formal theory or a definition of community psychology, and its predominant characteristic is that of a search for new paradigms, for new ways of understanding *and* of doing. Within this general theme the outlines of a new paradigm, a new perspective, are emerging. *The defining aspects of the perspective are cultural relativity, diversity, and ecology: the fit between persons and environments.*

An ecological viewpoint, which borrows terminology from fields other than psychology, includes more than an emphasis on person–environment fit, but that phrase captures an important aspect of the orientation. The term *ecology* has been used by many writers, both in psychology and other disciplines, who do not always mean the same thing. Originating in biology and coming to social science through sociology, it has been used in psychology in various contexts. The details of the viewpoint are spelled out more directly in other parts of this book and especially in Chapter V, but it may be useful to anticipate some of the general points to be made:

1. For the present, the ecological viewpoint should be regarded as an orientation emphasizing *relationships* among persons and their social and physical environment. Conceptually the term implies that there are neither inadequate persons nor inadequate environments, but rather that the fit between persons and environments may be in relative accord or discord (Kelly, 1969; Murrell, 1973).

2. In terms of *action* the ecological viewpoint will emphasize, in this volume, creation of alternatives by locating and developing existing resources and strengths, rather than by

---

[1]See, for example, the definition offered by Zax and Specter (1974): "Community psychology is regarded as an approach to human behavior problems that emphasizes contributions made to their development by environmental forces as well as the potential contributions to be made toward their alleviation by the use of these forces."

looking for weaknesses of people and/or communities.

3. In *value terms* an ecological viewpoint implies that differences among people and communities may be desirable, and that the resources of society should not be allocated on the basis of a single standard of competence. All of the above suggests a value system based on cultural relativity and diversity.

Here a cautionary note must be sounded. Often the activities of psychologists, including some community psychologists, have not followed from a perspective of cultural relativity, diversity, and ecology, and in some ways it is presumptuous to call these the defining themes of the field. What is intended here is to make this point: Community psychology will need to adopt such a perspective if it is to be more than an enforcing arm of a single set of standards as the only way to obtain the resources of society. Throughout this book the case for the value of this perspective will be made. In each of the content areas reviewed, the need for a culturally relativistic viewpoint, which accepts the value of human diversity and the right of people to choose their own goals and life-styles while still maintaining their fair share of society's material and psychological resources, is emphasized. In each case we shall examine the dominant psychological paradigm for viewing man, and argue that an ecological perspective, focusing on the match or "fit" between persons and environments, rather than on "fixing up" those who are seen as inferior, or trying to make all people the same by controlling their environments, is the most sensible perspective for a psychology of the community.

In this book the meaning of community is best represented by the second definition cited in this chapter heading. Particularly emphasized is the idea that a community is a subgroup within society, which is perceived or perceives itself as distinct in some respects from the larger society. More specifically, community psychology is concerned with the well-being of many different subcommunities within the larger social order. It is virtually impossible to have a large society made up of diverse individuals and subgroups

without accepting the fact of social conflict. Consequently, if such conflicts are to be resolved by non-violent means, then political activity is a necessary fact, and everyone, including the social scientists, be it out of choice or circumstance, is on one side or another. "The fundamental conflicts of human life are not between competing ideas, one 'true' and the other 'false'—but rather between those who hold power and use it to oppress others, and those who are oppressed by power and seek to free themselves of it" (Szasz, 1970, p. 63). That is the pessimism of community psychology.

Community psychology is interested in social change, particularly in those systems of society where psychologists are active participants. Change in society involves relationships among its component parts, encompassing those of individuals to social systems such as schools, hospitals, and courts, as well as to other individuals. Change toward a maximally equitable distribution of psychological as well as material resources is sought. That goal is clearly an expression of a set of values that follows from the perspective of cultural relativity, support for diversity, and an ecological view of man. The process is open-ended, however, for the goal can never be completely accomplished, and social change will always be necessary. Today's solutions will become tomorrow's problems—this is the reality of community psychology.

What is the place of psychological science in the pursuit of such values? That is the subject of this book, but at the outset some crucial points should be made clear. In its broadest sense, community psychology is concerned with the application of social science to both persons and environments. Its history lies in the applied traditions of medicine, particularly psychiatry, and in psychology, social work, and education. These are the human service fields, and basic to any definition of community psychology is an emphasis on development of human resources. Despite the fact that in their most recent past psychiatry, clinical psychology, and social work have focused on the intrapsychic problems of individuals, there is no break with earlier tradition when community psychology emphasizes the social environment rather than intrapsychic factors as a determinant of human well-being. That idea has been influential in psychiatry at least as early as the eighteenth century (Rosen, 1959); nor, today, is that idea unique to community psychology.

A second emphasis of community psychology, however, is the belief that traditional ways of developing human resources, which rely on individual clients finding their way into the service or social control network after they are already in difficulty, are not an efficient, effective, or equitable way to function. Rather, community psychology favors bringing services, or preferably resources, directly to the local community and to those individuals in need; or preventing difficulties prior to their onset by creating change in the various social systems of society that are theoretically implicated as causes of difficulty for community members. This brings community psychology into the political as well as the human resources realm. Although there are now attempts to broaden the theoretical and conceptual base of community psychology so as to include various sociological and political-economic lines of thought more consistent with a community, rather than an individual view of man, these academic disciplines do not have a tradition of intervention. At its essence community psychology requires application as well as analysis. If the analysis leads to political action, so must the activities of the community psychologist. Conceptualization is common, new theory is sought after, new viewpoints are developed; but no one defines herself or himself as a community psychologist unless involved in some form of social intervention. There are also attempts to bring law and urban planning into community psychology because of their history of involvement in the real world, but these disciplines are not based on a tradition of empirical research, and community psychology is as much founded on a tradition of research as one of action. Community psychologists view themselves as scientists, albeit applied scientists, and here the ecological view of human behavior begins to take on importance as a scientific-psychological approach that is not inconsistent with the values of cultural relativity and diversity.

There are a number of other characteristics that help to define community psychology, and

many of these are presented by example throughout this book. For the purpose of an introduction to the assumptions under which community psychology operates, the emphasis of self-identification with developing human resources, sometimes requiring political involvement as well as science, is most important. *It is these three frequently conflicting sets of concerns in which community psychology resides: human resource development, political activity, and science.* Viewed through a perspective respectful of human diversity, cultural relativity, and ecology, community psychology is potentially a contributing force for social change.

The comfortable combination of human resource development, a willingness to engage in the political activity necessary to implement new programs or to encourage social change, and a belief in science, is not easy to accomplish. Advocates of each of these approaches to the world are normally quite critical of one another. The helping professions and agents of social control are necessarily concerned with individual here-and-now problems and actions of clients, patients, or deviants. Their aim is to reduce individual discomfort and deviance, and to maintain the social order.

Political activists, regardless of their preference for maintenance of the status quo or for change toward more or less social control, are frequently critical of the helping professionals and agents of control as concerned with "band-aid" symptomatic approaches rather than underlying problematic policies and systems. The professional service deliverers are critical of the political activists as unprofessional and unconcerned with real problems of human misery and human need. Both are critical of the social scientist as a sheltered, ivory-tower academic. Scientists are in turn critical of political activists and helping professionals who are seen as operating on the basis of unproven hypotheses, ineffective methods of unproven value, and poorly conceptualized strategies.

All three of these rivals compete for public respect, sanction, and money. For community psychology to try to bring these competing concerns together in a single movement creates a number of advantages as well as difficulties. To satisfy all of these aims simultaneously is virtually impossible. The individual community psychologist then must be flexible enough not only to move from one approach to the other as the situation requires, but also be prepared to deal with legitimate concerns about the particular aspect ignored at any moment in time. *As a discipline, however, community psychology must ultimately accept responsibility for human resource development, political activity, and scientific method.*

Despite the traditional antagonism between advocates of these three value systems they may not really be so different as appears on the surface. Bringing them together has the advantage of revealing not only new perspectives through which to view their common concern—the well-being of man and society—but also showing how their advocates can help, rather than attack each other.

In order to facilitate communication among these three potentially powerful allies it is important for their adherents to recognize a mutual need. New scientific information cannot be useful unless it is implemented, and it cannot be implemented without the existence of various forms of political activity and competent people who use the information. The value of services provided or systems implemented cannot be assessed or improved without the use of scientific method in the field and in the laboratory. The new information in turn cannot be used without further political activity, competent professional implementers, and so on. The traditional method of diffusing scientific information by publication in professional journals is often so slow in dissemination as to be useless, or not effective at all (Fairweather, Sanders, & Tornatzky, 1974).

Community psychology takes three elements—science, human resource development, and politics—and tries to facilitate their interaction to not only mutual advantage, but to the advantage of the larger community and its many subcommunities. To begin, then, it is useful to recognize that science, politics, and development of resources are not necessarily so independent of each other as first appears. Each is influenced by social and historical forces, and adherents of each are subject to personal values and beliefs that mediate these forces. To under-

stand this as something to make explicit rather than hide under the guise of objective and absolute truth is as important for social science as for politics. The problems of human living and social well-being are simply not independent of social forces and values, which change over time. This argument will be pursued in detail in Chapter II.

The remainder of this chapter is divided into four sections. The first is a sequential presentation of some historical events that have led to community psychology. This will provide some sense of how we got to where we are, although it will necessarily be schematic and appear more linear than it really has been. The second section develops the first by discussing how important social-political activities in the 1960s have influenced community psychology. The third section is a discussion of the importance of psychological paradigms for the activities of the applied psychologist, and explains the reason why community psychology is presented in this book as a search for new paradigms. The final section details the values implied by a psychology based on cultural relativity, ecology, and diversity.

A Chronology of Events Leading to Community Psychology

Comunity psychology is, then, a direct product of our attempt to deal with the behavior of those individuals who do not fit into society. In a sense it is a history of the attempt to deal with marginal people who either reject or are rejected by society. Although there have been influences from the study of psychology as it relates to "everyman," these influences are fragmentary and peripheral to the mainstream of historical development. The roots of community psychology are in clinical psychology, which in turn is rooted in psychiatry—a medical specialty aimed at the diagnosis and treatment of "abnormal" behavior. To be sure, clinical psychology is also rooted in the academic study of human behavior and the study of individual differences, but its special emphasis has always been the abnormal, the so-called "pathological," and the deviant.

Historical accounts of the attempt by Western civilization to deal with deviance usually begin with the observation that in earlier times bizarre behavior was considered to be an indication of demonic possession. From Hippocrates (circa 377 B.C.) to Galen (circa A.D. 200) early Greek and Roman thought viewed disorders of the mind as appropriate for scientific-medical study. This is contrasted with both the prehistory of not dealing with such problems at all (other than to consider them sacred, mysterious, and spiritual) and the dark ages of medicine following Galen (Zilboorg, 1941). The decline of the medical study of deviance is directly related to the rise of Christianity as a secular power, such that the Middle Ages are characterized by an increasing relationship between deviance and devils. If the deviants were not considered possessed they were considered criminals, and treated either to prison or exorcism. There are numerous accounts of earlier cruel and unusual punishments, and the occasional physician who cried out against such practices—men like Paracelsus, Agrippa, Vives, and Johann Weyer are dramatically portrayed in Zilboorg's *History of Medical Psychology* (1941) as voices of humanitarian scientists in times of superstition. The publication of *Malleus Maleficarum*, a late fifteenth-century text on the diagnosis and treatment of witchcraft, was the culmination of the theory of demonology. Endorsed by Pope Innocent VIII as a means of ridding the world of heresy, and later by the Faculty of Theology at the University of Cologne, and Maximilian, the King of Rome, this became the textbook of the Inquisition. Written by two Dominican Brothers, Johann Sprenger and Heinrich Kraemer, it deals with three things: the existence of witchcraft, its diagnosis, and its treatment. Those who denied witchcraft were themselves guilty of heresy, a fact that leads some (Szasz, 1970) to compare such reasoning with the present-day practice of psychiatry, which sometimes causes those who are called mentally ill but deny it to be labeled "insane" by virtue of their own denial.[2]

The advancement of medical psychology in the eighteenth and early nineteenth centuries is represented in France by the efforts of men like Philippe Pinel, who is credited with unchaining the emotionally disturbed and giving them humane hospital care. Another story of which modern psychiatry is equally proud is of the New World's Benjamin Rush (1745–1815), who founded American psychiatry and perpetuated the idea that emotional disorder is an illness. Ironically, much of the treatment prescribed by such medical men was not so different in kind from the earlier cruelty. Bloodletting, dunking in vats of water, and intimidation were commonly prescribed. At the same time, a brief period of what is known as moral treatment developed in America. Owing its philosophy to Pinel's example, this means of treatment relied on small-group institutional care for the insane, a treatment that was feasible because the population density was low, and mental illness was not considered a major social problem.

Colonial American communities tended to care for their own deviants without the need for special places to house them. When confinement did begin it was not so much a function of medical advances (Grobb, 1973) as it was of the need to change social welfare policies as the population of the cities grew. At first the institutions were undifferentiated and cared for any kind of helpless indigent member of the community. The first institution in America to devote itself exclusively to care of the sick and the mentally ill was the Pennsylvania Hospital in Philadelphia, established in the 1750s. At first the hospital's regulations limited its use to the "curable;" its population was quite small, and it housed both the wealthy and the poor. By the beginning of the nineteenth century, as the growth of the urban population increased, so did the popula-

---

[2]The history of bigotry, prejudice, and cultural bias found in the story of Sprenger and Kraemer is one that psychiatric historians look back on with a sense of superiority. There is heavy irony in comparing these two statements by Zilboorg (1941): ". . . despite our conviction of being right, a future

Galileo or Newton of psychiatry will find it necessary to judge us . . . as we ourselves judge [earlier] prejudices . . . " (pp. 511–512). This he writes, having earlier described Sprenger and Kraemer as "methodical and persistent Germans" (p. 147). Perhaps this is not surprising for a psychiatric historian educated in Russia and the United States and writing in the 1940s. It does, however, serve as a reminder that even the critics of bigotry and advocates of science are subject to cultural bias, values, and personal beliefs.

tion of institutions. Funds became increasingly more difficult to obtain, and public and private facilities became separated. The moral treatment methods of Pinel and Rush were largely limited to the people of financial means who were seen to benefit from humane but disciplined interaction with the physicians of their own social class. More a social philosophy than a medically based treatment, it was destined to disappear as the size and nature of hospital populations changed.

By the time that Dorothea L. Dix would campaign in the mid-1800s for the release of mental patients from jails, and before a nation-wide system of public mental hospitals could be instituted, both the number and the kind of patients had changed drastically. As the number of immigrants to the United States increased, so did the numbers of poor and foreign-born in the mental hospitals. Increasing costs, economic inflation, and loss of public support led hospitals to adopt a gradual change from a treatment orientation to a business administration philosophy, and by the 1860s the typical American psychiatric journal was more a business management publication than a clinical or scientific journal. With the decline of treatment and the increase of custodial care came a corresponding decline in discharges and the resultant accumulation of chronic patients (Rappaport, Chinsky, & Cowen, 1971). From the end of the nineteenth century through the present day, the history of mental hospitals has been a cyclical one of exposé and reform followed by a return to previous conditions of stagnation and deterioration (Rappaport & Chinsky, 1974).

In 1908 Clifford Beers published a book called *The Mind that Found Itself*, which told of his experiences as a hospitalized mental patient. This book was a stimulus for the mental hygiene movement in America, and later led to the formation of the National Committee for Mental Health, which quickly became concerned with proper medical examination of immigrants and with the expansion of state responsibility in the care of mental patients. Today the Committee's offspring, the National Association for Mental Health, publishes a journal, *Mental Hygiene,* and works largely in the area of public education. "Ring the bell for mental health" is their most frequently heard slogan. Despite continuous reforms, the public mental hospitals to this day create more problems than they solve.

Goffman (1961) and Kesey (1962), one as a sociologist and the other as a novelist, have perhaps the best descriptions of the ways in which mental institutions have created what Goffman (1961) calls "institutionalism." This refers to the kind of behavior among inmates that enables them to withdraw into themselves, fit into the routine of a custodial hospital, and avoid the experiences necessary to function in the outside world. Clearly the system of mental hospitals has failed as a means for solving the problems of emotional disturbance. Currently they serve a social function only as places to put those with whom we do not know how to deal, and who are therefore deemed incompetent to function on their own. In other words, hospitals remove such people from public view . . . and public conscience. It is partly out of unhappiness with this state of affairs that community psychology has grown, first as community mental health and later as community psychology per se. More about the relationship between community mental health and community psychology will be said in Chapter III.

In the first half of this century psychiatry was greatly influenced by Sigmund Freud. Today his ideas are so pervasive as to constitute the popular beliefs about human psychology. Everyone knows about the unconscious and repression of early infantile sexuality. Individual psychodynamic psychotherapy has become the preferred means of treatment for emotional problems. In private practice, and in outpatient public practice, psychotherapy is sold or given away to thousands of people each year. Variants of psychoanalysis and a long list of "humanistic" conceptions of psychotheraphy (the most influential being those directly or indirectly derived from Carl Rogers' client-centered approach) have joined a diverse treatment armamentarium. Therapies now include methods of individual treatment that reject Freud and honor B. F. Skinner or other "behaviorists," who are more concerned with overt rather than covert behavior. There are other variants of psychotheraphy as well, but what they all have in common is a professional talking as an expert to a client, usually in the expert's office, about the client's personal problems and about ways to view the problems or things to do about them.

The effectiveness of these means of individual treatment, a complicated issue in its own right, requires a volume to itself in order to be judged fairly, and is at best controversial. A general conclusion that might be agreed upon is something like the following: Taken as a whole, the effectiveness of psychotherapy cannot really be judged. There are too many different kinds of therapy and too many different kinds of people doing it and receiving it. A better question asks what works best, for whom, and under what conditions (Kiesler, 1966, 1971; Paul, 1969a). The idea that we need to consider therapist variables, client variables, and treatment variables, is widely accepted (Bergin & Garfield, 1971; Meltzoff & Kornreich, 1970). The idea that what may help some may hurt others is also commonly recognized, such that evaluations of outcome based on a large number of clients whose improvement scores on some criteria are lumped together is questioned in favor of an individual analysis of each client (Bergin, 1966; Sidman, 1960). Although these arguments certainly lead to important research concerning individual psychotherapy, others argue that psychotherapy is at least not yet of such proven value as to justify its support as the major mode of treatment advocated by the mental health professions. This argument is a second influence on the development of community psychology.

Even if psychotherapy were 100 percent effective, some argue that the demand for treatment and the need for mental health professionals are so great as to make training of adequate numbers of professionals virtually impossible (Albee, 1959; Arnhoff, Rubinstein, & Speisman, 1969). That is, training psychotherapists takes 4 to 8 years of graduate education and frequently involves training in the skills of medicine or research not directly relevant to psychotherapy. Only at that point can professionals then treat individual patients on a one-to-one basis, after the clients already have severe problems, and after the patients manage to find their way to a therapist. Certainly it is an inefficient delivery system for mental health

care. Others argue that the reach of services is so limited to young, adult, verbal, intelligent, successful, white, middle-class, urban people as to be useless as a solution for those most in need (Cowen, Gardner, & Zax, 1967). Schofield (1964), among others, has distinguished between demand for services and need. Although the former is easy to assess by looking at the number of people who request services, the latter is more difficult to define. Many estimate need for services to be as much as six to twenty times the expressed demand (Nichols, 1963). Mental health professionals doing psychotherapy can never hope to have enough manpower to meet the demand, let alone the need for services. This line of reasoning is a third influence on the development of community psychology. It has led to a widespread use of "nonprofessional" mental health workers.

Nonprofessionals as mental health workers have a long history in America, although it is one that was forgotten as mental health work became a profession early in this century. In the first third of the century there were at least two related developments of importance to the history of the helping professions: the settlement house movement, which was developed by those interested in socialization of immigrants to America; and the child guidance movement, which was concerned with child-rearing practices and family adjustment. Both movements were influential in the development of social work as a profession (Levine & Levine, 1970; see Chapter II, p. 47). The settlement house movement, which provided social services of various kinds offered by volunteer nonprofessional help-givers, was peopled by workers who literally moved into the neighborhoods of immigrant target populations. This movement is most important as an example of an early attempt to deal with the social adjustment of nonmainstream American subculture by means of direct participation in the political and social processes that make up the psychological environment. Despite this early beginning, social work, which grew out of this movement into a profession, quickly became, like psychiatry in America, psychoanalytic and oriented toward individual psychotherapy and casework. It was not until the 1960s, for largely political reasons, with a few scattered exceptions along the way, that many of the early ideas of the settlement house movement were to reemerge in social work and psychology as well. We shall take up this reemergence shortly.

Professional Psychology

Psychology in the meantime was following other directions. Experimental psychology developed out of physiology and philosophy. Those who were interested in applied psychology early in this century were heavily influenced by the psychometric tradition and the study of individual differences. As we shall see, this usually meant comparison of individuals in a rank-order fashion based on a set of criteria of the ideal man.

Francis Galton, the English psychometrician and advocate of eugenics, is among the early founders of the psychometric approach. In America it was the psychology of James McKeen Cattell that began the tradition. In both places it owed its philosophy to Darwin. Here in the study of individual differences was the perfect combination of laboratory measurement methods developed in the German physiological tradition and philosophical ideas concerning how man "ought" to be. America was the ideal place for Darwin's theory of evolution to take hold. The half-myth–half-truth of the opportunity to conquer new frontiers and win new fortunes for those who were strong enough in a new country, regardless of prior social position, fit with the notion of natural selection as it became interpreted by social darwinism. People differed in their natural abilities, and these abilities, in a society supposedly free of hereditary social position, determined one's success in society. Consequently, the abilities that were important for success were obviously those held by successful people. That the society's choice to reward some abilities as opposed to others was socially determined, as opposed to being a fact of the "nature of man," eluded its adherents. People differ in their "natural" abilities, and psychologists now believed that they could measure these abilities.

Cattell, credited by Boring (1950) in his *History of Experimental Psychology* with the entrepreneurial skills necessary for the widespread development of American academic psychology, was an important figure in the founding of what is called the "functional" school of psychology, the forerunner of behaviorism. Boring (1950) defined a functionalist, as opposed to a "structuralist," as one interested in more than description—one who asks "why," one who is interested in prediction and causality, and one who is concerned about the future. Applied psychology is necessarily functional because it is concerned with future success in living. This kind of psychology developed out of the psychometric tradition and led to the functional "tools" of applied psychology: child psychology, educational psychology, and the mental tests (Boring, 1950). It ultimately led to clinical and community psychology as well. Such a psychology is, as Boring (1950) notes, the perfect American psychology. It adapts to the *zeitgeist* or the temper of the times. It is concerned with being useful. How it is used is probably more determined by the political, moral, and ethical beliefs of the day than the state of psychological knowledge, because the essence of such a psychology is pragmatism. It can be used for implementing social policies while appearing to be scientifically objective. For example, one can test or train toward any criterion valued by a society. In so doing the tester uses scientific methods but need not question the criterion for competence, so long as it is agreed upon by the larger society.

Cattell's students, among them Robert S. Woodworth and Edward L. Thorndike, were the early leaders of a functional psychology that led to the establishment of psychologists as "mental test" experts, a name coined by Cattell. The testing movement, as Boring (1950) describes it, was a progression of ideas moving from Galton in the 1880s to Cattell in the 1890s and Alfred Binet in the 1900s. Here is a good example of its pragmatism. Binet developed his IQ test for the French government in order to identify children who were "feeble-minded" and provide them with special instruction. In America that test and others derived from it have been used to limit immigration of undesirables; to justify limiting educational opportunity for those who are labeled, at a very early age, to be incapable of learning; to isolate people in institutions; and to justify a number of other similar "social welfare" policies. By 1910 G. M. Whipple had published a *Manual of Mental and Physical Tests* that included over fifty of them.

Parallel with the testing movement was the development of educational psychology under G. Stanley Hall, who applied a psychological interpretation of Darwin's ideas about evolution to individual development, and who perhaps more than any other American can be credited, quite literally, with bringing Freud to America. Hall's work was important in the establishment of a professional foundation for educational psychology through his legitimization of applied work with children and adolescents. Although William James and John Dewey were the philosophers of the soon-to-emerge functional school of American psychology, it was E. L. Thorndike, whose publications on *Educational Psychology* in 1903 and *Mental and Social Measurement* in 1904 tied together the academic study of individual differences and the emerging educational psychology fostered by G. S. Hall. From Hall there was encouragement for psychologists to engage in the real world of applied child psychology and education. From Thorndike there was the means to apply the thinking of psychometrics to educational matters. That Hall and the psychometricians believed in social darwinism is not to be forgotten if we are to understand today's psychometric tradition. The psychology of individual differences often ignores this fact, and by accepting established, current, socially defined criteria as the only legitimate bases for the study of differences among people, psychometry often implicitly supports the status quo rather than the psychology of social change and awareness of philosophical assumptions that John Dewey preached. Community psychologists interested in social change must be aware of this fact in their traditions.

After Binet developed his intelligence test in France it was a Hall student, Henry H. Goddard, who introduced it to America and established

psychologists as experts on the "feeble-minded." This work was carried on by Edgar Doll, Goddard's successor at the Vineland Training School in New Jersey. Although Goddard was also an important figure in the use of mental tests to screen out "undesirable" European immigrants, it was the work of Lewis Terman, through his revisions of the Binet scale in 1916 and again in 1937, which spread the intelligence testing movement among American psychologists.

Although all of the individuals named here, and many others, were important to applied American psychology, it was a social-political event—World War I—which, by creating a perceived necessity, fostered widespread acceptance for the use of mental tests. Faced with the need to classify a large number of recruits for appropriate jobs, and to eliminate the intellectually incompetent, the Army Group Tests of Intelligence were developed and refined under the leadership of heretofore experimental psychologists such as Robert Yerkes and Carl Brigham. Now applied psychology began to gain acceptance in the public mind, an acceptance that would later lead to other uses for such tests (see Chapter II, pp. 32–33). Such an impact on the nation's view of psychology, and its subsequent growth, would not be seen again until World War II.

Until the Second World War, clinical psychologists outside the psychometric tradition worked primarily with problems of childhood. In 1896 Lightner Witmer opened the first psychological clinic at the University of Pennsylvania in Philadelphia. Witmer's clinic was primarily concerned with children's neurological and intellectual problems, rather than social adjustment. Historians of clinical psychology (Reisman, 1966; Watson, 1953) credit this clinic with less influence on the subsequent development of clinical psychology than the one later opened in 1909 in Chicago. William Healy, a psychiatrist, and Grace Fernald, a psychologist, opened the Juvenile Psychopathic Institute, primarily concerned with social adjustment and juvenile delinquency. Influenced by Freud's psychodynamic psychology, their approach is credited with leading to the child guidance movement and the establishment of other similar clinics. The child guidance movement was fostered by the National Committee for Mental Hygiene, which had been stimulated by Clifford Beers' book, and was supported by the renowned psychiatrist, Aldoph Meyer, and the Harvard psychologist, William James. The child guidance movement boomed in the 1920s, along with the organization of the "team" approach to treatment, which combined the skills of psychiatrist, psychologist, and social worker, and focused on the child–school and child–family relationship. Even here, however, the psychologist was basically a testing specialist who worked in schools and with handicapped children.

Psychologists who worked with adults later began to develop tools for the measurement of personality as well as intelligence. As psychodynamic psychology took hold of psychiatry psychologists began to use Rorschach's inkblots as a diagnostic testing instrument, and were influenced by L. K. Frank's (1939) projective hypothesis, as well as various "objective" tests of personality. They became expert diagnosticians in the mental health movement. The validity of such diagnosis is beyond the scope of this book, but, as with psychotherapy, it is controversial at best.

In the first third of the century clinical psychology as a profession was both small and isolated from the mainstream of academic psychology. In 1917 Leta S. Hollingworth organized a group within the American Psychological Association (APA) interested in psychology as a profession. This group later became the section of clinical psychology. In the 1930s the America Association for Applied Psychology was organized with a large number of non-APA members. At that time, unless one had published post-Ph.D. research, full membership in APA was not granted. The Association for Applied Psychology did not join with the APA until 1945. In the meantime World War II took place, and again the face of professional clinical psychology was changed by political and social events.

According to Reisman (1966) there were about 1700 psychologists who served in World War II. They were young (average age 32) and just reaching the prime of their careers. The war experience in applying psychology apparently changed many of their career interests. At the outset 90 percent were in academic positions, but by the end of the war many were interested in continuing with clinical work after their discharge. These young psychologists had worked on such applied problems as the design of instrument panels, and the testing and selection of personnel for various special positions. Serving on discharge boards, many had even become involved in counselling and psychotherapy when large numbers of men needed help in readjusting to civilian life. Apparently the psychologists liked such work. But more important than their interest was America's perceived need.

Many returning veterans were psychiatric casualties. The Veterans Administration (VA) alone needed thousands of psychologists to help staff their hospitals, so they began a program to support the training of clinical psychologists as a means of increasing the number of mental health professionals. It is here that the histories of psychiatry and clinical psychology began to blend together. During the 1930s clinical psychology was, as Robert Watson (1962) has described it, "child," "psychological," and "clinical" as contrasted with "adult," "psychiatric," and "institutional." The latter description became predominant following the Second World War. Until this change, however, psychiatry and psychology were largely separate in their domains. Now they were thrown together, not for reasons of scientific advancement but rather, for perceived social necessity. With the Congressional passage of a National Mental Health Act in 1946 clinical psychology blossomed as a professsion. It was to those whose history was in philosophy and physiology, whose greatest moments were in academia, whose accomplishments were in education, testing, and child development that the United States Government turned for mental health services for large numbers of psychological casualties of war. Now psychology was seen as psychiatry's handmaiden in the war on mental illness.

As the millions classified by psychologists on intelligence and personality tests during the war returned to domestic life, many problems of adjustment ensued. The Veterans Administration set up programs to train interns and finance the academic training of psychologists. It was an economic boom for psychology and stimulated rapid growth of the professsion. The number of students who came into graduate schools in clinical psychology began to exceed the number in experimental psychology. The National Mental Health Act of 1946 created the National Institute of Mental Health, and along with it a support system for the training of psychologists. Since that year the federal government has given training grants to psychology departments, enabling students to have financial support and departments to expand their staff and facilities. Once again, it was the perceived social need of the time, not great scientific discovery, that led to the growth of the profession.

In 1949 the United States Public Health Service sponsored a conference in Boulder, Colorado, which set the model for training of a professional clinical psychologist, a model that was to be followed for at least the next 25 years. This approach, which has come to be known as the "scientist-professional," emphasizes research skills and training in testing and psychotherapy. The Ph.D., a research degree, became the defining degree for clinical psychology, and to this day a doctoral degree remains necessary for full membership in the APA.[3] In the 1950s the most economically lucrative positions for psychologists involved work with adults in hospitals, medical schools, and industry. Beginning to challenge psychiatrists for the right to do psychotherapy, psychologists today are at home in a realm where they are recognized as both competent and independent.

Thus it was not long before psychology, a discipline with a long history of independence, would emerge as more than a handmaiden of psychiatry, and people such as George Albee, a

former president of the American Psychological Association, would call for psychology's own "place to stand," independent of the medical profession. Today the Division of Clinical Psychology is the largest in the APA. An offshoot public policy organization is, at the time of this writing, lobbying for the inclusion of psychologists in federal medical-psychiatric insurance plans as legitimate treaters of "mental illness."

In recent years the professional practice of psychology has emerged as a full-fledged specialty of psychology, even including the first signs of total professionalization based on identity as a service profession rather than a research profession. In 1968 the University of Illinois, while retaining its Ph.D. training, added its Doctor of Psychology program (Peterson, 1968a), which awards a doctoral degree for service competence rather than performance of research. Professional schools of psychology, which grant similar degrees, have developed in California, New Jersey, and Texas. Although hardly noncontroversial among psychologists, it is probably safe to predict that in 25 years professional psychology will be quite well established as a socially recognized and legitimate endeavor, independent of research psychology. The merits of such developments are debatable, and this is not the place to do more than simply note them as landmarks in the establishment of psychology as a helping profession similar in its service aims to psychiatry and social work.

The Boulder model is still predominant, but it is beginning to slip as is evidenced by the outcome of a 1973 conference on the training of clinical psychologists convened at Vail, Colorado. In addition to supporting the Doctor of Psychology degree, many new issues of professional practice and training, which had emerged in the 1960s, have been discussed in its controversial report (Korman, 1974). These issues include subdoctoral training and training for minority groups who have been largely excluded from a profession that frequently professes concern with their special problems. The outcome of that conference is not yet clear, and it may be more of a reflection of current controversy than a blueprint for the future. (See also Chapter XI.)

---

[3]At this writing that requirement is being challenged off and on by those in favor of extending full membership to Masters-level psychologists, who have grown in number in recent years.

In 1955, ten years after World War II, the United States Congress passed the Mental Health Study Act which established a Joint Commission on Mental Health and Illness. This commission, on which psychologists were significant members, published ten monographs and a final report, *Action for Mental Health* (1961), which evaluated the then current status of mental health services in the United States. The final recommendations of this report are attributed by many to be the direct stimulus for the development of community mental health, and therefore indirectly, community psychology. The details of this report are considered in Chapter III. The most direct social consequence of the Commission's report was its recommendation concerning reduction of the patient population in state hospitals. In 1963 the report led to the so-called "Kennedy Bill," which called for the construction of community mental health centers to serve specified geographic communities with "comprehensive care." The basic principle of such centers was to be the early detection and treatment of acute mental illness, by means of a delivery system that would provide services locally and avoid the necessity of removing those with problems from their home community. The aim is to avoid the buildup of chronic patients residing in large state institutions. This legislation was followed by staffing funds in 1965, and between 1965 and 1971 a number of such centers were either built (300) or funded (420) (Bloom, 1973; Golann & Eisdorfer, 1972).

Because the principle of comprehensive community care has been interpreted as concern with the general well-being of a community, it has led to public discussion, for the first time in the history of the mental health professions, of who shall determine the nature of such care. The American Psychological Association has taken an official position with regard to such centers, including endorsement of the principle of community resident participation in decision making (Smith & Hobbs, 1966). There has been much reaction to this, some of which we will also consider in Chapters III and IX. Here we note the development of community mental health centers and the issue of community participation

as stimuli for a conference among psychologists who were interested in the problems of community mental health.

In 1965 several psychologists, some already working in community mental health centers, met in Boston to discuss the education of psychologists for community mental health. This meeting has been credited with the birth of community psychology (Hersch, 1969: Zax & Specter, 1974). The attendants at the Boston Conference were already dissatisfied with the limits imposed by a concern only with mental health problems per se, and called for community psychologists to be active participants in the more general problems of society. In 1966 they published a report of the conference (Bennett, Anderson, Cooper, Hassol, Klein, & Rosenblum, 1966) calling for the community psychologist to be a social change agent, a political activist, and a "participant-conceptualizer."

As many psychologists began to identify with the community mental health movement professionally, and with the goals of the Boston conferees, the establishment of a Division of Community Psychology within the APA followed. In 1965 the first journal devoted to community mental health was published (*The Community Mental Health Journal*). It was not long before Cowen (1973) would convince the editors of the *Annual Review of Psychology* that rather than limit its review of techniques for "change" to a chapter on psychotherapy, one on *Social and Community Intervention* should be introduced. At about the same time the *American Journal of Community Psychology* appeared under the editorship of Charles D. Spielberger.

All the trappings of an independent approach to psychology are now evident. Several collections of readings have appeared (e.g., Cowen, Gardner, & Zax, 1967; Bindman & Spiegel, 1969; Cook, 1970; Denner & Price, 1973), as have original works on community psychology such as Sarason's extended essay (see Chapter VI), Murrell's viewpoint (Chapters V and VII), and the first attempt at a "textbook" cataloging a broad range of community psychology endeavors (Zax & Specter, 1974). In 1970 a book on training appeared (Iscoe & Spielberger, 1970), and in 1972 a *Handbook of Community Mental Health* (Golann & Eisdorfer, 1972) was published. Community psychology in one form or another is now taught in many psychology departments despite some confusion as to what it is. These events mark the onset rather than the culmination of community psychology. It is only now that the discipline is ready to explore and develop its own directions, conceptions, and practices, as well as to explore input from areas outside of psychology per se.

Professional developments since the 1961 Joint Commission report have, of course, not happened in isolation from developments in the larger society. As we get closer to the present it is more difficult to understand such social influences, but some of their effects are already quite clear.

Social-Political Events of the 1960s

While the federal government was encouraging expansion of mental health services on a geographical community basis, and professionals participating in such mental health centers were beginning to be interested in a broad range of social problems not limited to the traditional concerns with "mental health" narrowly defined, there had been rising in parallel a grass-roots movement for social justice among American Blacks. Stimulated by the hope engendered from the 1954 Supreme Court decision calling for school desegregation, the movement began in the southern part of the United States. Inspired by the nonviolent protest ideology of the Congress on Racial Equality (CORE) and by Martin Luther King, Jr., it rapidly built to a national momentum. The broad outlines of the Civil Rights Movement in legislation, voter registration, and human services are well known. The optimistic approach to social change of the Kennedy Administration in the 1960s, later attempted in principle by the Johnson Administration, gave the first part of the decade a sense of high hope and expectation for genuine solutions to the problems of poverty and racial injustice. As this optimism began to wane, and the programs and promises fell short of the expecta-

tions, an angry and resentful atmosphere emerged in America. Political assassination of civil right leaders, government officials, and those in symbolic positions, combined with a general social unrest typified by civil disorders. Social disruption rocked many of America's largest cities. At the same time the college campuses, with the unjust war in Viet Nam as their issue, carried on parallel activism. An "urban crisis" was seen by everyone. Black leaders, seeking new ways, began to turn to solutions in the political process, and won many victories, perhaps more as a function of default than real success. White Americans began to move out of the cities, and the new Black mayors were left with political control over inadequate resources. Dissatisfaction with the result of the efforts of the past 20 years led many to the ideology of Black Power and separatism, positions that have had profound and positive psychological implications for self concept, even if they were not always necessarily economically sound. For the first time Black Americans in large numbers were saying out loud "we are worthwhile; we can control our own lives and our own destiny; we may need resources but we do not need paternalism." Here is where the situation seems to be at the present time; power and control are the issues, together with access to the resources of society. Community psychology has come to life in this atmosphere.

The political events glossed over too quickly above have had an impact on the activities and thinking of applied psychologists and mental health professionals at least equal to that of the earlier world wars and the professional developments leading to community mental health centers. The psychologists at the 1965 conference in Boston were able to advocate political action with regard to the social problems of society because they were influenced by the times in which they were living. In the 1960s, applied psychology, social work, and all the mental health professions experienced a reemergence of the political and social reform fervor of the settlement house movement. Once again, as after World War II, the federal government assumed responsibility for a new war, a "War on Poverty." But the times were different. In the early part of the century the settlement house movement was largely a private citizen, nonprofessional one. Since then the growth of the "helping professions" has been rapid. These professional helpers have become the only people seen as competent to deliver social services. Helpgiving is professionalized, in part as a function of the growth of the educational establishment and the governmental policy of regulating social welfare. The reintroduction of nonprofessionals to the social welfare activities of the nation has been one of the major aspects of community mental health and community psychology (see Chapter XI).

In 1957, when the Soviet Union launched its space satellite "Sputnik" a panic emerged in American science and education. The federal government devoted itself to the "space race" and universities turned out aerospace engineers and received massive financial support for the "hard sciences." Not many years later the "urban crisis" was perceived as a threat to American security and a demand for "solutions" to human problems created support for the social sciences and the "helping professions" similar to earlier support for the space industry. More and more money became available for programs run by social scientists dealing with urban issues. The expectation for success was expressed in naive clichés such as "any country that can put a man on the moon certainly ought to be able to solve its more immediate social problems." American pragmatism went to work most directly in its War on Poverty. Many social scientists were hired as consultants and program developers for government-sponsored education and social service agencies. The federal government's response to complaints of social and educational inequality was to make a concerted effort to create a new matrix of programs for social good, independent of the existing social service network.

The traditional American philosophy of giving dissidents a "piece of the action" was a core concept in the War on Poverty. Rather than reform existing social systems, a politically difficult strategy, new ones were created under the guise of "maximum feasible participation" of community residents in their own problem solving. Community action programs with representation of local community residents on decision-making boards were instituted. Indigenous nonprofessional community workers were hired, supposedly to provide needed services, and a culture of programs grew up around them. Typically, vocal residents of local poor communities were paid as "workers" to "organize" the community. The War on Poverty was legislated in the 1964 Economic Opportunity Act, and administered by the federal government's Office of Economic Opportunity. Its most visible programs have been Head Start, an education program for "disadvantaged" preschoolers; Upward Bound, a college preparation program for high school students; and various programs of "community action."

Kenneth B. Clark and Jeannette Hopkins (1969) have analyzed this movement, and point out that the policies it represented did not develop in isolation from the history of social welfare in America. They identify the President's Committee on Juvenile Delinquency, organized under John F. Kennedy and chaired by Robert F. Kennedy, as the source of a model for such programs. This committee supported the New York City programs called Mobilization for Youth and Harlem Youth Opportunities Unlimited (HARYOU). Both were a product of a theory of delinquency put forth by two sociologists, Richard Cloward and Lloyd Ohlin (1960), who saw delinquency to be a result of the blocking of social and economic opportunity that would enable the poor to obtain middle-class possessions. "The essence of this approach was that juvenile delinquency had to be understood in terms of larger and pervasive community problems, and could be controlled only through programs designed to ameliorate these relevant problems and pathologies" (Clark & Hopkins, 1969, p. 4). The basic recommendation which grew out of the HARYOU experience of the early 1960s was that social action, conducted by the people themselves, could be a major factor in positive social change. Clark and Hopkins (1969, pp. 5–6) go on to observe that:

. . . this emphasis on social action and social change precipitated the dilemma which has pervaded the anti-poverty program; namely, that it simultaneously demanded the mobilization of the people of a depressed community for social action and social change, and sought to finance such programs through federal and local funds. This remains a fundamental problem . . . concerning the feasibility and realism of expecting political institutions and governmental agencies to finance a serious program of community social action which would necessarily involve political confrontation and the possibility of abrasive conflict between those forces seeking fundamental changes and those forces required to resist such changes.

As might be expected from such difficulties inherent in the War on Poverty, today the Office of Economic Opportunity is disbanded and its programs that survive do so less as a hope for the future than as a reminder of failure. Moynihan (1969), as well as Clark and Hopkins (1969), has written a postmortem on the War on Poverty. His analysis of the failure emphasizes confusion in the meaning of community participation and community action, terms that have never been well defined, and have apparently been interpreted to mean very different things to different people. This led to confusion and false expectations for genuine social change. To such observations might be added the additional note that the War on Poverty was also burdened with the traditional aim of the helping professions: *to make everyone the same according to a single standard*. It could not help but fail.

Some of the issues and programs developed out of the community action model will be reviewed in other chapters; here the point is that such activities and ideology have had a profound influence on the development of community psychology, which was just emerging in the mid-1960s. Golann and Eisdorfer (1972) have pointed out that the issue of the 1970s for both the mental health field and the social welfare arena is one of power and conflict. Just as mental health has led to community mental health and later to community psychology, the concerns first voiced as a need for local community care have been restated as the need to prevent problems in living by changing the social conditions that create them (see Chapter III). The development of an ideology of prevention has come into conflict with the traditional aims of

"cure" for mental illness. The community mental health centers have been under increasing pressure to be responsive to lay, as opposed to professional, control. Just who should exercise the community control is an issue for community mental health centers in exactly the same way that it has become an issue in education, city government, and federal programs for poor communities. Such conflict reminds us that *programs of social welfare are essentially based on social values*. "To a considerable extent there has been a recognition of the social relativism of deviance and the need to redefine or indeed to question whether behavior previously identified as a reflection of individual psychopathology is not societally determined. Mental health according to this view is a concern with maximizing the effectiveness of all" (Golann & Eisdorfer, 1972, p. 15).

In the above analysis we can see the basic problems of community psychology: (1) the conflict between individual and subcommunity rights with the concerns of the larger society for social order and control; (2) the problem of cultural relativity and its conflict with the tradition of a single standard for social behavior; (3) the need for a psychology of person-environment fit, which not only recognizes diversity as legitimate, but also provides resources and alternatives to foster it. In order to have a chance to solve such problems community psychologists must search for new paradigms to guide research and conceptualization. The next section discusses the importance of the search for new paradigms.

The Power of Paradigms[4]

It is only recently that Thomas Kuhn (1962, 1970) has challenged the prevailing belief that science progresses by a linear accumulation of

---

[4]For the reader interested in philosophy of science as such, this section will not do justice to Kuhn's analysis. His work, *The Structure of Scientific Revolutions* (Kuhn, 1970, 2d ed.), is now widely available as a 210-page paperback, and must be read in the original to be appreciated. It is concerned with far more than this text presents, and is written with due consideration for many of the philosophical problems with which it is

knowledge toward some objective called "truth." Rather, he has argued, science develops by means of successive "crises" and "revolutions." This may be understood as a process involving first the inability of a prevailing paradigm to continue to solve important problems which the community of scientists thinks ought to be solvable (the crisis), and next the development and adoption of a new paradigm coincident with the rejection of the other (the revolution). He likens scientific revolutions to political revolutions, created by a small group of believers and resisted by the prevailing institutions until popular acclaim can no longer hold back the new order. The new paradigm creates a whole new way of looking at the world, and once it is adopted the world itself literally is not the same for those who believe in the paradigm. The results of such paradigm shifts may be large scientific revolutions involving many scientists, or they may be small revolutions in the continuing evolution of science toward more and more useful science, rather than necessarily toward a closer representation of "reality." In this view the usefulness of science is determined by its ability to solve problems. Briefly, what Kuhn calls "normal science" involves scientists working on problems ("puzzle solving") that the community of scientists view as worthy of study by their discipline or subdiscipline. The scientist uses theory, conception, methods, and instruments that are deemed appropriate to the currently agreed-upon paradigm. When a crisis occurs because the paradigm is not working, normal science ceases to be effective and, unless a new paradigm is advocated and accepted, the field is in chaos.

The term *paradigm* is used to convey a number of things, and it has stimulated philosophical controversy as to its precise mean-

ing. For our purposes a paradigm may be understood simply as a set of shared ways of viewing a world of concern. To qualify as a paradigm the view must have a group of adherents in the scientific community who follow certain rules and are guided by the paradigm to the study of certain unresolved though, hopefully, resolvable problems. Social science, including psychology, may not have any true paradigms in the strict sense of the word. It may yet be in a "pre-paradigm" stage wherein various schools come and go and compete, and there is no single agreed-upon paradigm through which to view the world. This is similar to a state of crisis, which occurs less frequently in the more mature physical sciences. For this reason some (e.g., Price, 1972) have preferred to speak of models, metaphors, or perspectives for social science. For Kuhn a paradigm is necessary for normal science to operate because normal science pushes the details, assumptions, and applications of a paradigm to its logical end until a new crisis emerges. Psychology, with or without paradigms, tries to follow normal science and we will not be concerned here which term— model, metaphor, perspective, or paradigm—is preferred; they each convey the sense in which it is necessary to understand what community psychology is currently about. The terms are therefore used almost interchangeably in this book, a use that is philosophically imprecise, but will nevertheless serve its function here. The term paradigm is chosen in this section because it is genuine paradigms for which we are searching. Along the way we may have something less, but that is what we endeavor to find.

When adopting a paradigm the scientist adopts along with it a set of rules for problem solving, or doing normal science, as well as a set of permissible problems. Some problems are excluded as outside the realm of the paradigm, others as uninteresting, and still others as impossible to solve and therefore not of scientific concern, by definition.

It is important to understand that a paradigm does not mean simply a way to interpret the objective data on which all can agree, but rather that the same data viewed through different paradigms will actually lead scientists to *see* dif-

---

concerned. The work is used here as a set of ideas and vocabulary providing a format for description of the current state in which a community of scientists finds itself.

Several months after this chapter was written I came across a book by Jessie Bernard (1973), *The Sociology of Community*. In that volume Bernard, following Kuhn, draws the same conclusion about sociology that has been drawn here about psychology: it is in serious need of new paradigms to help us to understand the processes shaping communities today.

ferent things. That is, the paradigm allows one to be open to see things that literally could not have been seen before. The paradigm does not permit one to ever see the world or one's discipline exactly the way one did before the paradigm was accepted. For example, imagine that the familiar Gestalt figure-ground reversal figure in which one can first see a vase and then see two faces were such that once one is seen the other cannot be, and if the second were later seen, the first would now be impossible to ever see again. Another example provided by Kuhn is the well-known Bruner and Postman (1949) experiment in which subjects are shown playing cards at high speed, but slow enough so that they can see and report them accurately. Included in the series of cards is a new one such as a red six of spades or a black four of hearts. The anomalous cards are almost always identified as normal cards (e.g., the red six of spades as a six of hearts). Subjects "see" what they expect to see, given their perceptual readiness. Other examples are provided by Kuhn that are more directly relevant to the scientist's observations. For example, once Galileo had the paradigm of the pendulum he was able to see a rock suspended from a string differently than he could before. Prior to the discovery that Uranus is a planet it had been seen many times before as a star. It was only after it was viewed as a planet that some twenty new planets were found in the next several decades. None had been found in the decades preceding the discovery even though the same equipment had been used.

To bring examples closer to our concern here, when medical scientists began to view deviant behavior as illness rather than as demonic possission did they "see" exactly the same things they had seen before? They no longer saw devils, but now saw symptoms of illness. This is more than simple interpretation. If the same deviant behaviors were to be viewed as rational we would "see" something altogether different. Similarly, if intelligence is viewed as a fixed ability, then improvement on IQ tests is seen as an artifact. If intelligence is viewed as learning with experience, then the same test improvement *is* intelligence. If performance on standardized tests has no meaning in a paradigm for

intelligence then one will not see in performance on such tests anything of importance. Or again, is the motor behavior of a problem child in a school classroom "hyperactive"? Only if such a label is in our paradigm for children's behavior. If it is not, then we will see the child's behavior differently. For example, one paradigm might say the teacher reinforces that child for motor activity by paying a great deal of attention to it. Another might say there is a need in the child's class to arrange the physical environment and teaching methods such that children can move around without distrubing others. The examples could go on and on. We will encounter many in this book.

Given the above view of how a scientific community is influenced by its paradigms, what importance does this have for community psychology in particular? Community psychology is in a state of scientific crisis. It is searching for paradigms. In virtually every content area of concern the psychological paradigms that have guided problem selection, research, training, and application are viewed by community psychologists as failing. The rules for doing normal science are not providing answers to the puzzles that community psychologists now define as worth solving. In each of the content areas reviewed in this book the same theme will be repeated. First, we will define a problem area of interest to community psychology. Second, the prevalent paradigm for normal science and application within that area will be generated. Third, we will review the results of the application of the current paradigm, and find that its failure to provide problem solutions has led to a crisis. Finally, the beginnings of a new paradigm will be offered.

Community psychology is in a total state of crisis because the members of its scientific community have been willing to go, quite literally, to "forbidden turf." They have left the domain of individual psychology and entered the larger world of social systems.

One of the things a paradigm provides for a scientific community is what Kuhn calls a criterion for choosing problems assumed to have solutions. The problems to which the paradigm leads are the only problems that the appropriate scientific community will consider to be scientific, or worthy of its members' attention. In Kuhn's words:

. . . other problems, including many that had previously been standard, are rejected as metaphysical, or the concern of another discipline, or sometimes as just too problematic to be worth the time. A paradigm can, for that matter, even insulate the community from those socially important problems that are not reducible to the puzzle form, because they cannot be stated in terms of the conceptual and instrumental tools the paradigm supplies. Such problems can be a distraction . . . one of the reasons why normal science seems to progress so rapidly is that its practitioners concentrate on problems that only their own lack of ingenuity should keep from solving (Kuhn, p. 37).

Community psychologists have broken this rule. They have overstepped the limits of the available psychological paradigms and are now interested in social change, social justice, politics, economic and social systems as well as individuals. Try as they do to implement them, the paradigms of psychology and the helping professions will simply not stretch far enough to allow us to even expect a solution to many of the content areas (puzzles) which the Boston Conference psychologists hoped they would solve. In every area there is a search for a new paradigm. Even more confusing to this picture is the fact that old paradigms cannot simply be discarded. They must be replaced with something that works better. In the meantime community psychologists struggle on with paradigms that we all know are failing. What is important to understand here is that the paradigms of psychology have simply never been designed to account for the problems that community psychology wants to solve.

Psychology is full of paradigms of the person. When psychologists, especially clinical or applied psychologists, realized the importance of the environment or the situation, that in itself created crisis and revolution. Currently behaviorism has sent clinical psychology reeling with innovation. As we will discover in Chapter IV, however, behaviorism and even environmental psychology (Chapter V) is still seen through the eyes of a psychological-scientific community trained within a tradition, a set, a perspective, a world view, or if you will, a paradigm, which sees everything in terms of individuals and their adjustment to a single standard. The effect of the environment on the person is what is studied, and adjustment to society is the aim. The problem areas selected by community psychology are quite simply beyond the "rules of the game" for existing psychological paradigms; and therefore the community psychologist's colleagues will say: "that sounds like social work" or "that's politics, not science," or "psychology can't deal with that." Hebb (1974), the distinguished scientist and former president of the APA, aptly puts the attitude:

It is to the literary world, not to psychological science, that you go to learn how to live with people, how to make love, how not to make enemies; to find out what grief does to people, or the stoicism that is possible in the endurance of pain, or how if you're lucky you may die with dignity; to see how corrosive the effects of jealousy can be, or how power corrupts or does not corrupt. For such knowledge and understanding of the human species, don't look in my Textbook of Psychology (or anyone else's), try Lear and Othello and Hamlet (p. 74).

Community psychology goes much farther outside of Hebb's paradigm than he fears—outside the individual altogether and into relationships between the institutions of society. Individual psychology just won't do. Nor will a psychology based on one idealized standard of man. Both are characteristic of psychology's current paradigms. They have led us to rank-order people and to declare them as more or less valuable, rather than to maximize each person's opportunity. If the aim of community psychology is to maximize opportunity for all, then scientific paradigms, which apply rank-ordering principles based on individual differences and a single standard of competence, are inherently not capable of solving the problems of community psychology. Although our current paradigms of individual difference could possibly be reconstructed so as to be consistent with a community psychology, they have functionally been associated with limiting opportunity and supporting the status quo for so long that they must now be rejected in favor of a new paradigm which explicitly favors social change. The resultant search for new paradigms is frantic and fed by the continual rediscovery that the old paradigms are failing with the new problems.

There remains at least one other important element to our understanding of the function of paradigms—they are never completely successful. They function in a more or less successful fashion. If a paradigm were completely successful it would no longer be of scientific interest because it would not point the scientist to unsolved problems. It would then become the province of technology. A scientific paradigm, rather than a guide to technology, serves as a guide to new puzzles. In this sense then, we must understand that some parts of the prevalent paradigms of psychology—perhaps we can think of these parts as conceptual elements or ideas—are at least partially successful, and more importantly for the scientific enterprise, lend a reasonable expectancy for further success in dealing with some of the problems chosen by community psychology. That is, psychology does have some useful theory, conception, methods, instruments, and data to help solve some of the problems of interest to community psychology. Recognizing this, that was the first intention in writing this book. Many of these useful elements are included in this book, and there are probably others that are not included. There are certainly those in the realm of methodology for research and they can be obtained from the many excellent research methods volumes that already exist for the social sciences. Because this book cannot be a review of all of psychology, let alone all of social science, hopefully many readers will know of additional ideas relevant to the concerns of community psychology and will use them, together with whatever understanding of the problems this book may provide.

Finally, one may ask, "What contribution does this book have to the search for new paradigms?" The answer must paradoxically be both modest and grandiose. According to Kuhn's analysis, new paradigms are at first rarely able to account for very much puzzle solving. At first they may be even less successful

than the existing paradigms. Nevertheless, a paradigm will be a candidate for adoption if for some reason enough scientists believe in it and take a risk, against all reasonable odds (since most paradigms fail) that the paradigm is worth testing systematically over the years of hard work that must follow. This book is, in part, a plea for the community of scientists to take such risks. The basic outline of a new paradigm is now perceptible, but it needs to be developed by the process of normal science. The modest aim with grand hope is for the next generation of community psychologists to adopt a set of criteria, given below, to guide in their search for new paradigms.

Why should the scientist take such a risk? Kuhn again is helpful, if not complete, in understanding this. The first step has to do with the scientist's recognition of the existence of a crisis, and in part this book tries to demonstrate that a crisis does exist. Normal science will resist this, as it must in order to push to its limits the utility of its current paradigms. Individual scientists are trained not to abandon existing paradigms, but rather to operate within them. Most scientists spend their entire professional life doing normal science. As Kuhn notes, revolutions are usually created by the paradigms of younger scientists in whom the existing paradigms are not yet ingrained so deeply, or by those who switch from one field to another. Fortunately, perhaps, a massive number of psychologists have shifted from one field (essentially clinical psychology) to another—community psychology.

The individual scientist will first begin to feel uneasy when his paradigm does not solve problems that are expected to be solved by it. As he continues to deal with the problem, in order to develop new paradigms he will need to abandon older ones. Paradigm shift is destructive as well as constructive. For example, belief in congenitally fixed intelligence had to be discarded before the effects of learning experiences on intellectual performance could be taken seriously. Today the paradigm of "cultural deprivation," which supposedly creates intellectual deficit and thus accounts for the failure of poor children in public school, is failing, as we shall see in Chapters VII and VIII. To accept a new paradigm this one will need to be discarded. The same is true in mental health, where the illness model is failing. Failure of all paradigms which discourage diversity and what Kittrie (1971) calls "the right to be different" is apparent in every content area.

Again, why should a scientist take the risk of a new paradigm? The old paradigm will only be discarded if it does not work for a problem which is of profound importance to the scientist in question. Second, there must be a substitute available, if not, the scientist in crisis will ". . . often seem a man searching at random, trying experiments just to see what will happen, looking for an effect whose nature he cannot quite guess" (Kuhn, 1970, p. 87).

If a new paradigm emerges it will clash with the existing paradigm; the two will be incompatible. The choice between the two, however, will not be made by a simple look at the results of normal science. The choice more often will be made only by relying on faith, persuasion, and values. This is a very important aspect of Kuhn's analysis of scientific communities. The essential point he makes is that true paradigm clashes involve disagreement about basic assumptions (biases, beliefs, values) or the "givens" necessary to any paradigm. When the advocates of two paradigms cannot concede the basic assumptions of the other, all further normal scientific debate is irrelevant, even though they both may share a similar respect for the process of science.

Kuhn notes several specific reasons why "proofs" cannot resolve a paradigm clash. Frequently the adherents of different paradigms will not agree on what problems are legitimate. Often, the new paradigm will incorporate terms and methods of the old and use these in a different way. Communication between the two will be difficult. In a sense they will "practice their trades in different worlds." In Kuhn's words:

Both are looking at the world, and what they look at has not changed. But in some areas they see different things, and they see them in different relation one to the other. That is why a law that cannot even be demonstrated to one group of scientists may occasionally seem intuitively obvious to another. *Equally, it is why, before they can hope to communicate fully, one group or the other must experience the conversion that we have been calling a paradigm shift"* (Kuhn, 1970, p. 150, italics added).

On what basis may a scientist experience such a conversion? Kuhn answers that often there are few early converts, but those who are, sometimes claim to be able to solve heretofore insoluble problems. These claims notwithstanding, the accuracy of the claim is often minimal, since a new paradigm will leave many questions unanswered, and rarely is a new paradigm as well developed as an older one. Sometimes the paradigm draws on evidence from its success with other problems. Sometimes the new theory is "neater" or more aesthetically appealing, although Kuhn notes that such arguments are less effective in science than in mathematics. The usual situation seems to be that the new paradigm is at first no better at solving the problem, and if all new paradigms were to be judged by that criterion at the start there would be very few major revolutions. "Instead, the issue is which paradigm should in the future guide research in problems of which neither competitor can yet claim to resolve completely . . . that decision must be based less on past achievement than on future promise . . . The man who embraces a new paradigm at an early stage must often do so in defiance of the evidence provided by problem solving. He must, that is, have faith that the new paradigm will succeed with the many large problems that confront it, knowing only that the older paradigm has failed with a few. *A decision of that kind can only be made on faith"* (Kuhn, 1970, p. 154, italics added).

The faith proposed here is a faith in the possibility of a society that is consistent with a belief in the worth of all people, even if they differ from some idealized model of what man "ought" to be. This is essentially a value position. The basic values argued for here include a respect for diversity and for the right of people to be different without fear of loss of material and psychological well-being. As noted in the beginning of this chapter, its corollary is of equal importance. People must also have the right to be the same. Traditional psychology paradigms share an emphasis on individual differences and a tendency to compare people with one another by rank-ordering them on traits or skills or ideals that are held to be of absolute value. Translated into the ''helping professions'' such beliefs are based on the *faith* that those in power hold the right answer as to how one should live. ''Help'' means to make deviants of any variety and for any reason just like those who are in power. The current paradigms are based on a faith in authority. The one offered in this book is based on a faith in the people themselves.

The Values of Cultural Relativity and Diversity as a Base for the Ecological Viewpoint

In American psychology the traditional paradigms adopt an implicit faith that the single standard of white, middle-class society is, on an absolute basis, superior to all others. At the same time, because rank-ordering is built into these psychological paradigms, some will always be on the top and others in the middle and still others on the bottom. Being born into a white, middle-class home will automatically increase one's chances of not being on the bottom. The basic contradictions in such a system render its professed aims of equal opportunity to life, liberty, and happiness virtually impossible. American psychology's paradigms are historically so tied to such contradictions that they are necessarily a function of them. Within such paradigms and their hidden social values the aims of community psychology described in this chapter are totally impossible to accomplish; thus, the crisis and the search for new paradigms. In education, in mental health, in employment, in living environments, and in the legal system, equal access to psychological and material resources is incompatible with a distribution of resources on the basis of rank-ordering people against a single standard of competence. As we examine the dominant paradigms offered by psychology as a helping profession we will discover that they are closely associated with a recognition of, but a disrespect for, individual and cultural differences. *No matter how humanitarian the aims, it is the way*

such paradigms function which destine them to failure from a community psychology perspective. The community psychologist cannot reform the entire society, but the activities of community psychology can be based on a value system, *as well as* a scientific paradigm, consistent with the aims of such reform.

In this book the broad outlines of a new paradigm will appear. The paradigm is not invented here, but one that has been suggested by others, rarely in this context, and rarely as one that necessarily must replace the older paradigms of psychology if a true psychology for the community is to emerge. The basic values in which this paradigm puts its faith are exactly opposite to those of traditional applied psychology. They are respect for human diversity, the right to be different, and the belief that human problems are those of person-environment fit, rather than of incompetent (inferior) people or inferior psychological and cultural environments.[5]

The model offered here is an ecological one. It is a viewpoint rather than a fully developed paradigm. It is today only the beginning of a paradigm for psychology. Its principles, derived from other fields, are rudimentary; the work of normal science based on a model of human ecology remains to be done, but the promise is immense. It can be a morally and ethically responsible paradigm if it rejects the need for rank-ordering of people on a single criterion, and instead posits maximization of each person's potential for living according to a standard of life selected by the persons themselves, not by those in power. In application it must aim at fostering the availability of alternative environments for each person, and recognize that the diversity of human beings and of cultures requires such a view. The role of the helping pro-

---

[5]Obviously there are physical limits to this notion. For example, an environment in which food and shelter are not provided may be thought of as inferior. The issue here is one of psychological and cultural environments which can only be judged by relative, not absolute values. The danger in comparing inadequate physical aspects of an environment to the psychological environment is exemplified by the use of constructs such as ''cultural deprivation'' (see Chapters VII and VIII).

fessions within this ecological paradigm must be to help develop resources and alternatives for those who are now denied any opportunity other than the single "choice" of mainstream society, which for them does not work.[6]

Rather than trying to fit everyone into a single way of life, the community psychologist must become an agent of the local community. This will often require the community psychologist to work toward providing socially marginal people with the resources, the power, and the control over their own lives, which is necessary for a society of diversity rather than of conformity. Clearly the community psychologist is in no position to redistribute the resources of society, but he or she is in a position not to continue to support the rank-ordering of people on the basis of a standard of conformity, which provides a legitimized psychological basis for the inequitable distribution of resources. Rather than seek to diagnose and repair "deficits" the community psychologist can help to identify strengths and develop resources.

The adoption of an ecological viewpoint would have a number of implications for psychology, and specific examples are presented in later chapters. Here it is necessary to understand the general value position that such a paradigm requires, because it can only lead to genuine social change if it includes, along with scientific assumptions, the values of diversity and cultural relativity. *Unless these values are an explicit part of the paradigm, it runs the risk of leading to old solutions with new names.*

There are both ecomomic and cultural aspects to the values on which a new paradigm must be based. The value position advocated here is neither traditional social welfare-liberal nor individualistic-conservative, but rather leads one to a fairly unique sort of social politics. To clarify these politics it is helpful to first give some stereotypes.

In America, stereotypically, an individualistic-conservative might be thought of as one who favors individual responsibility and respects individual and local community differences and rights over those of the larger society (the federal government). A social welfare-liberal tends to favor the good of the larger society over the rights of local communities to impose their own values. This liberal usually favors centralized social welfare programs, while conservatives tend to dislike such programs. A liberal generally believes in equal treatment for everyone based on a set of public standards. Discrimination against or for someone on the basis of race, religion, age, and so on, is frowned upon. The tremendous disillusionment between Black Power advocates and liberals is in part a function of the difficulty for many liberals to accept what may be viewed as "separatism." Despite a humanitarian outlook, to many political liberals a Black Power advocate is a "bigot in reverse." The political conservative, on the other hand, while often opposed to public welfare programs, seems not to mind separatism or local community control. "Let each community live as it likes, so long as we don't have to support them."

There are two basic dimensions fused in the above descriptions. One is the *economic policy dimension*, the other the *cultural value dimension*. The conservative economic position favors individual responsibility as opposed to societal responsibility for economic welfare. The liberal economic position favors societal economic responsibility. With regard to cultural values, the liberal, while "tolerating" differences (e.g., one should not discriminate because of them), seeks a unified society with one standard by which all people can be fairly judged. Each person has a right to private beliefs, but judgments of competence, and therefore employment and educational opportunity, must be based on the same standards for all. More important, the liberal tends to support a system in which the federal government helps everyone to adapt to the prevailing culture. "We should all be part of a common society of people," it is argued. The conservative on the cultural value dimension is much more inclined to support diversity, believ-

---

[6]The ecological paradigm, as we shall see in Chapters V and VI, can be applied as a means to adjust persons to environments or environments to people, but also allows for the possibility that neither solution is adequate, and that entirely new environments, created by, and in the control of, people who are different from the mainstream are desirable.

ing one's own values are better, but differences among local communities, cultures, and people are a fact of life not to be tampered with by "big government."

The specific social values argued for here are those that cross these two stereotypes. It is an individualistic-conservative cultural position and a social welfare-liberal economic policy. Diversity and cultural relativity are supported. Each community has a right to maintain its own values and style and to control its own institutions. There is a respect for individual differences. At the same time, the economic policy is one of social responsibility and shared resources equitably distributed. There are no inferior persons or cultures and each has a right to be judged by its own standards and to receive a fair share of the resources of the larger society. It is a mixture of conservative respect for individuals with liberal social responsibility. It is an ideal, not a panacea, but the implications for a psychology based on this ideal are profoundly different from a psychology based on conformity, a single standard for competence, and rank-ordering of people.

What is suggested here is a paradigm based on an ecological view of people, combined with the values of cultural relativity and social responsibility. As Kuhn (1970, p. 149) has observed, "Copernicus' innovation was not simply to move the earth. Rather it was a whole new way of regarding the problems of physics and astronomy, one that necessarily changed the meaning of both 'earth' and 'motion'." For community psychology, a paradigm based on ecology and on the values described above does not simply take into account person and environment, rather it is a whole new way of regarding the problems of applied psychology and social change. *Such a viewpoint frees community psychology from the need to make everyone fit into a single environment in order to live a decent life, but not from the responsibility of providing resources to make it possible.*

As the following chapters review the success of the older paradigms that have tried to make everyone "fit in," it will be demostrated that in each instance the older paradigm is inadequate for accomplishing the aims of community

psychology set forth in this chapter. Consequently, the success of that demonstration is dependent on accepting the value system presented here. If one prefers a single standard and rank-ordering of people as the desirable goal for society, then the evidence presented will not be convincing. As Kuhn has indicated, a paradigm shift is based on other than proof. If, however, the basic values advocated here are accepted, then the problems for community psychology to solve are those of how to live with diversity rather than how to extinguish it, and the ecological paradigm can be shown to have promise.

The next chapter is an attempt to show that in the helping professions the paradigms chosen have always been a function of the underlying value system of their adherents. The view of history as a chronology presented in the first part of this chapter is at best only a "cover story" which has provided an introduction. The appearance of community psychology as a logical outgrowth of the mental health movement is neither true nor false; it is rather one perspective through which to view history. As we shall see in Chapter II, the helping professions have never been based on the orderly accumulation of value-free knowledge.

The major theme of the next chapter is that the beliefs and actions of scientists and professionals are a function of more than their data. This is so for the nature of the research they conduct, the problems they investigate, the conclusions they reach, and the social policy they advocate or imply. The views and behavior of people in the role of scientist, no less than those in the role of political advocate, are at least a function of two influences other than the information they accumulate: the social forces operative at that moment in history, mediated through personal values and beliefs, and the paradigms available for the conduct of research and practice in their particular discipline. This is true for all of science, although here we are concerned with its particular manifestation in the science of psychology, and especially in the practice of psychology which has come to be known by the work of service-oriented professionals, including psychologists, psychiatrists, social workers, educators and other social scientists. The influence of social forces through values and be-liefs is pervasive but often difficult to notice in the work of the natural scientist. It is easier to discover its influence on the social sciences be-cause of the nature of the subject matter, and most easy to identify in applied social science, because that is where positions must be clarified in order to be implemented.[7]

Community psychology as a science-profession was born in part as a consequence of the social forces operative in American society and the human service professions at the begin-ning of the second half of this century, and in part as a consequence of dissatisfaction with existing paradigms for the application of psychology to new problem areas. This chapter was concerned with a history of events that have led to community psychology. The next chapter is about the ways in which social forces and values have historically shaped social science and the helping professions.

---

[7]Although the influence of social forces and paradigms can be argued to be so for all of science (cf. Kuhn, 1970), here we are concerned with social science and its application. Consequently, for the sake of the present discussion the terms science and scientist used throughout this and the next chapters may be limited to social science and social scientists without changing the meaning of the position presented or the conclusions reached.

THE SOCIAL AND HISTORICAL CONTEXT: Values, Faith, and the Helping Professions

> . . . historians of the future will point out that we too lived by myths.
> —*Herbert J. Muller*

> What needs to be stressed is the intimate relationship between the philosophy of man prevailing in a given historical period and the assumptions concerning the deviant person. What is of importance is the relationship between these assumptions and the institutionalized practices that have developed for coping with deviance.
> —*Jules D. Holzberg*

It is common to begin textbooks with a chapter placing the current view of a field of study into sequential historical perspective. That was in part the aim of Chapter I. The aim of this chapter is slightly different in that it is less concerned with a time line of historical "fact" and reporting of specific events. Chapter I is misleading if it makes the history of the helping professions appear to be orderly and rational. Some events become historical fact as a function being remembered, recorded, written about, and interpreted. Other events are ignored and do not become facts. The recent emergence of Black American history, regarded for so long as nonhistory, is one good example. The way events are put together is as much a function of the interpreter and the community of historians as the events themselves. Such a view is similar to the one presented by Carr (1961) in a little book called *What is History?* His answer to his own question is that historical fact is something different from truth. This account will be no different. It will express a point of view rather than a set of truths. It is expected that the viewpoint will have heuristic value. That is, it will describe how the social sciences and the helping professions are influenced by faith, social forces, and values.

This chapter presents the following points:

1. All of man's quest for understanding, including science, and particularly social science, can be shown to be influenced by social forces, mediated through personal values and beliefs. We shall consider several analyses as examples of that theme, leading to the inevitable conclusion that the helping professions are so affected by current social forces that there is little sense in the argument that direct political action on the part of social scientists is "unprofessional." The passive acceptance of status quo social forces is viewed as equally political as active intervention aimed at social change. The alternative presented here is not to deny such influence, not to condemn it, but rather to recognize that applied social science and the human service professions are inherently political. This requires scientist-professionals to examine their own values, and to present

them clearly and explicitly so as not to deceive themselves or the community they wish to serve.

2. Although the traditional view is that the nonapplied psychologist is less influenced by social forces, the fact is that *both* "basic" and applied psychology have been influenced directly and indirectly by historical events, cultural biases, and values.

3. We review some "historical notes" on the determinants of mental health practices which will demonstrate that the actual *content* of the "best scientific and professional practices" is often influenced by social forces, fads, and biases of influential leaders, as much as by scientific advancement.

4. Community psychology can best deal with the moral, ethical, and value questions of human welfare through an appreciation of the multiple communities that make up a society. Such an appreciation requires the cultivation of diversity and strength building, two themes that are repeated throughout this book. The scientific methods used by community psychology are most likely to keep the moral and ethical questions in mind when they are seen through a perspective based on cultural relativity and an ecological view of human behavior, both of which are concerned with person-environment fit, rather than with evaluative labeling of people or environments.

Social Forces, Values, and Belief in Science

Science and the professions it supports are influenced by social forces both within the community of scientists and within the larger society. For the purpose of this discussion, *social forces* are defined rather loosely as *political, social, cultural, and economic factors and their complex interaction extant in a society, or a segment of society, at a given moment in history*. These forces are mediated to scientific behavior by way of personal values and beliefs of individual scientists. There are both local and national aspects of social forces, and sometimes

these are thought of as largely political in nature, separate from the work of scientists. It is often thought to be demeaning for scientists to engage in attempts to participate in the shaping of these forces, or to be influenced by them. The argument is that scientists may participate in social policy debate as citizens, but not as scientists, and that their actual work as scientists is not influenced by other than "scientific method." In fact, scientists, like other members of society, are shaped by social forces regardless of their willingness, and as they participate in society they also help to shape it. This participation can be active (usually to change or create a social policy) or passive (usually to accept an existing social policy). Because it is difficult to see outside of one's own time, people are shaped by social forces even when they are unaware of them. History is usually clearest (if not necessarily accurate) in retrospect rather than in contemporary historical accounts. Phenomenologically it is difficult for people to recognize the social forces influencing their behavior, attitudes, and beliefs because these forces are often diffused and are mixed with the common-sense beliefs of the time. We cannot easily become "unstuck" in time, and we pay little attention to the importance of when we live on how we think. In the unwritten code of the scientist there is a belief that denies this influence. Science deals with "objective truth," or at least the search for it, and science is therefore supposedly above the influence of contemporary events.

The "leap of faith" taken by Christians who believe in God and the teachings of Christ as recorded in the Bible later permits a number of quite logical conclusions about how to live, find truth, happiness, justice, and so on. The "leap of faith" of the social scientists who have all been trained in similar places, have read similar textbooks, and who have viewed the world for many years from a common perspective, such that most accept a number of common assumptions, including mathematical and statistical procedures as a way to make sense of complex information about humanity, also permits certain "logical" conclusions. But they are only logical if the basic assumptions are accepted. Within a given science or profession there are frequently conflicting sets of theory and interpretation to ''explain'' the same data. ''Schools'' with particular biases develop, especially in the social sciences. Sects of scientists proliferate like sects of religion. Each sect tends to view the world of concern with somewhat different ''assumptions.'' Scientists prefer to call biases and values ''assumptions,'' but the terminology should not disguise the fact that they are beliefs. The history of science is scattered with such discarded beliefs. Today's truth is tomorrow's phlogiston.

It is not often admitted that the choice of science as a system in which one has faith must be seen as simply that: a choice based on faith. Science is one system for ordering the world. It seems to work well for the natural sciences, and perhaps less well for the social sciences. Social science, despite its effort to be empirical, may actually involve new ways of viewing things already known, at least as much as new discoveries. If that is true, then there are, of course, a number of ways outside of science to help humanity view itself. A writer such as Kafka may say as much about us as a scientist studying alienation and anxiety. Does Shakespeare's literature say any less about us than Freud or Skinner? The choice between methods of understanding lies in a ''leap of faith'' to science, religion, art, or some other system. Once the leap is made each has its own logic. Today most psychologists believe in science. The rules of science therefore govern many of the conceptions and actions of community psychologists. However, this should not hide the fact that the issues of concern to psychologists are basically those of human welfare. The American Psychological Association prints each month the following statement on the title page of its official publication, *The American Psychologist:* ''The purpose of the APA is to advance psychology as a science and as a means of promoting human welfare.'' The statement means that while the method endorsed is science, the questions addressed are necessarily moral, ethical, and value questions. What constitutes human welfare cannot be viewed in any other way. It is impossible to escape this fact, even when it is disguised by scientific language which calls value judgments ''assumptions'' or is hidden in laboratory research which is less open to public view than applied research.

As psychology moves from the biological to the social, and from the theoretical to the applied, the questions dealt with (and the answers given) are increasingly more obvious as value positions. All views of how people ought to be are by nature value statements subject to the beliefs of their advocates. When one moves from theory to application they also become action statements, again subject to the beliefs of their advocates. Consequently, psychologists must openly admit this influence, try to make their values, beliefs, and cultural biases as clear as possible, and try to understand the social forces influencing their work.

Much of applied psychology, which includes community psychology, is concerned with how best to implement those things already known. Thus, applied psychology is in a kind of ''double jeopardy.'' On the one hand its ''facts'' are subject to cultural biases, values, and beliefs. On the other hand the methods and aims for application of these ''facts'' are also subject to values, beliefs, and cultural perspectives. For example, if a social scientist observes, by collection of empirical data, that children who do well in public school tend to have a positive self-concept, that ''fact'' may have more to say about how positive self-concept is defined by the psychologist than it does about the child or the process of feeling good about one's self. If an applied psychologist takes this fact and tries to implement a program which aims to improve the self-concept of children by helping them to do well in school, he implicitly accepts the notion that positive self-concept should be a function of doing well in school. Although he may justify his work with children on the basis of the scientific fact of a relationship between positive self-concept and doing well in school, in so doing he often tends to ignore the basic value position this reflects, that is, self-concept and school performance ought to covary.

Trimble (1974) has made the same point more concrete in reporting on the self-image of native American Indians who are observed to have high rates of alcoholism and suicide. As he notes, many psychologists assume that American Indians have a low sense of self-esteem because of their association with such "negative" behaviors. However, in his survey of over 1000 native Americans from five major tribes, he found that their reported self-esteem is quite high. In interpreting these results, Trimble concludes that the native American culture may not label as negative the same behaviors which the mainstream culture calls negative. Other behaviors, such as courage or the lack of it, may be more important to self-esteem than drunkenness or the lack of it. Although these are rather straightforward examples, the same process holds, as we shall see in this chapter, for less obvious examples.

It is ironic that social scientists are frequently less willing than physical scientists to admit to being influenced by the very processes which social science is about! Yates (1974), for example, in reviewing a recent book on *Behavior Influence and Personality* (Krasner & Ullmann, 1973), takes issue with the authors' contention that science, and particularly psychology, is relative, rather than absolute, and that the scientist fulfills a role by following a current methodology and a value system. Yates calls this "dangerous nonsense" and argues that there can be a universally valid body of knowledge by citing work from the physical sciences such as Newton's laws of motion. Although he means this to concern psychology, since it is a review of a book about psychology in a journal written for psychologists, Yates does not cite an example of "universal knowledge" from the social sciences.

It is important for community psychologists to straightforwardly recognize the influence of social forces and not be apologetic about having values or participating in the political process. It is important for community psychologists to recognize, and to tell nonscientists, that contrary to popular belief, scientists, and therefore the practice of science, are subject to values, biases, and faith, just as are any people engaged in any form of human endeavor. No person, even when acting in the role of scientist, can avoid making human judgments that are influenced by one's own values, culture, and "common sense." Sometimes the values are explicit, more frequently they are implicit. When the values are consistent with a prevailing status quo they are less likely to be recognized as value judgments than when they challenge an established way of viewing the world.

Community psychology is by its very nature dedicated to a challenge of the status quo. The challenge is to applied work in public settings as well as to science practiced in more controlled settings. Community psychology requires testing in the real world, and leaves its practitioner open to the claim that "you are operating on personal values rather than on science." One aim of this chapter, and other parts of this book, is to present the view that values and science are not contradictory. That is, a scientist has values, no more right than anyone else's, and these values influence the scientist's work and ideas. Furthermore, this is unavoidable, especially in applied activities based on social science, and should be made public rather than hidden.

The more the scientist operates in the real world the more difficult it is to hide the influence of values and beliefs. Perry London (1965) has argued that psychotherapists cannot help but influence the values of their clients and that they have a responsibility to inform them about their biases before the fact. Community psychology, more often concerned with entire populations and social systems than individuals, is even more public, and the practitioner will similarly need to clarify his or her values to those affected by an intervention. It is less usual to expect laboratory scientists to make their values and biases explicit, yet it is their data and interpretations that presumably serve as a basis for applied social science. The totally objective social scientist simply does not exist except as a theoretical model.

The Applied Versus "Basic" Dichotomy As It Affects the Psychologist Interested in Social Change

There is, within the social sciences, a kind of hierarchical distinction drawn between so-called scientists and practitioners. The practitioners, while they presumably base their interventions on knowledge of research, must also deal with problems for which the data are at best inconclusive, and activities are often based on hypotheses rather than fact; at worst research may be almost nonexistent. In applying psychology, researchers and practitioners are necessarily responding to the press of current events. This is almost a definition of applied psychology. Consequently, there must be an obvious influence of contemporary needs, values, beliefs, as well as political and economic aims. Applied psychology is a servant of these aims. This open responsiveness to contemporary issues creates a conflict in values which one sees repeated over and over again within the profession of psychology.

Because psychology has developed out of an academic and research tradition based in philosophy and physiology, even those who apply psychology to contemporary problems see themselves as "scientist-practitioners." The ideal of this model is one of objective tester of reality, with the data of a value-free investigation objectively gathered and applied dispassionately. Applied psychology is frequently thought of as not different in its ideal from experimental psychology, but simply as a means of going the next step. This ideal is popular not only among the applied scientists, but among laymen as well. Within psychology the bias of the scientific establishment leads to a kind of hierarchy of scientific respectability which places experimental science at the top, descriptive science somewhere below, and application at the bottom. Applied social scientists are now in a peculiar position. Although the physical scientist, who serves as the model of objective science, can apply many of the neccessary controls for a truly experimental science, and the psychologist who confines his work to the laboratory can presumably approximate this, the applied psychologist is forced to make a number of compromises with the ideal model in order to conduct research, and even more to apply it. There are various means for approximation, many detailed by Donald T. Campbell and Julian Stanley (1966) under the rubric of "quasi-experimental" research designs. Others have

proposed a set of methodologies called *program evaluation* (Shulberg, Sheldon, & Baker, 1969; Struening & Guttentag, 1975; Weiss, 1972). But ultimately the applied researcher is always in a "one-down" position when judged by the criteria of "pure science."

Unfortunately, testing in the real world frequently requires so much compromise of the experimental model as to always be in a weak inferential position. On the other hand, laboratory research is often so far removed from the real world as to be in an equally weak position when application is required. There seems to be an inverse relationship between scientific "rigor" and relevance to the real world. Clinical psychology has dealt with this problem since its existence; community psychology, which has a considerably broader scope and far fewer traditions is, with little question, in a "one-down" position with regard to these issues, even when compared to research in clinical psychology, let alone experimental psychology.

When a psychologist performs an experiment in the laboratory there are few questions with which he or she must deal outside of those that other psychologists of similar interests, background, and biases raise. This creates the illusion of objectivity. The further away one moves from the safety of the laboratory the more open one is to questions from a wider audience who do not necessarily share one's assumptions. To do research in a mental hospital there are a number of ethical and procedural standards that must be met. But again the reviewers are usually of like mind with the researcher. As one moves to other social systems, such as schools (educational research has its own set of rules), and as one moves out to less traditional settings in the natural environment, the rules and assumptions become less clear and a number of legitimate questions can be raised by an increasing number of people affected directly or indirectly by the work. There are no fewer biases held by psychologists doing laboratory research than there are by those in community psychology. The difference lies in the publicness of the research, the number of people and special interests touched upon, and in the potential for immediate social influence.

When one collects data in the "field" rather than the laboratory, even if it is descriptive data, and particularly when it is data to evaluate an attempt to change things, the influence of political-social forces becomes most apparent. Not only does the researcher need to accommodate to various influential forces quite directly in order to be permitted to do research, but also the predetermined biases of the researcher become more obvious. The ways in which he has been influenced by social forces around him all his life are more apparent than if he is doing laboratory research. They are not more influential, simply more apparent.

A psychologist who wants to examine the effects of cooperation and competition is rarely asked what right she has to study this in a social-psychological, small-group laboratory experiment. But the same psychologist, if she wishes to do research on the effects of cooperation in schools, will need to establish a school that operates by the principles she wants to examine. This will require political behavior at the local level, because she will have to create the program before she can evaluate it. If she stays in the laboratory she may never have to be politically active, and her own political biases that shape her research can be kept quite to herself. She would, of course, have to give up the test of her ideas in the real world, unless she were lucky enough to find a reformer somewhere who approximated her ideas and who would allow her to conduct a "quasi-experiment" (Campbell, 1969).

What this means is that the applied psychologist interested in social *change*, or in examining the effects of a program not already in existence, is not only in a one-down position because he is an applied rather than a "pure" researcher, but he must also openly enter the political market place in order to test his ideas. He must make his values clear, and he must be politically active if he is to be permitted the opportunity to test them out. The alternative is to never test his ideas. Since, in American society, the right to try out new ideas for social policy is under political control, the community psychologist who wants to obtain empirical data will necessarily be a political activist, either in a confined setting such as a school or in the larger community, depending on what sort of programs he is proposing. To *implement* new programs, as well as to invent them, is seen as the responsibility of the community psychologist (Fairweather, Sanders, & Tornatzky, 1974).

When Is a Scientist Political?

Although most psychologists and scientists verbally state that to be politically active and to respond to the immediate needs of society is inappropriate to the scientific enterprise, this attitude is not reflected in our actual history. Robert Reiff (1971a) has argued this point cogently when he pointed out that the history of the behavioral scientist's involvement in politics and public policy in the United States shows increases during war time, or when there is a threat to the perceived well-being of society. During World War II, many of the "pure" scientists were willing to become applied when they considered the need for assessment of military personnel vital. In times when they do not perceive a crisis these same scientists argue for nonpolitical involvement in public policy. Who (which scientist) gets involved in political interventions and public policy depends on who sees the problems as sufficiently important to demand action as opposed to reflection. The willingness to be involved in such action is in part a function of the values one holds. The more a scientist feels personally concerned with an issue, the more likely he is to act rather than reflect. During World War II, most psychologists did not refuse to do applied work on the basis of ethics or lack of data. The political situation affected them directly. Those who identify with the problems of the poor and minority groups are more likely to be involved in political and scientific work with such problems. During the late 1960s and early 1970s many students went on "strike" for changes in the university system. Some professors joined them and others argued that it was inappropriate for a professor to be involved in such political activity. As funds for salary raises to professors have been reduced in the 1970s more seem willing to join unions and threaten strikes themselves. If the political issue is relevant to the scientist, he is more likely to participate. It has far more to do with values than with data.

Although social forces and values affect the viewpoints, interpretations, and models of basic as well as applied social science, this is always more obvious in the work of the applied psychologist. However, even within applied psychology those who are involved in programs for social change are more likely to be labeled as "political" than are those who work for programs of social control. In some measure, the scientist who works with grass-roots people, or from the bottom up, rather than with the governmental or established agencies of social control, is viewed as more political than his government agency counterpart. The real difference may be in their status quo versus change politics, but they are both political.

Even avowedly antipolitical social scientists have been influenced in their scientific work by their personal value system and by contemporary social forces. Leon J. Kamin (1974a),[1] in a recent paper on "Heredity, intelligence, politics, and psychology," has noted the political involvement of some of the most esteemed of American psychologists early in this century. He reviews, for example, some of the activities of the renowned psychologist, Henry Goddard, who became involved in the effort to limit European immigration to the United States. Goddard used "mental tests" to examine large numbers of immigrants and concluded that 83 percent of Jews, 80 percent of Hungarians, 79 percent of Italians, and 87 percent of Russians were "feeble minded." Congress used his data in 1924 to limit immigration of "undesirables."

Under the direction of Robert M. Yerkes, a psychologist renowned in the annals of experimental psychology and social science, the Army's World War I testing program results were published by the American Academy of Sciences in 1921. Kamin notes that the results not only provided evidence for the low intelligence

of Blacks, but were used in the most important political battle of the day, the debate over admission of immigrants by quota. Under Yerkes' leadership and with the assistance of scientists from the Eugenics Research Association, a committee of scientists, ". . . in an effort to take the national debate over immigration 'out of politics' and to place it on a 'scientific basis,' began to support relevant research" (cited in Kamin, 1974a, p. 4). They sponsored the work of Carl Brigham who reanalyzed the army data on intelligence of immigrants. Brigham found that immigrants who had been in the country 16–20 years were as bright as native-born Americans. However, those who were recent arrivals were classified as feeble-minded. Brigham argued that he was measuring native intelligence, and the reason for the better showing of the longer residing immigrants was that most had come from England, Scandinavia, and Germany, whereas the more recent were from Southeastern Europe. The decline was seen as due to a decrease in "Nordic blood." As Kamin notes, Brigham went on to add, in a classic disavowal of political activity, that:

We are incorporating the negro into our racial stock, while all of Europe is comparatively free from this taint . . . *The steps that should be taken must of course be dictated by science and not by political expediency* . . . and the revision of the immigration and naturalization laws will only afford slight relief . . . the really important steps are those looking toward prevention of the continued propagation of defective strains in the present population (Carl Brigham, cited in Kamin, 1974a, italics added).

Not only does Kamin show, by citing Congressional testimony from scientists, how this and other similarly value-laden interpretations of scientific research helped establish immigration quotas, but he notes, not incidentally, that Brigham later became an important office holder in the American Psychological Association, and served on the College Entrance Examination Board where he devised and developed the Scholastic Aptitude Test.

If men like Yerkes, Goddard, and Brigham had decided that the intelligence test data used to justify limited immigration were actually so cul-

---

[1]Kamin has recently expanded on his observations in a book, *The Science and Politics of IQ*. Potomac, Maryland: Lawrence Erlbaum Associates, 1974b.

turally biased as to be unfair and unscientific, and had used their considerable influence to argue for more opportunities for immigrants, one wonders what their fate in the history of social science might have been. The fact that they supported the dominant political viewpoint of their time does not make their actions any less political, but they are remembered as experimental scientists, not as political polemicists.

This same point has been well made by opponents of military research who have taken university scientists to task for accepting "defense contracts" which support improved war machines in the name of science. Unfortunately, because it is more disguised, it is less often realized that those who receive grants from the Department of Health, Education, and Welfare, including this author, have also worked for the government and consequently are often agents of social control.

This argument does not state that social control through health, education, and welfare programs is necessarily wrong, but simply notes that such scientific and applied work is just as much in the realm of politics and values as work with grass-roots groups who seek direct political change. To support a status quo political system, or a psychology of adjustment to things the way they are, is just as political, even if less obviously so, as supporting a change in political and social systems. Is work with a grass-roots group of Black youth who want to organize and protest their treatment in school any more political than consulting with the school system to develop a plan to control those same children by use of behavior modification aimed at social control, or therapy groups which give them some place other than the public domain to vent their anger? Albee (1969) has noted that as long as mental health deals with therapies it is not threatening to the existing social structure. But when the problems are conceptualized as a result of inadequate, unequal, and destructive social systems it becomes a threat to the existing political-economic system. Thus, those who respond to contemporary problems are often seen as political, and those who ignore them are not. Actually, all human service professionals are

political, differing only in which politics they are responsive to.

Halleck (1971) has recently argued this same point and noted his own growing awareness that ". . . a psychiatrist who recognizes the oppressive nature of his patient's external environment must decide whether or not he should do something to change it, not only for those who are his patients, but for everyone who suffers from the same environment" (p. 31). Halleck goes on to argue that psychiatric practice is essentially political in nature:

Psychiatry was never an ethically or politically neutral profession. Value systems, usually implicit rather than explicit, have always dominated the practices of different schools of psychiatry . . . The person who is preoccupied with internal problems is likely to be less inclined to confront social systems . . . so long as treatment does not encourage the patient to examine or confront his environment and so long as treatment protects those who have adversely affected that patient from considering their own behavior, the net effect of treatment is to strengthen the status quo . . . *there is no way in which the psychiatrist can deal with behavior that is partly generated by a social system without either strengthening or altering that system. Every encounter with a psychiatrist, therefore, has political implications* . . . once this fact is appreciated, the psychiatrist's search for political neutrality begins to appear illusory (Halleck, 1971, pp. 34–36, italics in original).

Some (Szasz, 1970) have argued that institutional psychiatry, which involves involuntary hospital commitment, is politically motivated and repressive in the same sense that the inquisition repressed religious deviance. Halleck (1971) goes further to argue that all of psychiatry is a political weapon. He notes that:

In treating a patient (or—in the case of community psychiatry—in dealing with any mental health problem) the psychiatrist chooses his own modes of treatment; he is not required to explain either the values or political philosophies that govern his choice. Some psychiatrists are conservative; most are liberal, and a few are radicals. The extent to which a psychiatrist's political or moral belief systems affect his choice of a particular therapeutic approach is rarely acknowledged or appreciated. He merely insists that his primary goal is preventing mental illness (p. 88).

Ronald Leifer (1969) has also argued that the human service professions have always been agents of social and political control "in the name of mental health." He calls psychiatry social control disguised as medicine, and notes that the factors that are usually credited with leading to community psychiatry are merely historical events that have not been causative. The events that are usually cited, as was noted in Chapter I, include increased public recognition of mental health needs, the increasing role of the federal government in health care, and new developments in medicine and psychiatric practice. Community mental health has, Leifer notes, focused on programs for improvement or abolition of mental hospitals, construction of mental health centers to serve geographically proximal communities, and programs to prevent "mental illness." He interprets these activities as manifestations of a ". . . social movement with a long history. Its development is related to profound changes in the character of modern social and political life—changes in national character, national purpose, and public policy" (p. 214).

Leifer's essential argument is that the change of emphasis in psychiatry from hospital confinement to community treatment is a reflection of a change in governmental public policy from obvious maltreatment and oppression of the poor to welfare programs, *rather than a change in basic medical knowledge*. He notes that treatment of the mentally ill in America and Europe has always been through the control of deviance. Public mental hospitals evolved from prisons and poorhouses, and policies for operation of public hospitals have always been a function of public policy toward the poor, not scientific discovery. The same system has evolved into the modern welfare system of which community mental health programs are a recent extension. Leifer views the localization of community mental health programs as an extension of social control over deviants by means of surveillance, rather than true medical advances. He sees danger not in the expression of such political values, but rather in disguising these values as medically and scientifically based, and advocates frank admission by psychiatrists of their

political biases and values in favor of social control.

The way in which Leifer views community psychiatry and community mental health is as a movement directed by the state to control its deviants, and he shows how this is hidden by medical or sociological terminology. Interestingly, many of the mental health workers who participate in the community mental health system would view themselves as apolitical, or certainly not as political activists. If Leifer's view is adopted they, just as much as an organizer in a radical grass-roots movement, or a conservative policeman, must be viewed as agents of political mission, regardless of their avowed interest in mental health rather than politics.

Anyone who has ever tried to implement a new program of mental health service not consistent with the status quo, or who has engaged in the delicate game of "grantsmenship" (a euphemism for the politics of economic support for research or service programs), will recognize that current political forces are influential in determining success. The actual content and feasibility of mental health service programs are necessarily affected by the economics and politics of health, education, and welfare, at least as much as they are affected by scientific merit. Funding agencies set priorities. These priorities are a function of governmental policies. Individual scientists are usually selected to serve as consultants on grant applications, and, not surprisingly, they have biases, beliefs, and values. Usually those selected to serve on review panels are well-known, established scientists or professionals whose position is therefore most often representative of the status quo prevailing beliefs. New ideas, particularly if they challenge those in power, be it the scientists, the mental health professionals, or the political administration, are difficult to finance. Anthony Graziano (1969) has illustrated this reality in a detailed case history of an attempt to establish a new mental health program based on what he viewed as recent advances in psychological research.

Graziano describes the experience of a group who wanted to provide new mental health services in a community already controlled by a mental health establishment. By applying the ground rules of currently acceptable scientific decision making, if this new approach had been compared with the success of the established approach, the weight of evidence would have been strongly in favor of the new approach. However, the skills of politics, rather than those of science or medicine were necessary for obtaining funding to establish the new program. The governmental agents did not ask for rational scientific comparison. Rather, power and social control were the determining factors. The established professionals whose control was being challenged were called upon as the only legitimate evaluators of the program proposed by this new group. The new service was automatically referred to the control of those whom they challenged, since the established professionals were considered to be the best judges, apparently on the basis of their social position. Despite outside and independent positive evaluation, the new program was rejected for funding because, argues Graziano, it threatened the status quo continuation of the local mental health establishment.

Graziano has drawn some general conclusions from this experience. The major lesson he presents is that turning innovative ideas into innovative programs requires "a good deal more than humanitarian beliefs and scientific objectivity" (1969, p. 13). Rather, he argues, political knowhow is essential. Here we see the link between social science and development of human resources: politics. To *implement* a program requires political action, particularly if that program is one which challenges existing power relationships in a community. Graziano argues that the mental health power structure (and this could be generalized to any social system) spends the major portion of its efforts in maintaining itself. He gives it the motto "Innovation without change," and describes the typical established power as supporting words that sound like innovation, and actions that do not lead to it. To challenge the controlling system one must become political. "Contemporary American mental health professions base their major decisions neither on science nor humanitarianism, and certainly not on honest self-appraisal, but on everyday politics of bureaucratic survival in

local communities" (Graziano, 1969, p.1). Only the psychologist who openly recognizes this can engage in the political activity necessary for *implementation* of new ideas. Community psychology must be political because applied social science is political by definition.

A note of caution: To declare one's values openly and to work for their implementation politically must not be confused with professing truth (Sarason, 1975). Flexibility and openness to new ideas will need to be continually fostered if one is to avoid setting up a new status quo. It will always be easier to see the ways in which social and historical forces influence applied scientists than the ways in which they influence laboratory researchers. Does this mean that the psychologist who does laboratory research, or who does not care to work for social change, either because he likes things the way they are, or because he deems it inappropriate, or not worth his time, is less a product of and influenced by his society? Probably not. It is important to realize that nonapplied social scientists are just as "culture bound" and tied to both their history and their society.

The Influence of Contemporary and Historical Forces on "Basic" Psychology

It may be argued that the really basic procedures of science and verifiability are different from particular theories. All scientists tend to agree on the "rules of science" even when they differ in their interpretation of data. But even the procedures which are said to lead to verifiability are based on faith and tradition. The continued replication of an experiment which finds results "statistically significant" such that the chances are one in twenty that the result is random convinces us that the result means something, in that it is *generally* reproducible *under the same conditions*. Unfortunately, not only are there few such consistent replications in the social sciences, but those found frequently account for only a small portion of the data, and are often suspect beyond the specific (usually laboratory) conditions under which they were obtained.

Recently a small number of psychologists have emerged who question the adequacy of scientific aims borrowed from the natural sciences as appropriate to the social sciences. The major issues raised center on the observation that, unlike the physical universe, social behavior changes quite rapidly over a relatively short time span, and may make "universal behavioral laws" impossible to find. This position has been well presented from three entirely different and independent perspectives by Lee Cronbach, Kenneth Gergin, and Klaus Riegel.

Cronbach's Analysis of the Quest for Universal Laws

In 1957 Lee J. Cronbach presented a very influential paper which argued for the combination of experimental and correlational research in what he calls aptitude by treatment interactions. The question such research asks is "how do the same experimental treatments affect people with different individual characteristics?" Today this is a very common sort of research design in psychology. In 1975, coming back to his earlier suggestion in an address to the APA on receipt of a Distinguished Scientific Contribution Award, Cronbach noted that looking at these simple interactions is probably an insufficient means of understanding since behavior is so complicated that many other uncontrolled factors are usually operative in an experiment. In Cronbach's (1975) words, "An ability by treatment interaction can be taken as a general conclusion only if it is not in turn moderated by futher variables . . . However far we carry our analysis—to the third-order or fifth-order or any other—untested interactions of still higher order can be envisioned."

Going further, he argues that laboratory experimentation may not even be a good first approximation of real world relationships in that experimental generalizations assume that, "all other things being equal," a treatment effect accounts for a given result. However, in the real world other things are rarely equal, and most frequently we are not even aware of what the "other things" are. Finally, Cronbach notes what he calls "time as a source of interactions."

Over time, empirical relationships change. For example, DDT is no longer effective because mosquitos have adapted to it. As the economy and community attitudes change, social psychology changes. Even the position of the stars change over time. Culture changes, and "the more open a system the shorter the half-life of relations within it are likely to be."

The argument that psychological reality is not fixed over time, nor is it independent of cultural and attitudinal changes, is one which is emerging here and there among psychologists, although it is contradictory to the standard model of science as a search for enduring empirical relationships. Cronbach now suggests that psychology may be realistically thought of as interpretation in a social context, rather than as a search for timeless generalization. Again, in his words:

Social scientists are rightly proud of the discipline we draw from the natural science side of our ancestry. Scientific discipline is what we uniquely add to the time-honored ways of studying man. Too narrow an identification with science, however, has fixed our eyes upon an inappropriate goal. The goal of our work . . . is not to amass generalization atop which a theoretical tower can someday be erected . . . The special task of the social scientist in each generation is to pin down contemporary facts. Beyond that, he shares with the humanistic scholar and the artist in an effort to gain insight into contemporary relationships, and to realign the culture's view of man with present realities (Cronbach, 1975, p. 126).

It is not much of a step from this contextual view of psychology to recognize that even the publication of data is influenced by values, biases, and social influences. The tradition, for example, of publishing only results that are positive tends to bias the journals that scientists read in favor of data that support a prevailing status quo. In the same way, since journal reviewers are typically those already well established in a field, the tendency is to accept articles for publication that support the existing rather than new paradigms. That is in part why each new school of psychology finds it necessary to create its own journal. Likewise, the social meaning and interpretation of data, once published, are also functions of current social values.

A few simple examples will clarify this latter point. If Blacks are consistently found to score lower than whites on intelligence measures used by American psychologists for most of the twentieth century, what does that mean, and what social policy does it imply? There have been many different answers to that question, often put forth by scientists who share a respect for the basic procedures of science. These answers range from refusal to offer any policy (which is the same as saying "do what has traditionally been done") to radical proposals for change, ranging from eugenics through cultural enrichment and educational reform, to banning the use of tests. The social policies offered are more a function of values and beliefs than of data. The policies most popular are a function of the times in which one lives, such that the same data can be used to support genetic inferiority, environmental causality, or invalidity of tests, depending on one's politics and on current popular beliefs. The beliefs are rationalized by data, but they remain rooted in values.

A recent example of the same phenomenon was presented by the American Psychiatric Association which has now determined *by popular vote of its membership* that homosexuality is no longer to be considered a disease. The sudden "curing" of many heretofore "sick" people is a consequence of the Gay Liberation Movement and current liberal sexual attitudes, rather than scientific advances. This is not an isolated example. "More than a century ago Dr. Oliver Wendel Holmes observed that 'medicine, professedly founded on observation, is as sensitive to outside influence, political, religious, philosophical, imaginative, as is the barometer to the changes of atmospheric density. Theoretically it ought to go on in its own straightforward inductive path, without regard to changes in government or to fluctuation of public opinion. But [actually there is] a closer relation between Medical Sciences and the condition of society and the general thought of the time than would at first be suspect' " (cited in Grobb, 1973).

There is danger in saying this if it is interpreted to mean that scientific method has no place in psychology. Psychology must operate within the best scientific methodology available.

Unfortunately, the best is not always the most popular, and the methodology is at best only a *tool* for research. Faith in that tool is simply an example of a belief, a value. The methods of science are based on assumptions and faith just as are the methods of religion. The tools of science can be used within very different value systems and yield very different interpretations of exactly the same data. The data themselves can be changed depending on how they are collected and analyzed. Collection and analysis are open to the influence of value and belief just as are interpretations of the data. The point is simply that social scientists need not be embarrassed by belief in a social value system; nor should they be embarrassed by the fact that they are "true believers" and have "faith" in science. Nor should social scientists be embarrassed by the fact that they function within a particular time, culture, and history. *Rather, all this needs to be admitted so that it can be taken into account.* It is a bit like the existential argument that to find meaning in life people must first recognize the absurdity and meaninglessness of their existence. Then they are free to find their own meaning. For social science to make sense of itself it must recognize its culture boundness, and try to take into account the fact that scientists are not immune from the social process they study, including cultural transmission, tradition, conformity, political ideology, and even errors of judgment. Putting numbers on beliefs may make us able to obtain a mean, but it does not make these beliefs any less a function of social forces.

Gergin's View of Social Psychology as Contemporary History

Kenneth Gergin (1973), a consulting editor for the *Journal of Personality and Social Psychology* at the time, has argued that although methods of research in social psychology, an area which aspires to the model of the natural sciences, are scientific in character, its theories and ideas about social behavior are essentially reflections of contemporary history. "It is the rare social psychologist whose values do not influence the subject of his research, his methods of observation, or the terms of description" (p. 311). Individual difference research, for example, places those most like the researcher in the best light. The more similar the subject is in education, sex, and values to the psychologist, the more positively he is described. Models of social interaction as well as individual personality variables are based on value judgments. Conformity, authoritarianism, aggression, and other such concepts are not value-free, and are either highly regarded or not depending on the culture. As Gergin notes, the authoritarian personality is looked down upon in American psychology, but has been praised in German society (Jaensch, 1938).

Wiggins, Jones, and Wasserman (1975) recently found that Whites and Blacks view the term "aggressive" quite differently, with Blacks rating it more positively than Whites. Further examination showed that Whites view the term to mean physical aggressiveness, and Blacks see it to mean gaining active control over one's environment. The meaning of such words is always culture bound. Unless psychologists recognize this they may reify the meaning and make improper inferences about people. Even when careful methods are used to collect data the discussions of results often employ words as if they have a meaning that is not culture-bound. Gergin gives some excellent examples:

> . . . self-esteem could be termed egotism, need for approval could be translated as need for social integration; cognitive differentiation as hair-splitting; creativity as deviance; and internal control as egocentricity . . . if our values were otherwise conformity could be viewed as pro-solidarity behavior . . . (1973, p. 312).

Gergin goes on to argue that social psychology does not operate in a vacuum; as it influences humanity's view of itself via dissemination of theories of social behavior the very nature and influence of the variables described change the way they affect its behavior. To know that psychologists think that people repress sexuality leads to attempts to deal with it openly. To know about reinforcement as a way to control behavior leads them to resist such control. The more powerful a theory of social behavior, the more aware people become of it, and paradoxically, the more they change in reaction to the previously understood social influences. Gergin argues that this is most true in areas of concern to the public. Learned ways of behaving in social situations are a function of culture. As culture changes so must these ways of behaving. Gergin, like Cronbach, argues that the study of social psychology is essentially an historical account of contemporary affairs. He asserts that although the prejudice of academic psychologists is against applied research because it is assumed to be of only transient value, and "pure research" is seen as contributing to "basic and enduring knowledge," this is false, and he argues for a change of the intention of social psychological research from prediction and control to "sensitization." "Whether it be in the domain of public policy or personal relationships, social psychology can sharpen one's sensitivity to subtle influences and pinpoint assumptions about behavior that have not proved useful in the past" (Gergin, p. 317).

Because the processes of social psychological concern are not locked into the biology of the organism they are subject to what Gergin calls "enlightenment effects." Making people aware of their current behavior patterns and social influences on them, he argues, will aid in changing the influence itself. A good example is the much noted practice of institutional racism. Raising the consciousness of people with regard to the subtle ways social institutions discriminate against minority groups is an important step in changing this fact. Social psychology, argues Gergin, should study changing patterns over time, as the major share of the variance of social behavior is due to historically dependent dispositions.

Basically, what Gergin is saying is that even social psychologists opposed to applied research are culture-bound and influenced by the social forces around them. These forces change over time, and the psychologists themselves, even as their subjects, are products of their time and their history. He urges social psychologists to embrace this fact and not only admit it, but make use of it to better understand their own data in light of political, economic, and historical reality.

Gergin's (1973) paper has not been accepted without criticism. Typical is Schlenker's (1974) response appearing in the same journal. His counter-argument is essentially a statement asserting the *possibility* of a social science with enduring laws and abstract generalizations that are not time- or culture-bound. Schlenker's position is that a nontime-bound science of social behavior is not illogical and could be constructed, despite the fact that social science differs from natural science in a number of ways. For example, he shows that the nature of the open systems affecting social behavior means only that experimentation is difficult, not that there are no regularities. He also makes a useful distinction between empirical generalizations and higher order abstract theories which shows that the former are possible as a means of avoiding the culture-boundness of the latter.

Regardless of one's position as to the *possibility* of timeless and universal laws of behavior, Gergin's paper makes it clear that much of social psychology has in fact been culture- and time-bound. To recognize this one need not reject the possibility of finding, or the desirability of a search for, universals. It does, however, focus on the problem of cultural and historical relativity. This is a particularly acute problem when one applies social science, since it is in application that one must deal with current reality rather than theoretical possibility. But it is not limited to applied social science. The cultural and historical biases imposed by social forces on "basic" as well as applied science are considerable.

Riegel's View of the Influence of Social Forces on Basic Psychology

A third analysis, similar in some ways to Cronbach's and to Gergin's, but more sweeping in its historical scope, has been offered by Riegel (1972) to demonstrate the "Influence of Economic and Political Ideologies on the Development of Developmental Psychology." His general thesis is that the economic and cultural conditions of society provide a basis for the direction and growth of its science. Specifically, Riegel argues that two considerably different views of developmental psychology have

evolved as a consequence of two distinct political-economic traditions: the "capitalistic" popular in the Anglo-American world, and the Continental European "mercantilistic-social-istic."

The capitalist tradition, out of which grew Darwin's notions of the "struggle for survival," was supportive of a reemergence of the philosopher Hobbes' argument that man is essentially competitive, and established social order only as a means for protection of self and property. The result of these two lines of thinking in what came to be known as "Social Darwinism" (Spencer, 1897) with its emphasis on "successful survivors" was the natural conclusion by capitalist societies that the best of men are "white middle-class adults, most likely engaged in manufacturing or business enterprises" (Riegel, 1972, p. 130). In short, it is a rationalization of why the ruling class rules. Riegel argues that this philosophy was perfect for a society such as England with its history of entrepreneurial competition, manufacturing, hunting, and breeding, and led to a view of deviance of any kind from the standard as inferior. ". . . children are regarded as incomplete adults; old persons as deficient; criminals, mental defectives, colonial subjects and non-whites as far below the rank of white middle-class adults" (Riegel, 1972, p. 130).

In psychology, as we have seen in Chapter I, this view has been expressed through the tradition of individual difference research, stimulated in England by Francis Galton's eugenics and Pearsons' psychometrics. G. Stanley Hall, in America early in this century, while accepting the idea of inheritance of acquired characteristics, emphasized environmental rather than genetic factors, and helped to shift explanations of deviance from totally genetic explanations to socially malleable differences. Nevertheless, the essential tradition established in both England and America, regardless of attributed causality, is one of comparison of groups to a single standard or ideal.

The interpretation of Hall's idea that each person "recapitulates" evolution in his own individual development, but is malleable, particularly during adolescence, led educational reformers in America to a psychological justification of the need for assimilation of immigrants to the standard, largely through forced public education. ''. . . boys clubs (stimulated by Hall's psychology) and public school athletic directors, conceived of sports, quite explicitly, as a modern means of indoctrinating alien lower-class youngsters with conventional American pieties on patriotism and mobility . . .'' (Schlossman, 1973, p. 147).

Functionally, the explanation of differences as caused by either genetic or environmental factors matters little so long as differences from the standard continue to be regarded as inferior. Riegel (1972) sees this tradition of comparison to a single, dominant-group ideal, expressed in psychology by individual and group difference research, as in large measure a function of the competitive-capitalistic tradition in which it has developed, and which it in turn helps to justify. If the poor and other deviants do badly on psychological tests, it is no wonder that they are poor. They simply have either bad genes or bad environments. We shall see later in this book, particularly in Chapters VII and VIII, how pervasive this point of view still is.

A different type of developmental psychology grew out of the political-economic traditions which Riegel calls ''mercantilistic-socialistic.'' His analysis of political-economic life in Europe, particularly France and parts of Germany and Italy, sees these countries as essentially land powers dominated by land-owning aristocrats. Their large armies and courts made manufacturing necessary, but it was supervised by the state. Merchants who were too successful were suppressed, but as manufacturing increased, a middle class was added to the social classes of aristocracy and peasantry. Nevertheless, they were less well off than the aristocrats, and eventually this helped lead to the French Revolution. Riegel sees the existence of specific classes, and the absence of cross-class competition, as creating conservative attempts to justify that particular social order; consequently, unlike England, a social and educational philosophy which emphasized multi-cultural differences developed. Riegel notes that Rousseau, for instance, outlined an educational philosophy in which a child is compared only to his peer group, and gave support for the romantic notion

of the ''noble savage.'' Men are seen as basically good and as born equal. Civilization creates group differences. Out of the tradition of preserving the child's desirable natural state for as long as possible grew the educational traditions of Montessori (1870–1952), Pestalozzi's (1746–1827) child-centered ''kindergarten,'' and the ''youth'' or ''back to nature'' movements which, unlike the American scouting programs, were totally youth operated. Spranger (1882–1963), an influential developmental psychologist who emphasized sympathetic understanding of deviance, was a participant in this movement, and Riegel sees him as typical. Piaget's developmental psychology grows out of this tradition emphasizing stages of development, each to be understood in its own terms, rather than in comparison with other stages.

Finally, Riegel notes the recent influence of continental European psychology in America, which he interprets as supportive of a more individual appreciation of deviance and subculture, with a diversity of standards. He cautions, however, that in its extreme, this view can be supportive of classes and castes, and argues for a combination of the two traditions of developmental psychology through an ''interaction or relational model.'' He cites some attempts to develop such an ''interaction paradigm'' in ecology and in the social psychology of Kurt Lewin (1936). Basically, this idea is an attempt to separate the specific content of development from the *process* of development. It is an attempt to understand development in a context, rather than by analysis of its elements. In short, people may differ with regard to what they know and do as a function of their social context, but the assumed meaning of those differences may say more about the observers than about the observed.

The essence of Riegel's viewpoint, in his words, is that:

. . . our sciences, as much as our children, do not develop in a sociocultural vacuum; . . . it is naive, irrelevant, and irresponsible to anchor our efforts upon an abstract truth criterion traditionally conceived as either ''god-given'' or as provided by ''scientific facts'' and ''nature itself.'' Truth and knowledge are also functions of the actions taken and of the actions they demand. These actions are determined by the economic and political ideologies of the societies in which we live (Riegel, 1972, p. 140).

The foregoing analyses by Cronbach, Gergin, and Riegel lay open to question the argument that social science is ever free from the influence of time, history, politics, economics, and cultural tradition. Although the influences are somewhat indirect and serve to set certain tones, limits, and broad ideological guidelines for so-called "basic" research, the influences are just as powerful, even if more subtle, than those on the applied scientist.

Historical Notes on the Determinants of Mental Health Practices

Examining the historical events of the mental health professions allows us, in various ways, to understand the profession's current activity. We have seen in Chapter I that a chronology of events is one way to view history. A second has been to examine the influence of social forces, mediated through values and beliefs. We have discussed how the content of scientific and professional belief is influenced by political attitudes favoring or rejecting the status quo (Halleck; Liefer). We have seen how contemporary events change "truth" (Gergin); how economic systems influence psychological method (Riegel); and how professional practice is influenced by the tendency to preserve power and control rather than to be scientific and humanitarian (Graziano). There remains at least one other historical perspective to further muddy the waters of objectivity: how the actual content of the "best scientific, professional, and mental health practices" change with the winds of fad, the whims of political leaders, and the current views of "proper" behavior, rather than the orderly flow of scientific advancement.

Fads, Political Leaders, and Scientific "Breakthroughs"

Ruth Caplan (1969), in detailing the history of American psychiatry in nineteenth-century America, presents the view that psychiatrists, even as today, were concerned with the role of environment in the creation of mental illness. She provides many examples of similarity between nineteenth-century belief and today's mental health movement:

The early nineteenth-century practitioners . . . were eager to manipulate facets of both extramural and institutional life in order to encourage optimum conditions for the prevention of mental disorder, for early case finding, and rapid treatment, and for averting relapses among discharged patients. They tended to reach these objectives first in programs directed toward the lay community, second in the organization of institutions, and third in the interface of these two milieux (Caplan, 1969, p. 10).

The obvious similarity between this and the current view of community mental health centers (see Chapter III) is so close as to be interchangeable. Nineteenth-century psychiatrists were particularly concerned with children and therefore sought prevention of illness through public education. Parent groups, based on cultivation of "intellectual and moral character" believed to directly affect the brain, were popular. "Defective education and injudicious early training" were thought to be the prime causes of insanity. The major reference groups for American psychiatry during this period were lawyers, doctors, clergymen, and educated merchants who composed the upper-middle-class society. Parents were warned against leaving their children in the care of others, and early education at home was considered paramount. In general, the advice of the period favored clean, regular habits of life, and the Puritan Ethic of the time. The recent interest in early education, in day care, and in preschools shows the same concern today, only the proper contents, agents, and targets for such education are changed. The agents are now professionals as well as parents, and education is aimed at the lower classes rather than exclusively at the middle class (see Chapters VII and VIII). More important is that the content now reflects current views of what makes a child worthwhile—that is, doing well in academic school work rather than the earlier "moral training."

In Ruth Caplan's view of nineteenth-century psychiatry, based on the beliefs and practices of those in the medical professions, the physician's belief in environmental factors as a cause of mental illness ultimately led to confinement as a means for dealing with insanity. Although it was rationalized that isolating the mentally ill in environments which removed them from pressures of the world that might "bruise the brain," such treatment also served a social purpose in justifying the removal of undesirables.

In the early days of the nineteenth century insanity was believed to be curable by means of "moral treatment" and the provision of small-group social interaction in a relaxed environment. Later, disillusionment with such treatment came as a function of the unwillingness of American society to apply the expensive procedures of moral treatment to an increasing population of lower-social-class immigrants. Throughout the nineteenth century mental diseases, although considered to reflect brain damage, were believed to be envionmentally determined, yet specific ideas for treatment came and went and seemed to have less to do with their actual value as treatment than with their cost and social utility as a means of isolation and punishment (treatment) of deviants.

After the middle of the nineteenth century, when large numbers of immigrants and the poor began to fill the mental hospitals, there was a corresponding decrease in funds available for such services. "Moral treatment had been created to serve an elite group of patients, well-mannered, clean, self-supporting Protestant artisans and farmers who shared their superintendent's adherence to the gospel of work and to the value of worship and education" (Caplan, 1969, p. 73). In the years 1839 to 1844 nearly 80,000 immigrant German and Irish poor entered the United States. Many wondered if the Irish were not more prone to disorder than other "races." Not only did they have to deal with ethnic prejudice when they encountered psychiatry, but there were few who understood their culture. Isaac Ray, a renowned physician and hospital superintendent wrote of them in 1863 (cited in Caplan, 1969):

In endeavoring to restore the disordered mind of the clodhopper, who has scarcely an idea beyond that of his manual employment, the great difficulty is to find some available point from which constructive influences may be projected. He dislikes reading, he

never learned amusement, he feels no interest in the affairs of the world, and unless the circumstances allow some kind of bodily labor, his mind must remain in a state of solitary isolation, brooding over its morbid fancies, and utterly incompetent to initiate any recuperative movement (p. 74).

In the 1950s Hollingshead and Redlich (1958) published their famous study of differential psychiatric treatment and diagnosis by social class. They found that those diagnosed as schizophrenic were more likely to be lower-class people, and that these lower-class clients were most often hospitalized and treated with physical methods rather than with psychotherapy, which was the preferred method for middle-class clients. Grobb (1973), in a review of mental institutions in America, found that the same phenomenon occurred over one hundred years earlier. Many American psychiatrists, among them, not surprisingly, Isaac Ray, supported the idea of differential treatment by separation of paying and nonpaying clients:

. . . patients from the "poor and laboring class" required less attention than those from "educated and affluent" backgrounds. The former were used to working and were content with simple pleasures such as a walk in the country or performing small tasks. The latter, on the other hand, could only be satisfied by long and repeated interviews with the superintendent. Each class, therefore, required different forms of therapy (Ray, cited in Grobb, 1973).

This reasoning led to support for "separate but equal" facilities.

Eventually, as foreigners were overrepresented in hospitals, there was a loss of public support for psychiatry, and consequently, a loss of resources and difficulty attracting good young physicians to its practice. In the latter nineteenth century the rise of social darwinism and the continued influx of immigrants led psychiatry in two directions. One was to support mental institutions as a means of removing the undesirables from the community. The second was to encourage reform activities to prevent the spread of alcoholism, tobacco, and masturbation, believed to be a cause of insanity. Many medical scientists lobbied for legislation and worked for "public education" on these matters. Like the modern community mental health reformer, the social darwinist-psychiatrist sought to work on two fronts—on the one hand to hospitalize those deviants already sick, and on the other to clean up the environment. Although they believed that poor environments were passed on biologically, and today's environmental reformers believe in cultural transmission, the similarity is obvious. Many who now advocate parent education in child-rearing practices and proper assimilation of the lower classes to middle-class culture, so as to eradicate differences from the mainstream culture, do so on the grounds of mental health.

Caplan, in summarizing much of the failure of nineteenth-century psychiatry, points to several "traits" characteristic of psychiatry which seem to recur periodically, even today. One is the tendency to support panaceas and to oversell a given treatment, only to be disappointed by its later failure. For example, in 1874 the Association of Hospital Superintendents endorsed the use of chloral hydrate in mental institutions, without regard for many of its detrimental effects. Even the use of "cautions" in the endorsement was eliminated. A second tendency was to support particular treatments by investing huge amounts of manpower and resources, even when they were untested. This recurrent tendency, which remains operative in the mental health movement, seems to operate through the occurrence of fads, or what are frequently called "priorities." A priority is a euphemism which enables a granting agency to say "do this if you want money." Frequently the "this" is the latest panacea or research problem that is currently embarrassing the political administration.

Government leaders, particularly those in positions of high symbolic value (e.g., kings, presidents) can influence the practices of mental health by both direct (with financial support) and indirect means (through the weight of their opinions and concerns in public statements). This influence is easily translated into "priorities." Two very good, yet very different examples of this phenomenon can be drawn from England and the United States some two hundred years apart.

King George III, who reigned in Britain at the time of the American Revolution, is known to have been subject to periods of insanity, or frequent occurrences of bizarre behavior. Many physicians of the time who would not have been otherwise concerned about the treatment of "incurable disease" were attracted to its study, particularly since all sorts of notable people suddenly began to hear about and manifest similar symptoms. Even the specific treatment that the King received became a fad among physicians. His doctors, influenced by the belief that removing the patient from all familiar sights and sounds cuts off the possibility of ruminating on disturbing matters, prescribed a complete change of scene. This was soon to become the preferred mode of treatment for the fashionably insane. From this idea the notion of institutionalization is not far removed (Caplan, 1968a).

Some two hundred years after King George III, the then President of the United States, John F. Kennedy, was to have a widespread effect on the mental health movement in his country. Quite by accident of history a man who during his short stay in the White House (1960–1963) reached, through his personal appeal, almost legendary status, had a sister who is mentally retarded. Kennedy's personal interest in retardation research and programs of service, rather than "scientific breakthroughs," profoundly influenced levels of funding and research in retardation during the 1960s. Much of this research has been a search for medical causes of retardation, although there is some reason to believe such programs may be fruitless (Albee, 1968 a).

Benjamin Rush, a signer of the American Declaration of Independence, is one of the most influential men in the history of American psychiatry and provides another example of personal influence. He represents the enlightened medical-psychiatric thought of the late eighteenth and early nineteenth centuries, as well as an important early link to government. In part as a function of his political influence, as well as his intellectual leadership, many of his ideas were widely accepted and implemented by American psychiatry. If all men were created equal, as stated in the Declaration of Independence, it must follow that their environment molded them to their differential status in society. However, this view was functionally not so equalitarian as it may first appear. Throughout the nineteenth century, either through belief in the inheritance of characteristics acquired as a function of the environment and culture of one's forebearers, or later through belief in one kind of social darwinism or another, the assertion was held that through natural selection one reached one's place in society. Much of the impact of these views was to mute the implications of environmental determinism and to justify social class inequality while sounding equalitarian. Rush, for example, like his contemporaries, was faced with a peculiarly difficult contradiction in the beliefs expressed by the Declaration of Independence and the simultaneous existence of slavery in America. Thomas Szasz (1970) is enlightening in his description of how Rush managed to deal with the contradition.

As Szasz shows, Rush was a master at interpreting social, political, and moral beliefs in terms of medicine. He presented a view which accepted the Black man as a person, but at the same time stigmatized him as a carrier of hereditary disease. In 1792 Rush encountered a Black man who was suffering from a disease now known as vitiligo, which causes loss of pigmentation, such that some areas of the skin appear white. Believing this to be a spontaneous "cure" of his blackness, Rush wrote a paper on the cause of the "disease." In his view of "Negritude" Rush rejected the popular belief that God made the Negro black as indication of his inferiority; or that he is black by nature; but rather argued that he suffers from a disease. Both his facial features and skin color are a function of the affliction of his ancestors with leprosy. It is a symptom, now passed on by inheritance, and no longer infectious to others, except by producing children. Here, Szasz notes, was the perfect scientific-medical model of illness which enabled the physician to justify a social evil and support a status quo while appearing to be humanitarian and scientific. It is similar in function to today's sociological explanations of inferior Black culture. Today, by attributing many of the problems of living which Blacks face to poor mothering or bad environments, the

behavioral scientist is able to deny genetic inferiority, but functionally justify the societal scapegoating of Black Americans. Rush's conclusion from his "medical analysis" was that although Whites should not intermarry with Blacks, they should be humanitarian and should attempt to cure the disease!

It must be recalled that Rush was a leading *scientific* as well as a political figure of his day. His textbook *Medical Inquiries and Observations upon Diseases of the Mind*, published in 1813, was the most influential book in American psychiatry during the nineteenth century. Many of his medical methods of care, such as blood letting, dunking, and confinement, were quite popular and hailed as scientific advances over earlier religious practices for mental treatment.

One of the most striking examples of treatment fads occurred at the beginning of this century and is described in a full chapter by Caplan (1969). The superintendent of Manhattan State Hospital on Ward's Island, New York, fearing an epidemic of tuberculosis, erected tents on the hospital grounds in order to alleviate overcrowding. All living and dining facilities for a group of twenty patients were moved to the tent. There was great attention paid to this experiment, including regular scrubbing and spraying, and the provision of an excellent set of meals. Although intended to be a preventive measure against tuberculosis, the physicians were surprised to find improved behavior among the small group of patients. Only after patients were returned to the hospital wards did many relapse. Case histories and publications followed, lauding the newly discovered treatment. Improvement was attributed to sunlight, open air, and the change in environment. The hospital began to remove other patients from the overcrowded wards to tents of twenty or so inmates. They were even given the opportunity to decorate and participate in designing their new environment. Staff were assigned so that patients now had more frequent and easy contact with doctors. Photographs were taken, and the outside world acknowledged them. Patients housed in the wards were soon also given more opportunity to get "fresh air," considered to be a major factor in the recovery. They began to be sent out for long walks. More publications followed, the word spread. The idea began to take hold in other places including Illinois, Ohio, and California. Tents were lauded for their low cost as a means of setting up new units. With customary overenthusiasm and misunderstanding, however, as the idea spread it was also misused such that the small group, excitement, and patient participation in setting up and running the camps were lost. Eventually the camps became large, overcrowded, and routine, with necessary staff shortages, and the entire atmosphere reverted to the style of the buildings. Tent treatment was soon found to be ineffective and disappeared.

Since then there have been other fads, sometimes lauded as panaceas. The use of brain surgery was extensive in the mid-twentieth century. Shock treatments continue to be used today. Drugs are frequently administered in large and routine doses as "maintenance" for chronic patients despite their failure as treatment (e.g., Anthony *et al.*, 1972; see also chapter IX).

The advent of the community mental health movement, which has focused in part on opening up the back wards of large hospitals to release chronic patients, has, to the extent that many hospitals have suddenly "dumped" patients into the community, been unfortunate in recent years. Interestingly, the same hospital which developed tent treatment was recently reported in the *New York Times* (October 20, 1974) to be unable to maintain the free movement of a large patient population housed there. As a function of the community mental health movement many patients had been let out of locked wards to move freely about the community. Many were found to get into various kinds of difficulty and the staff was calling for more "security," that is, locked wards, guards, and so on, according to the newspaper report. Here again seems to be the misuse of an idea. To some, release to the community apparently means simply opening the doors and not providing preparation or necessary resources. The same phenomena occur as halfway houses, places where small groups of patients can live together in the community, are shown to be an effective means to return them to community living. There is danger that such settings will be

misused as their adoption increases. As Fairweather (see Chapter IX) has shown, these settings, to be successful, require a number of carefully administered characteristics. In cases where patients have been released to "group homes" without proper administration or preparation disaster has resulted. Sometimes the concept is so misapplied that patients have been sent to large (200–500 persons) "hotels" to live on their own. As we shall see in Chapter IX many patients can live on their own if the environment is properly set up so as to get them started toward true independent living. But the fad of simply letting patients out to live together, unprepared after years of confinement, and without resources, creates chaos. What the *New York Times* was seeing, of course, was a reaction to that chaos which will likely lead to a return to the wards of hospitals, rather than provision of proper supports.

Similar misuse of promising ideas occurs frequently. The idea of nonprofessionals as mental health workers (see Chapter XI) is often misused. Behavior modification (see Chapter IV) is another modern example. Initially shown to be effective in maintaining socially acceptable behavior under carefully administered conditions of hospital living, the fad has caught on. Many hospitals now have such "behavior-mod" units which are only that in name. The general ideas of reward and punishment are sometimes applied without proper training of staff in administering a system which only on the face of it seems easy to apply. The techniques have spread to schools and prisons as well, and are frequently so misused as to properly arouse public anger and prohibition (Murphy, 1974; *Time*, 1974). Fads of the mental health movement continue to be uncritically applied by the so-called helping professions even in the "age of science."

Caplan (1969) notes several other historical characteristics of the helping professions. One is the tendency to meet public criticism by denial, defensiveness, and withdrawal. This is again being witnessed as our mental hospitals misapply today's "truths." If it continues, professionals may once again retreat, and take their patients along with them, behind the walls of institutions where the public cannot see them. Although emptying the mental hospitals and getting community input in mental health programs are the current stated goals of community mental health, the consumer still has little real impact on psychiatry and mental health practice. Local community control of mental health programs has never really been implemented for several reasons, some of which are discussed in later chapters. Here we simply note that the realities of the situation do not match the rhetoric. Rather, there is a tendency to accept secondary goals and to confuse ends and means. Clean hospitals, quiet wards, and correct staff procedures are settled for.

Finally, Caplan notes, there has been a neglect of the social history of psychiatry. Rather than understanding the social and political forces that have shaped its history, psychiatry has tended to view itself from the eyes of its great men and their "scientific advances" (e.g., see Zilboorg, 1941). This view has prevented modern psychiatry from understanding its relationship to the social environment with which it has been theoretically concerned.

Recently, others have attempted to understand the mental health movement from a broader perspective of social history (Foucault, 1965; Grobb, 1973; Rothman, 1971; Szasz, 1970). Although Caplan began in that direction, her view is largely focused on developments within the mental health profession itself, and centers on the beliefs and practices of psychiatrists. Daniel J. Rothman (1971) approaches some of the same events from the perspective of American history, and focuses particularly on the question "Why did Americans in the Jacksonian Era suddenly begin to construct and support institutions for deviant and dependent members of the community?" He notes, with the irony of historical perspective, that the builders considered the asylums to be instances of reform in the care of mental patients and to be based on scientific and medical advances. He questions why American society was ready to adopt such measures as asylums and prisons when in earlier days there had been none. The answers he finds are less a function of science or of the advances of medical treatment than a function of social values.

Asylums were a means to restore a kind of social balance to the newly founded American society. Like today's community mental health centers, which became popular in the 1960s during times of considerable social unrest, the asylum, in the 1800s, was a means of social control. The community mental health center movement of today was given tremendous support by its temporal association with the War on Poverty, which would help to assimilate the deviant poor into mainstream American society. The theories of insanity in the early 1800s, Rothman notes, also had more to do with social and political conditions than with medical discovery. The society which was trying to establish itself and its republican form of government in the eyes of the world needed a means of social control which appeared rational and humanitarian. The medical reformers of the day, in an effort to prevent epidemics of "insanity," tried to establish a kind of utopian environment which became the mental institution. Despite its obvious failure, the asylum has survived, partly as a means of keeping the poor and deviant away from the community at large, and partly through the ability of its proponents to protect and maintain themselves in the only way feasible—as a custodial institution.

Just as state-supported institutions boasted of keeping the paupers clean so too private ones found satisfaction in making the rich comfortable. . . . Once it gave up the claim of cure or rehabilitation, the asylum could concentrate on the "failure proof task of care for the chronic" . . . and thus maintain itself as an institution even if it lost its original aims (Rothman, 1971, pp. 278–282).

The Manufacture of Madness and Other Outgroups

The use of asylums as a convenient place to incarcerate immigrants, paupers, and undesirables is not new to America. Foucault (1965) has argued, in a review of the social use of the concept of insanity in Europe from 1500 to 1800, that society has always needed a scapegoat. For modern man the insane are the equivalent of lepers of the Middle Ages. He notes that the "great Reform" in Europe which eliminated jailing of the emotionally disturbed on the basis of demonology or criminality was followed by the "great Confinement" on the basis of disease.

Thomas S. Szasz (1970) presents a similar analysis in *The Manufacture of Madness*. His treatment of the social history of madness is perhaps the most pointed and critical study to date. It requires one to ask serious questions of our most cherished beliefs in the helping professions; it reverses our images and calls the "helper" the creator of madness who is rewarded by its creation and by its punishment (treatment) even as were witch-hunters and exorcists. To be sure, Szasz does not consider the individual psychiatrist to be evil in intention, but rather a well-meaning believer, a modern transformation of the religious zealot.[2] To rid the world of mental illness is equivalent to ridding the world of heresy. Both aims serve the purpose of scapegoating and protecting society symbolically as well as literally, by means of control of deviance.

Of all the social critics of the helping professions reviewed thus far, it is Szasz who leaves one most uncomfortable. It is easier to understand and agree with Szasz intellectually than it is to follow the implications of his arguments to their logical conclusion. He, like Leifer, Halleck, Caplan, Graziano, Rothman, and Foucault, raises intellectual arguments which question the social purpose of the helping professions; he points out their vested interests, their history of misguided beliefs, and their support for the status quo. Szasz also gives new ways to interpret the meaning of one's common sense belief in those whose ideas are in ascendance. But Szasz goes further. His arguments raise moral as well as intellectual questions for those who are in the professional practice of "helping." His analysis requires close examination by community psychology, for he questions if the aims of "community" can ever be reconciled with those of individual freedom.

The most striking thing about Szasz's work is the way he traces the history of the Inquisition and the mental health movement as one unbroken line of events, each movement serving the

same function at different times in history. People have always, since societies have been organized, needed a scapegoat to serve as both symbolic and literal validation of the group. The deviant is the scapegoat. Ritual destruction of humans and animals are found among all societies. Symbolically this is the way in which people have shifted the burden of evil, guilt, and suffering from the group to a nonmember. The Jewish custom of the sacrificial goat is later shifted to the story of Jesus as the scapegoat who died for all the sins of man. Once in ascendance, Christianity found scapegoats in those who did not believe—Jews and heretics. In Greece, the practice of sacrificing a deformed person in time of famine was common. In earlier times sacrifices were for religious reasons; today they are rationalized by medical-scientific terminology, but serve the same purpose: expulsion of evil through the sacrifice of one who is either not a group member or is defined as an outcast The justification is always technical (scientific), but the basis lies in a magical belief in expulsion of evil. The witch-hunter, the anti-Semite, the psychiatrist who confines deviants against their will, drugs them, and shocks them are each fighting evil. The ends justify the means. Society is "improved" through their work. In all cases the oppressor is unable to accept human differences. Everyone must be the same or the group is threatened. According to Szasz, by use of medical terminology the moral questions in such practices are avoided. By religious conversion Jews are saved, by treatment (social conversion) the "mentally ill" are saved. In both cases the group is unwilling to accept the deviant.

The crux of Szasz's argument lies in his belief that mental illness is a social invention used to stigmatize deviants. He is particularly concerned with the social function of institutional psychiatry, which is seen as an agent of the state to control the society even as the religious establishment did in earlier times. Psychiatry is the new priesthood, able to diagnose mental illness just as the witch-hunters diagnosed witches, and for the same reasons, now in medical rather than religious terms.

Szasz's idea that mental illness is a myth is often not well understood. That is, he does not

---

[2]Although he writes specifically about psychiatry, Szasz's arguments are intended to encompass the mental health professions more generally.

deny that some people are unhappy and unable to cope with their environments, but when this happens they are often condemned, stigmatized, and locked away against their will. This is even, or perhaps especially, the case for those who do not want "help." They are seen as "out of their mind," otherwise they would be just like us, or at least they would want to be.

Using Sartre's discussion of anti-Semitism as an exemplar of the process, Szasz points out that for some deviants there is no need to "diagnose" their difference; Blacks, for example, are readily identifiable in a white society, but for others—Jews or mental patients—the identification requires a social act on the part of others. His discussion of Sartre's analysis of anti-Semitism is instructive:

Although Sartre recognizes that Jews exist in the same way as homosexuals or depressed people exist, he asserts that "The Jew is one whom other men consider a Jew: that is the simple truth from which we must start . . . . It is the anti-Semite who makes the Jew." Now, of course, Sartre knows as well as anyone else that Jews may exist without anti-Semites. In saying that the anti-Semite "makes the Jew," he means the Jew *qua* social object upon whom the anti-Semite proposes to act in his own self-interest. This point cannot be emphasized too strongly about mental illness. It is one thing for an observer to say that someone is sad and thinks of killing himself—and do *nothing* about it; it is quite another to describe such a person as "suicidal" or "dangerous to himself"— and *lock him up in a hospital* (to cure the disease of depression, of which he considers suicidal ideas but a symptom). In the former sense, mental illness may be said to exist without the intervention of the psychiatrist; in the latter, it is created by the psychiatrist. As in the case of anti-Semitism, moreover, the psychiatrist creates mental patients as social objects so that he can act upon them in his own self-interest. That he conceals his self-interest as altruism need not detain us here, as it is but a fresh "therapeutic" justification of interpersonal coercion.

To the extent that people have characteristics that set them apart from others, the truly liberal and humane attitude toward these differences can only be one of acceptance. Sartre describes this in terms equally applicable to so-called mental patients. "In societies where women vote," he writes, "they are not asked to change their sex when they enter the voting booth . . . . When it is a question of the legal

rights of the Jew, and of the more obscure but equally indispensable rights that are not inscribed in any code, he must enjoy those rights not as a potential Christian but precisely as a French Jew. It is with his character, his customs, his tastes, his religion if he has one, his name, and his physical traits that we *must* accept him." To apply this attitude to the so-called mentally ill is not an easy task. Present-day American society shows not the slightest interest in even seeing the problem in this light, much less in so resolving it. It prefers the model of conversion and cure: As Benjamin Rush sought the solution of Negritude in vitiligo, we seek the solution of fear and futility, rage and sadness in Community Mental Health Centers (Szasz, pp. 273–274).

Szasz is specifically concerned with the involuntary patient—the homosexual, the drug addict, the alcoholic, the idiosyncratic person who is called schizophrenic and locked away against his will under the fallacious argument of physical dangerousness. He sees this to be a rationalization for the inability of society to tolerate differences that are a moral rather than a physical threat. This is the classic conflict between individual freedom and communal values and beliefs reenacted since the beginning of civilization. To see it in other terms than this, Szasz feels, obscures the real challenge for society—*to accept pluralism and individual differences, and to live in harmony with them.* These same concerns must be faced as community psychology approaches questions other than mental illness per se.

The history of the mental health movement finds an ever-increasing definition of the scope of mental illness (Zax & Cowen, 1972). The movement toward concern with the "well-being" of all members of society has served as justification for large-scale "helping programs." Many of these programs are administered by professional middle-class people who have little contact with or understanding of the people they presumably seek to help. Operationalized in the community mental health movement, and through various welfare programs, including those for early education such as Head Start, mental health consultation to schools, and extension of public health concepts to social phenomena, the network of people defined as in need is sometimes seen to be as high as one-third to one-half of the population (Cowen, Gardner, & Zax, 1967).

The poor are special targets of such efforts, often targeted for "programs" for which they neither volunteer nor in which they have a say. Many of the aims of such programs are to socialize everyone to a single standard of "model man" as defined by the mental health and the educational establishments. Even when people volunteer for such programs the values, aims, and ideologies of those in control are rarely obvious. This is not surprising because the programs are, on the face of it, for the "good" of the people, which needs little justification. When poor parents volunteer their child for the opportunity to prepare for school in a preschool program, the image is usually a false one presenting the road to success in America. Actually, either socialization to middle-class values or nothing occurs, and there is little guarantee of success in later school or life even for those who become socialized. These issues are discussed more fully in later chapters.

It is important to note here that the concepts of mental illness are increasingly being extended to embrace all forms of deviance including educational (to be a high school dropout is as much a stigma as to be sick). The education establishment is now coming together with the mental health establishment to foster this extension. Those who are deviant by not fitting in to the American middle-class school are, if not mentally ill, suffering from a social-intellectual pathology which because of their inferior environment, makes them at least stupid and unsocialized. Once again their "place" in society is justified in humanitarian terms.

Does Szasz have a solution? Because he writes from the perspective of the private-practicing psychodynamically oriented psychiatrist, his solution is essentially a "hands off" policy. Psychiatry should not be used to further the aims of the state, but only to be available for what he calls "contractual psychiatry," wherein individual patients seek individual treatment from a private practitioner. This places the mental health professional in the role of agent only for those who seek him out. What Szasz does not deal with are the large number of non-

middle-class people who, for various reasons, are socially marginal. He offers no assistance for the poor, the Black man, the oppressed minorities, or the unhappy who cannot afford the services he offers, and for whom those services may be largely irrelevant because they are inappropriate to their problems in living. Szasz offers sympathy to the victims of an unequal social system, but little else. He would not have us stigmatize them, but at the same time he offers no clue as to how to work for the social changes that are necessary to truly have a pluralistic society. Szasz is essentially ideological and not action oriented.

Community psychology, or more precisely, a psychology for the members of diverse communities, demands more. Passivity will not do. The lesson to be learned from Szasz is to recognize the traditional role of the helping professions as agents of the status quo. This means, once again, a willingness to examine one's values and to advocate them even when they are for social change rather than social stability. A community psychologist need not work to confine deviants, nor need he limit himself to individual psychotherapy. Rather, by identifying himself with various stigmatized grass-roots groups the community psychologist can work for social change together with those groups.

If community is defined not as a monolithic "other," representative only of prevailing values and powers, but is defined as a set of subgroups some of whom are in need of resources and assistance in establishing their place in the society, then the community psychologist may be free to work for social change. This requires a view of the world through a cultural relativist-ecological perspective which sees neither inferior people nor inferior environment (cultures).

The Emergence of Cultural Relativity and the Need for an Ecological Viewpoint

Others have also argued that the helping services have always been responsive to the political and economic conditions of society. In a recent historical analysis of the settlement-house move-ment, Levine and Levine (1970) detail the be-ginnings of social work in America. Their analysis has been cited as historically important for an understanding of current community psychology (Zax & Specter, 1974), community mental health (Hersch, 1972), and helping ser-vices for children (Mora, 1972). The idea of the settlement house, a place where well-off and idealistic social service volunteers could live and work to provide services for the working-class poor, was based on the notion that one had to live in a given community in order to under-stand its people. Neighborhood organization was seen as an important means of socialization. In America, during the late nineteenth and early twentieth centuries, frequently with religious aims, and often with the paramount idea of as-similation of immigrants into the American mainstream, many young, economically and educationally advantaged women became cru-saders for social reform through this move-ment. The workers in the settlement houses they established not only provided neighborhood so-cial, medical, and recreation services, but also joined in political activity for neighborhood im-provement, improvement of labor conditions, and legal rights of children. Although early ef-forts were based on reaching the children through volunteers who provided socioenviron-mental opportunities such as education and rec-reation, eventually the settlement houses came to be operated by professionals. As the child guidance movement developed, concurrent with the widespread acceptance of Freudian psychol-ogy, individual counseling of an intraphysic na-ture gained precedence over socioenvironmental reform activities.

In describing this history the Levines discuss the relationship between the political tenor of the times and the kinds of explanations and solu-tions offered for social problems by members of the helping professions. They see two classes of theory and help-giving activity which have al-ternated in popularity. One is the intrapsychic or individual explanation and intervention, the other is the environmental or situational. Each of these approaches is based on a social value system which dictates the activity of the profes-sional service deliverer. In the context of the individual approach, activity focuses on prob-lems believed to be idiosyncratic to the person in question. The individual's particular back-ground, experiences, learning history, genetic makeup, intrapsychic processes, personality, and so on, are attributed the major share of the cause for problems in living. In essence, it is a belief in the individual as totally responsible for his own actions. The environmental or situa-tional view emphasizes the social and environ-mental causes of problems in living, quite apart from individual makeup. The environmental view leads to activity aimed at reforming the social conditions, rather than the individual.

Similarly, the Levines note, the political tenor of the times may be described as generally conservative, or generally reform-oriented. They argue that the helping orientation, domi-nant during a given era, is a function of which political ideology has set the tone for the times. Although not a one-to-one correspondence, they document this relationship for the social history of the helping services which they have re-viewed. During times of political conser-vativism the intrapsychic orientation is most popular, whereas during times of political re-form the environmental approach is in ascen-dance.

Ira Goldenberg (1971), in the context of a description of his own program for social ac-tion (see Chapter X), has reflected similarly on the relationships between the tenor of the times and the history of clinical psychology, which, as we have seen in Chapter I, emerged as a profession just after the end of World War II. At that time there was an increas-ingly felt need for psychological services to be available to the many returning veterans, and there was a concerted effort to develop clinical psychology to assist the psychiatric profession. Goldenberg characterizes the development of clinical psychology in the 1940s, and 1950s, and 1960s as passing through three respective stages which mirrored the times: "frantic," "si-lent," and "action-oriented." Psychology had been called to the front during the war and, like the rest of the country, responded to the needs of war. As Reiff (1971a) noted, the cautious scientist became a self-proclaimed expert by necessity and joined other helping professionals in making decisions and providing service with less than certain knowledge. In the 1950s we became, along with Eisenhower, stabilized, conservative, and quiet. In the 1960s, aroused first by Kennedy's call to action and later by Johnson's War on Poverty, we again took up the call to arms with less than caution. The times had shifted from political conservatism to reform and psychological intervention became, as the Levines' historical analysis would predict, focused on environmental change. It was during the 1960s that community psychology was born.

Community psychology will be a "teenager" in the late 1970s and early 1980s. The outcome of its inevitable search for identity will in part be determined by the temper of the times. We already know that this decade is less openly action-oriented and more reflective. Conflicting groups have turned inward. In the 1970s a new awareness of our past has emerged which may help community psychology to break with the idea that either persons or their cultural environments are to "blame" for their problems in living. The concept of person-environment "fit" rather than inferior or superior people or cultures is beginning to take hold. Recognition of and support for diversity is emerging. A major political-social question for the rest of this century will involve the ability of diverse groups to "live and let live," and this will mean understanding that there are neither sick persons (in the social-psychological sense) nor inferior cultures.

American Blacks have helped to make all of the ethnic groups, as well as themselves, aware of the importance of diversity. There is now an inward and reflective atmosphere with a new respect for difference. Difference is even flaunted by some. The interest in nostalgia and looking back to the 1920s and 1930s in dress, style, movies, and television has been interpreted as a search for the simpler days; but it may also be seen as a search for our roots and our traditions.

Many Americans who do not identify with an ethnic or a minority group, a European country of family origin, or a religion, have a rela-

tively short American history. Those who see themselves as first and most basically American are left out of the diversity trend. To recall and explore the recent past in style and content seems to be an alternative to ethnic identification. In any case, it appears that the 1970s are a time in our social history when diversity and tradition are both being honored again. It is a time when one's belonging to a group with a past is honored.

In both academics and politics there is today a serious challenge to the American assimilationist ideology. Many do not want to enter a melting pot and lose their own diversity. There appears to be an increased tolerance for people (as it is expressed in the popular slang) "doing their own thing." Greely (1971) sees this in terms of cultural pluralism which derives out of what Edward Shils (1957) calls "primordial attachments" or a kind of natural sense of belonging out of which self-esteem is developed. Recognizing the traditional American (and academic) dislike for diversity, Greely is an advocate for ethnic pluralism. He views the American assimilationist ethic, which calls for everyone to be the same in order to live in harmony, as a kind of white, middle-class, Protestant imperialism. Similarly, he is critical of the Marxist thought which views ethnicity as a mask for class oppression. He argues that ethnic pluralism is healthy, and in fact, those Americans who have a strong identification with an ethnic group are not anti-Black, as they are painted in popular newspaper accounts. Rather, he argues, according to survey research, they are more pro-integration than the general population. Furthermore, he cites considerable data to support the argument that "ethnics are more likely to be politically liberal than Anglo-Saxon Americans of comparable social class, and the more ethnic a person is, the more he is likely to be 'liberal' " (Greely, 1971).

Arguing further that Americans live in relative peace among diversity, Greely concludes that it may well be that the answer to such peace is universal affluence. In other words, diversity is healthy in that it allows each individual a sense of personal identity, and it is workable, given enough physical resources to allow their equitable distribution. The popular picture of "ethnics" in conflict with Blacks is newsworthy, but occurs only when by accident of geography or political maneuver they are thrown into direct competition for limited resources. Greely believes that pluralism works in America because of denominational pluralism in religious tradition, supported by the American Constitution. He sees diverse groups in political, cultural, and social style living together in relative harmony. He goes so far as to view minorities, even Blacks, as better off in America than minorities in other countries ". . . diverse groups live together with at least some harmony and if not with justice, still at least with the conviction that justice (is) a reasonable expectation" (Greely, 1971). He sees the current interest in diversity, bolstered by the arrival of Black ethnicity, as legitimate. This leaves other groups who support (or oppose) this ethnicity, freer to admit and support their own diversity. "It has now . . . become official: it is all right for Blacks to have their own heritage, their own tradition, their own culture. If it is all right for the Blacks, then it ought to be all right for everyone else" (Greely, 1971).

If it is true that diversity, expressed in reverence for the traditions, skills, and experiences of the past, is the social theme of the 1970s, then there are several possible outcomes. On the one hand, appreciation of diversity may lead to a fairer amd more equitable distribution of psychological resources that is, self-esteem. But this need not necessarily lead to equitable distribution of physical resources. If the two distributions continue to be disparate, as indeed they are in the 1970s, as appreciation for diversity increases and power and economic relationships remain the same, then one might expect efforts to balance the psychological and material scales. The way this appears to be attempted in the 1970s is through internal efforts of ethnic, social, and religious groups to build their own strength. In the past, attempts to obtain resources involved largely assimilationist strategies, and the willingness to give up diversity to attain them. To build a society in which material resources and power are distributed in fair share to ethnic and minority groups, without

the loss of psychological identity and respect for diversity, requires a turning inward and solidarity among group members. They must take and not be given, they must do it in their style, not anyone else's. Social change no longer can exclude preservation of tradition and the contents of ethnic identity, but must retain such identity while seeking reorganization of the political, economic, and social relationships among groups. For community psychology this signals several implications. Progress in the 1970s will depend on a recognition of the strengths of special groups and support for diversity. A social view that is culturally relativistic and eschews comparison of all to a single standard must be developed. The political temper of the times demands control by diverse groups over their own destiny, rather than by a monolithic authority.

For community psychology, Greely's (1971) analysis is a step in the direction of the "rediscovery of diversity," but it falls short on several grounds. His analysis leads him to the conclusion that the attempt to organize "ethnics" is silly because they are already organized. Unfortunately, his use of the term "ethnic" is restricted to those groups who are traditionally identified as such by sociologists. That is why he appears to be satisfied with the way diversity works in America. Greely does not carry his analysis of diversity to its logical end point. Diversity implies that in order to truly have a society that both tolerates difference and does so with justice, there needs to be room for more than traditional ethnic difference. New groups of people who are different on other than an ethnic basis must be allowed to emerge.

The so-called "mental patients" who Szasz is so concerned about need the right to their individual differences without loss of their legal rights or the physical resources of society. Homosexuals may not be an ethnic group, but they certainly are different from the standard. They too need political, legal, and psychological resources. The individual "odd" mental patient needs the opportunity to live in a community which provides him the resources to which he is entitled as a member of the human race, even if he is a group of one. The alcoholic and the drug addict must not have their individual rights violated. Women, although not an ethnic group and not even a minority, may now appropriately be considered a "new minority." Greely does not even mention Puerto Ricans, Mexican-, or Native Americans.

In discussing the Black American, Greely (1971) smooths over the unjust and inequitable distribution of resources to which they are subjected. He, ironically, does not even touch on the pervasive inability of White Americans to consider the Black man in other than assimilationist terms. It is these groups of Americans, sometimes called the "new minorities," that community psychology, in order to be a true psychology of communities, must support. Community psychology is at its best when it is responsive to grass-roots groups who require not treatment, cure, or re-education, but support with political, social, and psychological resources. The perspective for community psychology must be one of support for cultural relativity, diversity, and equitable distribution of resources. Community psychology must be based first on a social and ethical value system which recognizes the right to be different; second, on an ecological perspective which views all people and all cultures as worthwhile in their own right; and third, on a belief in equal access to material and psychological resources.

CONCEPTIONS FROM COMMUNITY MENTAL HEALTH

Every institution states explicitly that it is a community facility, it exists because of and for the citizens of a particular geographic area. In reality, of course, the institution is usually physically and psychologically removed from the community . . . it is frequently viewed as an "alien body" in the community, and there is no basis for asserting that the citizens of the community in any way have any feeling of responsibility for and involvement in the institution.

—*Seymour B. Sarason*

To this point we have scanned a chronology of events leading to the community psychology movement, and have given multiple examples of how social forces, politics, and value systems have interacted to influence the activities and ideas of helping professionals. We have seen how community psychology may be characterized as a search for new paradigms to solve problems outside the scope of traditional psychology; and finally, we have explored the implications of cultural relativity, diversity, and person-environment fit as a value base for the new paradigm. We are now ready to explore the details of community psychology's closest relative—community mental health. This chapter is concerned with the assumptions and conceptions that have served as the basis for community mental health, the precursor to community psychology.

The Joint Commission Report

As noted in Chapter I, the 1961 report of the Joint Commission on Mental Illness and Health may be considered a direct stimulus which set the tone for the next 15 years of United States mental health policy. Although the movement

itself was overdetermined by social and professional developments, the report shaped a perspective for national mental health planning, and signaled the formal birth of the modern community mental health movement.

The Joint Commission was an interdisciplinary group whose members were appointed by the National Institute of Mental Health in cooperation with 36 different participating national health and social welfare agencies. These agencies ranged from the American Academy of Neurology through the Veterans Administration. There were 45 members of the commission—over half were M.D.s, but also included were nine laymen, one minister, one nurse, one educator, one occupational therapist, and five psychologists. The background research was accumulated in ten monographs and a final report. These eleven volumes are listed in Table III-1. As can be seen from a glance at the titles, the commission addressed itself to very broad policy implications in mental health planning at the national level. The final report, *Action for Mental Health* (1961), is really an abstract of these volumes, together with a set of recommendations.

The final report argues that a national mental health program requires solution of three problems: manpower, facilities, and cost. The rec-

TABLE III–1   **Monographs published by The Joint Commission on Mental Illness and Health**

Title	Author
Mental Health Manpower Trends	George W. Albee
The Role of Schools in Mental Health	Wesley Allinsmith & George W. Goethals
Economics of Mental Illness	Rashi Fein
Americans View Their Mental Health. A Nationwide Interview Survey	Gerald Gurin, Joseph Veroff, & Sheila Feld
Current Concepts of Positive Mental Health	Marie Jahoda
The Churches and Mental Health	Richard V. McCann
Epidemiology and Mental Illness	Richard J. Plunkett & John E. Gordon
Community Resources in Mental Health	Reginald Robinson, David F. DeMarche, & Mildred R. Wagle
New Perspectives on Mental Patient Care	Morris S. Schwartz *et al.*
Research Resources in Mental Health	William F. Soskin
Action for Mental Health: Final Report	Joint Commission on Mental Illness and Health

ommendations are accordingly concerned with "Pursuit of New Knowledge, Better Use of Knowledge and Experience, and the Cost." First, an investment in "basic research" and support for investigators is recommended. In addition, the establishment of research centers and research facilities is supported, especially in rural areas where such institutions are sparse. Interestingly, only 5 percent of the total mental health budget was suggested for research and training, despite this rhetoric.

Second, a broadening of the definition of who can legitimately participate in the delivery of mental health services is recommended. Treatment, it is argued, should depend on knowledge and training and not necessarily on formal degrees. The acceptance of nonmedical mental health workers, as well as volunteers, nonprofessionals, clergymen, physicians, and educators as legitimate members of the service network is advanced, although medical supervision is held to be necessary. In addition, an emphasis on recruitment and training of future mental health professionals is emphasized.

A third major set of recommendations includes the notion that persons who are emotionally disturbed should have services available to them, in their local community, as soon as the difficulty becomes apparent. Intervening during the early stages of mental illness, prior to its becoming severe, is seen as a way to prevent exacerbation of the problem and worsening of adjustment. The availability of emergency care for acute breakdowns is emphasized, and the key recommendation that ". . . *major mental illness is the core problem and unfinished business of the mental health movement . . .*" is put forth with such force as to become the guiding principle behind the later legislation that has encouraged reduction of the size of state hospital populations and the construction of comprehensive community mental health centers. Specifically, the report set the objective of one mental health clinic for every 50,000 people, expansion of services for children and adults, addition of psychiatric units to general hospitals, and the conversion of all state hospitals to 1000 beds or less. A major emphasis is placed on care for chronic mental patients, including after-care and rehabilitation. In overall emphasis the report tries to break down the barriers between the institution and the community through the use of programs such as day hospitals and night hospitals which would enable patients to live at home part of the time or to work if they are able. Halfway houses, foster family services, and the like are also encouraged.

A fourth set of recommendations is focused on the need for public information with regard to mental illness, and the need to publicly emphasize that many of the problems of the mentally ill are a result of social ostracism, rejection, and isolation. This aspect of the recommendations has not been as influential as some of the others, and although many of the large state hospitals have been reduced in size over the past 15 years, acceptance of identified patients in local communities has continued to be problematic (for an example of the problem in New York City, see Chapter II, p. 45).

A fifth set of recommendations is concerned with financing the delivery of mental health services. It is recommended that the federal government assume a large responsibility, while encouraging the states to share in the cost of new facilities. Support on the basis of merit as determined by the National Institute of Mental Health is recommended.

As a consequence of the Joint Commission's report, legislation was passed in the mid-1960s (see Chapter I, p. 13), which provided funds first for building new community mental health centers and later for staffing them. The guidelines for such comprehensive community mental health centers include five "essential" services (required for funding) and five "desirable" (optional) services. The basic services are: inpatient care for those who need 24-hour hospitalization; outpatient service for adults and children; partial care, such as day hospitals and night hospitals for those who can live at home in the evenings or work during the day; emergency services on a 24-hour basis; and consultation and education programs. The five additional services include a diagnostic service, social and vocational rehabilitation programs, prehospital care and post hospital after-care, training programs for mental health workers, and research and evaluation programs.

The community mental health centers legislation was met with a great deal of enthusiasm by the mental health professionals, an enthusiasm that was undoubtedly an honest response to a financial boom in the mental health field. Suddenly the funds for expansion of manpower and reach of services were to be provided. If local mental health groups would set up the required services they could now find new sources of building and staffing funds. The initial response to this boom included much enthusiasm and high hopes for successful community programs just at a time when many professionals were discouraged about the outcome of their previous efforts.

Guidelines for Community Mental Health and Community Mental Health Centers

Why is the Joint Commission report considered to be so important in the development of community mental health and community psychology? The reason has more to do with its political and financial impact on administrative and social policy than with its scientific content. The new policies advocated seemed to provide support for a number of ideas that already existed in the mental health field, but not widely implemented (e.g., Caplan's thinking described below) and, in addition, stimulated the energies and the thinking of many professionals who saw the report, perhaps unrealistically, as a mandate for genuine change. Initially, large numbers of professionals united behind the community mental health ideology. It has taken more than a decade for those engaged in such community work to begin to go in a number of separate ways. Today, as a consequence of differing success and failure, and the chance to concretize a vague set of recommendations, there are many different meanings to the term community mental health. In this chapter we shall try to sort them out systematically. Community psychology has grown out of this splitting apart of the community mental health movement, and to understand it we must understand its parent— community mental health. What were the conceptions that, beyond the promise of money, so excited the professional help givers?

One of the first to present a viewpoint for the movement was Nicholas Hobbs who, in a 1964 paper published by the *American Journal of Orthopsychiatry*, called community mental health the "third mental health revolution." Ever since Zilboorg's (1941) *History of Medical Psychology*, the first revolution in mental health had been considered the work of Pinel, Rush, and

Dix in humanizing treatment for the insane. The second revolution had been considered the introduction of Freud's thinking. Now Hobbs termed community mental health a third revolution. Specifically, he saw the concepts of public health, which emphasize prevention of disease and creation of a healthy environment, as entering into mental health work. He felt that now the mental health professions could be concerned not just with disease, but also with human well-being more generally. Mental illness, in Hobbs' view, ". . . is not the private organic misery of an individual but a social, ethical and moral problem, a responsibility of the total community." Citing the work of Hollingshead and Redlich (1958), which was an investigation of all persons who received psychiatric treatment in New Haven, Connecticut during a specified time period, Hobbs noted that although there was no relationship between psychiatric diagnosis and treatment, there was between social class and treatment received. Those from the lower classes received a quick and automatic chemical or electrical "treatment" while those in the higher socioeconomic classes received one-to-one psychotherapy. These data had been collected in 1950 and on the basis of 1960 data on the same patients (not then available to Hobbs) Meyers and Bean (1968) extended the analysis. They found that on a 10-year follow-up the lower the social class of the patients, the higher the proportion under hospital care, the fewer discharged, the fewer to receive psychotherapy, and the fewer to receive outpatient treatment. Among former patients, those in the upper and middle classes are more impaired psychologically, but less likely to have employment problems. The lower the social class the higher the proportion of socially isolated patients. In both the Hollingshead and Redlich and the Meyers and Bean studies such relationships were found for public hospitals and clinics. These data, together with George Albee's analysis of *Mental Health Manpower* (1959) trends, which demonstrated a critical professional manpower shortage, led Hobbs to conclude that new ways must be found to deliver services to the poor.

In some measure Hobbs in 1964 cited the goals for community mental health. He argued that the mental health specialist must be a broad humanist as well as a scientist "prepared to make decisions not only about the welfare of an individual but also about the kind of society that must be developed to nurture the greatest human fulfillment." Here mental health professionals were offered, at a time when the entire country perceived itself to be experiencing an urban crisis and many professionals were seeking "relevance," exactly the kind of role that could rally professional helpers behind the community mental health movement. The role was clear, but the means for accomplishing it were less clear. To be sure, Hobbs cautioned that comprehensive community mental health centers could turn out to be a failure, but optimism in the excitement of a new role overcame such cautions. Hobbs called for a training program for "ourselves" (the professionals) to prepare us to serve as planners and consultants to schools, churches, and other social institutions; to work with problems of delinquency, city planning, human ecology, and social change. He assumed that someone among the professionals knew what to teach and how to solve such social problems. He called for interdisciplinary cooperation, for use of nonprofessional mental health workers, and work through consultation to already established social institutions. Furthermore, he called for a public health emphasis which accentuates prevention and early detection of emotional disturbance, and a revision of the organizational structures for delivery of services, and for continuing research and education.

It should be clear from a comparison of Hobbs' writing with the Joint Commission report that Hobbs was overstepping the bounds of the mental health movement mandated by Congress. Yet it was his aims that attracted large numbers of professional help givers. By 1966 the American Psychological Association adopted, as its official position paper, a set of guidelines for community mental health centers authored by M. Brewster Smith and Nicholas Hobbs (1966). The basic assumptions of that paper were that the logic of community mental health was to move the care and treatment of the mentally ill into the local community and thereby avoid the disruption of normal patterns of living, and to strengthen the resources of the community in order to prevent mental disorder. Writing from the point of view of community members who are responsible for their own mental health care, Smith and Hobbs advocated the following kind of community mental health care.

First, *community control* is considered to be essential. The community is asked to accept responsibility for all its citizens, and this responsibility implies control over its own mental health programs. Second, the center is expected to be active in seeking to prevent emotional problems through programs of early detection and treatment, and by means of work with social agencies such as schools, police, industry, the courts, and community councils. The concept of personal illness is rejected in favor of an emphasis on the failure of social systems to provide a proper environment. The center staff should help the community's social systems to function effectively, and consequently goals and policies of the center are a matter for local control, with mental health professionals as consultants. As we shall see below, this recommendation has proven to be difficult to implement, and at best it has created controversy because professionals were accustomed to answering only to their colleagues; now they were being asked to be accountable to local citizens.

In terms of programs, the center is expected to go beyond direct patient services and to provide consultation to already existing social agencies as well as to help develop new community resources. By working with other community leaders the center staff is asked to provide a new perspective for all community activities. Coordination of all community services is sought such that information flows freely across agencies and social systems. Here the agency staff is asked to help monitor such communication. Such proposals get dangerously close to having the mental health center staff viewed as a kind of central clearing agency for all community activities, a proposal that many

other community agents may reject. But other aims are less controversial, if idealistic. One such aim is to reach those who are in need of services but who do not normally receive them, particularly the poor, and those other than the White, middle-class, adult, verbal, and successful clients of psychotherapists. This is recommended as best accomplished by developing new methods of treatment that are reality- and action-oriented rather than based on talk. Implied in such methods are programs of social action for employment, housing, and educational opportunity as legitimate mental health improvement activities. In this regard the use of nonprofessionals is emphasized. Methods, such as group treatment and on-the-spot consultation to those in a crisis, are emphasized, as are new services for children. An additional emphasis is on planning services for those that do not fit neatly into our existing programs—alcoholics, addicts, the aging, delinquents, and the mentally retarded. The skills required, it is acknowledged, may not be those of the therapist, but rather those of the social change agent. Finally, the recommendations support training of mental health workers as well as program evaluation and research.

For professionals seeking a cooperative and democratic base for community welfare, the above proposals, which have more to do with social values and social change than traditional mental health as adjustment to the status quo, provided a framework to unite themselves in a new movement for social justice. In the mid-1960s such an ideology was enthusiastically, if naively, embraced.

In 1967 APA's Division of Community Psychology appointed a Task Force on Community Mental Health which, in 1968, presented a summary report of *Priorities for Psychologists in Community Mental Health*. Following revisions, the report was endorsed by the Executive Committee of the division and published under the sponsorship of APA (Glidewell, 1971). That statement endorsed the position of Smith and Hobbs (1966) and extended it to apply to the work of psychologists outside of community mental health per se. In that statement one can observe the beginning evolution of community psychology toward increasing concern with social systems change and away from more traditional clinical services as such. The essence of the endorsed priorities is captured in Glidewell's (1971) summary statement:

Psychologists involved in community mental health should place the highest priority upon collaborative, self-modifying, social interventions to prevent disorders by facilitating the accomplishment of developmental tasks, especially in children. The training and retraining of psychologists competent to perform the roles required should be assigned a top priority by the American Psychological Association (p. 143).

These guidelines were based on a number of conclusions that had been reached by the task force, including the belief that individual human development progresses through a distinct set of "stages" wherein the successful completion of one stage is a prerequisite for the next.

The idea of stages has gained wide acceptance in both the realm of cognitive development, through the influence of Jean Piaget (Flavell, 1963) and J. McV. Hunt (1961), and in emotional-social development, through the influence of Erik Erikson (1950) and Robert White (1959). Although the exact age at which an individual passes through the stages of development is variable, the stages themselves are seen to be in invariant order, one building upon the next. Table III-2 presents the Piagetian stages of intellectual development and the Erikson stages of social-emotional development. These views of development are not presented here because the task force selected them as the ones to which all psychologists should ascribe; indeed, many disagree as to exactly what the "real" stages and developmental tasks are. Rather, the examples are presented here in order to give the reader some idea as to what the task force had in mind. Their essential conception is that all individuals must progress from infancy through childhood by learning progressively more complicated cognitive, social, and emotional tasks, and that successful learning of an earlier task is important for learning later tasks.

Theoretically there is some argument as to whether these stages of cognitive and emotional development are independent and universal, and

to what extent they are environmentally or biologically determined. But the task force seemed to make its recommendations on the belief that such stages are universal, and that successful completion of one stage is a prerequisite for passage to the next; and most importantly, successful accomplishment of each stage was taken to be environmentally determined. *Specifically, the view endorsed was that failure to master developmental tasks should not be considered to be the result of illness, but rather of failure of social systems to provide the necessary resources.* This view places responsibility for community mental health with the agents of socialization—families, schools, police, political and economic systems—rather than with the individual person. It was further implied that developmental problems appear at a high rate in many communities.

A second conclusion reached by the task force relates this view of developmental tasks and the role of social systems to its implications for social intervention by community mental health practitioners. The task force concluded that early detection and treatment of disorders of *high incidence*[1] have not led to a reduction in the rate of new cases in the field of physical health, and is not likely to lead to such a reduction in the field of mental health. Such methods, which rely heavily on individual treatment, may be useful for problems of low incidence, such as those caused by constitutional failure, because the time and manpower necessary for individual treatment are more likely to be found when the system is not overloaded. For psychologists interested in reducing the problems of accomplishing developmental tasks that are caused by failure of social systems such as education, housing, employment, and law, where the incidence and prevalence of difficulty are high, individual treatment holds less promise as a solution. This

---

[1] The terms *incidence* and *prevalence* are borrowed by community mental health from the field of public health. These terms refer to the existence of disorder in a given community during a given time period. Incidence is the number of new cases occurring during the specified time period, while prevalence is the total number of cases, both new and ongoing, active during the specified period of time.

Table III–2 Example of cognitive and social-emotional stages of development

Cognitive Stages of Development	Emotional-Social Stages of Development
Hypothesized by Piaget as universal and occurring in invariant order (adapted from Flavell, 1963)	Hypothesized by Erikson (1950) as universal and occurring in invariant order

Cognitive Stages of Development

I. *The period of sensory-motor intelligence (0–2 yrs.)*
Characterized by simple sensory motor adjustment to objects without symbolic manipulation at first.
Stage 1. reflexes provided at birth (0–1 mo.)
Stage 2. reflexes coordinated with one another (1–4 mos.)
Stage 3. orientation to objects and events outside one's own body (4–8 mos.)
Stage 4. development of intention (8–12 mos.)
Stage 5. pursuit of novelty (12–18 mos.)
Stage 6. internal symbolic representations (18 mos.–2 yrs.)
Special developments during this period—imitation, play, objects, space, causality, and time.

II. *The period of ireoperational thought (2–7 yrs.)*
In the first few years the child elaborates on the earlier abilities, in the fifth, sixth, and seventh year the child is more able to address himself to a specified task, and apply intelligence. The child becomes more flexible, and learns cognitive transformations and reversability.

III. *The period of concrete operations (7–11 yrs.)*
The child develops a cognitive system to organize the world. Logical operations of addition, subtraction, multiplication, and division, and other numerical relations. Developments of values and personal-social-affective components.

IV. *Period of formal operations (11 yrs. +)*
Child learns the real versus the possible; development of hypothetico-deductive reasoning; propositional thinking.

Emotional-Social Stages of Development

I. *Oral sensory stage*
Child develops basic trust

II. *Muscular anal stage*
Child learns autonomy

III. *Locomotor genital stage*
Child learns initiative versus guilt

IV. *Period of latency*
Child learns industry or inferiority

V. *Adolescence*
Develops identity or role confusion

VI. *Young adult*
Learning of intimacy as opposed to isolation

VII. *Adulthood*
Generativity versus stagnation

VIII. *Maturity*
Ego integrity versus despair

does not mean that individual treatment cannot be useful to a given person, but as a *social policy,* emphasis on such services is not likely to contribute to reduction of the appearance of the problem in the community.

In order to reduce the incidence of new cases, the logic of the above arguments led the task force to the conclusion that community mental health programs should be conducted through social interventions aimed at changing the social systems affecting children, so as to enhance the likelihood that these social systems, including the education, mental health, legal, housing, economic, and employment systems, will facilitate rather than inhibit accomplishment of developmental tasks. Psychologists are encouraged to conduct studies of experimental social intervention through collaborative efforts with school systems, police, political leaders, and other socialization agents so as to obtain feedback on the outcomes and effects of societal institutions and of community interventions. This latter aim is to go hand in hand with the accountability of psychologists and other community interventionists to the local community. Psychologists are further urged to take responsibility for advocating public policy, even to the point of political debate and confrontation.

Hidden in such recommendations are several value issues that must be made explicit. First, the definition of mental health, although avoided per se, is implied to encompass many life areas not traditionally thought of in that way. Educational, social, employment, and economic problems are now viewed as legitimate mental health concerns because each affects one's well-being or quality of life. If a child is not obtaining proper nutrition, his or her mental health may be impaired. If a child is not receiving an adequate education, mental health is likewise viewed as impaired. One begins to define ''mental health'' as a set of behaviors and resources that must be available to an individual in order that he or she have the necessary alternatives for coping with the multifaceted problems of living. Economic, educational, and social variables are viewed as having at least equal relevance to mental health as do psychological factors. If a child grows up believing he is incompetent (a psychological

problem) he is likely to have acquired fewer available alternative behaviors than if he feels competent; that is, his mental health is impaired. If he believes he is incompetent because of racial bias in public policy (a political problem), poverty (an economic problem), or inadequate opportunity to learn and develop through his home and peer relationships (an interpersonal problem), the resultant difficulties may be identical in that he will have acquired a reduced number of coping behaviors. Hence, urban problems such as job training, money, political representation, and education are in effect ''psychological'' and should be directly approached by psychologists.

Second, the assumption is made that social problems such as delinquency, educational failure, and poverty, now within the concerns of the mental health worker, can be reduced by providing resources that enhance the likelihood of accomplishment of developmental tasks. This further implies that those individuals who are poor, delinquent, or educational failures have not attained satisfactory development. Although this is no longer viewed as due to an illness, but rather as due to a failure of socialization, it nevertheless implies that the individual victims of social systems suffer from a *deficit* of some kind, whatever the reason. The aim of community mental health remains, therefore, the removal of deficits as measured by failure to fit into the expected societal norms. *The goal of community mental health is adjustment to the demands of society.*

As we shall see, community psychology has developed out of community mental health as an approach to community problems. It rejects the notion of deficits and argues that by applying the principles of person-environment fit, cultural relativity, and diversity, the problem of social intervention becomes one of providing material, educational, and psychological resources that support the right of individuals and subgroups of a community to live in ways that differ from the norms of the larger society. But this is moving ahead of our story. For now we must first detail the approach of community mental health, although we must also keep in mind that its aims are different from those of community psychology, and more like those of the traditional mental health movement. Only the methods of accomplishment are different. The social values of community mental health support the desirability of socializing everyone to the societal norm, despite a rhetoric of social systems change. What social systems change generally means is improvement of the effectiveness of socialization, rather than giving up its traditional aims. This, once again, brings us to the crucial issue of values. The values of community mental health are different from those of community psychology. From either viewpoint it is important for those who work in community settings both to be aware of those differences, and to be ethically responsible in informing one's clients.

The Ideology of Prevention

Thus far we have followed the policy statements that have helped to foster a community mental health ideology. What underlies much of this thinking has been the notion of *prevention* as opposed to amelioration of mental illness. This idea is directly borrowed from public health and is expressed well in the old cliche, "an ounce of prevention is worth a pound of cure." The idea is logical enough and seems to be a way to get around the problems of lack of manpower for treatment, ineffective treatment, and inability to reach large numbers of people in need. If a program for prevention of mental illness were successful it would presumably cut off the flow of patients, thereby reduce the patient load on professional care givers, and allow more time for the development of treatment strategies for those few who "slip through" the preventive efforts. The basic idea is illustrated well in a story that has been attributed to various origins, and has been elaborated and passed on orally: Imagine that you are out for a picnic on a pleasant spring day with a group of friends. You have just set out a checkered tablecloth with all manner of your favorite foods. You have situated yourself by the bank of a river, and as you are about to bite into a sandwich a cry is heard from the river. "Help, help!" the screamer yells. Putting down your sandwich you tear off your shoes and

clothes and dive in to rescue a drowning victim, apply artificial respiration, and prepare to return to your picnic. Suddenly two people call out "help, help!" You dive in again and pull them out, one on each arm. But as you return there are three or four others calling for help. Again you return, but this time, tired and overwhelmed by several people at once, you let a few slip away. Again, now in larger numbers, people call for help, but you cannot handle very many. You are only one person and you don't even swim very well yourself. Your friends don't swim at all, but as they watch you one has a bright idea. "Why not go upstream and find out who is pushing these people in?" That is what prevention is all about.

In the public health field the notion of prevention owes its origin to the control of contagious diseases such as smallpox. The development of a vaccination which could inoculate a community against the possibility of contracting a disease is most likely when the cause or etiology of the disease is known. But even where the etiology is unknown, as was the case with malaria and cholera, epidemiological studies which located the rate and distribution of illness have provided clues to its prevention. With malaria, the suspected relationship of the disease to the swamps, even without isolating the specific carrier, led to sanitation measures which prevented spread of the disease. Mervyn Susser (1968), an epidemiologist at Columbia University's School of Public Health, has pointed out that Edwin Chadwick advocated the independent circulation of water and sewage on the basis of a mistaken theory of disease, and although he opposed the germ theory, his sanitary innovations may have prevented more disease than any other single public health measure.

As we have seen in the history of the mental health movement (Chapters I and II) the notion that easing of environmental pressures would lead to a reduced incidence of mental illness has long been with psychiatry. Yet methods for the prevention of mental illness have not been emphasized, partly because the causes are frequently seen to be very broad social-political and economic factors, beyond the reach of psychiatric practice.

The current preventive ideology in mental health owes its origin in this century to Adolph Meyer, although his ideas on the matter were largely ignored. Later, Eric Lindemann (1944) stimulated some attempts to develop a limited kind of preventive psychiatry by detailing methods for helping people who were experiencing a crisis situation, so as to avoid exacerbation of the problem. But it remained for the writings of Gerald Caplan, who has taken traditional public health concepts and applied them to the mental health field, to popularize the ideas of prevention among mental health professionals. What Caplan accomplished was a well-defined conceptualization of prevention in the realm of mental health, together with concrete examples of how this idealogy could influence the practice of psychiatry. He brought the concepts of prevention down from sociological analysis to explicit programs for action in a textbook, *Principles of Preventive Psychiatry* (1964).

Principles of Preventive Psychiatry

Caplan introduced to psychiatry a now popular threefold conceptualization of prevention. In so doing he helped to point psychiatry toward the view that mental health interventions of various kinds, some of which the professionals were already performing, could be delivered so as to be preventive in nature. The three types of prevention are called primary, secondary, and tertiary. It is easiest to describe these three kinds of preventive activities in reverse order, as they become decreasingly associated with those activities familiarly linked to traditional work of the metal health specialist.

Tertiary Prevention

The aim of tertiary prevention is to reduce the rate of mental disorders in a community. Basically, this term encompasses programs aimed at large-scale rehabilitation of people already suffering from mental disorder so as to reduce its duration and destructiveness. However, Caplan differentiates between the term "rehabilitation," which refers to work with individual clients, and tertiary prevention by which he means efforts to reduce the rate of problems in an entire community. To use a phrase now common in preventive psychiatry, "the community is the client." This definition implies large-scale programs of service, capable of effectively reaching the total population of identified mental patients. One of the key methods for such programming is the basis of one of the recommendations of the Joint Commission's report, and involves what is largely an administrative decision to remove as few patients as is possible from their homes and communities. This policy is designed to avoid the problem that Cumming and Cumming (1957) called "closing the ranks." When a patient is removed from his or her role in the family or work setting those individuals left to live without that person necessarily take over his or her role. The longer a patient is removed, the more difficult it is to return and continue with his or her former place in the world. Consequently, keeping in mind the need for tertiary prevention, a policy of local community care, day and night hospitals, and so on, maximizes the likelihood that such closing of the ranks will not occur, and helps reduce the detrimental social effects of mental illness. If this is instituted as a social policy the duration of problems experienced as a result of mental illness is likely to be reduced for the entire community.

The concept of tertiary prevention also has implications for the quality of hospital care per se. It implies that such programs will emphasize more than custodial care which simply maintains chronic patients on large wards. Rather, reform of the services offered to chronic patients includes innovative programs of rehabilitation such as milieu or socio-environmental treatment; token economies designed to teach adequate social functioning; use of volunteers and nonprofessional mental health workers, both in the hospital and in the community as "significant others" for those who are socially isolated; halfway houses; and vocational rehabilitation. Examples of these kinds of programs in the mental health system are presented in Chapters IV, IX, and XI.

Secondary Prevention

Secondary prevention refers to programs that reduce the rate of disorder by lowering its prevalence, or the number of identified cases in a given population "at risk." This reduction may come about either by altering the factors that lead to new cases, or by reducing the duration and severity of existing cases through early diagnosis and treatment. Generally, secondary prevention emphasizes the latter approach. Caplan points out that psychiatry has traditionally been concerned with diagnosis and treatment of individual clients. The difference from a secondary preventive view is that methods of individual treatment that deal with problems, albeit early and effectively, without reducing the total number of cases in the community, are not public health-oriented. In community mental health the community is the client, and methods of diagnosis and treatment, which reach large numbers of people so as to significantly improve the mental health statistics of a defined community, are sought. It will be recalled that the problems of training enough professional manpower to deliver services to meet the large demand and need for treatment, as well as the inability of traditional services to reach many potential patient groups because the clients reject psychotherapy, or the psychotherapists reject them, or both, were important elements in the development of community mental health. Programs of secondary prevention, consequently, are concerned not only with effective diagnosis and treatment of individuals, but also with maximization of resources to both reach and shorten the problems of mental illness, and thereby reduce the extent of the problems in a given community.

Secondary prevention, as opposed to tertiary prevention, rests upon the notion of identifying the problems early, before they become major mental illness. This has been interpreted in two ways. Often, it means early identification ontogenetically. As the *Priorities for Community Mental Health* statement of the Division of Community Psychology (Glidewell, 1971) presented it, the emphasis is on early identification in the life cycle. By emphasizing early intervention with children, aimed at providing enhanced opportunity to cope with developmental tasks, such programs should prevent later problems in living and thereby reduce both the incidence and the prevalence of mental disorder. Early diagnosis has also been interpreted to mean early in the "disease process," or at the first signs of disorder and prior to its exacerbation. This may involve detection of disorder in children, but it also includes detection of problems among adults before they reach severe proportions.

Caplan discusses several ways in which early detection may be accomplished. One is by sharpening diagnostic tools so as to identify the onset of emotional disorder from fewer and milder signs and symptoms. This method emphasizes testing procedures. For example, the use of tests such as the Minnesota Multiphasic Personality Inventory (MMPI), as a prescreening device in large organizations such as the army, may alert the psychiatrist to potential problems. Such a test can be administered to a large group of people in about 1½ hours. It has the advantage of "bandwidth," or the ability to efficiently cover a large number of areas of potential maladjustment. By using such a device as a screening technique, the mental health professional can then select for closer examination those individuals who appear to be in difficulty. Because such instruments lack "fidelity" in that they sacrifice individual accuracy and ability to detail specifics of a problem in favor of maximization of efficiency and global identification of problem groups, once a potential problem is identified a more careful evaluation by techniques such as an interview is necessary. Such a device is far from perfect as an early identification tool because it suffers from numerous psychometric and conceptual inadequacies which need not concern us here. (cf. Wiggins, 1973.) Nevertheless, with proper caution it can serve at least as a prescreening device. The MMPI is not necessarily the best example of such a technique, although it is widely used. The point here is that tests such as the MMPI are one way to try to identify, before the problems become obvious, the existence of maladjustment. Presumably the earlier it is diagnosed, the easier it will be to treat.

Other devices for early detection of potential problems have been developed specifically for programs of early detection among children. Cowen *et al.* (1973), working in a school setting because of its potential socializing power and its geographic convenience and amenability to program input, have systematized a method for teacher identification of potential maladjustment among elementary school children. In this setting they have developed the AML, a brief 11-item scale on which a teacher records the frequency of occurrence of symptoms of maladjustment for each student in a class. The scale was originally developed by the California State Department of Education, and was revised by Cowen and his associates. It has been found to show three stable factors of maladjustment, aggressive-outgoing, moody-internalized, and learning disability. It is very easy to administer, and takes only 30–60 seconds per child, or 20–30 minutes for an entire classroom. Cowen *et al.* (1973) have presented several studies of the AML which find it to be reliable and significantly related to other, more cumbersome measures of early maladjustment. The scale is shown to discriminate between children referred for special help to a mental health project and those not referred, and norms have been collected. Although the authors caution that the scale may miss some children who are experiencing difficulty, they recommend its use as a means for systematically and efficiently identifying from among a large pool those children who manifest warning signs and may therefore benefit from special attention. Such a detection device is a necessary prerequisite for developing programs of secondary prevention.

A second means of early detection noted by Caplan is to encourage early referral to treatment if a difficulty is suspected. Public education through the mass media is one such method of encouragement, and would include not only a description of symptoms but of where to go for help. Similarly, consultation with key persons in the community, such as physicians, teachers,

and clergymen, is recommended. The use of "walk-in clinics" as part of a general hospital is another method recommended for lowering the threshold between community and mental health agency contact. Finally, gearing diagnosis to specific treatment steps rather than separating the two functions is suggested.

Each of the above methods of identification is only useful if followed by prompt and effective treatment. This has several implications; one of which Caplan notes is that no more cases than can actually be treated in a given system should be identified by that system. Labeling someone as maladjusted without providing a positive alternative may create more harm than good. A related problem for community mental health is not to intervene in those cases where "spontaneous recovery" is likely. These cautions for programs of secondary prevention are not always followed because they require careful attention to treatment program outcome followed by feedback to, and modification of, the system's services. Although such aspects of secondary prevention programs are absolutely necessary in order to follow the best principles of community mental health, they are frequently relegated to the category of luxuries in mental health budgets. One of the aims of making the community mental health center staff accountable to residents of their "catchment area" is to encourage the collection of such data.

Primary Prevention

The final type of prevention discussed by Caplan leads to activities that deviate most sharply from the traditional methods of mental health professionals. It is primary prevention that, because of this deviation from tradition, has served as a bridge carrying some from community mental health activities to community psychology. For this reason primary prevention is the most important idea borrowed from community mental health by community psychologists. In a sense it is the starting point on a road toward the search for new paradigms from which there is no return. If the idea of primary prevention is followed to its logical conclusion the paradigms of mental health work and individual psychology will ultimately be found inadequate. One will find the aims of primary prevention to be either visionary, or abstract and futuristic (Cowen, 1973), and give them up in favor of more realistic goals, or instead search for new paradigms for solving the problems. But this was not always recognized, and in the beginning it was primary prevention within community mental health, largely as proposed by Caplan, which stimulated a great deal of thought and action.

Caplan's definition of primary prevention is difficult to improve upon:

Primary prevention is a community concept. It involves lowering the rate of new cases of mental disorder in a population over a certain period by counteracting harmful circumstances before they have had a chance to produce illness. It does not seek to prevent a specific person from becoming sick. Instead, it seeks to reduce the risk for a whole population, so that, although some may become ill, their number will be reduced. It thus contrasts with individual patient-oriented psychiatry, which focuses on a single person and deals with general influences only insofar as they are combined in his unique experience (Caplan, 1964, p. 26).

The emphasis in the above definition is the focus on ". . . counteracting harmful circumstances before they have had a chance to produce illness." This emphasis on before-the-fact intervention moves mental health workers into activities that are not traditionally within their domain, since the mental health system is designed to treat identified problems. By way of clarification, the term "illness" is used in the very broad sense mentioned earlier, such that a variety of social problems in living are included. However, it is mental illness per se that Caplan is interested in preventing. Caplan goes on to note that such a conception implies study, not only of illness, but also of health, a point that has, unfortunately, not often been emphasized. Programs for primary prevention are to be aimed at identifying both helpful and harmful environmental factors that influence a community's ability to cope with the stresses of life.

A Conceptual Model for Primary Prevention: Crisis Theory

Because the concept of primary prevention was relatively new to psychiatry, despite its existence for many years in the field of public health, Caplan begins his book with a conceptual model for primary prevention. Although he argues that we need not know the specific etiology of mental illness in order to develop programs for its prevention, he does acknowledge the need to make some educated guesses. In his view the members of a community all require what he calls "supplies" which he classes as physical, psychosocial, and sociocultural. The physical supplies include food, shelter, and sensory stimulation; psychosocial supplies include interpersonal interaction which stimulates cognitive and emotional development, and are ordinarily obtained from family, peers, church, and work. According to Caplan, proper development requires love, affection, and social control from appropriate authority as well as support for independence. Resistance to mental disorder is seen as dependent on the "health" of interpersonal relationships and defined by satisfaction of the above "needs." It is clear that this view largely reflects a particular set of social values, although they are values to which most people in our society subscribe.

It is in the realm of "sociocultural supplies" that Caplan makes one of his most tenuous assumptions, and where he, like many others before and since in the field of mental health, appears to be somewhat insensitive to the viability of cultural differences in providing psychological strengths. Sociocultural supplies, defined as influences on development and functioning exerted by the culture and the social structure, are seen in large measure to prescribe a person's path in life. Although there can be no argument with Caplan's assertion that a person born into a disadvantaged group may find fewer opportunities, he sees some cultures as having a negative effect on mental health. Implied in this assertion is that so-called socially disadvantaged groups do not provide adequate psychological resources, and that only those who share in the middle-class culture are mentally healthy. He goes on, for example, to argue that "the richer his cultural heritage, the more complicated are the problems he will probably have been taught to handle." In this argument there are subtle lines of ethnocentrism. It seems to be implied that some cultures are richer in heritage, and therefore richer in adaptive skills than others. Caplan is not simply saying that cultures differ, and that it may be difficult for a child brought up in a culture not in power to be successful in a society dominated by a different culture, but rather he seems to imply that some cultures (those that are dominant) are better per se, that is, more adaptive, or more mentally healthy than others. It might be argued that exactly the opposite is true, since members of a nondominant culture often need to learn to cope with more problems in living. Nevertheless, Caplan's view, it must be noted, is quite consistent with the aims of community mental health as observed earlier in this chapter, since the goal is to help all to adapt to the prevailing norms. The implications of this view, which are different from the view of community psychology, are not terribly explicit, and have only recently come to light in some of the writings of community psychologists to be reviewed in later chapters.

Caplan's emphasis on "supplies" as the basis for resistance to emotional disturbance is his view of etiology, and is the first part of his conceptual model. The second element in his model, and perhaps the most useful, is an emphasis on the significance of life crises. Some life crises are events that occur in the normal course of growth and appear during transitional periods from one stage of development to another. Progress through the eight stages of man discussed by Erikson (1950, see Table III-2) is thought of as marked by a series of *developmental crises*. The well-known idea of the adolescent identity crisis that all children are expected to experience is one example. Such developmental crises are to be expected to occur at predictable times in the individual's life as he or she passes from birth to maturity.

A second type of crisis Caplan terms *accidental*. These are the crises that appear at unpre-dictable times in one's life. They are a function of the stresses of life precipitated by a loss of any of the basic supplies—for example, loss or threat of loss of a loved one. The crisis can last from a few days to a few weeks, and resolution draws upon all the adaptive skills one has acquired. Although these crises are not as predictable as developmental crises, their occurrence in a given population can be statistically predicted. For example, one would expect the likelihood of the death of a spouse to increase with age, and since men have a shorter life expectancy more women than men can be expected to experience widowhood.

The importance of crises for individual treatment lies in the observation that during such periods, either developmental or accidental, the person is experiencing increased anxiety, looking for coping strategies, and in general is most susceptible to new learning. Even people normally resistant to influence are relatively more open to change. Depending on how such crises are handled, the person may emerge from them with either more or less adaptive skills. If a crisis is resolved with new insights and skills the person emerges as stronger and better able to deal with future crises. If the crisis is handled poorly, the person may be less able to function well in the future. In short, crises are turning points in people's lives. As Caplan notes, these phenomena have been recognized by novelists and dramatists who often focus on the person in crisis as he or she develops a new equilibrium changing them for better or worse. Because of this vulnerability, Caplan hypothesizes that "resistance to metal disorder can be increased by helping the individual extend his repertoire of effective problem-solving skills so that he will not need to use regressive, nonreality-based skills or socially unacceptable ways of dealing with predicaments which may lead to neurotic or psychotic symptoms as a way of avoiding or symbolically mastering his problems" (p. 37).

How a crisis is resolved is hypothesized to be a function of several factors including: (1) How similar crises were resolved in the past. (2) The solutions offered in one's cultural norms. (3) The kinds of advice and support offered by members of the family or other primary group. (4) The influence of key members in the community such as religious leaders, physicians, teachers, and even bartenders, shopkeepers, and newspaper advice columns. (5) The influence of professional mental health workers.

In most cases the outcome of a crisis is believed to be susceptible to influence by external intervention during the period of disequilibrium. Theoretically the person experiences a heightened desire for help, which evokes helping behavior from others, to which he is more susceptible than under normal conditions. Consequently, the importance of crises for a theory of preventive psychiatry lies in the observation that several of the factors listed above that affect crisis resolution can be influenced by deployment of the mental health resources of a community.

Caplan's Program for Primary Prevention

The two basic approaches to deployment of mental health resources so as to assist in provision of supplies and in crisis resolution, involve what Caplan calls programs of social action and programs of interpersonal action. The former aim to change the organization of community services and policies, the latter to change particular key individuals. Social action programs, in turn, are divided into two classes: those that provide supplies, and those that assist in crisis resolution.

Social action programs to enhance the provision of physical supplies include organizing a campaign to prevent children in a slum environment from ingesting lead paint, to establish prenatal services and well-baby clinics in communities that lack such services, and to consult with city planners to include psychological as well as physical needs in their plans. With regard to social action for the provision of psychosocial supplies Caplan emphasizes "safeguarding of family integrity." Examples include consultation with legislators and planners to provide work opportunities near residential areas, homemaker services for working mothers, and

parent education in child care. In the realm of sociocultural supplies examples include working for legislation that modifies retirement laws that force people to cease being productive; change of welfare policies that penalize a person for earning extra money; and provision of recreational and social facilities. Other examples include attempts to influence the educational system which is viewed as a prime agent, together with the family, of socialization, as well as programs to influence employment opportunity and the work environment.

Although Caplan emphasizes consultation with those at the top of the social hierarchy, others have emphasized community consultation at the grass-roots level to accomplish similar aims. Peck, Kaplan, and Roman (1966), for example, view grass-roots community action groups as contributing not only to the accomplishment of social and political aims, but as participating in a process by which the poor and the powerless may learn to gain control over their external environment. In this regard Caplan's suggestions are much more conservative than the term social action implies, and he falls short of recommending that mental health specialists serve as advocates for grass-roots groups. Rather, he views social action as working for changes through established and powerful community leaders. The role requires making one's self a resource person who gives politicians and administrators an understanding of the human needs of their constituents. Advice and intervention are to be restricted to subjects "relevant to achievement of professional goals."

In Caplan's words:

The need for professional self-awareness and self-control in this area is similar to that which is familiar to us in our interaction with individual patients. The difference is that the therapeutic role of the psychiatrist has become well defined . . . the role of the preventive psychiatrist in social action is relatively new, and its development must be carefully watched to insure adequate professional safeguards (Caplan, 1964, p. 67).

Once again, it is emphasized that primary prevention of emotional disorder, even when it involves social change, means change through the process of established political channels, such that social agencies provide better and more efficient means for socialization. The psychiatrist in this role is clearly accountable to the agents of socialization rather than to grass-roots people. Although the professional presumably works in the best interest of grass-roots groups, these groups themselves are not the decision makers. The one role that is perhaps an exception to these basic guidelines is as an agent who may use his consultation and therapeutic skills to help community members improve their problem-solving skills and "cooperative patterns of dealing with community problems." It is not clear whether Caplan means to support actual grass-roots community decision making, or simply to help them use reasoning to understand the problems of established institutions so as to fit in and be less troublesome.

The second type of social action involves improvement of the population's ability to adjust during the life crises. This is to be provided by "attenuation of the hazardous circumstance, and . . . provision of services to foster healthy coping." Several steps are identified in such programs. First, the hazardous circumstances in a given community need to be identified, together with those people who are "at risk." For example, people who are at an age when developmental crises are likely to occur can be expected to be at risk. Those who are beginning school, retiring, recently engaged, pregnant, and so on, are examples. Next, locating such people in schools, hospitals, churches, and divorce courts is necessary. Other examples are families about to be moved as a consequence of urban renewal, and those experiencing the death of a loved one. Provision of services will require the mental health professional to be mindful of the prerogatives of other professionals and to learn the skills of effective consultation. Social action of this type often tries to influence policy changes by eliciting the cooperation of those community agents who normally are in control or helping establish services that are lacking, such as homemaker services or chapters of Parents Without Partners, a self-help group for single parent families.

Other programs that can be established by cooperation with other professionals, such as school officials, include bringing mental health training into the academic curriculum through programs such as Ojemann's (Ojemann, Levitt, Lyle, & Whiteside, 1955) which is aimed at teaching children to analyze problem situations. Spivack and Shure (1974), for example, have detailed a program for teaching problem solving to preschool children. Allen *et al.* (1976) have recently extended such training to an elementary school setting, and Berck (1976a) has extended it to teaching interpersonal problem solving to children in transition from an elementary school to a junior high school. Each of these programs is described in Chapter IX.

The other major method of preventive intervention is by means of interpersonal action to change key persons in a community. Methods and techniques aimed at the maximization of impact are suggested. Consultation to a well-baby clinic to help physicians provide services for mothers is one example. In addition, education to increase the awareness of mental health problems and methods for key community people who are in roles of authority is suggested. This includes policemen, industry foremen, administrators, wardens, officers in the armed forces, and political leaders. Here the aim is not to relieve them of individual "cases," but rather to assist in helping the authorities to deal with such people themselves. Toward this end Caplan details several different types and methods of mental health consultation (see Chapter IX).

A Summary of the Community Mental Health Ideology

To this point we have considered many of the ideas that have been put together to form the basis for what is called the community mental health movement. Although there are many formal definitions of community mental health (e.g., Goldston, 1965), perhaps the best single description is provided by Bloom (1973) who has summarized the field in terms of its actual activities, and has discussed a number of dimensions on which community mental health may be differentiated from traditional, clinically oriented services. These dimensions are presented and elaborated in Table III-3. Examination of Table III-3 will find that the nine dimensions on which Bloom describes community mental health each implies a criticism of traditional mental health services, and each leads the community-oriented professional to seek new ways to deal with mental health planning and service delivery. It may further be observed that each of the distinctions deals with practical matters of service delivery rather than with theoretical conceptions of human behavior. Thus, community mental health is described in terms of its location and level of intervention, the type of service and the way it is delivered, its mental health planning strategy, its sources of manpower and locus of decision making. The one exception which bears on conception or theory, rather than practice, lies in its assumptions about etiology. Environmental as opposed to intrapsychic variables are emphasized. This emphasis, however, does not really describe community mental health because such conceptions of environment causality are now prominent in much of psychology. The areas of behavior modification, social learning theory, and environmental psychology identify much more justifiably with such conceptions. Psychologists in these areas have, far more carefully than those in community mental health, presented theory and research addressed to the influences of environment on behavior. Similarly, those who have addressed themselves to social ecology and general systems theory have contributed much to our understanding of environment and behavior. This research will be considered in appropriate places in later chapters. At this point it is important to note that *the contribution of community mental health has been more in the realm of new attitudes about service delivery than in conceptions of human behavior.* Consequently, many of the community mental health professionals borrow their conceptions from individual psychology.

Notwithstanding the emphasis on environmental etiology suggested by many community-oriented professionals, many others who identify with community mental health as a professional practice retain their earlier conceptions of human behavior as largely intrapsychically determined. There are at least three reasons for this. First, as noted above, the real emphasis in community mental health has been on where and how services are delivered so as to reach larger numbers of people in the population. Consequently, many professionals have been able to follow the prescriptions of community mental health without changing how they think about problems in living or what they actually do when they reach a target population. For many, community mental health is simply more available psychotherapy, perhaps briefer in nature (Romano, 1967). A second and related reason is that the movement has grown so rapidly and encompasses so many professionals that it includes many very different kinds of people and activities. In part, the second reason is a consequence of the first. Since community mental health ideology has not emphasized theory, it has remained open to may divergent viewpoints. Both of these reasons have combined with a third: The sudden infusion of financial and physical resources for those willing to call their activities ''community mental health'' has encouraged ''innovation'' and relabeling without real change in basic beliefs or activities.

The result of these developments is a fair amount of confusion as to what exactly constitutes the practices of community mental health. If so many different kinds of professionals, often with divergent views of human behavior, identify with the movement, how can it be defined? Phrased otherwise, how can one know what a psychologist who says that she or he practices community mental health actually does?

A Schema for Models of Mental Health Services

Rappaport and Chinsky (1974) have proposed that community mental health is much more an attitude than a particular body of knowledge. The attitude is expressed in many of the statements reviewed above. The emphasis on preven-

TABLE III–3 Dimensions of community mental health versus clinically oriented services.*

Dimensions of Comparison	Community Mental Health	Traditional Clinical Services
1. Location of intervention	Practice in the community	Practice in institutional mental health settings
2. Level of intervention	Emphasis on a total or defined community (e.g., a catchment area, or population at risk)	Emphasis on individual clients
3. Type of services	Emphasis on preventive services	Emphasis on therapeutic services
4. How service is delivered	Emphasis on indirect services through consultation and education	Emphasis on direct clinical services to clients
5. Strategies of service	Strategies aimed at reaching large numbers of people, including brief psychotherapy and crisis intervention	Emphasis on extended psychotherapy
6. Kind of planning	Rational planning aimed at specification of unmet needs, high-risk populations, and coordinated services	Unplanned, individual services with no overall community coordination; a "free enterprise" system
7. Source of manpower	Mental health professionals together with new, including nonprofessional, sources of manpower, such as college students and persons indigenous to the target group	Traditional mental health professionals (psychiatrists, psychologists, social workers)
8. Locus of decision making	Shared responsibility for control and decision making with regard to mental health programs between community and professionals	Professional control of all mental health services
9. Etiological assumptions	Environmental causes of mental disorder	Intrapsychic causes of mental disorder

*Derived from Bloom, 1973.

tion, new treatment methods, and a commitment to deal with previously untreated segments of the population are examples. In each of these ways, however, community mental health represents a new orientation rather than specific advances in the technology of treatment. It is a social as opposed to a scientific movement. Within these rather broad guidelines for community mental health, a community psychologist may have any of several theoretical conceptions of human behavior often borrowed from individual psychology, and ranging from the orthodox psychoanalytic to operant behaviorism. To describe exactly what the community mental health specialist does when she seeks to reach out into the community, Rappaport and Chinsky (1974) have proposed a schema for models of mental health service delivery.

The type of care offered by a member or an institution of the helping professions will be determined by the model subscribed to for mental health service. Every model for mental health service, regardless of its content, can be divided into two basic components—a *conceptual component* and a *style of delivery component*. The term model is used here in its broadest sense to refer *only* to a combination of these two components. We are only dealing with a *model* for mental health service when we consider *both* a *conceptual* component and a *style of delivery* component. The conceptual component refers to that aspect of the model which dictates the empirical data base, theoretical notions and basic assumptions for understanding human behavior. One might consider the conceptual component of a model for mental health service its theory of human behavior. Thus, in recent years there has been much criticizing of the so-called "medical model" (Turner & Cumming, 1967; Ullmann & Krasner, 1965). What is generally referred to by this term is either the use of disease notions in conceptualizing "problems in living" (Ullmann & Krasner, 1969) or an emphasis on repairing those who already have significant problems (Cowen, 1973). Depending on whom one is reading, the medical model is criticized either because of the way it conceptualizes problems in living as similar to physical illness rather than as

learned and environmentally determined, or because it emphasizes a repairing rather than a preventive strategy and thus continues to support the traditional role of the professional as an expert who remains in his or her office waiting for those in need to seek services. Often, those who critique the medical model because of its conceptual failure ignore the problem of its professional role implications. Conversely, many who critique the role implications continue to base their conceptualizations on the traditional psychiatric theory of disease. Because these two dimensions have not always been explicitly separated, there is sometimes confusion as to what kind of mental health program is being advocated by "community mental health."

Following the definition above of a model for mental health service, what has been called the "medical model" elsewhere might be thought of as the medical or disease *conceptual component* because this is only one *part* of a model for mental health service. A list of conceptual components for mental health service models might include a behavioral conceptualization (Ullmann & Krasner, 1965; Ullmann & Krasner, 1969), a social learning conceptualization (Albee, 1968b; Bandura, 1967, 1969; Mischel, 1968), or a neurological conceptualization (Reitan, 1969). Such a list might also include several less easily described conceptualizations which utilize a number of insights about human behavior borrowed from several theoretical approaches that are relevant to specific settings such as mental hospitals, for example, a socioenvironmental conceptualization of ward management (Sanders, Smith, & Weinman, 1967). Other nonpsychological conceptual components include sociological approaches (Sheff, 1967) and even economic approaches to human behavior (Feuer, 1959). There are many other possible conceptualizations, some of which are combinations of the above, some of which are entirely independent. For example a recent monograph (L'Abate, 1969) detailed nine such conceptual components or, as the editor calls them, "models" for clinical psychology.

The second component of a model for mental health service—its *style of delivery*—is that segment of the model which dictates how the service called for by the conceptual component will be offered to the target population. In discussions of models in clinical psychology this component is most frequently omitted. It is generally taken for granted that the style of delivery of service should be the traditional one defined by the "doctor-patient relationship." This medical style of delivery is by far the one used most frequently. Even those who are critical of the medical *conceptual component*, such as behavior theorists, rarely consider, much less criticize, the medical *style of delivery*. Its primary characteristics include the "expert" or authority, who usually holds an M.D., Ph.D., or M.S.W. degree, and who is responsible for some form of diagnosis and prescription. This same person also usually administers treatment. Diagnosis and treatment usually take place in the expert's office or in a hospital. The expert passively waits for the client to find him. This style of delivery can be referred to as the *waiting-mode*.

An alternative style of delivery is the *seeking-mode*, which may, in fact, define community mental health. This is the new "attitude" mentioned above (p. 72). A service offered in the seeking-mode generally takes place outside of the expert's office or hospital. It may be delivered directly by any number of persons, either professional or nonprofessional. The professional generally assumes the role of consultant, program innovator, and evaluator. Service is frequently aimed at primary prevention or early detection and secondary prevention. The key aspect of the seeking-mode is the professional in a nontraditional role, developing and evaluating an innovative program which deals with some important community problem, outside the office or clinic. A neighborhood service center staffed by indigenous nonprofessionals is a good example of the seeking-mode (see Chapter XI). Here the professional reaches out of his traditional setting into the community by training others to deliver service. The role of the nonprofessional is one of direct service agent to the target population.

Given these two independent components—the conceptual and the style of delivery—the model for any given approach to mental health

service can be systematically described. In essence, any given conceptual component will be applied in either the waiting- or the seeking-mode. Table III-4 is an example of four possible models. The four depicted include:

1. *Disease conception-waiting mode*. Here lies the typical dynamically oriented psychotherapy. Emotional dysfunctions are seen conceptually as indicants of an ongoing pathological disease process which needs to be diagnosed and treated. Symptoms are surface manifestations of a disease process. The client comes to the office and is seen in a one-to-one or group therapy situation conducted by a waiting expert who is almost always a doctor, or at least a trained mental health professional. This includes the practice of what has been termed "insight" therapy.

2. *Behavioral conception-waiting mode*. Again, the client comes to the office to be diagnosed. Here the diagnosis may be in terms of delineation of the discriminative stimuli for anxiety, or description of environmental contingencies maintaining a deviant behavior. Problems in living are seen as learned. Principles such as reinforcement are important. The client finds the authority and is seen in the office or clinic by a doctor who administers the expert treatment (e.g., systematic desensitization).

3. *Disease conception-seeking mode*. Here the traditional public health paradigm is applied. Deviants are seen as ill, and the best way to deal with illness is through its prevention or early treatment. A medical association's public education concerning mental health issues is one approach to dealing with such problems. Another is for the trained professional to conduct traditional psychiatric treatment in places such as the public schools; or for medical centers to extend traditional services to the broader community in the form of approaches such as a 24-hour emergency department or brief psychotherapy (Romano, 1967).

4. *Behavioral conception-seeking mode*. Emotional dysfunctions are seen as learning dis-

TABLE III–4   Some possible models for mental health service.*

Conceptual Component**	Style of Delivery Component	
	Waiting-Mode	Seeking-Mode
Disease Conception	Mental illness and disease explanations of abnormal behavior. Dynamic or insight psychotherapy. Client finds the expert and is treated in the office or clinic.	Deviants are seen as ill. Prevention of illness is emphasized through public education. Extension of traditional treatment on a 24-hour or brief psychotherapy basis; training of nonprofessionals in "relationship" therapy. Use of preventive medicine such as prenatal care.
Behavioral Conception	Learning theory interpretation of emotional dysfunction. Client finds the expert and is treated in the office or clinic with techniques such as systematic desensitization and contingency management.	Learning theory interpretation of emotional dysfunction. Professional extends services into the community through public education; training of various nonprofessionals in behavior modification techniques and social learning principles.

*Adapted from Rappaport and Chinsky, 1974.
**Listed here as examples are only two of a large number of possible conceptual components borrowed from individual psychology. Likewise, the specific examples in each box of the table could be extended to include many others.

orders and the method of treatment is relearning or new learning. The principle of reinforcement, including social reinforcement, is important. The conception of human behavior is identical to the conception of the behaviorist who practices in the waiting-mode. In this model, however, the expert may serve primarily as a consultant to teachers (Becker, Madsen, Arnold, & Thomas, 1967), as a trainer of parents (Wahler, Winkel, Peterson, & Morrison, 1965), or trainer of any of a number of nonprofessionals who actually deliver the service (Guerney, 1969).

The four models for delivery of service represented here are only a few of the many possible. The number is limited only by the number of conceptual components developed, that is, the number of theories of human behavior that are in practice. Theoretically, any conceptual component can be applied in either the waiting- or seeking-mode. Nevertheless, each implies dealing with different variables and using different techniques. Social learning theory, for example (Bandura, 1969; Bandura & Walters, 1963), can be thought of as a variant of the behavioral conceptual component, as can a strict operant approach to human behavior. However, the implications for each of these variants in the

application of services for the community are different. Operant technology would suggest the use of shaping procedures in the one-to-one setting or training teachers to apply this technique in the classroom. Social learning theory might emphasize modeling techniques such as films and role playing (see Chapter IV). Regardless of the specific technology, however, each approach becomes community mental health when it reaches out of the traditional setting and seeks innovative ways to deliver service in the community.

Another conceptual mode is the sociological. This is almost necessarily delivered in the seeking-style. If one believes that the social systems impinging on individuals are a major cause of emotional dysfunction, then an active intervention of a nontraditional sort is obviously implied. This model, the *sociological conception-seeking mode*, is most closely allied to the primary prevention aspects of community mental health. The Lincoln Hospital program and the Woodlawn program described in Chapter IX (which define negotiating the social system as mental health-relevant) probably come close to such a model.

The style of delivery that eventually proves to be most effective in dealing with the mental health needs of society is likely to be the one that is applied in the seeking-mode. Such an approach is most likely to meet the demands of an urban society and seems necessary in order to break out of the endless mental health reform cycle described in Chapter I. The conceptual component with which it combines to form a model for delivery of service is as yet undetermined. The best evidence (although it is by no means conclusive) for effective techniques within the *waiting-mode* is that offered by the behaviorists (see Chapter IV). It may be that a variant of the behavioral conception, perhaps social learning theory as suggested by Albee (1968b) and behavior modification technology combined with a sociological conception, is most promising for the *seeking-mode* of community mental health. The application of sociological and social psychological theories of organizations and power might also be useful. However, only a good deal of future research contrasting and/or combining each of the possible conceptions will determine which is most effective for community mental health.

Finally, it should be noted that in each of the models for delivery of service described above there are common elements. On the one hand, all are conceptions about how *individual* behavior is determined. Second, each model aims to help individuals, sometimes a few, sometimes an entire population, *adjust to the prevailing standards of society*. Mental health is implicitly or explicitly measured by the degree to which a person can adjust to the norm, be it through insight or new learning, delivered by means of direct service or by influencing other socialization agents.

Where Does Community Mental Health Now Stand?

At this point we are prepared to ask two questions. First, what has community mental health accomplished? And second, how promising is it for the future?

One of the earliest critiques of the Joint Commission report and subsequent legislation, and still perhaps the most cogent, was put forth by Cowen (1967) in an influential volume produced as a result of a conference held at the University of Rochester in 1965. On the positive side, Cowen placed the commitment to research, and more importantly to making the mental health professions less "fraternity-like" by opening up participation to anyone who can be effective, including new sources of helping manpower such as college students and nonprofessionals indigenous to the target communities. A final positive point is the emphasis on reducing the population of state hospitals and on making services available earlier to more people. As Cowen pointed out, the terms prevention and community mental health appear frequently in the Joint Commision report, but it would be an error to assume that these were its primary emphases. More precisely, the emphasis was on treatment for those already identified as mentally ill. New proposals for treatment were not bold or challenging in terms of innovative ideas. The report was for "good" and against "evil," but failed to distinguish between new mental health programs for their own sake, and genuine innovation. The problem is one of quality as well as quantity, and in some ways the report fostered an "old wine in new bottles."

Cowen's critique has turned out to be somewhat prophetic in that during the almost two decades following the report the community mental health movement did not accomplish substantially more than the earlier mental health movement. It may have fostered an atmosphere of excitement and growth, but perhaps this has been little more than a feeling of change.

More recently, Cowen (1973) has once again surveyed the field and come to conclusions that support his earlier cautions. In a survey of papers published in the *Community Mental Health Journal* between its beginning and June 1971, he finds that using a criterion as simple as counting the papers in which there appear numbers and/or graphs to indicate that they are research reports, only 30 percent could be so classified, and most of these data were simply descriptive. Second, only 3 percent of all the articles even mentioned the idea of prevention. Similarly, *Golann's Coordinate Index Reference Guide to Community Mental Health* (1969) classified only 2 percent of the over 1500 studies cited as concerned with primary prevention. It is safe to observe that although prevention is important *conceptually,* it has not, in fact, been an emphasis in community mental health *practice.*

Forgetting ideological issues for the moment, what about the delivery of services per se? The development of community mental health centers nationally has been quick and probably inadequate. There is no evidence that the mental health of American communities has improved. The movement's greatest practical success may have been to open up careers or volunteer opportunities in mental health work for people with qualifications other than the traditional degree. This development, however, has been more a function of administrative decision than one of scientific-therapeutic breakthrough. It is based on a realization that psychiatric care has been "mythologized," and that clinical services can probably be delivered as well or better through selection of people on the basis of their personal characteristics and/or strategic position in relation to a given target population, than by advanced academic degrees. Even in this regard, however, the professional mental health groups are far from giving up their control of the mental health system, and so-called "nonprofessionals" clearly play a minor role in that system. (See Chapter XI for a discussion of these issues.)

One of the major aims of the community mental health movement was to reduce the numbers of people who are confined in large state mental hospitals. As Bloom (1973) has noted, this reduction actually began to take place as early as 1955 and continued to decline through 1971 by nearly 50 percent. The decline has been in spite of an actual increase in number of admissions, and can be attributed to a reduced length of hospitalization. This change is again by means of an administrative decision to implement a new social policy, rather than because of scientific-therapeutic breakthroughs.[2] There is no evidence that those released patients are

any better off at the time of release than were the patients who had earlier been confined for longer periods of time. Rather, by instituting a new social policy we have begun to remove a social problem caused by a social policy that could no longer be justified—long-term confinement. As we have seen in Chapters I and II, this is the way "advances" in mental health policy have traditionally occurred. Once again it points to the close relationship between mental health and social values. Even the reality of this statistic of reduced numbers of hospitalized patients has been questioned. Chu and Trotter (1974) argue that between 1966 and 1972 the number of state mental hospitals, the number of inpatients, and the expenditures for state hospitals have actually increased. Although probably a function of more admissions rather than long-term stay, the point remains that the state hospital system is still very much with us.

Perhaps more important than the above data are questions of effectiveness of care. Although many new buildings have been funded and old buildings renamed as "community mental health centers," many believe that a great deal of money has been largely wasted in the construction of unnecessary buildings. It is not clear why a set of programs that are supposed to become part of a community need to function in new buildings with their own separate identity. Sarason (1972) has raised, in another similar context, this very question concerning what he has termed "buildings as distractions." He has argued that new buildings generally perpetuate the problem of limited resources. They are very expensive and often cost more than the services provided in them. Second, buildings contribute to inadequate services by attracting attention to their planning and maintenance rather than to their programs; and finally, they separate the services from the larger society. In Sarason's (1972) words:

Every institution states explicitly that it is a community facility, it exists because of and for the citizens of a particular geographic area. In reality, of course, the institution is usually physically and psychologically removed from the community (or communities), it is frequently viewed as an "alien body" in the community, and there is no basis for asserting that the citizens

---

[2]Some will argue that it is a consequence of the psychotropic drugs, but the evidence for the effectiveness of drug treatment would lead to a conclusion that rather than effective treatment, drugs have served more as a means for professionals to feel better about releasing patients (cf: Paul, Tobias, & Holly, 1972).

of the community in any way have any feeling of responsibility for and involvement in the institution (p. 168).

Sarason goes on to point out how a new institution will first be looked to as the place to send all relevant problems and thus reduce rather than enhance community initiative. This further sets the stage for disillusionment when there are no more beds, programs are full, and the staff is overcommitted. He suggests that community mental health centers might better provide people to work in and with existing grass-roots groups, and to assist them in developing their own programs rather than to create a monolithic comprehensive community mental health center focused on programs of the professionals.

In 1974, Windle, Bass, and Taube, of the National Institute of Mental Health, reported on the results of several studies conducted under the sponsorship of NIMH for evaluation of the community mental health centers program. Although not definitive, those studies do convey a picture of where things stand today. Their report concerns itself with the "process goals" of the centers and presents data on several such goals, summarized below:

1. *Increased quantity and range of services*. In 1972 there were 493 funded community mental health centers, although there were 1498 nationally designated catchment areas. This means two-thirds of the nation's areas that were expected to develop a center have not done so. Nationally, there has been a rise in the numbers of people treated as outpatients. NIMH "estimates" that about one-third of the rise in areas that have centers can be attributed to the center's program. However, there has been no evaluation of quality of services.

2. *Less use of state mental hospitals*. The authors conclude that the data are "equivocal." There is some indication that areas that have community mental health centers have reduced the admission rate to state hospitals, but not the total number of residents, compared to areas without centers. There does appear to be some shift toward partial and outpatient care as opposed to total hospitalization.

3. *Responsiveness to needs*. More centers have been funded in designated "poverty areas" (52 percent) than in nonpoverty areas (23 percent). Although Windle, Bass, and Taube (1974) do not report evaluation of the poverty area centers, there is some indication that they may not be accomplishing what is intended. Sue, McKinney, Allen, and Hall (1974), for example, recently compared the services rendered to Black and White clients seen at 17 community mental health centers in the state of Washington. They found that Black clients were significantly more likely to be referred to a nonprofessional than to a professional psychiatrist, psychologist, or social worker. Although this in itself is not surprising, since the addition of such paraprofessionals to community mental health center staffs is designed as a means to reach larger numbers of minority group clients who will supposedly be more willing to work with a nonprofessional of similar social background, the outcome of such contacts is surprising. These researchers found that over half the Black clients failed to return after the first session. Although the precise reason for this apparent failure of the centers studied to be helpful to Blacks cannot be determined from this study, it is apparent that naming a facility a community mental health center and staffing it with paraprofessionals is not sufficient to reach large numbers of minority clients with the sort of help they are seeking.

4. *Accessibility of services*. Adults living in selected areas where there is a center were interviewed, and about one-third could name some mental health service. Half named their own center, but only half of those knew of its location. Perhaps more importantly, when presented with stories about people with problems and asked where they should go, only 3 percent chose the mental health center. The most frequently cited reasons for not going to the mental health centers were waiting lists, fear of stigma, and the need to make an advance appointment—the very things the center is supposed to overcome!

Cowen's (1967) earlier caution about "old wine in new bottles" comes to mind.

5. *Community participation*. Lack of community participation in policy making of any kind is the most frequently noted deficiency in the mental health centers site-visited by NIMH evaluators. Although most administrators said they did not oppose such participation, few did anything to encourage it. Even the number of volunteers working in centers has not shown a significant increase in recent years, although many do use some indigenous workers.

6. *Continuity of services*. Most centers lack sufficient arrangements for the provision of continuity of care, and interagency contact is often minimal. Other agencies seem to refer low-income people to the centers and make their own service less accessible, such that the community mental health center may actually *reduce* the number of available services for the poor.

The final section of the report suggests that evaluation methods are being encouraged, although quality of services at this time cannot be ascertained.

In summary this report, from the very agency which sponsors community mental health centers, is not encouraging. There has been little in the way of new concepts and approaches. Psychotherapy, testing, and work with individual clients who seek services continues to be the method of choice, and even the acceptable goals of the centers, and of NIMH. As can be seen from the above report, NIMH is primarily concerned with quantity and accessibility of services, rather than with change in content of the services. As we can see from Cowen's (1973) analysis, although many professionals now work in community mental health centers, most do not do anything different than they did before. Often the letter but not the spirit of community mental health is followed. This has led, in some instances, to a reduction in the number of long-term hospital residents by releasing people to questionable outpatient care (e.g., see *NY Times* report, Chapter II, p. 45). Here they may be placed in "shelter care

homes" which is often simply a move from a large back ward to a smaller ward in a new location. Often no new services are offered, nor are patients, except in the few experimental programs such as those reviewed in Chapter IX, either given preparation for their release, or true autonomy. Frequently, they are maintained by the same methods that failed earlier because they keep the patients dependent on the mental health system—once-a-week counseling and drug treatment. Kaplan (1975) has described this innovation without change in the Massachusetts mental health system. She reports how a state hospital began to reduce its inpatient census without really releasing clients and without any change in the activities of its professional staff. Patients were simply transferred to smaller community centers or set up in isolated living arrangements and maintained as "outpatients."

To be fair, the community mental health movement could be described as new and just beginning to get off the ground, but our analysis of the history, background, and goals of the movement makes such an assessment little more than a repeat of an historical rationalization. It is easy to predict that in 20 years there will be another expose of the system because there has been no real change in what Szasz (1970) would call the "manufacture of madness."

There are several basic reasons why neither the ideology nor the services of community mental health has been terribly successful in fulfilling the promise of the early 1960s. At least one of the reasons is that the style of delivery (called here the "waiting-mode") remains the most comfortable for mental health professionals. It is an accepted role to wait, diagnose, and treat rather than seek to prevent problems. Every year clinical psychology, psychiatry, and social work train far more professionals in these skills and attitudes than those with the skills and attitudes of a preventive model. Diagnosis and treatment is what the mental health professionals know how to do—the outcome of such work not withstanding. The public expects such services, and has been convinced of their value, although any professional in the privacy of his or her peers will understand that most services offered (although perhaps not his or her own) are oversold. Similarly, the rewards for individual treatment are direct as well as financially rewarding in our free enterprise health care system. The system enables persons with financial resources to quite literally buy the time of professionals. Of course, such facts of professional life were true prior to the community mental health movement, but that movement, to which many pay at least lip service, was supposedly designed to counteract such tendencies. Indeed, community mental health centers were supposed to be a new system for delivery of service. What has gone wrong?

A second aspect of the problem is conceptual rather than motivational. Even those who have accepted and engaged in an active style of delivery have continued to view human behavior in terms of individual variables and deliver individual services. This is true both for those who conceptualize problems in living as disease based, and those who view the problems as a function of learning—the two most accepted paradigms in the helping professions. So long as interventions are conceptualized solely in terms of individual behavior and are aimed at person-oriented prevention, even if applied to large populations by means other than one-to-one treatment, the psychologist will not develop effective programs of social change. *Systems do not necessarily function by the same principles that account for individual behavior*. What is required is systems-oriented prevention. This point is elaborated in Chapter V.

A third aspect of the problem is social values. So long as community mental health is aimed at adjustment of all to the norms of society, even if programs to foster such adjustment are applied to large populations and are based on a preventive ideology, the psychologist will be involved in programs to improve the socialization function of systems, rather than to change social systems themselves. So long as the goal of our social systems—to fit everyone to a single standard—remains unchallenged, the community mental health movement cannot be more successful than the mental health movements of the past. It is a goal that is virtually impossible to achieve. There will necessarily always be many people who, either by choice or by circumstance, are unable or unwilling to fit into mainstream society. There is no medical, behavioral, or scientific technology that will change this. The challenge for community psychology is to develop paradigms that help society to create viable alternative choices for those who are not in the mainstream. The challenge is to support a society in which diversity and cultural relativity are not simply abstractions to be supported in principle, but rather values to live by. The challenge is to create a society in which deviants are not only "tolerated" but allowed fair access to the resources of society—material and psychological—which really allow them to live with dignity even though they are different. Such a society requires a psychology of person-environment fit, rather than of adjustment, and this point must be underscored for community psychology. Before we turn to conceptions of community psychology, however, it is necessary to review some of the conceptions of individual psychology which, while incomplete in and of themselves, are useful to the community psychologist when thinking about individual behavior.

CONCEPTIONS FROM INDIVIDUAL PSYCHOLOGY USEFUL TO THE COMMUNITY PSYCHOLOGIST

The gods sit over the board, but it is men who move under their hands for the mating and the kill.

— *Merlin (Mary Stewart)*

There is no antidote to power but power, nor has there ever been . . . in order to defend individual freedom, it is necessary to enhance the power of individuals . . . . If behavior technology endangers freedom by giving refined power to controllers, then the antidote which promotes freedom is to give more refined power over their own behavior to those who are endangered.

— *Perry London*

The aim of this chapter is to present an orientation toward individual psychology consistent with community mental health and community psychology. In the preceding chapter we saw that even when a psychologist assumes an active style of delivery the service delivered often will be determined by how human behavior is conceptualized (see Table III-4, p. 74). The community mental health professional may be engaged in a preventively oriented program which provides crisis-oriented services to individuals before they experience persistent difficulty; or he may engage in a program designed to deliver services to an entire population, but the content (what actually transpires between the mental health helper and the target people) will be based on how individual behavior is understood. This is always so with *person-oriented prevention* such as community mental health programs. An examination of the principles and implications of individual psychology will also find that the community psychologist requires conceptualizations in addition to those at the individual

level, and that one must be careful not to apply thinking about individuals when the difficulty may actually be a function of other, systems-level variables. Nevertheless, the reverse is also true. Systems-level variables will not be helpful when dealing with individuals. Although many of the problems of community psychology are different from the problems of individual psychology (that is, they are systems-oriented rather than person-oriented), individual psychology is often implicit. It could not otherwise be given psychology's traditions. The challenge for community psychology is to apply the individual conceptions useful to *person-oriented prevention* in conjunction with the social change conceptions of *systems-oriented prevention* so as to create a psychology of the community rather than one limited to the individual.

It should be acknowledged at the outset of this chapter that *individual psychology cannot solve the puzzles of community change*. That is why community psychologists must search for new paradigms. Nevertheless, individual psychology can be consistent with community psychology. To be consistent means at least two things. First, because community psychology posits the salience of environmental causality, conceptions of individual behavior must be explicitly concerned with such factors. Second, to the extent that delivery of service is emphasized, the most effective and efficient methods need to be administered; that is, finding treatments that are not only based on knowledge of current environmental impact on individual behavior, but also those that show the most promise for creating change in the shortest time, with the least expenditure of professional manpower, and the greatest likelihood of reaching the most people. Although individual psychology cannot ever be a total answer to the problems of community psychology, or even to the problems of community mental health service delivery, it can serve as a sensible basis for service if it is consistent with the above aims. Such aims have also been the concern of social learning theory and behavior modification.

Social Learning and Behavior Modification

The social learning view of man, as an outgrowth of behaviorism, is currently and rapidly reaching a point of ascendance in modern clinical psychology. New papers and books advocating a behavioral conception of individual human beings appear almost every day. In applied work it is no longer surprising to find behavior modification techniques to be gaining increased acceptance among psychologists who find that it has a degree of pragmatic utility in their daily work. Demonstrations of the effectiveness of techniques such as systematic desensitization for the treatment of anxiety problems (Paul, 1966; Paul & Bernstein, 1973) and the use of reinforcement to teach retarded children and chronically hospitalized patients new skills, are well known (Ayllon & Azrin, 1968; Bijou, 1966; 1976). The thinking and treatment methods of behaviorists have now been systematically applied to almost every known clinical

problem of individual psychology (Bandura, 1968; Ullmann & Krasner, 1969; Yates, 1970) as well as to treatment of delinquents (e.g., Tharp & Wetzel, 1969), family therapy (Stuart, 1971), and other programs in nonmental health settings such as schools and prisons. Although applying the principles of behavior modification is more complicated than is apparent and requires a good deal of social skill, knowledge, and experience, the ideas on which the applications are based are quite understandable and in part account for its popularity. There are, of course, many subtle and complicated variants of the principles, and as research in human learning and individual behavior continues the variants become even more complicated, but to understand the essence of the social learning orientation is not difficult.[1]

Behaviorism is a reaction to the overemphasis on intrapsychic determinants and fixed traits which gripped psychology for many years. Its adherents among mental health professionals have argued that traditional methods of behavior change, which emphasize insight into the past, the relationship between therapist and client, and hypothetical internal determinants of behavior, not only ignore the effect of current environmental or situational factors on behavior, but are not effective in creating behavior change. This conclusion is similar to the one reached by those advocating community mental health. However, whereas community mental health has emphasized new styles of delivery, social learning and behavior modification have emphasized new conceptions and methods of treatment. As we have seen in Chapter III (Table

---

[1]The intent of this section is to provide only a few examples of the approach. For details, four books are especially recommended: Albert Bandura's (1969) *Principles of Behavior Modification;* L. P. Ullmann and L. Krasner's (1969) *A Psychological Approach to Abnormal Behavior;* Donald Peterson's (1968a) *The Clinical Study of Social Behavior;* and Walter Mischel's (1968) *Personality and Assessment.* A number of more simplified presentations are also available, including Ralph Schwitzgebel and David Kolb's (1974) *Changing Human Behavior.* For summaries specifically related to the psychotherapeutic situation see chapters by Leonard Krasner, by Albert Bandura, and by Gerald Patterson in Bergin and Garfield (1971).

III-4) both conception and style are vital elements in a model for delivery of service.

According to Bandura:

From a social-learning perspective, behaviors that may be detrimental to the individual or that depart widely from accepted social and ethical norms are considered not as manifestations of an underlying pathology but as ways, which the person has learned, of coping with environmental and self-imposed demands . . . . Considering the arbitrary relativistic nature of social judgment and definition of deviance, the main value of the normal versus abnormal dichotomy lies in guiding the social and legal actions of societal agents concerned with the maintenance of an efficiently functioning society. This dichotomy, however, has little theoretical significance, because no evidence exists that the behaviors so dichotomized are either qualitatively different or are under the control of fundamentally different variables (1969, p. 62).

Bandura (1969), in reviewing social learning theory and behavior modification, argues that all individual behavior is largely a function of the consequences of environmental control. This is the same assumption concerning environmental etiology made in community mental health (see Table III-3, p. 71). However, rather than stop at that, social learning theory goes on to explore how this environmental control works, and to base its methods of treatment on those details, rather than on traditional psychotherapy. Three "regulatory systems" are posited. The first includes mechanisms of external stimulus control by association with emotional responses, or contingencies of reward and punishment. A second involves feedback in the form of consequences of behavior, and the third involves "central mediational processes" such as learned hypotheses, rules, and strategies. Man is seen as in reciprocal interaction with his environment, and is neither a passive reactor nor internally impelled (Bandura, 1969).

Like any school of psychology, adherents of behaviorism span a continuum from rigid adherents who draw formal boundaries for "acceptable" research and practice to those who support the school's more general guidelines. In this chapter the term social learning theory will be used to refer to a general theoretical orientation through which individual behavior may be viewed, and behavior modification will refer to the application of this theoretical orientation to the creation of individual behavior change. Behavior therapy is distinguishable from behavior modification in at least two ways. As a style of delivery behavior therapy is generally limited to the traditional one-to-one or small group setting, while behavior modification is more frequently employed "in the field" or in the natural environment. Behavior modification, however, is also practiced in the traditional clinical setting. Conceptually, behavior therapy is not limited to but tends to employ the principles of learning associated with Pavlov's classical conditioning paradigm, although this is now expressed in more recent and sophisticated variations. The emphasis is on learning as a function of association between stimuli and responses connected in time, such as conditioned emotional reactions.

Behavior modification principles can be traced to E. L. Thorndike's early work on the law of effect, and to the behaviorism of John B. Watson, who was opposed to the study of subjective experience and favored limiting psychology to observable behavior. B. F. Skinner is, of course, the modern and most influential adherent of this view, and his work in instrumental or operant conditioning now represents the most extreme form of behaviorism. Its stated goal, as was Watson's, is the prediction and control of behavior. Its basic premise is that behavior is a function of its consequences. Knowledge about internal states of individual people is assumed unnecessary for the prediction and control of behavior. There are three major concepts in the operant approach: stimulus, response, and reinforcement. Although these are studied in various relationships to one another and in minute detail, for example by manipulating schedules (timing and amount) of reinforcement, for applied psychology the implications of the principles are straightforward. It is assumed that all behavior is under the control of environmental contingencies, or relationships among these three variables. The relationship can be manipulated by using both primary reinforcers, such as food, or secondary reinforcers, such as attention from others. Any response is assumed teachable by means of shaping or reinforcing successive approximations. To change behavior one needs to "diagnose" the environmental stimuli and discover the reinforcement which maintains an undesirable response. By elimination of reinforcement for undesirable behavior, coupled with the provision of a new "contingency," that is, reinforcement of a desired behavior, the individual should act differently. These ideas have been extremely useful in training retarded children (Bijou, 1966, 1976), and some of the most amazing progress in the history of psychology has derived from such programs. For the psychologist concerned with this important area of application an intimate knowledge of operant psychology in all its details is absolutely essential.

The operant approach has also been useful in work with conduct problems of young children in both the school and the home situation. Training teachers to apply the principles in the classroom has helped many to eliminate disruptive behavior and to enhance prosocial behavior (e.g., O'Leary & Becker, 1967; Walker & Buckley, 1972). Many child management books are now available (e.g., Becker, 1971; Patterson, 1971) for training parents to be systematic, consistent, and to reinforce desired as opposed to disruptive behavior of their children. For many troubled families this approach has avoided the need for long-term treatment and "deep" psychological explanations of why their child is misbehaving. By treating the "symptom" they have eliminated the problem —one of the major contributions of behavior modification. It has focused attention away from ill-defined and insoluble problems and concentrated attention on the careful and precise delineation of the behavior one wants to change. For example, the principle of extinction, which is simply that a behavior will cease if it is not reinforced, has been used to eliminate excessive crying among infants (Bandura & Walters, 1963). Imagine the worried parents of a new infant who cannot get the child to sleep through the night. The parents are tired and irritable in the morning. They fight with each other and are generally unhappy. Their marriage seems in difficulty and they visit a psychologist. A psychologist who views the situation through the eyes of an operant approach would be likely to advise the parents to be sure the child is not in physical distress and then let the child cry. They might be advised to chart how long the infant takes to stop crying each night. If they do not go in to comfort the child (i.e., do not reinforce crying) the behavior would be expected to first increase and then decrease more and more each day, and be eliminated in a very short time. Rather than explore the parents' "relationship" the psychologist would assume that their problems will dissipate as the child's behavior improves, since they will now get enough sleep, be less irritable, and so on. Similar programs of contingency management can be arranged for almost any behavior problem including less obvious problems such as depression (Ferster, 1973). In application to children, where its use is now prominent, the behavioral approach assumes that by manipulation of parental interaction with the child almost any child-rearing problem can be solved.

Gerald Patterson (1974) has recently reported a complicated set of investigations that are more relevant than the simple example above. Relying on principles of operant learning as the basis for treatment he has designed a series of procedures for use with young boys referred for conduct problems in both the classroom and the home environment. All children had an extensive and long history of difficulty, and many were from lower socioeconomic status families. Twenty-seven of the original group of 35 children completed the treatment procedures which included training parents by means of programmed texts, defining "target" behaviors to increase and decrease, parent training groups on how to apply contingencies, and live demonstrations by the researchers. About half the boys also received classroom treatment in which the research team set up an individual program for each child based on his receiving reinforcement for appropriate behavior in the classroom. The children's behavior was carefully observed both at home and in school before, during, and up to 12 months after the treatment program, which involved about 30 hours of professional time for each child in each setting. Patterson found that such interventions were "moderately successful" in reducing disruptive behavior and enhancing appropriate behavior, and that these results persisted over time.

Recall that these were children with a longstanding history of apparently "insoluble" conduct problems. Parents were found to change their behavior as a function of training, and the boys' home behavior showed a significant decrease in the level of deviance. Using a very detailed observational procedure in which the research team actually recorded the behavior of the child in the home setting, they found that up to 12 months after terminating their intervention the boys, as a group, were still behaving within the normal range, compared to a group of "normal" children, and two-thirds showed marked reduction in the behavior for which they had been referred (see Figure IV-1). All parents reported that the child was improved, and most felt that the entire family was better off. Data were also collected for six "waiting list" families at comparable time periods and showed no change. In the classroom, two-thirds of the boys showed behavior that was comparable to nonproblem peers, and interestingly, the behavior of the other (nontreated) children in the classroom also showed a significant improvement. Similar generalizations of effect on classroom peers have been reported by others (Reppucci & Reiss, 1970; Broden, Bruce, Mitchell, Carter, & Hall, 1970; Kazdin, 1973). One of the discouraging findings of Patterson's research is that lower-class membership was correlated ($r = .49$) with poor treatment outcome such that children of welfare mothers living alone and

feeling unable to cope were, as might be expected, the least improved. Others have argued that learning- or action-oriented treatments are more likely to be effective with the poor than are "talk-oriented" treatments. As we have seen in Chapter III, this is an issue of some importance to community mental health and is therefore considered in detail in the next section.

Treatment programs based on contingency management have also been widely used in total institutions such as mental hospitals by means of what have come to be known as "token economies" (Ayllon & Azrin, 1968; Atthowe & Krasner, 1968). The aim in such programs is to alter institutional practices in a given organization such that the behavior of all members will be affected. These programs are organized around three procedures derived from operant psychology (Bandura, 1969). First, desirable behaviors such as those necessary for "normal" day-to-day functioning are identified as "reinforceable responses." Second, a simulated currency is "earned" by performance of the identified appropriate behaviors. Third, the currency is exchangeable for rewards or privileges. Originally applied in mental hospitals with great success at changing the in-hospital behavior of very withdrawn and chronic patients, the procedures have more recently been applied to residential settings for delinquent boys and found to increase appropriate prosocial behavior far more effectively than most institutions for delinquents (Phillips, Phillips, Fixsen, & Wolf, 1972; see Chapter X). These procedures are easiest to apply when the target individuals are under complete control of the institution, and are most effective in improving in-institution behavior rather than in providing skills which are generalizable following release (Davidson & Seidman, 1974). Such programs are reviewed in more detail in later chapters concerned with mental health and legal system interventions. At this point it should be noted that the token economy is an organizational-level application of principles derived from the study of individual behavior.

Other behaviorists have taken a somewhat broader view of the processes involved in learning and many now include cognitive mediational

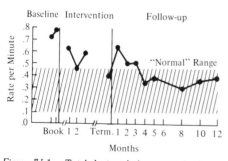

Figure IV-1. Total deviant behavior in the home. (Redrawn from Patterson, 1974.)

variables in their social learning theory, that is, unobservable internal responses that are said to mediate between stimuli and responses. Some even go so far as to argue that reinforcement, while it may *control* behavior, is not necessary for learning to take place. Bandura (1969), for example, has argued that vicarious learning (observing others) is a very important way in which people experience their world, and the direct experience of trial and error is not always necessary for learning to take place. He notes that a great deal of what a child learns is by observation and instruction rather than by direct experience. If this were not the case most children would not survive; trial and error learning would often lead to "extinction of the organism" rather than of the behavior. Most children avoid running out in the street in front of a car even though they have never been run over.

In an ingenious experiment which Bandura (1965) has called a case of "no-trial learning" he has distinguished between the acquisition (learning) of a response and its performance. He argues that although reinforcement does control performance, acquisition need not involve direct reinforcement, but rather can occur as a function of observation and resultant "symbolic processes." To demonstrate this Bandura (1965) showed a modeling film in which novel physical and verbal aggressive behaviors were exhibited to three different groups of children. One group was shown a film in which the model was rewarded for performing the aggressive behaviors, a second group was shown a film in which the model was punished for the same behaviors, and the third group saw a film in which there were no consequences following the model's performance of aggressive behavior. Following the viewing of the films, the children in the model-rewarded condition and in the no-consequences condition performed significantly more of the aggressive behaviors than children in the model-punished condition. Boys performed more of the modeled aggressive behaviors than girls. If the experiment had stopped at this point it would have simply served as a demonstration of the powerful effects of observational learning and reinforcement. However, Bandura then offered to *all* children highly attractive incentives

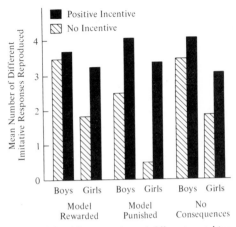

Figure IV-2. Mean number of different matching responses reproduced by children as a function of response consequences to the model and positive incentives. (Redrawn from Bandura, 1965.)

to perform the behaviors they had observed. As can be seen in Figure IV-2, these incentives eliminated the previous differences in performance. All children performed the modeled behaviors about equally, indicating that they had learned what to do by observation, but that actual performance is under the control of consequences. In addition, boys and girls each performed the modeled behavior about equally, indicating that given reinforcement for it, girls will be as aggressive as boys.

The above study is a good example of the fact that behavior can be learned by observation and controlled by reinforcement. Bandura (1969, 1971) and others (Rachman, 1972) have reviewed many applications of this modeling procedure to the treatment situation, including teaching young children to overcome phobias, using modeling as an effective device in teaching various kinds of prosocial behaviors to people who either do not know how to perform them or who are afraid to perform them, and training interpersonal skills. Sarason and Ganzer (1969) and others (see Chapter X) have applied such techniques to programs for delinquents. O'Connor and Rappaport (1970) have applied them to training "hard core" unemployed men, and O'Connor (1969, 1972) has used the procedure to teach young children, identified by teachers as social isolates, how to interact with other children.

O'Connor's work may be of particular importance to those interested in early detection and prevention of interpersonal difficulties among children. In a preliminary study, O'Connor (1969) asked nursery school teachers to identify children who demonstrated extreme social withdrawal in the classroom. He further observed the actual extent to which the children interacted with their peers, and then divided the children who were designated as ''social isolates'' into two groups. One group was shown a 23-minute modeling film in which young children were reinforced for interacting with one another in the classroom. A narrator pointed out each step of the interaction from initiation through completion, including the positive consequences. Each child in the modeling group viewed the film in a situation that focused his or her attention on the modeling, a step believed to be very important for acquisition, and the absence of which is presumed, together with social anxiety, to partially account for why withdrawn children appear unable to learn to interact by simply observing other children in the classroom. Children in the second group served as control subjects and were shown a film of dolphins with a musical soundtrack. Immediately following the films each child was observed in the classroom, and the number of interactions with other children was recorded. Figure IV-3 presents the results of this study. Children who had viewed the modeling film interacted with their peers as often as did other nonisolate children in the same classroom, while the control-group children continued to avoid social interaction.

The immediate question raised about these results is ''will they last?'' In order to answer this question O'Connor (1972) replicated the earlier study and found the identical outcome with nursery school children in another city. He added follow-up observations as well, and found that treated children continued to interact at normal levels, that is, comparable to nonisolate peers over three observations, each several weeks after viewing the modeling film.

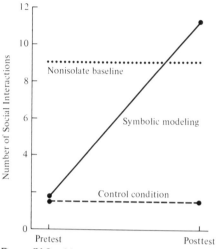

Figure IV-3. Mean number of social interactions displayed. (Redrawn from O'Connor, 1969.)

In most theories of child development and psychopathology it is assumed that withdrawal from social interaction is a poor prognostic sign for normal development. It is reasonable to assume that early detection and prevention of social withdrawal are extremely important for community mental health programs. The development of techniques that are easily administered, effective, and require a minimal investment of professional time is basic to such efforts. The use of filmed modeling appears to be a technique which community mental health professionals would be wise to investigate further.

Behavior Modification and Individual Treatment for the Poor

The current status of any method of treatment for lower socioeconomic class patients is by no means clear. Two recent articles by Lorion (1973, 1974) have added some understanding to the situation with regard to individual treatment for adults, and have indicated possible alternatives, including those based on social learning and behavior modification. Although it is well documented that lower-class clients drop out of traditional psychotherapy prematurely, or even before it begins, there is no consistent evidence that a patient's socioeconomic status is related to outcome for those who remain in treatment. Much of the argument that the poor are not good candidates for psychotherapy appears to come from characteristic reactions of the *therapists* to clients who are often seen as difficult to empathize with, "merely" seeking symptomatic relief, speak in crude language, and display sexual and aggressive behaviors. How much the high attrition rate for lower-class clients is a function of therapists who *perceive* them as "untreatable," rather than of the clients or the methods, is not known (Meltzoff & Kornreich, 1970; Heine & Trosman, 1960). Much of the attribution may be due to a self-fulfilling prophecy on the part of the therapists (Thomas & Sillen, 1972).

Often, lower-class clients are considered not to be "psychologically minded" and unwilling to participate in a treatment in which the authority does not tell them what to do. However, Lorion's (1974) review cites several recent studies of "help-seeking attitudes" among the poor and finds that when objective data, rather than therapist's observations, are reported, low-income applicants for treatment do not appear to hold attitudes that are more negative toward treatment than middle- or upper-income applicants. In addition, many clients from all income levels, not just lower-class clients, appear to want treatment to include direct advice and active support, although it appears that middle- and upper-class clients learn to give this up in favor of the therapist's expectation that psychotherapy will not be conducted this way. The data on outcome of traditional psychotherapy, confusing at best, leave open to question whose expectations are unrealistic, the client's or the therapist's.

In considering treatment alternatives, Lorion emphasizes that it is possible to modify treatment procedures so as to conform to the patient's expectations, rather than vice versa. Such changes are consistent with the community mental health emphasis on efficient use of scarce resources. Of special interest in this regard is the use of crisis intervention, brief psychotherapy, and behavior modification. Each of these tends to be congruent with expectations for a short-term treatment based on direct advice and support. Behavior modification in particular has focused attention on the details of setting specific behavioral goals contracted between client and therapist, and step-by-step actions to be taken. Given the desire for help with a particular problem, as Lorion notes, such methods should be more acceptable than "talk therapy" to lower-class clients who are often described as "concrete minded and less verbal" than upper-income groups. Although such characterizations of the lower-income client may not be more than a stereotype, which is probably a function of psychologists' social class bias and inability to communicate with people who are different from themselves, the observation that direct advice and action, as opposed to talking about past child-rearing, may be more acceptable is probably true. If upper-income clients, who are well read and informed about psychology and psychiatry, were not already oversold on the need for "deep" understanding of the "unconscious" or of their "relationships," but instead simply wanted sensible and effective ways to solve their problems in living, they too would probably prefer direct advice and action. The fact that middle- and upper-income clients can afford to take the time (because they have more money, can afford babysitters, or can more easily leave their jobs to keep treatment appointments) probably contributes to their willingness to gradually accept the long-term and nondirective nature of psychotherapy. On the other hand, lower-class patients often cannot afford to wait to be convinced (Bergin & Garfield, 1971).

Arnold Goldstein (1973) has recently described, in the greatest detail to date, a social learning approach to treatment for the poor. He calls the method "structured learning therapy," and it involves the use of social reinforcement, role playing, and modeling.

. . . the patient is provided with numerous, specific, detailed, and vivid displays of the specific interpersonal or personal skill we are seeking to teach him (i.e., modeling); he is given considerable opportunity, training and encouragement to behaviorally rehearse or practice the modeled behavior (i.e., role playing); and he is provided with positive feedback, approval, or reward as his enactments increasingly approximate those of the model (i.e., social reinforcement) (Gutride, Goldstein, & Hunter, 1973).

Such methods have been shown to be useful in teaching therapeutic skills to nonprofessionals such as prison guards, nurses, ministers, and college students; training employees in job skills (Goldstein & Sorcher, 1973); teaching schizophrenic patients interpersonal skills (Gutride, Goldstein, & Hunter, 1973); as well as in helping low-income clients (Goldstein, 1973).

In addition to the careful specification of agreed upon goals and steps toward their accomplishment, because a social-learning approach emphasizes environmental contingencies as opposed to intrapsychic conflicts, the behavior modifier must pay careful attention to real life constraints on people who are poor. "Behavioral norms" of a subculture must be understood (Lazarus, 1971; Lorion, 1974; Ullmann & Krasner, 1969) in order to design a workable behavioral treatment plan. With such an emphasis, behavior modification treatment should potentially be the kind of individual psychology on which a community mental health system may be built, because it would take into account the particular desires and goals of individual clients and their subcommunity. In addition to being an efficient method of individual treatment, the utility of techniques such as those developed by Patterson and others for home and school intervention lies in their potential as preventive measures. The techniques can be taught to teachers as well as to parents, and may enable them to deal with behavior problems before the child gets into severe difficulty. They also require far less time than traditional individual psychotherapy, and may be more effective as well. Also, by equipping the agents of socialization (parents and teachers) with such techniques, they should be able to apply them to future as well as present children.

There are two cautions that need to be stated with regard to behavior modification treatment for lower socioeconomic class children and adults. Those professionals who practice behavior therapy with adults are not necessarily any more comfortable with or accepting of lower-class patients than are traditional psychotherapists. In adult treatment, the self-fulfilling prophecy and negative expectations found to limit the availability of psychotherapy for lower-class clients are also potential dangers. All forms of psychotherapy are dependent to some extent on client motivation and therapist interpersonal skills (i.e., the ability to understand, listen to, and empathize with the client). Although these personality factors are not emphasized in behavior therapy, they are probably still necessary if not sufficient for the creation of behavior change. With this in mind, even though the behavior therapist may have useful skills and techniques, unless he or she is able to deal with lower-class clients on their own terms they are likely to run into the same difficulties that have inhibited traditional therapists from relating to lower-class clients. In any case, both the goals and language of treatment need to make sense to the client in his or her own terms. Although theoretically behavior modification requires the therapist to accept and understand the values and natural environment of his or her client, in practice this is not easy to achieve. Most behavior therapists, like traditional therapists, come from a middle-class background. They are just as likely as other therapists to select goals and operate on a value system which seeks to make all people conform to middle-class norms.

With regard to programs aimed at enhancing the ability of the agents of socialization, such as teachers, parents, probation officers, and so on, to train children, the dangers are similar to those in any community mental health program and have already been discussed in Chapter III. Behavior modification techniques, like all forms of therapy, can most easily be used to support a single standard of adjustment to middle-class norms. Some of these issues have been discussed within the behavior modification movement itself, and particularly well in a paper by Winett and Winkler (1972) entitled *Current behavior modification in the classroom: Be still, be quiet, be docile.* Winett and Winkler, while reviewing the effectiveness of behavior modification programs, have shown many to be based on keeping children obedient as opposed to helping them attain more meaningful educational goals. There is theoretically no reason why behavior modification procedures must be used in this way. Rather, once again the social values which underlie a mental health program are far more important to its aims than are the techniques used. These value questions will continue to concern us throughout this book, but are to some extent independent of the effectiveness of the socialization techniques, and in this regard behavior modification seems to be a set of tools that community mental health professionals cannot afford to ignore.

Difficulties in the Extension of Behavior Modification to Community Psychology

Despite its obvious usefulness to community mental health practice, social learning theory and behavior modification have some very important limits for community psychology, to the extent that it differs from community mental health. Although it will be useful to the community psychologist when thinking about individual behavior, it may actually be a distraction when thinking about community behavior.

As behavioral technology has grown in popularity, has been shown to be as good or better than other forms of individual treatment, and has been applied to problems in the natural environment (that is, to other than mental health settings and to settings not established for the purpose of behavior modification per se, but those which are a part of society's already established activities), some have seen the obvious link between this form of individual psychology and the aims of community psychology. Winett (1974) has suggested that contingency management in the control of important social, as opposed to individual, behaviors seems promising. He has cited several examples which, while at present are somewhat trivial, nevertheless make the point with regard to environmental pollution. Reinforcers have been used to encourage children to properly dispose of litter, and to encourage commuters to preserve gasoline and re-

duce pollution through the use of car pools by setting up a faster moving "priority lane" over a San Francisco bridge. Similarly, Meyers, Craighead, and Meyers (1974) cite other studies that found behavior modification useful in employment settings and in encouraging social integration of Black first graders in a White classroom (Hauserman, Walen, & Behling, 1973). They have argued that behavioral technology may be combined with community mental health to educate communities in such a way as to enhance their "self-control." They assume that by making people aware of how contingencies affect behavior, a community could systematically select the contingencies it wants to reinforce. Such analyses imply that we now have the scientific means to implement "new societies." Such thinking of course is not new for behaviorists. Skinner, as early as 1948 in *Walden Two*, and as recently as 1971, has suggested that behavior control can readily be applied to the creation of utopian societies.

There are at least four reasons why the application of behavior modification principles to the problems of community psychology may be unrealistic. The first reason is that the techniques are simply not as powerful and generalizable as they appear at first glance. Although behavior modification may be an effective means of controlling people in well-defined settings, and even of teaching specific behavior to individuals, the generalization of behavior from one setting to another is not shown to be terribly consistent. Successful programs using token systems in the control of institutional behaviors do not necessarily carry over to the far more complicated "real life" social environment. Society is an open rather than a closed system with continual new inputs, unlike the hospital or the classroom (Davidson & Seidman, 1974; see also Chapters IX and X). Second, although it is often brushed aside, the question of who controls the reinforcers cannot be overlooked. It is one thing to talk about a "community" setting its own contingencies, but quite another to change *who* in the community makes such decisions. This is simply a restatement of the need to distribute power more equitably and has little to do with behaviorism. It is reasonable to expect that those now in power are likely to continue to be in power unless that issue is dealt with directly. This is a question of social values, not of technology. As London (1969) has put it:

There is no antidote to power but power, nor has there ever been . . . in order to defend individual freedom, it is necessary to enhance the power of individuals . . . . If behavior technology endangers freedom by giving refined power to controllers, then the antidote which promotes freedom is to give more refined power over their own behavior to those who are endangered.

The socially marginal people who are now expected to conform to the status quo are not likely to be given power to set their own "schedules of reinforcement" or choose their own "desirable" behaviors simply because behavior modification has shown that systematic distribution of material resources is obviously important as a means of behavior control. If anything, this is likely to increase the control of those already in power. As we will see in the next chapter, community psychology must be concerned with the very issue of *who* controls the reinforcers, rather than with the obvious fact that rewards often control behavior. Behavior modification may give psychologists an acceptable vocabulary with which to say this, but it does not solve the problem by relabeling it. This leads us to the third reason why behavior modification technology will probably not solve the problems of community psychology: Because the principles are based on an analysis of individual behavior they may be misleading as a basis on which to understand the behavior of a community. This point is discussed in more detail in the next chapter as an "error of logical typing" (Watzlawick, Weakland, & Fisch, 1974).

Finally, the fourth reason why behavior modification is unlikely to serve as a basis for community psychology is more mundane—it may be impossible to implement. Reppucci and Saunders (1974) have recently discussed this very issue. They have noted what they call a "large gap" between what is real and what is imagined about the success of behavior modification. What is real consists of small-scale attempts to change the behavior of isolated units

of people; what is imagined in *Walden Two* (Skinner, 1948) and in *Beyond Freedom and Dignity* (Skinner, 1971) is quite another matter. They posit several reasons, extrapolating from their own work and that of others, as to why this gap exists, even for the successful application of behavior modification to relatively confined institutional settings such as hospitals, schools, and prisons, let alone the larger society.

(1) The problem of institutional constraints, or bureaucracy, is formidable. Most complex institutions have a great deal of "red tape" and diffusion of responsibility which makes control of a consistent set of contingencies very difficult. (2) External pressure from the larger society, especially on public institutions, is constantly changing and requires flexibility which is often incompatible with the needs of a behavior modification program. (3) The language of behavior modification is often not well received because it sounds "unhumanistic." (4) To implement a behavior modification program the staff of an organization must be trained and this is frequently difficult to accomplish because the contingencies on *their* behavior (the staff) are often outside the control of the behavior modifier (e.g., the staff may be civil service employees who are paid for behavior which is not necessarily the same behavior that the program organizer desires). (5) The institutions of society frequently function with less than optimal resources as compared to resources available in experimental research. This makes things possible in principle but not in reality. (6) The existing labels used to describe the activities of many organizations are often not specific and may lead to confusion. (7) The organizer of a behavior modification program may often be perceived as inflexible. (8) The organizer will therefore need to compromise many of the procedures that should work in principle.

Although each of these problems seems to be unrelated to psychology, Reppucci and Saunders (1974) feel that they are at least as important as is technology for effective programming and should be the subject matter of psychology. Behavior modification advocates seem to argue that all one needs is knowledge of learning principles in order to be effective. Reppucci and Saunders state that other kinds of knowledge and understanding are at least equally essential, but that the answers are not to be found in behavioral technology. Questions they raise are: where and how should one enter a setting? What is a realistic time perspective for change? What are the potential points of conflict in a social system? These are of importance to community rather than individual psychology. Reppucci (1973) has suggested that research in organizational psychology may help to answer such questions, and his observations in that regard are discussed in Chapter VI.

Seymour B. Sarason (1972) has addressed himself to similar questions with regard to what he calls "the creation of settings." He takes issue with Skinner's assumption that the scientific basis for creating new societies exists. He notes that Skinner's "data" are based on the study of single organisms, and as such the data fail to confront the issue of power and who controls it, or of how social institutions operate. Humans are fallible and, despite intentions, between principles and actions there lies the implementer's or the leader's capacity to "foul things up."

My objection to Skinner is not that his position is wrong but that it is incredibly incomplete. It solves the problem of the creation of settings by labeling it technological, a typically American solution to social problems. It pays homage to and genuflects before the experimental method and spirit as if that fully compensates for incomplete and inadequate observation and description of the problems under study. And by an exercise of assertion and faith the elegant simplicity of its principles is presented to us as isomorphic with the workings of the social world. Parsimony of principles is not an inherent virtue (Sarason, 1972, p. 264).

Sarason is more concerned with what is missing in Skinner's analysis than with what is included. He argues that if one is really interested in social engineering, the questions of social action, such as those raised by Reppucci and Saunders above, need to be understood.

A more modest view, and less utopian than Skinner's, of the implications of behavior modification for social change has been offered by Bandura (1969). His analysis seems to acknowledge that principles of individual behavior change are inadequate for the creation of social change, but nevertheless suggests that they may be useful in the armamentarium of the change agent when he does deal with individuals. To begin with, Bandura notes that socially significant changes require a great deal of time, energy, and resources, and that the beneficial outcomes are usually difficult to demonstrate until they have been tried. Most people will be skeptical of change until they have seen it to be rewarding. Furthermore, conventional behavior patterns are frequently supported by belief systems and moral codes. In addition, vested interests in preserving traditional prestige, power, and economic advantages are usually apparent to those in authority. It is clear from these statements that Bandura is not naive with regard to the difficulties of creating social change, nor is he saying anything much different from Reppucci and Saunders. However, he believes that principles of behavior modification are to some extent applicable to these problems. He notes that often attempts to change attitudes have been employed to create change, and that these efforts have generally not been adequate to the task. He favors an approach that is more optimistic, albeit realistic. He focuses on demonstrating new alternatives rather than on attacking old practices. His basic assumption is that social change will require the institution of new practices that are beneficial to the user, and that attitude change will then follow, rather than vice versa, or that the new practices will be construed in a way which now makes them acceptable. The key, however, is to demonstrate to the targets of change that new behaviors are beneficial to them.

Bandura has convincingly demonstrated that modeling is influential for the creation of individual behavior change and he argues, to the extent that social change can be facilitated by individual change, modeling is useful. Consequently, in order for new behaviors to be learned, models need to be provided, and because vicarious reinforcement can facilitate modeling effects the models also need to be rewarded publicly. In addition, new reinforcement contingencies that will favor adoption of the desired behaviors need to be introduced into the social system. This, of course, is not simple, but at least it gives the change agent some clear goals. It implies that even from the principles of individual behavior we now understand that change is often maintained by institutional practices. For example, if a university is serious about encouraging the recruitment of minority and women faculty members, then the contingencies on hiring need to reflect that desire. One way to do this would be to allow departments to have extra money for new faculty positions, contingent on the hiring of minority faculty. If this is modeled by some departments, others may follow when it is seen to be advantageous to do so. The same will be true in other employment situations. Often when an employer recruits minority employees in a business that has not had any previously, there are difficulties of adjustment between supervisors and the new employees. Often this has led to high turnover rates. To increase the likelihood of success one could make bonus payments to factory supervisors who retain minority employees. Such practices, of course, are not easily implemented. They need to be agreed to by those in power. However, it could be demonstrated that employers can save money by reducing turnover, and that recruitment of minority employees is good public relations, opens new markets, and so on.

Bandura further suggests that in cases where the advantages of new behavior are delayed it is necessary to provide intervening immediate incentives. Such incentives might include money, new social status, or leadership positions. For example, in employment programs the provision of tax incentives by the federal government to employers of minority people or the granting of training funds to universities with large numbers of minority students might be sensible. In creating change in organizations the establishment of new roles within the organization that are specifically concerned with the implementation of social changes may also be desirable. Here the problem of negative sanctions from envious or threatened peers is realistic, and points to the need of establishing interdependent contingencies based on group reinforcement. For exam-

ple, rather than reward the supervisor who retains minority employees, the group of people with whom minority members work might all be rewarded for their collective success.

Finally, Bandura suggests that under conditions where the change agents have no controlling or rewarding power they must establish their value by demonstrating that the practices they advocate will lead to favorable outcomes. However, this strategy has been questioned by others (e.g., Fairweather, Sanders, & Tornatsky, 1974) who argue that demonstration projects are not necessarily effective in the diffusion of an innovation (see Chapter VI). It is probably safe to conclude that Bandura has more insight about the reasons why principles of individual behavior change are difficult to apply when the goal is sociocultural change than he is about how to do it.

What has been said in this section is that social learning theory and behavior modification techniques can be used to accomplish individual behavior change, perhaps better than other known methods. Even so, these techniques are incomplete when a social organization or a community is the unit of study and the focus of change.

Personality Theory and Research

As might be expected, many of the conceptions of personality and social psychology have at least face-valid implications for both community mental health and community psychology. Some of the most interesting and literate descriptions of humanity by psychologists have been used to label the constructs of personality and social psychology. We could begin with the top of the alphabet and cite words such as achievement, affiliation, authority, competence, conformity, cooperation, and work our way down through "z." Most of these constructs have been studied in laboratory situations in order to make predictions about individual behavior. Nevertheless, the implications for real world behavior are often sensible, within the limits suggested by Gergin, Cronbach, and others (see

Chapter II). Despite the emphasis on laboratory research under very controlled conditions, with operational definitions of terms, the very words used often carry a good deal of "surplus meaning." Even the researchers who employ careful methodology are prone to extend it to the larger social environment when introducing their subject matter and discussing the meaning of their data. It is clear that the aims, if not the methods, of such research are to comment on real people in a real world of concern.

For many years personality theory was developed through real world observations, many of which later found their way into the laboratory for more precise study. The failure of such theorizing to predict behavior under laboratory experimentation (e.g., experimental studies of Freud's theory of personality) led to a general disavowal of "big theory," which attempts to explain all of man's behavior, in favor of delimited theory about some aspect of behavior based on empirical, often laboratory, research. It is increasingly difficult to put these delimited sets of empirical research into a unified understanding of man without reference to some theory or model of human behavior.

Personality research, theories, and conceptions hold a crucial place in psychology. They function like a bridge between the academic and the applied worlds, across which many psychologists move freely from laboratory research on one side to application and the "real" world on the other. The bridge seems to have been built by different people starting on either side of a chasm and not quite meeting somewhere in the middle. It is imperfect and does not quite fit together. But for the person of action a leap over the gap from one side to the other is not difficult, even at the risk of falling into the chasm below and probably not being rescued by colleagues on either side. Wiggins, Renner, Clore, and Rose (1971) have characterized the psychology of personality from the shores of academia to be dominated by four viewpoints, or paradigms, each with its own set of methods, procedures, and assumptions. The viewpoints they review are: the biological, which construes events in terms of early experience, genetic en-

dowment, and evolutionary background; the experimental, which construes personality in terms of learning, perceptual, and thought processes; the psychometric-trait viewpoint which views man in terms of his attributes studied by observation, self-report, and indirect assessment; and the social viewpoint which sees man in a social context and emphasizes models, roles, and culture. For community mental health and community psychology each of these ways of viewing man have contributed ideas, methods, and conceptions that are useful; but it is the social viewpoint that is of special relevance.

On the opposite shore from academia lies the real world, out of which have developed theories of personality designed not only to study and understand humanity, but also to help individuals deal with problems in living. Many such theories have been designed to account for humanity as a unified whole, and were initially developed by practitioners to aid in their own work. As Wiggins *et al.* (1971) note, "Personality theories provide a unique view of man that draws attention to certain variables or relationships that might otherwise not be considered." Both the viewpoints and the theories can serve that purpose for the community psychologist, and the aim of this section is to note some of the ideas that personality researchers have examined and that may alert the community psychologist to important concerns. Once again, it must be emphasized that personality research, based as it is on individual psychology, will not solve the puzzles of community change. The very questions personality theory and research ask are not those that need to be answered by community psychology. Rather, personality research may help to call attention to ways in which individuals may be viewed in relationship to society.

Rotter's Social Learning Theory: The Importance of Expectancy

As early as 1954, Julian Rotter was critical of the ways in which many clinical psychologists and personality theorists view people, assess their capacities, and design treatments. He was not only critical of traditional views and practices, but also offered a substitute based on what he called social learning theory (Rotter, 1954). Rotter, a clinical psychologist interested in personality theory and research, was perhaps the first to present a systematic statement of social learning theory as an alternative.[2] Although his view of the social learning process is considerably more "cognitive" and admits to more internal constructs than most behavior modification advocates feel comfortable with, the stated aim of the theory is to integrate the two major trends in American psychology—stimulus-response or reinforcement theories and cognitive or "field" theories (Rotter, 1975; Rotter, Chance, & Phares, 1972). Two of the theory's major contributions are a systematic use of the concepts of "situational specificity" and "expectancy."[3] The emphasis on situational specifity makes this theory compatible with behavior modification, and expectancy adds to it a number of important cognitive considerations.

For our purposes the logic of the theory is expressed sufficiently if it serves to focus our attention on the variable of *expectancy*. For example, the likelihood that a person will apply for a job may be seen as a function of the expectation that to apply will lead to obtaining the job, and the reinforcement value of having it. On the one hand we may assume reinforcement value to be related to the nature of the job, its social prestige, or the meaning of the job to one's self, one's peers, and one's culture, as well as to the job's material payoffs and its other characteristics (e.g., danger involved, difficulty of the work). On the other hand, assuming that reinforcement value is held constant, Rotter's social learning theory predicts that the *subjective expectation* one holds about the likelihood of obtaining the job will determine the likelihood that one applies for it. Similarly, in a school situation, the potential for studying may in part be a function of the reinforcement value of either getting good grades or learning some academic material. In either case, for people who are equal in ability and who view good grades or learning as highly valuable, the extent of study behavior may be a function of how likely each person *expects* studying to lead to the desired outcome. For some people other alternatives, such as cheating, may have a greater expectation for leading to the desired outcome. Similarly, staying in school in order to complete work for a degree will in part be a function of the expectation that getting the degree will lead to some desired outcome, such as obtaining a job or satisfying a parent.

Because *expectations are subjective probability statements*, they cannot be estimated by simply assessing the objective probability that a given behavior will lead to a given reinforce-

---

[2]Although many attribute this to Dollard and Miller (1950), because they attempted to account for psychodynamic theory in learning terms, they were actually translaters rather than introducers of a new paradigm.

[3]There are four major concepts in Rotter's social learning theory: behavior potential, expectancy, reinforcement value, and the psychological situation. Behavior potential (BP) is simply the probability that a given behavior will occur compared to other alternative behaviors. Behavior may be an internal cognitive response, as well as an observable response, and it is assumed that the principles that govern one govern the other. Expectancy is an extremely important part of Rotter's theory. It refers to the *subjective* probability held by a person that a given behavior will lead to a given reinforcement. Reinforcement value is taken to be independent of expectancy and to be the degree of preference one has for a given reinforcement from among all possible alternatives. Finally, the psychological situation refers to both the internal and the external environment, and interactions within and between each of them. Rotter does not simply mean the "stimuli," but rather he has a broader and more inclusive view (consequently one less specific than operant psychologists) of what constitutes a situation. For example, while Rotter would distinguish between behavior in a school situation, in a dating situation, and so on, operant psychologists will look for more detailed elements (the discriminative stimuli) within each situation.

Although not intended as precise mathematical statements, Rotter presents his theory in a series of basic formulas. The simplest formula (Rotter, Chance, & Phares, 1972, p. 14) is:

$$BP_{x, s_1, Ra} = f \left(E_{x, Ras_1} \ \& \ RV_{a, s_1} \right)$$

This means the potential for a given behavior x in situation 1 in relation to reinforcement a is a function of the expectation that behavior x in situation 1 will lead to the occurence of reinforcement a, and the value of reinforcement a in situation 1.

A more complicated statement which incorporates these basic ideas but refers to a broader range of related behaviors and situations has also been formulated, as have detailed analyses of reinforcement and reinforcement value.

ment. Subjective expectation is a function of two factors: generalized expectancy (GE) and specific expectancy (E').[4] Rotter, Chance, & Phares (1972, p. 25) give the following example: One's expectancy for winning a 100-yard dash, if he has never competed in a dash, is determined by his success at other athletic events. After competing in 100-yard dash races his expectation will increasingly be a function of success in that specific event. Similarly, a child who enters school for the first time will have a generalized expectation for the likelihood that he will succeed in school, based on previous experience in school-like situations and with adults. As he progresses in school, his expectancy for success will increasingly be a function of more specific experiences and experiences with teachers.[5]

Rotter believes that the major task in creating behavior change involves changing expectations because reinforcement value (the other crucial variable in his theory) is usually very stable. For example, if one is dealing with a teenager who shoplifts, he usually does so either because of the material reinforcement he can obtain, the social reinforcement he gets from his peers, or the attention of adults. It is probably difficult, if not useless, to try to begin by changing these values, or to introduce competing values such as morality, respect for property, and so on. Similarly, punishment, no matter how severe, is not likely to be effective in competing with such strong reinforcers. On the other hand, it makes more sense to try to increase the *expectation* that *alternative behaviors* may be more effective in obtaining the desired rewards.

Contingency management programs based on operant principles might be interpreted in this theory as effective (or generalizable to new situations) because they increase the expectation that a new behavior will lead to the desired rewards. In order to implement contingency management programs it is necessary to gain a good deal of control over the dispensing of reinforcement. When this is possible it is an efficient behavior control technique. Such control in the real world is often difficult if not impossible to obtain. Even if such control is obtained, as in institutional settings where contingency management programs can be quite effective, to the extent that the person perceives the contingencies as specific to the institution his behavior may not generalize to other situations in the real world. However, one's behavior will generalize when one's expectations for reinforcement in multiple situations in the real world are changed.

Theoretically, there are two kinds of generalized expectations. The first, discussed above, is generalized expectation for a particular kind of reinforcement. The second is called *generalized problem-solving expectation*. This involves expectations that generalize to a series of situations where the nature of the reinforcements themselves varies (Rotter, 1975). For example, a generalized expectation of looking for alternatives to solve problem situations is hypothesized as one important source of individual differences in behavior (Rotter, Chance, & Phares, 1972). Rotter's social learning theory emphasizes this kind of learning as a potentially powerful tool for changing behavior. Rotter (1970) has recently discussed and listed several implications of his social learning theory for the creation of individual behavior change:

1. Because the creation of behavior change involves a social influence process the techniques must be suitable to the target per-

---

[4]GE is a function of one's past experiences in related situations. For example, generalized expectancy for success in a mathematics course is a function of success in all previous school situations. E', on the other hand, is determined by past experience in situations perceived by the person as similar to the current situation; for example, success in other mathematics courses. To the extent that the person has no specific experience in a given situation, expectancy is a function of generalized experience.

[5]Again, the general proposition may be stated as a formula (Rotter, Chance, & Phares, 1972, p. 25):

$$E_{s_1} = f\left(E'_{s_1} \ \& \ \frac{GE}{N_{s_1}}\right)$$

or, an expectancy is a function of expectancy for a given reinforcement to occur as a function of previous experience in the same situation and as a function of experiences generalized from other situations divided by some function of the number of experiences in the given situation.

son. Most people will reject a technique that they do not find compatible with their view of themselves. Specific technique is therefore less important than general principles of social influence.

2. Social learning theory views behavior change from a problem-solving point of view. The major emphasis is on looking for alternative ways of reaching goals, thinking about consequences of behavior, discriminating between life situations, and recognizing the needs and atittudes of others, so as to anticipate their reactions.

3. To create constructive alternatives often requires that the change agent be active and use direct reinforcement. Although the specific methods of behavior modification are "happily included" these are seen as part of a more comprehensive approach.

4. Insight into the past is useful only if the person feels a need for it. It is more important to obtain insight into long-term future consequences of particular behavior, and into values and goals.

5. Emphasis is placed on understanding the behavior and motives of others, and of learning from them by means of modeling, direct instruction, and so on.

6. Real life experiences in many situations are more important in changing expectations and behavior than is "psychotherapy." Environmental manipulation, by obtaining cooperation of significant others to change their own behavior in relation to the target person, is often an effective technique. Hospitalization, imprisonment, or removal from the natural environment is viewed as potentially destructive and not helpful in teaching new ways to live in the world.

In discussing behavior change Rotter (1970) is explicit about his values, or the direction of such change. He believes that it is useful for persons to change toward "normalcy" or conformity to the way most people are, and that the change agent should be willing to accept some responsibility for implementing this. Specifically, the aim is to help the person find satisfaction, eliminate behaviors which are clearly detrimental to others, and to "carry his own weight" in society. However, as he notes, the social learning approach need not necessarily be used to implement these values. Rather, it could be used to support any social values selected.

Rotter's influence on personality theory is quite direct, although his influence on the development of behavior modification and behavioral treatment techniques is less so. Although not often acknowledged, Rotter's social learning theory is an anticipation of the more recent thinking in behavior modification. In some ways, as behaviorists find the need to account for more and more of the complexities of human functioning, including cognitive mediation between stimulus and response, Rotter's theory may be in advance of other behavioral approaches, rather than simply an anticipation (cf. Mischel, 1973).

In addition to using concepts such as reinforcement, which is consistent with behavior modification, Rotter's theory adds a number of other variables of concern, as well as a number of assumptions about human beings. First, he emphasizes that behavior is a function of the *interaction* of an individual and his environment. Although the words are familiar, the emphasis is both important and different from behavior modification. All behaviorists recognize the importance of "learning history" such that individuals are seen to enter a given situation with differential experiences; the operant approach stresses that indiyiduals vary with regard to what is reinforcing and tends to ignore other individual differences as either not important or not measurable. In part this is because behavior modification has been a reaction to the overreliance on person variables as opposed to environmental or situational factors in controlling behavior. Much of this reaction is based on the well-documented failure of traditional personality theory to specify individual differences in other than "fuzzy," often unreliable form. That approach tends to label people on "traits" and repeatedly finds that traits are not useful in predicting behavior (see Mischel, below). Rotter places one foot on each side of the issue of the importance of person variables as opposed to situational variables. Many of the recent criticisms of "trait theory" currently presented by behavior modification adherents were recognized by Rotter 25 years ago. His view has been that the problem is one of better conceptualizations and methodology of measurement, rather than that person variables should be discarded.

Rotter was also one of the first personality theorists to emphasize the importance of what he calls the "psychological situation," and in all of his theoretical statements situational variables are stressed. Although the importance of the situation is emphasized, for Rotter the situation is examined at a more molar level than for behavior modifiers. However, whereas behavior modification has emphasized the importance of small details of situational variation, Rotter has been more concerned with specification of the details of cognitive variables. Whereas behavior modification has tended to study and manipulate access to and conditions of reinforcement, Rotter and his colleagues have tended to study and manipulate specific cognitive variables. Both emphasize learning and the view that behavior is modifiable. Although both view history of the person as less important than current events in understanding or changing behavior, Rotter tends to rely more on historical information because of the greater emphasis on internalized individual differences. This is consistent with his view that behavior has consistency across situations, although he cautions that this does not mean that it is independent of the situation. John may be generally more aggressive than Bill, but that does not mean that in some situations Bill will not be more aggressive than John. Rotter's basic point of view has been both adopted and refined (although not always acknowledged) by other personality theorists, and before considering the implications of this viewpoint for community psychology, some of their refinements are considered below.

Cognitive Social Learning Theory and Ideographic Psychology

Although it is an old issue for psychology (Bem & Allen, 1974), the importance of situational variables in personality theory has been most explicitly argued in modern terms by Walter Mischel (1968, 1969, 1973). Most recently Mischel (1973) has described an approach he terms *cognitive social learning*. His viewpoint is an attempt, similar to Rotter's, to integrate reinforcement theory and cognitive theory. There are a number of similarities between Rotter and Mischel, and although Mischel adds some important modernizations, specifics, and refinements to social learning theory, his basic arguments are consistent with both behavior modification and Rotter's social learning theory.

In 1968 Mischel wrote what is probably the classic *tour de force* opposing traditional trait views of personality. The basis of his argument was a documentation of the failure of measured traits or hypothetical underlying predispositions to show more than a very limited cross-situational consistency. Since then there has been considerable controversy with regard to the importance of information about persons as opposed to information about situations for the prediction of human behavior. Out of this controversy the notion of "moderator variables" has been developed. This position argues that although there is consistency in a person's behavior, much of it is also affected by a host of variables (for example, IQ, sex, age, and many other person and situational factors that are different depending on what behavior is under study) such that there are severe limits to our ability to find behavioral consistency from general dispositions or traits.

Others have emphasized that the *interaction* of a person in a given context is a better predictor of behavior than either information about the person or the situation alone (Bowers, 1973). The crux of the interactionist argument comes from several sources. One is the finding that in quantitative terms the interaction of person and situational variables accounts for more behavioral variance than either variable alone (Bowers, 1973). A second source of the interactionist view is the observation from cognitive psychology that a person constructs his own view of the world, and this view is in constant interplay with new experiences. Persons are not only active in creating their own psychological situations, but they are also active in selecting the situations in which they find themselves (Bowers, 1973; Kelley & Stahelski, 1970; Wachtel, 1973). Although there appears to be considerable logical and empirical evidence that better *group* predictions can be made by knowing about both the person and the situations, as Mischel has argued, in the absence of the ability to predict *consistencies* in *individual* human behavior, interactionism is simply a "truism."

With the above in mind, in his more recent writing Mischel has attempted to bring person variables as well as situational variables into social learning theory, so as to focus on prediction of individual consistency. Although Mischel does not want to be accused of being a trait theorist, and is careful to argue that he views person variables such as expectancy as "specific (and modifiable) 'if-then' hypotheses about contingencies" he is not really far from an interactionist position. His cognitive social learning theory posits five general classes of person variables, or those that an individual has within herself or himself. These include *competencies* (both intellectual and social); learned *encoding strategies* and personal constructs which enable an individual to sort and categorize the world; *behavior-outcome and stimulus-outcome expectancies* which are similar to Rotter's specific expectancies; *subjective stimulus value* (similar to Rotter's reinforcement value); and *self-regulatory systems* which are learned rules for self-control and self-evaluation. He adds these person variables to the situational variables prominent in behavior modification, and interprets the specificity of behavior in a given situation to be governed by the sum of these person variables, or what he calls a person's *discriminative facility:* the ability to recognize and act on subtle situational differences. Although to a large extent the more powerful the stimulus variables the more they will be similarly viewed by different people, the situation is always interpreted by the person and it is necessary to approach behavioral prediction through the viewpoint of each individual person.

Mischel's most recent statements, then, have been interpreted as favoring an ideographic or individual view of personality, which assumes that although a person may be consistent with one's self, he or she is not necessarily consistent with other people. This view is opposed to a nomothetic view of personality, in which it is assumed that there are general traits that are universally important for everyone. The ideographic viewpoint has been eloquently presented by Bem and Allen (1974). They argue that some personality dimensions are important for some people and not others, and that if one asks people, they will be able to tell the researcher on what dimensions and in what situations they themselves will be consistent.

Bem and Allen (1974) present data to support their view. They divided research subjects (college students at Stanford) into two groups: those who had predicted that they would be consistent in multiple situations with regard to the traits of friendliness and conscientiousness in school work, and a second group who predicted that they would vary on these traits depending on the specific situation. These groups were then compared on actual consistency, by observing school-related behavior, performance in experimental situations, and by collecting ratings from the subjects themselves, their parents, and their peers. To test their own (the researchers') hypothesis that personal neatness should be related to conscientiousness the researchers also obtained observer's ratings of that characteristic. It was found that for those who expected themselves to be consistent there were significantly higher correlations between the various sources of information (indicating consistency in the different situations) than for those who did not expect themselves to be consistent. However, the relationship between self-predicted consistency and actual consistency in different situations did not hold for neatness when correlated with the other measures of conscientiousness. This last result is, in the authors' words "precisely . . . the main point of (their) article." They go on to note that:

. . . it is only we, the investigators, who think that school-related conscientiousness (returning evaluations and course readings) and personal neatness ought to belong in the same equivalence class. Our subjects do not, our low-variability subjects find them to be orthogonal . . . and our high variability subjects apparently have time to do their school work or to keep things neat and clean, but not both ($r = -.61$). . . . The moral of all this is that we need to move even further toward ideographic assessment . . . we have relinquished the presumption that all traits are relevant to all people, but stubbornly retained the right to dictate which behaviors and situations shall constitute the trait itself (Bem & Allen, 1974, p. 517).

For community psychology the implications of an ideographic individual psychology are profound. If one finds, from the study of college students at Stanford University, that the hypotheses of the experimenter who expects all his subjects to conform to his view of the world are less accurate than those of the experimenter who asks his subjects how they view the world, and adjusts his psychological predictions accordingly, how valid is a psychology which neglects the viewpoint of persons who are from social class, ethnic, and cultural backgrounds far more different from most psychology professors and professionals than are Stanford University students? Furthermore, although it may be all well and good for personality researchers to stop expecting their subjects to conform to their (the researchers') view of the world, what does this imply for those who expect all cultural, ethnic, and minority groups to conform to the standards of the single most powerful "experimenter" of them all, the socialization agent(s)? Such questions must be raised for the community psychologists whenever they engage in individual-level behavior change. If the questions are ignored the community psychologists may find their individual psychology to be inconsistent with their community psychology.

Some Implications of a Cognitive Social Learning Theory and an Ideographic Approach for Community Psychology

The strengths and weaknesses of both Rotter's and Mischel's social learning theory for community mental health as service delivery are similar to those already discussed for behavior modification. The emphasis on environmental process and active intervention is one which community mental health, to the extent that it focuses on individuals, should find compatible with its orientation. More importantly, for community psychology the cognitive social learning approach points toward a number of variables that have implications for social analysis and intervention. The notion of expectancy is one such variable.

Gurin and Gurin (1970) have used the concept of expectancy as a means to integrate the implications of research and intervention programs for the poor. They believe that expectancy is a variable which forces the psychologist to relate individual motivation to environmental analysis. Because expectancies are directly affected by immediate and objective rewards they are subject to situational changes. However, generalized expectancy is also a "residue of the past," and subjective expectancies cannot be presumed to change automatically with every situation. For the poor, expectancy has two kinds of psychological implications: (1) the problem of *low expectancy* that one will attain one's goal; (2) the feeling of *powerlessness*, which is related but not identical. Powerlessness, or the feeeling that one does not control one's own chances, is termed external locus of control in Rotter's theory, and is discussed in some detail below.

Following a review of studies that had attempted to change expectations, Gurin and Gurin (1970) have concluded that success experiences and changes in the objective opportunities available to people can be used to change expectancy for success when this is done under conditions where a person feels that the success came from his own skill and competence. However, they see danger in basing poverty interventions on an overly psychological approach which assumes the problems are *in* the poor. Rather, they see the problem in terms of a realistic match between subjective and objective expectancies. With regard to skills training programs for education and employment, on the subjective side, in order to increase generalized expectancy for success, the social relationship between trainer and trainee is crucial, and one must pay attention to the characteristics that make trainers creditable models. The implications of research on attitude change (Kelman, 1965) and on modeling (Bandura, 1969) in this regard appear to be congruent with the view of many that local community people need to be involved in programs as leaders and models for the poor. At the same time, it is important to recognize that studies of modeling have shown that an observer will imitate a model who *controls resources* that are valuable to the observer (Flanders, 1968). That is, programs which use indigenous nonprofessionals as trainers, but which do not provide these trainers with the actual power to provide resources, will probably be less than successful at creating behavior change[6] (see Clark & Hopkins' analysis of the War on Poverty in Chapter I, pp. 15–16).

On the other side of the coin—the objective probabilities—Gurin and Gurin make some important observations. First, studies of change in expectations (as well as those of modeling effects) assume a benign environment. In expectancy studies the implicit assumption is that success in life will follow from individual competence. In modeling studies it is assumed that the new positive behaviors will be reinforced by the natural environment. Unfortunately, such assumptions are often questionable with regard to the poor. It may be that the objective opportunities, or real world contingencies, are such that low expectancy for success among the poor is in fact realistic. The simple competence training approach to expectancies and training programs is therefore limited because it deals only with individuals. Thus far the studies of expectancy and modeling have not dealt with issues such as community control and social action aimed at changing the objective probabilities for success, or the real-life reinforcement contingencies.

Seidman and Rappaport (1974a) have recently extended the implications of the Gurin and Gurin (1970) analysis. They argue that one can deal with the problem of low expectations in two ways. One way is by working at changing the subjective probabilities that a given behavior, such as going to school, will lead to success in life and all the things one cares about. If a minority group member raises his or her

expectations in the absence of changes in the external, objective opportunity structure, where the real probabilites rather than the subjective probabilities lie, that person may be moving toward disappointment and failure. On the other hand, if there are changes in the external opportunity structure which are not perceived at the level of individual people, a minority group member may not take advantage of the changes. From this analysis it is clear that *social change will require multiple levels of intervention*.

Finally, if one takes seriously the implications of Bem and Allen's call for experimenters to stop expecting their subjects to conform to their preconceived notions of how everyone should view the world, and instead develop an ideographic psychology, the community psychologist is faced with a difficult task. The "experimenters" in community psychology are often the agents of socialization who, by the very nature of their task, do expect everyone to conform to their preconceived views. The Black child who speaks in Black dialect is often assumed to be stupid or apathetic about learning to read because the teacher does not understand that for that child Black dialect is the way one should speak (see Chapter VIII). The mental patient is assumed to be suffering from a disease and to be incompetent if he or she does not behave in *all* the ways which the professional mental health worker expects people to behave (see Chapter IX). Professionals even have a difficult time seeing "normal" behavior once a person is designated as abnormal (e.g., Rosenhan, 1973). Individual psychology, which is increasingly finding that an ideographic view of man is more sensible than expecting all to be the same, needs to be translated into a community psychology which does not expect all persons to conform to society's single standard of behavior in order to be allowed access to the resources of society.

Locus of Control, Learned Helplessness, and Power

One of the key linking variables between individual behavior and social systems is the concept of locus of control of reinforcement,

---

[6]This point will need to be stressed as we consider the strategies and tactics of community intervention, particularly those which suggest true autonomous community control.

developed in the context of cognitive social learning theory. Originally conceptualized by Rotter in order to account for the fact that increases and decreases in expectancy tended to vary depending on both the nature of the situation and on apparent consistent differences among people, the variable was thought of as a way to refine predictions concerning the relationship between expectations and reinforcement (Rotter, 1975). It has been defined as follows:

When a reinforcement is perceived by the subject as following some action of his own but not being entirely contingent upon his action, then, in our culture, it is typically perceived as the result of luck, chance, fate, as under the control of powerful others, or as unpredictable because of the great complexity of the forces surrounding him. When the event is interpreted in this way by an individual we have labeled this a belief in *external control*. If the person perceives that the event is contingent upon his own behavior or his own relatively permanent characteristics, we have termed this belief in *internal control* (Rotter, 1966, p. 1; 1975, p. 57).

This variable has been studied in two ways. One is by manipulating situations such that a task outcome is perceived by subjects as either under the control of luck and chance, or under the control of their own skill. The second way it has been studied is as an individual difference variable in which some people tend to have a generalized expectancy for external control of reinforcement, and others a generalized expectancy for internal control of reinforcement. For the latter method a self-report questionnaire has been developed (Rotter, 1966) which contains 23 items in a forced-choice format—the scale most often used in subsequent research, although other similar scales have been developed, including those for children. Although locus of control as a generalized expectancy has sometimes been treated as a typology, Rotter has explicitly disavowed such a use of the concept in favor of the view that the tendency to be internal of external is probably normally distributed in the general population.

Research on the locus of control dimension has been extensive. Throop and MacDonald (1971) cited over 300 articles, and Rotter (1975) estimated that over 600 studies have been conducted. Early reviews of the concept (Lefcourt, 1966; Rotter, 1966) have demonstrated that a person with a high expectancy for internal control of reinforcement is more likely than a person who expects external control of reinforcement to, among other positive behaviors, actively engage in mastering his environment, be more effective in influencing others, be higher in achievement orientation, and be more involved in social action. Lefcourt (1972) has again reviewed several major themes of this research, relating locus of control as an individual difference variable to social influence, cognitive activity, delay of gratification, achievement, success and failure, familial and social antecedents, and change in one's generalized expectancy for control of reinforcement itself. To understand the power of this variable it is necessary to recall that it was intended to measure a *generalized* rather than a specific expectancy, and to be used in predicting behavior in conjunction with reinforcement value and specific expectancy. Consequently, one would expect consistent but low-level prediction from this variable when studied alone. That in fact has been the case, and many studies have now shown that the conception of locus of control is indeed a useful way to improve behavioral prediction. People who tend to view their rewards as internally or externally controlled also tend to behave differently (Phares, 1973). What is important about this variable for community psychology is its connection to the sociological idea of power and its converse, alienation. Locus of control is one of the few variables in social science that may be shown to have a consistent relationship which ties research across levels of analysis. It is sometimes called by different names, but the idea is usually clear and consistent.

In a series of animal studies begun in 1953 by Richard Solomon and his colleagues (Seligman & Maier, 1967; Seligman, Maier, & Geer, 1968; Solomon, Kamin, & Wynne, 1953; Overmier & Seligman, 1967) a phenomenon with potentially important implications for the salience of locus of control has been uncovered. In the initial study Solomon *et al.* (1953) placed dogs in a shuttle box (a cage with two compartments separated by a partition over which a dog can jump). They arranged an experimental procedure in which first a buzzer rang and a gate between the two compartments was lifted. The buzzer rang for 10 seconds and then a shock was delivered to the floor of the compartment in which the dog had been placed. Following a series of trials during which the dogs engaged in wild movements and indicated that they were in severe distress, the dogs quickly learned that they could avoid shock by jumping into the other side of the box when the buzzer sounded. After only a few trials most dogs would jump into the second side long before the warning buzzer stopped. Later, the experimenters found that this avoidance behavior was almost impossible to extinguish. Even when they no longer applied shock to the first compartment the dogs continued to jump when the buzzer sounded.

In later studies, Seligman and others found that when they first put dogs in a situation which made the shock *inescapable*, by strapping the dogs into a harness which prevented jumping out of the first compartment, initially the dogs would react wildly, and then remain silent and passive, apparently resigned to the pain. Even when they then repeated the conditions of the first experiment, such that the dogs could avoid the shock by jumping over the barrier, those who had earlier experienced it as inescapable did nothing. Additional experiments showed that if there were 48 hours between the inescapable and the escapable condition the dogs would learn again to escape, but that if 24 hours after the first inescapable experience they again experienced an inescapable condition, chronic failure to escape ensued. Rather than try to escape, the dogs passively took up to 50 seconds of severe shock. Furthermore, if they accidentally jumped over the barrier, and thus escaped the shock, they would not necessarily do so on subsequent trials.

How do they account for this apparently maladaptive behavior? The researchers directly tested a number of alternative hypotheses including the suggestion that the dogs had learned a competing and incompatible response, or that they had adapted to the pain. The details of these experiments need not concern us here save to note that they found that neither hypothesis ac-

counted for their results. Rather, they offer a third hypothesis, that the animals who experienced inescapable shock learned that its termination was independent of their own responses or, what they suggested might be considered ''an expectation'' (Seligman, Maier, & Geer, 1968), that their behavior was unrelated to the shock. Animals that did not experience the inescapable condition learned, on the other hand, that their own behavior was directly responsible for avoidance of the shock. The similarity between these two different ways of dealing with shock, and Rotter's definition of internal and external locus of control is unmistakable. Developed in very different settings for very different reasons, the same phenomenon is observed. Both animals and people behave differently when they view the outcomes of a situation as related or unrelated to their own behavior.

After demonstrating this phenomenon, which they termed ''learned helplessness,'' Seligman and Maier (1967) went on to examine how this maladaptive behavior may be prevented. First they trained dogs under two different kinds of conditions. In one condition the dogs were put into the restraining harness which prevented escape from the shock compartment, but were able, by pressing a panel on either side of their heads to stop the shock. A second group, also put in the harness, was given exactly the same sequence and duration of shock as the first, but was unable to turn it off. Both groups were later compared with a group of dogs that had not been in harness, that is, those who had experienced the original situation (shock and freedom to avoid it by jumping over the partition). The animals who were not able to turn off the shock during training later demonstrated ''learned helplessness.'' The group that was able to turn off the shock, but not jump and avoid it altogether, later was able to avoid shock as well as the animals who had learned to avoid shock initially. They concluded that it was not the trauma of shock itself which created learned helplessness.

Because the behavior of the dogs who were unable to stop the shock during training was independent of the shock, they seem to have learned that there is no connection between their behavior and outcome in the shuttle-box situation. In Rotter's terms they seem to expect *external locus of control*. However, the dogs who had experienced the identical trauma during training, but who learned that they could control even if not avoid it, appear to have learned to expect *internal locus of control*. Later, when the "realities" are changed, they quickly learn to adapt and avoid the trauma. It appears that by learning that their behavior makes a difference these animals are better able to cope with a future situation realistically. The researchers consider this demonstration to be an analogy to "prevention." Experience in a world where, however painful, one is able to control personal outcomes is more likely to lead to later adaptive behavior than is experience in a world where one cannot control outcomes.

In a final study, Seligman *et al.* went on to investigate an analog to "treatment" for four dogs that had already acquired learned helplessness. After training the dogs to exhibit learned helplessness, and demonstrating that the behavior appeared to be stable, they used two different methods of "treatment." In one method the dogs were encouraged to escape shock on their own, by providing no barrier between the sides of the shuttle box and by "calling" them to the other side. Only one dog learned to avoid shock this way. The others learned to avoid shock when the experimenters forcibly pulled them to the "safe" side of the box (what they call an analog to "directive therapy"). Following this treatment the dogs that had previously demonstrated persistent learned helplessness were able to avoid future shocks 100 percent of the time.

It does not require a great deal of anthropomorphizing to recognize the implications of the above for human beings (cf. Seligman, 1975). Most theories of psychotherapy posit some form of internal locus of control as desirable. Many persons who are seen as "neurotic" or "psychotic" often act as if they suffer from a form of learned helplessness and are unable to see the connection between their behavior and the outcomes of their life. The goal of therapy is often to teach the connection, either by insight or by direct intervention. The relationship between internal locus of control and improvement in psychotherapy has been impressively demonstrated (Lefcourt, 1972). On the other hand, many people, particularly those who are poor, members of minority groups, or socially "marginal" and do not fit into the larger society (the "safe" side of the box) may in *reality* experience situations over which they have little or no personal control. Recall that for both "prevention" and "treatment" of learned helplessness two elements were required. One was that the subject learn that it *could* escape, but the second was a "system" in which escape was possible. The barrier had to be opened, the dogs had to be unharnessed. *If poverty, racism, and other social systems variables act as a harness, or as an inescapable barrier, it is reasonable to expect that they will create learned helplessness and alienation. As suggested by the Gurins above, social change will require interventions which reach beyond individuals and change real world possibilities.*

Although the need for interventions at both the individual and the systems level can only be assumed by analogy in animal research, studies of locus of control among adult humans are remarkably consistent with the implications drawn from that analogy. Using both Rotter's scale and special revisions of it several researchers have recently discovered that, rather than measuring a single dimension, the scale seems to reflect at least two "factors" of generalized expectancy (Gurin, Gurin, Lao, & Beattie, 1969; Lao, 1970; Mirels, 1970). On the one hand, a set of items that refer to belief in control of reinforcement in one's personal life and are empirically related to each other form a consistent factor (termed *personal control*). However, a second set of items that pertain to expectancy for control over social systems (termed *systems blame*) also appear to be logically and empirically related to each other and somewhat independent of the first factor. Personal control items are phrased in the first person; for example, "when I make plans I am almost certain I can make them work." Systems blame items are phrased in the third person and measure ideological belief about internal and external control; for example, "Many Negroes who don't do well in life do have good training, but the opportunity just always goes to whites" (Lao, 1970). Rather than refer to expectancy for internal or external locus of control per se, it appears that separately assessing these two factors may uncover clearer relationships between expectancy and behavior.[7]

With the above in mind, Rosina Lao conducted a very important study of over 1400 Black male college students from 10 different southern universities. She hypothesized that by assessing generalized expectations for each of the two factors separately she could better account for the behavior of the students she studied. Belief in internal control is almost always regarded as desirable. This is because belief in external control has usually been thought of as attributing outcomes to chance or luck. Lao now hypothesized that if belief in personal control were separated from belief in systems blame, and if questions on the systems blame factor reflected content issues such as in the example above, it may turn out that a belief in external control on the systems blame factor is more reality based than an internal belief, at least for southern Black students, and may therefore predict to positive behavior. She reasoned that externals on the systems blame factor should be more interested in collective social change strategies and in social action. Specifically, Lao predicted that while traditional positive behavior such as academic achievement might be more likely for Black students with a belief in *internal* personal control, the participation of southern Black students in efforts to change their social system (what she called innovative positive behavior) might actually be more likely for those who expressed belief in *external* locus of control on the systems blame factor.

Lao's results are consistent with her predictions. Personal control and systems blame were found to be independent factors. Students high on belief in internal personal control were found to have significantly better college entrance examination scores, better grade-point averages after one year in college, more confidence in their academic ability, and higher educational expectations and aspirations than students who believe in external personal control. These results are consistent with previous research demonstrating a similar relationship between internal locus of control and competence among White students. Direction of belief on the systems blame factor did not predict to academic competence measures. Students high or low on this factor were equally likely to be academically competent. On the other hand, those students who scored high on *external* locus of control with regard to the systems blame factor also reported that they favored collective approaches to the civil rights movement and preferred protest actions as opposed to negotiations significantly more than students who scored in the internal direction.

Lao has drawn several conclusions from these results. Most importantly, it appears that it is not necessarily desirable to always believe in internal control. Rather, if one regards *both* personal success and participation in social action as necessary for social change, a young Black person is more likely to be both competent and socially involved if she or he understands the distinction between these two. For community psychology this means that rather than simply focusing interventions on enhancing expectation of internal personal control and competence, it is desirable to focus educational and training programs on the distinction between personal and systems limitations, and on the need for a realistic assessment of beliefs and actions at *both* levels.

Such conclusions are related to the sociological and political concept of "power" and make possible a link between the two levels of analysis which may be helpful to community psychology. In the next chapter the concept of power is introduced as an important variable in the thinking of community psychologists. It is important to recognize that power can be interpreted in both the psychological and the political sense, and that these two are interrelated. On the one hand power means control over the out-

---

[7]Similar distinctions have been found useful in work with children. For example, Crandall, Katkovsky, and Crandall (1965), in studying belief about academic success, distinguish between external control by impersonal forces (chance or luck) and control through a teacher's behavior. They and others (Mischel, Zeiss, & Zeiss, 1973) also distinguish between locus of control attributed to positive and negative outcomes.

comes of one's own personal life, on the other hand it means social and political control over the institutions of which one is a part.

Melvin Seeman (1972) has discussed and documented the important relationship between locus of control as a psychological variable and power or powerlessness (often called *alienation* in sociological literature). It is his contention that Rotter's social learning theory can serve as a bridge between psychological and sociological analysis. In what is referred to as "mass society theory" it is assumed that alienation or powerlessness is produced by some kinds of social structures and not by others, and that alienation results in conformity and political passivity. Seeman cites as an example a study of the United Nations by Star and Hughes (1950) which found "widespread turning away from political knowledge" attributed to the conviction that there was nothing an ordinary person could do. Such descriptions call to mind the studies of learned helplessness. Rotter's social learning theory also assumes that learning which takes place under conditions perceived as externally rather than internally controlled will lead to a number of less than desirable outcomes. Both social learning theory and theories of mass society find that learning conditions perceived as outside of one's personal control often lead to apathy and reduced acquisition of information.

Because much of the data from social learning theory comes from laboratory research on learning under "chance" versus "skill" conditions and much of the data from sociology comes from a global analysis of social conditions, there is a gap between the two disciplines that may obscure important similarities. In an effort to fill this gap Seeman reports a series of investigations (Seeman & Evans, 1962; Seeman, 1963) that examined this variable in institutional settings, a kind of midpoint between psychology and sociology. In one study he found that tuberculosis patients, matched on socioeconomic variables and hospital history, differed in the extent of their knowledge about tuberculosis as a function of expectancy for control. Internals knew more than externals, a result that was attributed to reliance among the externals on experts and bureaucratic authority. Because this study could be interpreted as a demonstration of poor knowledge leading to external locus of control *or* external locus of control leading to poor knowledge, Seeman conducted a second study aimed at clarifying the direction of influence. This latter study was conducted in a reformatory and involved teaching three different kinds of new knowledge, each with a different potential for controlling one's destiny. Inmates were presented with descriptive information about the prison, information about factors influential in obtaining parole, and descriptive information about the long-range future of prison programs. He predicted that the concrete, useful information about parole, but not the descriptive information, would be learned better by those inmates who were high on the internal side of the locus of control scale than by those who saw themselves as powerless (externals). He found that locus of control and retention of descriptive information were uncorrelated, but that powerlessness and retention of information about parole, as predicted, were significantly and negatively correlated. However, the correction, while significant, was low ($r = -.23$).

In Rotter's theory, because behavior potential is a function of reinforcement value as well as expectancy, Seeman also assessed the extent to which inmates valued parole. He distinguished between two kinds of inmates, the "Square Johns" and the "Real Cons." The Square Johns accepted conventional ideas about prison rehabilitation and the value of parole, whereas the Real Cons identified with the prison culture and rejected the value of working for parole. Following Rotter's theory, he therefore predicted that learning differences with regard to parole information should be a function of powerlessness, or expectancy for external control, only for those who valued parole (the Square Johns). As predicted, he found that for the Real Cons retention of information and powerlessness were not significantly related ($r = -.16$) whereas for the Square Johns they were significantly related ($r = -.40$).

In a study with a similar rationale as the above Neal and Seeman (1964) examined the sociological prediction that alienation will be highest among those members of the work force who are unorganized, rather than among union members. Again, although that prediction was confirmed, it was accounted for, among both white collar and manual workers, by those who *valued* social and occupational mobility. Once again, as Gurin and Gurin (1970) have argued, it would appear that social intervention programs that attempt to increase expectations for success among members of the lower socioeconomic class are likely to lead to increased frustration and alienation unless such efforts are accompanied by changes in the objective probability for success, that is, structural changes in society which in fact increase the probability of success (for example, admission to unions).[8]

To summarize briefly, the concept of locus of control or "power" is one which seems to cut consistently across multiple levels of analysis. It is found to be important in both animal and individual human learning, as well as in theories of mass society.[9] For community psychology, a discipline interested in social change, this variable may be crucial in the design of social interventions. In the next two chapters the importance of the concept of power in social intervention is elaborated further.

Interpersonal Psychology and the Consequences of Labeling

Although still within the same tradition of understanding individual behavior, many psychologists have hypothesized the importance of other people (the person-environment) in determining one's behavior. In this context Robert

---

[8]Of related interest here is the intention of many "poverty programs" to increase the sense of control felt by members of a poor community by means of "maximum feasible participation" in program planning. Such programs have usually involved only a select few so-called "representatives" of the poor. Even for these select few the available research demonstrates that although they may experience an increased belief in activism and achievement, they will not necessarily come to feel less powerless. Rather, it may even increase their sense of powerlessness when not accompanied by genuine opportunities which meet their expectations (Zurcher, 1970).
[9]There is also some recent evidence from work with human subjects which indicates that learned helplessness may have physiological correlates (cf. Gatchel & Proctor, 1976).

Carson (1969) has reviewed what he calls interaction concepts of personality. He argues that human behavior cannot be understood other than in the context of social behavior, or as an interaction with other persons. Carson is writing in a tradition which he acknowledges as most directly traceable to the thinking of the psychiatrist Harry Stack Sullivan (1953) who early in this century hypothesized almost totally from observations of patients in his consulting room that human behavior is basically interpersonal in nature. Very briefly, Sullivan emphasized the importance of learned styles for obtaining interpersonal security, around which each person builds a characteristic way of interacting in social situations. He wrote in greatest detail about mother-child interactions and same-sex peer interactions as the context for learning how to behave in future interpersonal situations. The *Interpersonal Theory of Psychiatry* (1953) was a step "up" from totally intrapsychic explanations of behavior, and although Sullivan was most concerned with "abnormal" or deviant persons, his thinking has been applicable to normal development as well.

Carson (1969), in specifically taking the study of personality to an interpersonal context, moves the focus of research and observation to the interpersonal environment and makes explicit what behavior modification has largely ignored and what cognitive social learning theory implies. Although social learning theory is obviously a "social" rather than a strictly individual theory it does not explicitly take into account the behavior of "significant others" (a term coined by Sullivan) in any detail in its own right. In social learning theory, although behavior is obviously under social influence, the "others" are treated as similar to physical environment variables. They are the discriminative stimuli, the models, or the dispensers of reinforcement. Although it is recognized that the expectations which others hold for a given person, as well as the contingencies which they administer, influence behavior, emphasis is placed on a single direction of static influence rather than on a mutual influence process. Phrased otherwise, the principles of social learning are based on the behavior of a single person, while "others" behave only as environmental stimuli rather than as people. In his emphasis on interaction concepts of personality Carson moves the unit of study to the dyad, or the two-person level. As he presents it the focus is still on understanding an individual, and in many ways it is compatible with social learning theory, but it goes one step farther and includes other people as the key aspect of the environment, and as themselves modifiable. It may be thought of as a person-person environment theory.

There are four basic elements in Carson's interaction psychology. To begin, he sees interpersonal behavior as made up of learned ways of avoiding anxiety and seeking security. He recognizes "action learning" as well as "cognitive learning." By action learning he includes the principles useful in behavior modification and by cognitive learning he includes the same emphasis on expectancies and cognitions formulated by Rotter and more recently by Mischel. However, he is somewhat more specific about the process of cognition in that he draws on the work of Miller, Galanter, and Pribram (1960) in positing a view of the person as an active problem solver who formulates both images of himself in the world and plans for his own behavior. By the process of testing new informational input the person both modifies his plans and images and rejects disparate information. Although the details of the cognitive process are somewhat different for Rotter, Mischel, and Carson, the function of cognition in all three approaches is the same. It serves as the means by which people "problem solve" as they go about the business of living.

Carson adds to social learning theory two other ideas which he borrows from social psychology. As with social learning theory, the notion of reward is important. However, the emphasis in this interpersonal theory is on costs as well as rewards, measured by interpersonal outcomes. Here he is expanding on the ideas of Thibaut and Kelley (1959) who view interpersonal behavior as an "exchange" between people. Carson posits that interpersonal behavior is a function of the "payoff matrix" in which persons will seek to interact with people

who, and in ways which, increase their interpersonal satisfaction (increase their security and decrease their anxiety). Following Leary (1957), each person is said to desire "complementary" behavior from others, such that people are seen to both seek out those whose behavior is complementary to their own and to stimulate such behaviors in others. For example, a dominant person will both seek and create submissive behavior from others. The exact nature of this complementarity is quite complicated, but the details are of less interest here than the basic idea that behavior is viewed as interpersonally motivated and that personality or style of interpersonal behavior is viewed as a learned way to increase interpersonal security. These learned ways are cognitively mediated through a person's "images" which control their "plans" for behavior. In addition, established images and plans influence the way the person will process new situations and selectively attend to the environment so as to make input consistent with existing self-images and existing plans. In short, people seek a "fit" between their images and their interpersonal environment.

The fourth element in Carson's theory is "contractual arrangements." Through the development of (usually) implicit "contracts" for interpersonal behavior people come to expect each other to behave in a particular way. These contracts are similar to the norms and roles that control social behavior more generally. According to Carson, a person who is experiencing a problem in living, and who seeks psychotherapy, usually requires changes in his or her Images and Plans. Because Plans require behaviors to be consistent with one's Images, and the Image of Self in "disordered personality" is described as constricted and intolerant of experience that does not match, the role of the therapist is to provide the client with new learning experiences leading to a change in the Image, and as such, psychotherapy techniques include all those used by other theorists, but with an emphasis on the interpersonal influence process between therapist and client.

More important for community psychology than his interpretation of psychotherapy are two related implications which Carson draws from an interpersonal view of behavior, but which he leaves largely undeveloped. First, if behavior is to be understood in social-interpersonal terms, then identifying some people as disordered, abnormal, or deviant must be consistent with this view. Neither medical explanations nor learning explanations alone account for the social meaning of deviant behavior. Carson turns to sociological explanations of why some behavior is labeled as mentally ill, and other behavior is not. He follows the writing of Scheff (1966, 1967) and of Becker (1963) in arguing that a person is *labeled* as mentally ill. The criteria for the label are the products of social custom and convention, and will differ from one society to another. Such labels are based in part on violation of a given society's norms. But this is only part of the story, since many violations of norms are not labeled as mental illness (e.g., criminal acts). Scheff (1966) makes a distinction between those norms that are explicit, such as laws, and those that are so much a part of the culture as to be basic to its understanding of the world—for example, unwritten assumptions about reality and decency. In our society these "rules" include the norms of the work ethic, such that people who do not work are often labeled as "sick" or as suffering from some form of internalized disorder. Since deliberate violation is unthinkable, there is a search for explanations in the supernatural, the morality, or the health of the person. Violation of these unwritten norms is termed "residual rule-breaking." Although residual rule-breaking is a necessary condition for the label of "mental illness," it is not sufficient. Many "normal" people violate such rules and it is usually ignored or seen as transitory. For example, a wealthy person or a retired person need not work.

Following Becker (1963) and Scheff (1966) Carson finds the crucial step to be the *response of others* to deviance. Residual norm violation needs to be *labeled* before it becomes "mental illness." For example, a few years ago shoulder-length hair among males would have been considered a violation of the unwritten norms of sexual identity, and a man with long hair would have had an increased probability of being negatively labeled. Today it is often ignored. The person who walks down the street talking to himself will not be "mentally ill" unless other people pay attention to that talk, label it mental illness, and initiate a series of social actions and reactions. In Sheff's analysis this labeling is said to call attention to the residual norm violation and to amplify its occurrence through social feedback. In behavioral terms the attention is reinforcing and encourages the continuation of the deviance. Carson takes the idea a step farther and argues that the social response serves a purpose for the person in the same way that all interpersonal behavior does. Its persistence is explained as a behavior which gives the person the best "payoff" in terms of interpersonal security. Although to others who accept the residual rules as universal it often appears to be self-destructive, *it may be that deviant behavior is the best alternative available to a person* for coping with his or her problems in living. Rather than being viewed as sickness, the behavior can be seen as following the same principles that govern all interpersonal behavior: maximization of interpersonal payoff, given the alternatives available.

Carrying this reasoning to its logical conclusion, Murrell (1973) has pointed out that the problem is one of person-environment fit. When the available environmental alternatives and the behaviors available to persons do not match, that person will be forced to behave in ways that are objectively detrimental to himself and/or to others. Viewed in this way, the problem of intervening on behalf of deviants labeled "mentally ill" does not necessarily require changing the person, but could equally logically be viewed as a need to change the available environmental alternatives. The implications of this view are legion. The analysis can be extended to any form of deviance from mainstream society. Although the labels used may be something other than mental illness, the process is identical. For example, Scheff (1967) observes:

In order to understand the situation of the mentally ill, . . . one could profit by comparing their position with that of *other subordinate minorities*. Psychological processes such as stereotyping, projection, and stigmatization, and social processes such as rejection, segregation, and isolation characterize, to some degree, the orientation of the ingroup toward the outgroup *regardless of the basic distinction*" (Scheff, 1967, p. 4, italics added).

For many people who are not part of mainstream society, be they poor, minority group members, "mentally ill," or whatever, the problems they experience in our society may be a function of the lack of available alternatives in their society, and the insistence that they either "fit in" to those that are available or be punished by hospitalization, unemployment, lack of educational opportunity, and so on. Theoretically, an alternative to requiring that everyone fit in is that the society develop multiple paths for various people, congruent with their particular skills and style. The mental patient who cannot or will not engage in "normal" interpersonal relationships can be provided with a place in the community where he or she can live productively (see Chapter IX); the child who speaks Black dialect can be provided with a school that accepts and values his or her language and provides genuine educational opportunity (see Chapter VIII). Such alternatives, however, require a psychology of person-environment fit which respects both cultural variation and personal deviance as legitimate, and a social service network based on support for the strengths of people and communities rather than a total emphasis on changing everyone to fit into existing social organizations.

Even for those who see it as desirable for a person to learn to fit into society and who view psychotherapy as a viable way to learn how to fit in, the logic of an interpersonal view of human behavior, just as the logic of social learning theory, leads to the ultimate conclusion that environmental intervention beyond the single person is necessary. Carson notes, following his discussion of psychotherapy as a social influence process, that there is often a "fly in the ointment," such that

. . . more often than one likes to think—the psychotherapy client has become enmeshed in very complicated relationships . . . with other persons in his life . . . these other persons may not find the changes in the client to their liking, because they have come to depend for one reason or another on his enact-

ing his particular variety of disordered behavior . . . they therefore put enormous pressure on the client in order to force him back into his old ways (Carson, 1969, p. 293).

Carson observes that for persons with a "disordered personality" the significant people are often family members, and he notes the need for an interventionist to involve one's self in the social system of the family. He concludes that although how to do this may be as yet unresolved, the therapist "does *not* have the option of doing nothing" (Carson, 1969, p. 295, italics in original). Although this suggestion appears literally at the end of Carson's book, those who are concerned with problems within social systems other than the family, such as education and employment, cannot help but see the implications that are left undeveloped. The social interventionist here too does not have the option of doing nothing. The creation of new alternatives in the real world is obviously needed. To begin we need to examine the links between individual behavior and social process.

Role Theory and Community Psychology[10]

Theodore R. Sarbin, in applying the thinking of "role theory" to the problems of community psychology has provided a link between individual behavior and social process. His analysis

---

[10]It is tempting here to include all of social psychology because in many ways the variables that social psychologists have studied are potentially important as links. However, because social psychology has not generally been interested in intervention, much of the research needs to be "stretched" to be directly relevant. Sarbin's views are selected here because he has explicitly tried to apply them to the problems of community psychology, and because they are useful as a *general orientation* rather than a narrowly defined content area. For specific content areas other social psychological research is also relevant, and it appears in various appropriate places in this volume. Examples of research which is not reviewed, but which may be of use to community psychology for specific problems, include studies of helping behavior (Latané & Darley, 1970), obedience to authority (Milgram, 1974), attitude change (Fishbein & Ajzen, 1975), conformity and social influence (Sampson, 1971), as well as person-perception and attribution theory (Kelley, 1971). This list could be considerably longer, as a review of almost any social psychology textbook will reveal.

will once again lead to the same conclusion that other approaches reach when trying to deal with the human problems selected for study and intervention by community psychology: "The community psychologist, then, must be sensitive to the fact that the 'social systems' approach is more likely to achieve his goals than 'psyche systems' " (Sarbin, 1970, p. 111).

Sarbin (1970) begins by making what is a crucial point for social interventionists: It is imperative that the level of analysis and conceptions invoked are those that are applicable to the problem at hand. An error in applying conceptions that are based on a model not appropriate to the problem area of concern will lead to confusion and inability to solve problems. This same point will be reiterated in detail in the next chapter, and Sarbin serves as an anticipation of and transition to conceptions of community psychology.

In an effort to make more explicit the meaning of "environment" as a social-psychological term Sarbin has divided the psychological environment into what he conceptualizes as four "differentiated ecologies": the self-maintenance ecology, the social ecology, the normative ecology, and the transcendental ecology. Every person needs to "locate" herself or himself in each of these ecologies. When there is a difficulty in one of these realms the person may find intervention by others helpful, or the society may require it. Sarbin argues in a way that appreciates both the advantages and the limitations of various conceptions of personality and techniques of behavior change: depending on the goals of social intervention, or in his terms, depending on in which ecology one is trying to intervene, various methods and techniques are differentially appropriate. Each of the four ecologies is described in terms of one's relationship to it, and in terms of appropriate conceptions and change techniques (see Table IV-1).

The self-maintenance ecology requires the person to answer, in concrete terms, the question "What am I?" The answer is found in one's behavior and in the world of action. To function in this realm one requires discriminative skills and competencies similar to those described by Mischel (see above) as "discriminative facil-

ity." Failure in this realm leads to anxiety, cognitive disorder, and often to the label "mentally ill" or "retarded." The best methods for dealing with such problems are behavior modification and social learning techniques, where the aim is to teach new and change old behaviors.

The normative ecology requires the person to answer the question "How well am I performing?" The answer is found in understanding one's self, in accepting responsibility for one's actions, and in the "causes" of one's behavior. Sarbin believes that for such questions psychodynamic theory is appropriate and useful.

The transcendental ecology requires that one answer the question "What am I in relation to God, the universe, my ancestors, and so on?" Failure leads to doubt and obsession. The conceptions useful are humanistic-existential psychology, religion, and philosophy. Techniques of meditation and prayer as well as "therapy" can be used.

The social ecology requires that each person answer the question "Who am I in relationship to others?" The answers are found in social identity and social status. The problems that occur when people do not agree on the "place" they have been allocated to by others, or when some are arbitrarily allotted to a social identity and social status that is demeaning and lacks elements of personal choice and human rights, are those Sarbin sees as of concern to community psychology, and require not only change in the person, but *change in the social structure which dictates problematic role relationships.* "The targets (of change) are organizations of persons whose conduct is dysfunctional as a result of ecological misplacement or nonplacement" (Sarbin, 1970, p. 100). Phrased otherwise, the problems of community psychology are a function of the roles which a person is forced into and which provide no adequate alternatives. To understand this set of problems Sarbin proposes adoption of role theory and a model of social identity, a subject on which he has written for some years.

Role theory is based on the idea that much of man's social behavior is prescribed by his social role. Regardless of individual characteristics people are actors given a part to play in society.

TABLE IV-1 Problems, conceptions, change techniques, and aims appropriate to the four ecologies of the psychological environment.*

Psychological Ecologies	Problems for People	Concepts and Change Techniques Appropriate	Aims
Self-Maintenance Ecology	The person asks, "What am I?" Development of discriminative skills and competencies is required in a world of actions. Failure leads to anxiety, cognitive disorders, and the label "illness" or "retardation."	Behavior modification and cognitive social learning theory may be applicable to understand and help the person.	Acquisition of new and change of old behavior
Normative Ecology	The person asks, "How well am I performing?" Understanding of self and location of "causes" of behavior is crucial. Failure leads to disappointment and guilt.	Psychodynamic theory may be useful to understand and to help the person.	Understanding of self and acceptance of responsibility
Transcendental Ecology	The person asks, "What am I in relation to transcendental objects—God, the universe, mankind, my ancestors?" Failure leads to doubt and obsession.	Humanistic-existential psychology, religion, philosophy, meditation, and prayer may be useful.	Awareness and self-actualization
Social Ecology	The person asks, "Who am I in relationship to others?" Problems include social identity and social status. Failure leads to violation of expectations and social ills	Community psychology and social change may be necessary and useful.	Change in role relationships

*Derived from Sarbin, 1970.

As members of society their roles can only be understood in relationship to the roles played by others. To be a teacher requires a pupil, to be a boss requires a worker. The social structure dictates such relationships, and to understand them Sarbin postulates a three-dimensional model based on status, value, and involvement (Table IV-2).

The status dimension is described as a continuum ranging from *ascribed* to *achieved* status. Ascribed status is determined by factors over which the person has little or no choice— age, sex, race, family background, and so on. Examples are mother, son, adult, male. At the achieved end of the continuum are roles over which there is theoretically a higher element of choice, such as cheerleader, PTA member, athlete, teacher. These achieved statuses are obtained by various pathways including training, election, and other forms of personal achievement. Ascribed status is granted to everyone. Everyone is expected to perform in ways appropriate to his or her ascribed role, and is thereby granted minimal rights as a person. Achieved status is more limited and competitive and carries certain powers and social esteem. Each person's social identity is a function of performance in various roles along the continuum of ascribed and achieved status.

The value dimension is orthogonal to the status dimension. It has a neutral point and a positive and a negative end point, but the range of the value dimension is different in relationship to the ascribed and the achieved ends of the status dimension. Proper performance of the ascribed roles is valued neutrally. Everyone is expected to perform within the norms of his or her ascribed role. Performance in that role is never viewed as highly positive; it simply grants one status as a person. However, if the ascribed role is not performed as expected, the person is negatively valued and declared a kind of "nonperson." For example, in our society a mother is expected to care for her children. If she does, she is given neutral status, but if she does not she is regarded negatively and loses the minimal rights of personhood. On the other hand, achieved status roles range from neutral to positive. Nonperformance of an achieved role does not lead to exclusion from society. Failure, underachievement, and so on, are generally ignored by the community, which regards the person neutrally. However, performance of achieved status roles earns positive regard from society, including public recognition, money, and so on. The behavior expected of one who is performing an ascribed role is similar to Scheff's (see above) notion of residual norms. The person must perform within the expectations of her or his ascribed roles or she or he is labeled a nonperson—less than human, and thereby not eligible for achieved status. As Sarbin points out, the social-scientific vocabulary uses various labels that are euphemisms for negatively labeling those who are regarded as nonpersons: slum dwellers, underpriviledged, mental patients, and so on. *Once labeled, the person is likely to be treated negatively, so as to degrade him socially and reduce further the possibility of his obtaining achieved status.*

The third dimension in Sarbin's model is involvement. This is also described as on a continuum, and it varies from high to low involvement depending on the amount of time and energy one spends in the role. Ascribed roles permit little variation on the involvement dimension because the person is required to be in that role most of the time. Achieved roles permit greater variation with regard to involvement. One can work at achieved roles more or less,

TABLE IV-2   Sarbin's model of social identity.*

Dimension	*Range of Dimension*		
Status	Achieved roles (high choice) — — — —		Ascribed roles (low choice)
Value	Positive to neutral — — — — — — —		Neutral to negative (nonperson)
Involvement	High variation— — — — — — — —		Low variation

*Derived from Sarbin, 1970.

and generally they take up only a part of a person's life. The teacher or the doctor can leave the role when they choose. When a person is regarded totally on the basis of an ascribed role he or she is forced to be in it virtually all the time. The prisoner, the hospital patient, or the unemployed workers in urban ghettos are examples presented by Sarbin. A Black person in America is always Black. A child labeled "culturally disadvantaged" has no choice in the matter. Typically, opportunity for variation is low. As Sarbin notes, the social identity of a member of these classes of persons often does not include achieved roles, and although they are labeled by others their behavior is often explained as caused by deficiencies in themselves, which serve to justify their "place." To degrade a person a society need only remove from him or her the opportunity to enact roles of choice. The more she or he is forced into ascribed roles the less chance he or she has of being positively valued.[11]

It is the people who have "degraded social identities" who are the candidates for helping services and social interventions. A person who is forced to act in ascribed roles most of the time has less time for enacting achieved roles. He or she can only hope to be neutrally valued. *A person who is forced into his or her ascribed* roles most of the time can work for achieved roles only with a great deal of *strain,* often more than one could be expected to deal with. The Black student who is always viewed as "disadvantaged" will necessarily be under a great deal of

strain in the educational system, no matter how bright or competent she or he is. In addition, the social network of possibilites open to the degraded person is limited. They have fewer opportunities to engage in genuine positively valued roles. Consequently, "social and psychological intervention [must be] directed toward social subsystems, toward *all* persons enacting interrelated roles, the value declarers as well as the degraded persons" (Sarbin, 1970, p. 111, italics in original).

The implications from Sarbin's analysis are quite direct and similar to those drawn from research on locus of control, alienation, and power discussed in an earlier section of this chapter. *The aim of community psychology must be to identify and change those aspects of the social structure which degrade people.* Ideologically this will require a psychology of person-environment fit and respect for differences. At the level of social intervention it may mean the creation of viable alternative settings which provide pathways to achieved status. This is considerably easier to say than to do, but part of the task can be achieved by *not* doing as well as by doing. Rather than serve as agents of social degradation by labeling deviants and "treating" them with inappropriate techniques, social science, even if it did nothing to create new alternatives, could help to upgrade the status of many people by refusing to label them as stupid, sick, culturally disadvantaged, or criminals.[12] This argument is pursued in more detail in the next chapter.

---

[11]This point is exactly the one made by advocates of "women's liberation" when they call for choice in the roles available to women (and men). To a large extent they wish to reduce the power of sex to create ascribed roles.

[12]For a concrete example of how this thinking may be applied see the discussion of crimes whithout victims and of radical nonintervention presented in Chapter X. See also the discussion of a "community lodge" for mental patients (Chapter IX).

V

CONCEPTIONS OF SOCIAL INTERVENTION: Toward a Community Psychology

Belief in a golden age has provided mankind with solace in times of despair and élan during the expansive periods of history . . . the golden age means different things to different men, but the very belief in its existence implies the conviction that perfect health and happiness are birthrights of men. Yet, in reality, complete freedom from disease and from struggle is almost incompatible with the process of living.

—René Dubos

There can be no darker or more devastating tragedy than the death of man's faith in himself and in his power to direct his future.

—Saul Alinsky

Community psychologists have come to recognize that the paradigms of individual psychology fail as a basis for community change. At worst the variables suggested by individual psychology may confuse efforts to understand and design community change, at best they are simply incomplete. Nevertheless, community mental health borrows many of its conceptions from individual psychology. This observation has been an important stimulus for the development of community psychology as distinct from community mental health. Although some elements of individual psychology and community mental health are useful (as we have seen in the preceding chapter) individual psychology does not adequately address itself to the problem area. Thus the search for new paradigms.

The Transition from Community Mental Health to Community Psychology

The idea of primary prevention of mental illness has served as a stimulus for the development of community psychology. It is through the process of thinking about and trying to develop programs of primary prevention that some

psychologists have come to recognize the basic impossibility of such efforts so long as they are totally conceived within an individual psychology and focused on preventing mental illness. The community mental health paradigm is simply unable to solve the puzzles posed. For one thing, the term mental illness has no agreed upon meaning and, as we have seen, its broadening definition now includes in its suspected etiology any social process that reduces, for a given population, alternatives for dealing with problems in living. Many who began with an interest in community mental health have changed their focus to an even wider set of concerns, social well-being in general. Now of course, almost any profession sees itself as concerned with social well-being, and it will be recalled that the American Psychological Association has even included this concern in its official statement of purpose.

The difference for community psychologists is that they interpret a concern with social well-being to mean taking direct actions to reduce contemporary social ills. The questions asked are: "What can be done to change our social institutions so as to improve the quality of education for all children, reduce the problem of

114

crime and delinquency, improve housing, and eliminate racism, poverty, and social isolation?'' The step to such questions from a platform of primary prevention is not far because these are the suspected causes of the developmental crises and the problems in living that primary prevention seeks to reduce. Once one accepts the idea that the social institutions and ritual practices of our society create many of the problems in living which one wants to prevent, there are two questions that remain to be answered before proceeding with a social intervention: How do social institutions create problems in living? And its corollary, how can these institutions be changed? This chapter is devoted to a review of conceptions that are concerned with the first question, ''how do social institutions create problems in living?'' Methods of change are discussed in Chapter VI.

For community mental health professionals the process by which social institutions create problems in living is said to be by failing to accomplish their socialization functions. Because our schools, our courts, our mental health system, and so on are unable to reach, with effective services, those people who need socialization most (the target or ''at risk'' low-income, lower social class, and minority groups) they suffer from ''cultural deprivation,'' bad habits of living, and psychological deficits. The social interventions necessary are those that enhance the socialization functions of society. The aim is to help the teachers, probation officers, policemen, job counselors, and parents to do a better job at implementing the values and decisions of the prevailing power structure. This may be done by a reorganization of the system for delivery of services, or improvement of the services, or by direct training of the people administering the system. While individual psychology would focus on the products of the system, community mental health wants to prevent the products from having deficits as a function of slipping through the ''leaky umbrella'' of social services.

Community psychology, on the other hand, sees differently the process by which social systems create problems in living. Rather than as a failure of socialization, problems in living are seen to be a function of denial or lack of access to resources, both physical and psychological. This is created by a set of social systems that selectively withholds two essential ingredients for well-being: power and money. Poverty is explained, somewhat inelegantly, as the absence of money. Power is interpreted to be a variable of importance at multiple levels. On the one hand it is as straightforward as a feeling of control over the outcomes of one's own life, or what psychologists have termed internal locus of control of reinforcement (see Chapter IV). At another level power means social and political control of the institutions of which one is a part.

Everyone agrees that the processes identified in each of the two analyses above (community mental health and community psychology) are both objectively correct. Clearly our social institutions do fail to socialize to the predominant standards of our society large numbers of mental patients, lawbreakers, and educational failures, many of whom are poor, members of a minority group, live in inadequate housing arrangements, and have minimal job skills. It is also obvious that such people have no money and no power, in either sense of the term. Many are deviant from middle-class norms in life style, language, and other behavior. On what basis then does one psychologist, who is genuinely concerned about these problems, choose community mental health while another, equally concerned, chooses community psychology? Surely today it must be on the basis of science. But it is not. It is on the basis of values and faith that one selects from among these two paradigms, each with very different implications for social intervention.

As Kuhn (see Chapter I) has suggested, a paradigm choice is unresolvable on the basis of data. The data are not in question, rather it is the way to explain the data that is debated, and this debate is more akin to one's world view than to science. Are lack of power and money the cause or the effect of the leaky umbrella of services and the problems in living? Such a question is not answerable any more than are questions such as which came first, the chicken or the egg? We can explain fertilization, development of the embryo, hatching, and so on by scientific studies. We can even improve the process, but we can never know the answer to the etiology of chickens. If we want to start a chicken farm we will have to decide whether to get chickens or eggs, and the answer will be found by looking at pragmatics. Which is most likely to work? For solutions to our social problems, which paradigm shows the most promise for results? That, of course, is an empirical question. But we are not completely in the dark. The social problems of concern to community psychology are not new. The mental health and social welfare professions have had many years of dealing with them by means of socialization of all to a single standard and rejection of those who do not fit in. But what guarantee have we that a redistribution of power and money (or material and psychological resources to put it in terms of social science) will do any better? We can only offer values and faith. We know that the old paradigms are failing and as yet, we do not know that the new will solve the puzzles; however, we have reasons, some logical, some empirical and scientific, and many value-based, to see the promise of a new paradigm for social intervention. This is exactly, as Kuhn suggests, what all choices between paradigms are ultimately based on. What is proposed by community psychology is a paradigm of cultural relativity, ecology, and diversity as a value system on which to base social interventions aimed at equitable distribution of material and psychological resources, rather than on improved socialization of all to a single standard which then serves as a means for selective distribution of society's resources.

Once one makes this leap of faith to a new paradigm it is no longer possible to accept the goals of community mental health. Rather, one begins to ask questions that are very new for psychology, such as how can the *goals* of society's institutions themselves be changed? This requires political, economic, and sociological analysis in which psychology has little experience. Although the older paradigms, even those of public health, do focus on total populations, they have very little to say about values and *social* institutions. To convince a school system to serve as a base for administration of a polio

vaccination is not at all similar to convincing the same school system to end its practices of racial discrimation or to change its curriculum, no matter what evidence may exist for the likelihood of change leading to improved education. This will be true of any attempt at *social* change.

Unlike a technical innovation in medicine that may produce a new pill, social change will require change in the role relationships between people and people, and people and institutions. George Fairweather (1972), for example, notes that the resistance to change of racial practices in the South cannot be accounted for by a simple inability to accept innovation. New manufacturing techniques have been widely accepted by the same people. Rather, one must take account of the fact that acceptance of Blacks as equal in status requires a special kind of change, one based on a restructuring of role and status relationships. Similarly, a physician who will quickly accept the innovation of penicillin into his medical practice because it does not change his basic role relationship to his clients is not as likely to accept a medical innovation which requires a change in that social relationship. The American Medical Association's resistance to a system of national health care is a good example. *"Thus it appears axiomatic that an invention is acceptable to a society in direct proportion to the degree that the innovation does not require a change in the roles or social organization of that society"* (Fairweather, 1972, p. 7, italics in original). Some (Sarbin, 1970; see Chapter IV) have argued that the task for a community psychologist is exactly what Fairweather notes as so difficult to achieve, the restructuring of role relationships.

Blaming the Victim

In order to change social relationships one must either change the powerful and the powerless directly, or the social structures that support their relationship. In essence, one is faced with a choice between working with individuals or systems. We have already traced the logic, largely developed in public health and community mental health, behind working to change systems.

The fact remains, however, that in changing *social* systems one will inevitably force change on individuals, both the powerful and the powerless. The powerful will understandably resist such change, for it is clearly to their personal economic and social advantage to do so. But this will create a conflict for many who hold powerful positions in our society, and who at the same time regard themselves as progressive, liberal, and pro social change. The way in which this conflict has been resolved by well meaning people who do not personally wish to hurt anyone, who are often personally appalled at racism and the results of poverty and powerlessness, but yet stand to lose a great deal of their own power and economic advantage should there be a massive redistribution of resources, is what William Ryan (1971) has termed "blaming the victim." Ryan's book is a "paradigm buster" of the first order. Once one has read it the world of social intervention can never be viewed in quite the same way that it was before. It is a book to which community psychologists need pay particular attention.

In the introduction to the book Ryan cites his hoped-for audience: the concerned, politically liberal and responsible citizens cited above, who he feels are miseducated with regard to the causes of the problems which plague victims of slums—discrimination, educational failure, and exploitation. He tells us that we have been misled by an ideology. We see all the individual horror of our social systems in the stories of individual people, yet we fail to put it all together and so continue to see their problems as a need for rehabilitation, urban renewal, and provision of social services. We see deficits, cultural deprivation, and weakness created by bad social environments as the causes of the problems, and in so doing we blame the victims for their own victimization. How the victim-blaming process works and its consequences are the subject of Ryan's book. It tells us about what Ryan calls the "art of savage discovery" or how we identify the victims by automatically labeling strangers (people who are different from ourselves) as savages. We have many ways to identify them. Psychological tests, observations of their life style and their "lower-class" values, as well as stereotypes and myths about their motivation or lack of it, their inability to delay gratification, their promiscuity, and their supposed inability to deal with the abstract. In Ryan's words:

The formula for action becomes extraordinarily simple: Change the victim. All of this happens so smoothly that it seems downright rational. First, identify a social problem. Second, study those affected by the problem and discover in what ways they are different from the rest of us as a consequence of deprivation and injustice. Third, define the differences as the cause of the social problem itself. Finally, of course, assign a government bureaucrat to invent a humanitarian action program to correct the differences (Ryan, 1971, p. 8).

In the view of the victim blamer the poor child is said to contain, within himself, the cause of his inability to read and write well. Slum parents presumably do not talk to their children, and if they do talk, they do not talk properly. They do not know how to raise their own children. The child is said to be impulse ridden and culturally disadvantaged. We are told to confine our attention to the child's failure rather than to the schools the child attends and to the fact that after spending ten thousand hours in the company of professional educators the child still cannot read. Cultural deprivation explains it all. The "Negro family" is part of it. The stereotyped matriarchial, fatherless family, where presumably most children are illegitimate (Ryan wonders how a human being can be illegitimate) and all women promiscuous, is described as the cause of the problem. Ryan demonstrates the selective reporting of births to unmarried women as a function of economics. He shows how differential access to birth control devices, abortion and adoption services, as well as differential economic opportunities for potential fathers to support a family, account for the differential rates of births to unmarried women of different social classes. He shows how "illegitimacy" is a function of economics rather than morals, life style, or differential rates of sexual activity.

The children of poor and Black families do not often grow up to be all-American boys and girls. They have a relatively high rate of contact with the law, and Ryan shows how this is a function of law enforcement practices which make the probability of arrest higher for *any* Black person than for most criminals. Despite the fact that large numbers of their parents enroll them in tutoring programs and express the desire for them to go to college, Black children are said not to be interested in education. This is documented by their owning fewer encyclopedias and making less concrete plans to attend college than their middle-class counterparts (e.g., Coleman, 1966, perhaps the most widely cited source for such statements). No one seems to wonder if a poor family can afford either an encyclopedia or the tuition to go to school.

These same children supposedly grow up to have poor motivation for health care, although lack of money to obtain it is overlooked. Public education rather than change in the gross inequities of the free enterprise system of health services is advocated. Presumably this will change their willingness to tolerate the well-documented differences between the "clinic" and the private health services offered to the affluent. In the mental health system the same inequities as a function of social class have already been noted, and Ryan shows how they are repeated in public housing programs as urban renewal reduces rather than increases the number of housing units available to the poor, while high rent housing is government subsidized. He describes the nonenforcement of housing code violations, most of which are structural and therefore the responsibility of the landlords, coupled with blaming its victims for not keeping their homes in adequate repair.

The victim-blaming analysis is always cloaked in genuine humanitarianism and deep concern. Clearly it is not their "fault." References to innate or genetic defects are strongly denied. Negroes are not born inferior, we are told; they become that way as a function of environmental circumstances and their family life. Nevertheless they are defective and the cause of the defect is in them, although it got there through their environment. *The genetic and the environmental victim-blaming strategies are functionally equivalent.* They both justify not changing the society, but rather, its victims.

Here we see illustrated a basic principle of an ecological analysis of systems, and although Ryan does not spell out the principle, it is helpful to do so.[1]

Every system will tend to functionally maintain itself. If an input is changed, the system will tend to compensate for this by changing somewhere else, so as to keep the output unchanged. As genetic explanations of inferiority have gone out of vogue they no longer serve the purpose as a socially acceptable means of justifying the lack of resources our society has provided to Black people. Environmental causality is now the preferred explanation. This is the change of input to the system. However, the way this explanation is *used* (compensated for) makes it functionally equivalent to earlier genetic explanations. An analysis of the system (or the functional relationships between people and institutions) finds that it is creating the same output despite an *apparent* change. Black people still have limited access to the resources of society, even though this is now explained in a currently acceptable way. Ecological systems analysis leads one to conclude that the component system relationships (e.g., distribution of resources, such as money and power, and social relationships) themselves must be changed in order to alter its output. We shall return to this point shortly.

In the victim-blaming strategy frequently recommended programs are compensatory education to improve the skills and attitudes of the ghetto child, and education of the parents to use "proper" child-rearing methods. The school system itself is not questioned. In such programs, the basic relationships between people in the system remain unchanged. Chapters VII and VIII of this book are a detailed analysis of the rationale, outcomes, and problems of such strategies, and present a set of alternative approaches.

This process of blaming the victim Ryan calls an "ideology" (a paradigm in the terminology of this book). It involves a belief system, a way of viewing reality, and serves a func-

---

[1]Details of the principles of ecological and systems analysis are presented in the final section of this chapter.

tion. Ryan argues that although it is not necessarily intentional, it serves the class interests of those who practice it. The norms of society are taken as a given, and deviation from those norms is a function of failure of socialization. Again, in Ryan's words:

In defining social problems in this way the social pathologists are, of course, ignoring a whole set of factors that ordinarily might be considered relevant— for instance, unequal distribution of income, social stratification, political struggle, ethnic and racial group conflict, and inequality of power. Their ideology concentrates almost exclusively on the failure of the deviant. To the extent that society plays any part in social problems, it is said to have somehow failed to socialize the individual, to teach him how to adjust to circumstances, which, though far from perfect, are gradually changing for the better (p. 14).

For Ryan, blaming the victim ranks with social darwinism as an "ideological monstrosity," and in discussing this he makes a very important point. Such thinking has not been constructed by monsters, nor without every sign of valid scholarship, science, and data. The view is most often academically and socially respectable and even holds a position of "exclusive validity." Disagreement is unrespectable or radical, and risks being called irresponsible.

Such an ideology Ryan views as a way to reconcile one's own self-interest with humanitarian impulses. Basically, for those who like the social system the way it is, at least for themselves, yet see the effects of poverty and inequality, there are two obvious alternatives, both of which are viewed as "extremes." To be openly reactionary and repressive so as to view social inequality as a necessary by-product of a basically good system is often incompatible with progressive middle-class morality. On the other hand, to be radical and support radical social and economic change (i.e., that which changes basic relationships within the system) threatens one's own well-being. A more equitable distribution of income necessarily will mean less for those now in privileged or solidly middle-class positions. We have seen the rejection of both "extremes" in the resounding political defeat of Barry Goldwater on the right and George McGovern on the left (although neither position

was really as extreme as imagined). Both struck fear in the heart of the liberal and the middle-of-the-road American. The resolution of these two "extremes" is a compromise. The victims' problems are seen as a result of apathy, ignorance, and lower-class culture. The solution is to make the victims less vulnerable and to send them into battle with better weapons and a higher level of morale. The solutions are job skills, education, better values, habits of thrift, and foresight. Victim blamers, argues Ryan, are all passing judgment on themselves and concluding that the problems are in the *past* inequities of society, they themselves are "not guilty." This enables one to "help" the poor without threatening one's own privileged status. "They will be entitled to what I have as soon as they are just like me."

In Praise of Loot and Clout

In order to be consistent with an ecological and systems analysis as detailed later in this chapter, Ryan's attribution of victim-blaming strategies to individual motivation (conscious or not) is somewhat beside the point. Perhaps a better way to understand the process is as a natural consequence of any social system's efforts to maintain itself, as an ecological and systems analysis would assume. The historical patterns examined in Chapter II, particularly the analyses offered by Szasz, Riegel, Foucault, Rothman, and Lieffer, would emphasize the importance of such a blaming-the-victim paradigm in maintaining one of the key functions of society—a perpetuation of itself in unaltered form. In order to accomplish this aim, deviants of any kind must be rejected and/or socialized. These historical analyses have shown that such a process has been a consistent aspect of society. It is probably an unavoidable principle of all organizations and institutions; and although the specific means and rationale have changed over time, blaming the victim and the environment is simply its newest expression. To change this process the very goals of society must be questioned and its basic social relationships altered directly. Ryan is well aware of this and his suggestions for change are twofold. He terms his program for social change "In praise of loot and clout."

His basic argument is that life style is a function of money and power (in both the psychological and the political sense noted in Chapter IV) and is an adaptation to whatever the particular stresses of living happen to be. These stresses are a function of the resources available. Money and power lead to life style changes and not vice versa. The history of our failure to change behavior through insight and attitude change is well known. It is now clear that attitudes follow behavior (e.g., Wicker, 1969a) and similarly, life style is a function of resources available. Two examples offered by Ryan are instructive:

Is it possible that the sociologists, in wealthy universities, who talk so wisely about the sexual standards and behavior of the poor, do not know that flocks of their coed students swallow the Pill every day? And that they do so because they can afford to get the prescription from their private physicians? And that a poor single working girl is not going to get that service at a city hospital? (Ryan, 1971, p. 238.)

And again,

No reasonable person could spend five minutes in the out-patient clinic or emergency room of a general hospital—particularly a public hospital—and another five minutes in the waiting room of a highly competent internist, or pediatrician, or gynecologist, and not come away with some pretty strong hunches about why the rich are healthier and longer-lived than the poor (p. 239).

Lee Rainwater (1968), a sociologist who views the problems of poverty in a way similar to Ryan, that is, as "symptoms" of a lack of money, has drawn out the social policy implications of this and other views of the poor. He identifies two predominant sociological explanations of poverty. The most popular is Merton's (1957) which emphasizes "opportunity." The lower class is viewed as ordinary people caught in unfavorable circumstances and unable to obtain the same things everyone desires. Consequently, they require job training, education, and counseling to make them aware of opportunities. However, in pursuing this strategy one becomes aware of the many obstacles to making

opportunities realistically available and eventually one must focus on what he calls "the failures and incompetence of the institutional framework that theoretically has the task of equality of opportunity" (Rainwater, 1968, p. 249). This was the perspective of the War on Poverty run by the Office of Economic Opportunity—provide the opportunity for escape from poverty. According to Rainwater's analysis, this view of everyone as basically the same and only needing opportunity is false; it will not work because lower-class people will make realistic adaptations to the actual situation of deprivation, and this will interfere with such programs by making them unattractive and distrusted. For example, a well-known program of job training, the *Opportunities Industrialization Center,* located in many city ghetto areas, has a difficult time in some of these cities recruiting men to their training programs. I have interviewed many of the men who are the potential targets in my own community and they are well aware that job training is usually not tied to obtaining a meaningful job because such jobs often do not exist. Consequently, to the outside observer these unemployed men appear apathetic, unable to delay gratification, and so on. A similar and more detailed analysis of this problem has been presented by Eliot Liebow (1967) who spent many months living with "street people" in Washington, D.C. His book is one of the rare accounts of the situation as viewed by the people rather than by the professionals.

The second popular sociological explanation is similar to what Ryan has called blaming the victim. In this view the problem is one of lower-class subculture and values. The policy implications stress, as we have seen, culture and personality change, or the interruption of transmission of lower-class culture from one generation to the next. Special education programs such as Head Start, parent education, and prevocational training in speech, dress, and so on, are emphasized. Taking an anthropological viewpoint, Rainwater argues that one must predict that such efforts by outside educational interventions are doomed to failure. There is no incentive to change without significant change in the realities of the situation. In his view, the adaptation of poor people is seen as a mark of their ability to problem-solve in order to minimize real life difficulties. To change would be both stupid and unrealistic. In addition, a realistic assessment of either the Merton or the blaming-the-victim strategy must take into account the "middle-class caretaker culture," and its inability to offer services that are not demeaning. As Rainwater notes, "anthropologists have been traditionally distrustful of the culture-change potential of missionaries; it is not difficult for them to see the analogous situation involved in many community-action programs, guided self-help, and education-for-the-disadvantaged programs" (1968, p. 251). He concludes that if ". . . lower-class people are eventually to be enabled to take advantage of 'opportunities' to participate in conventional society and to earn their own way in it, *this change can only come about through a change in the social and ecological situation to which lower-class people must adapt*" (Rainwater, 1968, p. 251, italics in original).

Rainwater offers his own analysis of the problem as a third alternative. He sees the lower-class person as suffering from *relative*, rather than absolute deprivation of resources. It is not simply how little he has, but rather, how little in comparison to the middle class. He is so far removed that he cannot feel part of mainstream society. Rainwater's solution, like Ryan's, is "a resource equalization strategy." Rather than the usual view that social welfare means every family has at least a *minimal* standard of living, he proposes that social welfare requires every family to have at least an *average* standard of living. Minimal standards are concerned with animal survival needs; our social welfare programs must be more respectful of everyone's right to live as a *person*. His proposal is that a floor on income not be based on an absolute amount of money, but rather on an amount relative to the median income for the nation; that is, relative to other families. He focuses on changing the *shape* of the distribution of family income. At present, income distribution is diamond shaped, with some families at

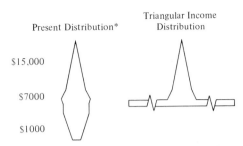

Figure V-1. Present (1965) and more equal income distribution, using 1965 nonfarm income distribution for illustration.* While the exact figures are out of date, they serve to illustrate the approximate shape of actual and proposed income distributions. (Redrawn from Rainwater, 1968.)

the top and some at the bottom, while most are in between. His proposal is to increase the income of those at the bottom so that the shape of the distribution becomes triangular (see Figure V-1). Such a plan should be implemented to provide the maximum amount of freedom, such that it is based on income for heads of families, not the total family income. Those who want more money can decide on the basis of personal costs and values if it is wise for both husband and wife or an older child to work. Size of family can also be left a personal option by excluding it from consideration in income allotment. Since income would be based on the average family, each can decide how many children to have on some basis other than its effect on income. The characteristics of this form of social welfare program, emphasizing a triangular distribution of family income, are noted by Rainwater as:

1. The median income is the bottom income class.
2. There are fewer people at each successive higher income level.

This distribution preserves the American desire that it should be possible to strive for materially rewarded success, but does away with the circumstance of some families as so far down the ladder that questions of motivation become meaningless. In order to work, the plan would need to allocate resources directly to families, and not through training or socialization programs. If society is willing to do it, Rainwater argues, this would by definition eliminate relative poverty. If society is not willing to do this, argues Rainwater, poverty cannot be eliminated, since it is in fact a condition of relative, rather than absolute deprivation.

Such a system as the one described above would be best attached to employment rather than to income supplement practices. This would mean that all jobs would pay no less than the average income for the nation. Such a plan would, of course, have profound implications for other relationships in our society, and that is exactly the point. For one thing it would mean that working at any job would guarantee a person's family a standard of living that would be relatively comparable to mainstream America's standard of living. This would increase the likelihood that persons would select jobs on the basis of their content rather than their salary. More people would be likely to find jobs they like and give up those they dislike but now cannot afford to give up.

Often the unemployed lower social class person is criticized for not taking an available low-status job. Many people do not take such jobs because the minimum wage they earn in them does not change their relative deprivation. If such jobs earned an average wage, rather than a minimum, more people would take them. This means that a waitress, a dishwasher, a worker in a small factory, a clerical worker, and a teacher might each make the same amount of money. It may even mean that lower status jobs would pay more money, in order to attract necessary workers. Some in currently higher paying jobs may not like the fact that a less well-trained person makes as much money as he does. Essentially the differential pay between many skilled and unskilled jobs would be eliminated. It might be argued that this would reduce the incentive for learning a skill. However, stated in positive terms, it might create a society in which people learn a skill because they like the job rather than because they need the money. Likewise, people would go to school in order to learn something in which they are interested, or pursue an educa-

tion for its own sake, rather than simply for financial reasons. It would separate educational and financial incentives. The gross national product might decline, but some might argue that this is a "healthier" way to organize a society. Job characteristics and personal preferences and interests, rather than financial payoff, become the motivation for work and for education. As René Dubos (1974a, 1974b), Professor Emeritus at Rockefeller University and renowned public health physician and Pulitzer Prize winning author, has put it, "The next fifty years must not be an extrapolation of today, but an original mode of life that seeks qualitative rather than quantitative growth."

There are other, perhaps "radical" economic implications. Jobs would need to be made available, probably through governmental agencies, that would pay no less than the average wage. This would mean higher taxes and a planned economy, but that is the price for elimination of poverty. Fairweather (1972) has suggested that another way to increase jobs is to rotate people on a 3- or 4-day work week. Furthermore, businesses, both small and large, would need to pay all of their employees at least an average wage. This would necessarily mean a reduction of their percentage of profit. Again, that is the price to pay for a more equitable distribution of resources. The cost in money is a reduction at the top and an equalization at the bottom. The cost in the social status of median income people is that now they will not earn more than a person working in a job that has less social prestige.

These are radical proposals that would require a great deal of political, economic, and value change in our society. However, a systems analysis leads us to conclude that such a basic rearrangement of our goals and social relationships is the only step that can break the natural tendency of a system to perpetuate itself unchanged. These changes are obviously not the kind that psychologists or other social scientists have either the power or the ability to implement. They are the kind that will need to evolve as our society asks itself what end product we really desire. The role of the social scientist in such a plan, however, is important. The necessary steps in a reformation of society's goals and social relationships include an *awareness of the alternatives* and an assessment of the likely outcomes of programs. So long as social science and the helping professions support, either implicitly or explicitly, a blaming-the-victim strategy, they will perpetuate the current social problems they say they want to eliminate. Psychology and the other social sciences have a responsibility to make as clear as possible the implications and values supported by their programs. Although a set of values, goals, and programs similar to the ones presented here may be rejected by many as undesirable, social science cannot honestly argue that currently acceptable programs, which blame victims for social processes, are likely to solve the problems of poverty and powerlessness. *Society may choose not to change, but the choice should be made without the cover of rationalizations from social science.*

The public and the policy makers need to know that current programs will support things as they are, rather than as we say we want them to be. The value choices and goals for our society need to be made consciously rather than covered by rationalizations from a social science which simply allows us to feel like responsible and concerned citizens. If society is going to choose one set of values over another, these choices and outcomes should be made explicit by social science. Although it is not legitimate for social scientists to impose values and programs (nor is it politically feasible), it is quite legitimate to make the values and likely outcomes clear. That, in fact, is the business of social science. There is no guarantee that society will support the values expressed here, but it is certain that if social science and the helping professions simply continue to support things the way they are, by making directly or indirectly false promises of change, change will never occur. One way in which a community psychology may participate in the change process is by publicly examining the values supported by current community welfare programs and by presenting new programs, with the values of each made

clear. Social welfare, like it or not, is a function of social values. It is on the basis of a clear assessment of the values which lie behind our programs that social science can contribute to social change.[2]

Power and Control

The methods of social change described above are analytical. There is also a second way for community psychology to participate in social change—by direct intervention. For community psychology, direct intervention must be on the basis of psychological rather than economic analysis, and this leads us to the second component in Ryan's proposals, "clout." Clout means power, and as we have already noted earlier in this chapter, power has at least two aspects, political and psychological. It includes the power to control the social institutions that affect one's life, and the psychological well-being that comes from a sense of internal locus of control over the outcomes of one's actions. The importance of internal locus of control as a psychological variable was discussed in Chapter IV. Here we are concerned with *power as a resource,* perhaps even more basic than money as a resource. This variable is of such importance to community psychology that it serves as a basis for many of the action programs reviewed in the chapters that follow.

According to Ryan, a primary cause of social problems is powerlessness; its cure is a redistribution of power. The absence of power is what he sees behind the so-called characteristics of the poor—apathy, fatalism, and pessimism. The cure lies not only in analysis, but also in direct action. In educational programs this means putting control of the institutions directly

---

[2]A recent analysis by an economist (Gordon, 1973), which suggests the need for a "planned economy" combined with what he calls "democratic control of our working and political lives" has spelled out in detail other implications of current and possible economic policy from the viewpoint of economic theory. Recognizing that such a society can easily be labeled "utopian," he counters that it is the mainstream economists who are utopian for dreaming that our present economic system could possibly work!

in the hands of local community people. One such plan is offered in Chapter VIII. Ryan has suggested a similar plan in which financial resources would be tied to individuals rather than to the school system. Each child would have the right to attend the school of his or her choice, and schools would compete for students by offering educational alternatives. The power to choose would lead to the power to control because schools would need to be directly accountable to the students and their parents. Although quality control could be maintained by centralized standards of educational outcome, the day-to-day issues of administration, teacher-student interaction, and style of instruction are suggested as appropriate for local community (neighborhood) control. These issues are discussed more fully in the last section of Chapter VIII.

In the legal system Ryan suggests a local neighborhood community police force, rather than a centralized agency of social control. He also suggests a reform of bail-bond procedures (see Chapter X for a discussion of these and similar programs). In the mental health system (see Chapter IX) a redistribution of power would mean a system that would allow deviants the right to be different and would support their efforts at independence rather than dependence. In housing, programs that maximize individual control based on the right to adequate homes and independent choice would be emphasized.

Basic to each of the programs which Ryan suggests is an issue which he presents in terms of an old song: "It's not only what you do, but the way you do it." The issue of accountability and planning has emerged in American social welfare programs. Everyone now believes in the principles. However, what is not agreed upon is who should plan and to whom they should be accountable. Ryan argues that "rational or not, centralized social accounting will do nothing to alter the powerlessness and the exclusion of the poor, the oppressed, and the alienated. It will do nothing to solve the problem of what might be called the 'Giving Enemy' " (Ryan, 1971, p. 264).

What does Ryan mean by the Giving Enemy? He describes this enemy as the public service agent who gives people what they have, but at the same time robs them of dignity and a personal sense of control. He patrols our streets, but acts rude. In the classroom he is an agent of education and socialization, but often seems more interested in homogenization and in social control than in learning. He seems to dislike some children and their families because they do not fit into a set of predetermined standards of behavior. He sees that welfare checks come every month, but wants to regulate their use. He represents the depersonalized delivery of human services. The defects in a system which creates the Giving Enemy are structural. Ryan cites five problems:

1. The problem of centralization. Authority, decision making, and accountability are centered so far from the person-to-person touchstone of services that they appear to be invisible.
2. The lack of citizen participation. The same citizens who are accused of apathy complain of being excluded.
3. The lack of true comprehensive planning. Although within their own domains each service is planned, across domains there is anarchy. Each service, mental health, education, social welfare, physical health, and so on is independent of all others and totally out of touch with the local citizens.
4. The lack of accountability to grass-roots people. Accountability is simply an abstract virtue which is not translated to include the recipients of supplied services.
5. This misguided "Giving Enemy" himself who blames the victims for their own victimization.

Ryan's solutions to these problems lie in a political-community organization proposal. He advocates the development of new mechanisms of government at the neighborhood level: elected district or neighborhood councils, social planning, and accountability boards. There are also a number of implications from his analysis for the direct actions of professionals who are now the Giving Enemy. The programs that are advocated for improving social welfare must take into account the importance of power at both the psychological and the political level. In the chapters that follow programs that have been cognizant of this dimension either explicitly or implicitly are reviewed. Together they constitute the beginnings of an empirical base for a community psychology based on cultural relativity, ecological systems change, and support for human diversity and independence. These values lead to a set of programs that fosters independence and personal control rather than a dependence on services. They are supported by a psychology of strengths rather than of weaknesses.

A Community Strengths Approach to Social Intervention

Before we can turn to the action-specific strategies and tactics necessary for the work of community psychology, additional characteristics of the search for new paradigms require discussion. One such characteristic is a shift in emphasis away from programs for prevention of illness and toward programs, structures, and institutions to support the *strengths* of diverse communities. Such a shift is both subtle and profound. Although at first glance it will appear to be only a semantic distinction, it is in fact not trivial.

Nevitt Sanford (1972) has recently raised the question "is the concept of prevention necessary or useful?" He has asserted that because "mental illness" is not a set of specific disorders with specific causes, to assume that specific disorders can be prevented, as in the physical health model, is probably a mistake. Indeed, René Dubos (1959) has questioned whether or not physical illness itself can be altogether eliminated. Sanford proposes that our planned actions be focused on promotion of the potential for human development in general, or nonspecific forms of prevention, which means enhancing the *possibilities* for growth. He goes on to argue for a set of social-psychological goals which will articulate what positive things a person can become, and which will require a reconsideration of our values now often based on a narrow interpretation of human potential. For example,

Sanford notes that often the development of "competence" is suggested as a goal of development, yet such goals are frequently narrowly defined and independent of other qualities. More importantly, competence is most often defined in such a way as to be a form of discrimination against ethnic minorities by use of what we have been calling in this book the "single standard."

In contemporary American society young people of ethnic minorities live in a predominantly White society which tells them on the one hand to conform to majority culture and on the other that they cannot do so because, by White "standards," they are inferior. Sanford is concerned with how, in such a contemporary atmosphere, the needs of young people can be met by educational institutions. He argues that self-esteem as opposed to self-contempt is the crucial variable. People must be permitted to live in an environment that affirms who they are, especially in their "formative years." He cites the report of Ortega (1969) that "Spanish-speaking Americans who emerged as leaders in the Southwest lived during their formative years in Chicano enclaves where they were relatively untroubled by intrusions of 'Anglo' culture—until they had enough security in their identity to enable them to cope with the surrounding dominant culture" (Sanford, 1972, p. 468). Such reasoning is supportive of the efforts of Black people to preserve and create a cultural heritage of their own. Before one can become a "citizen of the world" one must have a secure sense of one's own culture. Finally, Sanford argues, community-run schools and ethnic studies programs within schools and colleges are highly significant as institutions for strength building:

. . . it seems unfair to label as "racism in reverse" or as "separatism" the efforts of these minorities to establish some cultural basis for identity and pride . . . [people require] both cultural identity and the freedom to go where they please. Educational programs for ethnic identity can even be . . . carried out in integrated institutions provided these schools are not run by white people for the benefit of white people, and provided white people do not say in effect "we'll accept them when they become like us" nor feel guilty or anxious everytime minority students are observed to stick together—in the cafeteria, or on the playground, or in classes of their own (Sanford, 1972, p. 469).

Rappaport, Davidson, Wilson, and Mitchell (1975) have described a training program for psychologists which seeks to aid in the development of existing community strengths (see Chapter XI). In order to build on the cultural values and strengths that already exist in a minority community they have argued that it is necessary to support them with resources rather than to attack weaknesses as perceived by the majority (Seidman & Rappaport, 1974). They have argued that we need programs which provide for "cultural amplifiers" or those aspects of technology which enable a community to transfer skills from areas of already existing competence to new ones. There is a need for conceptions, resources, and programs that provide an alternative to a blaming-the-victim-environment ideology.

Philip L. Berck (1976b) has carried this notion further in what he has called "an experimental community strengths model for social change." In examining the possibilities for social intervention, one dimension of analysis Berck cites is what he calls the "scope of the change strategy." At one end this scope includes comprehensive plans for entire cities and regions where, as Ryan has noted, "target" individuals are excluded from the decision-making process. Such attempts at social intervention most often benefit the power elite. At the other extreme is the individual intervention which, while it maximizes single-person input, is not only infeasible for reasons of efficiency, but also tends to label the person as deficited and to blame him for his own victimization. Berck argues for interventions aimed at what Sarason (1972) has termed the "setting" or the organization, the neighborhood or social subsystem. As Ryan has suggested in his notion of elected district councils, such a scope has the advantage of affecting multiple individuals, is aimed at systematic changes, and includes the target group in decision making. To this Berck adds the observation that not only does it affect multiple individuals, but "new members" as well. Such efforts may be aimed at the creation of new settings or the creation of change in existing settings (see Chapter VI for an elaboration of the strategies and tactics of this approach).

One obvious result of such a system of planning would be a fostering of a *diversity* of settings in which multiple life styles and goals are accepted as legitimate. How such a social order can be maintained and integrated is an important and unresolved question for community psychology; and if community psychology is to be more than utopian, this question must be dealt with. However, the only way to deal with it realistically is to try to implement such a society through the creation of settings, and to evaluate and modify their functioning. To continue to support a single standard, rank-ordered society, which plans without diversity and tries to fit everyone into the plan, is to assure more of the same problems that now plague us.

The second dimension Berck (1976b) introduces is what he calls the "perspective of the change strategy." This idea is very much like Kuhn's notion of the paradigm in that a change in perspective will change the way one "sees" the world of concern. Berck argues that how the interventionist defines and conceptualizes the issues will have a major impact on what follows.

The first step in such definition and conceptualization is selection of a "difficulty area." Here the change agent becomes familiar with both the clientele and the history of the situation. The agent helps to set objectives that are a combination of personal interests and those of the constituents. Traditionally, Berck notes, a plan is aimed at *problem* definition. "Who isn't getting what from whom. Where are the deficits in the system, and how can they be most efficiently eradicated? Thus, the traditional problem definition strategy inplies a remedial change strategy, 'fixing what needs fixing'" (Berck, 1976b). It is here, Berck asserts, in the tradition of conceptualizing change as remediation and designing interventions as reactions to *problems*, that the change agent often assumes a perspective that literally blinds him to multiple possibilities for genuine alteration of system output.

In developing this idea Berck draws heavily on the thinking of Watzlawick, Weakland, and Fisch (1974) who have presented a theory of change based on the kind of ecological systems analysis introduced into the behavioral sciences by Gregory Bateson (1972). Their ideas concerning the need for a change agent to step outside the usual ways of viewing a difficulty area, so as to take a new perspective, are also consistent with Kuhn's analysis of the importance of paradigms, and extends the same idea beyond the community of scientists to the community of all people. Their analysis leads us again to the importance of community psychology's search for new paradgms, and their view of the process of change is presented in detail below. For our present purposes it is sufficient to invoke their notion of the difference between *first-order change,* which may be thought of as change within a system that only looks like change but is really not, and change in the "rules of the game" or *second-order change,* which they define as genuine change in a system.

In applying the notion of second-order change, Berck (1976b) uses the principles suggested by Watzlawick *et al.* to argue that one way to create genuine change or change in the "rules of the game" for social welfare programs is to redefine the difficulty area for social intervention in terms of strengths rather than weaknesses. Ask "what resources exist and how can these resources be bolstered?" rather than "what is the deficit?" This reformulation makes several paradoxical assumptions. It assumes that the targets of a social intervention have competencies that are more important to understand and to work with than the weaknesses that have made them a target in the first place. In some instances the "weaknesses" are not even real, as for example with the so-called culturally deprived child, and are only a problem because they do not fit into the existing solutions (see Chapters VII and VIII). In other cases, as with the chronic mental patient, there may be some very real deficits that are less important than the strengths that are usually ignored (see Chapter IX). Such an approach has a number of crucial implications for the "message" given to the target person. The expectations communicated to the persons are that they are competent, adequate, perhaps different, but not deficient or maladjusted.

Berck (1976b) has provided us with an ex-cellent example of the differing implications for action from a "problems" as opposed to a "strengths" perspective:

Viewing an example through these two different perspectives might serve to clarify the distinctions. Suppose the innovator is interested in the educative system in a community and, through the immersion process, it becomes apparent that a difficulty area within the present system involves low attendance rates for a subpopulation of students. Given the problem or weaknesses approach to defining target areas of intervention, a reasonable . . . (goal) might be . . . to increase the attendance of those students. One might look at the history of attempts to maintain attendance rates (e.g., truancy laws and police involvement, or parent conferences) and conclude that what is needed are more of those strategies, e.g., more stringent laws, or conferences with more parents more frequently. These would be true first-order change attempts; they would more than likely exacerbate the difficulty, by defining the subpopulation as law breakers as well as low attenders.

An innovator with more foresight (still working within the constraints of the weaknesses model) might see through these "more of the same" first-order change strategies and explore new and better ways of increasing attendance. But in so doing, the innovator still assumes that there is something inherently wrong with the students' nonattending behavior, and what is called for is a corrective action. While the innovator may think he or she is working for the students as clientele (helping them get the education they deserve), it is probably more accurate to describe the clientele as some combination of the school system, parents, and perhaps even the police.

From the strengths perspective an entirely different picture emerges. The first step in examining the same difficulty area is to identify strengths in the system involved, especially strengths in the consumers: the students. The most obvious strength is the clients' awareness that the present school system has little to offer them. Immediately strategies to create alternative settings (that may offer something useful to the clientele) come to mind, which ironically, might involve even further reduction of attendance rates, or complete withdrawal from the public school system. Alternatively, one might conclude that enhancing one of the present school system's strengths, a diverse curriculum, might be another viable strategy.

Reemphasis of the major "side-effect" of this perspective is warranted, that is, the nature of the expectations placed on the target of change. For the students, the strengths perspective no longer identifies them as misfits. Rather, since concentration centers on what developable resources they posess, the metacommunication is that they are basically worthwhile people. Rather than blaming the victim of the system, and rather than blaming the system for lack of accommodation, no blame is leveled at all. As illustrated by the curriculum enhancement strategy, the metacommunication to the current school system is "you have a good thing because you have all these other students interested enough to attend; let's enhance your basic resource, a diverse curriculum." The metacommunication of the deficit approach is "your curriculum is deficient because you don't offer anything to these certain kids, so we'll try to construct something you *can* offer them!"

Berck (1976b), as noted above, goes on to elaborate on the possible strategies of change that are implied in his analysis. He makes a distinction between strategies aimed at the individual and those where the scope of the intervention is a social system. This distinction may now be combined with the second—the perspective of change as one which frames the difficulty in terms of strengths or weaknesses. The result is a two-by-two table (Table V-1). Strategies aimed at the individual level and which take a weakness perspective include the traditional forms of psychotherapy, as well as behavior modification, which is typically aimed at amelioration of some deficit thought to be a consequence of faulty learning, and which can now be "unlearned" as a new set of behaviors is taught. Tutoring programs are similar in that they focus on 'fixing-up" an individual who needs special attention. Individual interventions may also be taken from a strengths perspective—the most common is of course the vocational counseling

paradigm in which the couselor helps the person select an area of work or training most suitable to individual needs, abilities, and aspirations. Child advocacy, a more recent addition to the social welfare armementarium, is aimed at assisting a particular child to obtain the resources of the community. It might involve a professional or a nonprofessional helping the person to negotiate with teachers, judges, welfare workers, or whomever, and assumes that the child has strengths and assets that will blossom if the child is given legal and other rights.

As we have already seen, community mental health is an attempt to intervene at the systems, rather than the individual level. Unfortunately, many of its conceptions are borrowed from traditional individual psychology and are seen through an individual weakness perspective. This leads to programs aimed at repairing the deficits, albeit now among large numbers of people, or entire populations, which are presumed to limit their ability to adapt to the prevailing social norms. Berck also places incremental planning in the same category, from the field of Urban Planning. This is aimed at finding the maximum benefits of a system through continual analysis of what is not working. Its focus is on system feedback and correction and its goal is system maintenance. Finally, Berck sees community psychology as ideally a systems-level change strategy which analyzes systems in terms of strengths and resources. Advocacy planning, built on the strengths of the group advocated for, is similar. Important in such an approach is the emphasis on allocation of resources—material and psychological. Power and control, money and independence are the

TABLE V-1   A two-dimensional model of change strategies.*

Perspective of the Intervention	Scope of the Intervention	
	Individual	*Social System*
Strengths	Vocational counseling Child advocacy	Community psychology Advocacy planning
Weaknesses	Psychotherapy Behavior modification Tutoring	Community mental health Incrementalist planning

*From Berck, 1976b.

resources. It is assumed in this model that the target group already has within its own members the ability to use the resources, but that their major problems are a function of lack of access—a systems rather than an individual difficulty. Such a social intervention strategy may require community organization and social advocacy as detailed in Chapter VI, as well as the interventionist to work directly with grass-roots people.

For the would-be change agent of any variety the question "how?," that is, what to do when trying to create change, is a major issue. This question has preoccupied the helping professions and is a question that seeks a technology. It assumes that the goal is known and the motivation for change present, although these must be assessed and stimulated as necessary preconditions. The change agent who focuses on individuals wants person P to stop behaving or feeling like X, Y, and Z and/or to begin doing and feeling like E, F, and G. The change agent builds a bridge for person P from point A to point B. The problem viewed in this way is modeled after the engineer who builds a bridge to get from point A to point B. The question, "How do I build the bridge?" is answered by a technology that applies general laws to a particular problem. Some therapists of course view their bridge building as more art than science, and indeed bridges were built before they were understood. Nevertheless, for the artist or the technician the question "how?" is based on some theory of bridge building, or, in this case, methods of therapy based on one or more theories of individual human behavior. The change agent may select from among the many conceptual modes (see Table III-4) available to psychology. This is a matter of faith in one conceptualization or the other, although empirical evidence will be presented, and scientific methodology applied to evaluate and justify the choice. For the passive change agent, working only with individuals, waiting in his or her office or clinic for the clients to present themselves, the answer to the question "how?" is supplied by individual psychological conceptions. As we have seen in Table III-4, for the active style of delivery the conception of individual behavior will also be important in determining how the change agent intervenes, or what is actually done with individuals. But for the community psychologist there are additional questions to answer, such as "where," as well as "how" to intervene.

Levels of Organization

In an effort to develop paradigms that would help answer the question "where," and to take community-level variables into account, Robert Reiff convened, at his Institute for Community Intervention in New York City, a group of community psychologists who met for periodic seminars. [3] Beginning with Reiff's notion that the social order of a society is made up of a series of increasingly complex levels of organization, the group developed the implications of this thinking for a psychology of community change. Seidman and Rappaport (1974b) have presented some of this thinking in what they call a *conceptual-methodological schema*.

It has been posited that the "social order" may be described in terms of its levels of organization and scaled by varying degrees of complexity. In this schema one may think about the society as a series of increasingly complex levels of organization. Each level serves as a potential point of intervention, as well as a potential point for assessment. Interventions at one level may also have effects at other levels. Consider, for example, the following schema, in order of increasing organizational complexity:

1. individual level
2. group level
3. organizational level
4. institutional level
5. community level
6. societal level

The relationships within and between levels may be thought to make up a given "social order," at a moment in time (cf. Reiff, 1971b).

Given the community mental health professional's training in a "clinical model," which

---

[3]These seminars under the direction of Robert Reiff included a number of his postdoctoral students and Morton Bard, James G. Kelly, Ramsay Leim, Jerry Osterweil, Julian Rappaport, and William Ryan.

deals primarily in conceptions of individuals and small groups (levels 1 and 2, above), Seidman and Rappaport (1974b) have reasoned that it may be difficult to deal with problems at the other levels. It may be, for example, that the principles and techniques that make sense at the individual level (e.g., personality theory, principles of learning, and behavior modification) are not necessarily operative at other levels. For example, organizations may be best understood on the basis of principles and variables that are different from those useful in understanding individual behavior. Indeed, the two levels probably interact (Watson, 1971) to produce both social and psychological effects.

It is also possible, even without a detailed understanding of each level, to use this conceptualization in order to make clear the need to assess an intervention, regardless of the level at which it occurs, at levels other than the actual point of intervention, or what Kelly (1971) terms its "radiating" impact. If community psychology is really interested in social systems change, it must be concerned with the impact of its interventions at multiple levels—in order to have maximum societal impact as well as to develop assessment and conceptual tools which would enable evaluation of preventive interventions. For example, an intervention such as the use of college students as companions for teenage probationers should have impact not only on the target child, but also on the court system as an organization. Judges should be more willing to give probation than to institutionalize offenders, if the program has an effect on the court system. Likewise, the positive effects of a program for juvenile delinquents should have a "spillover effect" on peers, classmates, and neighbors. This schema is illustrated in what Seidman and Rappaport (1974b) have called the *educational pyramid*, and is described in Chapter XI.

Models of Community Change

Although the above schema clarifies both potential points of intervention and observation for the community psychologist as well as the need

to operate and observe at multiple levels, it still does not speak to the question of exactly what *form* a community intervention should take, or what theory of individual and community behavior it should be based on. As we have already seen, psychology has many conceptions of individual behavior but few of community behavior, since this is a relatively new problem area.[4] Kenneth Heller (1970) has attempted to classify some of the more recent activities of both community mental health professionals and community psychologists in order to deal with exactly this question: What are the conceptions of community as opposed to individual change which may serve as a basis for community psychology? He has identified four community models and their assumptions about the change process. From his work it is possible to derive some of the activities implied for community psychology. Heller's models and assumptions, together with their implied activities, are presented in Table V-2.[5]

The *consultation model* is based largely on Caplan's rationale, already presented in Chapter III. Its basic assumptions about mental health revolve around the belief that the organizations of society are crucial in the socialization process, and that change is largely a function of key individuals in those organizations. The activities of the community mental health worker are therefore focused on consultation to key persons in the established settings, and they are the target of change. Specific methods of consultation have been suggested by many different writers, and some of these are reviewed in Chapter IX.

The *organization development model* is based on the assumption that the mental health of a community is largely a function of the

---

[4]Community psychology is concerned with intervention and action as well as analysis. Although social psychology and sociology have both been concerned with community behavior, most of their analyses have not involved actual interventions. A notable exception is organizational psychology, discussed in the next chapter.

[5]Heller's four models of community change are presented here as an introduction to the problem area, and as a means of concretizing the importance of level of analysis. A more detailed discussion of the strategies and tactics of community change models is presented in Chapter VI.

characteristics of its organizations, particularly in the work setting. Emphasis is on open communication between leaders and co-workers. The basic methods of intervention are communication groups and organizational consultation (see Chapter VI).

Although the first two models identified by Heller focus attention of the community psychologist on work with established organizations and leaders, the second two are more concerned with activities directed toward grassroots people, or those who are not in powerful positions of social control. In the consultation and the organization development models the community worker is accountable to the leadership in established settings of work, socialization, and social control. Often the community psychologist will be hired by the established leaders, and almost always will have worked out a contractual arrangement with that leadership in which the goals of the organization are taken as givens, while the means for accomplishing these goals are the focus of change. Change is aimed at efficiency and effectiveness in bringing the members of the organization under social control. This may involve helping students to adjust to school, men to the assembly line, or helping community members and policemen to understand and cooperate with one another. The *status quo* aims of socialization to predominant social values is taken for granted, if not often made explicit.

In the second two models emphasis begins to shift away from traditional mental health adjustment toward what has been called advocacy and accountability to grass-roots people (Rappaport & O'Connor, 1972). In the *parallel institutions model,* or what Sarason (1972) has termed "the creation of settings," it is assumed that the social institutions available to many people are incapable of meeting their human needs; perhaps such institutions are even oppressive and destructive for those people who do not "fit in." Although it may be possible to work with leaders of these organizations to create more humane and less rigid institutions, it is usually seen as more feasible to develop separate facilities now under the control of previously powerless people. Examples of this kind

of community psychology are presented in Chapter VI and in subsequent chapters.

The *community organization and social advocacy model* shares some of the basic assumptions of the parallel institutions model, but differs with regard to assumptions about change and therefore community activities. In this model the aim is to help heretofore powerless people gain control over the existing social institutions affecting their lives. Examples of such activities are also presented in Chapter VI and in subsequent chapters, and constitute one means of gaining local community control of educational institutions as already presented in Chapter VIII.

As can be seen from these concrete examples, the community psychologist is interested in changes at multiple levels of societal organization, ranging from individual and small group change through organizational, institutional, and community change. Behavior and change at each level may be governed by different principles, and therefore the community psychologist needs to have conceptions of change at more than the individual level. Heller's tabulation of some of the models of *community* change with which the social interventionist has been concerned helps to demonstrate the importance of the questions "how" and "where" for community psychology.

For the community psychologist the question "how?" must be answered in conjunction with the question "where?" The Watzlawick, Wakeland, and Fisch (1974) application of the Theory of Groups and the Theory of Logical Types, presented below, shows us the importance of how one answers such questions for the creation of change. If a given solution is applied to a difficulty at the wrong level, what they call an "error of logical typing," the solution applied will either create a "game without end," because the change generated will always be first-order change, or the solution will exacerbate the difficulty and create a problem rather than solve one. No matter how useful one's conceptual mode is for a technology of change at a given level, *if change at that level is not appropriate for solution of the difficulty the solution itself becomes a problem.*

TABLE V–2   Heller's community change models and assumptions*

	Mental Health Assumptions	Assumptions about the Change Process	Implied Activities of the Community Psychologist
Consultation Model	Primary care-givers and other community leaders will perform their service and socialization functions better and will develop more effective and psychologically sound programs if they learn to understand and deal with the social and emotional components of the problems with which their clients confront them. Programs can be developed in organizations responsible for the quality of human life that will reduce or prevent the build-up of psychiatric casualties.	As is true for all community leaders, care-givers usually represent community sentiments with great accuracy and if removed would be replaced in all likelihood by personnel with similar values. Care-givers try to do their best within the limits of their ability, training, and experience. They will be responsive to attempts to help them improve their job functioning as long as personal or organizational constraints are not excessive. Institutions and individuals are capable of change. Methods of consultation are available to deal with personal or institutional constraints that develop over time in any bureaucratic structure.	Consult with key community leaders. Teachers, policemen, administrators, and other persons in positions of authority are the targets of change. Public education is emphasized. Apply Caplan's principles of preventive psychiatry. (See Chapter III.)
Organizational Development Model	Decentralization of decision making within institutions. Understanding, open communication, and the ability to deal with the social and emotional components of one's own daily life and work situation leads to increased productivity, satisfaction, and mental health.	Fully aware and interpersonally honest personnel will lead to more humane and effective institutions and organizations.	Organizational consultation. Conduct communication training for leaders of established organizations. Use various techniques of organization development. (See Chapter VI.)

*Adapted from Heller, 1970.

The Theory of Groups and the Theory of Logical Types

Relying upon mathematical logic, Watzlawick *et al*. (1974) propose that change of any kind may be understood by analogy in terms of the *Theory of Groups* and the *Theory of Logical Types*. It is their contention that principles derived from these theories are applicable to any kind of change. According to the Theory of Groups, any group is composed of members who are alike in one common characteristic, and their "actual nature" other than that characteristic is irrelevant for the theory. They cite four

	Mental Health Assumptions	*Assumptions about the Change Process*	*Implied Activities of the Community Psychologist*
Parallel Institutions Model	Whether due to bureaucratic complexity, size, or general insensitivity to the human condition, existing institutions and personnel within them are often incapable of responding to the needs of large segments of the population. Oppressive institutions are particularly neglectful of psychological needs, so that mental health problems are created by these institutions where none would have existed otherwise.	In some instances it may be sufficient to train a new cadre of personnel of moral purpose, capable of responding with warmth and sincerity. However, when organizational rigidity is great, separate facilities under the control of the previously disenfranchised groups may be necessary.	Creation of alternative settings. Work with established leaders as well as grass-roots people. (See Chapter VI.)
Community Organization and Social Advocacy Model	Possessing the resources to determine one's own fate leads to better mental health than having no resources for self-sufficiency or self-determination. All members of the community should have the same ability to deal with mental health problems. They will have that ability if community resources are shared equally among all. Organizations are neglectful of psychological needs because they are set up to control rather than serve their supposed constituencies.	Those in power will not voluntarily give up their control and exclusive utilization of community resources. Resources can only be seized from them by a counter-political force of sufficient strength.	Social and political action; community organization and work at the grass-roots level as well as with established leaders. (See Chapter VI.)

properties of groups derived from the theory, and give many examples of how the properties may be applied to human interaction.

The first property states that the outcome of a combination of two or more members of a group is itself a member of the group. This allows for many changes within the group, but makes it impossible for a member to be outside the group. If, for example, as in our society, groups are defined on the basis of race or role, any attempt to change a member of a given group so as to have him behave more like a member of another group will create change internal to the group, but the member will still not be placed outside the group of which he is a member. The Black child who is a participant in a preschool education program will still be a Black child, and to the extent that Black children experience difficulty in public school as a function of being a group member, that difficulty will not be eliminated. Conversely, the White teacher who is a member of the group "Whites" may become "educated" to problems of racial discrimination, but will still be a member of the group of Whites. Similarly, the group of "students" and the group of "teachers" will be defined in terms of their relationship to one another, regardless of any behavior on the part of any member of either group. The role behavior of teachers gives them decision-making power over students. A democratic or authoritarian teacher is only more or less so relative to other group members. A student cannot be the teacher, even when the teacher uses students as teachers for other students, so long as the defining characteristic of teacher is the power to make decisions about the students. A teacher in our current public school system cannot avoid this because it is a group characteristic.

A second property of a group is that it may combine members in a varying sequence and yet the outcome of the combination remains the same. In our example above, the Black child with a preschool education may initially do better in school than another member of his group (he may change his rank-order within the group) but the *outcome for the group* will remain the same. Most Blacks will continue to experience more difficulty in school than most Whites if the difficulty is a function of their group membership and resultant racial discrimination. Again, a given teacher in a public school may be relatively less authoritarian with his students than other teachers, but this will not change the outcome for the group. Teachers as a group will still be in authority because this is the characteristic of the group "teachers in public schools."

Third, a group contains an identity member (in mathematics, for addition the member is zero while for multiplication it is one) such that combination with this member maintains the member's identity. In groups of Blacks or

Whites in our society skin color is the identity member, and any combination of characteristics with skin color will not change one's identity. Again, to paraphrase the well known, a teacher is a teacher is a teacher, regardless of other behaviors. Fourth, in any group every member has its reciprocal. In our examples White is the reciprocal of Black, and student the reciprocal of teacher.

Watzlawick *et al.* argue that these postulates of Group Theory help to explain why change within a given group makes no difference to the group. For example, changes in the educational accomplishments of individual Black students will not change the outcomes of education for people who are members of the group "Black." They will still find it difficult, as a group, to find jobs and other resources so long as group (racial) discrimination is the controlling variable. Likewise, changes in individual teachers will not change the group "teachers" so long as schools are structured as they now are.

To these principles Watzlawick *et al.* add the axioms of the Theory of Logical Types. In this theory all components are referred to as members and the totality itself is called a class. An essential axiom of the Theory of Logical Types is that whatever involves all of the collection must not be one of the collection (Watzlawick *et al.*, p. 6). Mankind is all individuals, but mankind itself in not an individual, and here they make an important observation for community psychology:

> Any attempt to deal with one in terms of the other is doomed to lead to nonsense and confusion. For example, the economic behavior of the population of a large city cannot be understood in terms of the behavior of one inhabitant multiplied by, say four million . . . a population of four million is not just quantitatively but qualitatively different from an individual, because it involves systems of interaction among individuals. Similarly, while the individual members of a species are usually endowed with very specific survival mechanisms, it is well known that the entire species may race head long towards extinction—and the human species is probably no exception (Watzlawick *et al.*, 1974, p. 6).

Confusing a member with a class is common to behavioral science and is a point that was made earlier in this chapter (p. 129) by emphasizing that the social order is composed of levels of organization, the principles of which vary from one level to another. In order to effect change at a societal level, for example, it may not be adequate to apply the principles of individual psychology. This is an important reason for the failure of psychology's paradigms of individual behavior to solve the puzzles of community psychology, which require change at other than the individual level.

According to the Theory of Logical Types, levels of analysis must be kept strictly apart in order to prevent confusion. Going from one level to another requires a "shift, a jump, a discontinuity or transformation" of utmost importance. It is a way out of the "rules," which apply to a given level and to a group and allows one out of the system that is unchangeable by its own rules. In our examples above, jumping to a level of analysis other than that focused on changes in the individual members of a group such as Black people, or poor people, or individual teachers, would instead allow one to look for change in the "rules of the game" which maintain *relationships* between Blacks and Whites and teachers and students.

First-order Change and Second-order Change

Following these principles Watzlawick *et al.* (1974) posit two general kinds of change. One, which is understood by Group Theory, is change within a system that itself stays invariant. Helping individuals to adapt to a system may be thought of as exemplary. It is very close to what Ryan (1971) means by "blaming the victim." In this analysis within-group change is called *first-order change*. The second type of change, referred to as *second-order change*, is one whose occurrence changes the system itself. It is the way out of changes that do not really change things. Groups are invariant in terms of first-order change (the more things change the more they remain the same). However, if one is able to jump levels, to second-order change, or *change the rules that govern relationships between groups*, then "real" change is possible.

Watzlawick *et al.* compare first- and second-order change by asking us to consider a person having a nightmare. The person can do a number of things within the nightmare itself, but no change of behavior within the nightmare will free the person from it. The way out of the dream is to change the rules—that is, stop dreaming. Consider the large number of people who live the nightmare of being Black and poor within our system of rules for allocation of physical, material, and psychological resources. Being White and rich allows the best opportunities for well-being. The group which is defined by the characteristics Black and poor, according to the principles of Group Theory, cannot end its nightmare by changing behavior within the nightmare (the system and its rules). It is only by changing the system, that is, its rules for allocation of resources and well-being to those who are Black and poor, or by a *second-order change*, that the group may escape. Individual members within the group may be rearranged by first-order change; that is, a given member may become relatively better off than another, but in terms of the group this will be no change at all.

Because second-order change does not follow the rules on which everyone has heretofore agreed it often requires actions that are illogical and seem to violate "common sense." Watzlawick *et al.* provide many examples in which common sense solutions fail to solve human problems. They cite three common ways in which these solution errors occur: (1) action is necessary but not taken, (2) action is taken where it should not be, and (3) "an error in logical typing is committed and the Game Without End established . . . by action taken at the wrong level."

This last type of solution is of most interest to us here. In an earlier section of this chapter (p. 118) we noted that the change from a genetic to an environmental explanation of social problems is *functionally* no change at all—it continues to blame the victims for their own victimization. In Watzlawick's terms this "change" in explanation has two characteristics that explain why it is not change at all. On the one hand it can be seen as a first-order change, wherein the rules of the system are left unaltered; now we simply have a new "explanation" for why some do not "make it" by those rules. Second, this may be seen as an "error of logical typing" in which a systems level problem, allocation of resources, is "dealt with" by means of an individual level solution—providing cultural and educational "enrichment" programs. It establishes a "Game Without End" in that all change will be no change because it is the wrong kind of change, and more and more of it will be called for without success. As we shall see in Chapters VII and VIII this is exactly the outcome of programs of preschool education for the "disadvantaged" which can never get beyond first-order change because they are solutions aimed at individual members rather than at the rules of the game.

In presenting their ideas about second-order change Watzlawick *et al.* argue that genuine (second-order) change is most often found to occur as a function of actions applied to the *solution* rather than to the difficulty itself.[6] This is because the "solution" is often the cause of the problem, despite the fact that first-order solutions always appear to be based on common sense. Second-order change, often appearing illogical because it does not accept the rules, avoids the trap of endless solutions within the system. Much of the work of community psychology may be thought of as attempts to change the solutions to human difficulties which do not solve the difficulties, and may even exacerbate them. In working for second-order change, community psychologists may often appear "illogical," in Watzlawick's terms, since they will question the rules. Others may even call community psychology "radical" because in seeking second-order change the accepted tenets of social systems must necessarily be questioned. Watzlawick provides some examples that will be helpful.

The legalization of marijuana, whose effects are not certain but probably are not worse than other now legal drugs, might not only decrease its use, but would end the consequences of its legal suppression. The consequences of its sup-

pression may be worse than the consequences of its use. The well-known history of the prohibition of alcohol and its consequences seems to be "proof" of such reasoning. At the same time, the legalization of something one wants to reduce appears to be paradoxical or illogical. Nevertheless, by examining the difficulty at the next level of analysis one is able to observe that such laws are not only unenforceable, except in ways which discriminate against some members of the population, but in fact contribute to the difficulties one wants to eliminate. The solution creates a problem which exacerbates the difficulty. (See also Chapter X, especially the discussion of victimless crimes.)

A second example, offered from Watzlawick's work with probation officers, involves the desirability for the legal offender to trust his probation officer. Both parties know, however, that the officer is not only a helper, but also an agent of the state. This illogical relationship is dealt with by advising the officer to tell his clients "you should never fully trust me or tell me everything." The probation officer's paradoxical statement, which seems to be the opposite of what he wants, makes him trustworthy because he has declared himself untrustworthy (which in fact is true).

These two examples are what Watzlawick *et al.* call problem resolution by paradox. Such thinking is aimed at those situations where the common sense solution is to try to prevent a difficulty by introduction of its opposite, which usually provides only the illusion of a solution. Rather than stopping the use of marijuana, the law simply limits the choices available to "break the law or not." Its legalization on the other hand creates multiple alternatives for how it will be used. In the case of the probation officer, saying "trust me" (his aim) would make the officer untrustworthy, since everyone knows he is an agent of the authorities. Saying "do not trust me" makes available to the probationer the *possibility* of trust, since the officer is seen to tell the truth.

Watzlawick *et al.* present many other examples and techniques from interpersonal relationships, the specifics of which need not concern us here. Rather, we can draw implications from

---

[6]These authors make a distinction here between a difficulty and a problem. A difficulty is the situation which one wants to change. A problem is the outcome of attempted solutions (often quite logical) which do not solve the difficulty, and often exacerbate it.

their analysis for community psychology. One such implication is directly taken from their recommendation that change agents need to investigate the solutions offered so far, because they may be creating the problem and exacerbating the difficulty. The history of the helping professions (see Chapter II) has shown us that we tend to repeat the solutions of the past in a "Game Without End." As Watzlawick *et al.* put it:

The handling of many fundamental social problems—e.g., poverty, aging, crime—is customarily approached by separating these difficulties as entities unto themselves, as almost diagnostic categories referring to essentially quite disparate problems and requiring very different solutions. The next step then is to create enormous physical and administrative structures and whole industries of expertise, producing increased incompetence in even vaster numbers of individuals. We see this as a basically counterproductive approach to such social needs, an approach that requires a massive deviant population to support the raison d'etre of these monolithic agencies and departments (p. 159).

In the mental health system our aims are presumably to increase the independence and functioning of people who have problems in living. In order to do this we have set up a system which follows from common sense. The system provides "psychological support" for those people viewed as incompetent to make their own decisions. They are isolated and protected from the real world until they are "ready for it." We have already seen how the large mental hospital has failed in this regard, and how community mental health programs have been instituted as a means of providing services in the community. Unfortunately, such programs tend to provide services that continue to be based on the assumption that the way to enhance independence is to take away the client's responsibilities until he is ready for them, or to solve the problem of the large mental hospital by simply releasing its residents, or to train them in a controlled setting and then release them to an uncontrolled setting; or to provide them with drugs to reduce anxiety. Each of these methods follows from an individual analysis of "mental health," and can produce only first-order change. To produce second-order change the system itself must be changed.

We need to examine in what ways the mental health rules of the game label deviance as illness, isolate deviants, and take away, rather than provide, the resources necessary for independence. Paradoxically, to foster independence a system may need to be organized around a set of rules that provides the necessary support in terms of physical resources, and then allows the "incompetents" to make their own decisions and find psychological independence for themselves. Jobs, money, and personal control over the decisions that affect one's life may be a prerequisite for mental health, rather than a consequence of it. The implications of this thinking and the work of those who have begun to explore it are discussed more fully in Chapter IX.

In the educational system many of our social welfare programs are focused on providing educational opportunities for "disadvantaged" or "deprived" children. Most of these programs view the child as the problem and try to change the child to fit into the educational system. Often the family is blamed for the child's lack of preparation for school. Such programs are doomed to first-order change. In order to obtain second-order change, the educational system's rules of the game need to be changed. Here again issues of diversity, power, and control will be crucial. Paradoxically, the poor and the uneducated, rather than the "experts," may need to control the education of their children if their children are to benefit from the schools they attend. These issues are examined in Chapter VIII. Likewise, in the legal system (Chapter X) and in housing and employment many of the problems with which community psychology is concerned may be a function of our solutions rather than the apparent difficulties. Once again, second-order change may require a change in the rules of the game. To reiterate, if change techniques are based on principles and levels of intervention (the how and the where) that are inappropriate for the difficulty area, the solution itself may create or exacerbate the original problem. In a sense this is a problem of mis-diagnosis, and of what might be thought of as iatrogenic effects, or negative effects which are an unintended result of treatment. A final example will be helpful at this point.

Timothy Wolfred (1974; Wolfred & Davidson, 1977) has recently reported the outcome of a program designed to prevent the need for institutionalization of young children who had come into contact with the law for a variety of reasons. Most of these children were school truants or runaways and had committed various juvenile offenses. They were often difficult to control and disrespectful of teachers and parents. Many had been in and out of various foster homes. Following some of the most promising research on individual treatment, a program was set up to help these youngsters based on the principles of behavior modification and social learning which systematically applied reinforcement for positive behavior on a carefully worked out individual basis. Each child was admitted to a residential setting for a period not to exceed 90 days, was evaluated, and a "program" was set up so that the child's behavior was carefully monitored. Performance goals in school and in daily behavior were set, and rewards made contingent on their completion. Almost all of the children met the goals set for them during the time they were in the program, including school attendance and conduct goals.

The assumptions of this behavior modification program were that the children would learn prosocial behaviors that would socialize them and enable them to live in the community without further difficulty. Wolfred wanted to test this logical assumption and set up a program evaluation study. Because this program was operating in a small city, almost all the referrals received were admitted. This made a true control group (referred but not admitted) impossible to find. Consequently, he found a comparable group of children in a nearby city which had no similar program. He selected a group of children who were matched on demographic and situational characteristics to the children admitted to his program, and who local authorities said they would refer if there were a program. Follow-up data as much as nine months later were collected on all identified children in both cities. Much to the surprise of the research team the children who were "untreated" were significantly more likely to be living in a foster home or with their family, while the treated children were more likely to be in an institution. This occurred de-

spite the fact that the children in the treatment program were successful in completing the goals of their program. That is, their individual behavior had improved while being treated, and was certainly no *worse* than the behavior of the comparable children. What had happened?

First, it should be clear that the behavior modification program was successful. That is, each child did change his or her behavior in conduct areas where previous difficulty had been encountered. Theoretically, this should have led to their return to the community and to greater success at meeting its demands. It is a good example of "an error of logical typing." The intervention was apparently applied to a difficulty which requires change at the institutional and community level, rather than at the individual level. By focusing attention on the individual children the program seems to have communicated to the responsible agencies of the community that these individual children were "bad," "deficited," "delinquent," or whatever label one prefers. They were then sent to a residential-institutional setting which removed them from the community and took pressure off the local agencies to find a noninstitutional placement. The children in the other city were more often placed in community homes despite the fact that the agency resources and people were quite comparable to those in the "treatment" city. In the treatment city the "solution" to a difficulty may have actually exacerbated the problem which it was designed to alleviate, by labeling children and by making their institutionalization more rather than less acceptable.

It is to the credit of the program's administrators that once this outcome was realized they began to change their focus to work with other local child welfare agencies to find community placements, including group homes where a small number of children who cannot be placed in a foster home can live together with a house parent. The efforts now are to demonstrate to others that these children are not different from their own, and that they need to be provided with alternative settings in the community where they can learn to live on their own as legitimate members. Similar examples are abundant in the realm of hospital care for "mental illness" in which individual people are often treated and released only to return to the hospital when they find no way to fit into the larger social system (see Chapter IX).

In order to cope with community difficulties, the psychologist must be prepared to work simultaneously at multiple levels of society. Depending on the particular difficulty and on the local situation, he or she will need to apply appropriate measures based on assumptions about community, organizational, and institutional change. Individual change procedures may be helpful and even necessary for dealing with some individual problems. It may be that behavior modification is useful for individual behavior change. But not all community problems are individual. Often they require change at other levels. Sometimes working to change individuals not only diverts resources, but also exacerbates the problem. In later chapters we shall see how the work aimed at individual preschool education for poor and minority group children has diverted attention from change in the school system itself, which may actually be the source of the problem.

Programs called "prevention" are not necessarily programs applied at the appropriate level. Often programs such as the one reported by Wolfred above or those described as preschool intervention are justified because they presumably deal with large numbers of children before they are in serious emotional, legal, or educational difficulty; that is, they are programs to "prevent" the difficulty. Nevertheless, it should be clear that such preventive programs may still commit an error of logical typing by assuming that community difficulty may be solved by working only at the individual level. It is often likely that both individual and community level interventions are required, and it is community, organizational, and institutional change which is most frequently ignored.

Conceptions of Environments and Systems: The Ecological Paradigm as a Conceptual Alternative

In order to focus attention on community change at other than the individual level certain assumptions about individuals, different from those that

are made in programs of individual change, are necessary. To begin with, an emphasis on the strengths of the individual people in a system is required. This is the view taken by Berck and by Sanford above. An assumption is made that given available resources or alternatives most individuals will solve their own problems in living. One need not deny the possible utility of individual help, but emphasis is on already existing strengths and skills which may come to the surface in an environment other than the one normally provided by predominant systems. Here again the emphasis on strengths leads to a psychology based on values of person-environment fit rather than on changing all to fit into one "best" environment.

A psychology of person-environment fit requires some attention to the principles by which environments operate, and must begin with an observation of environments and systems rather than of persons. Some of these conceptions begin with observations of the physical environment, others begin with individual perceptions of the environment, and still others, rather than beginning with observations of people within a system, start from variables and principles which are system properties independent of people and applicable to all systems. For example, Watzlawick's application of the Theory of Groups and the Theory of Logical Types is a form of systems analysis without reference to people. It is in this sense a metatheory, or a theory about all systems and the *rules* by which they function, rather than about a specific system. Such analyses may then be applied to prediction about behavior within a given system, including one where the elements are persons.

Much of the thinking of this sort is derived, at the most general level, from the biological sciences (Bertalanffy, 1968), and from information theory and cybernetics (Bateson, 1972). At a less general level are principles of social ecology derived from biological ecology, and at a more person-oriented level are notions of environmental psychology and social science observation in the natural environment (Willems & Raush, 1969). Each of these approaches is quite different, with its own set of methodology and concepts, yet for the community psychologist they share a common directional focus. To a greater degree than most purely psychological paradigms, including the behavioral, the observer looks outside of persons to assess environmental variables.

Rudolph Moos (1973, 1974a) has recently surveyed several different approaches to the assessment of human environments. In his review he cites two approaches that have already been discussed with regard to community psychology. One is the identification of reinforcement contingencies, or a functional analysis of the relationship between specific situations (environments) and behavior. This is based on the behavior modification–social learning paradigm discussed in Chapter IV. A second viewpoint identified by Moos is what he calls the "average background characteristics," or a view of the environment as a function of aggregate person characteristics. The variables in this approach include intelligence, occupation, education, sex, and personality assessment. The implications of this view of "environment" appear to be consistent with traditional person-oriented psychological interventions. The third approach is *organizational psychology* reviewed in Chapter VI, which is devoted to strategies and tactics of intervention.[7] A fourth approach to environmental assessment involves measurement of the geographical, physical, and architectural (or man-made) environment. This approach is discussed below as *environmental psychology*. A fifth view is Roger Barker's *ecological psychology*, and a sixth involves measurement of *organization climate* through the perceptions of participants or observers. To this list may be added a seventh viewpoint known as *general systems theory* and an eighth known as *social ecology*. What follows is a discussion of these latter viewpoints: environmental psychology, ecological psychology, general systems theory, and social ecology.

In describing these viewpoints it will be clear that they are primarily conceptual in nature and have had little direct connection to actual community interventions. Nevertheless, there is some variation in this regard, and the implications of each viewpoint for community intervention will be noted as each is discussed. The paradigms may be thought of as on a continuum away from traditional psychology. The one closest to traditional psychology is environmental psychology. Its nearest relative is probably operant psychology and cognitive social learning theory in that, as the name suggests, they share an emphasis on careful descriptions of environmental variables. Environmental psychology, however, tends to focus on the more purely physical characteristics of the environment.

Environmental Psychology

Environmental psychology has recently been presented in collections of readings (Proshansky, Ittelson, & Rivlin, 1970; Wohlwill & Carson, 1972) and in a chapter of the *Annual Review of Psychology* (Craik, 1973). It is a somewhat difficult field to summarize in that empirical studies covering a wide variety of variables far outnumber theoretical systems for organizing them. Craik's (1973) review chapter is less than ten pages long, but has an equal number of pages devoted to a list of 280 references. This field is noted for its multidisciplinary character, with contributions from researchers in sociology, geography, planning, architecture, and anthropology. Craik's classification of topics researched includes environmental assessment, which for psychologists means a careful analysis of physical-spatial properties and the use of space; perception of the environment by people of varying personal and demographic characteristics; and environmental decision making with regard to planning the physical environment, including residential, institutional, and recreational environments. This latter topic brings the research closest to applications of relevance to community psychology.

According to Proshansky *et al.* (1970) there are several distinctive features of what he calls "environmental science." These are summarized as a study of "man-ordered" environments. Ironically, although environmental psychology has served as a means by which

---

[7]Although the distinction between conceptions and strategies and tactics is somewhat arbitrary, organizational psychology has tended to tie its thinking more directly to intervention than the other orientations reviewed in this section.

psychologists have begun to consider the impact of the physical environment on people, for the other disciplines it is a means by which they can begin to consider the person variables that have historically been ignored or assumed to be unimportant (e.g., in areas such as urban planning and architectural design). The two broad classes of environmental psychology include research on "environmental quality" and on the impact of architectural and spatial arrangements on people. Specific content areas that have occupied the attention of environmental psychologists have included the effects of crowding on mice and humans, air and noise pollution, and the impact of architecture on behavior in institutional settings, including mental hospitals and prisons.

Theoretically, although such research of the design of "ideal" physical environments to meet the chosen behavioral goals for planners and controllers of organizations is feasible, most of the work of environmental psychologists remains at the level of descriptive research rather than direct action. Wohlwill and Carson (1972) suggest that the "payoff" from such research will lie in the formulation of laws and regulations concerning land usage and access, use of space, and maintenance of environmental quality. Other applications might involve planning and redesign of buildings for residential, recreational, educational, or mental health service on the basis of empirical research. For example, if amount of social interaction is a variable of importance in a given setting, knowing what kind of buildings and room arrangements increase or decrease such interactions would allow for better planning of man-made environments.

The sort of information that environmental psychology accumulates with regard to organizational settings is typified by the work of Ittelson, Proshansky, and Rivlin, (1970, 1972). These researchers examined four different psychiatric units in three hospitals, two wards of a state hospital, and units in a city and a private hospital. They categorized the nature and location of social behavior, given differential physical arrangements. For example, they recorded the use of bedroom space as a function of the number of persons assigned to the bedroom and found that when one to three persons were assigned to a single bedroom, activities were more varied than when larger numbers of people were assigned to the same bedroom. Social as opposed to isolated activity was also more frequent with smaller room assignments. From this and similar data they have argued that most of the withdrawn behavior shown by patients took place in the presence of others, that is, when they did not have the physical option of being alone. Contrary to folklore of the psychiatric ward, it is the large occupancy room which provokes withdrawal. Similar kinds of information have been offered by Glaser (1972) with regard to prison living arrangements. He suggests, for example, that the practice of housing delinquents or "training school" inmates in dormitories is actually one factor in the spread of criminal attitudes and behavior, and that single rooms or cells not only permit privacy, but reduce the likelihood of such criminal influence on younger inmates. Private rooms may also foster more rehabilitative activities such as reading.

Little attention has been paid to how research documenting a relationship between physical environment and human behavior can be translated into effective action. The methods advocated for dissemination and use of such information are not dissimilar from those normally used by social scientists, that is, publication of results or direct input to planners. Depending on the kind of information generated, the target of change may vary. If patient or inmate room assignments can be feasibly changed it may not be too difficult to encourage an organization to participate in research on the effects of different assignments, or to simply supply information generated elsewhere and encourage them to use it. When remodeling of a physical environment is needed the target of information would likely be at higher levels of the organization, although support from lower-level personnel who have participated in accumulation of data would also probably be a sensible tactic. Obviously, the planning of new buildings would require providing input to architects and higher level administrators.

The translation of data, such as the behavioral effects of environmental pollution, into organizational planning and change actions are not confronted by environmental psychologists in other than a superficial way. Swan (1972), for example, reports a review of professional journals to discover the suggested role of the public in promoting environmental quality and participation in decision making. He found three types of articles. One type suggests public opinion polls to determine the significance of the problem. As he points out, such polls may be used to justify no change, since many people will have "adapted" to poor environmental conditions and in a sense be willing to live with them. A second type of article Swan terms a "rhetorical plea" for consideration of the public in management; and the third type he found is concerned with how to run effective campaigns for bond elections to support environmental improvement. He found no discussion of public involvement before such decisions are made, and he suggests that participation of the public in such problem solving is essential. In this regard a recent article by Abram and Rosinger (1972) suggests that the means to improvement of environmental quality lie in the public education domain where attitudes and values of the public can be assessed and influenced.

Summarizing, the general position in this field with regard to change strategies seems to be one of support for research on the behavioral impact of architecture, physical characteristics, and environmental quality, with dissemination of that research by means of professional journals and education of both the planners and the public. In that sense it is a data-based strategy as described in Chapter VI, although often the psychologist will be an unaffiliated rather than an affiliated change agent (see p. 202). It is assumed that accurate information disseminated through the usual channels of public and scientific communication will lead to social change.

For community psychology the importance of the work of environmental psychologists lies less in the realm of strategies and tactics than in the explicit study of physical variables as they affect human behavior. Such data may serve as a rational basis for goal selection in the planning and change of living environments. The orientation is presented in this section because it is a step in the direction of exploring behavior in its environmental context, and as such it is a conceptual stepping stone to the next level of analysis, broadly represented by the term ecological psychology.

Ecological Psychology

The ecological viewpoint in psychology has been championed for many years by Roger Barker and his colleagues and students at the University of Kansas. The term "ecological" as associated with Barker has a very special kind of meaning which is more specialized than the way it has been used in this volume. The ecological approach to community psychology as used in this book has emphasized a view of *social intervention* stressing the *creation of alternatives* to maximize *person-environment fit*. In that regard some of the work of Barker is relevant, but it does not have a one-to-one correspondence with our use of the term. He is less concerned with intervention than with description. The relevance of Barker, for our purposes, lies in his emphasis on the importance of understanding behavioral "rules" in the natural setting where behavior takes place, rather than in the laboratory or in some idealized notion of how people should behave (see also Price & Blashfield, 1975).

Much of Barker's contribution lies in the conception and theory of *behavior settings* (Barker, 1968) and in methods for their assessment. A behavior setting is defined by one or more regularly occuring "standing patterns" of behavior that are "self-generated," that is, not arranged artificially by a researcher. A standing pattern is one that has definite time and space characteristics and does not depend on specific persons. The behavior persists even when persons change. For example, a basketball game or a worship service are behavior settings. The *milieu* is a part of the behavior setting and it includes its physical, temporal, and spacial aspects. The behavior and the milieu of a setting are seen as interdependent. For Barker, the importance of ecological psychology follows from the belief that the laws that govern individual behavior are different from those that govern behavior settings, and behavior settings are seen to account for a great deal of human behavior in the natural environment. By this reasoning one can never understand the real world if one only studies people characteristics or contrived settings and manipulations.

Barker provides an example which presents his argument that a "new science" of human ecology needs to be developed. Suppose someone who had never seen a baseball game wanted to understand the environment of a baseball player. The person might examine the first baseman through field glasses and view the player's behavior as he interacts with balls thrown and caught, players passing by, and so on, but the viewer would never understand the game itself. One might interview the first baseman and understand the player's aspirations, perceptions, and so on, but the interviewer could never know about the game itself. Rather, Barker argues, the observer would learn more about the game if he blotted out the player and observed the game around him. In this view the players are interchangeable. Again, to understand a school environment the teachers and pupils are viewed as interchangable. It is the behavior setting of the classroom that determines most of what happens there.

In essence, Barker's emphasis is on observing the rules that govern behavior settings of various types. The rules are to be discovered by examining settings rather than the people. His most recent work (Barker & Schoggen, 1973) is a comparison of behavior settings in an American and an English town, and describes in some detail the differences in number and kind of behavior settings available in each town. For example, children and adolescents in the midwestern town are shown to have more important and powerful positions in the behavior settings of their town. In the midwest more settings are child centered. Such empirical-descriptive accounts of the environment, which took over ten years to compile, are taken to be necessary to understand what really goes on in a natural environment. In this regard Barker suggests that field stations need to be set up in various communities to collect information about ongoing behavior over a long period of time.

Some of Barker's early work (Barker & Gump, 1964) was focused on public schools. Although not initially aimed at applied issues, the work does have many implications for the design of school environments, and serves as an example of an ecological approach to questions such as the effect of size of schools on their inhabitants. If translated into planning and action these data could be useful to educators, administrators, and communities in determining size of their schools. With this in mind it has been summarized by Gump (1974).

These researchers studied 13 schools in Kansas, ranging in size from 35 to 2287 students. In each school they classified the variety of subject matter offered to students. As can be seen in Figure V-2, as size of school increases so does variety of instruction; however, it takes large increases in size to get relatively small increases in variety. Perhaps of more interest is the fact that individual students in large schools do not actually attend a larger variety of classes than those in small schools. What is theoretically "available" is not the same as what actually happens for a given student. Rather, in larger schools not all offerings are available to all students, and some students tended to "specialize," for example in mathematics or music. Contrary to expectation, children in small schools actually participated in a larger variety of classes. As Gump points out, the question "which is better?" depends on what the goals are. Do we seek more opportunity for "specialists" or a broader academic experience for the general student body?

Size of School	Variety of Instruction
Median	Median
Very Small (2) 40	12.5
88	13.5
Moderate (2) 185	16.5
Large (2) 339	21.5
Larger (1) 945	23
Largest (2) 2105	28.5

Figure V-2. Does increasing school size produce a corresponding increase in variety of instruction? (Redrawn from Gump, 1974.)

Similar data were observed with regard to extracurricular activities such as student council meetings, class plays, athletic events, and clubs. Although there were over four times the number of activities available in a big school, variety of participation for any given person was actually larger in the small schools. More importantly, in the large school a sizable minority attended very few activities. In essense, in a large school some proportion of the student body tends to get lost. In this same vein the researchers examined the opportunity of students in large or small schools to be performers in activities as opposed to observers. They found that although more settings (activities) theoretically were available to students in the large schools, the number of settings engaged in per student was actually far greater in the small schools. For example, in one large school 794 juniors were exposed to 189 settings and each student averaged 3.5 performances over a three-month period. In the small schools, with an average of 23 juniors, there was exposure to only 48 settings, but an average of 8.6 performances per student. Most interesting was the fact that in the large school 28 percent of the juniors performed in no activities, while in the small school only 2 percent were nonperformers. Again, the large school created a group of "outsiders."

Similarly, the nature of the satisfactions expressed by students in small schools tended to emphasize competence rather than vicarious enjoyment because more of them actually participated in activities. In addition, students in the small schools, *regardless of their academic standing,* expressed the feeling that their school depended on them to perform in activities. They felt more community responsibility than students in the large schools. In large schools the academically marginal were also socially marginal. Gump argues that the problem in large schools is not one of teacher or administrator behavior which excludes students but rather, as an organization increases in size "selection into" and "selection out of" works automatically. Again, as schools increase in size so does the percentage of drop-outs.

The implications of these data are clear, yet the tendency in most locations is to consolidate rather than retain small schools, usually for reason of cost and perceived need for specialized instruction. However, the social cost may be far greater than is often realized. In our cities the tendency to have very large public schools not only removes many students from participation but may also remove the school from the control of and identification with its local community, an issue which is discussed in some detail in Chapter VIII.[8]

On the basis of their research in schools, Barker and his colleagues have concluded that the size of an organization is of marked importance for the behavior and satisfaction of its members. Specifically, they hypothesize that organizations that are "undermanned" encourage members to take positions of responsibility and engage in a wider range of behavior than organizations that are "overmanned." Alan Wicker (1969b) has extended the findings of Barker and Gump to religious institutions and found that size of church membership seems to create similar effects. This research has expanded the above findings to middle-aged adults as well as adolescents, and included behavioral measures such as attendance and monetary contributions to the church, as well as self-report data. In addition, all churches studied by Wicker were in the same urban area, so that the results of differences could not be attributed to urban or rural locations, which might have accounted for the results of the earlier school research.

Wicker found that individual members of small churches took part in more activities, had more leadership positions, attended church more often, and contributed more money than members of large churches. Table V-3 presents the mean data for a sample of people from large and small churches. He also found similar correlational data when he examined over 100 churches ranging in size from 23 to over 1500 members. As Wicker notes, the results of his research fit very nicely with the research of others who find

---

[8]It might also be noted that this same tendency to "consolidate" schools has also been the trend in many rural areas.

TABLE V–3   Behaviors in support of church behavior settings.*

Behavior	Large church (N = 34)	Small church (N = 30)	t
Sunday worship services attendance	15.8	24.8	3.30*****
No. behavior settings entered	7.4	9.2	1.11
No. kinds of behavior settings entered	4.6	6.2	1.81***
No. behavior settings in which S was a worker or leader	2.6	4.0	1.35**
No. behavior settings in which S was a leader	2	1.1	3.00*****
No. hours spent in behavior settings	29.2	43.5	1.90***
Amount of money pledged, 1966–1967	$128	$214	2.92*****
Amount of money given, 1966–1967	$111	$187	2.53****
Amount of money pledged, 1967–1968	$137	$255	2.83*****

*From Wicker, 1969b.
Note: All *t* tests are one-tailed. The time periods for the above behaviors were as follows: Sunday worship service attendance, September 1966, through May 1967 (39 Sundays); participation in church behavior settings, January 1, 1967, through April 15, 1967 (15 weeks); contributions to the church, June 1, 1966, through May 31, 1967 (52 weeks).
**p < .10.
***p < .05.
****p < .01.
*****p < .005.

that small organizational units have lower absence and turnover rates than large units (Porter & Lawler, 1965) and with the work of Latané and Darley (1970) who find that the likelihood that people will come to the aid of others in distress is increased as the number of others present is reduced.

For community psychology the content implications of this research are clear. Some (see Sarason, Chapter VI) have hypothesized that the major problem for community psychology to solve is how to foster a "sense of community." The importance of sense of community, of internal locus of control, of power versus alienation, and of under- versus overmanned organizations all seem to fit together to suggest a desirable goal direction for community psychology. The Barker and Gump and the Wicker data would seem to indicate that small organizations enable greater participation of more members in key roles and may be a crucial variable in creating a sense of community. Although Barker and his associates have not concerned themselves with the strategies and tactics of changing or creating such organizations, their research does point to the sense of the strategy and tactics

reviewed in Chapter VI under the headings "Creation of Alternative Settings" and "Community Organization and Social Advocacy." These strategies expressly aim to involve local members of a community in the control of their own social institutions.

Organizational Climate

Another way in which organizational environments have been studied is provided by the work of Rudolph Moos and his colleagues, and has been described as assessment of "organizational climate" (Moos & Insel, 1974). Following the work of Barker and of Mischel (see Chapter IV), Insel and Moos (1974) suggest that the social demands of a situation or an environment account for more of what goes on in a given setting than the personality of the individuals. This has led them to a view of environment *as perceived* by the persons in it. In that regard those using the organizational climate approach differ from both environmental psychology and Barker's ecological psychology whose adherents, like behavior modification advocates, prefer to describe the environment by means of observers other than the actual members. These latter researchers will observe the frequency of a given behavior, where and when it takes place, and so on, relying on trained observers. The organizational climate approach favors a description of the environment from the point of view of the participants rather than from an "objective" observer; it is an interesting combination of phenomonology and environmental psychology. Moos has constructed several *Social Climate Scales* (1974b) for the assessment of nine different environments, classified as four types: (a) treatment environments: hospital-based treatment programs and community-based treatment programs; (b) total institutions: juvenile and adult correctional facilities and military companies; (c) educational environments: university student living groups, junior high and high school classrooms; (d) community settings: social, task-oriented, and therapeutic groups, industrial and work milieus, families. For each of these identified environments Moos and his colleagues have created a scale which enables description of the environment from different points of view; for example, members (students, inmates, or patients) versus administrators and staff.

The characteristics of the environments studied have been classified by Moos into three broad categories: relationship, personal development or goal orientation, and system maintenance and change. Table V-4 presents the dimensions of each environment studied and classified according to their hypothesized function (relationship, personal development, or system maintenance). The names of the specific dimensions in Table V-4 are the scales on which members rate social climate. The scales falling under the relationship category have to do with the extent of interpersonal support perceived by the members. Personal development refers to the perceived opportunity for growth and self-esteem, while system maintenance and change assesses perceived orderliness, clarity of expectations, and responsiveness to change. Keep in mind that these perceptions are not necessarily veridical. For example, an environment may be viewed by its members as responsive to change,

but may not actually be so. Also, the final description of the environment is a sum of its members, such that not all individuals view it exactly as its mean description.

According to Moos (1974b) each of the Social Climate Scales is fairly independent and only moderately related to other organizational characteristics such as size of the organization or background of its members. He argues that the scales add information, not otherwise available, about how the organization is viewed by its participants. Furthermore, he argues that the scales have been shown to discriminate between different environments, and that differences on the dimensions make a difference in the behavior of their members. He cites a fair amount of research evidence supportive of the conclusion that different environments have different consequences for their members.[9]

At present it is not clear that the dimensions Moos has identified and scaled are really independent either of each other or of characteristics of the persons completing the scales, or exactly how much individual behavior and/or organizational outcome can be accounted for by the scales, or what other more specific aspects of social climate can be identified. Many of these questions have to do with the psychometric properties of the assessment instrument, and constitute a fertile field for future research (cf. Alden, 1975). For our present purpose (a review of conceptions useful to study of the environment) these questions can be put aside to examine the implications of this way of conceptualizing.

Trickett (Trickett & Moos, 1974) has argued that the task for the community psychologist is to develop a "framework" in which to view environments so as to assess both the structure and function of settings, and the probable con-

---

[9]For example, dropout rates, release rates, and stay in the community after release have been related to the climate scales (Moos, Shelton, & Petty, 1973). Similar data for effectiveness of military training environments have also been reported by Insel and Moos (1974). Trickett and Moos (1974) have recently reported on the relationship between rule clarity and student satisfactions, among other climate variables. For a bibliography see Moos (1974b).

TABLE V–4 **Similarities of social climate dimensions across environments.***

Type of Environment	Relationship Dimensions	Personal Development Dimensions	System Maintenance and System Change Dimensions
Treatment			
Hospital and community programs	Involvement Support Spontaneity	Autonomy Practical orientation Personal problem orientation Anger and aggression	Order and organization Clarity Control
Total Institutions			
Correctional institutions	Involvement Support Expressiveness	Autonomy Practical orientation Personal problem orientation	Order and organization Clarity Control
Military companies	Involvement Peer cohesion Officer support	Personal status	Order and organization Clarity Officer control
Educational			
University student living groups	Involvement Emotional support	Independence Traditional social orientation Competition Academic achievement Intellectuality	Order and organization Student Influence Innovation
Junior high and high school classrooms	Involvement Affiliation Teacher support	Task orientation Competition	Order and organization Rule clarity Teacher control Innovation
Community Settings			
Work milieus	Involvement Peer cohesion Staff support	Task orientation Competition	Work pressure Clarity Control Innovation Physical comfort
Social, task-oriented, and therapeutic groups	Cohesiveness Leader support Expressiveness	Independence Task orientation Self-discovery Anger and aggression	Order and organization Leader control Innovation
Families	Cohesiveness Expressiveness Conflict	Independence Achievement orientation Intellectual-cultural orientation Active recreational orientation Moral-religious emphasis	Organization Control

*From Moos, 1974b.

sequences of change. In this context he has studied the relationship of different kinds of classroom environments to student reactions in the class. Trickett argues that if one can specify "desired outcomes," then it is possible to examine the sort of classroom environments likely to produce them, and he suggests that the Social Climate Scales can be used to assess discrepancy between desired environment and perceived environment. For example, if an organization wants its members to perceive the environment as supportive, but finds that they do not, such data can serve as a basis for introducing structural changes.

Insel and Moos (1974) suggest four steps in facilitating social change in "small environments with a high frequency of interactions among milieu members." First, every member reports on his or her view of the environment. The Social Climate Scales serve here as a convenient means of systematizing the views. Each member also reports on how an ideal environment should be; for example, their goals and values are assessed. Again, this is done by use of rephrased versions of the scales. Next, individual feedback is given with emphasis on how various subgroups differ in their perceptions; for example, doctors versus nurses, managers versus line workers, or students versus teachers. Attention is also paid to differences in the "real" and the "ideal." Planning for changes agreed to as a consequence of such feedback is conducted in small groups with the aid of a "facilitator." Change is assessed by repeating the scales continuously as feedback. "This methodology is linked with concepts of problem-solving, coping, and adaptive behavior" (Insel & Moos, 1974).

The above methods of introducing change into organizations are essentially the same as those of organizational psychology, to be reviewed in Chapter VI. The prime strategy suggested is *data-based diagnositc surveys and systematic feedback* combined with the techniques of *organization development*. The major contribution of organizational climate scales to change strategies is as an assessment device which uses dimensions of description appropriate to the goals of human service organizations, a notable lack in organizational psychology which has tended to focus on production-oriented businesses. It is assumed that the community psychologist is either affiliated with the organization or contracted as a change agent. Questions such as what to do when the goals or values of the organization cannot be agreed upon, or when a minority in the organization is excluded, are not dealt with. Although perceptions of the organization by its members are related to outcomes of the organization there is no connection made between the desirable perceptions and how to create an organization that fosters them, other than to suggest that members participate in the decision making. How organizations function so as to create their outcome is not emphasized. In this context we turn now to a related viewpoint which has attempted to analyze more explicitly the *process* of organizational functioning.

General Systems Theory

Similar to the Watzlawick, Wakeland, and Fisch view of change, the conceptions of general systems theory are the most abstract to be reviewed thus far. They are more totally outside the realm of person variables than any of the other conceptions and, like the Theory of Groups and the Theory of Logical Types, are concerned with the "rules of the game." The concern of general systems theory is to describe how a system works by means of principles applicable to all systems. The viewpoints of biological ecology, information theory, cybernetics, and decision theory are included in this set of conceptions which has been used to understand families, organizations, institutions, and even world politics (Bateson, 1972). Systems theorists have not been directly concerned with the problems of community psychology, indeed most are not even psychologists, although some have used systems theory and the social psychology of organizations in conjunction (Katz & Kahn, 1966). Fortunately, a community psychologist, Stanley Murrell (1973), has recently reviewed general systems theory from the viewpoint of community psychology, and he has helped to concretize many of its general theoretical notions, together with implications for the community interventionist. Although most of the examples used here are different from Murrell's, his writing has made the task of understanding the implications of general systems theory considerably easier than would have been without his book.

As Murrell notes, a key aspect of general systems theory is the distinction between "open" and "closed" systems. Openness is probably a characteristic of all *social* systems; that is, a social system is in constant interplay with its surrounding environment. This is similar to the view suggested by social ecology below, and assumes that a school, a hospital, or any other organization must be understood in relationship to its larger environment. Katz and Kahn (1966) suggest that open systems continually take in and give out information. Information is viewed as similar to energy in a physical system. The *input* of information is transformed by the system's internal workings (its *throughput*) to create *output,* which is its product delivered to the environment, and which in turn *recycles* back to the system.[10] For example, a school trains a student who goes out to the community to work at a job; the former student earns money, pays taxes, and the taxes are used to support the school. Similarly, the schools teach students to read and write; some of them in turn read and write information which is sent back into the school and used by new students. If a school system excludes a student or does not prepare the student for the larger environment, that student experiences difficulty in the community, which in turn may create problems for the school, and so on. If a school is not responsive to its community's needs for training it will ultimately have difficulty with that community. For example, if a community requires a set of vocational courses or college preparation courses for its students, but this is not perceived

or responded to, the school will lose some of its usefulness to that community.

Open systems are said to tend toward increasing complexity and to store energy. In so doing an open system tends to develop the means to maintain itself, even if its original purpose is gone. For example, the mental hospital, despite widespread belief that it is counterproductive, has stored energy in various ways. It has developed roles and jobs and public support and expectations for its use. The only way it could be eliminated would be to change the rules for mental health system maintenance, that is, to stop training people to work in mental hospitals and allocating funds for their activities. However, part of the system now includes the legislative mental health lobby and the training establishments which continually turn out new workers. This in turn supports the training programs which get money from the legislature because of the perceived need for training of mental hospital personnel, and enables the trainers to expand their own staff, and so on. The same process is true for any system.

An open system is said to be in *dynamic equilibrium*—it continually makes gradual adjustments. However, it is assumed that adjustments which are too abrupt will create a reaction in the opposite direction so as to reestablish equilibrium. When the equilibrium is disrupted, the basic character of the system is threatened. Murrell suggests that in planning interventions this must be taken into account, lest a "backlash" be created to reestablish equilibrium. Others might argue that in some circumstances, such conflict is desirable, particularly if one wants to threaten the "basic character" of a system. For example, the systems which maintained segregation and voter exclusion of Blacks in the South were effectively changed by tactics which created abrupt disruption during the 1960's, after gradual changes had not been adequate. This principle highlights an important question for community psychology: "How much and how rapid a change is desirable?" The answer will depend on local conditions, but the principle is important. It highlights the conflict between those who argue

---

[10]This observation is similar to the principle of cycling of resources which is noted by social ecologists and reviewed below.

for gradual change and those who favor abrupt system disruption. These differing points of view have not been tested for effectiveness under differing circumstances, and at present they are logical rather than empirically based preferences.

Open systems are also said to become *differentiated* over time, that is, to develop specialized and insulated components. Some systems components have a great deal of influence on others, and some do not. Consequently, for systems intervention to be effective one needs to know *where* to intervene in a given system. For example, if a school's social service staff (psychologists, social workers) is isolated from the major functions of the school (e.g., what goes on in the classroom), no amount of "in-service training" or consultation for that staff will be as effective as will direct consultation to the teachers. On the other hand, in a school where the social service staff is actively influential, systems intervention may focus on them as a means to influence change. In other cases, where the aim may be to encourage the educational system to be responsive to local community members whose children attend the school, new channels may need to be created to break down the differentiation.

Another characteristic of open systems is called *equifinality*. As Murrell puts it, ". . . different internal states may result in the same end condition." Murrell suggests that this should alert the change agent to the fact that a "symptom" can be caused by many different mechanisms, and one cannot assume causality. This principle is similar to Graziano's notion of innovation without change and Watzlawick's "first-order change." It seems to suggest that many interventions which look like they should create change may not actually do so, and the community psychologist needs to examine the "rules of the game" before taking action. Examples of this could fill an entire book, and indeed it is the subject of one (Watzlawick *et al.*, 1974, see above).

Feedback, a concept borrowed from cybernetics, is an important notion for systems theory. There are two kinds of feedback—positive and negative. The former tells the system to keep going the way it is headed, the latter tells it to go back in the other direction. The thermostat is a classic example of a feedback mechanism used to keep a heating system within a desired range of temperature. Positive feedback tells the heater to keep going, negative feedback says stop. It is actually possible for feedback to get out of hand by keeping a system on course. One example Murrell cites is the child who is punished for academic performance which results in reduced motivation and further poor performance and on and on.

Often the feedback to a system is not current because there is a time lag. For example, by the time the thermostat registers the temperature in the room and tells the heater to stop, the actual temperature may be beyond the desired level. Consequently, feedback mechanisms may, either because they are insensitive, or too slow, or unable to anticipate side effects, mislead a system to continue on a course of action which is destructive to itself. More importantly, once the thermostat is set it does not make decisions about what the desired temperature should be; it simply keeps the system on its course.

In social systems the above is also true. Here, however, social values (rules for playing the game) will determine the "thermostat" settings. Gregory Bateson (1972) has discussed this very point and suggests that the importance of cybernetics for understanding social systems is exactly this fact. The thermostat represents the rules of the game, or the "bias" of the system. He notes that the state departments of many nations use game theory and computers to develop international policy. They identify the rules of the game, quantify and feed in the variables, and look for the best decision under the *current rules*. Those rules are thus reified, supported and affirmed as the ones to play by. "I submit," says Bateson, ". . . that what is wrong with the international field is that the rules need changing. The question is not what is the best thing to do within the rules as they are at the moment. The question is how we can get away from the rules within which we have been operating . . . ." (Bateson, 1972, p. 477.) The same is true for many of the social systems designed for health, education and welfare. We may need to set the thermostat with differnt values and priorities.

In sum, the principles of general systems theory, in addition to providing an orientation which helps us to look beyond specifics to the implications of an action for an entire system, focus the attention of community psychology on several questions of importance for any intervention. They tell us that in addition to deciding how to intervene in a system we need also to consider *where* to intervene, what the *side effects* may be, and how *abruptly* or *gradually* to introduce a change. Finally, the rules of the game, or the social priorities, need to be considered as changeable. The social values, or the rules of the game suggested in this book, are cultural relativity, diversity, and person-environment fit. However, whereas general systems theory provides a useful orientation, it lacks the specificity necessary for designing actual interventions. The final set of conceptions to be reviewed in this chapter, those of social ecology, have been used by some to apply principles similar to those of general systems theory to more specifically human systems and to social interventions.

Social Ecology

Social ecology has its conceptual foundations in biology, and was later extended into a model of human ecology used productively by sociologists. The first popular extension from plant to human organization was made by Park and Burgess (1921). This sociological-ecological model has been summarized in a recent critical analysis by Bernard (1973). She cites several emphases of the model as it has been used in sociology. One is examination of the distribution of land use as a resource. A second is the concept of community structure, which predicted changing patterns of urban growth; and the third emphasis is on the *processes* which were hypothesized to account for land use and patterns of urban growth. In this paradigm urban land use was expected to develop in systematic nonrandom patterns; for example, in concentric circles around a central business district, evolving into five "zones" of differential use. The

processes by which this occurs are described by analogies borrowed from biological ecology and are assumed to result from the natual competition for land use. *Competition* is said to result in *segregation* of land-use districts, followed by *invasion,* and ultimately a *succession* of land uses in the same space. This model was used to account for the predictable invasion by business into the immediately surrounding geographical areas, and invasion, over time, into the neighborhood of one ethnic group by another. "The whole set of processes—competition, segregation, invasion, and succession—was assumed to be as natural as the process by which fauna and flora related to one another in nature" (Bernard, 1973, p. 39).

Bernard goes on to describe this sociological paradigm as one deeply founded in the capitalistic ideology of individual initiative, free of government intervention. People were assumed to select where to live and where to establish their business on the basis of a "free market." Initially the paradigm was able to account for the rise of slums and the movement of ethnic groups from one location to another on their way "up" as the process of succession worked. In 1939 Faris and Dunham used the ecological model to relate mental disorder to the "natural areas" of a city's living patterns, showing prevalence of disorder to be highest in the inner city areas and to decrease as one moves out from the center of a city. According to Bernard, the paradigm began to fail to work for sociology when the "free market" policies of American economics began to be controlled by regulated monopolies, corporations, and the federal government. Intervention decisions to zone, plan cities, encourage roads, build homes, institute urban renewal, and so on, made the predictions of ecological sociology based on a so-called "free market" inaccurate. More importantly, competition did not operate as the model suggested. Black families with resources were unable to buy and move into new areas. The pattern of succession therefore broke down. Even the affluent Blacks were unable to move progressively out of the center city. "Community structure that had been relatively permeable . . . (with respect to other minority groups) rigidified when the Black man's turn came'' (Bernard, 1973). The so-called "natural" ecological processes failed to operate.

As the term ecology began to enter the vocabulary of psychologists it first took on a rather general meaning, which suggested that attention need be paid to one's place in the complexity of social systems and to ways in which systems themselves work. In the broadest sense it seemed to be a restatement of the "behavior is a function of person and environment" model of social psychology made popular by Kurt Lewin (1936) and lately reemerging in clinical psychology (see Chapter IV). Once again, an emphasis on "environment" which had been ignored by psychology was reemphasized. However, social ecology, although often difficult to pin down with regard to concrete actions of application, has evolved into a considerably more and different set of conceptions than simply an emphasis on "environment" or "social systems." The paradigm views environment neither in the minute sense of "stimuli" as suggested by behaviorists, nor in the often vague and unspecified sense of social forces. In one sense it is a refinement of the preventive orientation adopted by community mental health, but with some important differences.

As Trickett, Kelly, and Todd (1972) point out, community mental health has tended to view prevention as a search for *the* cause and *a* treatment rather than as a way of viewing humans in their natural environment with all the complexities and interactions of their past, present, and future experience and surroundings— social, physical, and psychological. Viewed in this way, social ecology suggests not discrete interventions aimed to solve specific isolated problems so much as a set of activities to foster the development of an organization or a community. Development suggests an ongoing natural process. Part of the difficulty in establishing social ecology as a paradigm of use to community psychology and the helping professions is exactly this aspect of it. It requires a shift from the design of treatments to the design of social interventions that will foster natural developmental processes. Although it suggests

general processes of systems functioning and questions to be asked, the viewpoint tends to emphasize empirical description of local conditions and makes it difficult to generalize from one place to another. It is a general orientation rather than a specific technology. It emphasizes description of a setting and its distribution of resources. The helping professions are not used to thinking about ways to mobilize existing community resources.

Social ecology is based on a longitudinal study of each locale analyzing its used and unused human resources and linkages between these resources. It involves planning and anticipation of impact on all parts of a given system. It requires understanding of people, but in the context of their particular setting and its resources and demands. It requires understanding of the way the organizations function and of the interaction of persons and surroundings. In the same sense, implied by Barker's notion of behavior settings, persons are not independent of the setting, they are a part of it, although as it unfolds in applied work social ecology seems to be more interested in person variables in their own right than is Barker's ecological approach. In some ways social ecology is an attempt to change the "rules" for viewing communities by looking at them at another level of analysis, exactly in the sense that Watzlawick suggests. In another sense it requires a genuine "paradigm shift" in Kuhn's terms, because the person and the environment are no longer viewed as independent or even as simply interactive—they are one unit of analysis. What is most difficult to understand is that the "principles" it seeks are general modes of functioning rather than specific technologies.

Just as sociologists applied the terms of biological ecology to their analysis of community development, so too psychologists relied on these terms to suggest principles of development in organizations and communities. The principles must be thought of as orienting "axioms" rather than as empirically verified (Trickett, Kelly, & Todd, 1972). There is always some danger in the application of an analogy from one field to another, yet the function of a paradigm is served well if it helps to organize thought and research and to generate testable hypotheses and actions. A large step in this direction has been fostered by the work of James G. Kelly and his colleagues, although as will be apparent below there is a great deal of "normal science" yet to be done if the paradigm is to become well established.

One of the most well-known observations of biological ecology, thanks to the recent interest in environmental pollution and conservation of natural resources, is that the introduction of change into a system will be likely to have multiple effects on that system, in addition to the one intended. Once noted, this apparently simple observation has profound implications. In terms of the ecology of the physical environment it is now well understood that use of chemicals in agriculture, leading to disruption of natural water supply and so on, has effects on our environment that may make the long-term value of such activities questionable. Fairweather (1972), for example, has noted that the use of fertilizers and pesticides so as to create apples unblemished by worm holes (desired by American consumers), has profound and hidden cost. The chemicals are carried by rainfall to rivers and lakes, upsetting the balance and growth of plants and bacteria, which in turn affects the oxygen content of the water and kills the fish—an unintended result of a presumably positive intervention. Even before such observations were popularly recognized Kelly (1966) was suggesting that the same phenomenon may be applicable to human systems, and cautioned that the development of community mental health centers aimed at providing new services may affect other services in unpredictable ways. We have since seen this illustrated in the mental health system. As community mental health centers have been developed, many communities have assumed that they would serve the poor who had admittedly received a small share of adequate services. But as community mental health centers fail to serve the poor who are now turned away (referred to the centers) by other services whose workers expect the center to perform that function, the unexpected effect of a new service may actually be to *reduce services* (see Chapter III, p. 78). A similar example was provided above (p. 138) in the experience of Wolfred (1974; Wolfred & Davidson, 1977) with regard to the impact of a new program for service to juveniles which actually resulted in more use of institutionalization by the community.

A second "primary feature" of the ecological analysis emphasized by Kelly is to redefine behavior not as sick or well, but as an outcome of interaction between a person and the social system. Adaptive behavior is seen to be a function of the requirements of the particular social setting, and as such cannot be viewed in absolute terms. This of course has been a major emphasis throughout this volume. Person-environment fit is viewed as a more sensible way to understand human adaptation. For example, the students in Barker and Gump's big school or small school could not be understood without reference to their particular ecological system. The kinds of behaviors adaptive in each school would be different. Similarly, Kelly's own research in high schools is designed to examine the ecological constraints or adaptation of its members. His major hypothesis is contained in a definition of adaptation:

Adaptation is viewed as specific to a particular social setting, and as dependent upon the congruence between the particular coping styles, that is, individual preferences for mastering the environment, and the normative requirements of the environment. Thus, a particular set of coping styles will be relevant to adaptation in one environment but not in another (Kelly, 1969).

In pursuit of this hypothesis Kelly has studied, over a period of years, two high school environments. The schools were selected on the basis of different "rates of exchange." In one school turnover rate of members was 42 percent per year, in the other less than 10 percent. He termed these schools *fluid* and *constant* and predicted differential impact on students. For example, he expected that the fluid school would result in changing social groups with membership based on competence, whereas in the constant environment there would result an unchanging status differential once established. People would be more likely to "locate themselves" rather than to "develop." The constant environment, he predicted, would be more preoccupied with deviant behavior, given its relative consistency.

In order to assess the environment and its members Kelly has developed measures of individual "coping style" to assess *anticipation* of future, *exploration* or preference for novel experiences, *locus of control* (see Chapter IV), and *social effectiveness*. He has also observed behavior in various school settings (principal's office, lavatories, hallways, and cafeterias), and interviewed individual students. Kelly's findings reported to date are supportive of his general hypotheses. Persons high in preference for exploratory behavior improve in their competence more in a fluid than in a constant environment, while the reverse is true for those who do not prefer exploration. In the constant school, life revolves around fixed status and group membership. In the halls both male and female students are observed to dress in more varied ways in the fluid school, and the halls are also noisier. Size of natural grouping is different in each school, as are rates of entering the principal's office and of talking to him or her. In the fluid school group membership varied more. Responses to new students in the constant school are found to be cautious. Only if the new student is dressed "properly" and is willing to become absorbed into the dominant pattern is the student accepted. In the fluid setting there is a more open set of options for new students and a wider range of possible entry points. In addition, high "explorers" are more likely to be labeled as "deviant" by the faculty in the constant environment than in the fluid environment.

The aim of Kelly's research has been to develop "preventive interventions" or ways to plan school interventions to help avoid difficulties for students. He believes that this can only be done if one first understands the natural environment or ecological constraints of a school. For example, he would expect fluid and constant schools and large and small schools to differ in the ways in which they offer help and in the kinds of services they require.

In an effort to further refine the ecological model Kelly and his colleagues (Trickett, Kelly,

& Todd, 1972; Mills & Kelly, 1972) have specified a set of "ecological principles" derived from the biological study of "ecosystems." The principles are offered as guideposts for assessment, planning, and intervention. They have been defined and explicated most recently in the context of community development and the development of high school envrionments.

The Principle of Interdependence.   This is a formal statement of the first observation cited above with regard to social ecology. ". . . Whenever any component of a natural ecosystem is changed there are alterations in the relationships between all other components in the ecosystem" (Trickett, Kelly, & Todd, 1972). Translated into programs for fostering development of organizations or communities this principle suggests that development of new resources requires the creation of new relationships between components of a system. This in turn means that the entire system must be well understood before intervening in it. Such understanding can only come from careful observation of the locale, not from a priori assumptions. For a community it means that new relationships must evolve from those already existing (Mills & Kelly, 1972); for an organization such as a school it means that new services must be based on understanding current and possible resources, including an historical understanding of that organization. Here one needs to know about the interdependence of roles of key persons in the system and the possibility for new options. For both local communities and organizations the crucial links between them and the larger community need careful analysis. The principle could be translated into an apparently simple imperative—"know the system before you try to change it." The problem from an action point of view is that it is not always clear when one does really "know" the system. It therefore could serve as a rationalization for inaction. There are some guidelines for assessment which suggest that key questions involve actual and potential roles of members, the resources and rules for their distribution, as well as the relationship of the setting to its surrounding environments. Trickett, Kelly, and Todd (1972) suggest many specific questions to be asked using the high school as an example, but it is clear that these are hypotheses and that the specifics to be examined will vary from place to place.

The Principle of Cycling of Resources. Just as the natural ecosystem is energized by the sun's light which is converted by plants and in turn eaten by animals, so too an organization or a community is said to distribute its *resources* by various rules, both formal and informal. These rules, which will vary from locale to locale, need to be understood before intervention can be designed. In essence, the intervener needs to evaluate possible new ways in which the organization can use its resources, including its people, so as to encourage development. For example, how are the secretaries and janitorial staff of a school used, and in what ways could their roles be changed to redistribute resources that are currently unused? Likewise, what resources are available but unmobilized in a given community? This principle, which makes explicit an emphasis on locating resources, is an orientation that is quite different from that suggested by the helping profession's typical paradigm. By the very nature of the helping paradigm's intention to deliver services the community is encouraged to rely on the helper rather than their own resources. As Kaswan (1975) has recently put it: "Both the reliance on expertise as the valued basis for problem solving and the institutionalization of service settings lessen the purposefulness and the need for interdependence among people in the community." The principle of cycling of resources suggests that the aim of the interventionist is to mobilize and help to redistribute existing resources, a viewpoint consistent with a strengths rather than a deficits model.

The Principle of Adaptation. This principle suggests that there is a continual development or change process always operating, and that people in an organization or a community are both influenced by it and in turn influence it. Each environment requires somewhat specific adaptive skills; for example, Kelly's "explorers" do better in his fluid school than in his constant school. Similarly, knowledge of Black dialect may be an important competence for teachers, as well as students, in one school and not another. In order to understand an organization or a community the adaptive skills it demands need to be described. These skills will vary from one setting to another and because people function in more than one system, may make conflicting demands on members. For example, the competencies necessary to adapt to a school environment may be in conflict with those necessary to survive in one's community. Consequently, the relationships between school and community, in terms of adaptive skills, need to be carefully assessed.

This point of view is at variance with current thinking which defines successful socialization in terms of functions internal to the organization. One premise of the ecological point of view is that maladaptive behavior in one setting may affect successful adaptation in a new setting. Upon the basis of this idea, the design for interventions must include ways to identify the diverse requirements of the social structure and the varieties of responses to such structures to which the student will be asked to adapt (Trickett, Kelly & Todd, 1972, p. 396).

The same principle as applied to a community suggests that "a primary method of inducing change in the direction of development is to provide the community with a greater variety of *niches*, or functional roles, while not directly threatening the status of those roles already legitimatized in the community" (Mills & Kelly, 1972). This suggestion is extremely important as a basis for the development of alternative settings which provide a community with the opportunity to develop and use its resources. Such programs are discussed in Chapter VI.

The Principle of Succession. This principle emphasizes the continual change of communities by means of what has been called "dynamic equilibrium." That is, the apparent steady state of a community is actually, when viewed in a longitudinal time perspective, a response to continual inputs and adaptations. It means that not only is a time perspective necessary to understand an organization and a community, but also that it is possible to anticipate rate and direction of change. For example, the sociological-ecology model was quite good at predicting the changes in neighborhoods, as ethnic groups gained a foothold in society, until a new and unanticipated factor was introduced into the system—racism. In order to assist in the development of a community or an organization, it is necessary to understand both its own direction of development and that of its surrounding community. Trickett, Kelly, and Todd suggest that such understanding can enable an organization to adapt to changes by translating it into new roles. If a school is able to adjust its curriculum to its community's development it can better prepare students for entry to that community. For the interventionist this means a focus away from working for changes in how individual people view their world (intrapsychic concerns) toward how the roles and structures of the organization "hook up" to resources of the community, such as jobs.

Some Implications of Social Ecology. To summarize the implications of this orientation Trickett, Kelly, and Todd suggest that interventions should be based on an understanding of *local* conditions and on a *longitudinal* assessment of the organization in the community; they should focus on anticipating effects of the intervention on all the members of a setting and use a wide variety of strategies and tactics for creating change. Trickett *et al.* further suggest that *accountability* requires this orientation which focuses on a local situation and is concerned with its future side effects rather than short-run data analysis. To these observations might be added the fact that such an orientation implies that given the opportunity to develop and use its own resources a community will adapt to its environment, and often the job of community development will require the interventionist to assist in the location and development of such resources. In doing this the psychologist is less likely to discover specific treatments for specific problems than to provide a *method of analysis* based on the principles cited above, which helps to discover and mobilize resources.

To some extent the academic research traditions of psychology do not reward the activities as described above. Psychology has tended to reward the search for universal "laws" based on classic controlled experiments and to encourage immediate evaluation and publication. To develop an ecological approach will require both a commitment to long-term work with a community and evaluation research which, if fruitful, will take years rather than weeks or months to complete. Even when completed, such research, although it may document general orienting principles, is unlikely to be directly applicable in terms of specific technology or "facts" for other communities. Rather, the sense in which it may contribute to social science as well as community development will be much more in terms suggested by Cronbach and Gergin in Chapter II, that is, as adding to our understanding of contemporary society. In that sense community psychology may be more like history, philosophy, and literature than like physics. Such a viewpoint, it must be emphasized, is *not* anti-research. It is pro-research. However, it does suggest that we may need a different kind of research than that emphasized by the standard experimental methods, or even by the quasi-experimental or program evaluation type (e.g., Campbell, 1969). It suggests research with more emphasis on long-term projects and use of ongoing description and feedback in *collaboration* with target people. That is, it may not be possible to isolate *the* controlling variables in an intervention, so much as to delimit a set of ongoing *processes* useful in understanding and developing communities. This does not preclude specifying the criteria for change, nor systematically and carefully observing the outcomes of actions taken.

In terms of research, what we now must recognize is that the traditional ideal of applying laboratory verified hypotheses to field settings is unrealistic as a means of developing community psychology. Rather than only transferring the results of laboratory studies to the natural environment, we will need to both generate and test hypotheses in the very settings we wish to change. This will require intimate first-hand knowledge of both the settings and the people who reside in them. In this sense, the combining of psychological methodologies and conceptions with those of other disciplines that deal with the same issues is highly desirable. Anthropology, as one example, may have a great deal to tell us about social ecology (cf., Cohen, 1976). However, we must also recognize that no single discipline really has the "answers" to our questions. If this is true, although we can now see a conceptual starting point for community psychology, the work of normal science, as we push the paradigm to its limits, is still very much before us.

The community psychologist is interested in change at multiple levels of society and therefore requires conceptions that go beyond the individual. Individual change is not necessarily the most useful target if one is interested in second-order (genuine) change in the rules of the game. Community psychology often seeks changes at the organizational and the institutional level and presumes that individual and community strengths will appear as resources are made available. Necessary resources are often in the form of material and psychological power. Power is conceptualized as both political and psychological. To obtain such power, organizational change, as well as the creation of parallel institutions and programs of social advocacy are often useful. The chapters that follow present guidelines for action programs based on this kind of community psychology. We turn now to a consideration of the concrete *strategies* and *tactics* of such community intervention.

STRATEGIES AND TACTICS
OF SOCIAL INTERVENTION

We are a people upon experiments . . . [I protest] against that unkind, ungrateful, and impolite custom of ridiculing unsuccessful experiments. . . . I am led to this reflection by the present domestic state of America, because it will unavoidably happen, that before we can arrive at that perfection of things which other nations have acquired, many hopes will fail, many whimsical attempts become fortunate, and many reasonable ones end in error and expense.

—*Thomas Paine*

Obviously, in planning a new system, [we] would have to examine many candidates-ideas and reexamine our value system to determine what it is we really want to maximize. Not easy work, to say the least.

—*Garrett Hardin*

In the preceding chapter it was noted that there are two ways in which community psychology may contribute to social change. One way to contribute is through public analysis of social policy. The second, with which this chapter is concerned, is by direct action, evaluation of outcomes, and diffusion of information and innovation. Direct action serves as a link between analysis and policy recommendations. It is from the tradition of an empirical and experimental rather than a purely observational-analytic science that community psychology has emerged. Although the methods of the experimental approach cannot be accepted completely for the problems of community psychology, the general attitude of experimentation, which calls for direct comparison of interventions, attempts to control as many extraneous factors as is feasible; and a healthy skepticism and consideration of alternative hypotheses requires that ideas be directly tested. In addition, community psychology has emerged from a human service tradition which places responsibility on professionals to do something directly about the social problems they observe. These two traditions combine to

lead community psychology into direct action.

The movement from analysis to action requires techniques for social intervention. Theoretically, such techniques should follow from conceptions about the level of society at which one is intervening. Conceptions of "how things work" at a given level of analysis should dictate strategies of intervention. The problem is often thought of as technological: "what change techniques, based on what conceptions, delivered how, when, where, and by whom, are appropriate and effective in changing what social systems, with what characteristics, given a particular level of analysis?" This is of course similar to the way questions of psychotherapy technique are now posed (Bergin & Garfield, 1971). It suggests that the problem is to fill in a kind of matrix of social situations, conceptions, levels of analysis, and intervention strategies such that given identified characteristics of a system one can look at the matrix to see that in such and such a situation the following techniques have been empirically demonstrated to have such and such a probability of obtaining a particular goal. It is tempting to say that this is a sensible way to look at the problem because it would make the process and aims of community psychology very similar to the process and aims of general psychology: to discover universal laws of behavior; and similar to clinical psychology: to develop change techniques from such laws. Only the content of problem areas under study would differ, and the underlying philosophy and method would remain unchanged. In some ways this is sensible. Attempts to fill in such a matrix probably should constitute much of the work of normal science in community psychology for the foreseeable future. Empirical data from different social interventions collected in defined systems, whose characteristics are well described, will clearly be of value. Nevertheless, it is difficult to be totally optimistic about the outcome of such normal science for at least two reasons. First, it may be impossible to conduct,[1] and second, it ignores one additional element—the influence of social values and goals on the selection of intervention techniques. Social values dictate goals, goals dictate the appropriate level of analysis, and in

turn the conceptions and strategies of intervention follow.

As we have seen in Chapter II, even for psychologists interested in individual behavior, the quest for universal laws seems to be ephemeral. Cronbach, Gergin, and others have suggested a different view—one which sees psychology as observing contemporary behavior in the context of contemporary social, cultural, and historical factors that may not necessarily be "truths" forever. If this view is accurate it may suggest a more appropriate way for social interventionists to approach the task of community change. In short, there are two perspectives that may be taken with regard to social intervention strategies and tactics. One is based on the assumption that certain principles which govern the functioning of the level of society at which one is working will dictate the methods appropriate to change at that level. For example, given organization "A" with structure "B," use technique "1" to accomplish goal "X." Knowing the principles operative at the given level of organization leads to appropriate

---

[1]Despite the value of such research, the genuine experimental test required to fill in such a matrix may be impossible to achieve because it would require direct comparison of strategies randomly assigned to similar systems, a situation which is rarely possible. While Campbell (1969, 1971) and others suggest ways to approximate this sort of research, such designs tend to capitalize on naturally occurring interventions rather than those predetermined by specific psychological principles or social change goals. Fairweather (as discussed later in this chapter) has come close to research which approximates the desirable, and he and other methodologists have suggested reasonable ways to approach such evaluation. There are now enough suggestions concerning methodology for comparison of interventions and analysis of outcome such that careful evaluation of direct action is theoretically always possible. The major reasons why it is not often done appear to be practical, ethical, and social rather than technological. Depending on where and with whom the interventionist is working, the need for evaluation, comparison, and resources for data collection and analysis must be more or less "sold," and as such requires social and interpersonal as well as scientific skill.

One additional point worth noting is that for some social interventions the evaluation of outcome may be obvious without complicated research design skills. To say this is undoubtedly a heresy, nevertheless, the point may be illustrated by example. Suppose a social interventionist working with a grass-roots group receiving public assistance was interested in helping to organize a welfare rights organization to obtain the maximum benefits to which they are legally entitled. Success would be obvious—whether the organization generated mem-

bership and results; that is, did the people obtain more resources? When the interventionist asks questions about the best ways to help organize other such groups in other settings, different tactics would need to be tried with similar groups and systematically compared. The chances are, however, that tactics will be determined by each specific situation rather than by general principles that can be *experimentally* tested. In some cases it might even be unethical to randomly assign tactics to groups. Certainly the various tactics could be described and analyzed as to effect within each intervention, and interventions could be evaluated with regard to other effects on participants, but is a classical experiment really necessary or possible? If the group gets organized and meets its goals, then that may be proof enough of outcome. Side issues of theoretical interest (for example, changes in the members' reported sense of personal control) can be investigated, but clearly these are of less significance than real-world changes that may only be *described* rather than experimented upon. To the obvious question, "why is this social science?" one can only answer that description and dissemination of information about how the organization was formed may be as useful to contemporary social science understanding and human welfare as true experiments which do not touch the real world. Program description in the model of the "case study" is, in this view, just as much a contribution to knowledge about contemporary society as laboratory experimentation. The important point for social science is that the intervention must be carefully described and evaluated, not that the evaluation necessarily be "experimental" in the narrow sense of the term.

strategies and tactics. The second perspective is that "principles" of functioning are not timeless, but rather change in ways that are not predictable. The specific strategies of social intervention, as well as the level of analysis selected, will be based, in this view, on the values and goals of the intervener, or on what the intervener wishes to accomplish, rather than on identifiable and objective "principles" of social change. In this view social values and goals are more important than the discovery of universal principles which govern social systems in determining level of analysis, conceptions, strategies, and tactics. Research is a straightforward evaluation of outcome rather than a search for universal principles.

In this chapter the view presented is a cross between the two perspectives above. Strategies and tactics of social intervention are seen to be affected both by the values and goals of the intervener and the level of analysis. If either the values and goals or the level of analysis are not considered explicitly the interventionist runs the risk of applying a tactic which may not only be ineffective in accomplishing the goals, but may even make matters worse from his or her own perspective. In sequence, the process suggested is that values and goals come first. These tend to influence one toward a given level of analysis. The levels include those noted in Chapter V (individual, group, organization, institution, community). Each level does function by principles that are not necessarily applicable to the other levels, and therefore requires study and conceptions of functioning and change appropriate to itself. Such conceptions may then lead to strategies and tactics for change. When the four factors (values/goals, level of analysis, conceptions, and strategies and tactics of social intervention) are inconsistent the outcomes are confusing and uninterpretable. When the interventionist confuses these four factors the risk of an error of logical typing and a game without end is increased (see Chapter V). It is only when the four factors are consistent with one another that they lead to useful information for social science and social policy, as well as to effective change strategies.

The Sources of Social Intervention Strategies

Within present-day community psychology there are four major sources of strategies and tactics for social intervention.[2] One source is individual clinical psychology and community mental health. This approach has already been discussed in Chapters III and IV. Summarizing, the underlying *values* and *goals* are that social problems are a function of the inability of some people, or even an entire subculture, to fit into the structures of society, or to be comfortable being different. People are seen to suffer from deficits. The place of applied behavioral science is to help as many people as possible adjust to the goals and norms of the small groups and organizations of which they are a part. The values of the institutions of society are basically benign and the organizations developed to accomplish these values do as good a job as one can expect, given human fallibility. If individuals differ from their society the problem is to decrease discomfort to self and others by changing or helping the person to live with the difference in a nondestructive way. These values and goals lead to an *individual level of analysis*. Understanding a person as an individual is the key to changing that person to be more competent, adaptive, fit in, and be comfortable with one's self and the available structures of society. The *conceptions* of individuals that have been developed range from the behavioral through the psychodynamic (see Chapter III, especially Table III-4). Depending on the specific problem this level of analysis may require, in Sarbin's terms (see Chapter IV, P. 110), helping persons to find their places in the self-maintenance, transcendental, or normative ecology. Social change is implied to be a summation of indi-

---

[2]There are a number of "theories of social change," but few which have been directly connected to intervention strategies. Some of these are theories of unplanned change, which assume that social change happens as a function of factors outside the realm of control. Others involve the application of direct force, that is, revolution. Here we are concerned with planned rational change and are limited to techniques that are nonviolent and have actually been used by social scientists in direct interventions.

vidual changes. Such conceptions lead to *person-centered strategies and tactics of intervention*. The community mental-health-oriented therapies such as brief treatment and crisis intervention (see Chapters III and IX) are examples. Training of new-person-power to work in the mental health field, as well as employment training for specific high risk individuals and other educational competence programs for children and for parents are also based on these values. The specific content of the interventions varies with the specific conception of how individual behavior works.

A second source of intervention strategies is interpersonal clinical psychology and community mental health. The *values* and *goals* of this viewpoint are related to, but somewhat different from, those of individual psychology. Social problems are viewed as created by interpersonal difficulties within primary groups, such as the family, peer, and work groups. Defects in the group rather than in the individual members are emphasized. Sometimes the problem is an inability of people in different groups to communicate with each other; for example, policemen and members of a given community. When these groups are not functioning well internally, or are in conflict with other groups, they not only have a negative impact on individual members, but also inhibit the ability of organizations to accomplish the necessary tasks for administering society's institutional values and goals. These values lead to a *small-group level of analysis*. If social problems are a function of interpersonal communication and conflict, understanding the dynamics of interpersonal relations and small-group interaction must be stressed. Two primary sources of *conceptions* are the group dynamics literature of social psychology and the group and family treatment literature derived from clinical psychology. Ecological principles can also be used to understand and adjust the functioning of the group and the person's place in it. *Strategies of social intervention* which follow from these values, level of analysis, and conceptions include family therapy, interpersonal communications training, sensitivity groups, and group therapy. It may

also suggest retraining of the agents of socialization to communicate more effectively with themselves and with the target people.

A third source of intervention strategies is the social psychology of organizations and various approaches to change suggested therein. The *values* and *goals* which underlie this source are based on the view that social problems are created by the organizations of society that fail to implement, as well as they might, the desirable values and goals of our social institutions.[3] Concrete organizations are imperfectly structured and administered such that they often fail to accomplish the values and goals of socialization as stipulated by work, education, health, and welfare institutions. The aim remains to enhance the likelihood that organizations will help individuals to fit into society; however, the problems are in the organizations themselves, rather than in the person. Less obvious, but often implied, is the emphasis on weakness and deficits of target people. This set of values leads to *systems-centered conceptions* from public health, social, and organizational psychology. Conceptions of the influence of deviant subcultures may be included. Power and alienation are posited as psychological variables. Social systems analysis, ecological, and environmental psychology may be used to understand and adjust the functioning of systems. The *strategies of social intervention* are those of public health and organization development. Systems-centered consultation and development of new structures, communication channels, and styles within existing organizations are emphasized. A vari-

---

[3]The distinction between *organizations* as specific facilities, usually but not necessarily contained within walls, which are the means by which society operates (e.g., a particular school and its practices) and *institutions*, or sets of social values, goals, and abstract procedures which tell organizations why they are there (e.g., the institution of public education and its values and biases) is important throughout this chapter. Schein's (1970) definition of an organization may be helpful here. He considers it to be ". . . the rational coordination of the activities of a number of people for the achievement of some common or explicit purpose or goal, through division of labor and function, and through a hierarchy of authority and responsibility." Note that for an organization the "common purpose or goal" remains implicit, and the emphasis is on *how* the organization goes about accomplishing it.

ety of organization development techniques (see below) is used. Programs of early identification of "high risk" persons in various locations, such as schools, the armed services, or in the general mental health system (i.e., by use of epidemiological techniques), are implemented. This strategy may be combined with secondary prevention which involves tactics such as development and introduction of new programs including any of the person or small-group-level strategies identified above.

The fourth source of social intervention strategies is based on a broad social analysis. The *values* and *goals* which underlie this source stem from a belief that social problems are created by our institutions rather than by persons, groups, or specific organizations. Although there are many problems in organizations that may be solved by specific changes, the real key to social change is in the culture, expectations, attitudes, values, goals, and the political-economic and social policy ideology of which institutions themselves are composed, and on which organizations are based. The distribution of power and other resources among the various communities of society is a crucial variable. Values supportive of diversity and the need for alternative pathways to success most strongly imply a search for environmental alternatives within a psychology of person-environment fit. Explicit emphasis is placed on the strengths of target people, cultural relativity, and the need for resources. This value system leads to an *institutional* and a *community level of analysis*. Because the institutions of society support and determine relationships within and between organizations and communities, these institutions hold the key to social change. Institutionally determined relationships limit the alternatives available to community members. The *conceptions* of this position are derived from various systems-centered social sciences. Power is a political and economic as well as a psychological variable. Principles of social action and community organization are emphasized. Because many people require new alternatives, an ecological viewpoint is useful to this value system and level of analysis. Two major classes of *social intervention strategies*

and tactics are the community organization–social advocacy model and the parallel institutions or creation of settings model (see also Table V-2). Tactics emphasize power, autonomy, and control by disenfranchised groups either within existing organizations or in newly created organizations. In either case the aim is to build organizations based on institutional assumptions different from those currently dominant in society. Choice between changing existing or creating new settings is a function of the specifics of the situation, which includes the resources of the particular group and the belief that existing structures ultimately will or will not yield power and control. These strategies and tactics may be combined with those at other levels of analysis, depending on the specific aims; and it is important to note that the change agent may need to work at multiple levels of analysis and intervention. In addition, any of the available research methods for collection of data leading to social policy recommendations and feedback for new intervention strategies may be applied at this level of analysis. Especially appropriate are methods typified by the unaffiliated data-based change agent, as discussed in the last section of this chapter.

These four sources of intervention strategies and tactics are summarized in Table VI-1. They are each based on a seeking- rather than a waiting-mode (see Table III-4). As one progresses from the individual to the community level of analysis, interventions at the lower levels are not necessarily precluded. Each higher level of analysis is inclusionary rather than exclusionary, such that the institutional and community level does not limit intervention to that level, but *includes the possibility of interventions at all levels,*[4] depending on the prob-

---

[4]There is danger in this statement if it leads the reader to conclude that one can create organizational or institutional change by *only* working at lower levels of analysis, or if it leads to confused goals. The intention of this statement is simply to acknowledge that higher levels of intervention will often require one to work with both individuals and small groups as part of an overall plan. For example, it may be helpful, when working toward organizational change, to find and work with members of the organization who share one's values and goals, or even to get more such people into the organization. Richard Price (personal communication) has

lem at hand. Often in practice the strategies of multiple levels of intervention are combined. However, the values which underlie the institutional and community level of analysis suggest that an intervention *limited* to a lower level of analysis may be incomplete. *The task for community psychology is to know when interventions based on conceptions from each level of analysis are appropriate to the goals.* Applying an intervention at the wrong level (an error of logical typing) will not create genuine (second-order) change. In this sense, one of the tasks of community psychology is to "diagnose" the appropriate level and "prescribe" an intervention suitable to change at that level.

For example, if I wish to change a school system so as to reduce the number of lower social class members who drop out of school, I first need to analyze the values behind such a desire. Do I view it as desirable for everyone to fit into the existing structures of the educational organization (the school)? Do I think the problem is a function of the child's inability to fit into the school (for whatever reason) or do I think it is due to the inflexibility of the school? If it is the child I want to change then I need to use an individual level of analysis, and conceptions of the person will lead to appropriate strategies and tactics of change. If I see the school as the source of the problem I need to ask myself if this school as an organization is structured such that it can efficiently accomplish the goals of socialization prescribed by the institution of public education. Strategies and tactics for changing the school as an organization will require a different level of analysis and be based on different conceptions than strategies for changing individuals.

In addition, I need to ask how I feel about the institutional values involved. Are the current values of public education as a social institution consistent with the sort of society I want to support? Do the problems of poor children in school reflect their deficits, deficits in the school as an

organization, or a lack of fit between the school's strengths and those of the children? Perhaps the problem is the development of educational alternatives for the children in question. What about the children and their families? Do they participate in decision making within the school? Do they have any power or control over the educational process, and do I believe that this is an important issue? If I do believe it is important then I may need to work at the level of institutional and/or community analysis. The strategies and tactics I use will then be based on conceptions considerably different from the other levels of analysis.

If I believe (in answer to the value question) that the problems of poor children in the educational system are in some part a function of their role relationships to that system and its distribution of resources, and if I try to change the system by strategies and techniques based on changing individual people, small groups, or even on principles for changing organizations, but exclude conceptions and strategies for changing the ideology of the educational institution, or the power and role relationships in the community, I may commit an error of logical typing. The outcomes of my intervention will not answer questions about which I am really concerned. If the problem I am interested in is a function of the problems that my values suggest, but that I have ignored in my level of analysis, conceptions, and intervention strategies, I can only create first-order, rather than second-order change. If I try to help children to fit into a system that I recognize is supportive of values and goals I view as the "real" problem, then I may be able to use principles derived from conceptions at levels other than institutional and community functioning; however, I cannot argue that I am working for social change of the institutions and communities of my society. If I do I will create confusion. The confusion lies in part with the somewhat nonspecific meaning of the term "social change." If social change is interpreted to mean fitting more people into the current social institutions, then this is a different definition from one based on social change viewed as changes in the social institutions themselves and the consequent relationships be-

---

pointed out that this has been called "ideological penetration." It must be emphasized that if the aim is organizational or institutional change, ideological penetration cannot be an end in itself, but only part of a larger intervention strategy.

TABLE VI–1 **Relationships between values and goals, level of analysis, conceptions, and strategies and tactics of social intervention***

Values and Goals	Level of Analysis**	Conceptions**	Strategies and Tactics***, ****
1. Social problems are a function of the inability of some people or even an entire subculture to fit into the structures of society, or to be comfortable being different. People have deficits. The place of applied behavioral science is to help as many people as possible adjust to the goals and norms of the small groups and organizations of which they are a part. The values of the institutions of society are basically benign and the organizations developed to accomplish these values do as good a job as one can expect, given human fallibility. If individuals differs from their society, the problem is to decrease discomfort to self and others by changing the persons or helping them to live with the difference in a nondestructive way.	*Individual level* of analysis is emphasized because understanding people is the key to changing them to be more competent, adaptive, fit in and be comfortable with themselves and the available structures of society.	Various individual conceptions ranging from behavioral through psychodynamic (see Chapters III and IV, especially Figure III-4). Depending on the specific problem this level of analysis may require, in Sarbin's terms (see Chapter IV, p. 109), helping individuals find their place in the self-maintenance, transcendental, or normative ecology. Social change is implied to be a summation of individual changes.	Person-centered interventions. Community-mental-health-oriented therapies such as brief treatment. Consultation to socialization agents. Crisis intervention. Training of new person power. Also includes employment training techniques for individuals as well as other educational programs for children and parents. The specific content varies with the specific conception of individual behavior.
2. Social problems are created by interpersonal difficulties, within primary groups such as the family, peer, and work groups. Deficits in the group rather than the individual members are emphasized. Sometimes the problem is seen as an inability of people in different groups to communicate with each other; for example, policemen and members of a given community. When these groups are not functioning well internally, or are in conflict with other groups, they not only have a negative impact on individual members, but inhibit the ability of organizations to accomplish the necessary tasks of administering society's institutional values and goals.	*Small group level* of analysis emphasized. Because the problems lie in interpersonal communication and conflict, understanding the dynamics of interpersonal relations and small group interaction is stressed.	Two primary sources of conceptions are the group dynamics literature of social psychology and the group and family treatment literature derived from clinical psychology. Ecological principles can be used to understand and adjust the functioning of the group.	Family therapy, interpersonal communications training, sensitivity groups, group therapy. May include retraining agents of socialization to communicate more effectively with themselves and with the target people.

TABLE VI–1 Cont.

Values and Goals	Level of Analysis**	Conceptions**	Strategies and Tactics***, ****
3. Social problems are created by the organizations of society which fail to implement, as well as they might, the desirable values and goals of our social institutions. Concrete organizations are imperfectly structured and administered such that they often fail to accomplish the values and goals of socialization as stipulated by work, education, health, and welfare institutions. The aim remains to enhance the likelihood that organizations will help individuals to fit into society; but the problems are in the organizations themselves, rather than in the person. Less obvious emphasis on weakness and deficits of targets, but often implied.	*Organizational level* of analysis. Because a great deal of behavior is under the control of the social structures of organizations, these structures and techniques for changing them are the key to solution of social problems.	Systems-centered conceptions from public health, social, and organizational psychology. May include conceptions of the influence of deviant subcultures and norms. Power and alienation are psychological rather than political variables. Principles of social systems analysis, ecological and environmental psychology applied to adjust the functioning of the organization.	Public health and organization development strategies. Systems-centered consultation. Development of new structures and communication channels and styles within existing organizations through use of various organization development techniques. Includes programs of early identification of "high risk" in various locations such as schools, and armed services, or in the general mental health system. The strategy of early identification may be combined with secondary prevention which usually involves tactics such as development and introduction of new programs including any of the person or small-group level strategies identified above.
4. Social problems are created by institutions rather than by persons, small groups, or by organizations. Although there are many problems in organizations that may be solved by specific changes, the real key to social change is in the attitudes, values, goals, and political-economic ideology and social policy of which the institutions themselves are composed and on which the organizations are based. The distribution of power (political as well as psychological) among various communities is an important variable. Values should be supportive of diversity and alternative pathways to success are needed. Explicit emphasis on strengths of target people, cultural relativity, and the need for resources.	*Institutional and community level* of analysis is emphasized because the institutions of society support and determine relationships within and between organizations and communities. These relationships limit the alternatives and the resources available to members, and therefore hold the key to social change.	Systems-centered conceptions from various social sciences. Power is a political-economic as well as a psychological variable. Principles of social action, social policy, and community organization are emphasized. Because many people require new alternatives, ecological principles applied to this value system and level of analysis lead to a search for new environmental alternatives.	Two major classes of social intervention are the community organization–social advocacy model and the parallel institutions or creation of settings model (see also Table V-2). Tactics emphasize · power, autonomy, and self-control of disenfranchised groups either with existing organizations or in newly created organizations. In either case, the aim is to build organizations based on institutional assumptions different from those currently dominant in society. Choice between changing existing or creating new settings is a function of the specifics of the situation, including the resources of

TABLE VI–1 Cont.

Values and Goals	Level of Analysis**	Conceptions**	Strategies and Tactics***, ****
4. (Cont.)			the particular group and the belief that existing structures ultimately will or will not yield power and control. May also use any of the strategies of change at other levels of analysis as well as any available research methods for data collection leading to social policy recommendations and feedback for new intervention strategies. Especially appropriate are the methods of the unaffiliated, data-based change agent.

*The social intervention strategies in this table all assume a seeking- rather than a waiting-mode, and an emphasis is on change through direct action. Ultimately each requires research and evaluation, although this is not always emphasized by adherents.
**The level of analysis may be cumulative as one goes down the column. Willingness to engage in strategies at the institutional and community level does not necessarily preclude a willingness to engage in strategies at other levels of analysis. In practice, often levels and strategies are combined.
***Examples presented include some of the major classes of strategies and tactics in which psychologists engage today. Other specific intervention forms are also logically possible. For example, urban planning programs of various kinds may be implemented at the organizational, institutional, or community level, the specifics of which will vary with the values of the planner as well as the perspective in the intervention as based on a strengths or a weaknesses model (see Table V-1).
****Public education and social policy recommendations, in various forms, aimed at spreading the values that underlie a particular strategy, so as to make the tactics themselves more acceptable, are techniques to which most change agents subscribe, and appear to be nonspecific with regard to values or level of analysis.

tween various communities. *Such distinctions are made on the basis of values and goals and only then lead to level of analysis, conceptions, strategies, and tactics of social intervention.*

It is quite reasonable to expect that the problems of community psychology will require intervention based on multiple levels of analysis and multiple conceptions appropriate to each level. In the example above I may need to change persons, organizations, and institutions. However, *the strategies and tactics of community psychology, although they do not exclude those at other levels of analysis, require conceptions, strategies, and tactics at the institutional and community level as well.* To this extent they imply a value system which questions the current institutional values and goals of society as well as the current relationships between the various communities of our society. Community psychology, viewed in this way, is a psychology

of social change which differs from one based on fitting people into existing structures. The remainder of this chapter considers some of the strategies and tactics of social intervention that have been based on an organizational, institutional, or community level of analysis.

Strategies and Tactics of Organizational Change

The essential strategy of organizational change is systems-centered consultation. Consultation is a somewhat catch-all term used by many different "experts" with very different ideas about what it is, how to do it, and how things work; that is, they have both differing values and differing theories. Many come from the ranks of the mental health professionals who have worked in various settings with the aim of enhancing the ability of individual caretakers and socialization agents to deliver mental health services either by training the individual agents to better understand the mental health needs of their clients, or by helping them to develop new service programs. Some of the activities of mental health consultation are reviewed in Chapter IX, which is concerned with interventions in the mental health system per se. Here we are more concerned with the other strategies and tactics suggested for creating change in organizations. These approaches are less concerned with improving "mental health" than with improving "effectiveness" of an organization more generally.

What exactly constitutes effectiveness is not an easy question to answer, but it seems that for most writers it includes the personal satisfaction of members of the organization as well as accomplishment of the organization's formal goals. The question posed is: "How can an organization maximize both of these?" As such, an *organizational psychology* has developed that tries to base its conceptions on ideas about how organizations function rather than on conceptions of how individuals function. Professionals concerned with organizational change have evolved out of social and industrial psychology into a separate professional group of applied social psychologists who consider their specialty area to be organizational psychology. More recently, a specialty within organizational psychology known as *Organization Development* has appeared. Organizational psychology has had widespread impact on its parents, social and industrial psychology, similar to the impact of community mental health on clinical psychology.

Organizational psychology is the major area within psychology that specifically seeks to understand how organizations work and how to help them to work better. As noted in Table VI-1, the values underlying this level of analysis imply that organizations hold the key to social change in that if they function effectively they will enhance their members' and their society's output, satisfaction, and progress. The goals of the organization are viewed as essentially benign (that is, the work, education, and other

social institutions on which they are based are not questioned). This is not to say that organizations do not create social problems, but rather that such problems can be reduced if the organizations are able to work better to accomplish their goals. In that sense it is a view compatible with the primary prevention goals of community mental health. As with individual psychology there is a very large set of specific studies on which organizational psychology is based, and several textbooks are available to the reader.[5] Rather than attempt a content review of this research our aim here is to consider the strategies and tactics for creating change that have been suggested by the writers, and to look for possible suggestions useful to community psychology. To begin we need to understand something of the context in which organizational psychology has developed and to understand the paradigm's viewpoint. An excellent overview of this development and viewpoint is provided by Edgar H. Schein (1970) and his analysis is reviewed below.

Although organizational psychology is concerned with many different kinds of organizations, including mutual benefit associations, business concerns, service organizations, and government organizations (Blau & Scott, 1962), a great deal of the work of organizational psychology has evolved out of the interest of industrial psychology in business concerns. Consequently, much of the vocabulary and measures of effectiveness have to do with management, work production, and job satisfaction. Nevertheless, techniques for analysis and stimulation of change in organizations whose "product" is human service, such as schools (see Schmuck, Runkel, & Langmeyer [1969] and below) have also been applied.

According to Schein (1970), although industrial psychologists began with attempts to help organizations in the assessment and selec-

---

[5]There are so many that it is impossible to list them all here. Some of the more well known include: Blake and Mouton (1964), Campbell, Dunnette, Lawler, and Weick (1970), Etzioni (1964), Fiedler (1967), Katz and Kahn (1966), Likert (1961), Lundgren (1974), March and Simon (1958), Schein (1970), Weick (1969).

tion of individual workers, they eventually became concerned with broader organizational problems such as design of the organization itself. Eventually they moved their interest to questions about the effects of formal rewards and punishments on productivity, and later began to examine the importance of social groups, both formal and informal, which create norms for work and other behavior in the organization. Ultimately the organization came to be regarded as a *system* that is more than the sum of its individuals, and psychologists began to ask how an organization can be designed to yield maximum output together with an internal environment that will help its members to grow and change over time. Organizational psychologists came to conclude, as have community psychologists, that *"the organization is a complex social system which must be studied as a social system if individual behavior within it is to be truly understood"* (Schein, 1970, p. 3, italics in original).

Some of the concrete problems to which organizational psychology has addressed itself are a function of the needs of the organization to recruit, select, and train people for its tasks. Because these goals have traditionally been seen as separate from the organization as a system, their accomplishment has sometimes ignored the human needs of employees and the impact of these procedures on their later view of the organization and their place in it. Questions revolving around the integration of selection procedures with later job requirements and how to train and develop employees while on the job so as to maximize their "human potential" have gained currency. The importance of the "psychological contract" between an organization and its employees and the organization's place in the external environment have also gained prominence. In short, one aim of organizational psychology is to train people, particularly the managers, to be active participants in an organization which, in order to survive in a rapidly changing world, requires them to be prepared for changes and innovations and to be good "diagnosticians" who can process new information and deal with employees and problems in an effective nonstereotyped way, while maximizing their own personal growth.

A subset of problems that organizational psychologists have studied are those involving groups and intergroup relationships. Because organizations have both formal and informal groups these two may sometimes conflict with one another. Formal groups are predictable from the structure of the organization; informal groups arise out of the structure *and* the human needs of members. In order to understand an organization it is important to understand the relationships within and between these two kinds of groups. Questions of leadership, communication, cooperation, and competition between groups have been extensively researched and various methods of reducing or avoiding conflict suggested. These methods range from techniques for training in interpersonal communication through establishment of organizational conditions which stimulate cooperation.

All of the above problems of an organization need to be understood, according to Schein, in terms of mutual dependencies. As he puts it, "empirical research studies have shown again and again how events in one part of the organization turn out to be linked to events in other parts or in the environment. Similarly, consultants have found how changes in one part of an organization produce unanticipated and often undesired changes in other parts" (Schein, 1970, p. 109). The similarity between this observation and the *principle of interdependence* derived from social ecology is obvious (see Chapter V, p. 154). It implies that an organization needs to be understood as a *process* rather than as a structure. How it works, how it is integrated, and how it communicates is more important, in this view, than its size, shape, function, or structure. Consequently, for many organizational psychologists the effectiveness of an organization is not measured by any one goal, but rather by its ability to adapt, grow, survive, and maintain itself regardless of its function. Questions of effectiveness are put in terms such as: How does the organization process information? Is the organization flexible and can it cope with changes in the external environment? In short, the "adaptive-coping cycle" is of major importance. Schein identifies six stages where problems may be identified and studied in that cycle.

1. Sensing changes in the environment. By what means and how accurate is the organization in monitoring the larger community which it serves? For a business the problem is one of anticipating product demand; for an educational institution it is not dissimilar in that the educational needs of the community need to be assessed.

2. Getting the information to the relevant parts of the organization. This is a very complicated matter. Often in a large organization because subunits are concerned with getting the information (for example, research and development teams) they may have difficulty communicating to the other units. Attitudes, self-images, and/or role relationships may need to be changed. This is not only true for business concerns. Especially in the mental health and education systems there is a separation between the developers of new information and the deliverers of service. Research journals tend to be read by the academic community and not by the deliverers of service, most of whom have learned their trade several years earlier.

3. Using the information once received by the organization. This is the key, of course, to organizational change. Resistance to change by those who are directly affected by it is one of the most "ubiquitous organizational phenomena" (Schein, 1970). Although Schein emphasizes business concerns, the same is again true for all organizations. Educational establishments, ironically, are just as resistant to the use of new information as are business establishments. Likewise, a mental health organization staffed by professionals who have obtained their degrees and nonprofessionals who have learned their roles several years ago can be quite resistant to change.

How can action, based on new data that suggest new methods and procedures that may require radical change in social and role relationships, be sold to established organizations? Schein suggests that the best evidence for how to overcome resistance supports the use of techniques that enable direct participation in decision making by those affected. Some of these techniques are considered below.

4. Insuring the impact of change on other subsystems and stabilizing the change. This stage requires consideration of where to intervene in the system. Should we be concerned with top-level managers alone, or need we deal with middle-managers as well? The answer will depend on the particular system, but it is clear that it is an important question. Is changing a principal or a guidance counselor enough to change a school, or are other changes also necessary? In the educational system the introduction of preschool programs for so-called "deprived" children, which has ignored the impact of the regular school system with which the child must later cope, is an example of this problem (see Chapter VII).

5. Exporting the new product, service, or information. For a business the problem is one of marketing and communicating the product's value. For an educational institution or a mental health or legal system it may not be so different. Here public education and social attitudes are of concern. For example, the idea that an identified mental patient or lawbreaker can function productively in the community needs to be sold to the residents. Likewise, a school needs to be viewed as creating a valuable product.

6. Obtaining feedback. This is crucial for an organization's ability to adapt and requires systematic evaluation and communication of the effects of its activities. It completes the loop back to stage 1, where the task is sensing changes in the environment which then must be acted upon.

According to Schein, in order for the organization to successfully complete all the above stages of coping it must not only take in and communicate information, but also have internal flexibility and good integration of its own subsystems, including a willingness to change based on an internal climate of support and freedom from threat. How to create such organizations is the goal of organizational psychology. What are the techniques that have been used?

The Technology of Social Intervention in Organizations

Hornstein, Bunker, Burke, Gindes, and Lewicki (1971) have recently reviewed the tactics for creating organizational change and classified them into several categories that are useful as a means of analysis. One set of tactics they have termed *individual* approaches. Here we find that some organizational consultants have used much the same methods as clinical psychologists. Depending on their particular theory of individual behavior the exact procedures vary, but they have all assumed that changes in key individuals can be summed to create institutional change. In general, the goals of the individual interventions have focused on feelings, values, attitudes, perceptions, skills, and actions of an organization's leaders and members. Some organizational psychologists, like those in community mental health, have used the analytic model, typified by Caplan and discussed in Chapter III. The behavioral model discussed in Chapter IV, which emphasizes direct training in relevant skills, just as it does in the clinical setting, has also been applied to individual employees in organizations. Other individual methods include an emphasis on information and knowledge and assume that providing information to key persons will create change. Many methods derived from group dynamics and the social psychology of small groups have also been applied. The use of so-called laboratory methods and sensitivity or T-groups to enhance communicaton in an organization has been very popular, aimed at developing the kind of "adaptive-coping cycle" suggested by Schein above.

A second set of methods has been termed *techno-structural*. Here the assumption is that the way the organization is structured is usually

a function of the job that needs to be done rather than the needs of the workers. As such, the problems of organizations are frequently due to a neglect of human needs. As Schein (1970) notes, the formal and informal systems may work at cross purposes; that is, the norms of the work groups that serve to satisfy the human needs may be at cross purposes with the formal structure of the organization. Consequently, the prescribed techniques rearrange the organization so that both are taken into consideration. This includes changes in group size, composition, physical arrangements, and task requirements. For example, Rice (1958) suggests, among other things, that tasks should be organized so that those involved can both complete the whole task and control their own activities. Schein suggests that intergroup competition is frequently an organizational problem and can be alleviated by structuring the organization so that departments are rewarded on the basis of contribution to overall effectiveness rather than simply their own. Other suggestions he derives from the literature of organizational functioning include arranging the formal groups so as to enhance high levels of interaction and frequent communication, giving rewards partly on the basis of the help groups give each other, rotating group members, and avoiding "win-lose" situations in which groups compete for a limited set of resources rather than sharing them equally.[6]

A third set of methods Hornstein *et al.* term *data-based*. Here the aim of the interventionist is not only to collect information, but to do it in such a way as to encourage its *use* by the members of the organization. They further identify two kinds of change agents who use this strategy. One is the *affiliated* change agent who is either a member of the organization or hired to fulfill a contract. The other is an *unaffiliated* change agent such as an investigative reporter or an independent social scientist. Ralph Nader's

[6]It is ironic that such suggestions, often adopted by an organization for its *internal* structure, are rarely considered by either consultants or organizational leaders with regard to their implications for the relationship *between* organizations or communities. When such suggestions are made for community relationships they are often labeled as some form of "socialism."

consumer advocate group is a good example of the unaffiliated change agent. They attempt to present data that will force the organization to change, either by stimulating legal sanctions or by means of public pressure. A more detailed discussion of the role of the social scientist as an unaffiliated data-based change agent is presented later in this chapter as a strategy for creating institutional change (p. 202).

The affiliated change agent uses data for two purposes. One is to present problems to the organization so as to stimulate solutions by the members, and the other is to provide a plan which it is assumed will be adopted by the organization because it is rational and backed with data. Affiliated data-based change agents often use four specific tactics identified by Hornstein *et al*. These include *diagnostic surveys* of both the internal and external effects of the system aimed at pinpointing where changes are needed. If no action follows from such surveys they can create more harm than good by raising expectations for change; Hornstein *et al.* suggest that they should always be combined with *systematic feedback* to the interviewees about the actions that follow from the survey. It is further suggested that surveys be conducted together with the members of the organization participating in the collection and interpretation of data so as to establish their legitimacy for further action. However, survey and feedback techniques used in this way will lack experimental "rigor." It will not be possible to sort out the impact of the data themselves from the effects of the collaboration of people with vested interests. Nevertheless, for such techniques the aims usually are to use the process of collaboration, rather than the data themselves, as a means for change, and thereby to create an atmosphere of problem solving within the organization. To evaluate the impact of the data collected per se, other research would need to be done, perhaps comparing collaborative and noncollaborative data collection in similar organizations.

This brings us to the third tactic of an affiliated data-based strategy which involves *evaluation research* aimed at demonstrating that a given set of actions creates a given effect. Unlike "true" experimental research the data

are not intended to pinpoint *why* it works, but rather simply that it is pragmatic in creating some desired effect. Finally, *action research* is defined by Hornstein as that which also seeks specific *causal factors* for the outcome of change and has been identified by others (see Sashkin, Morris, & Horst, below) as the kinds of data which are necessary for a science of organizational change. In order to conduct such research the evaluator often needs to limit participation of the clients so that the data are not "contaminated." It is assumed that later, when the data are revealed, people will respond to them because they are compelling, rather than because they identify with their collection and analysis. This is the sort of data that is held to be generalizable to other organizations because the methods used are based on an approximation of the experimental model.

Sashkin, Morris, and Horst (1973) have recently compared what they describe as five different "models" for *data-based strategies* and they make some useful distinctions with regard to the activities emphasized by each. Although they do not specifically consider the strategies as those of *affiliated* change agents, it is clear from their discussion that this is what they mean. Their comparison is based on what is done with the information collected. One model they term *research, development, and diffusion*. This is the typical demonstration study completed, published, and forgotten. It assumes that potential users will eventually find the data, and if the data are useful they will eventually be adopted by means of a rational process. No attention is paid to how to get the information to potential users and it is assumed that eventually it will diffuse itself.

A second model they term *social interaction and diffusion*. This is essentially a model based on providing consultation to key people in an organization by making information available to them. It is based on the idea of "gatekeepers" or "opinion leaders," people who theoretically influence others. The aim of this model is to find and influence such leaders who will then influence others. For example, providing conferences for teachers or offering continuing education programs will presumably attract such leaders who will bring the information back to their own organizations. The target of change is essentially a key individual.

Sashkin et al. call the third model *intervention theory and method*. This concentrates on the internal workings of a system and is essentially aimed at what Schein called the "adaptive-coping cycle" of the organization. The tasks of the interventionists are to generate problem-relevant data, obtain alternative solutions, and develop a shared commitment to decisions. It uses what Horstein et al. called diagnostic surveys and systematic feedback. It also uses confrontation meetings, T-groups, and the like. The aim is to change the *process* by which information is generated and acted on by an organization. It assumes that the organization can learn to solve its own problems if the process is modeled. The research generated is essentially "case study" and oriented to client training rather than to experimental research on change.

A fourth model is termed *planned change*. Like the intervention theory and method model it seeks to create a process in the organization that will enable it to develop its own solutions to future problems, but adds an emphasis on *action steps* which must be translated from the data collection and the process of interaction. It also emphasizes research which examines specific problem solutions, but not necessarily solutions which may be generalizable to other organizations. This seems to be the kind of research Hornstein et al. call "evaluation."

The fifth model is called *action research* and it is the same one identified by Hornstein as supposedly leading to a so-called scientific understanding of organizations. Although it seeks to generate a process within the organization and emphasizes the link between research and action in a continuous cycle, it is also aimed at generalizable knowledge of potential use to other organizations. A major question it asks is "how can research be designed so as to discover general rather than specific knowledge?" According to Sashkin et al., action research uses social science theory and the comparison of different techniques systematically. It is essentially thought of as true, or at least quasi-experimental research on organizations.

Whether or not so-called "action-research" really is able to find universal laws of organizational behavior is highly questionable for exactly the same reasons noted by Cronbach in Chapter II with regard to individual research conducted in a laboratory, but more so. It is highly unlikely that one ever identify all the causative variables in an organization's behavior, and quite likely that the exact causes of an outcome are impossible to isolate in the experimental sense of "knowing" how it works now and forever. Nevertheless, it is clear that *evaluation* by means of systematic comparisons of different techniques for problem solution in different systems is a useful goal, at least as feedback to the organization, and probably as a good example on which others can base hypotheses for their own action. In that sense, the comparison of these five models offered by Sashkin et al. is informative because they emphasize *change agent roles*. In so doing, the authors note three ways the affiliated change agent behaves. One is as a *consultant*, essentially in a role that tries to help find new solutions by using rational problem solving. The second role is as a *trainer*. Here the aim is to develop new skills, among the organization's members, which will lead to a continued ability to communicate and to solve future problems. The third role is as a *researcher*. One of the aims of this latter role is to model how to do systematic and careful evaluation and as such it overlaps with the training role. A second aim is to add to the "general knowledge" of social science. According to Sashkin et al. it is only the "action researcher" who performs all of the above roles and action research is therefore described as the desirable method for creating organizational change. They graphically depict the activity of the applied behavioral scientist in this role as a kind of center of the universe around which all of the above models for creation and evaluation of organizational change revolve (see Figure VI-1).

Figure VI-1 presents the change agent, or applied behavioral scientist, as what is termed a "knowledge linker" for information flow. Although the description is a bit grandiose, it does represent the ideal of the affiliated change agent

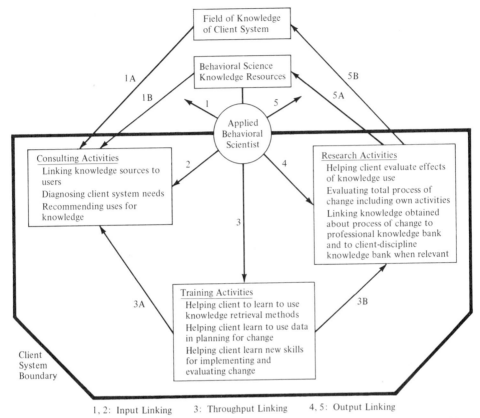

Figure VI-1. Data use and linking activities of the applied behavioral scientist. (Redrawn from Sashkin, Morris, & Horst, 1973.)

working in an applied setting, not only to improve his organization, but also to increase the general fund of knowledge available to others. One notable lack of this model is a set of values to guide the direction of social change. It is implied that the organization will necessarily have values and goals that lead not only to a better organization, but also to a better society. That may be questionable, and indeed is questioned by those who seek institutional as well as organizational change and by those who work from positions unaffiliated with the organizations they seek to change. These issues are elaborated in the appropriate section below.

A fourth set of methods identified by Hornstein *et al.* has been called *organization development* (OD), a term for a rather heterogeneous set of tactics aimed at the creation of or-

ganizational change of the sort described by Schein above and seems to rely on most of the activities Sashkin *et al.* identify in Figure VI-1. The tactics of OD, although they are essentially the same as those listed above, aim to create what Hornstein calls a *culture,* which "institutionalizes" their use, rather than a temporary intervention. There are many formal definitions of OD (Blake & Mouton, 1968; Beckhard, 1969; Bennis, 1966; Lippitt, 1969). The commonalities noted by Hornstein (p. 346) include: *intervention as an ongoing process of deliberate change efforts by means of behavioral science technology aimed at creating a process of cultural change which will institutionalize a means for regulating subsequent organizational behavior.*

Exactly what consultation, training, and research activities are engaged in is based on a "diagnosis" aimed at selecting a technique that will respond to or create a "felt need" for change among the members of an organization, facilitate change in the process by which decisions are made, and most importantly, involve the client group in planning and implementing change. Methods include interviews, group confrontation meetings, the development of intergroup competition and collaboration, problem-solving conferences, and diagnosis of managerial problems. An example of this latter technique, developed by Blake and Mouton (1964), is called the "managerial grid." It is a technique by which members of the organization complete a series of questions designed to help them diagnose and change their leadership styles. The grid presents, on one axis, descriptions of task-oriented leadership concerned only with "production" and on the other axis leadership concerned only with "people." The aim of the technique is to help members at all levels to move toward what is called "team management" or integration of task and human requirements.

Many of the techniques for organization development have been used by Schmuck, Runkel, and Langmeyer (1969) in an attempt to create change in a junior high school. Their award-winning research may serve here as an example of the application of such techniques. It also will demonstrate the difficulty involved in conducting adequate research that is generalizable to other organizations. They set out to use a strategy of intervention called "flexible organizational problem solving." Its basic aims were to train a school faculty in interpersonal communication skills so as to develop new norms for openness and helpfulness with each other. The strategy is based on McGregor's (1967) ideas, which focus on the provision of opportunities for members of an organization to "obtain intrinsic rewards from contributions to the success of the enterprise."

At first the interventionists invited faculty to present their frustrations, followed by a chance to practice problem solving to reduce these frustrations. Following the conclusions reached by Campbell and Dunnette (1968), who found

that T-groups that focus on personal growth away from the job rather than on application to job tasks per se, have little effect on organization development, they emphasized task-oriented groups in the actual school situation. They engaged in group activities with the entire staff, including teachers, administrators, secretaries, the head cook, and custodian. They also rotated sizes and membership in small group sessions, so that every pair of members interacted with each other as a means of reducing status barriers to communication. The specific aims were to establish a means for ongoing communication that would carry over to everyday activities, increase participation at regular faculty meetings, and include more faculty in decision making. In addition, they sought to model and train effective problem solving and testing of new ideas, followed by translation into actions. In essence they sought, by participation techniques, to create a culture that would help the staff continue to confront new problems and use new solutions. Specific skill training included paraphrasing, describing behavior and feelings, and checking perceptions with others.

The intervention took place in three parts. A six-day session in the fall, just prior to the onset of classes, a one and one-half day session in December, and a third day and one-half in February. The authors do not report exactly how or why they were invited to enter the school, but from their account it is clear that they were welcomed by people willing to work with them. The initial sessions used group exercises to increase awareness of organizational and interpersonal processes. These exercises and others are described in detail in a technical report (Langmeyer, Schmuck, & Runkel, 1970) and include activities such as the "five-square puzzle."

The five-square puzzle exercise demonstrates coordination or cooperation in a group task in which communication is nonverbal. It is administered to participants in groups of five, although other participants may act as observers. The participants are given parts of a puzzle which, when assembled, make five complete squares of equal dimensions. The task is finished when a completed square is put together in front of each person in the group. The rules are as follows: (1)

Each member must construct one square directly at his work place. (2) No member may talk, signal, or gesture in any way that would provide guidance, direction, or suggestion to any other group member. For example, no member may signal that he wants a piece from another member. (3) Any member may give any of his pieces to another member. (4) Each member's pieces must be in front of him at his work place except one that he is giving to another member. Only giving is allowed—no taking.

This exercise, of course, is difficult and frustrating for individuals who are accustomed to managing others. It is also very difficult for people who are accustomed to guiding themselves by watching for signals of the expectations of others, since the rules cut such signals to a minimum. To the extent that the rules are observed (and it is difficult for most participants to apply this self-discipline), the exercise focuses the attention of the participants on discovering the ways they can be helpful to the task. It points up the great difficulty experienced in letting other people do things their own way. It also points up the great reliance we put on language to influence the behavior of others. Finally, it provides a very useful amount of information about how members of the group act toward one another under the frustration the exercise produces. (Langmeyer, Schmuck, & Runkel, 1970, pp. 13–14.)

The above and other exercises were used for two days, and related, by discussion, to real problems in the school. The next four days of the initial session were devoted to problem solving of real issues raised by participants. The three issues that emerged were: insufficient role clarity, failure to use staff resources, and low staff involvement and participation at meetings. One subgroup attacked each of these problems using five steps of problem solving: (1) identifying the problem and behavioral description, (2) analyzing diagnostically, (3) brainstorming, (4) designing a concrete plan of action, and (5) trying out the plan in simulated activity. The initial week's session ended with a discussion of resources available, all members noting their own strengths and those of others.

Early in the fall all members were interviewed by the research team, and in December they all met again. In this second session the emphasis was on improving communication between teachers and administrators and on improving the problem-solving skill of the Princi-

pal's Advisory Committee, composed of teachers. Emphasis was placed on problem-solving techniques and feedback. One interesting technique used was the "fishbowl" in which the Principal's Advisory Committee met while everyone observed. Two or three empty chairs were left so that other people could come in and out of the discussion and later feedback was given to the committee by the observers. The last session, an evaluation and discussion of progress made by the group members, was held in February.

Schmuck et al. evaluated this intervention in several ways. One was by conducting interviews with teachers during the school year. Here they found that about one-third of them reported that they used, in their own classrooms, the communication exercises they had learned. The researchers also observed several "spontaneous" changes in the functioning of the school. For example, more teachers worked together in groups than had initially. The Advisory Committee was raised in status to a decision-making body of teachers. In addition, turnover rate of the school's staff was only 3 percent, compared to other schools in the district with a 10–16 percent turnover. Unfortunately, the researchers do not report the turnover rate for this school prior to the intervention, and leave open to question its initial comparability to other schools. Other observations include the school's use of more group sessions on their own, and diffusion of some of their innovative ideas to other schools in the district.

Schmuck et al. also compared the school with others identified as a kind of "control group." Unfortunately, this portion of their research is weak because the control group is composed of schools in other parts of the country that did not participate in training and on whom the researchers happened to have data. They say that the schools were demographically comparable, but no data are presented. At best this analysis is a weak comparison to a nonequivalent control group whose motivations for participation are unclear in comparison to the highly motivated experimental school. Nevertheless, the "control" schools do serve as a kind of baseline for comparison of changes in reported attitudes. They found that in the experimental school there were significantly more changes than in the "control" schools with regard to positive attitudes about the principal and the perceived worth and effectiveness of staff meetings. In addition, significantly more innovations in organizational structure were reported by the experimental school staff, and the staff reported being more open and helpful to each other than did the control schools' staffs.

From their findings these investigators recommend that others interested in organization development follow procedures that include all members of the faculty, use structured activities as an introduction and then move to less structured tasks, and rotate group membership. In addition, they suggest equal treatment for all ranks. Unfortunately, none of the techniques, all quite logical, was directly contrasted to others, so that one cannot conclude that these are the best methods, even if we accept the changes noted in the school as real and worthwhile. In essence, this study is a good example of the techniques used for organizational change and serves as a case study that may suggest hypotheses with regard to stimulation of internal change when a change agent is invited in by an organization. Finally, it must be noted that the kinds of changes sought in this study are fairly typical of those suggested by organization development advocates, in that they assume that if the staff can communicate better and be more satisfied they will also do a better job of teaching.

The above study is a concrete example of the value/goal of enhancing the functioning of the agents of socialization. The institutional values and goals were not called into question. There was no consideration of the actual product, that is, effect on the students, nor was there any attempt to include students or parents in the decision making and communication process. One wonders how welcome the researchers would have been had they insisted on inclusion of such people and measures. For our purposes, however, we can observe that the techniques they used do not necessarily exclude such participation or evaluation. Once again, inclusion or exclusion is a matter that is decided on prior

grounds, that is, how much one values it as important for social change and what is considered to be the *criterion of change*.

Organizational versus Institutional Change

Some of the value issues raised above have been more explicitly discussed in the context of organizational psychology by Reppucci (1973) who has generated what he considers to be a set of "general principles" for organizational intervention strategies. Reppucci is specifically concerned with creating change in human service organizations such as hospitals and prisons. He views the goal of such change to be the creation of a new culture in the institution, one which fosters a "sense of community," and in this context he makes an important point: ". . . organizational change consultants . . . provide . . . principles and useful information on how to change 'process' characteristics, i.e., communication patterns between staff members, *but they (do) not provide directive principles for changing content, e.g., the goals of an institution*" (Reppucci, 1973, p. 332, italics added). This means that when the goals as well as the processes of an organization are believed to require change, organizational psychology may be less helpful as a strategy. Here Reppucci is approaching the difference between organizational and institutional change, but although he has cited the problem accurately, his "general principles" remain largely focused on process goals once one has gained entry to an organization. He posits the following suggestions: (1) An organization needs a guiding philosophy, developed by all its members, to create a sense of hope for change. (2) An organizational structure is needed that will encourage consistency, communication, and cooperation. (3) Decision making must involve all levels of staff. (4) Each employee must be used according to one's strengths and qualifications regardless of formal degrees or job specifications. (5) The external community needs to be involved if one is to create long-term change (here he is referring to programs in mental health and corrections facilities that need to prepare residents for their return to the world; see Chapters IX and X). (6) A reasonable time perspective needs to be adopted for creation of change.

Reppucci (1973) provides an example of his own attempt to change a juvenile corrections facility by use of these principles (see also Chapter X); however, in that instance he was invited into the organization by the new director who essentially gave him and his colleagues the power, within some real-world constraints, to create changes on which the director was already sold. Little is said about the situation wherein the controllers of an organization do not adopt the same *content goals* as the interventionist, and where entry as well as goals are at issue. Nevertheless, some of the conditions under which Reppucci entered are instructive. The corrections facility was in great disarray and under a good deal of public pressure for change. A new director was appointed and, as part of his agreement to take over, obtained a commitment for an observation period for planning change and the right to bring in outside consultants who would operate within the value/goals listed as principles by Reppucci. Rather than rely on short-term demonstration projects financed by outside resources, an a priori agreement was reached to change the goals of the entire organization, using existing resources.

The success Reppucci reports in creating organizational change was probably as much a function of the above a priori agreement and set of entry conditions as the particular things done once he entered the organization. It is not that what was done with the organization, once in it, is unimportant, but simply that the initial agreement to change the goals of the organization itself may have been more important. Of some interest to community psychology would be knowledge about how to create the kind of *entry situations* in which there is a willingness to change the content of the organization's goals. Such a situation is not easy to create. It may require political and public activities that foster dissatisfaction with current goals, for example by using the strategies and tactics of an unaffiliated change agent or a community organizer-social advocate as described in later sections of this chapter.

At present, most of the strategies and tactics of organizational psychology are more akin to value statements about how organizations should operate *internally* than they are to specific strategies and tactics for getting those in power to agree to new outcome priorities. It is apparent that despite a perspective which recognizes the importance of a "system's analysis," much of the thinking of organizational psychology remains, like community mental health, both person-oriented and supportive of the status quo. In part this is because the aims of organizational psychology and community mental health are similar: to increase the internal effectiveness of organizations in producing their existing goals that are assumed to be benign. Depending on the organization this productivity may be measured by increased efficiency to socialize people, or to create a material product. In either case, organizational psychology usually aims to increase the efficiency and satisfaction of the employees of the organization, not the products or the consumers. We now have substituted a concern with the healthy person for a concern with the "healthy organization," but the organization itself is largely understood as person behavior in the aggregate, and moreover, its goals are rarely questioned.

There are two related issues of concern here, one is the process by which an organization is said to operate, the other is the goals that are supported. With regard to process, although the aim of change may theoretically be structural, interventions are generally conceived in terms of persons in groups, changes in openness, lines of communication and cooperation, leadership roles, and managerial styles. Change techniques are person-oriented. The criterion for change is measured as person variables summed across people and said to represent systems characteristics or changes in the *process* of interaction not change in the goals of the organization or the quality of the product. It is assumed that more satisfied workers will create better merchandise, a better student, or a "rehabilitated" mental patient or delinquent, but the aims of most organizational change strategies are to enhance the satisfaction and efficiency of the workers rather than the satisfaction or quality of their product.

Presumably, if teachers talk to each other and to the administrators and feel happy at their work they will do a better job; but the question remains, "what is a better job?" That issue is largely skirted by organizational psychology. If teachers and administrators all agree that the lower social class students in their school are incompetent because of their poor family background and that the school can operate most efficiently by putting these deviants in "special classes" and providing them with sensitivity groups (a "rap session") to express their anger, they can then go on their merry way with a happy organization and feel no need to change their goals (which tend to be education for the "good" or the "deserving" student).

When Schein describes the "internal organizational conditions" necessary for effective coping (see above), this sounds like a systems level analysis and a change in goals. Closer examination, however, reveals that it is a person level analysis in that the "conditions" are all based on how persons feel and behave and it is aimed at better accomplishing the existing goals (usually socialization and/or increased production). Organizational change consists of changing the attitudes, roles, and relationships of an organization's members, and how they use information and perform their tasks. Although it is argued that organizational change follows from an understanding of the organization as a system, most techniques for creating change are focused on how to induce individual or small-group communication. Structural change is expected to follow. All the techniques reviewed above turn out to be person-oriented. Even the so-called techno-structural approach is aimed at satisfaction of personal needs of the organization's members. In essence, although the general idea that all parts of the organization need to be considered together is invoked, one could observe people in an organization, intervene to change these people, and foster a different set of attitudes and interactions without ever dealing with principles or goals of change beyond these small groups.

Schein argues that "organizational effectiveness is a function of good communication, flexibility, creativity, and genuine psychological commitment . . ." and goes on to say that "the argument is not based on the assumption that this would be nice for people or make them feel better. Rather the argument is that systems *work better* if their parts are in good communication with each other, are committed, and are creative and flexible" (Schein, 1970, p. 129, italics in original). There is nothing wrong with this as a set of values for persons in an organization, but none of it really speaks to how systems themselves work and what the outcomes, values, and goals of an organization should be. Theoretically it could support the goals of a happy and efficient concentration camp! The fact remains that the organizations are seen to "work better" because they now more efficiently accomplish the accepted status quo values and goals.

Others interested in understanding and changing organizations have approached the problem from a somewhat different perspective. Rather than beginning with observations of people within a system, they begin with principles and variables that are system properties independent of people and applicable to all systems, including those that have no people in them. For example, the Watzlawick et al. (1974) application of the Theory of Groups and the Theory of Logical Types is a form of system analysis without regard to persons. The conceptions would apply to any system simply by virtue of its being a system, even if it did not contain people. It is, in this sense, a metatheory or a theory about systems, rather than about any specific system. This analysis may then be applied to understanding behavior within a given system, including one where the elements are persons. Similarly, social ecology and general systems theory are metatheories. They have in common a stress on *understanding and changing the rules and the goals* of the organization (see Chapter V).

The distinction between the two approaches (person-oriented versus systems-oriented) is both subtle and important. On the one hand, if a system is described in terms of summed individual behavior it is assumed that an understanding of individuals will lead to an understanding of systems. Perhaps more important for the strategies and tactics of change it is assumed that the interventionist will learn how to induce change, where to intervene in a system, and what to do by studying the behavior of individual people summed together. The statement that one is studying "system characteristics" is misleading and somewhat circular, in that the process requires observations of person behavior which is then simply restated as system behavior and used as an explanation for the same behavior already observed.

If, however, one takes the Watzlawick, the social ecology, or general systems theory paradigms with their emphasis on *rules of the game,* they inevitably lead to two questions: (1) "How are the resources distributed?" and (2) "What are the priorities, goals, or social values which 'set the thermostat'?" Such questions suggest an emphasis on institutional level changes, or those elements of a system on which organizations are based. The distribution of power, the values of conformity or diversity, and the availability of pathways to success built on the strengths of the supposed recipients of service (the products of the organization) come into prominence. These systems perspectives, focused on institutional change, or change in goals and priorities and rules of the game, at present constitute only a new way of viewing social organizations and communities. There is little if any normal science to "prove" that they can help to create genuine change. However, they do point one in a direction consistent with a reexamination of our social values, and appear to have the possibility of fostering second-order rather than first-order change if only because they are explicitly concerned with second-order change.

Such observations have not entirely escaped organizational psychologists, as a recent paper by Richard E. Walton (1972) on "frontiers beckoning the organizational psychologist" makes clear. Walton suggests that in addition to an organization's internal community, the change agent must begin to understand the linkage to external groups and to other organizations. He also recognizes that how to do this constitutes questions to be asked, rather than answers obtainable from current knowledge. His analysis of what he calls the "shift in source of legitimacy" is instructive.

As Walton notes, the idea of "community" is replacing the traditional basis of legitimacy in organizations: property rights, managerial prerogatives, and subordinates as the source of a superior's authority. These sources of legitimacy were historically based first on the belief in individual property rights during times of the country's growth, and later on a faith in managers or professionals as a desirable way to support productivity, technology, and continued growth. More recently, as reflected by organizational psychology, "participative management," as a means of achieving better production, has been emphasized but it has been assumed to be delegated authority and does not seriously challenge the ruling professionals. As the concept of "community" has emerged in recent years there is a growing feeling of the need to reorder priorities away from production for its own sake and toward the greater good of the outside environment and the members of the community in which an organization resides. Most important for our concerns is Walton's observation that:

Although hospitals, schools, and government agencies were founded not on property, but on some service principle enunciated by an enabling legislative group, the institutions appear to go through transitions similar to those of business organizations. First, their size and technical complexity promote the idea of prerogatives of doctors and administrators in hospitals, of teachers and administrators in schools, and of program heads and other administrators in government agencies. Second, the view that the authority of ranking officials is based on the consent of subordinates gained currency in these settings; thus participative methods were developed in teaching and therapy teams as well as in administrative processes. And finally, today both private and public organizations are faced with legitimacy claims from groups outside the organization. Neighborhood communities are today more likely to claim the right to prevent highway and airport extensions that alter community life, the right to control the local school curriculum, and the right to insist that hospitals be responsive to the needs of people in their immediate neighborhood (Walton, 1972, p. 603).

As the legitimacy of such claims by community representatives and consumers gains currency the very *criterion* by which an organization's success is to be judged comes into question. Is an organization successful if its employees and managers are satisfied because they like their jobs and they create a large margin of profit while polluting the local waterways? Is an organization successful if it excludes from its ranks minority employees or women? Is a school successful if it creates, along with its educational accomplishments, a large portion of alienated students? If a mental health system creates dependency on institutional care for large numbers of its clients is that success? Is a legal system that provides no positive alternatives and discriminates against the poor adequate? What purpose does the criminal justice system serve? Such questions lay open the very *institutional legitimacy* of our traditional organizations. To whom and to what values should they be responsive? For some, these questions lead to the argument that community organization and social advocacy by concerned groups of consumers and those directly affected by an organization are essential to the creation of genuine change. Because there are often multiple community and consumer groups with conflicting demands the inevitable result is a forcing to the front of social value, goal, and priority disagreements. Social values become openly discussed and the conflict is there for all to see. This makes many professionals uncomfortable, since we are all supposedly united in our common beliefs.

For those who take seriously the concern that many subgroups of our society are not well represented by prevailing organizations that are supposed to serve them there are two basic intervention strategies that have been developed, both with a similar rationale: the belief that social organizations are always controlled by values and power. The only reason organizations may seem not to be so controlled is that the "out-groups" are normally quiet. One strategy stresses the need to create alternative settings controlled by these out-groups and the other stresses the need to gain representation within existing organizations. In either case the aim is to build or rebuild organizations with a new constituency, new values, and new goals in mind. Choice between these two strategies depends on local conditions, resources, and belief or disbelief that existing organizations can be reformed to include out-group interests. Both strategies, from a psychological viewpoint, have the possibility of mobilizing and developing the strengths of people who have often been excluded from the power and resources of the larger society. Theoretically, either strategy should enhance the personal sense of power and control over one's life, and help to build a "sense of community" (Sarason, 1974, see below).

Institutional Change Strategies

The Creation of Alternative Settings

This strategy for social change encompasses a great many activities for differing purposes, with a wide variety of people, group sizes, and characteristics. Sarason (1972), whose approach is reviewed below, considers a setting to be created whenever "two or more people come together in new relationships over a sustained period of time in order to achieve certain goals." He formally includes everything from a marriage to a new society, but functionally his discussion of new settings is more pointed and specific to settings with which he is personally familiar as a professional—those with human service goals in health, education, and welfare.

Basic to this general strategy is a group of people with some common interest, who bring themselves together to plan, execute, and carry out a set of activities designed to accomplish either for themselves, for others, or with others, some goal normally under the control of decisions made by an existing authority or bureaucracy. Generally the group believes that the existing authority is not serving their needs or the needs of some identified target group. To accomplish its aims the group may exclude the entire larger society, or that segment of it normally in control of that realm which the group adopts as its concern. The group may interact with other organizations in its community, but it is, or seeks to be, structurally autonomous, with its own formal or informal culture and constitution (Sarason, 1974) or "rules of the game" by which it functions. In that sense it is an attempt at institutional change.

There are many different kinds of alternative settings and they cannot all, nor need they be, reviewed here. What is important to recognize is that collectively they may provide a viable strategy for social change at the institutional level, when designed and implemented so as to contain certain characteristics that are both logically compelling and (unlike most intervention strategies) have a reasonable degree of research support from multiple sources and perspectives.

Alternative settings, like traditional settings, span a continuum of personal involvement for their members. At one extreme are total living environments such as communes or utopian communities, wherein the members usually have come together because they already share some common, overriding value system or philosophy of life for which they are willing to give up their individuality. Such groups have had religious, political-economic (often socialist) or psychological (avoidance of alienation) motives. The most successful, in terms of becoming long-lasting total communities, have tended to emphasize certain common characteristics, including sacrifice of individual material possessions, renunciation of the outside world, and giving up of one's individuality in favor of the group's values and goals (Kanter, 1972). While of interest as model communities of various kinds, or as experiments in group relationships, such communes have tended to have little impact (usually by design) on the larger society, even when they have survived for long periods of time. What is perhaps most interesting about them from a psychological point of view is that they tend to be most successful during their early stages, when members are working together to build something. At this time the membership appears to be most committed (Kanter, 1972). They may or may not actually be accomplishing their aims, but the process of engaging in activities with a common end, in autonomous and cooperative fashion, seems to create group cohesion and feelings of excitement, direction, and purpose.

At the other end of the continuum of total personal involvement (in the sense of *living* with it) are numerous instances of alternative settings that are either permanent organizations or temporary, task-oriented groups of people who come together for an agreed-upon, time-limited, and goal-directed purpose. For example, a group may create a setting or an organization to elect someone outside of the major political party organizations to public office, or to pass a bond issue, or to raise funds for a charity. Another example is the National Organization of Women, an ongoing organization which takes on specific projects from time to time, such as support for laws concerned with women's rights. Common Cause, a loosely aligned citizen's group organized to influence the major political parties and legislators, is another example. Obviously the aim of such organizations, unlike the total-involvement living arrangement of a commune, is to have an impact on the larger society. Such groups are often organized for specific community action and social advocacy purposes around a given issue, and constitute a viable means of institutional, particularly legal, reform. The strategy has not often been used by psychologists, but it nevertheless remains as one that is both viable and researchable in local as well as national politics. Some of the specific tactics of this strategy, which include community organization techniques to *form* the group that will work for change, are considered below in the section on community organization.

A third kind of alternative setting is one in which a group of people seeks to take day-to-day control, administration, and decision making out of the hands of an established organization or agent of the social order and replace it with its own. The aim is often to set up some kind of parallel service organization such as a medical clinic, a program for retarded children, youth services such as drug counseling, programs for juveniles in legal difficulty, mental patients, and so on. This sort of setting actually encompasses three different types that appear to the casual observer to be similar, but on careful scrutiny turn out to be very different. The various types of parallel service settings can be distinguished by asking: "who is in control here and how are the relationships, rules of the game, and contracts between people different from those in the original setting?"

In one case, the most common, which we will term the *subunit* approach, a group within an existing organization decides to offer a new program, for example a day-treatment hospital for mental patients who are able to live at home, or an alternative school program for children who volunteer for it, or any one of a number of "new programs." If all we know about a new setting is that it is now an alternative to the traditional, we still do not know very much about it, and it may be an old wine in a new bottle. For example, a day hospital program for ex-hospitalized mental patients may look like a real innovation because now the clients go home at night; however, if the staff is still making decisions for the patients, keeping them in a dependent role, and so on, there is really little change in role relationships. Fairweather, Sanders, and Tornatzky (1974; see below) found, for example, in a national study of mental hospitals, that those that adopt "new" programs are not necessarily those that adopt genuine changes in role relationships and locus of decision making. Similarly, many schools now offer "alternative" programs that are under the control and decisions of a subgroup of the school's staff and administration, and may or may not be new in the sense of a new contract between students and teachers, or the roles of each in actual decision making.[7] This is not to say that all reforms and new programs within existing organizations and directed by the established professional or administrative regime are necessarily old wine in

new bottles; it does say, however, that an ecological analysis of the relationships, roles, rules, contracts, perceptions of the members, and so on, needs to be done before it can be established that it is indeed a "new" program. Labeling it new does not make it so.

A variant of the above type of alternative setting, the *new-unit* approach, is one in which a setting is established, not by a group who is employed by the existing organization, but rather by a new group of professionals who sets up a program essentially in competition with existing programs. They may base their service on the belief that they have a better technique, for example as Graziano's group did (see Chapter II, p. 34). In this instance they offered a service for autistic children, based on behavior modification rather than on psychoanalytic treatment. Other examples appear every day as new schools, services, and programs are established in all areas of human service and education. As with the subunit programs discussed above, these new-units may or may not alter the institutional, ideological, or value base of the program. They may or may not be based on new roles and relationships between people. Simply being under new leadership or using new techniques is no guarantee of a new "setting for the thermostat."

In either of the first two variants of alternative settings (the new-unit and the subunit) there *may be* a change in the status of the target people with regard to their autonomy, decision-making power, and role in the organization. The third variant of this strategy, the *autonomous setting,* is one in which the autonomy, power, and control of the organization are placed directly, overtly, and specifically in the hands of the people who are supposedly served by the setting. The role of the professional change agent is ideally one of catalyst, facilitator, guide, or consultant.[8]

---

[7]Alternative schools are a good example of the diversity of internal characteristics possible in a so-called alternative setting. Smith (1974) has described seven different kinds of alternative schools. The term, as he uses it, simply connotes the availability of any sort of learning experience in addition to the conventional one offered in a public school classroom, and wherein the child (or the parents) has a choice between one or the other. Many alternative schools are not autonomous units wherein the decision making is in the hands of students and/or parents, other than in the sense that they may choose to participate or not.

[8]Depending on the particular purposes of the setting, professional skills may be useful and the strategy does *not* deny them. Rather, the skills, be they curriculum development for a school, teaching of specific skills or competencies, or even the use of specialized techniques such as programmed learning or behavioral principles, are applied in a manner consistent with both the style and goals selected by the target group. This

In one example of this latter sort of alternative setting the professionals will plan their own withdrawal at a predetermined point in time; the emphasis of the planning is around control by the members themselves. Fairweather and his colleagues exemplified this approach when they set up an autonomous society of chronic mental patients who live and work in the community. The professionals moved from what they called an "era of maximum professional supervision" to one of "autonomy" (see Chapter IX). Goldenberg (1971), in his work with delinquent youth in which an alternative to the correctional facility was established, arranged a similar withdrawal for himself and has also emphasized a "horizontal" as opposed to a "pyramidal" organizational structure. In this setting the staff, regardless of educational status or job description, shared in decision making and responsibility. There was what he calls a "sharing of functions." Everyone prepared the meals, lived in, took multiple roles, shared administrative jobs, and conceptualized and planned program activities. They all knew that the director would leave and not be replaced by an outside professional who would come in and "run" things. The residents, young men in their mid- to late teens, were free to come and go as they pleased. They paid rent and participated in the program *with* the staff. From the outset this autonomous alternative setting explicitly changed the rules of the game. Further details and outcomes of this setting are presented in Chapter X.

Other alternative settings with a similar ideology have been described by Rappaport, Davidson, Wilson, and Mitchell (1975) who have developed an infant day-care center totally under the administrative control of local residents and teenage mothers, and a graphics and printing program for the circulation of ideas, news, and advertising among residents of a Black community. These programs, like Fairweather's and Goldenberg's, emphasize the existing strengths and abilities of target communities, *assuming that they need resources, but not control.*[9]

It is this last variant, the *autonomous alternative setting strategy,* that is of considerable interest to community psychology for several reasons. (1) Such programs, as noted above, are likely to be based on a strengths model in which the very people who are supposedly being "helped" are expected to build on the skills they already have; in short, their existing abilities are respected. (2) Such programs tend to assess the rules of the game, the role relationships, and who makes decisions. The goals and activities of the program become open to question and change by all, including the target people. (3) The essential paradox between the role of "helped" and the aim of development of autonomy in the target group is overcome from the outset. (4) Such programs lead away from the trap of first-order change and the "game without end" which usually follows when a new program is set up, planned, and run by one set of professionals who simply replace an original set. The strategy tries to get around the fact that the more things change the more they remain the same. (5) Such programs tend to encourage diversity because they do not necessarily accept a stereotyped status quo set of values by which to judge competence and success. Many of the goals are set by the members themselves. (6) A program in which recipients of service are also the decision makers is likely to be sensitive to the cultural relativity of its decisions.

Much of the sense of the autonomous alternative settings strategy, as well as many of the pitfalls of implementing it, have been discussed by Seymour B. Sarason in a set of companion volumes, *The Psychological Sense of Community* (1974) and *The Creation of Settings* (1972). Sarason's emphasis is on the universal need for a "readily available, mutually supportive network of relationships" as part of one's everyday life, or what he calls identification with an

---

strategy should not be interpreted as professional abdication of responsibility or "benign neglect." However, the professional teacher, psychologist, or whatever professional, must recognize that the need for resources and training, or the need for opportunity to develop in one area, does not negate the target group's abilities in other areas, or their right to self-determination and autonomy.

[9]See Chapter V, p. 126, and also Chapter XI for a discussion of the relationship between these programs and training in community psychology.

"overarching" set of values, a "psychological sense of community." In his view the professions of psychiatry and psychology have failed to recognize the importance of how culture and apparently nonpsychological factors (religion, demographic patterns, transportation systems, economics), contribute to one's sense of community and psychological well-being. Many of the conceptions reviewed in Chapter V are attempts by community psychology to move toward the kind of paradigms that Sarason suggests have been absent in traditional psychology. From his perspective, taking the concept of culture seriously requires an understanding of the history, structure, and interrelationships between a community's institutions and an understanding of how this is assimilated by individuals. The criterion by which he would have us judge the usefulness of our settings, regardless of their specific aims and characteristics, is the extent to which they "create the conditions in which people can experience a sense of community that permits a productive compromise between the needs of individuals and the achievement of group goals" (Sarason, 1974, p. 155). He goes on to suggest that the acceptance of this "overarching criterion" should change the strategies and tactics of social intervention.

Sarason describes, as have many others, how the legally and culturally sanctioned practice of segregating atypical individuals in isolated institutions and in "special classes" is not only inhumane, but destroys their sense of community as well. Although he is not always clear on this point, in that he emphasizes how the *separation* of people from their local community and the labeling of them as deviants tends to be destructive, he is also aware that *it is more than separation* which creates the horror of prisons, mental institutions, and so-called special classes. It is also a function of being deprived of any means to control one's fate—an elimination of the possibility of autonomy—and in a real sense the creation of conditions for learned helplessness (see Chapter IV, p. 101).

To the extent that this second aspect is recognized it must be understood that there is no guarantee that introducing drastic changes, or even destroying institutions which isolate people (mental hospitals, prisons, "special" classes) would necessarily find them replaced by settings that, even when "community based," will accomplish the overarching aim suggested as desirable. Much as is pointed out in the above discussion of the different types of alternative settings, Sarason points out how often new settings based on professional control and responsibility have failed to be "new" in the most meaningful sense of the term.

The psychological sense of community is neither panacea nor program: an agreement on values in no way insures that there will be agreement on what action is consistent with these values. Neither in logic nor reality does a particular value give rise to one and only one course of action, and the inability to recognize this—to confront the fact that there is always a universe of alternatives—is one of the causes of ineffective action . . . the way in which professionals think of community responsibility and of community needs dilutes rather than strengthens the psychological sense of community of the professionals themselves, of those they seek to help, and of those in the wider community (Sarason, 1974, p. 192).

Moving from the observation that "impeccable values are no guarantee that the actions to which they lead will be appropriate," Sarason is often at his best when he discusses why new settings so frequently fail. The difficulties he cites are multiple in nature and in some ways serve as a kind of prophetic guidebook for would-be creators of settings. In this sense Sarason's 1972 volume is more a set of warnings than a "how-to-do-it" list of tactics. To summarize his rich experiential language is very difficult, and one feels more like a translator than a reviewer. Nevertheless at least some of his observations can be extracted for the would-be creator of settings:

1. *Know the history and the culture of the place and the people who make up the new setting.* This includes a careful delineation of the relationship of the new to existing settings. This must be understood "before the beginning." To create a new setting implies dissatisfaction with the older settings, and therefore it begins in conflict. Be aware that

the new setting could inadvertently have many of the characteristics and problems of the old. Although a new value or ideology that clearly sets the new setting apart may be professed, one must also be concerned with the organizational similarity that may arise, as well as the fact that other organizations are likely to react to the new setting in ways that they have related to existing settings. These cautions lead to the suggestion that personal involvement may obscure what is going on ''out there,'' that problems cannot be put off to the future, ''when we are established,'' and that the problem is not how to keep the setting alive as much as how to keep it true to its goals and values.

2. *The importance of the leader and the core group goes beyond their personality or their competence.* The leader and the core group must be knowledgeable about all of the issues of history and culture noted above. They must recognize that they do not really begin at the beginning, but rather enter an historical process of tradition and practices. In selecting the core group to work in the setting the leader must recognize again that more than competence is involved—a new relationship is being established and the rules of the relationship need to be made explicit. A structure in which decision making separates leaders and members can lead to future problems. The leader and the core group need to explicitly plan for their own growth and development by means of an explicit consideration of the rules of the game, or the contract between themselves.

3. *Beware of the myth of unlimited resources and the distraction created by new buildings.* There tends to be, in the fervor of reform, a belief that it is possible to have enough money, time, energy, or people to really solve the problem. In the helping services this myth is perpetuated by goals that include an emphasis on professionals fixing people. The real questions of how resources will be allocated (determined by values and priorities) are hidden by this myth. Buildings not only divert resources and attention from the real aims of a setting, but tend to isolate both

staff and clients from the community of concern (see Chapter III, p. 76).

4. *Leaders tend to become isolated and out of touch.* Leaders need to structure their relationship with the members of the setting so as to explicitly encourage two-way communication.

5. *The need for renewal and external critics.* If the task is for a setting to be useful rather than to simply prolong its existence it should bring in outside critics whose commitment is to the goals of the setting, not to be loved. These critics might include both professionals and community residents.

6. *Social science does not now have an adequate knowledge base for telling us how to create a new setting that remains consistent with its own values.*

7. *The problems of a setting are never solved forever and are similar to the creation of a work of art.*

The suggestions that an alternative setting is, as a creative process, similar to a work of art and that we do not have an adequate knowledge base, do not imply that we cannot systematically study the process and refine our understanding of settings both internally and as a tool for social change. In that sense it should be clear that the strategy is always potentially researchable. To conduct research one needs to specify criteria by which the setting will be evaluated and the methods by which it will be understood. However, these are independent of the particular goals, strategies, and tactics of social intervention that may require a special kind of sensitivity to the local culture and its people. An effort to evaluate the outcomes of autonomous settings must include a continual awareness of the aims of a setting where personal and social control by the members, rather than necessarily adjustment to the dominant values of society, are the criteria.

Despite the difficulty of its implementation, the desirability of the *autonomous alternative setting* with the creation of a psychological sense of community as its goal has been recognized in contexts so numerous and varied as to lead one to wonder why it has not been more widely adopted, at least in principle.[10] Goldenberg (1974) has recently noted, with some chagrin, the reaction to his program:

The process of development as well as the results of the Residential Youth Center (RYC) have been presented in a variety of different publications . . . although a book recently published about the RYC has been rather favorably reviewed in a number of different journals (including some of our traditional "liberal" ones), I have been struck by how little attention reviewers have paid to some of the issues . . . even though (they) easily comprise two-thirds of the book's contents. It seems, rather, that reviewers . . . feel much more comfortable focusing attention on questions concerning clinical results for and on the target population than on the institutional and political implications of a setting developed, as the RYC was, as a reaction against the prevailing conceptions and internal processes that characterize most of our university departments and community agencies (Goldenberg, 1974, p. 169).

Despite this apparent ignoring of the implications of such a strategy, the issue which underlies it is not new; nor does it lack empirical support from research in other settings. Organizational psychologists have recognized the importance of "horizontal" or flat versus tall structure as an issue of concern for many years. Although there is some controversy over which is better for production and satisfaction in business organizations, many, as noted earlier in this chapter, suggest that horizontal (flat) structure and direct participation in decision making is desirable. Unfortunately, most of these organizational interventions have occurred in existing businesses, and there has been little transfer to human service organizations or to new settings. Perhaps more importantly, even when the ideas have been transposed to human service organizations they have often neglected to include the target community as participants (cf. Schmuck, Runkel, & Langmeyer, above). It is almost as if the employees and staff are seen as one kind of organism and the "recipients of service" as another kind.

Much supportive evidence for the role of autonomy in enhancing human functioning has already been reviewed in Chapter IV. To the work on internal locus of control, learned helplessness, and alienation can now be added the organizational psychologist's arguments, as well as the Fairweather and the Goldenberg programs which support the *autonomous alternative setting* as a strategy of social change, which is both consistent with the values presented in this book and empirically based.

There are many other sources of evidence, including the work of O. Hobart Mowrer (1975) with "integrity groups" for middle-class people. These groups bring people together in a given community and they are self-perpetuating and leaderless. They are designed to overcome, by means of developing communication links between people, the alienation that many of them feel, especially as a result of the decreased importance of family and religious organizations. Although data are minimal here, at least the self-reports of participants (many of them middle-class adults and college students), are suggestive of the conclusion that they fill a felt need. The same, of course, can be said of other variants of the "group movement." Their success as "genuine" therapy or mechanisms for behavior change notwithstanding, many people feel the need for such attempts to reduce their feelings of alienation and unhappiness. In a related vein, Tapp and Tapp (1972) have argued, on the basis of a review of the history of religious movements which clearly have had aims of social welfare and socialization similar to the helping professions, that the community psychology movement itself is an indication that the agencies of social control are heading toward greater tolerance for diversity. Presumably this

---

[10]It is interesting that the sense of this approach has probably had its greatest impact on nonprofessional groups who stand to lose little from its implementation, as opposed to professionals who stand to lose power, control, and prestige. Alcoholics Anonymous and Synanon, the well-known drug treatment program, are good examples of programs that operate entirely autonomously. Although their effectiveness compared to some "ideal" of success is not necessarily established, it is quite clear that they do no worse, and probably do better, than the existing professional approaches. Similarly, the "helper therapy principle" or the fact that self-help groups often lead to improvement in the psychological well-being of the helpers themselves, even when the very helpers viewed in other paradigms could be the recipients of service, seems to only exist in the awareness of professionals as a kind of interesting curiosity, with few if any implications for professional activity.

will lead to increased numbers of autonomous alternative settings.

A final note with additonal empirical support for the positive outcomes likely to accrue from the development of autonomous alternative settings among ethnic groups, a special case of such settings, is found in a review of history and laboratory and field studies of group cohesiveness (Guttentag, 1970). According to Guttentag's review, the small-group literature from social psychology suggests that especially low-status persons find group membership to be subjectively and objectively advantageous. Protected by the group, such people often feel better able to reject the majority norms and express their hostility and self-direction, rather than turning it toward self-hatred. Such groups also have greater real power (as a kind of collective bargaining organization) and also work more productively. Although they do not necessarily problem solve "better," they do develop a sense of autonomy, freedom of expression, and support for the efforts of their members as judged by their own criteria. Guttentag's historical analysis of religious and ethnic movements shows that although these groups may withdraw from the larger society, they also are less likely to depend on it for welfare programs, and less likely to show personal maladjustment such as alcoholism and suicide. Finally, they tend to consider themselves superior rather than inferior. She goes on to observe that:

In the past, an important characteristic of groups which have maintained ethnic cohesiveness, despite poverty, has been their control over, and responsibility for, educational, social, and some economic self-help functions . . . . In any struggle over power, money, or control, the individual, especially the poor individual, is helpless against an organization; it is organizations that interplay with, bargain with, and acquire power from organizations (Guttentag, 1970, p. 126).

Guttentag confronts the same question that Goldenberg asked. In light of all this evidence (and remember, her evidence is from a whole set of empirical research and historical analysis different from Goldenberg's and from that reviewed in Chapter IV), why have social scientists not emphasized the positive effects of group cohesiveness among ethnic minorities? She offers several interpretations. First, in a discussion of power and control one is generally forced to be either for or against the dominant authority, and social scientists of this generation (as opposed to those who wrote in the 1940s) have no personal experience in the struggle for ethnic identity. Very few are Black, Mexican-American, or native American, the groups that are in the forefront of the current struggle for power and identity. Inadvertently, social scientists may take a perspective which stresses collective goals of the larger society on the assumption that working together is "good" and being apart is "bad." Second, according to Guttentag, the literature on social change is influenced by a nineteenth-century idea of progress which assumes that we are always evolving toward a better and more just society, and that elimination of group tension and conflict is desirable. She questions the validity of this argument and cites Amir's[11] (1969) review of ethnic relations, which finds that simple integration between ethnic groups does not necessarily lead to the presumed positive effects.

Guttentag's conclusions with regard to strategies for social change are similar to those who argue for alternative autonomous settings as opposed to traditional organizational reform:

Government strategies in which help has been given to the poor individual or nuclear family by government-run agencies have not been markedly successful. It is reasonable to suppose that the overall goals of the society will be more readily furthered through the promotion of ethnic cohesiveness among poor minorities. Cohesiveness leads to organized attempts to gain economic and social control. And this struggle in turn promotes greater cohesiveness. It is only in organized groups that the poor have some chance of wresting power from government. Control over economic and social functions in a context of cohesiveness not only reduces some of the psychological

---

[11]Amir found that contrary to the myth of integration (or the "contact hypothesis," which assumes that interaction with other groups leads to better relationships), merely putting people of different ethnic backgrounds together is no guarantee of positive changes in attitudes or behaviors. Rather, the outcome depends on a variety of conditions (he summarizes eight) such that the assumption that contact necessarily lessens conflict is viewed as naive.

disadvantage of being poor but provides at least one avenue for achieving power and rising out of poverty (Guttentag, 1970, p. 128).

The final section of this chapter describes some of the strategies and tactics of institutional change that have emphasized data collection and research together with the creation of alternative autonomous settings. Before we turn to that approach we need to consider a second set of strategies and tactics for institutional change— community organization and social advocacy. This approach is aimed at creating societal awareness, entry conditions, and establishing the structures and social organization necessary for "out-groups" to influence the existing organizations of society. It is a second strategy that may be useful when one seeks a more equitable share of social power and resources for those members of society who do not now fit into existing structures.

Community Organization and Social Advocacy

As we move to the strategy and tactics of community organization and social advocacy our concerns shift away from questions such as: What is the best way to deliver a service?; what is the most efficient and effective way to run an organization?; and what social welfare programs are the most effective? Instead, there is an implicit assumption that such questions are either irrelevant or that the answers are already known. The answers may be considered "known" on the basis of previous research which has demonstrated a superior way to deal with a social problem (e.g., see Fairweather's approach below), or they may be considered known on the basis of face-valid, usually value-based assumptions about how things "should" be.

A community organization and social advocacy intervention, which aims to increase the number of jobs held by minority group members or by women, will usually not be based on the assumption that they will necessarily do a better job for an employer than his current employees, but rather that they have a "right" to jobs because of their status as human beings, citizens, and community members. This declaration of

"rights" is taken to be an absolute, in the same sense that the American Declaration of Independence could assert unalienable rights. Some of these rights are based on legal precedents, for example, the right to nondiscrimination in education and employment, but their real basis lies in a much deeper sense of one's view of justice. It is the spirit of the law rather than its letter that is the major justification for this strategy. For that reason those engaging in the community organization–social advocacy approach will not always be satisfied by formal compliance with law (although that is sometimes its short-run aim) and will often push for changes in the law itself or in the informal procedures by which a society functions. In this sense it is a strategy rooted in a desire for change in the very institutions of society.

A second rationale for social advocacy programs may be the unequal distribution of wealth, viewed as a function of the institutional practices of our economic system, and may serve as justification for social interventions aimed at changes in that system. We are speaking here of reforms, rather than revolution, and most concrete goals sought turn out to be quite specific. Consider the fact that a social movement for the establishment of national health insurance changes the basic relationships between our economic system and our health care system, yet many people who advocate such institutional change are far from revolutionary. The same may be said for those who seek local community control of schools and of health and welfare agencies. Revolution *could* be a strategy used to obtain such goals, but the strategy is not a goal in and of itself. Community organization and social advocacy is similarly a strategy, rather than itself a goal. The goals of such a strategy can vary as much as there is variance in a person's values, ideals, and sense of justice. What is specific about this strategy is that it assumes that power resides in social organization and in the assertion of one's "rights," however defined. For a community psychology, which may concern itself with the poor, the powerless, the deviants, and the excluded communities of society, the strategy also assumes that such power and control is an unrealized potential, an untapped human resource that can be stimulated to create change. Implicit is the assumption that the very stimulation of such human resources will create positive effects among the members of the community. For some it will enhance self-esteem, for others it will reduce alienation, and for still others it will simply give them access to material resources. But these are all side effects. The real aims are to create basic structural changes that will ultimately affect everyone in the community, not only the direct participants in the strategy.

Community organization–social advocacy is a strategy for social change in the best traditions of American political organizations. So-called machine politics have always used it and it was learned very early in the experience of American immigrant ethnic groups. One of the first things the immigrant learned was how to obtain resources through political organization. Alistair Cooke (1973) puts it succinctly as he describes early twentieth-century immigrant neighborhoods in America:

In exchange for your vote, a quid pro quo so elementary that it was only rarely hinted at, he (the neighborhood politican) would do his damnedest to get you a job, he would fish your son out of trouble, he would hound the landlord to repair the stove or the bath tub . . . . In bad times he brought up coal and food. He knew when the baby was coming and he got the doctor. These were not casual good deeds. They were the daily grind of a system as subtle and firm as the lineaments of city geography that dictated it (Cooke, 1973, p. 288).

That "subtile and firm" system was, and in many cities today still is, a tightly organized unit from block to precinct to ward to city and county. Today purely ethnic political organization has partially given way to social class and occupational organization, but the principle remains: organization is power.

Organization was also used by immigrants to gain economic and human rights for working people, through the labor union movement. Again, as Cooke describes the phenomenon:

. . . the immigrant did not stay cowed forever. Henry Frick, Carnegie's bosom partner in his steel enterprises, was a fanatical opponent of labor unions, but

he was quick to see that the latest wave of immigrants could be employed as strikebreakers. One year he employed Hungarians to break a strike. But within a year or two he had to hire Italians to break a strike of Hungarians . . . . In an irritable moment Frick got off a profound remark. "The immigrant," he complained, "however illiterate or ignorant he may be, always learns too soon" (Cooke, 1973, p. 293).

Just as the principle of succession broke down for sociological predictions of neighborhood change when the Black man's turn came (see Chapter V, p. 151), the principle of succession also broke down when applied to the Black person's participation in the American political system and in the labor union movement. The root causes of racism and the historical experience of slavery are beyond the scope of this volume, yet it is clear to even the casual observer of American history that the social forces and institutional structures of our society have retained a special set of "rules of the game" for Black Americans. The rules are those applied to deviants, and that, of course, is the answer to that continual question, "why don't they, like the immigrants, pick themselves up by their bootstraps?"

The understanding of these rules, and the need to step outside of them in order to reestablish our basic social institutions, is a crucial task for social science. In this regard there is a very important debate that has been taking place among the social scientists and activists. Some argue that the issues of institutional social change can be dealt with only on a social-class basis (as in the Marxian analysis); others argue that it is an ethnic or racist phenomenon to be dealt with by gaining ethnic independence (e.g., the Black Nationalists). Although the two viewpoints probably each have validity, and undoubtedly interact in as yet undetermined ways, the position taken in this section of this book is that ethnic organization is a first step toward institutional change.

Regardless of whether it ultimately turns out that basic institutional change requires the kind of class analysis and struggle posited by the so-called radical economists (e.g., Anderson, 1974), or that the American capitalist system is able to bend with social change and not break, the basis for a coalition of lower-class people in a planned economy, or for obtaining resources in a free-market economy, must come from a condition in which each of the participants occupies a position of strength. Political power, like psychological power, must be taken—it cannot be given. Today's ethnic minorities—Blacks, Puerto Ricans, Mexican-Americans, and native Americans—like others who are "different" for whatever reason, must establish their own sense of self-esteem and their own basis of power and control as a precondition to equal status with other ethnic minorities, and ultimately with the majority. They must gain control over the institutions and organizations that affect their lives and thus acquire money, power, and human rights. It requires community organization and social advocacy.

The place of the social scientist in these avowedly political endeavors is not different from his or her place as a consultant to established political organizations. The community psychologist may serve as a resource to communities that are seeking social change in exactly the same way that the psychologist traditionally serves as a resource to established organizations and governments. The community psychologist can use research skills to collect data, provide feedback, analyze social policy, and so on, in all the ways suggested earlier in this chapter. The community psychologist can also provide evaluation of strategies for diffusion of innovations (see Fairweather, below) and can use whatever knowledge, skills, and procedures social science has to offer by making them available to grass-roots people in a coalition of science and communities seeking social change.

The tools of science need not be used to support established priorities. They can also be used to create new ones. The fact is, as discussed in Chapter II, all of social science is political and value-based. There is no legitimate or logical reason why social science cannot be made available to those who would change the society rather than those who would maintain the status quo. There are some reality-based reasons why this is difficult. One is money. Who pays the bills for research and the salaries of social scientists working with grass-roots

groups? Another problem is that most social scientists reflexively value the maintenance of social order. In addition to these factors most social scientists, not unlike other White middle-class people, are more comfortable working in their own communities and feel uncomfortable particularly in the Black community. This often serves as a rationalization for keeping away. It is confused with the need for community control as expressed by many members of the emerging ethnic leadership. However, community control only means that leadership, goals, values, priorities, and decisions about their own life should be made by community members and not by professional outsiders. That does not mean exclusion of the resources that can be provided and assistance that can be given. A consultant to the White House recommends, but does not decide. There is no reason why a grass-roots group should not be given the same respect.

In part, the problem for the so-called helping professionals has been that they dislike working for others. They prefer the illusion of independence masked by an underlying, unstated agreement about the aims of their work. When the aims, values, and goals of the social scientists are called into question they have a difficult time. The high-status professionals (as a group) do not really believe that they are the servants of their clients. When the clients are "just like" them the conflict of "who is running the show" need not emerge, but when the clients are different from the social scientist or helping professional the issue raises its ugly head. That in part accounts for the social scientist's inability to provide even adequate therapeutic services for low-income clients (see Chapters III and IV).

It may be that for those who would work for a change in the rules of the game, for second-order change, or change in basic social institutions, the first step will need to be taken "at home." To assist in community development may require a different role relationship to our "clients." Perhaps even the word client is a subtle but lethal assumption. Perhaps we need to work as partners for social change, each of us contributing whatever skills we have, always under the guidance of as democratic and representative a set of priorities as is possible. The issue of "democratic or representative," however, may need to be dealt with by defining each community of concern as the very people *directly* affected by any social program—the children and the parents of a given school, the actual clients of a mental health service, and so on—rather than some diffuse idea of "the community."

The role of the service professional in this strategy is to assist people in obtaining their rights and in mobilizing their resources. The role of the researcher becomes one of evaluating the effectiveness of different ways to do this. As conceptualizers the researchers develop a *theory of action*, and as experimenters they test out the theory by involving themselves in real-world social interventions. Most people who have involved themselves in social advocacy and community organization have not been research-oriented. Many of the "principles" they advocate are on the basis of nonsystematic experience. Nevertheless, such experience may be a valid basis for future action and, when well documented, has genuine empirical validity as case studies. Even when such principles are viewed as hypotheses for action there is no reason why they cannot be systematically studied and compared in future social interventions.

Toward a Theory of Action[12]

Social Work Views

In the remainder of this section the aim is to describe the nature of the various activities of those who have engaged in the community

organization–social advocacy role, and to draw from these experiences suggestions for tactics that may be applied and evaluated in the future. The most extensive suggestions in this area come from social work and from the writing of independent people who are outside the mainstream of identified professions. Although neither group has emphasized empirical research, there is a considerable amount of careful description of real-world programs that has been largely ignored by psychologists. That writing constitutes a first step toward the development of a theory of action, or a systematic way to initiate and to evaluate social change tactics. One of the important observations that may be gleaned from this literature is the fact that the suggestions for action are quite congruent with the suggestions supported by the empirical research reviewed in the last section of this chapter. In some ways what has been documented with research is what many people engaged in action programs have always known. It adds a good deal of validity to their suggestions in that it broadens their sphere of application.

Perhaps the most comprehensive and systematic overview of the field of community organization has been presented by Robert Perlman and Arnold Gurin (1972). Working on a project sponsored by the Council for Social Work Education these authors and their staff have combined an empirical and a theoretical approach to describing the activities of actual practitioners in the field. They have compiled a volume of analysis based on interviews throughout the country with many community organizers. In addition to their overview, a companion volume of case studies, illustrating actual programs, has been compiled (Ecklein & Lauffer, 1972). Together these volumes summarize a wealth of material for the prospective interventionist-researcher, and serve as a practical guide to how community organizers have worked.

Perlman and Gurin suggest that community organizers and social planners approach the world from a stance that anticipates social problems, rather than simply reacting to them once manifest. Historically, they view the strategy as rooted in the middle-class reform activities of Americans earlier in this century. Out of this

---

[12]A recent volume by Rothman (1974) came to my attention too late for a detailed description in this chapter and appears to be an important reference compendium of "action principles" which should not be ignored by future community psychologists. Rothman has examined and abstracted the literature of relevant journals in applied anthropology, political science, social psychology, sociology, education, city planning, community mental health, public administration, public health, and social work between 1964 and 1970. From the relevant studies he has abstracted *generalizations* and *action guidelines* covering practitioner roles, organizational contexts, technology and personnel in organizations, political and legislative behavior, citizen participation, social movements, social change process, and many other topics. He includes, for each topic, an extensive bibliography.

initially informal beginning were developed professions and organizations for social reform. Paradoxically, the reforms become institutionalized because ". . . the hallmark of the agitators' success is the establishment of some new entity—an organization, a program, a new piece of legislation" (Perlman & Gurin, p. 25). Once established the new entity quickly becomes part of the status quo, and over time rigidifies and becomes less responsive to new social requirements. It is with this in mind that one must understand that the need for social change is an ongoing, never-ending process. The work of the change agent is never completed. In a sense one works against oneself to establish organizations that, if successful in gaining effectiveness, will ultimately require change themselves. Perhaps one of the best examples of this is the American labor union movement. Originally a force for genuine social change at the institutional level, unions today are among the strongest supporters of the status quo. With regard to minority groups the unions in many ways hold a key, even more important than the employers, to opening up jobs.

As Perlman and Gurin view the history of community organization they note a continuum of concerns ranging from the involvement of people in self-help groups to the coordination of institutional resources for the provision of services. They have described what they term four "views of practice" that have characterized community organization and planning: (1) strengthening community participation and integration so as to encourage cooperation among various groups and agencies; (2) enhancing coping capacities by means of communication skills and problem solving among community groups; (3) improving social conditions and services by defining needs, setting goals, and mobilizing resources through changes in social policy; (4) advancing the interests of "disadvantaged" groups by increasing their power, their share of resources, decision making, and status (Perlman & Gurin, 1972).

The first approach, strengthening participation and integration of a community, is essentially a "process" approach. It views community development in a way similar to organiza-

tion development (see above, p. 173). By means such as the formation of a "community association" which represents diverse community groups and interests the organizer tries to build between-group cooperation. Perlman and Gurin identify several roles for this organizer. The organizer may serve as a *guide*, an *enabler*, an *expert* who recommends but does not decide; he may provide service in a kind of *social therapy* which helps different groups to reach understanding. The organizer in this role needs to understand a community's history, structure, demographics, and values.

The second approach, enhancing coping ability, is similar to the first and places the organizer in the role of feedback agent, provider of information, and promoter of intergroup communication. The organizer is a *catalyst* and *expert* with information to share, as well as an *implementer* who helps create new abilities in a community, and a *researcher* who evaluates outcomes. The third view, the improving of social conditions and services approach, is a social planning model in which the planners try to change the policies of existing organizations by means of social influence. They will use any "pathway" available in a given situation—obligations, friendship, persuasion, selling, coercion, and inducement are cited. The planner will do this by means of any resources; for example, money, personal energy, popularity, political standing, professional expertise, or whatever. The aim is to influence the prevailing powers to change their policies toward a given direction. Fairweather's (see next section) use of data and action, and his principle of perseverance are good examples of a program aimed at influencing the powers of an organization to provide more adequate services.

It is the fourth approach, advancing the interests of "disadvantaged" groups, that is of major concern to us in this section. The aim of this approach, as summarized by Perlman and Gurin, is to involve the poor in decision making, both to overcome their alienation and to realign the distribution of power and resources in the larger community. They cite two primary goals: one is to gain a "larger share of the goods and services dispensed by agencies" and the other is to arouse people to organize and to take action to obtain the first goal. The role of the organizer is as a *broker* who puts people in touch with resources they may have difficulty locating, as well as an *advocate* who argues the correctness of a position and challenges the existing institutions together with the community members. The organizer is a *participant* whose expertise is available to client interests. The organizer is not impartial, but rather goal directed and is an *activist*, helping to organize rent strikes, presenting grievances, and demanding "rights" considered to be denied. The research that is needed for this approach is focused on evaluation of the most effective *tactics* for obtaining goals in given situations. The usefulness of the change agent to the community is clearly measured by effectiveness in obtaining concrete goals. The change agent's usefulness to social science is in the ability to evaluate outcomes and clearly describe strategies and tactics based on an understanding of how communities function.

The social scientist in the role of advocate is a kind of borderline member of two worlds with one foot in the respectability of dominant organizations, be they university settings, government agencies, foundations, or service organizations. Short of this, the organizer-advocate-social scientist needs some form of popular support. This kind of relationship to dominant organizations is necessary in order to have access to some form of power and resources—people, money, information, or simply status. The access can be a function of legitimacy as a scientist or as a social policy analyst, or as a person with a constituency. Some basis for legitimate power is necessary. For the social scientist it may come by having a formal degree which enables one to obtain a legitimate social position. The other foot must be in the community of concern. The organizer cannot be so much a part of established institutions that he will be out of touch with the constituency. The balance between these two worlds is often difficult to maintain because the organizer becomes an outsider in both worlds. It is an uncomfortable social role; often it is necessary to shift between identification with the insider and the outsider, depending on the specifics of the situation and the changes generated over time.

An analysis of the various *methods* of community organization and social planning has also been offered by Rothman (1968). He describes three models found in the literature and experience of organizers, and distinguishes between them on 12 different dimensions. Table VI-2 presents these models—termed *locality development, social planning,* and *social action* —and compares them on the relevant dimensions. Table VI-3 presents concrete examples of each. Examination of Tables VI-2 and VI-3 will reveal that the social planning model is similar to the community mental health model, *locality development* is similar to organization development, but with an emphasis on the entire community, and *social action* focuses on grass-roots disenfranchised groups. Rothman's tables are self-explanatory and descriptive. As one reads through them it is important to note that Rothman suggests that beyond understanding the basic assumptions of each model the organizer should be familiar enough with the strengths and weaknesses of each, and the local conditions at the time, so as to be able to *select a tactic that is appropriate to the time and place*, rather than to be committed to one model. He suggests several guidelines for such selection.

1. In the event of a homogenous population of consensus among a community, or when the aims are to enhance responsibility and competence of existing groups, locality development is suggested.

2. If problems are routine and simply require intelligent use of existing information the social planning approach is most sensible.

3. When subgroups are in a conflict that is unlikely to be resolved by discussion of factual information, or when the aim is to create long-range structural and institutional changes, social action may be preferable. This approach may also be necessary when there are no existing groups who represent a given segment of the population.

4. The organizer should assess the situation by taking a problem-solving stance to determine which approach is best for the current situation.

TABLE VI–2   Three models of community organization practice according to selected practice variables.*

	Model A (Locality Development)	Model B (Social Planning)	Model C (Social Action)
1. Goal categories of community action	Self-help; community capacity and integration (process goals)	Problem-solving with regard to substantive community problems (task goals)	Shifting of power relationships and resources; basic institutional change (task or process goals)
2. Assumptions concerning community structure and problem conditions	Community eclipsed, anomie; lack of relationships and democratic problem-solving capacities: static traditional community	Substantive social problems: mental and physical health, housing, recreation	Disadvantaged populations, social injustice, deprivation, inequity
3. Basic change strategy	Broad cross section of people involved in determining and solving their problems	Fact-gathering about problems and decisions on the most rational course of action	Crystallization of issues and organization of people to take action against enemy targets
4. Characteristic change tactics and techniques	Consensus: communication among community groups and interests; groups discussion	Consensus or conflict	Conflict or contest: confrontation, direct action
5. Salient practitioner roles	Enabler-catalyst, coordinator; teacher of problem-solving skills and ethical values	Fact-gatherer and analyst, program implementer, facilitator	Activist-advocate: agitator, broker, negotiator, partisan
6. Medium of change	Manipulation of small task-oriented groups	Manipulation of formal organizations and of data	Manipulation of mass organizations and political processes
7. Orientation toward power structure(s)	Members of power structure as collaborators in a common venture	Power structure as employers and sponsors	Power structure as external target of action: oppressors to be coerced or overturned
8. Boundary definition of the community client system or constituency	Total geographic community	Total community or community segment (including "functional" community)	Community segment
9. Assumptions regarding interests of community subparts	Common interests or reconcilable differences	Interests reconcilable or in conflict	Conflicting interests which are not easily reconcilable: scarce resources
10. Conception of the public interest	Rationalist-unitary	Idealist-unitary	Realist-individualist
11. Conception of the client population or constituency	Citizens	Consumers	Victims
12. Conception of client role	Participants in interactional problem-solving process	Consumers or recipients	Employers, constituents, members

*From Rothman, 1968.

TABLE VI–3   Some personnel aspects of community organization models.*

	Model A (Locality Development)	Model B (Social Planning)	Model C (Social Action)
Agency type	Settlement houses, overseas community development: Peace Corps, Friends Service Committee	Welfare council, city planning board, federal bureaucracy	Alinsky, civil rights, Black Power, New Left, welfare rights, cause and social movement groups, trade unions
Practice positions	Village worker, neighborhood worker, consultant to community development team, agricultural extension worker	Planning division head, planner	Local organizer
Professional analog	Adult educator, nonclinical group worker, group dynamics professional, agricultural extension worker	Demographer, social survey specialist, public administrator, hospital planning specialist	Labor organizer, civil rights worker, welfare rights organizer

*From Rothman, 1968.

5. The organizer should be prepared to switch from one model to another as the situation changes, and to use them all in conjunction. For example, a phasing may be desirable wherein one begins with social action, gains support and resources, and moves to social planning.

Perlman and Gurin (1972) suggest that the activities of the organizer require what they call a *social problem-solving process*. They suggest that this process involves both analytical and interactional tasks which are connected in parallel steps that proceed as follows: (1) defining the problem; (2) building structure; (3) formulating policy; (4) implementing plans; and (5) monitoring. Table VI-4 presents the details of this process as they view it.

It will be clear from a reading of Table VI-4 that the steps suggested are essentially logical problem solving made explicit. There is no special ability required other than a careful analysis followed by implementing steps. The job is not easy, but it is not mystical, and does not require great technological or scientific expertise (with the possible exception of methods for careful evaluation and monitoring of outcomes), but careful, logical, and planful actions, with a sensitivity to diverse people and social situations.

Within such an orientation the specific tactics one uses will be dependent on the local situation, and it is literally impossible to list or even imagine all possible tactics here. It is possible to note some tactics which have been most commonly used by organizers, with varying degrees of success.

The View of Activists

The Ecklein and Lauffer (1972) volume of case studies describes the use of tactics such as community surveys, the formation of block clubs, tenant organization, rent strikes, grantsmanship, planning organizations, leadership training, and many other specific tactics that are as various as are the content aims. Biddle and Biddle (1968) have put together a training guide for local workers which discusses multiple roles and skills. Another excellent book, available in a 300-page paperback, has been put together by a group known as the "O.M. Collective." They claim to represent leaders from among ethnic, labor, women, and student groups, as well as doctors, professors, and lawyers. Their writing, entitled *The Organizer's Manual* (1971), is explicit, logical, and informative to the novice. It includes a bibliography of books and organizations for further reference.

TABLE VI–4 Analytical and interactional tasks by phases of problem solving.*

	Analytical Tasks	*Interactional Tasks*
1. Defining the problem	In preliminary terms studying and describing the problematic aspects of a situation. Conceptualizing the system of relevant actors. Assessing what opportunities and limits are set by the organization employing the practitioner and by other actors.	Eliciting and receiving information, grievances, and preferences from those experiencing the problem and other sources
2. Building structure	Determining the nature of the practitioner's relationship to various actors. Deciding on types of structures to be developed. Choosing people for roles as experts, communicators, influencers, and the like.	Establishing formal and informal communication lines. Recruiting people into the selected structures and roles and obtaining their commitments to address the problem.
3. Formulating policy	Analyzing past efforts to deal with the problem. Developing alternative goals and strategies, assessing their possible consequences and feasibility. Selecting one or more for recommendations to decision makers.	Communicating alternative goals and strategies to selected actors. Promoting their expression of preferences and testing acceptance of various alternatives. Assisting decision makers to choose.
4. Implementing plans	Specifying what tasks need to be performed to achieve agreed-upon goals, by whom, when, and with what resources and procedures.	Presenting requirements to decision makers, overcoming resistances, and obtaining commitments to the program. Marshalling resources and putting procedures into operation.
5. Monitoring	Designing a system for collecting information on operations. Analyzing feedback data and specifying adjustments needed and/or new problems that require planning and action.	Obtaining information from relevant actors based on their experience. Communicating findings and recommendations and preparing actors for a new round of decisions to be made.

*From Perlman & Gurin, 1972.

The book covers such topics as small-group and grass-roots organizing, fund raising, self- and mass-education, and development of alternative settings with various content aims including drug programs, learning centers, tenants unions, and youth services.[13] It also reviews specific tactics such as marches and sit-ins, strikes, and boycotts. Finally, the authors discuss the use of "establishment" organizations and some of the special problems of working with specific groups of people. As its authors note, "the book was not spun out of an ideology, nor founded on a systematic theoretical analysis . . . (but rather) is a practical, how to do it (set of) suggestions."

It is informative to compare some of the O.M. Collective's suggestions, based on a wealth of practical experience, with the suggestions offered as "principles" by Fairweather (see the last section of this chapter) who has completed an extensive empirical research project using sophisticated research design and statistical analysis in order to assess the best

[13]In the area of organizing youth services an excellent description of the development of multiple services for adolescents on a small or zero budget, together with a consideration of political problems and a theory of adolescence, has been written by Gross (1975).

methods for diffusion of an innovation. Although there is not agreement on every point, the basic sets of suggestions are quite compatible with Fairweather's work and indicate that there are many ways in which one can learn useful information, not all of which are under the control of standard "scientific methods." Some of the suggestions from the O.M. Collective with regard to strategy and tactics of both organizing and of negotiating with those in power are:

1. "Organizations live in action and die in committee." This means, quite explicitly, that involving the members in concrete activity and specific tasks rather than in long discussion is a more effective tool for generating results. The same priciple is one of the prime findings of Fairweather's research discussed in the next section, and has also been suggested by many others (see p. 210).
2. Actions should be organized not only to accomplish specific aims, but also so that the organization can learn, through feedback from outcomes, how to do it better.
3. Try to get as many different people and groups involved as possible, by encouraging small-group participation.
4. Select an issue for organization of the group that relates to current concrete problems as they (the members) view them, and that can be used to expand actions to other issues. Pick clear issues, not abstractions.
5. Be sure that you and your group are knowledgeable about the issues and the history of the problem before you start.
6. Make your goals clear and specific. Write them down.
7. Timing is essential. Arrange actions in a sequence.
8. Start with small actions and those that are likely to lead to success and the building of a base of support.
9. Good small-group structure (communication, cohesiveness, and commitment) will be necessary to overcome setbacks.
10. Learn from failure.
11. In negotiating with those in power demand more than you want, so as to leave room for compromise.
12. Know as much as you can about the people you are trying to influence.
13. Stick to your principles and demands; do not compromise on the crucial principles.
14. Be skeptical.
15. Avoid being talked into forming "committees" to consider the demands.
16. If you are winning, allow the opponent to save face.
17. Plan ahead. Every power structure will resist change. Do not base your campaign on reaction to resistance. Rather, base it on the issues, analysis, and carefully planned actions.

They make many other suggestions, but these are illustrative and will provide a sufficient example for comparison to the research findings presented in the last section of this chapter.

The Alinsky Approach

Another writer who has suggested "principles" for community organization is Saul Alinsky (1971). His activities, which grew out of an early involvement as a labor organizer, led to the develpment of the *Industrial Areas Foundation*, a group devoted to organizing various "have-not" communities. They have most recently developed a training institute for community leaders and have focused on the need for middle-class groups to organize and confront their own set of economic, social, and political issues. The tactics of the Alinsky strategy in poor communities have been highly publicized and analyzed by many. They are aimed at the creation of what he calls "mass organization," and have recently been summarized by Robert Perlman (1972).

Using the example of Alinsky's involvement in Rochester, New York, during the mid-1960s, Perlman cites several steps by which the Alinsky approach operates: (1) It requires a base of support and resources outside the low-income target community. Supporters must guarantee, for a specified period of time, to provide the financial resources to pay salaries and operate an organization over which they will have no "say." In Rochester this support was provided by a council of churches that raised $100,000. This initial requirement is a part of the larger requirement that the organizer be invited in by the local people. In order to be invited, the organizer obviously first needs to have been proven to be a person in whom the group can have faith. More on this is presented below. (2) By setting preconditions to coming into a community Alinsky's approach begins to organize before the organizer arrives. (3) The organizer helps to meet the preconditions by holding preliminary meetings, polarizing issues, and identifying the "enemy." (4) The organizer suggests, as examples to stimulate thinking, the kinds of issues and tactics that might be used. (5) The tactics described and used often involve a principle that might be called "creative surprise." For example, Alinsky described to the Rochester group how he had organized 3000 Blacks in Chicago to go to one of the department stores, make small C.O.D. purchases to tie up its trucks, and then refuse the packages when delivered. The presence of large numbers of Blacks at the store also scared away many White customers. This was followed by negotiation for over 100 jobs for Black workers. (6) Alinsky views violence as a consequence of lack of organization. Organization leads to power (and he means both political and psychological power) and eliminates the need for violence. (7) His approach is not a program, but a *process* in which he offers technical assistance; he models and trains by demonstrating alternatives and assisting local leadership without selecting its goals. (8) The Alinsky-organizer, very early in the process, works to develop a "core group" and to convert issues to actions. (9) The aim is often to push people to take actions when they might normally be hesitant. This requires selection of several small goals likely to be successfully accomplished early, and aims toward increasing the perception of power among the group and among outsiders. (10) The shift of power in a community is the goal rather than some specific policy change. (11) Concrete programs are a means rather than an end in themselves. (12) The organizer remains a background figure who advises the core group.

In order to grasp the flavor of Alinsky's approach it is really necessary to experience his methods directly, although his writing does capture some of the charismatic ability to stimulate action. In his last book, *Rules for Radicals*, Alinsky (1971) relates in a rambling conversational style many of his thoughts about community organization. It is impossible to reproduce all of them, but a sampling of his ideas, presented below, will help to grasp some of the flavor of his approach.

Rules for Radicals is concerned with how to develop "mass organizations to seize power." It is not ideological, except that it is *for* change, which means in this context, a redistribution of power. To do this, Alinsky asserts, one must be able to take control over events and learn how to organize others to use their *potential* power. In an open society this means that there is no "fixed truth," and one takes a stance of "irreverence" toward the rules of the game. One must operate from the belief that "if people have the power to act, in the long run they will, most of the time, reach the right decisions. The alternative would be a rule by the elite . . .'' (Alinsky, 1971, p. 11). The job is to organize the people in whom one believes. One begins where these people are, rather than by imposing ideas to which they do not subscribe. This requires knowing the people.

Alinsky describes what amounts to the ecological principle of *interdependence* and the understanding that for every positive there is a negative, and that change is a process that is never completed. "The positive of today is the negative of tomorrow," and the most we can hope for is to understand the *probable* outcomes of our actions. The organizer is a pragmatist who views the means and ends in strategic terms rather than as moral absolutes. Alinsky views a concern with the morals of a tactic in some abstract sense such as "I agree with the ends but not the means" as a luxury that can only be afforded when multiple means are available. He lists several "rules of ethics" such as "you do what you can with what you have and clothe it with moral garments." However, it is clear from a careful reading of his pragmatics that there are certain overarching values that are literally the ideals of American democracy—freedom, equality, and justice. To maximize these values one cannot compromise them. However, one can make strategic compromises in negotiations. Alinsky's tactics are nonviolent and include negotiations because he views the organizing process to be most effective when dealing with our system in a nonviolent way. Nevertheless, his tactics are far from reticent. They confront, push, and demand action by placing others in embarrassing and uncomfortable situations. Conflict is viewed as necessary and desirable in a democracy.

Alinsky is not fond of academically trained professionals. He is highly critical of those trained to be "community organizers" by schools of social work. He sees them as failing, as a group, to understand that no situation ever repeats itself and that tactics cannot be learned by memorizing a vocabulary from courses in community organization. He also argues that social workers have a difficult time "repudiating" the two or three years of professional training which forced them into a given mold. The same, of course, is true of all professionals and one of the problems of which community psychology must be aware is the tendency to rigidify and develop a specific professional approach.

Alinsky describes the ideal qualities of the organizer as curiosity, irreverence, and imagination. It is likely, however, that persons who are really good, in a creative sense, at any task, share these qualities to some extent. To these qualities he adds that the organizer must be a "political-schizoid." By this he means that the organizer must polarize issues to create action. People will act when they are sure they are 100 percent on the side of "good," and the enemy is 100 percent evil. But the organizer must also know that in fact this is not really true. There is no all good or all evil, there are only degrees, and while *acting* as if this is not so, he must *know* that it is, lest he become a "true believer" and be unable to maintain flexibility.

We noted above that the Alinsky approach to organizing requires that the organizer be invited into the community. This, however, is not interpreted to mean that one is necessarily passive about obtaining an invitation. Consequently, Alinsky is concerned with how one creates the necessary entry conditions. In this regard his approach is to establish an identity on the basis of the experience of the people. One cannot simply be on the side of good, but rather must develop a reputation that by one's actions and statements, shows people he or she is against what they are against and for what they are for. Because the poor and the powerless often fear power and doubt their own judgment, the organizer must create a situation wherein the power being attacked acts fearful of him or her. By "baiting" the powerful and being branded a "dangerous enemy" who is feared, the organizer can stimulate credibility among the powerless. A reputation is, of course, helpful, but Alinsky also addresses the problem of how to get invited without a reputation. He suggests that by asking questions which stimulate others the organizer begins a process:

> The organizer's job is to inseminate an invitation for himself, to agitate, introduce ideas, get people pregnant with hope and a desire for change and to identify you as the person most qualified for this purpose. Here the tool of the organizer, in the agitation leading to the invitation as well as actual organization and education of local leadership, is the use of the question, the Socratic Method (Alinsky, 1971, p. 103).

Here is an example of a dialogue which Alinsky (1971, p. 103) presents:

ORGANIZER: Do you live over in that slummy building?
ANSWER: Yeah, what about it?
ORGANIZER: What the hell do you live there for?
ANSWER: What do you mean, what do I live there for? Where else am I going to live? I'm on welfare.
ORGANIZER: Oh, you mean you pay rent in that place?
ANSWER: Come on, is this a put-on? Very funny! You know where you can live for free?
ORGANIZER: Hmmm. That place looks like it's crawling with rats and bugs.
ANSWER: It sure is.
ORGANIZER: Did you ever try to get that landlord to do anything about it?
ANSWER: Try to get him to do anything about anything! If you don't like it, get out. That's all he has to say. There are plenty more waiting.
ORGANIZER: What if you didn't pay your rent?

ANSWER: They'd throw us out in ten minutes.

ORGANIZER: Hum. What if nobody in that building paid their rent?

ANSWER: Well, they'd start to throw . . . Hey, you know, they'd have trouble throwing everybody out, wouldn't they?

ORGANIZER: Yeah, I guess they would.

ANSWER: Hey, you know, maybe you got something—say, I'd like you to meet some of my friends. How about a drink?

In the beginning the community members will not be likely to know what they want. There will be stereotyped ideas and confusion because, argues Alinsky, only when people believe that they have the power to act will they really think about how to act. People need to have a reason for thinking. In the early days organizers, in Alinsky's style, are "out front," they "take the shit" and protect people. If they fail it is their fault, if they succeed it is the group's success. Later they need to know how to withdraw from the leadership role as others become willing to take risks. Organizations need to be based on multiple issues and actions. *"Organizations need action as an individual needs oxygen"* (Alinsky, 1971, p. 120, italics added). Continuous action requires multiple issues. In his chapter on tactics, Alinsky (1971, pp. 127–130) is clear that there are only general principles that can be kept in mind and adapted to the specifics of a situation. He lists several "rules":

1. Power is not only what you have, but what the enemy thinks you have. It is derived from money and/or people.
2. Never go outside the experience of your people.
3. Wherever possible go outside the experience of the enemy.
4. Make the enemy live up to its own book of rules.
5. Ridicule is man's most potent weapon.
6. A good tactic is one that your people enjoy.
7. A tactic that drags on too long becomes a drag.
8. Keep the pressure on.
9. The threat is usually more terrifying than the thing itself.
10. The major premise for tactics is the development of operations that will maintain a constant pressure upon the opposition.
11. If you push a negative hard and deep enough it will break through to its counterside.
12. The price of a successful attack is a constructive alternative.
13. Pick the target, freeze it, personalize it, and polarize it.

A Multiple Strategy-Environmental Resources Model

Most of the tactics discussed thus far in this section have been aimed at the organization of communities by social advocates. An advocate, however, may work at multiple levels of intervention. Recently Davidson and Rapp (1976) have detailed what they call an environmental resources conception of social advocacy. Although this is specifically discussed by them in the context of child advocacy, the reasoning is quite applicable to the decision making required by any social advocate, and helps to clarify some of the assumptions and processes required for the selection of a given level of intervention. Their conception of human behavior as a function of *resources available* to people and groups explicitly rejects the paradigms of individual or environmental deficit and supports the viewpoint taken in this volume—a pluralistic society that values equal access to resources. In this view *all* persons have a right to the resources of society, and the problem for an advocate is to decide how to assist a given person or group in obtaining their rights and resources. This environmental resources conception requires the kind of ecological analysis suggested in Chapter V, and is implemented as a social intervention by means of what Davidson and Rapp term a *multiple strategy model*, which is a nine-step problem-solving process (see Figure VI-2). The stages of this model are interrelated and contain feedback loops as indicated by double arrows in Figure VI-2.

The nine steps of the model are in three general phases: primary assessment, strategy selection, and implementation. During the assessment phase the advocate assesses the needs of the target group as they and others see them, together with the possible resources for obtaining these needs. This step involves identification

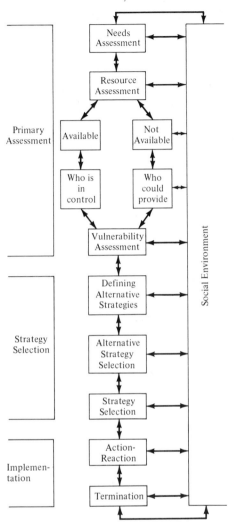

Figure VI-2. A multiple strategy model of social advocacy. (Redrawn from Davidson & Rapp, 1976.)

of as many resources as possible by brainstorming, interviewing, investigative reporting, or any other means. Who controls the needed resources is determined next, followed by an assessment of how to get the resources. This "vulnerability assessment" means considering what possible pathways of influence are available to obtain the resources from those who control them. Some of the questions to be asked are: What are the controllers' vested interests, ideology, and values? To whom are they responsive?

How can new resources be found and stimulated? This is followed by the development of alternative strategies, ranging from "positive" (gaining the favor of the resource controller) to "neutral" (consultation to the controller aimed at influence) to "negative" (taking direct and aggressive action, as in the Alinsky conflict approach). The third phase involves implementation, monitoring, and feedback so as to adopt new strategies as the situation changes.

To this rational problem-solving approach Davidson and Rapp add an important and often ignored consideration of the *level of analysis and intervention*. Depending on the particular situation, one may wish to be an advocate for a given *person*, in order to assist in gaining needed resources. For example, a child who is expelled from a school or who is having difficulty with a given teacher may be assisted by a child advocate who helps him to gain access to the school's and the community's resources, rather than one who serves as a "therapist." Alternatively, the advocate may intervene at the *administrative* (organizational) level. Here the aim is to create a more general effect on a given organization which holds the resources needed by an entire group of people. Finally, they cite the *policy level,* the level we have called in this book the *institutional level*.

The most important point of the above model is that within the social advocacy approach, positive, neutral, or negative strategies may be combined with individual, administrative, or policy strategies as the situation requires. Selection of the strategy combination is dependent on application of the environmental resources-oriented problem-solving model described above, rather than on traditional psychological or sociological paradigms.

Regardless of the level of intervention, or the strategy selected, this approach to social advocacy focuses on the resources of a community and on how to obtain them. It is particularly suited, as a model for social intervention, to the conceptions of social ecology and social systems theory described in Chapter V. The combination of theory, problem solving, and action devoted to locating, developing, and redistributing environmental resources avoids the need for blaming victims or environments, focuses on strengths, and responds to unique cultural needs and assets. It suggests, indeed it requires, a careful evaluation and selection of the appropriate level of intervention rather than focusing on only one level. It might even suggest intervention at multiple levels simultaneously, and requires examination of effects and outcomes at multiple levels of organization. It encourages exploration of novel rather than stereotyped solutions, including those suggested by the target group itself.

Unaffiliated Data-based Strategies of Social Intervention

Although identified by Hornstein *et al.* (1971) as a method for creating organizational change, the use of data-based strategies by unaffiliated change agents, such as consumer groups and university researchers, is included at the institutional and community analysis level because of its potential for influencing goals and priorities. The unaffiliated change agent who is database–oriented may use experimental research, surveys, or public records. All the methods of research are possible in *combination* with any other change technique. This change agent will often aim data at those not in direct control of organizations, such as legislators or the general public. Often data are communicated by the mass media rather than through professional journals. The data may be used either to persuade by evidence, or simply to provide a rallying point for action. Such strategies are aimed at *value/goal* changes or changes in the priorities of organizations, for example, making a safer automobile, not polluting the environment, expanding services to ignored groups, hiring minority people or women, and so on. Hornstein *et al.* (1971) point out that for this latter function the data must be *unambiguous, dramatic,* and *comprehensible.* These characteristics of data are not often found in traditional academic research. However, there is no reason why all of the methods of research available to social science cannot be brought to bear on the collection of data with stimulation of social change as its objective, and a clear presentation to the public as its style.

Research on persuasive communication suggests that it is best accepted if the communicator is viewed as both prestigious and objective. Here, of course, is an opportunity for social scientists to enter the real world, and this strategy is extremely important for university-based community psychologists who are unaffiliated with any established group. The strategy is generally applicable to all levels of analysis because data can be collected on a range of activities from individual level through community level, each with implications for social policy. The kind of data collected will determine the level of analysis for which they are appropriate. Consequently, the level of change sought should be determined and the nature of the data to be collected considered *before* the investigation is carried out. A common mistake is to base community level social policy on individual level data that happen to be available. For example, educational policy has sometimes been determined on the basis of individual academic performance rather than evaluation of educational institutions. This has led to programs, such as Head Start, which are incapable of solving the educational problems they set out to attack because they work at the wrong level (see Chapters VII and VIII).

The use of data to influence the basic values of our social institutions and the relationships among our various communities, or to establish a basis for change of priorities in our organizations, is essentially *a political use of social science methodology.* Such clearly political behavior is new to psychology only as a formal and sanctioned activity. In Chapter II we saw that historically data have often been used in this way. The use of intelligence test data by psychologists in order to influence congressional action on immigration policy during the 1920s is one example (Kamin, 1974).

This is perhaps a good place to reemphasize that all strategies and tactics, including the collection of data, can be used to influence social policy in any direction. The direction will depend on the values of the presenter. This is an assertion clearly not shared by those who view social science as a search for "truth." Data should, in this view, "speak for themselves" and tell the researcher what to recommend, rather than prove the researcher's predetermined views. Unfortunately, research methods in the social sciences lend themselves to objective "truths" of only a limited variety. First, data are rarely unambiguous, dramatic, and comprehensible. It is only the *interpretation* of data that meets these needs. Consequently *any* social policy recommendation is less than "pure." Second, and most important, *the very data collected as the criteria can change the outcomes of research.* For example, the Coleman report (1966) data on poor families' interest in education for their children were "objective" in that they counted the number of lower-class families who owned encyclopedias and who made concrete plans for their children to attend college. There can be no question of the objectivity of such measures. However, a different index, such as the number of parents who enroll their children in tutoring programs, might find different and equally "objective" results (see Chapter V, p. 118).

Social science data are so much a function of what measures one uses that "truth" is hardly what is commonly meant by the term. It literally becomes necessary to ask "truth by what criterion?" The answer to that question is heavily influenced by the values of the respondent. It must be made clear that what is suggested by this discussion is not that social scientists lie or deliberately distort, but rather that the names of the variables they study do not necessarily reflect the meaning of the data (see the discussion of Gergin in Chapter II, p. 38). That is, two pieces of social science research that are equally good methodologically may lead to very different conclusions, depending on the criterion measures used. Criterion measures most commonly used are those that reflect status quo social values. However, the researcher interested in change can use different criteria while remaining both scientific and objective.

The work of Labov and of Ginsburg, reviewed in Chapter VIII, finds that Black children are quite verbal and use language well. The same children tested by the criterion of standard IQ tests are found to be "nonverbal." Who is correct? Who has the truth? Clearly there are different truths that represent different values and meanings of the term "verbal ability." This is always the case, and social change by means

of data-based strategies suggests that such strategies may be helpful by using criteria that represent values consistent with the desired change.

A second example is provided by the work of Fairweather, reviewed below and in Chapter IX. He finds that he can keep people who are identified as chronically "mentally ill" living and working in a community by providing them with the opportunity and resources to function on their own in their own subcommunity. Nevertheless, many of these people are still "mentally ill" by other criteria such as psychological tests. Some current psychiatric theories have used similar tests of "psychological well-being" as a criterion for program evaluation, and would conclude that these patients remain ill. Fairweather argues that the criterion should be "can they, given the physical resources and autonomy, live outside the hospital?" Who is right? Data will not answer that question—only values will. In this case the community needs to tolerate deviants living together on "the outside," if Fairweather's research is to be convincing. In essence, the role of the unaffiliated data-based change agent is to present information in as clear and decisive a way as is possible, so as to convince the public, the press, and the controllers of the organization that new goals are sensible. Ralph Nader's success with consumer advocacy remains a fine example of this approach. Presumably, public interest research scientists could follow a similar strategy. Unfortunately, information once obtained is often not effective in creating change in and of itself, and political lobbying and other forms of dissemination are usually also necessary.

At the level of institutional change the two major classes of strategy reviewed in the preceding sections of this chapter—the creation of settings and community organization–social advocacy—may be combined with the data-based unaffiliated change agent approach. Ideally, any strategy would be carefully evaluated for both feedback purposes and as a means of dissemination of information. In reality this is rare. Here is one area where community psychologists may be able to make an important normal science contribution. Most of the change agents who have been involved in the creation of settings and social advocacy strategies have not been research-oriented social scientists. To the extent that community psychology brings its research interest and skills to these strategies and tactics it can yield important information on the creation of social change and build an empirically based theory of action. In this section that approach is specifically discussed. A data-based strategy for social change, which combines with the autonomous alternative settings model described earlier in this chapter, is best represented by the work of George W. Fairweather and his colleagues (Fairweather, 1967, 1972; Fairweather, Sanders, Cressler, and Maynard, 1969; Fairweather, Sanders, & Tornatzky, 1974). This approach has explicitly combined research methods and the creation of alternative settings. Fairweather calls the approach *experimental social innovation*. He has presented this strategy in the context of methods for social change and argues that it is the most promising available.[14]

The Fairweather Approach to Social Change

Fairweather (1972) suggests that historically the two most popular ways to create social change have been violent action or nonviolent protest. He finds violent strategies to be ineffective in creating genuine solutions to problems of social well-being for several reasons, including the fact that violence creates roles for people that are not functional once the violence is ended, and that such a means of creating social change is not compatible with the goals of human well-being. Consequently, if a democratic, nonviolent, and open society is desired, vio-

lence can at best serve only to draw attention to the current problems and cannot provide new solutions. It can overthrow existing rulers, but in itself will not create a better society. On the other hand, he views most nonviolent protest methods, such as demonstrations, as basically aimed at attitude change which in itself is ineffective as a solution to social problems. Nonviolence also does not necessarily lead one to the best solutions. Rather, Fairweather favors the systematic development of *innovations* and argues that the development of an atmosphere of continuous problem solving and change is required. By innovations he means new ways of doing things that have been demonstrated to work better than present ways.

Like technical innovations, a social innovation is an invention, or a new way of accomplishing some aim. However, social innovations often constitute a change in the role relationships between members of a society and therefore are more difficult to implement, even after they are discovered to be useful. Part of the difficulty lies in the criterion for usefulness. For Fairweather this criterion is useful to the *target people* rather than to the controllers of existing services. For example, if providing a group of chronic mental patients with a place to live and the means to operate a small business (resources), as well as *autonomy* from mental health professionals, were shown to be more effective and less expensive as a means to rehabilitation than current confinement and control, this would be more difficult to implement than if a pill were discovered to have the same results. This is because the autonomy solution would require a new role relationship between identified deviants and professionals now in control of them. The professional and the mental health status hierarchy become less important and lose power and control. Implementation of such changes requires more than their invention. If it is to be adopted, a social innovation needs to be met by a receptive society and requires an advocate or a salesperson who may or may not be the same person as the inventor. It is how to create this atmosphere of acceptance and what to do when advocating an innovation that Fairweather is concerned with.

---

[14]Fairweather's work is exemplary as an application of both the alternative setting approach and of work within the mental health system. In this section we will focus primarily on his development of a general strategy for social intervention which is applicable across content areas. His work as it pertains to the mental health system specifically is detailed in Chapter IX.

Donald Campbell (1969, 1971) has also presented a data-based approach which emphasizes methodology, but it is largely in a context of specific suggestions for research designs to evaluate existing programs rather than for *creating* social change.

To fully understand experimental social innovation as a strategy for social change the values that underlie the approach must be understood. For Fairweather, these values cannot be dismissed from the methods. He posits several biological "rights" of humans (e.g., to eat well, drink pure water, breathe clean air, live in decent shelter, and so on) as well as several social values. These include the right to love self and others, have human dignity and worth, true justice, individuality, and to live in a cooperative society. From this set of values he concludes that scientists are responsible for the use to which their technology is put, and that the role of the scientist cannot end with invention of techniques, but must include the assurance that inventions are put to a use consistent with these values. That is, the scientist must seek social change through direct action, not merely verbal statements, and the scientist is required to participate in *implementation* of the discoveries.

In addition to the above values Fairweather puts a great deal of emphasis on scientific method. ". . . there will always be others equally virtuous who believe that their own solutions to the problem will yield much better results. No person, however virtuous or insightful, can know the results of an innovation before that innovation is placed in action and evaluated" (Fairweather, 1972, p. 13). In this view the task of the social scientist is to conduct constant research on contemporary problems, so as to first find new ways to solve the problems and then to implement these new ways by encouraging their adoption by the larger society. Once adopted, the innovations are in turn investigated, improved, and so on, in continuous fashion. The process is as follows: a problem is defined; current knowledge of it is assessed from experts, books, and the people affected; several different solutions are devised; an experimental design comparing solutions is instituted in the natural environment; the outcomes of each solution are observed over a long enough period of time to permit selection of the "best" solution by researchers who are also responsible for the well-being of the people under study; and the "best" solution according to appropriate criteria is then disseminated to other places.

Clearly Fairweather has faith in the experimental model and although he recognizes the inability to pinpoint exact and universal cause and effect from a social experiment in the natural environment, the point emphasized is that evaluation of the outcome by agreed-upon criteria that reflect the well-being of the *target people* is absolutely necessary for social innovation to solve human problems. We need to know what the probable outcomes of our social innovations are before we engage in them on a large scale. Ironically, most existing status quo programs have never been evaluated. Nevertheless, to replace them with other unevaluated programs seems senseless from this viewpoint.

The kinds of social innovations that Fairweather is suggesting are considerably different from those suggested by organizational psychology. He is clearly interested in changing the priorities and goals or *social institutions* on which organizations are based, rather than with enhancing their ability to do their job more efficiently, or to keep their employees satisfied. This is what is meant by a social innovation. He suggests, for example, comparing an open-admissions policy with current practices in universities. He suggests comparing different kinds of public schools, including those based on student and/or community control. He also suggests the development of Black-owned businesses and community-controlled police forces, all to be tested against the standard models. What is important here is that while he wants experimental tests to be an integral part of his social change strategy, an equally important element of his approach is to develop "alternative social models" for the benefit of their targets. In developing these alternative models it is suggested that the change agent include, from the start, representatives of the so-called problem population as well as representatives who control the resources and the power to make decisions. When conflicts occur over the best model to implement, Fairweather's suggestion is to directly put the ideas to experimental test, with the provision that no model is admissible that the problem population itself would be unwilling to support. Although he subscribes to experimental test, there are some value-based "givens" in this approach. These "givens" appear to be consistent with the values of this book and also appear to emphasize independent and autonomous control by target people. Fairweather is approaching organizational change from the view of an outsider, not committed to the organization, but rather committed to getting the organization to implement an innovation in its priorities which is of maximum benefit to the *consumer* (student, mental patient, legal offender). The job of the change agent then becomes persuading the organizations to adopt the model that is best for the consumer, even if this requires changes in the organization's status quo.

The exact research methods suggested by Fairweather need not concern us here; they are all of the commonly known procedures available to social science. The difference in Fairweather's use of these methods is that he finds that they can be implemented in a straightforward fashion to compare alternative interventions, so that a social change agent can systematically observe the outcomes of her or his efforts. Perhaps even more important is what he uses these methods to accomplish. Donald Campbell (1969, 1971), who is perhaps the best-known advocate of the experimenting society and who has detailed many methods for assessing programs in the natural environment, is more representative of the "standard model" psychologist. He suggests that the researcher is essentially one who has a ". . .goal of learning more than we do now from the innovations decided upon by the political process" (Campbell, 1971). In this view, although the methodology of research is essentially the same as Fairweather's, the role of the scientist is only as an evaluator of the outcome of decisions made in the political process that is presumably outside the scientist's domain. For Fairweather, these two roles are not separable. Development and implementation of the very programs to be tested are both viewed as the responsibility of the scientist, equal to his responsibility for evaluation of their outcomes.

In pursuing these roles Fairweather's suggestion is that the initial program be small, because it might fail, but once the best alternative is discovered (as defined by criteria in the consumer's, not necessarily the professional's, interest) the role of the change agent is to implement it in other settings. "Best," of course, is relative and will require continual evaluation. To this point social science outcome research is theoretically compatible with experimental social innovation. Researchers often contrast alternative methods of treatment or teaching techniques; however, Fairweather goes much further. He suggests that if one has found something that works better for the consumer it is his or her responsibility to get it implemented, even if this requires changing existing organizations. It is at this point that he is concerned with institutional change. How can an experimental social innovator create change in a social organization when that change may itself challenge the status quo of the organization?

Fairweather's own innovation research, which has focused on the mental health system, is detailed in Chapter IX. In brief, he finds that the creation of small-group, independent living and work facilities, over which chronic mental patients have *autonomous control,* is a far more effective means of keeping patients living productively in the community (and costs less), than keeping them confined in a hospital and then sent out on their own to return for weekly outpatient visits to a therapist, or to pick up their tranquilizers. Armed with this finding he set about to understand how to disseminate the innovation, or to create change in the nation's mental health organizations. Ironically, he was not able to convince the very organization in which he developed the innovation to adopt it as a permanent program. *"Apparently, experimenting with a new social treatment program is one process: incorporating it into the ongoing treatment programs in quite another"* (Fairweather *et al.*, 1974, p. 10). It was at this point in his own work that Fairweather began to ask what techniques, strategies, and tactics could be used to incorporate new programs into existing organizations, and true to form he conducted an experiment to find out.

In detailing the experimental social innovation approach to social change Fairweather argues that although innovators will run "head on" into all of the active and passive resistance to change that society can muster, there is one advantage not usually available to social change advocates—actual experimental evidence that shows the new model to be better than the old. In a sense this argument is similar to the moral persuasion arguments of others in that it relies to some extent on the good intentions of those in power to act if not morally, at least rationally, because they see both their responsibility and the "best" solution available. This is a point to which we shall return in discussing the shortcomings of Fairweather's approach to social change.

In pursuing the aims of social change Fairweather is consistent in his belief that compromise of the new model must be minimal. In order to serve the public rather than the controllers of the organization who will adopt the innovation, compromise to simply make people in high-status positions "feel better" is unacceptable if the model is to work. For example, if the genuine autonomy of mental patients is a key part of the program, as it is disseminated it cannot fall under the control of mental health professionals, even if that is the only basis on which they will implement it. He provides another example:

If . . . a new secondary high school program designed for maximum student governance is found to decrease dramatically the number of school drop outs (a desirable outcome) in a minority community and to implement the same model in another area of the city the school board requires much more control by the teachers than existed in the prototype model, the resulting modification might destroy the reduction in drop out rate because the variable of student autonomy, which was the most important variable in the original model, would have been lost (Fairweather, 1972, pp. 32–33).

The first step in Fairweather's strategy involves contacting and involving the powerful and the controllers as well as the citizens and persons directly affected by the problem under study. Before an innovation can be implemented the advocate must gain the support of at least some groups, organizations, and citizens. For example, a new program in the public schools would require some support from the school board, the teachers, the parents, and the students. As Fairweather notes, there has been little scientific study of how to obtain such support, and he began to study that question in the context of changing mental hospitals. He views the problem of implementing an innovation as having three broad steps. The first involves *entry into the system*. The decisions that need to be made involve who to contact and at what level of the system. After questions of entry, the advocate needs to decide how to *pursuade* the target population to adopt the innovation, and finally how to *put the innovation into action*. The exact strategies and tactics will depend both on the specific system and the nature of the particular program. If one seeks change in a school policy involving the recommendations of students about the purchase of textbooks, the point of entry, methods of persuasion, and implementation may be different from those used by one seeking to implement a new program for mental patients in the local hospital. The exact methods that work at one time and in one place may never be the same, and to this extent "social change theories can be written only in the broadest terms" (Fairweather, 1972). This is a point that needs emphasis with regard to strategies and tactics because in this realm the variety of situations that a change agent is likely to meet is so multivariate and changing that the ideal of a universal set of strategies and tactics is senseless. Nevertheless, it may be possible to delimit a systematic set of principles as guidelines. Fairweather's work suggests that each step can be empirically tested so as to evaluate outcome.

The following experiment, designed to spread the use of autonomous living units for chronic patients, is exemplary of the experimental social innovation approach. Fairweather and his colleagues decided to contact, by a personal telephone call, almost every mental hospital in the United States. During this telephone conversation the researchers discussed the results of their early studies which had demonstrated the effectiveness of their plan for treatment of chronic patients, and offered to a representative of the hospital the opportunity to explore its possible value to that hospital. They offered each hospital either a *brochure* detailing the ideas and the outcomes of previous work, a *workshop* to be presented by a member of the research team who would visit the hospital, or to help set up a *demonstration unit* in the hospital in order to try out, in a pilot study, its feasibility. These telephone presentations actually constituted the first part of an experiment. The researchers arranged their calls in an experimental design such that the contact was made to each of five levels of "status hierarchy" including hospital superintendents, chiefs of psychiatry, psychology, social work, and nursing. The status of the contact person was systematically varied in conjunction with several variables including whether the hospital was urban or rural, state or federal. In addition, they systematically varied the offer of a brochure, a workshop, or a demonstration. This experimental design, aimed at assessing the relationship between the above factors and willingness to allow *entry* to the innovators, is depicted in Figure VI-3.

Following this entry experiment the researchers actually presented the offered service (a brochure sent to individual staff members from a list sent by the contact person, a workshop at the hospital, or help in setting up a de-

monstration ward) to those hospitals that had agreed to it. This constituted the second part of the experiment, in which they assessed how many hospitals in each condition were then willing to actually try to set up the new treatment program. The third step involved what they call the "adopting phase" and here again methods were experimentally contrasted. Each hospital that expressed a willingness to adopt the program was matched with another hospital, and one of the pair was given a detailed manual telling them, step by step, how to do it. The second was provided with an "action consultant" who would aid them in carrying out the plan. Finally, each hospital was followed for two years to see what happened.

The overall outcome of this experiment is summarized in Table VI-5. The results were as follows: Far more of the hospitals agreed to allow entry to their system when the entry itself was low cost in terms of commitment (a brochure or a workshop). More than two-thirds of the hospitals that were offered these services agreed to accept them; however, less than one-fourth of the hospitals that were asked to set up a demonstration ward agreed to entry. These

Social Status

		1 Supt.		2 Psychiatry		3 Psychology		4 Soc. Work		5 Nursing		N
Brochure	State	8	7	8	7	8	7	8	7	8	7	75
												85
	Fed.	1	1	1	1	1	1	1	1	1	1	10
Action Workshop	State	8	7	8	7	8	7	8	7	8	7	75
												85
	Fed.	1	1	1	1	1	1	1	1	1	1	10
Demonstration	State	8	7	8	7	8	7	8	7	8	7	75
												85
	Fed.	1	1	1	1	1	1	1	1	1	1	10
		Urban	Rural	Urban	Rural	Urban	Rural	Urban	Rural	Urban	Rural	
	N	51		51		51		51		51		255

Figure VI-3.   Experimental design showing the social status, action, urban-rural, and state-federal variables. (Redrawn from Fairweather, Sanders, & Tornatzky, 1974.)

TABLE VI–5. Number of hospitals adopting the fairweather innovation.*

	Mode of Presentation					
	Brochure		*Workshop*		*Demonstration Ward*	
Outcome	*(N)*	*(%)***	*(N)*	*(%)*	*(N)*	*(%)*
Total contacted by telephone	85	100	85	100	85	100
Rejection of entry	26	30	17	20	64	75
Permitted entry only	55	65	58	68	12	14
Permitted entry *and* later agreed to attempt adoption	4	5	10	12	9	11

*Adapted from Fairweather, Sanders, & Tornatzky, 1974.
**Percentage of total contacted in each condition.

findings, although not surprising in themselves, take on added importance when considered in relation to others. Of the 59 hospitals agreeing to be sent the brochure only four (7 percent) later agreed to adopt the new program; and of the 68 agreeing to the workshop only 10 (15 percent) later agreed to adopt. Although only 21 hospitals agreed to a demonstration ward, 9, or 43 percent, later decided to actually adopt the project. What this seems to indicate is that although an initial request for a substantial *active commitment* will be rejected by about 75 percent of the organizations contacted, of those that do make the commitment a substantial proportion is likely to actually adopt the innovation. Although a passive commitment to reading material and workshops allows entry to more organizations, the potential for change by these means is very small. Fairweather suggests that a combination of approaches may be necessary to create change. For example, one might get a foot in the door with a brochure or a workshop and then follow it up with a request for a demonstration project. It is clear that the passive approach (brochures and workshops) to change, the most common way that new findings are now disseminated, is ineffective as a means of adoption.

This argument that the key elements in creating social change are *active intervention* by the advocate and an *action commitment* by the recipient is bolstered by several other results of the Fairweather experiment. First, none of the demographic characteristics of the hospitals (e.g., urban versus rural, state- versus federally-funded) predicted to their acceptance or rejection of the innovation; nor did the status of the person contacted (e.g., nurse, social worker, psychologist, or physician). All were equally likely to accept or reject the offer. Nor were the financial resources available to the hospital predictive of adoption. Finally, of those hospitals that did agree to try adoption those that were given an *action consultant*, who met with them and helped them to implement the project, were found to be significantly more successful in implementation of the program than those hospitals that were provided with a detailed manual.[15] Again, the manual is most similar to the ways in which new information is transmitted in the standard publish-and-forget-it format. Actually going out to help others implement an innovation is rare for most researchers.

This experiment also involved a very detailed description of each hospital and its activities, discussions, diaries, demographics, and other data on hospital characteristics which enabled the research team to get a better understanding of the *process* involved in creating change. Using a cluster analysis to search for the variables that relate to change, they found that although the adoption of social change was dependent on "participative decision-making" in the workshop and brochure conditions, in the *action-oriented approach* of the demonstration ward (which was the most successful in creating adoption) minimal discussion and maximum ac-

[15]Despite variability in the experience of the three different consultants, all were found to be equally effective, and the researchers suggest that the role is more an encourager or a sounding board and perhaps a "pusher" rather than a technical expert.

tion take place. As they conclude, "it appears that the response to active intervention is an action response with a minimum amount of discussion while the reaction to verbal intervention is a verbal response culminating in the promotion of discussion within the organization" (Fairweather *et al.*, 1974, p. 103). They also found that high-change hospitals (those that were most successful in creating the new program) had a viable small group that identified with the new program and supported one another in action, rather than in discussion; and that greater movement toward development of the program was associated with hospitals that involved local community residents in planning.

The argument that *action* creates change has been suggested by others as well, although generally without empirical support. For example, Weick (1969), an organizational psychologist who is quite critical of much of his field, has suggested as one hypothesis with regard to organizing that even "chaotic action is preferable to orderly inaction" (Weick, 1969, p. 107). In his view action helps to clarify where the organization is going, whereas inaction is difficult to order meaningfully. The argument is also supportable by the evidence that attitudes follow behavior change rather than vice versa (Mischel, 1968; Wicker, 1969a). Finally, many other community organizers have suggested this approach for some time, although without "hard" data. *The Organizer's Manual* (1971), reviewed in a previous section, suggests in the very first sentence of the chapter on strategy and tactics that "organizations live in action and die in committee" (p. 105).

There are at least two negative findings in Fairweather's research that are of great importance and should not be overlooked. On the one hand, those hospitals that adopted the innovation did so because of the small, committed action group, and there was little evidence of a generalization to the entire hospital. The new programs tended to lead a rather isolated existence. To the extent that total organizational change is a goal, this experiment failed to produce it. In a similar vein, it should be recalled that of the 255 hospitals contacted in this study, less than 10 percent ultimately agreed to even

try the innovation, despite the fact of research evidence demonstrating its effectiveness. This brings us to face squarely the fact that demonstration of a best solution for the supposed recipients of service is inadequate as a means of social change. It also limits some of the findings of Fairweather's research to those organizations in the mental health system that are willing to make some active commitment, and that number is very small indeed. Finally, Fairweather makes the important point that many of the hospitals which did not adopt the innovation describe themselves as innovative because they frequently try out "new programs." He argues that a close look at these new programs shows that they almost always are limited to those that do not change the basic social relationships between patients and professionals; that is, they do not allow patient autonomy, or a change in the "rules of the game."

Despite the above shortcomings of this study, of which Fairweather and his colleagues are well aware, to provide definitive how-to-do-it answers, they do suggest several "principles" to be followed by experimental social innovators as guidelines for action. These principles can be viewed as one step toward a psychology of social change:

1. *The principle of perseverance.* This is, as anyone who has ever tried to do anything in the community is well aware, of major importance. The reality is that a great deal of constant and ongoing effort is necessary to obtain even the smallest movement. Fairweather's book provides those interested with many suggestions, by example, of how to push, pull, and stick to it.

2. *The principles of discontinuity and independence.* There is, in the results of this study, little relationship between the resources (salary, budget, space, staff size) and the acceptance of innovation. In a sense this can be translated to "where there is a will there is a way!" Forget the problem of scarce resources and instead find someone in the institution with the will, and help that person to organize and create a group for change based on action. Resources need not come from

allocations of large amounts of money. Similarly, in this study there was no relationship between the general social climate or the geographical location and willingness to adopt the innovation. Once again, action is emphasized. Although initially one may need to convince supporters, the real challenge is to move them from a recognition of the solution toward action to implement it.

3. *The principle of outside intervention.* Fairweather suggests that the role of the intervener must be to serve as an active, personally involved worker who encourages others on the one hand to view the project as their own, but on the other hand who keeps it consistent with its major ingredients. The actual style of the outside change agent is less important than the ability to keep up the morale of the change group. Directive and nondirective styles are equally effective so long as they are persistent and stress actions.

4. *The principle of action-oriented intervention.* Strategies based on tasks to be accomplished and behaviors to be completed work better than those aimed at attitude change.

5. *The foot in the door principle.* A strategy of gradually moving from discussion to behavioral commitment is suggested. For example, the researchers hypothesize that they might have been successful if they had gone back to those who refused a demonstration unit and offered them a workshop, followed by a new request for a demonstration unit. It should be emphasized, however, that the danger here is that the advocate will be satisfied with verbal commitment. Although one may need to start where the organization is willing to let one in, a continual push for action is essential.

6. *Do not be constrained by the power structure.* Those in higher status positions are no more essential to change than those in lower levels. Find whoever is willing to change and start there. Change can start from the bottom as well as the top.

7. *The principle of participation.* Get as many groups as possible involved; the innovation will not automatically diffuse.

8. *The principle of group action.* A group that is cohesive and committed must be developed. The members can come from any status level.

Other principles they suggest are that resistance to change is proportional to the role change required; continuous experimentation and feedback evaluation is essential; and the creation of "diffusion centers" for identification of those who want to "spread the word" to others is needed.

Most of the suggestions are based on a sensible combination of empirical data and astute observation. They are perhaps surprisingly similar to the suggestions of others who have engaged in active community change efforts even without conducting formal research (see the section on community organization and social advocacy, above). In a sense we have here empirical verification of the need for *more* than data. True we do need data, but alone they are not enough. Consider, for example, the fact that the number of hospitals studied by Fairweather that were actually willing to change was very low, indicating that a data-based approach to social change is unlikely in and of itself to be terribly successful, even when evidence for the effectiveness of the new solution is good. More to the point is the fact that the controllers of our hospital systems did not really have a basic clash of values with the innovators. That is, everyone could agree that the aim of assisting mental patients to be able to function independently is at least theoretically sensible and indeed is the *job* of our institutions. Resistance to change may have been based on fear of loss of status, or dislike of intrusion, or any number of unspoken resentments, even including an honest disbelief that the solution suggested really is the best. But even so, the major *intention* of the advocates for social change is difficult to argue against because it is theoretically the same as the hospital's. What if the aims or values of a social change agent are also challenged?

For example, suppose it could be demonstrated that members of a given minority community have a high unemployment rate, and that a large local firm, by providing jobs for these unemployed people, could reduce their poverty, enhance their well-being, and so on. In so doing the firm would perhaps initially reduce its margin of profit because it would need to invest in the training of new employees, establishment of a mechanism to assist the other employees and managers to deal with resentment, and so on. It might even turn out that the profits are permanently reduced because more people are employed than are needed. We are not talking about eliminating profit, simply reducing it. Such a program would, seemingly without question, benefit the currently unemployed workers. Here then we will observe a basic clash in values and priorities—is the company free to exclude currently unemployed workers if it infringes on their (the company's) profits? Some would argue that a reduction in profit would be, for many large firms, no greater than that incurred by advertising, or contributions to political campaigns, or public relations programs. Yet here, where the basic values are in question—human welfare versus economic growth—the resistance to change might be expected to include all of the resistance met by Fairweather in the mental hospitals, and more. The experience of Saul Alinsky in Rochester, New York, in attempting to convince the Eastman Kodak Company, an international corporation, to hire 500 Black workers is a case in point. Kodak did not leap at this chance to "do good" despite a minimal loss of profit that might have followed. Alinsky and other social change agents therefore find it necessary to use other strategies than (or in addition to) presentation of data.

This same fact is repeated even in institutions not based on profit. Public schools are often unresponsive to the expressed needs of students who do not want to do things in the traditional way. No amount of data on effectiveness of community-controlled schools or student participation in decision making as a means to keep students in school is going to change the fact that most public school systems do not want parents and students telling them what to teach or how to teach it. In order to get the data necessary to show that local community

control really can work (remember "work" means accomplish what the community members want, not necessarily what the professionals want) political movements based on community organization and social advocacy are necessary. Similarly, in the field of health delivery, physicians will fight to preserve a "free enterprise system" that everyone knows does not serve the poor. How can they be convinced to change? Clearly we need to develop techniques for social advocacy and community organization in which the values of human welfare are presented as top priority, and in which political activity is necessary. Perhaps the strategies and tactics do need to be evaluated for outcome, but they also clearly need to be implemented.

Zuñiga (1975) has recently discussed "the experimenting society" approach to evaluation research which supposedly looks at the outcomes of social programs from a politically neutral base, in which the scientist is supposedly value-free. He has shown, using his experience in Chile during the period from 1970–73, when political upheaval was high, that this model, with its assumptions of a stable social-political base, could not work. The academic researcher was forced to take sides in order to conduct research. In the field of community psychology the same is also true. Scientists can and should evaluate the solutions they propose, but they also must adopt a set of social values which rejects the status quo when it is detrimental to the community as judged by the community. Community here has a very specific meaning. It refers to the people directly affected by a social program: the students and their parents, the patients, the welfare recipients, or whomever. It is with these values in mind that some have proposed strategies and tactics of social intervention that are thought of as political. It is important to remember that none of them is necessarily opposed to research to determine effectiveness, and the community psychologist who combines research skills with these strategies and tactics will be breaking new ground.

The remaining chapters of this volume are concerned with some of the specific content areas that have been of interest to community psychologists. It should be clear to the reader that the potential areas of interest represent a much wider set of concerns than those reviewed here. The areas selected—education, mental health, the legal system, and the training of professional and nonprofesssional change agents—are presented because they are among those most widely influenced by traditional helping professionals, and the need for new paradigms, conceptions, and actions is acute.

INTERVENTIONS IN THE EDUCATIONAL SYSTEM: Preschool Programs and the Failure of a Paradigm

The particular types of symptom—behavior accompanying the individual who is an economic failure . . . are all determined by . . . an individual constitution inadequate to meet the demands made upon him.

—*Chester Carlisle*

These children of poverty lack . . . many opportunities to develop cognitive skills. They lack especially the circumstances which foster linquistic skills, numerical skills, and the syntax of standard language in which abstractions of cognitive content are couched.

—*J. McV. Hunt*

People, more often than not, do what is expected of them . . . one person's expectation for another person's behavior can quite unwittingly become a more accurate prediction simply for its having been made.

—*Robert Rosenthal and Lenore Jacobson*

The Social Context of Applied Child Psychology

Prior to the social and political events of the 1960s the mental health movement had lost touch with problems of early childhood (see Chapter I). Although American psychiatry has always been interested in children, the dominant psychoanalytic model has suggested that childhood be dealt with in reminiscence rather than in fact. Early in the twentieth century, largely through the settlement houses, social work developed as a profession concerned with children and families; but, as social workers also began to adopt a psychoanalytic model of case work, they became less concerned with direct treatment of the young child. It was primarily through the child guidance movement that mental health workers started to deliver children's services. However, even when the movement was fully operating the services it delivered were limited to severely disturbed children or to

school-age children from middle- and working-class homes. With the possible exception of test developers, until recently, applied psychologists have had little contact with preschool children of normal development and of those outside the middle class. In 1959 Alan Ross, writing on the practice of clinical child psychology, noted:

. . . the present situation represents a complete reversal of conditions which prevailed up to the Second World War. Before that time, what training there was for clinical psychologists emphasized work with children at the expense of training for clinical work with adults. With the wartime demand for more clinical psychologists and the training programs which were developed in response to this need, work with adults became increasingly stressed, until today we see the pendulum at the extreme where the training of a clinical psychologist may include only incidental experience with children (Ross, 1959, pp. 9–10).

Partly as a consequence of the community mental health emphasis on prevention, of the women's liberation movement emphasizing services for children (particularly day care for the children of working mothers), and of the demand for improved education services to the children of the poor, children of normal development, from nonmiddle-class homes, have been thrust upon the helping professions. Through the interest of the federal government and the consequent availability of research and program grants, these recent sociopolitical events have fostered an interest in children among the mental health professions.

In 1965 the Joint Commission on Mental Health of Children, appointed by Congress, conducted a three-year study of the problems of children and youth, and in 1970 released its report *Crisis in Child Mental Health: Challenge for the 1970s*. Although the report is a variety of suggestions and arguments from very diverse theoretical perspectives, its major themes reflect the sociopolitical concerns of the last ten to fifteen years: community care, the importance of schools, participation of youth in work and other aspects of community life, supportive services for the poor, and programs of child advocacy. Although these concerns have been reflected, the way to implement such services is far from clear. As one reviewer has noted, "The system for dealing with children is not much of a system. It is largely a set of independently knowing, independently acting professional individuals. To invert a famous description of the United States Navy, it is a system designed by idiots requiring execution by geniuses" (White, 1974, p. 500).

Beyond the community psychologists' logical interest in prevention, and therefore in childhood, the child psychologists' academic interest in early education, or the behaviorists' interest in classroom and home contingency management, psychologists have begun to have the opportunity to intervene in the real world of preschoolers more as a function of social and political circumstances than out of a logical effort to apply their scientific results. As contact increases between the appliers of psychology and the normal preschool children outside of the middle class, one questions how prepared the deliverers of service are to deal with such populations. With the exception of intellectual test development that finds no relationship to later measured intelligence (Bayley, 1955, 1965; McCall, Applebaum, & Hogarty, 1973), and work with retarded children, infant work has been largely left to experimental child psychologists rather than to interventionists. Applied child psychology is largely undeveloped beyond the operant approach to behavior management. Training programs in applied child psychology are not only rare, but have focused on middle-class or institutional problems of emotional disturbance and older children. Those who have studied the younger child have tended to be either experimental child psychologists, not interested in the practical problems of intervention, and/or those concerned with middle-class children who are convenient experimental subjects. As applied psychologists turn to the children of the poor the psychologists carry with them a number of disadvantages. They are used to thinking in terms of pathology and disturbance rather than normality. They look for problems as opposed to strengths. They are experienced with middle-class children, both their own and those they have seen in traditional clinics and read about in textbooks. Finally, they are guided by theories of development that are based on a number of implicit assumptions and research strategies with which many are unfamiliar.

Although child psychology is obviously important, community psychologists rarely have been devoted to the study of child development per se. Certainly many have focused on interventions aimed specifically at the problems of childhood, either in the public school system (Zax & Cowen, 1969) or for retarded and emotionally disturbed children (Hobbs, 1968); but these programs are more interventionist than aimed at theory development or a study of the processes of child development. Most rely on theories of development posited by child psychologists and work at interventions based on the premises of current developmental and child psychology. In this way community psychologists are aided by a massive set of empirical data and theory that has implications for their own work. This is clearly an efficient strategy because the study of developmental process is a lifetime of work in itself. At the same time, many of the assumptions behind the work of others may not be obvious to community interventionists. The sensible and efficient reliance on child psychology as a basis for application has disadvantages as well as advantages. That is, the community psychologist is faced with the problem of existing paradigms which tends to support a status quo that they themselves may actually wish to change. To both use and direct the paradigms toward change require a keen understanding of the paradigmatic assumptions as they relate to the community psychologists' aims.

Child Psychology's Paradigms

This chapter, as well as the one that follows, includes a review of some of the paradigms of child psychology as they have influenced community intervention. For the community psychologist, the paradigms that have influenced programs of early childhood education for so-called disadvantaged children are most relevant. The popular rationale for such programs is that by enhancing the child's intellectual and social adjustment to the demands of childhood, and particularly of school, the child will be more likely to meet the later demands of modern society, make a better life, and so on. This is a reflection of the American ideal that education, individual competence, and hard work will insure a bright future. It is the political base which supports preschool education programs for the poor. Because a relatively large proportion of Black and other minority-group children suffer from poverty in America, early education interventions based on this rationale have been most concerned with them.

In the ideology of prevention (a major concept in the thinking of community psychologists), the notion of early intervention in the life of so-called high-risk populations is both logical and compelling. Because it is difficult for the psychologist interested in "prevention" to find the targets before they have identifiable problems, the logical set borrowed from public health is to intervene with these high-risk groups before the fact; that is, to intervene with those overrepresented in the population identified as having the problems one wishes to prevent. Demographically, the poor, and therefore a large number of Black and other minority-group children, are overrepresented among those who fail in school. Consequently, Black children become the "at risk" target group of many preventive interventions. Indeed, the term "disadvantaged" has become almost a code word for "Black." In this way the preventive ideology applied to educational problems and Black children has a politically feasible basis because it overlaps with the popular American ideals.

In order to intervene and prevent educational failure among the "at risk" target group one needs to have at least a hunch as to etiology. Because most psychologists and educators reject a genetic basis for the etiology of school failure, environmental factors are hypothesized. If the psychologists focused on economics or politics, they would be less likely to maintain the political and financial base of support deemed necessary for community intervention and research. Therefore, the psychologists and educators, who are conditioned to think of individual rather than social variables anyway, and who are concerned with success in school for poor children, focus on individual educational attitudes and learning experiences that are thought to contribute to the poor child's inadequate school adjustment.

Given this social context, interest, and rationale, it is not surprising that much of community psychology is influenced by child psychology. Because the child spends a great deal of time in school and because a large part of the child's task is intellectual development, it is also not surprising that the paradigms of individual intelligence, education, and learning, prominent in child psychology, have had a great influence on community interventions. Unfortunately, the data base upon which such community programs rest is not always well examined. Even more important, the implications of such interventions are not always clear. A number of assumptions about poor children that have gained popular acceptance are sometimes applied uncritically. It is the intention of this chapter, and the next one, to review some of these assumptions and to contrast them with new ways to think about the education and intellectual performance of so-called disadvantaged children. The major paradigm to be considered here is the *environmentalist-early experience* model of intellectual development and the community interventions based upon it. This model has recently been questioned by those who favor what we shall call a *cultural-relativist* viewpoint, and by those who posit an *ecological-environmental resources* paradigm. Both of these latter approaches challenge some of the basic assumptions of the environmentalist-early experience paradigm and will be considered in the next chapter as they relate to an educational context.

In order to challenge the environmentalist-early experience paradigm it will be necessary first to show that it does not work; that is, the interventions based on it do not have their predicted outcome. Then we must understand both its scientific and its logical basis. This paradigm is currently in ascendance among psychologists and it influences community interventions in both direct and subtle ways. It is the "common sense" of psychologists, and it represents a particular value ideology which is, as noted above, also politically feasible. To reject such a strongly held paradigm requires a detailed understanding of it. This chapter begins with a consideration of the broad outlines of the paradigm, and follows with a review of the outcome of work guided by it. The next chapter examines why the paradigm fails and presents an alternative viewpoint.

The Paradigm of Early Experience and Its Analogical Relationship to Community Intervention

The most popular model of child development is that of the child as an interacter with the environment. Even the newborn is no longer thought of as passive. The child is seen as curious and seeking slightly more complex stimulation than previously found (Berlyne, 1960; Hershenson, Munsinger, & Kessen, 1965). An emphasis on experience, learning, and environmental determinism is the most widely held philosophical position in modern psychology. This position,

which in child psychology comes directly out of the work of Hebb (1949), Hunt (1961), and Piaget (Flavell, 1963), is generally thought to be politically liberal. It fits well with the ethic of "all men are created equal" and at the same time it supports the belief that the sort of environment in which one interacts is highly influential in the development of one's equal potential, intellectually and otherwise. This position apparently removes at least some of the responsibility and "blame" for poor development from the individual and places the blame on the environment, including the social environment, over which one may have little or no control. In the broadest sense who can argue with the assertion, made popular by Kurt Lewin, that behavior is a function of the person and the environment? Given this general proposition, however, we must ask the details of it. What are its implications and what procedures for psychological intervention and social change follow from it? None necessarily. It is too general a proposition. The answers to such questions with regard to early education are a function of two sets of often unstated assumptions that, although they reject heredity as the prime factor in cognitive development, are not always so equalitarian as is implied. The first set comes from experimental and child psychology, and usually includes the following reasoning.

Consider the fact that perceptual skills are learned by infants. Such skills can be shown to be a function of the child's experience with the environment. Add to this the idea that the child is an active seeker of such stimulation. Next, include the observation that when children or animals are deprived of the opportunity to seek stimulation or experience their physical environment, or are not provided with adequate physical care, they do not develop expected perceptual, motor, and cognitive abilities. Such children tend not to perform perceptual and intellectual tasks as well as nondeprived children. There is now very good evidence for this set of observations.[1]

---

[1] See a later section of this chapter, *Enrichment and Deprivation As it Affects Intelligence and Behavior*.

The second set of assumptions is largely inferential and comes from popular sociology and journalism (e.g., Harrington, 1962). The first observation in this set of assumptions is that children raised in economically deprived environments are *culturally deprived* (an analogy to physical deprivation) presumably because they do not live in the same sort of environment in which middle-class children live. That is, lower-class parents are assumed to have different values, reward different behaviors, and interact differently with their children than do middle-class parents. Many Black children, of course, are disadvantaged or deprived because their parents are poor. But this analysis is not really concerned with their economic deprivation. Its focus is on cultural deprivation. There is an analogy drawn between physical deprivation and the withholding of middle-class culture. The conclusion is that because poor children are deprived of correct experience and culture, they will therefore suffer from "deficits" analogous to those suffered from physical deprivation. Because perceptual and motor development is the basis for later cognitive development, psychologists then extend the presumed deficits into language, thought, and intellectual development. Consequently, if we can intervene early enough in childhood, it is argued, we can overcome this deprivation and prevent failure in school, unemployment, and social maladjustment. These ideas have become very popular in applied community work, due in great measure to the writing of J. McVicker Hunt. Hunt brought the two sets of ideas together—those from experimental psychology and those from popular sociology—in scientifically respectable form as a means of arguing against the idea that intelligence is fixed and unchangeable.

J. McVicker Hunt: Intelligence and Experience

The progression of ideas is cyclical. New paradigms, those which break down limits to our thinking, tend to become new limits. The breaker of the status quo becomes the status quo. Iconoclasts become icons. So it is with the notion of intelligence and experience. J.

McVicker Hunt is probably most responsible for the breakdown in the thinking of applied psychologists and educators of the notion of fixed intelligence. He brought together, in a most influential book, *Intelligence and Experience* (Hunt, 1961), a wealth of data and argument that presented to the early educational interventionists of the 1960s and 1970s a scientifically respectable base for the argument that intelligence is not fixed at birth, is largely environmentally determined, and that early experience is crucial in its development. We will review some of the data concerned with the effects of early experience later in this chapter, but it will be useful to review Hunt's position in some detail first because it is extremely influential. We shall see that it has helped to break down the beliefs which inhibited efforts to improve the environmental opportunities of those who were labeled as "low IQ." It brought the work of Hebb, of the animal researchers, and the orphanage researchers to the attention of a broad audience of applied psychologists. It also helped to focus American psychologists on the thinking of Piaget. Later, the case became overstated and through poor analogy it has functionally limited our interventions, but that is moving ahead of our story.

In his 1961 book Hunt observed that during the first half of this century, with their emphasis on hereditary and/or fixed intelligence and maturation, psychologists discouraged early education programs, warned parents not to overstimulate their children, and encouraged an overemphasis on selection as opposed to training. The testing movement in America was perpetuated by those who believed in fixed intelligence and was bolstered by the finding that close relatives' IQ scores correlate higher with each other than with those not closely related. Evidence from twins reared apart and from infant tests showing lack of correlation to adult intelligence was largely ignored or misinterpreted. Orphanage studies were explained away be selection factors in the samples and changes in IQ following nursery school were blamed on poor research designs. Hunt points out that some of this was a function of the tendency to generalize "the conceptual set of seeing dimensions of objects as immutable to seeing the characteristics of organisms and persons as also immutable'' (Hunt, 1961, p. 349). This is exactly the paradigmatic assumption which Hunt helped to break down. Belief in predetermined development became, in Hunt's words, ''common sense belief''; ''loose analogical reasoning'' from comparative psychology supported this belief. Hunt helped to point out the fallacies, but as we shall see his arguments have now become a new ''common sense'' and are applied to new problems via similarly loose analogical reasoning that is largely value ridden and ignores legitimate cultural differences.

Hunt attributed to Donald O. Hebb a major share of the influence leading to new conceptions of intelligence which emphasize central processes and experiences. He also relied on Harlow's work on learning sets, Pribram's computer analogy and information processing ideas, and Miller, Galanter, and Pribram's (1960) model of information processing. But more importantly, he used Piaget's observations and the implications of these for developmental and educational psychology. The importance of experience with the environment for building cognitive structures called ''schemas'' (emphasized by Piaget) involves a number of themes that Hunt helped to make popular. Some of these, now very much a part of the changed common sense thinking among psychologists about intelligence, include: (1) The idea of progressive change in the internalized structures of behavior and thought as the child develops. (2) The belief in a fixed order of development (stages). This does not necessarily mean a fixed rate of development, only that some elements must be learned before others. (3) The importance of the dual process of assimilation and accommodation which makes intellectual development dependent on an interaction of the child with the environment. Hunt tied this notion very nicely to the work of Hebb and to animal studies of early experience as well as to studies of sensory deprivation in orphanages. He also raised the possibility that the effects of early experience are reversible. A related and often ignored implication from Piaget is the importance of the match between internal schema and external stimula-

tion. The same environment may not be equally useful for all children. (4) The belief that thought is originated in action, basic to both Piaget and Hebb, was emphasized by Hunt. Learning requires doing, or experience with the environment. Both Hebb and Piaget see perception as the starting point.

All of these observations made it clear that intellectual development requires experience and sensory stimulation. They offered a sound basis for change in our institutional settings and for a better understanding of the intellectual processes. All of these observations have also been important in setting the stage for programs of early intervention with the poor, made possible by political events of the 1960s. During the decade following the publication of *Intelligence and Experience,* Hunt continued to write about, to pursue the issues, and to help develop the analogy which has set the most recent paradigm, now entrenched in the thinking of environmentally oriented psychologists. Much of this thinking was put together in a collection of papers called *The Challenge of Incompetence and Poverty* (Hunt, 1969).

Programs of early intervention are based on the belief that the children of the poor are like the children living in deprived sensory environments, such as institutions; or like animals in deprivation experiments. For example, Hunt (1969, p. 39) observed that ''The difference between the culturally deprived and the culturally privileged is, for children, analogous to the difference between cage-reared and pet-reared rats and dogs.'' Presumably this refers to a lack of opportunity for poor children to interact with their environment, or an inferior environment with which to interact. On what is such an analogy based? Does it make sense? To answer these questions we turn first to a review of the outcome studies that have been based on this paradigm. Although there have been many other studies, those reviewed here serve to present a picture that is increasingly clear to those involved in programs of early education: preschool intervention based on the environmentalist-early experience paradigm is failing to produce the expected outcomes. After reviewing these outcome studies, the final sections of this chapter and the following chapter explore the scientific and logical basis for the early experience paradigm and present an alternative.

Outcome Studies of Early Childhood Intervention Programs

Ever since the mid-1960s, when President Lyndon Johnson established the federal government's Office of Economic Opportunity (OEO), the subject of preschool educational programs has been popular and controversial. OEO's efforts in preschool education predate widespread impact of the Women's Rights Movement on the middle class. Consequently Project Head Start, one of OEO's major efforts, was developed specifically for "disadvantaged" children. In the 1960s Black Americans were just beginning to have their civil rights recognized in legislation, and the education establishment was turned to as implementer of a newly asserted equalitarian social policy. Head Start was a key component of this social policy. The policy was announced in 1964 and became operational in 1965. It was intended to overcome the widespread observation that poor children seem to enter school less well prepared for their tasks than middle-class children. It was logically based on the belief that intelligence is a function of early experience, and on the findings of apparently successful programs of compensatory education (Bereiter & Engleman, 1966; Gray & Klaus, 1965). Head Start was a politically popular program aimed at "maximum feasible participation" of the poor in their own betterment. OEO gave local Head Start centers individual control of the specifics of their program, with a very general set of guidelines for the provision of preschool experience to the youngsters of the poor. The programs established varied in length of the day and the number of weeks, from a summer through the entire academic year. The teachers' background, experience, and ratio to students varied from center to center. The specific techniques and goals were idiosyncratic, although most programs focused on "supportive, unstructured socialization," and included care of physical and medical needs as well as school preparation and adjustment aims.

Evaluation of Head Start Programs

Although there have been many studies of individual Head Start programs, with varying specific results (see Cicirelli, Evans, & Schiller, 1970, for a list of references) there appears to be a substantial convergence of conclusions not dissimilar to those offered in a national study undertaken by the Westinghouse Learning Corporation and Ohio University (1969). That study has been controversial with regard to the implications of its findings (cf. Hellmuth, 1970), but the findings themselves are fairly clear, if paradoxically consistent with both the positive and the negative results of other studies. Most of the argument has, as might be expected, focused on the policy implications of the complex outcomes. The methodology of the national study has been both attacked and defended, and the results appear to be open to interpretation with regard to educational and social policy. Such interpretation is in some measure a function of the values of the interpreter. A summary of the study's major findings seems to show that Head Start can be useful in some ways to some children, but it is not as totally successful as might be hoped. It is probably a mistake to consider all Head Start programs to be comparable. Positive effects, when they occur, seem to appear early in the child's public school experience, but have not been found to be stable. In later grades children who were in Head Start programs are not distinguishable from those who were not.

The Westinghouse/Ohio study was specifically designed to assess "overall effectiveness" of Head Start. Herein lies much of the subsequent criticism of its results. On such an overall national evaluation the specifics, which programs are accomplishing what results, are frequently obscured for the sake of a general conclusion, and as such the study loses much of its scientific and technical value. When different kinds of centers using different kinds of methods are lumped together the educational value of specific techniques, contents, and approaches is lost.

The Westinghouse/Ohio study examined several thousand children from 104 of the thousands of centers, which by 1970 were serving over three million children. Using a post-treatment-only research design, the evaluators identified children in the first, second, and third grades who had been enrolled in Head Start and compared them with similar children who had not been in Head Start. The use of a post-only design rather than a "true" experimental design (asking for volunteers first and then randomly assigning some to treatment and some to no treatment, using pre- and post-measures) is one of the major research flaws. Nevertheless, the authors of the report point out that such "true" experimental design is frequently impossible to implement and that to demand it would have made the study impossible to conduct. Unfortunately, without knowing how motivation to participate, or the children's pre–Head Start performance, affected post scores, the study could not be as decisive an evaluation as its authors wished.

The 104 centers studied were randomly selected from among a total of 12,927 centers. Approximately 70 percent of the 104 were summer programs and 30 percent were year long. The centers studied did not equally represent all the geographical areas of the country, nor was the racial composition of the sample proportional to the racial composition of the almost 13,000 centers in the total population. This has been pointed out as a limit to the study's claim to estimate overall national effectiveness (Smith & Bissell, 1970).

Once a center was selected for study, a random sample of children who had attended its program was selected. A comparable non–Head Start group was selected such that: the comparison group had lived in the target area from the time of the program until the study was completed; would have been eligible for Head Start (i.e., the family met federal poverty program characteristics); attended the same school system as the Head Start participants; and had no preschool experience. The major problem with this selection procedure is that the comparison group had not volunteered their children for Head Start. This motivational factor is confounded in analyzing the treatment effects. Other differences also exist between the Head Start and non–Head Start samples, and although some of these are taken into account through the use of co-variance analysis, which statistically controls for sample differences, this is not a completely satisfactory procedure and further weakens the study.

The results of the Westinghouse/Ohio study (1969) are reported in a massive two-volume report and only the highlights are mentioned here. About half of the Head Start program directors indicated, in responses to a questionnaire, that the child's self-worth, confidence, and self-acceptance were the most important program aims. Only 20 percent said improved language ability was their top priority. Despite this, much of the public expectation for Head Start as well as its evaluation is based on academic measures. Black children constituted more than half of the youngsters studied, and over 92 percent were from families where the parents held jobs at or below the unskilled worker category. One of the areas in which the program had been undoubtedly successful was to provide medical and dental care for large numbers of these children who might not have received such care. Additionally, the parents of the children are reported to have liked the program (Kirshner Associates, 1970).

With regard to the educational benefit of the Head Start programs the data are less clear. The study used several kinds of measures including reading readiness, achievement, self-concept, and behavior ratings, and compared experimental and "control" children at the end of grades 1, 2, and 3. The overall analysis indicated very few group differences and led the authors to conclude that the Head Start program had only a small impact on some of the children, in some portions of the sample, on one of the cognitive measures (Cicirelli, Evans, & Schiller, 1970). They have concluded that the changes are so small as to have no practical significance. Some (Campbell & Eriebacher, 1970) have argued that statistical artifacts, such as regression effects, actually make the data appear worse than they are. Others (e.g., Smith & Bissel, 1970) have reanalyzed and reinterpreted portions of the data and argue that some centers, particularly the urban Black centers, were more successful than others. The changes in reading readiness among first-graders were large enough so as to have practical significance—children in Head Start were less likely to be classified as low on reading readiness than were controls. The first-grade children who were in the most successful urban Black centers placed in the 48th percentile on national norms, while the control children were only at the 32nd percentile. No such differences appear for children in grades two and three.

Thus, the national Head Start evaluation seems to indicate a fair amount of consumer satisfaction. Families who participated liked it. The program provides medical and dental care as well as day care for low-income families. Data on educational effectiveness are not convincing, although it appears that some centers are better than others. This is not surprising because each center is autonomous in terms of staff qualifications, aims, and techniques used. It is not reasonable to try to draw general conclusions from what amounts to varied programs. On the other hand, assuming the best results, the educational outcomes demonstrated seem to be limited to an initial improvement among first-graders in urban Black centers, an improvement that is not maintained compared to control children in later school years.

Some (Smith & Bissel, 1970) argue that studies such as the Westinghouse/Ohio Head Start evaluation cannot be useful because they are too accepting of constraints which make a "true" experimental design impossible. The study's authors (Cicirelli, Evans, & Schiller, 1970) defend this type of research on the grounds that unless evaluators are willing to adapt to the conditions of the real world there can be no hope for input to national policy. It is likely that when researchers do adapt to the real world they can learn to do so with a minimal sacrifice of experimental rigor. The only way this will be learned, however, is to gain experience with the problems by involvement in them. This is one important task for community

psychology. At the same time, it is also necessary for the community psychologist to be aware of more carefully designed experimental studies. In that way national evaluations and policy research can be bolstered by careful methodology in relatively more controlled settings. Just as the clinician benefits from looking at laboratory data in conjunction with his consulting room observations, so too can the community psychologist benefit from the combination of real world quasi-experiments (which will necessarily be only suggestive) together with more "clean" experimental research. The experimental research will necessarily be limited by a smaller number of subjects and the particular implementation skills of the administrator who may not be comparable to the next administrator who carries out a similar program.

Experiments can frequently have a good deal of internal validity (for example, they follow correct experimental procedures) and still lack external or ecological validity. Often they may not represent all the complexities of the real world. However, when experimental studies converge on the same kinds of outcome as the more global evaluations it becomes possible to get a handle on a complex world. We now turn to some of the relatively more controlled studies of the outcome of early education programs. The studies reviewed include those most frequently presented as evidence for the value of preschool education for "disadvantaged" children. There are very few with adequate follow-up data, but they do seem to converge on a consistent result: the early educational gains, which a carefully operated program can accomplish, tend to disappear as the child progresses in school. Although some gains on paper and pencil tests can last for a number of years, it is not clear what these gains mean in terms of real success or failure in school. It will be important to note that it is not that preschool programs are ineffective in teaching, but that learning what is taught does not enhance the likelihood of doing well in later school years.[2]

---

[2]Although there are many other preschool programs in the literature that are not reviewed here, the overall findings and conclusions are not different from those presented in this chapter.

Outcomes of Specific Intervention Programs

Bereiter and Englemann's Direct Instruction Program. One of the most widely acclaimed programs for preschool education is the use of a detailed content curriculum broken down into small steps similar to programmed learning. This is combined with procedures of behavior modification relying on immediate reinforcement for correct responses. The teacher, working with a small group of children, gives each child a focused, high level of attention, and elicits verbal behavior in an effort to shape and reward correct responses. These responses are designed to shape concepts believed to be necessary for school success. Bereiter and Englemann (1966) have detailed much of the rationale and method of this approach, and Englemann (1969) has continued to detail many of the techniques and curriculum ideas in mathematics and reading. These interventionists have argued that "disadvantaged" children need to "catch up" in abilities necessary for school success. This requires an above-normal rate of progress, with an emphasis on content different from that required for middle-class children. The emphasis on social-emotional adjustment in the traditional nursery school classroom is dropped in favor of intense academic work. The basic argument is that children of the poor suffer from a cognitive deficit.

There are standards of knowledge and ability which are consistently held to be valuable in the schools, and any child in the schools who falls short of these standards by reason of his particular cultural background may be said to be culturally deprived. It does not matter that he may have other knowledge and other skills which in other contexts might be valued more highly. There are no schools in our society in which knowledge and skills peculiar to lower-class groups are valued and fostered (Bereiter & Englemann, 1966, p. 24).

They argue that this "deficit" is a function of what the child has learned, and that lower-class children have not learned the proper content; in particular they have not learned the proper use of language. It is not grammar, but the use of language that the lower-class child is seen to lack. ". . . he does not learn how to use language for obtaining and transmitting information, for monitoring his own behavior, and for carrying on verbal reasoning. In short, he fails to master the cognitive uses of language" (Bereiter & Englemann, 1966, p. 42). They argue explicitly against the belief that lower-class children suffer from social and emotional deprivation or maladjustment, and are critical of preschool programs based on such rationale. They view the lower-class child as suffering from a language-based cognitive deficit requiring programmed language instruction in small groups, with focused attention on each child.

Englemann (1970) has reported an evaluation of this approach which was tested on four-year-old children who were eligible for Head Start. All children were pretested on the Stanford-Binet Intelligence Test and categorized as medium and low intelligence. Equal proportions from each category were assigned to experimental (total $N = 15$) and comparison classes ($N = 28$), balancing the number of Blacks and Whites, and males and females. In addition, a group of 15 middle-class children was taken into the program and compared with a similar group enrolled in a local Montessori school. Experimental children were in the Bereiter-Englemann preschool for two years, and comparison children were in a traditional preschool emphasizing self-image, expression, and play for one year. In the second year they attended public school kindergarten classes. All children were later compared on IQ and achievement tests. Results of the IQ comparison between the two disadvantaged groups are presented in Figure VII-1. As can be seen in this figure, the experimental children scored higher on IQ than the other "disadvantaged" children, although it is interesting that the IQ of the "control group," who is supposedly suffering from a cognitive deficit, is about average compared to national norms. On achievement tests all experimental subjects scored above the grade level that would be expected of the "average" child, and the IQ and achievement scores of the treated middle-class children were at about the same level as the treated "disadvantaged" children, although En-

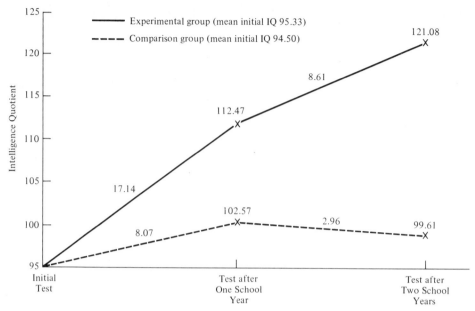

Figure VII-1. IQ comparision of experimental (Bereiter-Englemann training) and control children. (Redrawn from Englemann, 1970.)

glemann does not report statistical comparisons. The Montessori children's achievement scores were lower than the experimental middle-class children's scores.

A separate report by Bereiter (1968) does present a statistical comparison between two groups of "disadvantaged" children matched on IQ, socioeconomic status, and race. These children were randomly assigned to the structured learning program or to a variety of "educational games." Bereiter finds significant differences between the two groups, on a variety of academic achievement measures, favoring the children in the structured program. Neither Bereiter (1968) nor Englemann (1970) presents follow-up data collected after the program's conclusion. Englemann explicitly argues that such data say nothing about the effect of the preschool interventions. If children do not maintain their gains then that is seen as the fault of their school instructors, who are obviously not teaching them properly. It is argued that in order to maintain educational gains schools need to teach effectively at each level, an observation

which seems to contradict the "cognitive deficit" hypothesis to which the authors subscribe.

Bereiter (1972a) has recently reviewed evaluation studies of compensatory education and has concluded that the Bereiter-Englemann program has more impact on IQ and achievement than traditional nursery schools. However, the impact is not necessarily greater than other programs with a similarly strong instruction emphasis. He emphasizes that long-term effects are as good as can be expected and that permanent gains require "follow-through." This in fact has led to extensions of the Bereiter-Englemann methods into elementary school curricula. He has argued that we need to dispel the illusion that the early years of intellectual development are magic and that the "way to make the preschool learning more useful is to alter the actual course of subsequent school events so as to make use of it" (Bereiter, 1972a, p. 18). Again, Bereiter and Englemann never discuss the apparent contradiction between viewing the "disadvantaged" child as suffering from a cognitive deficit and at the same time arguing that the way to improve the child's school performance is to change what goes on in school.

The Karnes Studies: From Preschool to Home Intervention. Merle Karnes and her associates at the University of Illinois Institute for Research on Exceptional Children report one of the few comparative studies of preschool intervention programs (Karnes, Teska, & Hodgins, 1970). They were interested in the relative effectiveness of four different preschool programs ranging from a highly structured experimental curriculum similar to Bereiter and Englemann's and operated by the investigators, through a Montessori program operated by the Montessori Society which focused on "spontaneous choice" of "approved" materials. The teacher in this latter program is expected to structure the environment but, unlike the experimental program, not the specific interactions with the child. A third program, referred to as "community-integrated," was less structured than the first two. It was a "traditional nursery school," operated by community groups, with predominantly middle-class children, into which 16 disadvantaged children were placed (two to four in each of four centers). The aim of this program was to provide disadvantaged children with a peer model who already had developed adequate verbal and cognitive skills. Supposedly, being middle class assured that the peer models would be more "adequate" than the "disadvantaged" children. Finally, a "traditional" program was operated by the investigators. This involved daily sessions with a 1:5 ratio of teachers to children, as in the experimental program. The other two programs had a larger number of children per teacher.

The traditional program involved B.A.-level teachers in preprogram training, while the experimental program teachers were given weekly in-service training. The other two programs were left as they are normally run by the community groups. Goals of the traditional program emphasized personal, social, motor, and general language development on an informal basis, and was viewed as the least structured of the four comparison programs. The experimental program emphasized the "language deficits" of poor children and a great deal of small-group and one-to-one instruction occurred.

Subjects for all programs were recruited from the local school authorities and the State Department of Public Aid. They were "judged by authorities to be economically and educationally disadvantaged." All were approximately four years old. All children were pretested on the Stanford-Binet and divided into three groups: IQ above 100, between 99 and 90, and between 89 and 70. About equal numbers from each of these groups were then assigned to one of the four preschool programs. The mean IQ was about 95, so that this subject population, which is said to represent children who are supposedly culturally disadvantaged and suffering from cognitive deficits, is well within the normal range of IQ.

At the end of the seven to eight months of preschool each child was evaluated on the Stanford-Binet IQ Test, the Illinois Test of Psycholinguistic Abilities (ITPA), the Peabody Picture Vocabulary Test, and the Frostig Developmental Test of Visual Perception. Examiners were not informed of the child's program assignment. On the IQ test the experimental program children performed significantly better than the other three program children, but all groups had improved IQ scores, the mean now being 98.4 for the community-integrated group, 99.6 for the Montessori, 102.6 for the traditional, and 110.3 for the experimental program. The ITPA found a similar ordering with the experimental program children gaining the most in language development and the traditional program children gaining the next largest amount. The other two programs showed smaller and less consistent gains on language measures. Statistical tests between groups, however, are not reported. Experimental and traditional programs found the most gain in the picture vocabulary test and the experimental program children were better than all others on the perception test.

Karnes *et al.* (1970) explain these results as follows: Although structure per se is not the most important element in a program for "disadvantaged" preschoolers, the opportunity to develop language, an area in which these children presumably have a deficit, is very important. Observations of the children in each of the programs are offered to show that both the traditional and the experimental program emphasized verbalization from the children, whereas the two other programs did not. An alternative explanation of the results is that the two new programs, both of which were operated and controlled by the researchers, selected and trained staff and infused enthusiasm about the children's ability more than the older established programs. Here teachers were not part of an exciting experiment. As we shall see, this hypothesis of teacher enthusiasm and expectation has been offered by the author of another comparative study (Weikart, 1972) and it is supported by evidence from studies focused on expectation and school achievement per se. It could also be recalled that *all* groups were functioning well within the normal range of IQ, and one would not expect these children to fail in school on the basis of intellectual deficit.

In a second study of preschool intervention Karnes, Teska, Hodgins, and Badger (1970) evaluated the use of mothers as the prime agents of teaching. This approach represents a trend toward moving the locus of intervention from the preschool to the home environment (Ricciuti, 1974), a trend which, as we shall see in the next chapter, is not entirely without controversy.

In this study mothers from "disadvantaged families" were provided with a "sequential educational program" for use in the home. They were taught how to use positive reinforcement and also participated in weekly meetings designed to "foster a sense of dignity and worth." Twenty women with infants between 13 and 27 months of age were referred by the Offices of the State Aid to Dependent Children Program or the Department of Public Health, presumably because they were children of poor, Black parents and were therefore "high risk." Mothers attended a two-hour training and discussion meeting each week for seven or eight months in each of two years. They were paid $1.50 per hour and provided with transportation. Each woman was given toys to implement the instruc-

tional program. Fifteen of twenty mothers completed the program which operated for a total of 15 months. Fourteen were Black, one Caucasian, and the age range was from 22 to 55 years. The mean education was 9.5 years and the mean number of children was 4.9. With one exception all families had an income of less than $4000 per year. Only two of the mothers were employed full time. The children did not attend preschool during the program.

A control group was not selected until the time of post-evaluations, but at that time each experimental child was roughly matched with a control who had been previously tested for another project. Therefore this nonequivalent control group unfortunately was not matched on mother's motivation to participate. To partially account for this, a subgroup of six siblings of experimental families was compared to the target children. All children were tested at the program's conclusion on the Stanford-Binet and the ITPA. The experimental children scored significantly better than their "matched controls" and also significantly better than sibling controls on both measures. No follow-up data are reported.

Two studies, one by Schaefer and Aaronson (1970) and one by Levinstein (1969) are reported in Zax and Specter (1974) and are similar in their results to the Karnes *et al.* (1970) study. Levinstein found that children of mothers taught to interact with their child around verbal activities scored higher on IQ and vocabulary tests than control children. No follow-up data are reported. Schaefer and Aaronson used college student tutors five days per week for Black children from "disadvantaged" homes in Washington, D.C. The tutors worked with children for fifteen months until they were three years old and were compared with a control group who were tested but received no special attention. Tutored children were found to have higher IQ scores at 21, 27, and 36 months with better scores for those children rated as having a better mother-child relationship. Again, follow-up data are not provided.

It seems clear from these studies that providing preschoolers with a specific set of carefully taught academic experiences, similar to that measured by IQ tests, whether it is provided in a school setting or in a home, by professional teachers, college students, or mothers of the children, *can* improve the child's performance on IQ test measures taken at the conclusion of the intervention. Clearly, so-called disadvantaged children can learn such content. However, the questions that remain are serious ones. Some are psychological questions, others are social policy questions. What does an improved IQ test score mean? Do the results hold up over time? Does later school performance appear to be enhanced? Are the children really suffering from a deficit? The early experience programs reviewed so far are inadequate to answer these questions.

Preschool Programs for Other Minority-group Children: Three Examples.   The programs discussed thus far have centered on Black children. Similar outcomes have been found for other minority group children. Walter Plant and Mara Southern (1972) have reported a longitudinal investigation of a two-year preschool program for "disadvantaged" Mexican-American children. In two successive years they identified and tested groups of children in a California community. Each of the two identified groups participated in a ten-week, every day, summer preschool program for two years prior to their entrance to kindergarten. These children were later compared to similar nonparticipants in the same school district. Because of the close-knit family and community life of these children, two additional comparison groups were selected from a different California community, and also tested, but not given the summer program.

The "teachers" in the program were Mexican-American high school students, fluent in English and Spanish, who served as small-group leaders. They were supervised by "master teachers" selected from the public school as "one of the best" primary-grade teachers. This use of indigenous nonprofessional manpower is an efficient, as well as a necessary system because the children could not speak English. The material taught was similar to that used by Klaus and Gray (1968), which is described below, and emphasized perceptual-motor skills, concept formation, and language. Reinforcement with concrete reward and praise was emphasized at first; later reliance was placed on verbal reinforcement alone. Material was programmed in small progressive steps so that each child could experience success and learn "persistence."

All children were later tested on a series of intelligence and language tests, and school achievement data were collected. Despite a good deal of subject attrition, some general results are apparent. The treated students were performing better than their untreated peers on all tests at the time of entrance to kindergarten; however, none of the later school achievement measures found differences between groups. *It is apparent that the nonprofessional teachers did their job, but that this was not sufficient to change the ultimate impact of the school system.* The authors attribute this result, similar to results found with Head Start children, to the failure of continuing the "special program" into the elementary school years. They do not question why the school itself cannot adapt to the needs of children who apparently can be successfully taught by high school students!

McAfee (1972) also has reported an evaluation of a program for preschoolers of Spanish, Spanish-Indian, and Mexican background residing in a Colorado community. The curriculum materials and philosophy of education in this program, however, were based on what might be thought of as a more "child-centered" approach. This program emphasized the child's active role in choice of activities, and encouraged the child to experiment with his or her own interests rather than on the basis of external rewards. The teacher must be sensitive to the child's interests and develop programs to fit the child's and the family's needs. Individual children, in two different years of the preschool, were shown to make improvements in IQ and "task accomplishment" measures; however, no control-group data are presented. In a longitudinal study, children who completed the program were compared to a group "similar in cultural and sociological background." Unfortunately, in order to find a comparison group without preschool experience McAfee had to recruit them from small towns and rural areas close to the Colorado city in which the preschoolers lived, and no data are presented on initial comparability of the groups. Preschool attenders were found to have better attendance records in public school as well as better scores on some achievement tests. However, teacher ratings of students on academic standing in arithmetic, reading, independence, and attention span did not differentiate between the treated and untreated groups, nor did a self-concept measure.

Neither of these studies with Mexican-American children contradicts the observation that preschool education is not effective in changing the later outcome of public school for so-called disadvantaged children. McAfee suggests that a major problem is the education of teachers to be sensitive to the students' needs rather than to the children's adjustment to school. Plant and Southern conjecture that for Mexican-American children cultural differences may be even more of a problem in school than for Black children. Again, many questions are left unanswered. It appears that early advances in IQ-measured "intelligence" do not necessarily predict to later school performance, and at the same time it is not clear from such studies why this is the case.

One of the most often voiced hypotheses to account for such results is that because the child lives with a lower-class (inadequate) family, the family is unable or unwilling to sustain the child's intellectual gains. A program for American Indian children, operated by the Mormon church, is based on such a rationale. This program places foster children from American Indian reservations in the homes of White middle-class families during the academic year while they attend middle-class schools. The children return home only for summer vacation. Cundick, Gottfredson, and Willson (1974) recently looked at the IQ and achievement scores of 84 children who had participated in the program for five or more years. They found no changes in IQ and a *decline* in achievement test scores the longer children remained in the program.

As the authors point out, those who believe in an environmental-deficit model must understand that mere placement from one environment to another will not be sufficient for educa-

tional success. Interestingly, the major interpretation to which the early experience-environmentalist model leads the authors is that perhaps the return home in the summer negated the effects of living with a middle-class family for nine months of the year! Again, the paradigm seems to be lacking in explanatory value because it ignores the obvious impact of the school system itself.

The Early Training Project.   The Early Training Project, conducted in Tennessee by Susan Gray and Rupert Klaus, is probably the most adequately researched program of early education with respect to effects over time and the diffusion of those effects within and between families. The project has been reported in three separate papers. The initial presentation by Gray and Klaus appeared in 1965 and described the results up to school entrance; in 1968 Klaus and Gray wrote a lengthy monograph detailing the rationale and procedures, together with a follow-up of the children at the end of the second grade. In 1970 Gray and Klaus presented data on the same children at the end of the fourth grade.

The aim of these researchers was to design a project whose procedures would be general enough to be used by others, and which would overcome the "progressive retardation in the public school careers of children living in deprived circumstances" (Gray & Klaus, 1970, p. 910). They selected 61 Black children from families with an income below $3000 per year, with parents' education eighth grade or below, who worked at unskilled or semi-skilled jobs and resided in poor housing. In one-third of the homes no father was present. All children lived in a city of 25,000 in Tennessee, and were divided into three groups: the first (T-1) attended three ten-week summers of preschool and their mothers participated in three years of weekly meetings with a trained home visitor. The second group (T-2) began a year later and had two summers of preschool and two years of home visits; the third was a local control group (LC) tested but not treated; and the fourth was a "distal" control group (DC), selected from a similar Black ghetto area of a nearby city. This latter nonequivalent control group was selected because the researchers wanted to examine the "spillover" effects on neighbors of the treated children (i.e., the local control group children) compared to those who had no chance to be affected by interactions with the parents of treated children.

The rationale for the program was to change attitudes about achievement in school-related activities, in delay of gratification, in persistence (particularly of the parents), and to overcome presumed deficits in the children with regard to perceptual and cognitive development and language.

The program procedures, described in Klaus and Gray (1968), involved small groups of children, teachers, and assistant teachers, emphasizing verbal interaction and using systematic reinforcement and individual contingencies. The material was similar to that used in most nursery schools but was used "systematically," following the techniques described in Gray, Klaus, Miller, and Forrester (1966). The home visitor served as a liaison between school and home, providing opportunities for "catharsis." The visitor taught the parents to work with their children.

The results of this early educational intervention find that the treated groups, taken together, score significantly better than the untreated control groups on the Stanford-Binet IQ Test at the time of entrance to school, after the second, and again after the fourth grade. Interestingly, however, these IQ scores actually tend to rise slightly and then decline for all groups, with the *drop-off* being less for the treatment groups. At initial testing, the range of IQ scores for the four groups was from 92.5, for T-2, to 85.4 for LC, although at the end of the fourth grade the range was from 90.2 for T-2 to 77.7 for DC. The LC group scored about the same as they did at the outset (IQ: 84.9). Although the program seems to have kept IQ fairly stable for the treated groups the significant differences, even comparing the worst group to the best, are quite small, and actually represent simply a few more answers on a standardized test. On the Peabody Picture Vocabulary Test the treatment groups scored significantly better

than the control groups until second grade, but by the fourth grade the differences were no longer significant. On school achievement tests the experimental children did better at the end of first grade on three of four, and at the end of grade 2 they did better on two tests, and at the end of grade 4 there were no significant differences.

These results are reminiscent of those found for Head Start programs. Hints of early gains on school-related measures seem to disappear as the child continues in school.

In comparing the local and the distal controls, Gray and Klaus (1970) find that there is less decline (not statistically significant) for local controls on the IQ measure, and that local controls were performing better than distal controls on several achievement measures in the second grade, but on only one achievement measure in the fourth grade. This effect, which the authors call "horizontal diffusion" (influence on neighbors' children), seems to decline over time.

Finally, the authors note "vertical diffusion" effects, that is, impact on younger siblings of treated children. They find some effects on the Stanford-Binet IQ Test, which indicate that the siblings closest in age to the treated siblings tended to have higher IQ scores than siblings of the control children.

Gray and Klaus (1970) conclude that the intervention, although it has initial impact, is not sufficient to overcome "the massive effects of a low income home . . . surely it would be foolish not to realize that, without massive changes in the life situation of the child, home circumstances will continue to have adverse effect upon the child's performance" (p. 92).

Baratz and Baratz (1970) interpret the above findings somewhat differently. They argue that the initial increase in performance is a function of the poor Black child's initial contact with White middle-class culture. The decline is a function of the fact that simple contact with a system not dealing effectively with their needs is insufficient to enhance their further education. It is interesting that Gray and Klaus do not conclude that the schools are failing to provide adequate education for the children. They conclude that the *parents* are not preparing the children for school. It may be that the early experience-environmentalist paradigm, which is behind such programs of preschool intervention, limits the hypotheses available to the researchers to account for their data. The only acceptable way to account for failure within the paradigm is to hypothesize deficits in the children and their families. Hypothesizing difficulties in the school system, rather than the children, appears to require the ability to question the "rules of the game." These are points to which we shall return in the next chapter. They are crucial for the community psychologist.

The results of outcome studies such as those reviewed above appear to be inadequate to answer many questions of concern to community psychology. In order to understand why the children of the poor fail in school, despite successful preschool experience, a more detailed examination of the processes and procedures of our current educational programs is required.

The Ypsilanti Perry Preschool Project and Observations on the Self-fulfilling Prophecy

David Weikart of the High/Scope Educational Research Foundation (1972) has recently presented follow-up data on a preschool program run in Ypsilanti, Michigan, and reported earlier in preliminary form (Weikart, 1967). Weikart (1972) addresses himself to three questions: Does preschool education matter for disadvantaged children; if so, does curriculum matter; and finally, does staff make a difference?

Weikart (1972), in an attempt to place his own research in perspective, has distinguished between the different sort of preschool programs that have appeared in the literature and has classified them on two dimensions: the role of the teacher in relation to the role of the child and the role of the initiator as opposed to the role of the responder. Figure VII-2 is a diagram of these dimensions on which various preschool programs may be classified. There are four basic program types according to this analysis. One, referred to as *custodial care*, simply involves

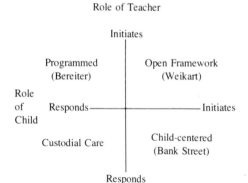

Figure VII-2.   Preschool curricula models.
(Adapted from Weikart, 1972.)

physical protection of the child. It is a teacher responds–child responds program which involves no particular programming or effort on the part of either.

In the teacher initiates–child responds quadrant of Figure VII-2 are "programmed" preschools such as Bereiter and Englemann's. The curricula are aimed at specific educational goals and the skills necessary for school success. The program is rigidly structured. The teacher dominates the interactions with specific procedures, equipment, and materials. They are what Weikart calls "teacher proof." If one follows the curricula every step is set and the teacher always knows what to do. These sorts of programs are most easily transferred to new settings and presumably new content can always be added. They tend to be learning theory based, usually within a behavior modification approach.

The teacher initiates–child initiates quadrant is called "open framework" and focuses upon specific goals theoretically related to cognitive development. This method is usually based on Jean Piaget's ideas, some of which were briefly described earlier in this chapter and in Chapter III. The aim is to involve the child in direct experience and action. There is no training in specific academic skills such as reading or arithmetic. These skills are seen to develop from more basic cognitive skills. The theory gives the teacher a framework for curricula, but he or she then develops specific activities within that framework. People rather than equipment are emphasized. Children are encouraged not to repeat answers, but to develop concepts through actual experience. One of the program's advantages is the teacher's personal involvement in the specifics of the curriculum planning, guided by theory. Emphasis is on intellectual rather than social-emotional growth. This presumably frees it from cultural bias and specific content based on middle-class language. Presumably the process of intellectual development is independent of the content of a curriculum. An example of such a program is Weikart's Ypsilanti Perry Preschool Project (1967, 1972), to be described below.

The fourth quadrant is represented by child initiates-teacher responds and is called *child-centered*. This includes the bulk of the traditional nursery school and Head Start programs. Social-emotional growth, free play, and theories of emotional development are emphasized. The Bank Street College of Education program is an excellent example of this child-centered model and is well described by Shapiro and Biber:

. . . cognitive functions—acquiring and ordering information, judging, reasoning, problem solving, using a system of symbols—cannot be separated from the growth of personal and interpersonal processes—the development of self-esteem and a sense of identity, internalization of impulse control, capacity for autonomous response, relatedness to other people (1972, p. 61).

For example, Shapiro and Biber (1972, pp. 62–63) list the following as goals: strengthen commitment to and pleasure in word learning; broaden sensitivity to experience; promote intellectual mastery; integrate affect and cognition; nurture self-esteem; encourage interaction with people; promote the capacity to participate in the social order. The style of intervention is theoretically open to the particular needs of the individual child. For example, Shapiro and Biber note that:

Current research and theory are far from providing a clearcut picture of a deprivation syndrome. As professional people, committed both to social values and social science, we must overhaul some of our conventional procedures and ways of thinking. In working with poor children and families we need to be aware of our own cultural biases. This is not a question of merely remembering that lower-class life style has its virtues too, but of being aware that psychology has never been as good at predicting strength and the ability to overcome adversity as it has in accounting for weakness and malfunction (1972, p. 79).

Although the ideals are valid, one of the difficulties of such programs is that they are fairly nonspecific in terms of how such values are implemented. This probably depends a great deal on the personal values of the teachers. This general orientation is the most common among preschool and nursery school teachers and is what researchers refer to as "traditional programs."

As a first step in his research Weikart (1972) began with a study of the effectiveness of an "open framework" two-year project for children from "disadvantaged" families. Similar to the Early Training Project (Gray & Klaus, described above), the program consisted of daily class and weekly home visits. The actual program was in operation for five years and still continues to collect follow-up data on the children. Matched on IQ and socioeconomic status, the children were then randomly assigned to an experimental or a control group and tested on a variety of intelligence, language, and achievement measures each year. The curriculum is described by Weikart as falling in the open framework quadrant of Figure VII-2. It is based on Piaget's notions and has "cognitive objectives." The curriculum is described in detail in Weikart, Rogers, Adcock, and McClelland (1971). Verbal stimulation and learning "concepts" through activity, rather than social behavior, are reported to be the program's emphasis, together with encouraging the mothers to participate.

Five pairs of experimental and control groups were provided with the program so that each independent group was small and that the overall results are actually for the same study replicated five times, or in what Weikart refers to as five "waves." The findings are that experimental children, immediately following the intervention, scored higher on the Stanford-Binet IQ Test than controls, but these results disappeared by the third grade (see Figure VII-

3). Achievement test differences favoring the experimental children appeared in the first and third grades (see Figure VII-4), and finally, through the third year, experimentals were rated better on academic, emotional, and social development by their elementary school teachers. Weikart conservatively concludes that a program wherein researchers have good control over the implementation of the project can have demonstrable impact on children, at least in the primary grades. He notes, however, that this conclusion has ecological validity only for special research projects and cannot be generalized to all preschool programs.

In an effort to give his research more generalizable utility and to understand more about the process of early education, Weikart goes on to describe a second-step project comparing three kinds of programs described above: the programmed, the open framework, and the child-centered (see Figure VII-2). Each of these was instituted at the Ypsilanti preschool for three- and four-year-old children from "disadvantaged" families. The programmed curriculum was based on Bereiter's approach (Bereiter & Englemann, 1966). The open framework was Weikart's own program described above, and the child-centered was one aimed at social emotional, rather than "cogni-

tive" goals. He reports, contrary to his own expectation that the child-centered program would not do as well, that each of these programs was about equally successful through the first year of operation, all showing large IQ gains. The following year, children in the child-centered program did less well than those in the other two.

By means of a careful analysis of diary reports of teachers, Weikart shows how the decline in the child-centered program may have been a function of the loss of enthusiasm by the teachers who began to see it as the "control group" in a setting where emphasis was placed on more clearly academic programs. He goes on to argue that the operation of a program so that it and the children are carefully attended to is more important than the exact curriculum, and the curriculum is useful primarily for the teachers' own guidance and organization of the day. He emphasizes the need for an enthusiastic staff, actively involved in a program, with *high expectations for the children as the crucial educational variable.*

At this point one may hypothesize that the failure of the children of the poor to do well in public elementary schools, despite their ability to learn and perform successfully in special preschool programs, may be related to the expectations that teachers in the public schools hold for

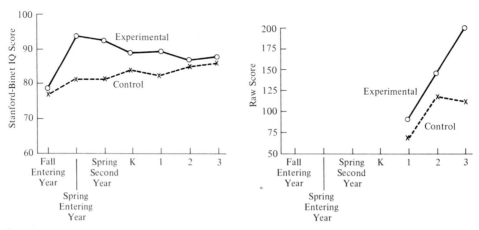

Figure VII-3.   Graph of Stanford-Binet group means: experimental versus control.   *Figure VII-4.*   Graph of achievement tests group means: experimental versus control. (Both adapted from Weikart, 1972.)

such children. One hypothesis is that the dissipation of the effects of preschool programs is mediated, at least in part, by the expectations that the teachers hold for the students. The kind of enthusiasm, identified by Weikart as so crucial, may be absent in the public schools attended by the children of the poor.

Rosenthal and Jacobson (1968), in their well-known study of the "pygmalian effect," find that IQ changes and achievement among elementary school children can in some cases be attributed to teacher expectations, even in the absence of a direct intervention with the children, and are supportive of Weikart's hypothesis. This research is a good example of the movement of an observation out of the laboratory into the real world. Rosenthal (1966) was originally interested in how an experimenter's hypotheses influence the outcome of laboratory results with both human and animal subjects. Extending the idea of the self-fulfilling prophesy to teachers and children he and Lenore Jacobson carried out the following study.

All children in a 650-student elementary school with a minority (about one-sixth) of Mexican-American children were given an IQ test which was represented to the teachers as a predictor of intellectual "blooming." The researchers randomly selected approximately 20 percent of the children in each classroom and told their teachers that the test indicated that these children were about to "bloom" academically. All children were retested after one semester, one year, and two years (after they had passed on to a new teacher). After one year the "bloomers," particularly those in first and second grade, were shown to have made greater IQ gains than the other children (47 percent improved by as much as 20 IQ points). In the second year the older children showed greater gains in IQ, while the younger children failed to maintain their gains with a new teacher. The school used a "track" system with a fast, medium, and slow track. The gains in IQ were initially most evident for children in the medium track and this continued to be the case in the second year. In both years the Mexican-American children who were "bloomers" showed the greatest IQ gains.

This was shown to relate to "Mexican-ness" of the children's faces. The authors' conjecture that this result may have been a function of surprise that these children were "bloomers," which led to increased interest in them, and so on. Bloomers also showed greater gains in reading grades and achievement tests. Children who were "bloomers" were also rated as more curious and better on personality and social adjustment measures.

These and similar results have been questioned as to methodology and appropriate statistical analyses (Barber & Silver, 1968). Nevertheless, they appear to be about as good as those presented to demonstrate the utility of early education. Similar results have been found for children who were in a class with the same teacher who taught an older sibling (Seaver, 1973). Expectancy effects as a function of race have also been demonstrated for student-teacher rating of elementary school children (Rubovits & Maher, 1973) and ratings of work performance of employees (Rotter & Rotter, 1968). It appears that the above data, together with observations of people such as Weikart (1972) and Rist (1970, see below) cannot be ignored as a simple artifact.

Rist (1970) in particular has noted how the process of expectation seems to work on the classroom behaviors of teacher and student. In an observational study of the effects of social class upon teacher behavior with children from kindergarten through first and second grade, Rist found that very early in the child's career (by the eighth day of kindergarten) teachers placed children in "ability" groups that reflected social class, rather than performance, and that these groups remained together in later school years. He further observed how the teacher's behavior as well as the child's interactions with one's peers served to influence the child's later lack of achievement. Interestingly, all the students in this study were Black, as were the teachers, yet Rist demonstrates how the teachers' preferences for middle-class behavior and appearance, similar to their own and their "reference group," led not only to negative labels for children from the lowest socioeconomic strata, but also to differential patterns of behavioral interaction in the classroom. These teacher behaviors tended to discourage the "lowest" group of children from participation in the class, and modeled similar negative behavior from peers, directed toward the economically poorest children. The teachers actually taught less directly to these children and inadvertently made it impossible for them to improve their performance. Not surprisingly, over time, they performed less well than their higher socioeconomic status peers.

Thus far in this chapter we have reviewed the broad outlines of the environmentalist-early experience model, which is behind preschool educational interventions, and have sampled the results of such programs. It is obvious from the sample of outcome studies that the early experience paradigm, which focuses on supposed deficits of children and their poor preparation for school, has not led to intervention programs that enable the child to perform successfully once he or she enters the public school system. *It is not that such children do not learn from special preschool programs, but what they learn does not matter once they get into the public school.* Possible contributors to public school failure include teacher expectations and self-fulfilling prophecy as well as the possibility that the school is not prepared for the students, rather than vice versa. As we have seen, however, the early experience paradigm finds no place for such hypotheses.

We turn next to a more detailed review of the scientific underpinnings of the early experience paradigm. Although the interventions based on this paradigm have not been shown to solve the problem of school failure, it is possible that the paradigm itself is not at fault, but that practical applications of it have simply been inadequate.[3] However, a closer look at the scientific basis for the paradigm itself (presented below) and the mistaken assumptions on which it rests make that possibility tenuous.

---

[3]I am grateful to Professor Richard Price, of the University of Michigan, for clarifying this point.

How Shall We Account for the Outcomes of Preschool Education?

As demonstrated in the preceding sections, programs for preschool intervention based on the early experience paradigm have failed to produce the predicted positive scholastic outcomes. Consequently, a reconsideration of the paradigm itself seems to be necessary. Currently three sorts of psychological explanations are given for the failure of many poor children to perform well in public school, with or without preschool experience. In gross terms these explanations may be thought of as the genetic, the early experience-environmentalist, and the ecological explanations.

The literature on heredity and environment which represents psychology's traditional battle between the genetic and the environmental points of view was most recently stimulated by Arthur Jensen in a paper which appeared in the *Harvard Educational Review* (1969). In that paper, Jensen challenged the prevailing notion that environment is the most important determinant of intelligence. His argument is complex and he has since expanded on it in several publications (e.g., Jensen, 1973a, 1973b, 1973c). However, with regard to early intervention programs there are three general points on which his argument seems to rest. First, he argues that compensatory education has failed to produce lasting effects on children's IQ and achievement. Secondly, he believes that compensatory education has failed because such programs have been based on faulty assumptions concerning the importance of environment over heredity. He believes that genes are more important than experience. He sees proper environment as perhaps necessary but not sufficient for competent intellectual development. Finally, Jensen argues that the poor child, because of inheritance, is better at one kind of learning (associative) than at other kinds (conceptual). In other words, the children of the poor are seen as better at memory tasks than at reasoning ability. This leads Jensen to conclude that the poor are more likely to succeed at school tasks that are specific rather than general, and he asserts that ". . .

accordingly, the ideal of equality of educational opportunity should not be interpreted as uniformity of facilities, instructional techniques, and education aims for all children. Diversity rather than uniformity of approaches and aims would seem to be the key to making education rewarding for children of different patterns of ability. The reality of individual differences then need not mean educational rewards for some children and frustration and defeat for others" (Jensen, 1969, p. 117). A similar position, as well as an interesting report of the social conflict created by advocating it, is presented in Herrnstein (1973).

Jensen's position has been controversial primarily because of his assertion that heredity is the major factor in intelligence, and that the kind of intellectual ability one possesses is a function of race and/or social class. Many have criticized Jensen on both scientific and social value grounds. The bulk of an issue of the *Harvard Educational Review* (1969) contains seven critiques by well-known psychologists and other social scientists.

The environmentalist-early experience explanation for the failure of lower-socioeconomic-class children in public school and for the poor outcomes of preschool education is to posit an extension of the model described earlier in this chapter. In summary, lower-class children are seen as suffering from cognitive deficits as a function of their presumably inadequate early experience. Despite the effective intervention of psychologists and educators, which can temporarily improve IQ test scores, these children fail in school because they continue to live in a deprived home environment. The little bit of inoculation they receive in a preschool program is seen as too little too late. Perhaps all children of the poor should, at birth, be assigned to a tutor who will visit the home each day, teach parents how to raise their children, and generally enrich the environment. An alternative is to continue preschool education into the elementary school years and beyond; essentially to operate a kind of parallel school system for "deprived" children.

In this chapter we cannot fully consider the details of the heredity-environment argument, but it is safe to say that in this, the last half of the twentieth century, the environmentalist's position with regard to intelligence is in ascendance. Most social and behavioral scientists emphasize environmental factors and few believe that heredity is the major controlling variable in intellectual performance. Hirsch (1970) has argued that the notion of "heritability" has been misunderstood by those who have argued that genes account for the largest amount of variance in measured IQ. Kamin (1974) has presented a strong critique of the twin and other studies which supposedly support a genetic basis for intelligence. Together, these two authors present much of the current criticism of the genetic-determinant position. This does not deny heredity as a factor; it is simply a statement of belief in its relative importance.

Perhaps the most sensible reason for rejecting genetic explanations of intelligence, aside from the scientific merit of the arguments, is one offered by an eminent behavioral-geneticist who is also a psychologist, Jerry Hirsch (personal communication). Hirsch has pointed out that intelligence is a variable that currently has only a social definition, with no demonstrated basis in biological functioning. That is, currently one is judged as intelligent or not purely on the basis of observable social behavior (a phenotype). There is no identifiable genotype for intelligence and no adequate biological definition of intelligence which relates it to what its social meaning implies. To search for the genetic basis of intelligence one needs to examine variables that grow out of the geneticists' studies, rather than try to fit social definitions into biological terms. It is likely to turn out, Hirsch feels, in some distant time, that the genetic basis of intelligence will require a redefinition of intelligence, with far less social content and surplus meaning. For example, it may be definable in terms of genotypic biochemical processes with no direct bearing on phenotypic behavior considered to be important in current ideas about intelligence.

Regardless of the outcome of the genetics-environment debate, for the community psychologist the genetic position is currently of less practical importance than the environmentalist position. The environmentalists currently dominate psychological thought and interventionist programs. For that reason community psychologists need to understand the environmentalists' position in detail, beyond simply seeing it as an alternative to the genetic position.

A third paradigm, the ecological, although available for some time, is newly emerging in psychology. It is critical of both the environmentalists and the geneticists. In important ways the position overlaps with a cultural-relativist value system. Both argue that the genetic and the early experience models are *functionally discriminatory* in that they lead to social policies that degrade differences among people, and accept only one standard of performance, the one held by the dominant social group. The cultural-relativist position is not popular among social scientists and is particularly ignored by most psychologists because it is based on arguments about the relative merits of values and beliefs. The position states that even scientists have values and these values influence their scientific work (for example, in the selection of criteria for intelligence) even when the scientists are unaware of such influence. Psychology has explicitly sought the physical science model of observable and objective "truth," and rejected the idea of cultural relativity that anthropologists, perhaps because of their cross-cultural and historical emphasis, have been more likely to embrace. Psychology grew out of a tradition of seeing fixed traits and abilities and into an era emphasizing the importance of learning. This view of behavior as changeable has sometimes overlooked the difference between the *process* of learning and the content of what is learned. In both the genetic and environmental view of human behavior the tendency has been to compare people on a single criterion. Although differences are accounted for by positing differential mechanisms, that is, inheritance as opposed to experience, difference still equals deficit. The functional similarity between the genetic and the environmental position becomes most apparent when the environmental experiences are posited to occur very early in life, to be transmitted by one's family, and to have

long-lasting effects. Under these circumstances little functional difference exist between the two positions. They both serve to rationalize existing social conditions.

The ecological model is more receptive to a culturally relativist viewpoint, in that person-environment fit and acquisition of resources is emphasized. Failure of the poor child to perform well in school is seen to be a function of the unavailability of a school environment suitable to that child's skills and style. The broad outlines of this paradigm have been presented earlier and its implications for the educational system are presented in the next chapter.

Because the environmentalist-early experience paradigm is the most widely accepted viewpoint and is the often unstated basis on which preschool education programs to "prepare" the child for school (such as those reviewed above) have been assumed to be necessary, we now turn to a detailed consideration of the evidence behind it. There are literally hundreds of studies in this area, and the remainder of this chapter is necessarily exemplary rather than comprehensive. The aim is to trace the source of the evidence from which an analogy is drawn between the need for early sensory stimulation and the assumption of cognitive deficit among the children of the poor.

The belief that poor children suffer from intellectual deficit as a function of their early experience is based on several converging sets of scientific research that have been brought together by people such as Hunt (1969). Basic to the paradigm is an understanding of *perceptual development* as the first step in intellectual development. Given this connection, one source of evidence for the importance of early sensory experience comes from studies of the effect of early visual and motor stimulation on perceptual development among both infants and animals. A second source of evidence comes from studies of *environmental enrichment* and *deprivation* on brain development and problem solving in animals, as well as observations of intellectual and behavioral deficit among *stimulation-deprived* children. The third source of evidence comes from studies of IQ, language development, and social class (see Chapter VIII).

Conclusions from the Study of Infant Perception

There is now a vast amount of evidence from the study of infant perception which indicates that experience with the physical environment is necessary for the development of basic perceptual abilities (Cohen, 1973; Fantz, 1964; Hebb, 1949; Held & Hein, 1963; Hershenson, 1965; Jeffery & Cohen, 1971; Reingold, Stanley, & Cooley, 1962; Riesen, 1975; Salapatek & Kessen, 1966). Indeed, early experience does affect development. However, we must be careful to understand exactly what the nature of such necessary experience appears to be. The evidence from the research cited above is that the opportunity to look at visual stimuli is necessary for perceptual development, and perhaps for visual memory. The opportunity to have motor experience together with visual experience is necessary for the development of coordinated perceptual-motor abilities. A child reared in total darkness, or with no chance to move about, would probably be "deprived" of vital experiences and would develop perceptual deficits, perhaps even leading to cognitive deficits. What has *not* been demonstrated is that the exact nature of the stimulus materials matters. That is, psychologists have not studied infants who were looking at objects found in middle- rather than lower-class homes, or moving about a room with objects that are new or old. Rather, *early experience research shows the need for some kind of visual stimulation.*

Unfortunately, this evidence is frequently misinterpreted to mean that *particular* kinds of content are necessary. That is, there is no reason to conclude that playing with expensive rounded, wooden "educational" toys or with mobiles will lead to greater perceptual, motor, or cognitive growth than playing with an old cardboard box, a pot and pan, or a chewing gum wrapper. Nor is there any reason to believe that the content of perception has anything to do with quality. Nevertheless, this research literature has often been cited as part of the basis for the argument that children of the poor, those who do not have middle-class "advantages," are likely to develop cognitive deficits (e.g., Hunt,

1969). The reasoning goes something like the following:

We know that intelligence begins with perceptual development. We know that perceptual development requires adequate stimulation (from research such as the above). Poor and uneducated parents probably do not provide adequate stimulation. We "know" also that poor children suffer from cognitive deficits because their IQ scores and performance in school are poor. Therefore (by circular reasoning and faulty analogy) it is concluded that these children must suffer from inadequate early stimulation. Consequently, they fail in school.

Research on perceptual development per se is not the only basis for assuming that children of the poor suffer from intellectual deficits, but it is one important set of studies out of which this reasoning has developed. There are other lines of research as well, and these will be reviewed in the remainder of this chapter and in the one that follows.

Enrichment and Deprivation as They Affect Intelligence and Behavior: Animal and Human Studies

The Berkeley Studies

Hebb's (1949) work on early environmental stimulation and basic perceptual processes said to underlie intelligence is probably the modern father of the study of such effects. The idea was not new, but Hebb brought it to modern scientific attention and gained a general psychological audience. Later work, perhaps equally influential in extending the paradigm of the importance of early stimulation for intellectual development is that of David Krech and Mark Rosenzweig and their colleagues at the University of California, Berkeley. They have conducted a series of studies, linked together in the fashion of programmatic research. This work has supported the general hypothesis that changes in the brain underlie changes in learning ability brought about by experience (Rosenzweig, 1966). Their studies demonstrate, with a good deal of conclusiveness, that rats raised under conditions which include a varied and complex physical environment (what they call an *enrichment* condition, which may or may not include specific problem-solving training) are better problem solvers (they make fewer errors in difficult discrimination tasks involving reversal learning) than are rats raised under *impoverished* conditions (less complexity of physical environment and in isolation from other rats).

Figure VII-5 presents the data from one such study (Krech, Rosenzweig, & Bennet, 1962) in which light and dark were alternated as correct responses to a discrimination learning task. This study is typical of the careful research conducted. For example, the enriched and the impoverished rats are paired littermates, each pair from a different litter. This controls for inheritance in a way only possible in animal research. All the rats were given the opportunity to explore the criterion situation many times before testing, therefore eliminating exploration as a reason for higher error scores for the impoverished rats. All animals were coded so that

the experimenter did not know the prior training condition. Animals were food deprived so as to provide heightened motivation. As can be seen from Figure VII-5, the enrichment condition rats, who had been exposed to the complex environment for 30 days after weaning, performed better on reversal discrimination than did their littermates kept in isolation for the same 30 days. The only test on which this did not hold was the easiest to solve problem.

In addition to these behavioral differences, the research team has extensively studied changes in the rat's brains. This, in fact, has been their major focus. They find that rats raised in an enriched physical environment develop greater cortical brain weight, apparently due to stimulated growth of the glial cells (thought to nourish the neurons) as well as increased chemical activity of the central nervous system. Furthermore, the enriched group has a high correlation between behavioral scores on the discrimination learning test and the measure of brain weight and central nervous system activity. Finally, they find that these physical effects of early experience are not immutable; the changes induced by the enrichment environment can be lost and the impoverished animal's brain can be changed by later enrichment (Krech, Rosenzweig, & Bennet, 1962.).

The above results have been extended to show that at least some of the effects are due to simply having animals live together in groups of 12; adding "toys" contributes still more. They have also been replicated and extended by other researchers in many settings. (See Newton & Levine, 1968, for a partial list as well as a recent book edited by Riesen, 1975.) This research evidence is published in multiple technical journals and dissertations, but many of its conclusions have been brought together and presented to a more general readership (Rosenzweig, 1966) and to the Division of Developmental Psychology of the American Psychological Association. The intention of such a presentation to a group of scientists primarily interested in young children is obvious. Although the authors have personally been cautious in extending the implications of their work, it has been influential in providing scientific logic and respectability to

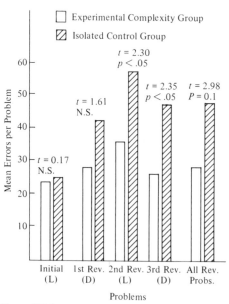

Figure VII-5. Mean errors per problem made by rats of the EC and IC groups. (Redrawn from Krech, Rosenzweig, & Bennet, 1962.)

early intervention programs for the so-called disadvantaged child. Once again, however, it should be noted that what has been demonstrated is that physical stimulation per se "enriches" the environment, and that this is better for cognitive development than isolation and lack of stimulation. There is no evidence that stimulation of equal physical value, but varying in content, leads to differential development.

Studies of infant stimulation with human subjects are necessarily less well controlled than the Berkeley experiments but, nevertheless, they are sufficient in number to lend some support to at least the behavioral conclusions of the animal researchers. Bronfenbrenner (1968), reviewing over 150 studies of early deprivation in mammals, concluded that his comparative analysis clearly indicated that humans and primates bear a striking similarity in the need for stimulation and attachment to others. Of course, most of the human work comes from studies of institutionalized children in places such as orphanages and hospitals because few would purposely create a deprived condition for children. By studying the effects of institutionalization and enrichment programs in places where the environment is relatively controlled and probably less adequate than in the noninstitutional setting, much has been learned about the importance of early experience for normal motor, perceptual, and cognitive development.

Studies of Institutionalization

One of the earliest (thirteenth century) recorded observations of deprivation in children is the report of an attempt by Frederick II to raise infants without the usual mothering. He wanted to see what language the children would "naturally" speak. Unfortunately, the children all died (Rose & McLaughlin, 1949). More modern reports include Itard's (1801) book on the "Wild Boy" (republished in 1962). This volume contains the observations of a French physician who tried to socialize a young boy who had been raised in the wilderness. It is a powerful and exciting story that director François Truffaut made into a movie (*The Wild Child*). More recent case reports have appeared in the

psychological literature on occasion, but there have also been a number of systematic observations and experiments. The Spitz studies of "anaclitic depression" (Spitz, 1945, 1946), for example, found that children who spent the first year of their life in institutions which did not provide adequate maternal care were withdrawn, emotionless, and frequently retarded intellectually and motorically. The studies were more observational than experimental and of course could not "prove" that the lack of adequate mothering was the "cause" of the behavior observed. Selection factors determining which infants are institutionalized and which stay longest might account for the poor appearance of the institutional children.

More systematic observation, including comparative data between institutionalized and noninstitutionalized children, is presented by Dennis and Najarian (1957). These researchers observed children in an institution in Beirut, Lebanon, which had a ratio of only one adult to 10 infants. The children were all institutionalized shortly after birth and had little opportunity for stimulation or adult-child interaction. In early months children were swaddled, with little opportunity for movement. For many months they simply lay in their cribs. The children between 2 and 12 months were given the Cattell Infant Scale and those between 4½ and 6 years were given a draw-a-man test, the Knox Cube Test, and a maze test. These children were compared to a sample of children brought to the Well Baby Clinic of the American University of Beirut Hospital. At two months of age, for almost every one of the institutionalized children, test scores were below those of the comparison group. However, the mean for the institutionalized children was "normal." Retardation as measured by the test given appeared between 3 and 12 months, apparently due to an almost total lack of learning opportunity, and the mean developmental quotient dropped to 65 for the institutionalized children. Nevertheless, by age 4½ to 6 years, when children were less restricted and interacted with each other, performance returned to only slightly below normal. The authors point out that the children had little language experience and probably would not have done well on language tests, but the authors question whether their early deprivation created irrevocable general retardation. The children apparently could do those things with which they had experience, such as use pencils and understand spatial relations. This study, frequently cited as documentation of the detrimental effects of reduced early infant stimulation, actually shows that, at least when such effects are not of the sort which involve physical abuse, they are reversible and children do not lose their capacity for learning what they later experience.

Better evidence for the effects of early childhood deprivation comes from comparative studies as opposed to simple observation of a supposedly deprived setting. Dennis (1960) compared children in two different institutions in Iran. In one setting children were deprived of the chance to practice creeping; more than half were never placed on their stomachs. They were not given toys and the ratio of adults to children was one to eight. These children were compared to children from a second institution with a staff ratio of one adult for every three children, where learning and interaction opportunities were more available. Most children had been in their respective institutions from birth to two years, and comparison with regard to motor development and emotional behavior all greatly favored the adequate environment children as opposed to the deprived children.

More recently, Dennis (1973) has reported on a study which took advantage of a "natural experiment" when a Lebanese social agency changed its policy for the care of foundlings. Although for many years they would institutionalize such children (and Dennis was able to examine the effects of this institutionalization) they later began a policy of adoption. He found that children adopted during the first two years of life overcame initial retardation and soon had a normal IQ. Those who were not adopted had low IQs. Furthermore, the earlier the adoption the better the child's later IQ. Children adopted after the age of two years continued to develop, but never fully reversed the retardation.

Even stronger evidence for the effects of early deprivation comes from experimental studies that explicitly attempt to improve the status of institutionalized children. These studies employ a comparable control group. The well-known study by Skeels and Dye (1939) and the follow-up by Skeels (1965) provide an unusual set of data. Although not a true experimental study and not answering questions about how it works, the data dramatically demonstrated the differential effects of various levels of early stimulation and child-adult interaction as well as the malleability of measured intelligence. They found that children who had been labeled as "feebleminded" and institutionalized, but who were later transferred and placed in the care of older and brighter children, showed substantial IQ gains relative to control children who remained in the original program (these children actually showed a decrease in IQ). Follow-up data on these children as adults found that none of the experimental children was institutionalized, and many were married and had children.

As with the Dennis (1960) observation that some institutions are better than others, the Skeels and Dye study is not simply an indictment of care in institutions. Mussen, Conger, and Kagen (1963), in their review of child development and personality, find that the negative effects of institutionalization cannot be simply attributed to institutionalization per se, but are more likely a function of the exact opportunities for physical stimulation and social interaction. They cite Brackbill's report on nursery schools in the Soviet Union, which pay a great deal of attention to verbal and motor stimulation, and find no adverse effects. Similarly, multiple mothering has not been found to account for adverse effects. Rabin (1958) has even suggested that it may be beneficial. Others, such as Casler (1968), reviewing the effect of perceptual (sensory) deprivation as opposed to maternal or social deprivation, find that there is no evidence that social stimulation is best administered by a loving mother or a mother figure. Although it can be argued that a mother is more likely to care, communicate, and provide such stimulation, there is no evidence that this is necessarily so. It may even be that multiple (but physically adequate) mothering is better in some ways for preparing a child for the diverse world. What does seem to account for the negative effects of institutional care is extreme sensory deprivation, little opportunity for visual experience, and little or no handling by and interaction with adults.

These studies are all remarkably consistent in showing the powerful effects of stimulation on learning. The lack of visual and motor experience inhibits perceptual development, while enhanced stimulation speeds up such development. Taken together, the work from animal and human perception studies in the field and the laboratory, animal research in perception, behavior and brain chemistry, as well as observational and experimental research with humans, finds a strong network of evidence supporting the importance of early sensory and motor stimulation for normal development, but *no evidence that the content or style of stimulation, given equal physical properties, matters.*

General Conclusions

Greenough (1976), in a recent review of the effects of experience and training on the brains of experimental animals, has come to the following general conclusions. First, all animals seem to require certain basic perceptual experiences in order to develop perceptual and motor abilities, or what he calls "perceptual constancies." Thus, for example, specific experience with the perceptual world of objects, coordinated with movement, is necessary for normal development (e.g., Held & Hein, 1963). Some of these physical experiences may need to be acquired at critical periods of development. Greenough calls a second level of experience "world constancy," or learning general rules about how the world works; for example, there are contingencies between one's behavior and certain outcomes. A third level may involve information about a particular environment and how to cope with its particular characteristics. These latter two areas of development do not

seem to be so dependent on critical periods of development as much as on specific experiences. The first level might be thought of as building the necessary equipment, the second two as using the equipment to function in one's later environment.

Perhaps there is confusion between these levels of experience when the analogy to "cultural deprivation" is drawn from studies of physical deprivation. Although physical deprivation does have deficit-creating effects (i.e., it reduces the effectiveness of the equipment) the learning of specific environments probably does not. Given the basic sensory experience, an animal or a person can probably later learn the characteristics of whatever environment he is placed in, although he would obviously need to acquire the information that others who have lived in it longer already have. There is no reason to assume that he could not acquire it if it were presented to him. These generalized conclusions need to be understood carefully. What are the implications for early intervention programs with children and for community psychology as a whole?

Another Look at the Analogy

Having carefully looked at the paradigm of perceptual development and the research on which need for enriched early experience is based, we are now in a position to answer the question raised earlier in this chapter. Is the analogy between sensory deprivation and so-called cultural deprivation a legitimate one?

From the perception studies we can see that organisms need to interact with the physical environment in order to develop cognitive and motor abilities. Children need physical (visual and motor) stimulation. It also appears that different cultures provide different contents of perception, although the perceptual process itself appears to be the same (Campbell, Segall, & Herskovits, 1966). In the human deprivation studies children raised in institutions are the deprived subjects. As infants they are cared for impersonally and there is usually a poor staff-to-resident ratio. The children lie in cribs all day, with little environmental stimulation. They are swaddled so as to limit movement, or placed in neutral, uninteresting surroundings, not surprisingly like a hospital. In animal research the subjects are usually isolated, not handled, and live in empty cages. In the enriched conditions, both animal and human, a wide array of visual patterns, handling, and sensory stimulation are provided. Opportunities to interact with subjects, experimenters, or caretakers are provided. The difference between deprivation and enrichment, then, is the lack or the inclusion of sensory stimulation and social interaction, what might be thought of as Greenough's (1976) first level of experience, noted above.

Anyone who has ever spent any time in the homes of the so-called culturally deprived children and in the homes of Black children who do poorly in school will find an analogy to lack of sensory stimulation and social isolation as an explanation for poor school performance to be absurd. These homes are not like institutions or cages. The children hardly need ''mobiles'' for increasing visual stimulation, as they undoubtedly would if raised in an institution. Furthermore, the absurd stereotype that parents do not attend to their children has no basis in fact except for those children whose families are so poor as to be malnourished. In some recognition of this problem, Hunt has considered the possibility that the problem may be one of overstimulation (Hunt, 1969) which leads to habituation! Others (e.g., Bernstein, 1961)[4] question the ''quality'' of the stimulation. This, however, does not fit well with the research on which early intervention programs are supposedly based. Although the research indicates a need for providing children with sensory input, this is not a problem for the poor. What seems to differ between middle-class and poor families is the *content* of their environment. That is, they learn different things but they seem to learn their respective content equally well.

The argument presented by Hunt and by Bernstein (1961) is one in which children who

do not have the same *content* of experience as middle-class children (studies do show class difference in content of experience; e.g., Hess & Baer, 1968) are thought to be deprived in an analogous fashion as those deprived of the *process* that develops from experience with the environment. Studies supporting the effects of early deprivations, however, present data finding the need for development of perceptual and cognitive *process*, via sensory stimulation, *not* a *particular content*. There have been no studies which show that one environmental experience is superior to another, unless they provide unequal amounts of physical stimulation. Given adequate physical stimulation, the process of perceptual-intellectual development seems to be similar, although the specific content will, of course, differ. Enriching the environment of orphanage-reared children did not find that the enrichment needed to be in standard English. There is every reason to believe that children would develop their perceptual and cognitive processes with stimulation in any language and with visual stimulation by any content other than nothing. Yet Hunt and others make a tremendous leap from comparisons of no stimulation and much stimulation to the need for specific (middle-class) content as necessary for proper development.

Those who have reviewed the effects of cultural influences also find that perceptual *contents* are learned differentially; for example, susceptibility to illusions (Campbell, *et al.,* 1966), social perceptions (Malpass & Kravitz, 1969), eidetic imagery (Leask, Haber, & Haber, 1969), but the *process* is the same. Despite these findings, blaming of the environment based on sensory stimulation research, while it avoids genetic explanations of ''deficit,'' nevertheless blames the nonmiddle-class parent for not providing middle-class content and views middle-class content as ''correct.'' If the *content* of their knowledge is different from middle-class, it is assumed that the *process* of their thought is inferior; this is said to explain why children from nonmiddle-class homes do poorly in school.

The analogy from deprived of stimulation to deprived of culture is faulty. Everyone has a

---

[4]Berstein has recently changed his position, although his earlier work is still frequently cited (see Chapter XIII).

culture. Cultures may differ, but difference does not equal deficit. This is a simple, well-known, and unfortunately ignored anthropological observation. Perhaps it is the schools that do poorly because they present content totally outside the realm of experience of many of the children, and then blame the child and family for inadequate preparation at home. They may say that it is not the child's fault that he or she is stupid, but it is assumed that without the middle-class content one must be less intelligent. One wonders how much poor children do know that is never discussed in school. As we shall see in Chapter XIII, they probably know a great deal. Although Hunt has helped to break down the fixed intelligence idea, he accepts, as do most early interventionists, the correctness and necessity of the content of the middle class. He does not question the criterion for intelligence or the institutional assumptions of our public schools and their "rules of the game."

This distinction between the ability to learn as a function of adequate stimulation (process development) and what one has already learned as a function of environment (content) is more than trivial. To expect a child from a poor family to be just as bright and capable as a child from a middle-class family, even though he now knows different things, is very different from assuming that the child has not developed the ability to learn (process). The expectations one has for the child as well as the procedures one uses to teach are profoundly different. We have already seen how expectations may be self-fulfilling, and in the next chapter we will consider some of the teaching implications.

This chapter has reviewed the line of reasoning for cultural deprivation based on an analogy to physical deprivation and found the evidence wanting. There are also other lines of reasoning that are given to support the analogy. These are based on variables such as language and intelligence, in which once again it is argued that difference from a standard is equal to a deficit. The next chapter reviews this line of reasoning.

INTELLIGENCE, LANGUAGE, CULTURAL RELATIVISM, AND THE PROBLEM OF THE CRITERION: Alternatives for Community Psychology and the Educational System

I've often thought there ought to be a manual to hand to little kids . . . . And one thing I would really like to tell them about is cultural relativity. I didn't learn until I was in college about all the other cultures, and I should have learned that in the first grade. A first grader should understand that his or her culture isn't a natural invention; that there are thousands of other cultures and they all work pretty well; that all cultures function on faith rather than truth; that there are lots of alternatives to our own society. Cultural relativity is defensible and attractive. It's also a source of hope. It means we don't have to continue this way if we don't like it.

—*Kurt Vonnegut, Jr.*

In Chapter VII we saw that preschool interventions based on the early experience paradigm have failed to produce expected results. Also, studies of physical deprivation and perception on which the paradigm is based are not supportive of the analogy to cultural deprivation. A final set of studies on which the paradigm rests includes those based on class differences in intelligence and language development. Consequently, we turn to a consideration of the criteria by which children are compared in our educational system. In so doing we will discover that there are many faulty assumptions behind the belief that the lower-class child is either verbally deficient or unable to reason properly. Finally, we will consider an alternative paradigm.

Part of the reason why the culture and knowledge of the poor, especially of the Black poor, is ignored lies in a peculiarly ethnocentric view of what constitutes intelligence. Psychologists with their tests and educators with their curriculum have reflected, perhaps not surprisingly, American mainstream culture. Intelligence tests select, order, and label children on a continuum that begins and ends in the content of middle-class values. These same values are represented in the curriculum of our public schools and one is then used to validate the other. Intelligence tests predict school performance better than any other single predictor. Those who do well in school are relatively more successful in American mainstream society; therefore common sense views them as more intelligent. The environmentalists recognize that this "intelligence" is acquired by experience, but accept the content of middle-class experience as more intelligent, better and right, as opposed to the content of nonmiddle-class culture. The fact that this is a matter of values is overlooked. If a child tests at a high IQ and does not perform well in school the child is considered to be an "underachiever." If tested at an "average" level and successful in school, the child is an "overachiever" presumably not as smart as he or she seems to be. The test is the criterion. The criterion is validated by performance in school and on similar tests with identical cultural biases.

There are specific things to know in our society (content) and if one knows them one does well on intelligence tests. To know them one must learn from the content of middle-class life. If one knows other things—about the numbers game, pimps, drugs, music, sports, hair styling, survival on the streets, auto mechanics, farming, sex, and so on—these things do not count as "intelligence." Many psychologists and educators do not seem to understand cultural relativism. As Melville Herskovits, the noted anthropologist, warned, "we are beguiled by a fallacious concept of cultural inferiority and superiority, and then replace racism by 'culturalism' " (Herskovits, 1972, p. 189).

IQ scores are based on middle-class content, are reified as intelligence, and are the criteria by which children are compared and by which the outcomes of educational interventions are determined. It is through the paradigm of culturalism that the environmentalists *functionally* inhibit social change just as the fixed IQ advocates did. Although we now recognize that environment makes intelligence malleable, we also suggest that some environments are "better" than others. We forget that the content of these better environments, given an adequate physical experience, is a matter of values, culture, and belief. We confuse content with process. Learning and cognitive abilities become confused with the learning of specific contents.

Donald T. Campbell (1972) has pointed out how psychologists often ignore or are unaware of the philosophers of science from Hume through Popper, Polany, Toulmin, and Kuhn. These philosophers have shown that the logic of science rests on a number of assumptions about truth that are articles of faith. Without realizing it, the social scientist is a biased observer and much of this bias is a function of ethnocentrism. The scientist is a product of one's culture. When one encounters differing patterns of judgment in another culture these often are viewed as erroneous.

. . . we are overconfident . . . we exaggerate the degree to which external truths have been revealed and underestimate the extent to which scientific decisions are made on biasing grounds of tradition, authority, ingroup solidarity, conformity pressures, and the like. . . . the message needs restating, both for the social scientist and for the general public, as there are no signs of abatement in the cultural and moral arrogance of those cultures with the greatest military and economic power (Campbell, 1972, pp. xvii & xxiii).

The work of the community psychologist in the search for new paradigms must include the restatement of this message. In work with the poor, and especially when intelligence is at issue, the community psychologist cannot accept a culturally biased, ethnocentric view of cognitive ability.

Hunt (1969) argues that the substantial correlation between socioeconomic status and competence is "abundantly clear." But closer examination of his argument reveals that it is based on two sorts of related evidence: IQ scores and middle-class values expressed in the *content* of child-rearing practices. Although he and other environmentalists (Deutsch, 1965; Hess & Shipman, 1965) have been most active in setting the aims, method, and criteria for programs of early intervention, oppose the idea of fixed intelligence, and substitute the provision of "better" environments, they do not acknowledge the cultural bias they perpetuate.

There is in the writing of the early intervention-environmentalists little questioning of the criteria by which to judge competence. Blame for failure does shift from genes to environments, but it may more properly rest with the criteria by which people are judged and therefore made to fail. The schools and society that perpetuate punishment for difference close off opportunities for those who do not fit in. This is not a question of educational method, but a question of values.

We have argued earlier in this volume that the community psychologist cannot back away from such questions. He or she must always, in research as well as in community intervention, spell out the values that guide the work. Only then can appropriate kinds and levels of intervention be selected. To fail to do so will increase the likelihood of a game without end and an error of logical typing (see Chapters V and

VI). The community psychologist must straightforwardly address value questions, but in order to do so he or she must also completely understand the scientific paradigm behind which such questions hide. Therefore we now turn to a consideration of the paradigm of intelligence, for it is frequently the criterion by which people and programs are judged.

Intelligence as a Construct

It is remarkable that in the many years that have elapsed since the appearance of Donald Hebb's *The Organization of Behavior* (1949), contemporary views of intelligence not only reflect the same questions to which Hebb addressed himself, but are still giving approximately the same answers. Although Hebb's is not the first, the most articulated, nor the most widely cited theory of intelligence, his view is quite representative of current thinking, particularly with regard to the effect of experience on intelligence. He has discussed this issue quite lucidly. If we understand Hebb's view of intelligence and experience we will understand the basic paradigm as it is currently applied. Regardless of the specifics of other theories of intelligence there are a number of agreements with Hebb's ideas that transcend these differences. The subtle differences in theories of intelligence are more interesting to other psychologists than they are to the community. Regardless of theoretical differences, all of psychology's *uses* of the idea of intelligence seem to have similar functional effects. Once again, the power of the paradigm within which much of our work and thought is constrained seems to allow for change in the specific content of research, but not in the outer limits of the meaning of intelligence or its use. The paradigm in this case is the very notion of the existence of such a thing as intelligence and the belief that it can be measured, and that this measurement is useful.

Most psychologists, of course, now recognize that intelligence is simply a construct and not an entity. That is, intelligence cannot be seen or touched or felt, it can only be inferred. Contrary to its popular meaning IQ does not even estimate native capacity. It is questionable if there is such a thing as "native" capacity, or if there is, its limits are so broad as not to be functionally meaningful. In fact, one of psychology's detrimental contributions to the world may be perpetuation among both educators and the general public of the belief that intelligence can really be measured and represented in an IQ score or a set of statements in a test report. Many children have been both socially labeled and limited by an educational system and a society that discriminates against them for their supposed lack of intellectual capacity. They simply may not be able to perform on a given measure which may not even test what the labelers believe it tests. We now seem to have decided that the way to teach is to classify as smart (gifted), normal, or stupid (retarded), and then to maintain "appropriate expectations." Once classified it is difficult to "jump" groups (cf. Rist, 1970, and Chapter VII).

Perhaps the best discussions of the general notion of a construct have been presented by Cronbach and Meehl (1955); Campbell and Fiske (1959); and Loevinger (1957). The details of these discussions are extremely important for an understanding of modern psychological thought. For our purposes, however, the general conceptions put forth will suffice because it is the limits of the paradigm not the details in which we are interested. In general, the idea of construct validity is one which permits the scientist to study and make inferences about unobservable psychological processes. One way to do this is to apply the philosophy of science called *operationism*. This leads to a use of various observable measures of performance, each hypothesized to be an "operational definition" of some unobservable psychological quality. If, by use of multiple measures, there is convergence, or consistency in the results, the construct's validity is said to be supported.

The observables said to measure some unobservable psychological quality are hypothesized to vary in specific ways if they truly represent the construct. If, through a series of experiments and observations of the various observable operations, these are seen to vary in predicted ways, then this evidence is said to add together to support the validity (usefulness or heuristic value) of the construct itself. The basic aim is to enable one to make future predictions about future observable behaviors which should be related or unrelated to the construct. Intelligence is one such construct of which there are many in psychology and in this book.

For example, the ability to remember and repeat a series of numbers, the ability to put blocks together to match a design, and knowing when George Washington was born are operations believed to be a sample from some larger set of abilities that are theoretically related to an unobservable called intelligence. The ultimate in operationism is the belief that intelligence is "what the intelligence test measures." Although this is only half-believed, theoretically, by most psychologists, it is clearly the message they have communicated to teachers and to the general public. The operations that are said to measure intelligence are not expected to be related to other constructs such as political beliefs, personality, or culture. If correlated with these variables the correlation is expected to be low. The measure of intelligence should not relate to other measures not presumed to represent intelligence. This is called *discriminant validity*. At the same time, different measures of intellectual ability should be relatively highly related. This is called *convergent validity*. Because similar methods of measurement are frequently related to one another (just because the methods are similar, regardless of content), to best establish the validity of a construct it should be measured with different kinds of assessment devices, for example, questionnaires, behavioral observations, and performance tests. That enables one to exclude from the correlations some of the covariation due to the method of measurement rather than the construct itself.

If intelligence is not innate capacity, and it is not directly observable, then what is it? There are many theories of intelligence in psychology and the aim is not to review those here, but to present the way the construct is functionally used by psychologists and educators in general, and to see the relationship between this *use* and our programs of early intervention and public education. The thesis is that this general use of the paradigm of intelligence greatly influences applied psychology. Hebb's discussion of intelligence is representative of this general use of the term by psychologists and it represents well the boundary conditions of the paradigm, regardless of one's specific theory of intelligence. Even though Hebb's theory is based on his neurological model, and many other theories do not discuss such a model, they nevertheless end up *using* the construct of intelligence in similar ways. This is especially true of applied psychologists who normally function out of a generalized conglomeration of theories of intelligence that have certain assumptions in common.

Hebb's View of Intelligence: An Example of the Paradigm

Hebb articulated two components of intelligent behavior. One component, which he calls intelligence type A, is thought to be a factor of heredity. The second, type B, is a function of experience. For Hebb, type A is the *capacity* to elaborate perceptions and conceptual activities. Type B is described as the extent to which type A is *actually* elaborated. Type B is supposedly not limited to a specific situation or occupation, but is thought to enter into "many human activities"; it includes "concepts of number, of causal relations, and so on" (Hebb, 1949, p. 294).

This is the first limit of the current intelligence paradigm on our psychological thinking. What exactly are these "common human activities"? What are the abilities implied in Hebb's "and so on"? The specific answers of course vary from one psychologist to another. However, by examining theories of intelligence, and particularly tests of intelligence and their specific items (the observable operations said to represent the construct), we find a common assumption. Those elements presumed common to "human activities" are largely those most common in the experience of White, middle-class Americans. An anthropologist's perspective would find such tests to be quite culturally idiosyncratic. It is clear from Hebb's viewpoint that he is aware of this, and that he intends the notion of intelligence type B to represent a *process* of conceptual elaboration rather than a content. However, because the theoretical process cannot be measured directly (it is a construct) it is virtually impossible to make its measurement content-free. Once content (tests of performance said to represent ability) is introduced in order to allow measurement, the notion of intelligence is immediately a function of those contents.

Although it might be argued that the *construct* of intelligence makes sense, and that the processes that make it up are culturally free, once one tries to operationalize the construct or the processes, the measures selected are necessarily culturally biased. Different contents will necessarily be chosen to represent "common human activities" by people from different cultures. The content may be a sample of intelligent behaviors in one cultural perspective, but not in others. This cannot be avoided. Campbell (1972, p. xx) cites the anthropologist Herskovits who made the same point in 1927:

. . . it has been found that the American Indians usually rate somewhat lower in psychological tests than Whites, and that this holds true when the tests are of a non-language variety, where the use of words is reduced to a minimum. But the consideration of the fact that the tests ordinarily used have been constructed by persons of a background different from that of the subjects is usually overlooked; and were there to be presented, for consideration as to what is wrong with a given picture, a six-clawed bear rather than a netless tennis court, one wonders whether the city-dwelling White might not be at a loss rather than the Indians.

It is agreed that there is no such thing as a "culture-free" test, even of intelligence type B. It is also true that there is no feasible way to test intelligence type A, at least none of which we are currently aware. Hebb separates types A and B to make exactly this point, one which is commonly accepted by psychologists: We cannot measure innate capacity, we can only estimate acquired intelligence. However, neither Hebb nor the many others who *use* the construct seem to recognize the confounding of process and content in all known measures of intelligence type B. Each of these operational measures is said to represent a process (intelli-

gence). In fact they only measure content (learned, culturally desirable abilities, attitudes, and information). If one has the slightest doubt about this it would be worthwhile to examine the items on the Wechsler intelligence scales for children and adults (cf. Cronbach, 1970). Herbert Ginsburg (1972) also has an excellent description of what really goes on during administration of the Stanford-Binet Intelligence Test and what these items are like.

Hebb goes on to argue that if one realizes the distinction between intelligence A and B and that the ". . . *effects of early experience are more or less generalized and permanent* one can concede a major effect of early experience on the IQ and still leave the IQ its constancy and validity as an index of future performance" (p. 295, italics added).

Here we have the second limiting assumption of the intelligence paradigm. The above quote from Hebb is exactly the way in which most psychologists on the side of environmental versus hereditary determinism of intelligence see the matter. They reject the evidence that intelligence tests measure innate ability but accept the notion that they do measure type B intelligence. They also accept the notion that type B intelligence is in large measure a function of early experience which is generalized and, if not permanent, at least difficult to change.

Recent cross-cultural evidence (Kagan & Klein, 1973) finds this position to be untenable. Kagan and Klein compared Guatemalan infants brought up in a child-rearing environment more like that of deprived infants in orphanages than like the environment of the American middle-class child. Children are left alone, rarely spoken to or played with, have no toys, and are only given adequate physical care. Their mothers apparently treat them this way because they have found that their children grow and develop adequately anyway. Kagan and Klein (1973) found that such children were apathetic; on tests of recall and recognition, perceptual abilities, and conceptual inference, they performed markedly inferior to American children. However, at ages 10 or 11 Guatemalan children performed as well as American children on these same tests, their earlier "retardation" notwithstanding. Similar reversible "retardation" was found by Dennis and Narjarian (1957) (see Chapter VII) for orphanage-reared children, by Suomi and Harlow (1972) with monkeys originally deprived and later placed with young female monkeys, and by Cairns and Nakelski (1971) with rats first isolated and then placed in groups. "There is no reason to assume that the caterpillar who metamorphoses a bit earlier than his kin is a better adapted or more efficient butterfly" (Kagan & Klein, 1973, p. 957).

Hebb's assumptions about the effect of early experience are, however, still held by the environmentalist paradigm. As a result, we find that for the applied psychologist such an early experience argument is *exactly the same in its implications* as the hereditary determinant argument. It serves the purpose of allowing the "liberal" to be against racist (genetic difference) arguments to account for intelligence test differences and failures in the public school; but at the same time its implications for social policy are only superficially different from the heredity position. It leads directly to conclusions of intractable and negative social conditions, unchangeable short of disruption of family life, and annihilation of existing culture, especially for poor, Black families.[1] It implies that early learning of the wrong *content* (culture) necessarily means that *process* (the ability to learn) is damaged. For example, Whimbey (1974), who views intelligence as a "learned skill and not a genetic gift" argues that "it is important to recognize that children come to school with varying IQs—that they do differ, as Jensen points out, in 'the ability to learn traditional scholastic subjects.' " He goes on to review two prominent environmentally based training programs for the "disadvantaged" (see Chapter VII): Carl Bereiter and Seigfried Englemann's *Teaching Disadvantaged Children in the Preschool* (1966)[2] and Bloom and Broder's *The Problem Solving Process of College Students* (1950). Both are based on a study of *errors* made in school situations. These "errors" are then traced to "three principle causes: inadequate attention to details, inadequate use of prior knowledge, and absence of step by step analysis."

These approaches emphasize the use of school content as if it totally represents the ability to think. They never consider how these children think in other situations, or with other than school content, or with children and adults of background and language similar to their own. They ascribe to these children, in general, an impulsive "one shot" approach to problem solving which may be totally a function of the school situation and have nothing to do with ability or style of thought in other situations. What follows from this position is fairly typical of the early experience-culturally disadvantaged theorists. They argue that ". . . certain types of parent-child verbal interactions . . . (are the) crucial advantage provided by middle-class homes . . . . Lacking such background, culturally disadvantaged preschoolers need direct training in *thinking* and in *language skills* . . ." (Whimbey, 1974, p. 51, italics added). The implication (actually, it is not implied, it is directly stated) is that children who are not doing things the way the school defines them to be correct are not able to *think* correctly. Not thinking in this way and not learning the particular contents of middle-class school systems is equal to being stupid.

Furthermore, the child is stupid because the parents are stupid (not through genetic transmission, of course; they do not know enough to teach their children the proper way to think). Finally, if we (White professional educators) do not do something about it early it will be irreversible. The process of thinking, one is told, can only be taught in the style of middle-class America. If one accepts this view it is surprising that people in other times and places, non-Western people, and those culturally different, were and are able to survive without such help. This is the most blatant kind of cultural ethnocentricity imaginable. It is not only a plea for socialization to the trappings of White middle-class America, but a demand that the children even think like the White, middle class.

---

[1]For example, see Scarr & Weinberg (1976).

[2]Bereiter (1972b, 1973) has recently attempted to clarify his position to avoid what he feels is a misunderstanding of his philosophy of education. He currently views the use of his methods as a means for socialization to middle-class norms to be a misapplication. His recent disclaimer notwithstanding, Bereiter's early work has in fact been used as indicated here. For a brief review of his recent statements on philosophy of education, see p. 257).

A careful reading of the method and style of teaching advocated will lead us to conclude that it is not thinking alone that is intended here, but the *right answers* as well. The right answers, as defined in school, are seen as the most important goal of education.

Herbert Ginsburg's Analysis of "The Myth of the Deprived Child"

In a recent book, appropriately titled *The Myth of the Deprived Child*, Herbert Ginsburg (1972) has put together an extensive critique of the thinking behind programs aimed at early educational interventions for the poor. This analysis, by a child psychologist, is one which community psycholigists must understand if they are to seek out new paradigms for social change with regard to the children of the poor. Ginsburg challenges the existing paradigm for such interventions on several grounds, and his book is worth close examination here. Its over-200 pages include a very detailed analysis of case study as well as group data, and anyone considering an educational program for the poor would do well to read this book first.

Beginning with the assumption that educational priorities are properly a function of community values, the selection of which is more political than psychological in nature, he nevertheless offers the argument that the practice of education, whatever its aims, must be based on a sound understanding of child development. It is this understanding which Ginsburg presents as he critiques earlier work. He views most current approaches to education for the poor child as essentially unable to challenge the rules of the educational game because they are based on faulty assumptions concerning the *existence* of deficits and the acquisition of knowledge. Although many psychologists differ on the nature of the deficit, they assume that the poor child does indeed suffer from some form of cognitive inadequacy. As we have seen, the environmentalists emphasize factors other than heredity, but still emphasize deficit, usually in the form of language and thinking abilities. As

we have also seen, even the environmentalists fail to appreciate the richness of the lower-class environment, and Ginsburg notes that deprivation is assumed:

Certainly a slum is not a pleasant place to live in, and certainly the middle class does not approve of much that goes on there. But this does not necessarily imply that the slum is not a stimulating environment in its own way. Like other environments, it contains sounds and shapes and it presents obstacles to surmount. In some respects, living in the slum requires a sharper intellect than that required to survive in middle-class suburbs. . . . The real issue is not why poor children are deficient, but why they develop as well as they do (Ginsburg, 1972, p. 15).

Beginning with an analysis of the items on standardized IQ tests, Ginsburg explodes several myths about IQ: it is a unitary ability, it reflects real intellectual differences, it measures competence, and it measures innate ability, unaffected by experience. As we have seen, only the last of these myths is rejected by the early interventionists; the others remain as part of their paradigm. As is clear from Chapter VII, intelligence tests remain the commonly used measure of educational outcomes and ability.

Ginsburg shows how inadequately the differences in IQ scores actually reflect the ability to think and the competence to do. He shows how IQ scores are affected by motivational factors and standardized situations which favor the style of the middle-class child and hurt the poor. His analysis of the failure of IQ tests to reflect real abilities is important, but Ginsburg's real contribution lies in his analysis of language and thinking differences between the middle- and the lower-class child. Just as Chapter VII of this book has emphasized the faulty analogy from sensory to cultural deprivation, Ginsburg emphasizes the faulty assumption that language differences between middle- and lower-class children indicate that lower-class children are either verbally deficient or less able to think.

Most of the interventionists who are concerned with influencing the child's language development base their assumptions of a deficit on the work of Bernstein (1961). He has argued that middle-class language is superior to lower-class language in the reasoning ability it reflects. Therefore, many of the environmentalists (Bereiter & Englemann, 1966; Hunt, 1969) base their programs around teaching "correct" language and "competence" according to middle-class standard English. Ginsburg has reviewed several normative studies of the language of the poor (Loban, 1963, 1966; Templin, 1957) and finds that there are actually very few social class differences in language. When there are differences these can often be accounted for by methodological problems in the study. Furthermore, such differences are not shown to relate to competence. Others (Robinson, 1965) find that poor children are often *capable* of performing like middle-class children, but frequently do not do so in standard school-like situations.

The most important work reviewed by Ginsburg is Labov's (Labov, Cohen, Rubins, & Lewis, 1968; Labov, 1974). Labov has, in the context of examining the syntax of nonstandard, Black-dialect English, tape recorded conversations among Black, teenage gang members in Philadelphia. These children, many of whom are considered nonverbal in school, are shown not only to use language with a consistent grammar (albeit different from standard English), but also to have a rich tradition for the use of language in their street culture. Their language is complex, abstract, and reflects a set of values and ideas not likely to be sympathetically viewed by middle-class teachers. When tested in school these children perform poorly; when tested in their own locale, under circumstances designed not for a standardized test, but to examine their capabilities, performance is not "deficient" (Labov, 1974).

Carrying the argument still further, Ginsburg goes on to examine the hypothesis that poor children are intellectually deficient by evaluating their performance on the intellectual tasks developed by Piaget. He argues that these tasks more accurately reflect thinking ability than do standard IQ tests and that they have been demonstrated to reflect cross-cultural developmental level. Furthermore, Ginsburg finds, in five different major cross-cultural studies, that social class differences on these tasks are not found to be crucial (Goodnow, 1962; Price-Williams, 1961; Vernon, 1965a, 1965b; Greenfield, 1966; Opper, 1971).

The ages at which children learn the Piagetian tasks may not be precisely the same in Geneva as in Hong Kong, but in both cases cognitive development seems to follow the same general course. . . . Some studies show no social-class differences in intellect, other studies show minor differences. . . . Surely the *content* of poor children's thought must include unique features. Poor children in the ghetto often know about the numbers racket, whereas middle-class children may think of numbers in the context of ordering lollipops" (Ginsburg, 1972, p. 138).

In summarizing studies of intellectual development Ginsburg concludes that poor children's intellect is adequate because; they are active learners (as are all children), their environment is adequate to promote the necessities of cognitive activity, they do not require direct teaching from parents in order to acquire the necessary (Piagetian) cognitive skills for intellectual development, and they develop some strengths (different from middle-class strengths) as a function of their distinctive environment. Unfortunately, the language and intellectual skills that poor children do have are frequently ignored by the schools they attend. Finally, Ginsburg proposes "open schools" as a possible solution. We will return to this suggestion in the section on *Alternatives* (below).

The Social Pathology Hypothesis

When a psychologist rejects the idea that intelligence tests measure inherited capacity and tries to account for both test differences and performance in school on the basis of early experience with the environment, the sorts of variables postulated to account for poor performance include sociocultural, familial, and physical environment. For psychologists this frequently leads to a discussion of the poor socialization of "disadvantaged" children. Hess and Baer (1968) in an edited volume on early childhood education present much of the thinking in this area, which takes deficits in the children as a given. Summarizing the discussion following a conference on early education they found that the major issue raised was ". . . where and how time and effort are best spent in educational programs, particularly those involving intervention with the disadvantaged" (p. 227). Two alternative hypotheses were discussed.

The deficit model asserts that lack of stimulation leads to retardation in time or even lack of appearance of a certain skill . . . opposing it is the cumulative model which asserts that the damage done by deprivation is not specific, but that the degree of retardation and the nature of the deficit change with prolonged deprivation . . . a variant of the cumulative model is the socialization model . . . (the child) learns the wrong behaviors and develops inappropriate skills (p. 228).

Finally,

. . . the family—especially the disadvantaged family—must be considered as a source in understanding early development, and included in programs with the child who becomes the subject of an educational intervention program (p. 230).

The overriding thread of this summary statement is an emphasis on the so-called deprived child's poor socialization and consequent lack of abilities. These elements—intellectual ability, socialization, and stimulation—are always intertwined. The emphasis is on early experience rather than genetics, but the effect is the same. Take the children of the poor (and this always includes Black children) into programs that change their socialization. Make them think and act like middle-class children. Change their parents, if you can, so that they help in the obliteration of their own culture. Then the children will do better in White, middle-class schools. Assimilate the deviant culture.

Baratz and Baratz (1970) have written probably the clearest analysis of the above kind of thinking in a paper aptly entitled *Early Childhood Invervention: The Social Science Base of Institutional Racism*. Their analysis merits careful review. They argue that an ethnocentric view of the Black community, such as the one presented above, produces a distorted image of that community. They are particularly critical of programs concerned with altering the child's home environment and child-rearing with the idea in mind that such interventions will improve cognitive and language abilities. They note that these abilities, although different in content, are not shown to be inferior.

One of the crucial observations which Baratz and Baratz make is that what they call the "social pathology model" underlies Head Start-type projects, a name they use as a rubric for preschool programs for "deprived" children. Such a model denies strengths within the Black community and inadvertently advocates annihilation of a cultural system not understood by most social scientists. Such programs are founded on the belief that the early experiences of "culturally disadvantaged" children are inferior to those of White middle-class children. ". . . research on the Negro has been guided by an ethnocentric liberal ideology which denies cultural differences and thus acts against the best interests of the people it wishes to understand and eventually help" (Baratz & Baratz, 1970, p. 31). This ethnocentricity is based on at least two assumptions: the belief that to be different is to be inferior, and that there is no such thing as Black culture.

The first assumption is rarely stated explicitly; it is usually only assumed. But the second assumption is often voiced (see, for example, Glaser & Moynihan, 1963). LeRoi Jones (1963), the Black poet, in *Blues People* takes up the second assumption—there is no Black culture. He traces, through the development of Black music in America, a good deal of this "nonexistent" culture, including language and thought. Kochman (1972) also details some of the systems of communication, language, and style of American Black culture. The language is shown to be different, but nevertheless to be as complex and adequate as "standard" English. Very few scientists who design intervention programs for Black people recognize, much less understand, Black culture or language. For a White social scientist to do so requires an immersion in the culture that few are willing to experience (cf. Liebow, 1967). When social scientists view Black culture they rarely can see beyond the surface appearance of similarity to

White society. What the Black person has chosen and been allowed to show is superficial similarity. It is the rich underbelly of culture that is not obvious to those unattuned to it.

The label of racist has been generally reserved for those who see Black inferiority as genetically determined. At the same time, the liberal social scientist posits familial transmission to account for "deficits" and "inferiority" among Black children. "The major differences between the genetic model and the social pathology model (e.g., via cultural transmisson) lies in the attribution of causality, *not* in the analysis of the behaviors observed as sick, pathological, deviant, or underdeveloped" (Baratz & Baratz, 1970, p. 32). Baratz and Baratz present evidence not only of this view, but of the *nonexistence of the need to account for any deficit.* They cite the recent work in language acquisition which finds "ghetto dialect" to be a fully developed syntactically sound language with its own rules. Nevertheless, many deprivation theorists continue to argue that Blacks lack language development.[3]

The social pathologists also seem to argue for the idea that specific *content* of learning and language is necessary for the *process* of learning to take place. They imply that it is less intelligent to join a gang or become a person who learns to survive on the streets than to learn to study or to become a social worker. They do not acknowledge that what is different are the values and *what* is learned, not the intellectual process. It would be interesting to see a White middle-class engineer take an intelligence test to see if he could survive on the ghetto streets. The engineer would probably fail and if forced to spend six hours a day in a small room with people who all spoke in Black dialect the engineer might even have difficulty understanding them. But it would be wrong to see him as stupid, or to blame his mother for not teaching him how to survive. Yet the assumption is that the ghetto mother does not provide her child with adequate

language, social and sensory stimulation. To anyone who has ever lived with people in a Black ghetto this is an absurdity. But, of course, few social scientists have lived in a Black ghetto.

If the evidence behind the early experience paradigm is not adequate to explain differences on intelligence tests and in school performance, why is it so readily accepted? The answer may lie in the value system it supports. Social scientists like to think of themselves as value-free adherents of scientific objectivity, even though the very processes they study are value-laden. In fact, this position enables the liberal social scientist to be comfortably nonracist, but still see people who are different as inferior. "Of course," they say, "it is no fault of their own, it is just their poor environment." Social scientists can then engage in "helping" programs to alter that environment by socializing poor children and their parents. When such strategies do not work, that is, when there is little or no improvement in school performance, it is always assumed that they did not start early enough, or stay long enough, or intervene in enough of the child's social spheres. If it is a school intervention that fails then one needs to work in the home or vice versa; and if the program was in both the home and the school then the peer group gets the blame for failure; or perhaps the group's historical background which does not support the proper culture, that is, the cultural transmission hypothesis gets the blame. In any case, the only route to success is to be exactly like White middle-class children.

Baratz and Baratz account for the failure of compensatory education in the following way. Their account is based on two major points: First, as we have seen in Chapter VII, preschool programs based on the idea that poor or inadequate stimulation needs to be overcome show, after an initial spurt in IQ, no differential effects for experimental as opposed to control children. Baratz and Baratz see these data as largely a methodological artifact in which the "gains" are a function of initial contact with the mainstream culture, that is, becoming accustomed to the school situation. For Head Start

---

[3]Further evidence for the language ability of those who speak Black dialect is presented in a later section of this chapter concerned with *psychoeducational alternatives,* p. 257.

children such gains occur early but, because the school does not continue to help the child intertwine his culture with the middle-class culture, the gains cease. Non-Head-Start children also experience the gain on initial contact with the new culture, but likewise are not assisted in expanding on this learning. By the end of the primary grades most children from minority groups fall behind, not because they are less intelligent, or because their parents are inadequate, or because they lack early stimulation, but because the *school fails* to teach by using the child's already existing knowledge and language ability. There is no systematic attempt to help the child learn the new culture by relating it to one's own. This is the Baratzes' second point. Schools do not use the system that the child already has available because they view it as pathological. Indeed, schools try to destroy that system and language rather than use it. Finally, the failure of such approaches leads to certain "inevitable hypotheses" (Caldwell, 1968) which, because the failure is defined as the child's rather than the school's, leads to attempts to move intervention further and further back in time for example, to infancy, or even ultimately to a rejection of environmental determinism in favor of genetics (e.g., Jensen, 1969).

If the above arguments are accepted, the logical question that arises is something like the following: OK, so poor Blacks are different, not inferior; they can think just as well as Whites and in some situations even better. This difference is based on culture, and in the abstract one culture and language is as good as another. Values are only values and one set is not objectively better than another. But in our society some values, those held by the majority, lead to success and specific kinds of skills necessary for equal opportunity. Therefore, we better teach these skills.

Here our knowledge about principles of learning, child development, behavioral assessment, research, and language acquisition may be useful and constructive; but only if we are also willing to permit value changes, alter power and control relationships, and develop new paradigms aimed at less ethnocentricity and

more diversity rather than simple assimilation. These issues are taken up in the remainder of this chapter.

Alternatives to the "Disadvantaged" Paradigm

Socialization, the Ecological Viewpoint, and Community Psychology

If we are to overcome the ethnocentricity dominating our educational system, a viewpoint other than one that emphasizes a single correct environment and the molding of individuals to fit into it must be developed. Cultural relativism and diversity require a paradigm that emphasizes the use of strengths and resources and the importance of the fit between persons and social systems. Community psychology must develop such a viewpoint to be viable; the broad outlines of the paradigm are beginning to appear.

Robert Reiff (1967), who was influential in the early development of community psychology, has written about "Socialization in an Urban Setting." He was concerned with the school's place in the socialization process of Black children residing in a ghetto area. Rather than focus on individuals, Reiff suggests that we look at settings as systems for socialization. The three settings he identifies are the family, the peer group, and the educational system. He views each of these as independent, with its own unique form of organization, territory, and socialization functions or goals. The family is seen to prepare the child to love, the peers to play, and the educational system to work. The child enters each system at a different age, and each system is characterized by a different mode of expression which corresponds to its function. Each system also has its own history and heritage, and in urban Black ghettos the educational system is based on a history and heritage alien to the family and the peer group.

For socialization to operate smoothly (i.e., to prepare the child for life) the three systems must work well together. In middle-class society this is generally the case because the goals of the three correspond to the goals of society as a whole. In the Black community this is not necessarily the case. Often the family and the peer systems are of the ghetto, while the educational system is controlled by outside powers. Often the family and peer group do not see the possibility of really obtaining work in the larger community and the function of school as a preparation for work is not objectively true. One need only look at older friends to see this fact. Often the peer group is the predominate force, and the family can accommodate itself to this; but the school remains inflexible and seeks only to assimilate, never to accommodate.

Rather than changing the family and the peer group, Reiff suggests changing the educational system. The current educational system has little relevance to real problems in living. In short, Reiff's description finds the educational system to be ethnocentric and not meaningful to the skills and needs of the Black children it is supposed to serve. He suggests changes in the school's disciplinary and rule structure, allowing more student decision making, using the street culture as a learning laboratory, including street leaders as teachers. He suggests transferring the functions of school to recreation centers and storefronts; instead of punishing children for the expression of their culture, reward it. This necessitates the involvement of parents in the control of their own neighborhood schools, and is a suggestion to which we shall return.

Stanley Murrell (1973) is one of the few psychologists who both views himself as primarily a community psychologist and who has attempted to explicitly relate child development to community intervention based on an ecological point of view. Murrell emphasizes explicitly, as do most community psychologists implicitly, the influence of the social systems network on child development. He begins to make this assumed input concrete. Although he does not go terribly far, he at least begins to develop a view of child development congruent with the community psychology movement. Stressing the relationship between the development of what he calls *personal problem management strategies* (or coping styles) and the network of social systems, Murrell begins with the family system and

describes it primarily in terms of selective reinforcement and punishment leading the child toward particular "solutions complementary to family responses to him." Murrell is relying heavily here on the work of the psychiatrist Harry Stack Sullivan, and more directly on Robert Carson's (1969) interpersonal psychology (see Chapter IV). Emphasizing the family influences, together with the notion of social norms for survival and affiliation, the developmental sequence then moves on to the school years, and here additional social systems demands are made on the child. Together, the school and the peer group create new "role expectancies" as the child becomes older. The possible positive and negative effects of the classroom system's demands on children, particularly those whose family system demands are at variance with the school system demands, are stressed. Here Murrell's view is similar to Reiff's view of the socialization process.

Using the notion of "intersystem accommodation" Murrell notes that the child must learn to make adjustments in his problem-management strategies. The child may have to subordinate the demands of one system in favor of another. Even when physically at home, the school has an effect on the child, and vice versa. The "forces" of values, expectations, and other unverbalized rules are powerful. How well the child manages to negotiate these systems in part depends on how congruent or incongruent such systems are with each other and with the child's already developed coping style. This "fit" is what Murrell calls *degree of psychosocial accord*. Congruent with a cultural relativist point of view rather than with a description of a person as pathological, or a system as malignant, Murrell, borrowing from Kelly (see Chapter V), views the interaction between the two as in relative degrees of psychosocial accord or discord.

Persons with more limited resources or more atypical problem-management programs will have less choice of systems; there will be fewer systems that can provide them with good fits. For example, if persons labeled "schizophrenic" are found to have physiological conditions that make them more vulnerable to stress than most people, their resources and problem-management programs will require a low stress systems network. The cause of the problem is still located in the discordant fit, and the reduction of the problem is to be found in more consonant person-system fits (Murrell, 1973, p. 82).

Murrell does not discuss in any detail the problem of restricted access to social systems because of *attributed* rather than "real" personal characteristics nor does he discuss the role of *positive* differences among people not tolerated by society. These should function in a similar manner with regard to the accord or discord between persons and systems. For example, if a person does not fit into the employment systems available because he or she has been labeled delinquent or criminal rather than because he or she is incompetent for work, or if a child does not fit into the educational system because he or she speaks Black dialect rather than standard English, the problem of psychosocial accord is a functional reality, although it may be "caused" by no fault, or "deficit," of the individual. Rigid systems may make differences among people into "problems." The traditional view is that those who do not fit are at fault and need to be changed. The "systems-fit" view is that this is only one explanation and option among many. Murrell does list the options for dealing with psychological discord so as to imply that differences among people may indeed be legitimate. The strategies he lists include: (1) improving individual or population resources, (2) relocating the individual, (3) modifying system responses, (4) modifying systems structure, and (5) creating new systems (Murrell, 1973, p. 86). These strategies are fairly representative of the range of community psychologists' solutions for dealing with such problems, and they are not limited to changing *people* to "fit in."

Although only a beginning, Murrell's discussion of child development is somewhat nonspecific with regard to the process and the details. He is careful to emphasize social systems and interpersonal communication; however, he relegates the first year of life and learning to "simple association between external stimuli and internal states" (p. 70). The first year of life is probably more complicated than this and it needs to be understood, particularly for dealing with questions of preventive inter-

ventions with children. Similarly, he has little to say about the specifics of programs in schools. Again, rather than turn to community psychology per se, we are forced to combine this perspective with the larger body of psychological research from child development and education.

What Does Child Psychology Suggest?

There is now a fair amount of consistent evidence as to what the effects of preschool education for poor children are likely to be. The poor child, like any other, will learn whatever content is taught well. If someone pays attention to teaching middle-class content useful on IQ and other school tests, the child will probably do better on those tests than children who do not experience that content. Furthermore, the more focused the academic attention and the better the expectations the child receives from a teacher (a parent, a professional teacher, or a college or high school-aged tutor), the more likely he is to learn the material. There are no data to indicate that these children think better, or are more intelligent, or even more academically successful than their peers. Although the content of middle class intelligence tests appears to be teachable, its utility beyond performance on similar tests is questionable. If specific attention to teaching such content is not continued, performance declines as the child progresses in a school where he or she is frequently ignored and expected to do poorly.

Chapter VII reviewed the literature supporting an analogy between physical and cultural deprivation, the analogy on which preschool interventions are based, and found it to be ill-conceived. In this chapter we have seen that many preschool programs are also based on an ethnocentric notion of intelligence and language which labels as social pathology those environments and abilities that are different from middle class. This suggests the need for a culturally relative point of view in educational programs for the poor, particularly the Black poor.

What kind of educational approach makes sense to the community psychologist who wants to overcome the problems of cultural bias in the educational system? To begin, the public education system itself is where the changes need to be located, not in isolated "special" programs. Second, the basic outlines of the program need to take into account observations such as those by Reiff and Murrell noted above. Although programs with this orientation have not been tested, they are at least consistent in opposing what we know is detrimental about the existing paradigms of education. The suggestions are at this point more in the form of boundary conditions than specific curricula or programs, but this is an important start.

The boundary conditions implied are that all children (with very few exceptions), regardless of the particular culture of their early experience, have probably had enough experience in looking, seeing, moving, thinking, and learning so that by the time they get to public school they have developed well enough to continue to learn. Ultimately, most children develop the intellectual structures necessary for functioning in their community (Kagan & Klein, 1973). Some children may know different culturally specific content than others, but the problem in the schools is that if one rank-orders children on one of these contents, those with the most experience with that particular content will be at the top and those with the least at the bottom. Regardless of one's intentions, such a system will communicate inferiority to some and superiority to others. Instead of doing this, child development and learning research (as well as common sense) tells us that schools need to deal with each child by assessing what the child *knows* (not what the child does not know) and starting from there. Cole and Bruner (1971), for example, have suggested that the focus in school should be on how to transfer skills from one area of competence to another. For example, if a child speaks in Black dialect it is obvious that the child is able to use language, albeit a somewhat different language than is valued in school. This makes it more difficult to read books in standard English, just as anyone would have more difficulty reading in a foreign language, or as a White person unaccustomed to Black dialect has difficulty understanding it. In this example one must recognize that the child does not have a deficit, but a skill to be built upon.

One can, for example, treat standard English for that child as a second language. To teach reading it might make sense to allow the child to read in Black dialect, a suggestion we shall consider further below.

Psychoeducational Alternatives

Carl Bereiter (1972b, 1973) has recently suggested that the educational system be divided into two separate elements. One would involve training and the second would involve what he calls "child care." Child care, in his definition, is the provision of opportunities for children to experience their world through interesting activities, thus providing opportunities for learning other than traditional academic skills. Training, on the other hand, is meant to include only those aspects of learning that are skills specific, such as reading and mathematics. He thinks that these can be taught by a specific set of procedures which structures the learning into discrete steps such as is done in the Bereiter-Englemann curriculum reviewed in Chapter VII. Although the specific procedures of this curriculum may not necessarily be the best for teaching reading and mathematics to all children, the idea of a separation of the skills training goals from other kinds of learning in school is an interesting one. This relegates the "skills" to a clear place with little confusion between them and the teaching of values. Methods such as those suggested by Reiff above could be applied to "child care," whereas with academic skills training, one could apply the idea of small steps, structured teaching procedures that pay attention to detail, reward of the child for success, and convey the expectation that each child can and will learn (which are probably the common elements in various successful teaching methods). To do this Bereiter suggests:

Take an ordinary old elementary school, announce to the teachers that they can have their choice between being child care workers and scholastic skill trainers. Put the child care workers on the ground floor and tell them that their job is not to educate children but simply provide them with an abundance of things to do in and out of school that will make for a good life. Put the trainers upstairs or in the basement. Assign them either language arts or arithmetic as their subject, and tell them to find a way to teach it successfully to any child who walks in the door, using no more than three hours of his time per week. Give the child care workers an ample equipment and field-trip budget and give the trainers some time off to be trained themselves in any teaching method of their choice (Bereiter, 1972b, p. 407).

The kind of school Bereiter suggests is one that would enable the learning of skills to be separated from the learning of values. Both the child care and the skills training could be better done than is now the case because the two would not be confounded. Each of them could also be best performed by teachers who are indigenous to the community. The child care activities would obviously be best performed by a teacher who could make access to the child's real life community a learning experience. But this would have different aims and methods from the teaching of academic skills. Skills training will require some technical expertise, but the question of importance is "what kind of expertise?"

In such a school the kinds of expertise and methods used for training are crucial. We have already suggested that skills be broken down into structured, small steps, children be systematically reinforced, and the expectation that each child will learn be conveyed. It is this last element which, for Black children, has important, and often ignored, psychoeducational and linguistic implications.

There is, in addition to Labov's work mentioned earlier, mounting evidence that Black children are already linguistically competent, even though their competence may be ignored by both standard tests and their teachers. Baratz (1969a), for example, found that although White children performed better than Black children on a task of sentence repetition when it was in standard English, Black children performed significantly better than White children when the test was in Black dialect. More recently, Hall and Freedle (1973) found the same results as Baratz (1969), and also found that those 8- to 10-year-old Blacks who improved at the same rate as Whites on tasks involving standard English, improved at a significantly greater rate when responding to nonstandard dialect. Furthermore, Blacks and Whites did equally

well in verbal comprehension and production tasks. In a second study, Hall, Reder, and Cole (1975) found that Black children from a large urban renewal complex in New York City's Harlem area, attending Head Start, when asked to recall a story in Black vernacular performed better than a group of White children attending a fee-paying coop nursery in Manhatten. When the children were asked to perform in standard English the White children did better. When probed with questions asked in the child's own dialect, the differences disappeared, suggesting that the information had been stored, but not produced unless the experimenter was speaking to the child "in his own language."

Obviously an approach which begins with the abilities children have requires teachers who respect the child and expect that child to be bright and able to learn. It also helps if the teacher understands the child's dialect. Skin color of the teacher is no guarantee of this (cf. Hall *et al.*, 1975; Rist, 1970). Cole and Bruner have also discussed what the anthropologists call *cultural amplifiers,* or those aspects of a technology which enable one to expand on the existing culture. Reading and mathematics, because they open a whole world of technological opportunities, can serve as cultural amplifiers for Black children without eradicating their culture. But to do this their culture must be respected and the skills for a technological society must be taught within the context of their life, not the life of a middle-class teacher.

Baratz (1969b) has observed that the literature on language of Black children comes from three sources: educators, psychologists, and linguists. Educators have traditionally assumed that Black children were "virtually verbally destitute, that is, they couldn't talk, and if they did, it was deviant speech filled with 'errors.' " Psychologists added the assumption that their speech was a deterrent to cognitive growth, and linguists appear to be astonished at the naivete of the psychologists' pronouncements. These latter researchers have found that Blacks use a "well-ordered, highly structured, highly developed language system which in many aspects is different from standard English" (Baratz, 1969b, p. 94, see also Labov, 1974). In short, there is no reason to assume that African Black children develop a language and Black inner city children do not. Contrary to the assumptions of many psychologists that Black children cannot discriminate (e.g., Deutsch, 1964), they respond to language on the basis of sound usage learned in their natural environment. Pronunciation and syntax in Black and standard dialect are different. The fact that *pin* and *pen* may be pronounced the same by a Black child does not reflect a problem in discrimination ability, only a difference in pronunciation between standard English and Black dialect.

Shuy (1969) has sufficiently posed the problem for educators. He argues that reading difficulty stems from a cultural difference in linguistic systems. When this interferes with the acquisition of reading skills there are two alternatives. One is to adjust the child to suit the materials. The other, favored by most linguists, is to realize that this sort of engineering is too slow moving to be effective, and that speaking standard English is not as important as learning to read. Changing the child is described as "educationally naive."

The notion that children in disadvantaged homes are the products of language deprivation seems to mean only that the investigators proved to be such a cultural barrier to the interviewee that informants were too frightened and awed to talk freely, or that the investigators simply asked the wrong questions (Shuy, 1969, p. 120).

This view is substantiated by Labov's (1974) recent data which find the residents in a Black ghetto to have both a complete and a systematic language.

Baratz and Shuy (1969) have presented a collection of papers about teaching Black children to read which starts from the assumption that one must deal with the role of the child's own language behavior in order to teach reading. Their book presents the work of linguists, rather than psychologists, who have argued that a reading program "is likely to be effective in proportion to its use of language habits that the student has acquired in speaking" (McDavid, 1969). Labov (1969) puts the position cogently when he asserts that ". . . ignorance of non-standard English rules on the part of teachers and text writers" is the major problem in teaching Black children to read.

A good example of the kind of teaching advocated above is presented by Kenneth Goodman (1969). He argues that preference for language dialect is relative, and that although some dialects may carry more social prestige than others, they are not necessarily more effective in communication. In his words,

. . . well-meaning adults, including teachers, who would never intentionally reject a child or any important characteristic of a child, such as the clothes he wears or the color of his skin, will immediately and emphatically reject his language. This hurts him far more than other kinds of rejection because it endangers the means which he depends on for communication and self-expression (Goodman, 1969, p. 16).

Because the language of a "divergent speaker" is just as functional and grammatical in its own terms as standard dialect, and a vital link between the person and those close to him, when the teacher "corrects" it, he contradicts the child's experience. School becomes a place where the teacher tells the child things that are not true and where people talk funny. Such ethnocentrism, argues Goodman, is tragic among educators. The child becomes marked as not only different but socially inferior, sloppy, careless, vulgar, and crude. "His best defense is to be silent."

One of the solutions Goodman suggests is based on the fact that although the printed word is standardized across dialects, pronunciation is not. Consequently, if the teacher allows children to read in their own dialect these children will have increased comprehension. How much comprehension is interfered with if the teacher insists on intonation patterns in oral reading that are unnatural, asks Goodman? Such instruction may not only be ineffective, but also confusing. He suggests three alternatives (1969, p. 25): (1) write new materials based on dialect; (2) teach children to speak the standard dialect before teaching reading; and (3) let the children read standard material in their own dialect. He sees the first alternative as impractical because of opposition among parents and educators, and the second as delaying reading too long, as well as trying to extinguish a language useful in communication outside of school. He recommends the third alternative, which avoids the problem of asking a child to accept a new dialect for learning and thereby avoids the implication that the language of his community is inferior. Such an alternative depends on acceptance by the school and by the teacher of the child's already existing language competence. ". . . the teacher must learn to understand and accept the children's language. He must study it carefully and become aware of (its) key elements" (Goodman, 1969, p. 28).

Labov (1969) has also extended the psycholinguistic facts to implications for teaching, and argues that the teacher and the student are ignorant of each other's system. The fact that the teacher has no systematic knowledge of the child's language leads the teacher to attribute "mistakes" to inadequate language, laziness and so on. Even teachers who are sincerely interested in the child cannot avoid the problem unless they understand the child's language. The teacher must be linguistically sophisticated to the differences or he will make serious errors in teaching reading. A child may read a word correctly (understand it) but simply pronounce it incorrectly. If this is the case, corrections will be confusing.

William Stewart (1969) has observed that Black language is not simply the hip talk of TV actors, or the vocabulary substitutions of ghetto slang. This is a very important point that has been misunderstood by many, including those who have developed so-called Black intelligence tests based on this vocabulary. Black dialect has its own syntax and is as complicated as any language. Thus the need for "preschool education" may be for the *teachers* to literally learn a new language (that of their students) before they try to teach them reading. Reading teachers will not only need to learn about programming language in systematic steps, reinforcement, and so on, which are really rather simple to teach and can be done with prepared curricula, but they also will need to learn the language of their students so that they can un-

derstand them. It may be that the easiest way to do this is to employ as teachers those who already understand and speak Black dialect.

There is no good reason why the style, language, and interests of the lower-class Black child cannot be made a legitimate part of school experiences in both skills training and in child care and social values. There are, however, some bad reasons. First, schools tend to be controlled by White middle-class people. Second, such styles and language frequently offend the teachers and administrators with whom the children must deal. Third, there are few, if any, curriculum materials or teaching methods and ideas now used that are appropriate for these children. This is not a question of putting pictures of Black children in the "Dick and Jane" books. It is a question of teacher and curriculum materials really understanding the language and style of the children and their families, and most important, of really liking it! It may be that to teach children well one needs not only to appreciate their style and abilities, but to like to interact with them and to expect them to do great things. If it works in preschools, why not in public schools?

The Problem of Political Reality

Although we can consider psychoeducational alternatives, we must recognize that the failure of the poor in school is at least as political as it is educational. To fail to analyze the problem at the institutional and community change level would lead us to commit an error of logical typing and enter a game without end (see Chapter V).

It is not surprising that American social policy should rely on educators for the implementation of programs aimed at equality. The American myth of success is one of the individual "bootstrapping" himself from poverty to wealth. One of the problems with this ideal for Blacks is the simple fact of racial discrimination, so well portrayed in the Fischetti cartoon (Figure VIII-1) of the Black man hanging with his arms over his head, held by handcuffs

© 1968 Chicago Daily News
Publishers-Hall Syndicate

WHY DON'T THEY LIFT THEMSELVES UP BY THEIR OWN BOOTSTRAPS LIKE WE DID?

labeled "White racism," and the caption: "Why don't they lift themselves up by their own bootstraps like we did?" But this is only a surface explanation. Its roots are in the social institutions that inadvertently support the status quo.

Outside of business success, education, particularly public education, has been the system for upward mobility available to the common person. Because the federal government's major operating rule is free business enterprise, where else would government programs for equality turn but to education? Education has traditionally been viewed as useful in the solution of real life American problems, as is typified in the state university systems. Originally established as agricultural schools, because that was the kind of technology our nation required, over the years these schools have turned to teacher education when we thought we needed more teachers, and developed aerospace engineers when we "needed" them. Most recently the community college has extended everyone's right to continue public education beyond grade school. This is seen as a kind of panacea in which one expects that post-high-school educa-

tion will lead to a good job and financial security.

For society, the role of education is to socialize and train for needed skills. Unfortunately, as post-high-school education becomes more and more available to everyone its use in our economic system declines. Because we have a system based on competition, someone must be on top, someone in the middle, and someone at the bottom. That is the nature of competition. Thus, the promise of education as the great equalizer cannot work—it is no longer selective. Now one needs an M.A. or other advanced degrees to be on top. If education is "given" to everyone and poor Blacks and other lower social class members gain access to it, education will inevitably have reduced value in the economic market place. The argument will be that "quality" of education has disappeared. In fact, it will simply be that the exclusiveness, the eliteness, is gone, and with it the mystique. This may have positive or negative outcomes. Perhaps real competence will be recognized with or without a degree, but if this is the case then the problem for the poor will not be to gain access to the right answers on tests, but to gain access to a system that allows them the opportunity to develop their own strengths and abilities by acquiring material resources.

Even today the practical value of education is greatly reduced. A college degree is no guarantee of a job or of the "good life," as some recent Black graduates have discovered. Nevertheless, the idea that preschool education is "what they need" continues because it fits well with the American Dream, and because it helps to cloud the economic and political power issues really involved in equality of opportunity. It is not surprising that American educators have accepted the role of provider of programs for the poor, regardless of the chance for genuine outcome. Along with this role comes power and money to the middleman, to the provider of "education," and to the bureaucracy, even if not to the supposed beneficiary. Moynihan (1965, 1969) is undoubtedly correct when he points to this misuse of money for the profit of the "helpers," despite the fact that his solution, which amounts to doing nothing, is at least as detrimental as the problem he notes.

With the invention of preschool education for the culturally deprived we have a new way to blame the poor for their own failure. We have "scientific" data to show that "you ain't got no culture." We offer something to the poor without changing the basic systems with which they need to deal. The educational establishment remains untouched while we develop preschools. Clearly, one reason why preschools, rather than reformed public schools, could develop is because grades one through twelve are under the control of state and local government. The federal government, even if it wanted to reform the public schools, could not do so without the cooperation of the education establishment in local communities. Implementing a massive nationwide program to appease the poor, who voiced loud protest over their condition in the 1960s, required the establishment of a new system of education not in direct confrontation with the already established system. Educators with method and psychologists with data were all too willing to get a piece of the action. When preschool "works" for a given child we find that

we have trained the child to be just like us. When preschool education fails, as it most often does, it is because the schools into which the children are deposited have not changed. Rather, they maintain the same biases, cultural ethnocentricity, and lack of respect for differences, and we conclude that poor children and their parents before them are stupid. We overlook the cultural biases and political facts that have predestined the failure.

Even if such programs were successful it is not likely that the middle class would now share the resources they hold so dear. As Richardson, Spears, and Richards (1972), in a review of race and intelligence, have noted, *the educational system mirrors society* and changes in society may therefore be reflected as changes in the educational system. However, it is unlikely that changes in the educational system will create changes in society.

These considerations are real constraints on the ability of psychologists and educators to change society. In a consideration of psychoeducational alternatives these political facts cannot be ignored by the community psychologist. To create social change, community psychology will need to engage in political battles at the local level. Politics as well as science must be accepted as a legitimate domain. New educational methods will not be adopted without their advocates' active participation in the political environment. Nor will the psychologists be able to act alone with the schools, unless they wish to perpetuate existing dogma under the guise of change. They will need the support of the local community because it is from the community that the political power for change, as well as the values to be reflected in schools, must derive. The psychologists will also need to realize that there are many local communities with conflicting values. They all have a right to exist. What we now need is the kind of psychoeducational paradigm that may permit the community psychologist to operate in a political world, full of value judgments and conflicting ideologies. These require the community interventionist to operate on the basis of assumptions that lead to respect for diverse backgrounds and the desire to seek out strengths rather than weaknesses.

To work in such a setting requires a view of social systems such as Reiff and Murrell and others (see Chapters V and VI) have suggested. Blame for failure, be it on individuals or environments, has no place. Community psychologists will also require techniques, implementation skills, knowledge of psycholinguistics, child development and education, as well as evaluation skills. But none of this will be useful unless it operates within a paradigm that can allow for both a cultural relativist view and a political reality. Such a paradigm, largely untested as an intervention strategy, and not terribly well articulated in this context, is the ecological paradigm, or more properly for its current stage of development within psychology, the ecological point of view.

Implications of the Community Psychology-Ecological Viewpoint

The ecological viewpoint has at least three related implications for the educational system. First, because it is based on the legitimacy of multiple kinds of people and multiple kinds of environments, it requires a perspective supportive of diversity. Second, it requires careful understanding of the experiences, strengths, and abilities of the target groups, and an accommodation of educational methodology to them rather than an assimilation of them to it. Third, because those currently in control of schools expect all children to fit into one environment or be labeled negatively, the paradigm necessitates community-based social action for its adoption and implementation.

As can be seen from Murrell's analysis, if the problem of maximization of resources requires that individuals be provided with systems into which they fit, then the problem for the educational system is to be adaptive enough so that different kinds of individuals are each provided with the opportunity to maximize their own potential. For such systems to be designed the targets of the educational system, including

minority groups, need to be a part of the planning and programming of the schools. They need to be teachers and administrators as well. But the inclusion of people not normally represented will not be enough. The idea of centralized educational systems will have to break down in favor of *neighborhood community control*. But this will also not be enough. The economic as well as the political power will need to be more equitably distributed. The role of psychologist and educator will need to include advocating politically for educational strategies based on the ecological viewpoint which stresses strengths and resources. The community psychologist will in turn need to be involved in public education aimed specifically at the acceptance of diversity. It is the public schools themselves, rather than preschool or parallel appendages, that must be changed. It is the institutions and the values of our educational system, rather than the students, that are "disadvantaged."

Suppose community control of schools in a poor Black neighborhood with enough resources to run an adequate school were provided. There is no reason to believe that the students would necessarily get a better education than they now do. The methods of teaching and the value system applied would also need drastic revision. Some of the kinds of revisions that are psychoeducationally sensible were noted in the preceding sections. More remains to be said because the community psychologist must also be concerned with social policy as well as educational curriculum.

Social Policy Implications

Almost everyone who has written about the problem of education and the lower-class child's failure arrives at a similar conclusion with regard to social policy. A careful look at what the various writers say, regardless of their bias for a genetic, an environmental, or an ecological viewpoint, finds that they all agree that the single model of schooling now offered is inadequate for many children. Jensen (1969) argues that all children are not the same and that individual differences must be acknowledged and accounted for in the education system (see Chapter VII, p. 235). Herrnstein (1973) similarly calls for diversity of education. They argue from a belief in genetic differences. The problem with their social policy is that it does not allow for individual choice. So long as presumed genetic inferiority or superiority is the basis of differential approaches to education, the values of a free society are in danger.

The environmentalists such as Hunt (1969) also argue for diversity in the educational system. But he is aiming at it from the viewpoint of Piaget and what he calls the "problem of the match." That is, depending on one's previous experience, and consequently on existing cognitive schema, a given environment may either be or not be a good match for enhancing intellectual development. His solution is to provide environments for poor children that give them the experiences (e.g., middle-class culture) that will prepare them for the school environment by building the appropriate cognitive schema. Ginsburg (1972), however, starting from exactly the same Piagetian observation with regard to the "problem of match" argues for changing the environment of the school to make it more adaptable to the varied children who enter, rather than trying to make all children the same. He proposes to do this through the establishment of "open schools" where the curriculum and methods are flexible according to the needs of the individual child. The system has goals but is not dominated by one method of accomplishing them. Unlike Jensen, he does not predetermine the kind of education each child should receive, but wants schools to flexibly adapt to children as they develop.

This requires a teacher with the utmost sensitivity and skill. He must first achieve an accurate perception of the child's interests and abilities and must then have the wit, often on the spur of the moment, to provide the necessary experiences, materials and opportunities. To accomplish this, the teacher must be open to almost any form of method or device . . . there is a sharing of power between the teacher and the student . . . . (Ginsburg, 1972, pp. 233–234).

The positions of Jensen, Hunt, and Ginsburg, then, are similar in their acceptance of diversity, but they differ in other ways. Jensen sees the determinants of diversity as genetic—individuals can do nothing to choose or prepare for a given kind of education other than the one they are predestined to be able to cope with. Hunt sees the problem of education as one which requires preparation of all children for the current school system by providing a "proper" preschool environment, that is, adapting them to it. Ginsburg prefers to make schools more flexible in adapting to varied children, rather than vice versa. The three are similar in that they only recognize but do not wish to deal with the politics of education.

The community psychologist who adopts an ecological viewpoint is also in agreement that diversity among children cannot be ignored. However, this diversity, from the community psychologist's perspective, involves politics as well as education, and leads to somewhat different solution from any of the others. To begin with, because the community psychologist sees the school as only one part of the community environment the psychologist must be willing to deal with the relationship between that school and the larger society. Although closest to Ginsburg's ideas, the concept of open schools now becomes the concept of *open school systems*. The school is simply seen as a reflection of the community and the aim of the community psychologist is to strengthen the community. The idea of the open school is too limited in its reliance on the individual skills and good intentions of particular teachers and administrators. The open school is difficult enough to implement when the individual differences of children from similar cultural and ethnic backgrounds are taken into account, but when the same teacher and resources are shared by children of differing cultures, languages, and style, the teacher would need to be super-human to really deal with all children in the warm, open, high-expectation-for-success way that Ginsburg describes. There is little reason to believe that any teacher is flexible enough to adapt to the multiple demands of a diversity of children at the same time. Even if a few such teachers could be found, the system needs to be workable for the average teacher. The teacher is as much a captive of cultural background and personal values as the students and the scientists. The school *system* needs to be *structurally* supportive of the special needs of diverse elements of its constituents. It is only through an educational *system* built on a *structural* support for diversity that we are free of the need for the teacher's individual good will.

Because the school is part of the community, and therefore an expression of it, the problem for poor and Black children in schools is the same as the problem for their parents in the larger community—they are ignored by those in power, they are devalued, regarded with scorn and negative bias, and in general have little power or influence. That is a simple fact. The poor, even in the Great Society years of Lyndon Johnson, and certainly now, lack control over and respect from the institutions that surround them. The school is simply one mirror reflecting this fact.

It is ironic that the most politically radical elements of society have come to realize that racial integration is not helpful to the Black child. They now favor community control of neighborhood schools where the local parents hire the teachers and the administrators, and consequently where there is mutual respect for the language and life style between the socialization agents and the students. Advocating this position always brings to mind the idea that this is the same as racism and segregation. But there are some major differences between this idea of community control and the older segregationist policies. First, segregation was forced from a central administration on everyone; the Black communities had no control over segregated schools. The policy of community control would give each neighborhood community its choice of school policy. It could be implemented such that each family has an option of sending its child to the community neighborhood school or some other. Second, the control over each school would come from within the local neighborhood. Hiring and firing, cur-

riculum, and so on would be determined by the people whose children attend the school. This was really always the American ideal and is the reason why schools are now under state as opposed to federal control. But as our communities have expanded in size, minorities and neighborhoods have gotten lost in an educational bureaucracy just as they do in a general election as opposed to a district election.

True community control would also be different from de facto segregation where Blacks and Whites are separated by city-county boundaries, because schools would also be decentralized in administration. School finances could still be allocated from state funds, but set by enrollment, rather than by wealth of parents, with sensible limits on size. States could even require minimal standards for reading and mathematics skills. Because it is the style and culture of the school that is really in question, additional skills could be emphasized differentially in given schools. This would assure a school *system* that was structurally maximally responsive to the local community residents whose children attend the school.

If such a school system were operative, then each independent school could determine its own style of operation, curriculum, and so on. Some communities (and remember here we are referring to the community as a functional unit made up of the children, parents, teachers, and administrators of each individual school) might choose to run the school with Ginsburg's model. Others may prefer a more structured-authoritarian model; still others a system with emphasis on vocational skills rather than traditional academics. Some might adopt Bereiter's idea of separating skills and child care. There is no reason to expect Black people not to want their children to learn to read, but there is every reason to expect that they will want it done effectively. They would not need to improve on current success very much to do a better job than our public schools now do. The point is that every individual community would be in control. This could only help to strengthen community identification, sense of personal worth, and cohesiveness. It seems perfectly within the

real meaning of a democratic society. This social policy seems to derive naturally out of current psychoeducational knowledge as well as
our basic American value system.[4]

What Is Acceptable and What Is Feasible?

Edward Banfield (1968) has noted that there is a
considerable difference between social policies
that are feasible and those that are acceptable. A
feasible social policy is one that would probably
work to accomplish its aims if it were implemented and is possible to implement because
it does not violate either the law or physical
reality. An *acceptable* social policy, however, is
one that people in authority are willing to carry
out. Although the policies described in this
chapter may be feasible, at present they are far
from acceptable in Banfield's sense of the term.
That is why community psychology needs to be
political. We must engage in the selling as well
as the testing of our ideas.

There are of course several political realities
that mitigate against adoption of the social policy described above. Most people with children
in school would probably accept such a policy if

it were well explained because it leaves the decisions up to them to make or defer to others.
However, a current educational power structure
lies between the idea and the people (Useem &
Useem, 1974). Entrenched and vested interests
of the educational establishment, the teachers'
unions, and ironically, the belief of local community members themselves that they can or
ought to have a viable say over their children's
education would need to be dealt with by the
community psychologist. The social policy advocated here, however, is not presented without
a recognition of Seymour Sarason's (1972) excellent presentation of the problems involved in
the creation of any new setting. Implementation
is much more difficult than ideology. At the
same time, community psychologists have at
least two responsibilities: one is the development and testing of new paradigms, the other is
the development of implementation strategies.
The policy presented here is intended not as a
panacea, but as an example of the kinds of questions with which community psychology must
grapple. The need for strategies and tactics of
implementation, as well as research and conceptualization, is imperative. The establishment of
social policy in the educational system based on
sound psychology and sound educational practice, together with maximum opportunity for all
children, requires that the community psychologist work with others in the political as
well as the educational sphere. The particular
strategies and tactics used, ranging from consultation to advocacy, or any others, will depend
on the local situation. In Chapter VI we reviewed some of the strategies and tactics that are
possible. But community psychologists must
deal with implementation issues in some way if
they are to be more than ivory tower academics
or agents of the status quo.

A final comment is necessary. This kind of
educational policy does not imply a panacea for
political-economic discrimination. It does not
provide jobs for all, nor does it end racism. It is
simply one step consistent with a culturally
pluralistic society. It makes schools more responsive to students and parents, but it does not
provide equality of opportunity in later years.
There remains the large problem of control over

---

[4]Two arguments against this proposal might be anticipated.
One suggests that "community control" has already been
tried and failed. Usually the attempts in New York City in the
1960s are cited. However, if one takes a close look at what
actually took place in those well-publicized efforts labeled
"community control," it becomes obvious that such programs were a good example of first-order change. Although it
looked like community control on the surface, control of hiring and finances was still very much centralized (cf., Fainstein & Fainstein, 1974; Greir, 1973). Even the attempts to
have a regional school board were far from what is proposed
here: that the parents and students in the *individual school* be
given *direct* control of policy, hiring, and finances. (See also
Chapter IX, pp. 299–304) for a discussion of similar issues in
the mental health system.)
A second objection is more difficult to resolve. It may be
argued that local community control will lead to isolation and
antipathy between groups, and serve to cut off minorities from
the larger society. The answer offered here is that if the local
control is genuine in that it includes control over resources
(not just the right to "advise"), it can serve to allow people to
come to the larger society as equals, rather than as underlings
to be "integrated." The position taken here is similar to the
one presented by Sanford (1972; see Chapter V, p. 125) which
asserts that before one can become a "citizen of the world"
one must have a secure sense of one's own culture.

money, business, jobs, universities, and other social institutions. If this social policy led to some schools being "written off" as inferior because they are different, then it could lead to more discrimination as the graduates enter the market place. Clearly, for such a social policy to work, jobs would need to depend on competence, not on where one happened to attend school.

An example of the potential problem is offered by Jerome Karabel (1974) in a recent analysis of the community college system.

Hailed as the "democratizers of higher education," community colleges are, in reality, a vital component of the class-based tracking system . . . with the push of the policy-planning elite for more career education, vocational training may well become more pervasive, and the community college will become even more a terminal rather than a transfer institution. These trends, often referred to as expressions of higher education's "diversity" and the community colleges' special and unique role, are the very processes which place the community college at the bottom of the class-based tracking system. The system of higher education's much-touted "diversity" is for the most part, hierarchy rather than genuine variety, a form of hierarchy which has more to do with social class than educational philosophy (pp. 138–139).

An educational system, such as the one suggested here, can only help to strengthen the sense of worth and accomplishment of individual students and the powerless. However, without a similar sharing of resources in the other social systems of society it will not go terribly far in making a more equitable society. As noted earlier, the educational system cannot be the equalizer of opportunity that American mythology proclaims it to be. The educational system is a function of the society, not vice versa. Nevertheless, if a social policy such as the one suggested here were to be implemented, it would reflect some significant changes in the attitudes of the larger society and might signal a new era in social relationships.

INTERVENTIONS IN THE
MENTAL HEALTH SYSTEM

. . . the world that thought to measure and justify madness through psychology must justify itself before madness . . . .

—*Michel Foucault*

Since every therapeutic program today has some measure of social defense as a motive, it would be quite easy to characterize the entire therapeutic state as a subterfuge for affecting social controls without guaranteeing constitutionally protected rights.

—*Nicholas N. Kittrie*

The mental health system has served as a spawning ground for community psychology. Dissatisfaction with all the failures of the helping professions can be found there. Its destructiveness of human individuality, its tendency to confinement and isolation tactics, and its inability to accept human differences are notorious characteristics. The predominant medical or disease model has been attacked on the basis of its conceptual failure as well as its style for delivery of services (see Chapter III). Hospital treatments and facilities have been reformed, exposed, and reformed over and over again. There is little point in documenting here the fact that long-term isolation of deviants in back wards is more destructive than constructive. The inaccessibility of services for the poor and the inferior quality of service when delivered has also been noted in earlier chapters. An overriding characteristic of the system is to label, in one way or another, as "inferior" or "deficited" those who do not fit into the larger society. The mental health system has reflected, perhaps more clearly than any other, the tendency for "solutions" to create more problems than they solve. Such problems go beyond conceptual failures, beyond technology, and extend to the basic *rules of the game* by which the system operates as an agent of social control. The need to reas-

sess the rules of the game and to find "illogical" or "paradoxical" solutions in the sense suggested by Watzlawick *et al*. (1974; see Chapter V) is clear.

It would require several volumes to review in any systematic way all of the successful and unsuccessful programs for the treatment of so-called mental illness. Instead, the aim of this chapter is to construct a picture of certain sensible directions for the future of the mental health system; directions that, one hopes, may be consistent with the values of this book and that may help to reassess the rules of the game. *In this volume the case has been made for an environmental resources and ecological systems conception of human behavior, with an emphasis on support for diversity, strengths, and autonomy. It is that direction toward which this chapter is pointed.*

This chapter also has certain limits that should be understood. The focus is, at one extreme, on interventions that are concerned with the identified deviants of society, that is those who are chronic patients and are either actually in a hospital now or who have been in and out many times. Most, but not all, of these people are also lower socioeconomic-status individuals. A second focus is on those who are in acute distress and run the risk of falling into the mental health system, then becoming like the first group. The third focus is on a consideration of the kind of mechanisms that can be made available to increase the likelihood that fewer people will need "services."

Absent from consideration here are helping services of an ongoing nature for people who are middle-class "neurotics" or those who are seeking meaning in life, and so on, but who continue to maintain themselves in society—working, living, and functioning outside the mental health system—except to the extent that they may seek out a therapist or counselor for psychological or interpersonal assistance. These latter services are not viewed as unimportant, but of lower priority than programs that seek to prevent or ameliorate isolation and deterioration of people who are withdrawn from the larger community and become its identified deviants. The aim is to get out and keep out of the mental health system as many people as is possible, and to increase the likelihood that those who do have contact with the system will function with as few limits to their autonomy as is feasible.[1]

As currently structured the mental health system is a complex network of independent but interlocking people and organizations. The rules of the game are largely informal and probably inadequate to protect the rights of those who become caught in the network (Ennis & Siegel, 1973). The rules are largely determined by the convenience of free enterprise professional practice, such that social and economic status determines what kind of "helper" one is likely to see, and what kind of treatment one receives. Financial status, including whether or not one has medical insurance, is an important factor in the system. In cases of serious emotional disturbance those with insurance who experience an acute episode of emotional difficulty are likely to be sent to a general hospital or to a private facility until the episode subsides; they are then released back to their family, if they have one. Those who are more isolated, or who do not seem to "recover" in the number of days for which they have insurance coverage, are likely to be sent to a state hospital or to a community mental health center. Middle-class clients may first be treated as outpatients, unless their behavior is suicidal or intolerable to others in their immediate environment. The poor tend to go to state hospitals or community mental health centers from the outset. Often, the contact route for the poor is a police complaint which leads to a referral to the local hospital or community mental health center (Lieberman, 1969). At the point of contact some diagnosis is usually made. It may involve personality testing and is usually followed by a label. If the label is schizophrenia, or some form of "character disorder" (a euphemism for nonmiddle-class behavior) the person stands a fair chance of long-term confinement, especially if he or she returns often.

The best way to get to a state hospital is to be poor, have a history of repeated contacts with the mental health system, and no private physician. Once hospitalized, the best way to stay in is to offend the staff by not being cooperative, not developing "insight," not behaving in prescribed docile ways, having few social relationships in the outside community, and having no job possibilities. Once in the state hospital one is part of a culture with its own special rules, roles, and norms. It has all the elements of a total society. The major treatments are drugs, electroshock, and/or some form of "socioenvironmental" treatment in which the living unit is supposed to help provide an opportunity to plan and reassess one's behavior. This is sometimes combined with an adaptation of "behavior modification," often a bastardization of the "token economy." In most hospitals, unless such programs are operated as careful experimental research units, they are often a poorly administered form of the ideas of reward for "prosocial" behavior. Staff who actually spend time with patients are usually poorly trained and poorly paid.

If released, drug therapy is a common form of treatment, perhaps with weekly or monthly

---

[1] Psychotherapists, like the priests of other times and places, are crucial to society. They serve a genuine function as consultants for those who experience personal problems in living. They probably function about as well as can be expected, and will continue to be of service to many people. Unfortunately, there is every reason to believe that the people to whom psychotherapy is useful already have relatively more resources than those to whom it is not useful. In general, the proposition that such help is most available and useful to those who need it the least (Cowen, Gardner, & Zax, 1967) continues to hold. Here we are concerned with those for whom such help is neither available nor successful.

outpatient visits to the hospital or local clinic to talk things over. There is little or no involvement in the client's ongoing life. Those who receive psychotherapy either instead of hospitalization, or following it, are usually the young, adult, verbal, successful, intelligent, middle-class clients. The specific kind of therapy is determined by the accident of whom one happens to visit, or who is assigned to the patient, rather than by particular patient characteristics and therapist skills. Most professionals will, in private, admit that if a member of their family were to seek psychotherapy they would refer on the basis of individual therapist skill. Unfortunately, most clients have no idea of the competence, therapeutic orientation, skills, or personal style of the individual they happen to contact. Failure of treatment is usually blamed on the client.

All of the above is admittedly an overdrawn and highly critical description. It is a generalization, but one which does hold in the experience of many people. Some will doubtless be helped along the way, but there is little evidence that they would not have recovered without the mental health network, and considerable evidence that the network may actually hurt others by dragging them into a complicated ordeal of "benevolent consumption." They are "protected" from themselves and the world, and are often caught in a Kafka-like game controlled by a difficult-to-pin-down bureaucracy clothed in jargon. If that description seems overdrawn in this enlightened day and age, when we all have read or seen performed Ken Kesey's *One Flew Over the Cuckoo's Nest*, it is worth considering the recent report of David Rosenhan (1973).

On Being Sane in Insane Places[2]

Beginning with the observation that what is considered normal and abnormal may be less a function of the person so labeled than of the system

that does the labeling, Rosenhan (1973) describes an experiment in which eight sane people were admitted to twelve different hospitals. These eight "pseudopatients" included people such as a psychology graduate student, a physician, a homemaker, a painter, and a psychiatrist. They were men and women who changed their reported names and occupations but not the report of their background, personal history, or interpersonal relationships. They each called a hospital for an appointment and complained about hearing voices. As soon as they were admitted to the hospital (apparently none was provided with an alternative to hospitalization, which is interesting in itself) they stopped feigning any symptoms, and behaved as they "normally" did. Although they followed all instructions on the unit (but did not swallow their medication), the pseudopatients also spent a great deal of time writing down their observations, at first secretly, but later openly, since no one seemed to mind. None of the pseudopatients knew when he or she would be released and all were told that they would have to get out on their own by convincing the hospital staff that they were sane. They all reported an immediate desire to leave and were described in hospital charts as friendly and cooperative.

The twelve hospitals were located in five different states and ranged from old to new. Some were research oriented, one was private, one university funded, and the others federal or state supported. They were fairly representative of places where one with an acute problem is likely to find one's self. The pseudopatients were not placed in a back ward "snake pit," but in a modern version of the enlightened psychiatric treatment unit—the kind of unit to which you would be likely to go if tomorrow you told a doctor that you were hearing voices and then never heard them again once in the hospital. What happens to people who make such a contact with the mental health system, even when they are competent, psychologically sound, and well-functioning adults who have never been hospitalized and who behave "normally" as soon as they are admitted?

First, all but one were admitted with a diagnosis of schizophrenia. None was detected as

[2]Although Rosenhan's report, described here, has been challenged (cf. Millon, 1975), it nevertheless serves as an extremely useful one which points out many of the problems of today's mental health system.

"normal." All, when released, were diagnosed as schizophrenic "in remission." The label schizophrenia, once given, remained with the person. Even when released they were still seen as "sick," although, of course, it was not now directly observable. The pseudopatients were kept in the hospital between 7 and 52 days, with the average length of stay being 19 days. One of the most interesting occurrences was that often the other hospital residents, but never the staff, questioned their "abnormality." Many of the patients guessed their purposes, but the staff at each hospital never did, either directly or indirectly by comment in the hospital charts. Rosenhan attributes this to the bias of the mental health system toward "seeing" illness. Once labeled, it is difficult to lose the label. In part this is accounted for by the medical model of physical illness, in which it is more harmful to fail to detect an illness than to detect one that is not there. Unfortunately, in the case of psychological diagnosis the opposite may be true because the negative effects of labeling create a number of detrimental social consequences including barriers to employment.

With the above in mind, Rosenhan conducted a second experiment in which the staff of a research and teaching hospital who knew about the first experiment was told that sometime during the next three months one or more pseudopatients would seek admission. Each staff member was asked to rate all 193 patients admitted during that time span on a ten point scale of confidence that the person was actually a pseudopatient. Forty-one patients were rated with high confidence, by at least one staff person, to be pseudopatients. Twenty-three were suspected by at least one psychiatrist, and 19 by one psychiatrist and one other staff member. Actually, no pseudopatients were sent to the hospital. Rosenhan sees this as an indication that the judgment of sanity may be more a reflection of the "payoff matrix" for decision making than of the behavior of the patients. When it is perceived as relatively more risky to find false positives the number of "insane" people may be "reduced." This says quite a lot about the current mental health system wherein the payoffs are to find illness and isolate deviance.

Perhaps even more interesting is how pseudopatients were perceived while in the hospital. The process is well described by Rosenhan as follows:

Once a person is designated abnormal, all of his other behaviors and characteristics are colored by that label. Indeed, that label is so powerful that many of the pseudopatients' normal behaviors were overlooked entirely or profoundly misinterpreted (1973, p. 253).

He describes how the patients' reports of their childhood were distorted in the records (later examined) to fit the current view of the dynamics of schizophrenia, and how their note taking was viewed as part of their "pathological" behavior. Ironically, it was interpreted by the other patients as an indication of their sanity; that is, many guessed that they were journalists or professors "checking up on the hospital." The pseudopatients also observed how, when "real" patients would react to mistreatment by a staff member, it would always be interpreted as the patients' fault. Patients diagnosed as schizophrenic are expected to remain so and to be incompetent. Rosenhan speculates that these expectations may actually become part of the patient's self-identity and that the future behavior of both the identified deviant and those who interact with him may be controlled by such expectations. His analysis is similar to Carson's and Scheff's (see Chapter IV, pp. 106–109).

During the average of 19 days that each pseudopatient spent in the hospital, what kind of treatment did he receive? By means of systematically recording, in four of the hospitals, observations of the pseudopatients, Rosenhan found that on the average attendants spent only 11.3 percent of their time out of the "cage" (a glass enclosure which serves as an office for the staff). Of this time, only a small fraction was spent talking with patients. Most of the time was used to perform custodial chores. For nurses the time spent out of the cage was even less (the actual amount was so brief that the number of times out was counted rather than the percentage of total time). During a typical daytime shift nurses came out to the unit only 11.5 times. Physicians were even less available. Only 6.7 times, on the average, did they appear on the unit. Most often they were seen only to arrive, go into their office, and later depart. On the average, pseudopatients spent 6.8 minutes per day in contact of any kind with psychiatrists, physicians, or psychologists.

Finally, Rosenhan also presents data on how the hospital system breeds disregard for patients as human beings. He compares an attempt by his pseudopatients to obtain information from various staff members to similar attempts to obtain information from a stranger in another setting. As can be seen in Table IX-1, when the pseudopatients attempted to ask a question of the psychiatrists, the nurses, or the attendants, the most frequent response was for the patients to be ignored. The questions asked were not disruptive or difficult, but simple information questions such as "when will I be presented at the staff meeting?" In order to contrast these reac-

tions to "normal" behavior with strangers, the research team sent a young woman into the hallways of Stanford University and The University Medical Center. She stopped several professors or physicians walking in the hall, and asked a series of six questions about directions and admission policies. In the medical center to some strangers she also mentioned that she was looking for an internist or a psychiatrist, and to others she did not. In contrast to the reaction accorded "mental patients" 100 percent of the professors stopped and talked, even when they were obviously heading somewhere or in a hurry. Similarly, there was an overwhelming tendency for physicians to stop and talk, although this was considerably less so if they were asked for a psychiatrist. It is clear from these data that a mental patient, especially if hospitalized, is relegated to the status of nonperson,

TABLE IX–1. **Self-initiated contact by pseudopatients with psychiatrists, nurses, and attendants, compared to contact with other groups.***

Contact	Psychiatric Hospitals		University Campus (non-medical)	University Medical Center		
					Physicians	
	(1)	(2)	(3)	(4)	(5)	(6)
	Psychiatrists	Nurses and Attendants	Faculty	"Looking for a Psychiatrist"	"Looking for an Internist"	No Additional Comment
Responses						
Moves on, head averted (%)	71	88	0	0	0	0
Makes eye contact (%)	23	10	0	11	0	0
Pauses and chats (%)	2	2	0	11	0	10
Stops and talks (%)	4	0.5	100	78	100	90
Mean number of questions answered (out of 6)	**	**	6	3.8	4.8	4.5
Respondents (No.)	13	47	14	18	15	10
Attempts (No.)	185	1283	14	18	15	10

*From Rosenhan, 1973.
**Not applicable.

even in the eyes of those who work in the hospital setting. One is far more likely to be treated as a person by walking up to a complete stranger!

Even these data, Rosenhan notes, do not convey the feeling of depersonalization and degradation experienced by the pseudopatients (and perhaps by the real patients as well). The hospital environment fosters a kind of disregard for human beings that can best be described in anecdotes and descriptions which have been written by others already noted (Kesey, 1962; Goffman, 1961). The difference here is that this is not a report from a large back ward of a state hospital housing thousands of chronic, withdrawn, already lost people; it is based on observations of units that supposedly "treat" those with acute problems in living. The question is not "how can we get such people to respond to us?" but "why are we not responsive to them?" Rosenhan suggests that one way to become responsive is to develop the behavior therapies and procedures of crisis intervention that deal in the real world with people "on the spot," rather than by labeling and sending them to a hospital. He also suggests the need for increasing awareness of how the mental health system uses the "Catch 22" phenomenon wherein the patient, once identified and labeled as abnormal, is always viewed as pathological. These suggestions are sensible enough; indeed they may be part of the solution (see below), but they will not suffice in and of themselves. Rather, we will need to create change at multiple levels and seriously question the current rules of the game by which the system operates. If we do not we are likely to continue the "game without end."

Where to Start: Closing Down the Mental Hospitals—A Five-year Plan

It is an unquestionable fact that state mental hospitals serve as storage houses for large numbers of human beings. Even with efforts since the mid-1950s and those subsequent to the Joint Commission Report of the early 1960s, the community mental health attempt to reduce the size of hospitals still leaves them as very much a part of the life of thousands of people (see Chapter III). There is no doubt that hospitals serve as "homes" for many who have learned a way of life and lack the resources to "make it" in the outside world. Many writers have described how the institution creates dependency, withdrawal, and degradation for thousands of persons each year. For thousands of others the "new" methods of day and night hospitals, halfway houses, and release to smaller living units "in the community" (often called shelter care homes) have been called a solution. It is clear from an examination of such solutions that although they go under similar names they actually represent a diversity of programs which vary in the extent of resident autonomy (see Chapter VI, p. 182), among other characteristics (Raush & Raush, 1968).

Before we consider such alternatives we need to begin where so many people are housed and literally deprived of contact with the outside world. In some ways one is tempted to suggest that the most therapeutic program would begin with helping the residents of mental hospitals to burn them down. Short of this, the question becomes how can we best empty the mental hospitals? It will require work at multiple levels of analysis. To begin at the institutional level, a social policy is required that explicitly, more so than the Joint Commisssion Report, prohibits their use. So long as they are available as an option they will be used. The systems analysis presented in Chapter V (see p. 149) led to the observation that as the mental health system stores energy for its own maintenance it creates subsystems that both train professionals and other levels of staff and lobby for its continuation through public funds, despite loss of effective function. Perhaps the only way to stop such a system is to cut off its life blood of public monies. In short, to reset the thermostat. One suggestion is that funds for mental hospitals and training of mental hospital staff be phased out, over, say, a period of five years. This would give the system enough time to find other placements for those now housed there and would be combined with the prohibition of any new admissions and the training of a different kind of mental health worker. At first such a plan may sound absurd because we are used to the idea that we *need* mental hospitals. As with most social policies that question the very rules of the game, such a policy may even appear to be illogical, if not downright unrealistic. Where will the severely disturbed go?

It can be shown that the use of mental hospitals is more a function of habit than necessity. There are many viable alternatives that could be implemented if we are willing to seriously consider the possibility of questioning current rules and roles. In order to break old habits new ones are required as substitutes. It is suggested that future mental health appropriations be used for the creation and implementation of alternatives that use community resources, rather than to sustain the current system which we already know fails. Over a period of five years it is suggested that federal and state mental health monies be increasingly spent to support the new alternatives proposed below, and decreasingly spent in the maintenance of mental hospitals. Although this policy may sound utopian it is clearly feasible if we choose to do it. With the creation of community mental health centers we have seen a similar shift in the resources from state hospitals. Unfortunately, such a shift was not far enough. Not only were state hospitals left functioning and available for use, but far too much money was spent to build new buildings and to staff them because that is what the rules of the game suggested. Rather, what is suggested here is that the mental health money be taken from the maintenance and staffing of such buildings and put into several new directions. These directions should be *incompatible* with current procedures. The addition of alternatives will not suffice. It must be a *substitution*. Such a policy requires that we do something first with those currently housed in the hospitals that we will close in five years. This can be accomplished in several steps, all of which have already been empirically demonstrated to work, given the will to do it.[3]

---

[3]It is possible that such a "radical" solution may ultimately be forced on the mental health professionals and legislators even if they do not plan it themselves. It may be decided indirectly in the courts. In recent years the issue of the "right to treatment" has been raised, and the courts have begun to find that the housing of a patient for an indefinite stay in a mental hospital may be unconstitutional. In short, the patient who is confined for reasons of "rehabilitation" has a right to receive treatment. The question at the time of this writing had just been ruled on by the Supreme Court, and although they ruled that at least in cases of involuntary commitment the patient has a "right to treatment," this is not likely to immediately resolve the issue.

One of the problems this ultimately poses is exactly how one can determine when "real treatment" (rather than confinement) is being conducted. Often in the history of the mental health movement what passes for treatment today is viewed as punishment tomorrow. If the courts do continue in this direction it may become necessary to demonstrate that a treatment is really rehabilitative, rather than custodial. Because there is no evidence that confinement is rehabilitative, the use of confinement may come to be seen as illegal, except for those who are committed for what amounts to a prison sentence for violation of the law. The number of such commitments relative to those now confined would be quite small. It has been estimated that 95 percent of those now confined are not legally dangerous to self or others (Mathews, 1975). If hospitals were found to be necessary for physical control of an acute episode (which is actually usually manageable by drug treatment) general hospitals, rather than mental hospitals, could be used for the few days that would be required.

Of related concern are the relatively small number of persons who suffer from a severe physical disability, such as brain damage, and may require nursing care. For this small number, whose problems are physical rather than social, the provision of institutional care may be required.

In-Hospital Treatment Programs

We could begin such a plan, as described above, by requiring all publicly supported hospitals to prepare 20 percent of their residents to leave the hospital within twelve months and to prepare the remaining patients in 20 percent "waves" for each of five years. It should be clear that this does *not* mean a "dumping" program in which people are released unprepared and unsupported into so-called shelter care homes that are nothing but small hospital wards. Rather, it means a shift of resources and efforts from custodial hospital care to development of community resources. What would such preparation require? From one point of view it would require the implementation of the best methods of hospital care now known, so as to bring currently chronic hospitalized patients up to a point where they are socialized enough to demonstrate at least minimal social skill; for example, they should be able to care for their own personal needs.

Perhaps the most detailed presentation of this viewpoint has been offered by Paul (1969b) in the context of attempts to rehabilitate chronic mental patients suffering from what has been termed the "social breakdown syndrome" (Gruenberg, 1967; Zusman, 1966), a condition in which long-term hospitalized patients are found to be withdrawn, apathetic, and lacking the necessary social skills for community living. Intrinsic to this view is the belief that a patient's behavior is not simply a function of intrapsychic personality characteristics; the hospital environment is also implicated as a major causative factor. Consistent with such a viewpoint, the argument for reform of mental hospitals is pursued in two directions. On the one hand it is suggested that "milieu" or "socioenvironmental" treatment programs, which involve various specific procedures differing from place to place but share certain common characteristics, are a promising way to reduce the social breakdown syndrome. The procedures that such programs share in common involve what amounts to an administrative structure: increasing contact between patients and lower-level ward staff, emphasizing positive expectations for the patients such that they are treated as people who are expected to be capable of functioning well and making independent decisions, and giving clear communications concerning role expectancies and responsibilities as well as increased autonomy. In short, it is a return to "moral treatment" (see Chapters I and II).

Ellsworth's (1968) program of hospital reform is exemplary in its emphasis on the changed roles of the hospital aides who, rather than serve in a custodial ward function, were changed from an average of 14 percent of their time spent in off-ward patient interaction to 69 percent. Ellsworth's research went on to demonstrate significant increases in discharge rates from the entire hospital as well as longer community stay and better adjustment in the community for experimental as compared to control patients. Sanders, Smith, and Weinman (1967) similarly developed a "socioenvironmental" treatment approach using college graduates with no prior experience in mental health and incorporating them as staff into a program which emphasized patient government, self-determination, and social interaction programs varying

in degree of structure. In general, they found improvement in social adjustment and psychiatric status to be most apparent for the more chronic patients in the most structured treatment. Similarly, Fairweather (1964) found that the development of small autonomous and patient-led groups in a mental hospital led to increased social activity and discharge rates. Unfortunately, many released patients later returned to the hospital, a result to which we will return shortly.

There have been many other milieu programs for chronic patients, with results similar to those noted above. Paul (1969b) has reviewed many of them, and concluded that such programs must be considered as a promising way to rehabilitate the chronic patient, at least to the point of "resocialization" (i.e., to where they are responsive enough to their environment to be considered as candidates for release).

A second major method of reform in mental hospital procedures involves programs such as those based on the social learning, behavior modification, and token economy procedures noted in Chapter IV (e.g., Ayllon & Azrin, 1968). Again, from Paul's (1969b) extensive review, it is clear that such procedures, when carefully implemented by a well-trained staff, have a demonstrated effectiveness in resocializing chronic patients to the point where their in-hospital behavior is acceptable and they can be considered candidates for release. As Paul notes, both the milieu and the social learning approaches, despite their success at improving in-hospital behavior, have failed to include provisions for community support and follow-up such that, after discharge, *failure to adjust to the demands of community living and return to the hospital are common*. Such failure tends to reinforce the view that we *need* hospitals for these patients to return to, since they "obviously" are unable to live outside of them. Paul's review suggests that this return is in part a function of the patients' unusual behavior that is not tolerated by community members, the lack of significant others for personal support, and the patients' lack of work and social participation skills. He suggests that hospital treatment programs should emphasize a set of training procedures that will specifically prepare the patient for a more successful return to community life. These procedures represent a summary of the best-known methods of in-hospital treatment for chronic patients, and are a markedly different set of procedures from those now implemented by most hospitals. They include the following steps:

1. Emphasize a "resident" rather than "patient" status through informal dress of staff, open channels of communication in all directions, and broad (but clear) authority structure.

2. Make clear, through a set of rules and attitudes, that the residents are responsible human beings; are expected to follow certain minimal rules of group living and are expected to do their share in participating in self-care, work, recreational, and social activities.

3. Utilize step systems which gradually increase the expectations placed on the residents in terms of their degree of independence and level of responsibility, with community return emphasized from the outset.

4. Encourage social interactions and skills provide a range of activities as well as regular large and small group meetings.

5. Emphasize clarity of communication, with concrete instruction in appropriate behavior and focus on utilitarian "action" rather than ad hominum "explanation."

6. Provide opportunity to practice vocational and housekeeping skills, with feedback, and specific training in marketable skills when needed.

7. Reacquaint residents with the "outside world" by exposing them to the community and bringing in community volunteers for discussions.

8. Identify the specific unique areas for change and support in concrete terms for each individual.

9. Prepare residents and significant-others to live in mutually supportive ways in the community through prerelease training and scheduled aftercare.

10. When no significant-other exists, follow Point 9 above, by training and releasing residents in groups of 2–3 as a "family" to provide significant-others for one another (Paul, 1969b, p. 91).[4]

Although the above suggestions are both sensible and have a good deal of empirical support, they also raise an important question for the community psychologist interested in the mental health system. Implicit in Paul's review and in each of his suggestions is an emphasis on intervention at the individual, small-group, and perhaps the organizational level. Institutional level changes in social policy and the rules of the game for dealing with deviants are not considered. The hospital is seen to properly serve as a base of operations around which milieu and behavioral programs are to be developed. Only later are patients expected to be discharged and supported in the community. Although such a sequential set of steps may be useful and necessary for the very chronic patients who are totally withdrawn because of their living in a hospital for many years, *it may be that for many current hospital residents, and certainly for potential future patients who are not now hospitalized, the hospital itself is an unnecessary step in the process.*

It is clear that so long as there are mental hospitals to which we can send patients they will

---

[4]In a recent comprehensive attempt to apply these suggestions Paul and his colleagues have engaged in a long-term evaluation study. At the time of this writing their work (G. L. Paul and R. J. Lentz (eds.), *Psychosocial Treatment of Chronically Institutionalized Mental Patients: A Comparative Study of Milieu vs. Social Learning Programs)* was in preparation for publication. Paul has reported that "the most effective intramural treatment was successful in improving the level of functioning of the most severely debilitated chronically institutionalized adult mental patients ever subjected to systematic study to the extent that 92.2 percent had been released to community placement and remained out of the hospital for a year and a half (at which time follow-up was terminated). The great majority of the latter patients were placed in private extended care facilities in the community (all had been previously rejected for such placement prior to the new treatment program); 11 percent of the original equated groups who received the new program improved sufficiently for independent release and self-support" (personal communication).

be used. That does not mean that such hospitals are necessary or desirable, nor does it preclude the use of any of the specific steps suggested by Paul with regard to the basic ingredients of positive expectations, patient autonomy, and systematic teaching of role skills at the individual level. In fact, implementing such steps as the training of role skills while the person is living in the community may actually be easier and more effective, although it will require a new set of rules and roles by which the mental health system operates.

A recent review of the efficacy of psychiatric rehabilitation (Anthony, Buell, Sharratt, & Althoff, 1972) lends considerable support to the suggestion that hospitalization may be, if not destructive, at least *irrelevant* to the ability of those with problems in living to learn to function in the real world. Anthony and his colleagues argue that the only legitimate criteria by which psychiatric treatment for discharged hospital patients may be judged are recidivism (percent of patients who return to the hospital) and post-hospital employment. In applying such criteria these authors are suggesting that real world access to resources, rather than some ill-defined interal intrapsychic "well-being" or adjustment to a hospital ward, is the proper aim of the mental health system with regard to those who suffer from severe problems in living.[5] That view is consistent with the values and orientation presented in this volume. It must be recalled that the criteria in part determine the outcome of program evaluation.

Anthony *et al.* review over 50 studies of rehabilitation methods and divide them into two general classes based on where the treatment takes place: in the hospital prior to discharge or on an outpatient basis. Each of these is contrasted with the *base rate* of recidivism and employment following hospitalization and traditional drug treatment and/or individual or group psychotherapy, the standard methods available in most hospitals. The base rate data for re-

cidivism one year after hospitalization, for psychiatric patients in general (usually diagnosed as schizophrenic) are from 30–50 percent, with 20–30 percent found to be employed full time. As patients become more chronic the figures indicate that the longer one is in the hospital the less likely is one to be discharged, or if discharged to remain out of the hospital and find employment. These figures are contrasted to special programs of in-hospital group therapy, work therapy, milieu, social learning or other in-hospital treatment. Although behavior in the hospital is shown to become more "pro-social," there is little demonstrated improvement in recidivism or employment rates. If these criteria are accepted as the legitimate value/goals then it is clear that *in-hospital treatments, regardless of their nature and effectiveness at improving hospital behavior, do not differentially affect the discharged patient's community functioning*.

In contrast to in-hospital treatment there are several other methods of treatment focused on post-discharge interventions. Among the most promising reviewed by Anthony *et al.* (1972) are two which appear to be effective: *aftercare follow-up counseling* and *autonomous alternative settings*. Although there is some evidence that attendance at a minimal contact drug maintenance aftercare clinic is related to reduced recidivism compared to base rates, these effects are difficult to interpret as due to aftercare per se because such data are often confounded with motivation to attend. That is, most studies include only those patients who elect to come to an outpatient clinic; the patients are presumably those most likely to work at remaining out of the hospital. As with other forms of therapy, those most in need probably stay away. Evaluation of more individual personal contact follow-up counseling programs, in which all patients discharged, not only those motivated to attend, are included in the results, provides stronger evidence for effectiveness.

One of the most interesting recent studies of this type was reported by Katkin, Ginsburg, Rifkin, and Scott (1971) who used supervised but untrained volunteer therapists (homemakers) in goal-oriented counseling which focused on

---

[5]Most programs that accept these criteria also turn out to cost less than those that rely on intrapsychic criteria and/or in-hospital behavior.

interpersonal and social problems. These researchers found recidivism rates for a population of diagnosed schizophrenic women with an average of 3.2 previous hospitalizations to be 11 percent compared to 34 percent for a demographically matched control group. The study's authors conclude that given appropriate supervision, nonprofessional therapeutic agents are able to reduce recidivism in a poor-risk population. Anthony et al. (1972), in their review of the study, further note that a key factor in this and other similar reports is that the counselor was flexible enough to provide *multiple levels of intervention*. The volunteers, unlike professionals, became involved in many aspects of the patients' lives, including advocating for them with various social agencies in order to obtain resources. This "unprofessional" attitude is one of the key aspects of the nonprofessional volunteer and is quite consistent with the *multiple strategy environmental resources model* presented in Chapter VI. It is also interesting as an example of how a community's human resources can be mobilized effectively (see also Chapter XI for a discussion of "nonprofessionals" per se).

A second post-discharge method of care reviewed by Anthony et al. is the "transitional facility," by which they include various halfway houses and other programs established as a step toward independent living outside the hospital. Such facilities are of two general types, those viewed as literally transitional and those developed as ongoing supportive living arrangements where a mental patient may reside with one or more other patients or a family. Anthony et al. find that although such facilities can keep patients out of the hospital, once they leave the facility they are just as likely to return as those who never received such treatment. It may be that autonomous settings that are oriented around autonomy of the target group living in mutual support are necessary as an ongoing arrangement in order to keep some people living and working in the community. As such, Anthony notes that their main benefits for mental patients tend to be more freedom and less stigma, while for society they are cheaper to operate than in-hospital programs.

It should be noted, then, that autonomous alternative settings for mental patients who require continual support are not mini-hospitals, but homes in the community that can be operated entirely by a small group of people who, like a family, continue to live together. Some or all the members may work and they can serve as psychological support for one another. They may be given various kinds of assistance by others such as training in employment skills but they do not require the usual professional activities of "treatment." Rather, the members may benefit from an environmental resources advocate who serves a facilitative rather than a controlling function (as in the Katkin program noted above). If judged by the traditional criteria of "psychological well-being" such residents may be found to be "sick" in the traditional sense. However, if judged by their ability to live with one another and to work and be largely self-supporting without a hospital, they may be found to be competent.

There is now reasonable evidence that most people who have traditionally had no alternative but to live in the confines and control of a mental institution can effectively reside in an autonomous alternative setting. In this regard there now appears to be evidence (see below) that hospitals may be irrelevant to the patients if they can be provided with genuine environmental resources and/or advocates who help them to establish a place in the world. Again, it must be noted that the criterion is living outside of a hospital, not some intrapsychic criterion of "health." It requires that we change our rules of the mental health game to focus on the right of people to be different without the risk of being confined. The criteria do not preclude the specific suggestions for work with individual people as suggested by Paul above.[6]

---

[6]In this regard the distinction between *subunit, new-unit,* and *autonomous setting* (see Chapter VI, p. 182) is crucial. It is only the autonomous setting that questions the rules of the game. Many so-called halfway houses (Raush & Raush, 1968) are simply new places for the traditional treatments. If autonomy is not a part of such settings they can become new forms of hospital confinement. This issue is elaborated in the next section.

Examples of Autonomy and Mobilization of Environmental Resources for Chronic Patients

The Community Lodge

Among the single most important pieces of research focused on change in the mental health system is the work of George W. Fairweather and his colleagues (Fairweather, Sanders, Maynard, & Cressler, 1969). After Fairweather discovered that a program of small-group autonomy within a mental hospital prepared patients for discharge, but failed to provide them with the resources to remain living productively in the community, he shifted his tactics to an experimental program designed to directly provide community resources. Chronic male patients residing in a VA hospital, who had participated in the in-hospital small-group treatment program, were assigned to participate, upon discharge, in development of a community resources program. This involved living on their own, in an autonomous alternative setting known as a "lodge," wherein the patients were taught to progressively take over administration of the setting, including the development of a patient-run small business (a janitorial service). Volunteers for the program were matched with similar patients and randomly assigned to either the autonomous setting or to the hospital's traditional aftercare programs, which generally include drug treatment and/or periodic contact with an outpatient clinic for some form of counseling. Nonvolunteers were also assigned to both the experimental and the control situations. Of the 334 patients involved in this study the experimentals and the controls were closely matched on a large number of relevant characteristics.

The key to the "lodge society" developed by Fairweather is its creation of a social system operating under rules considerably different from those normally controlling mental health programs. Fairweather emphasizes, like Sarbin (see Chapter IV) the need for providing currently "marginal persons" with a new social status. This requires the establishment of social systems that permit such status to develop. Table IX-2 graphically presents Fairweather's notions of the social statuses available to identified mental patients. He argues that the traditional rules of the game by which the mental health system operates leave no choice but to view identified patients as either "sick" or "well." Thus the rules provide no opportunity for those who have problems in living to develop their strengths and abilities through access to resources, although they should have the opportunity as adult citizens of a democratic society. In essence, the argument is that some people require a special situation in which they may have access to environmental resources that enable them to live as independently and successfully as they are able. Table IX-2 illustrates the lack of available status between being "sick or "well," with "well" defined as fitting into a single standard of competence. That is what the lodge society was designed to overcome. It is essentially an attempt to create an *autonomous setting* wherein people who do not fit into the standard social structures are given the opportunity to develop their own, suitable to their needs, without fear of confinement and control.[7] Implicit in this view is the belief that people need not be static in their social status; they should be provided with the opportunity to move from one status to another. The traditional mental health system makes this move very difficult.

Fairweather's lodge emphasizes a progressive program to provide community support through resources in the form of a patient-operated business and living situation. In this system the residents are expected to provide social and psychological support for each other, and the system itself requires that employment and other living responsibility be taken by the residents. The original testing of the plan was instituted so as to move from an initial period of maximum professional supervison, which involved help in setting up living and work rules,

---

[7]For a discussion of how the autonomous setting may differ from the typical halfway house, day or night hospital, see Chapter VI, pp. 182–183.

TABLE IX–2. Autonomy of mental patients' social status.*

| | None ←——— Dimension of Autonomy ———→ Complete | | | | | | |
| | Supervised institutional situation — The mental hospital | | Supervised community situations | | | Unsupervised community group situations | Partially autonomous individual status | Autonomous individual status |
	Closed locked ward	Open unlocked ward	Living situations (home care, day-care centers, day hospitals)	Work situations (sheltered workshops)	Combination of work-living situations	Discharged ex-patient-led group work-living situations—work in reference groups	Counseling or psychotherapy	No treatment
Social Situation								
Status Situation	Very limited adult rights and duties		Some adult rights and duties			Otherwise, full adult rights and duties	Otherwise, full adult rights and duties	Full adult rights and duties
Available Social Statuses	Sick person					(Usually unavailable) *Aim of the lodge society is to fill this cell*	Well person	

*Slightly modified from Fairweather *et al.*, 1969.

to a period of assistance from nonprofessionals, and finally to the development of self-governance and total autonomy.

Program evaluation was provided by periodic assessments of community tenure, employment status, as well as individual assessments of psychological well-being. Figures IX-1 and IX-2 graphically present a comparison of the lodge group and the control group on time spent in the community and time employed over a period ranging from six months after the lodge was established to seven months after it closed, a span of 40 months following initial patient discharge. It can be seen that the lodge group spent about 80 percent of its time living in the community (compared to about 20 percent for the controls). They were involved in full-time employment about 40 percent of the time (compared to almost no full-time employment for the control group). It should be noted, however, that once they left the lodge (this was permitted whenever they wished) they were usually not able to secure employment. Although these data are impressive with regard to the success of the

lodge as a viable substitute of an autonomous social system for hospital confinement, it is clear that it is not to be interpreted as a solution to "mental illness." Patients are not "cured" so much as they are able to live with considerably more freedom and autonomy. It should also be emphasized that the lodge costs far less to operate than traditional hospital care. Figure IX-3 presents data on cost per person per day for various kinds of treatment programs, including a lodge society operated by "experts," by lay people, or by the members themselves. Even when work income is not applied to the program support a lodge costs substantially less than other programs.

It is important to realize what Fairweather's work does not demonstrate. In addition to the fact that once they left the lodge most patients were not employed, Anthoney *et al.* (1972) point out that on actual recidivism (defined as number of patients who return at any time to the hospital) the experimental and control groups do not differ. Thus, even for those who can stay out of the hospital 80 percent of the time, *if a hospi-*

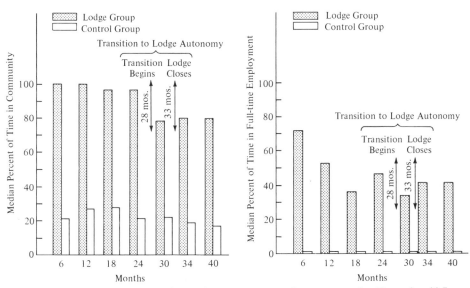

Figure IX-1. Comparison of lodge and control groups on time in the community for 40 months of follow-up.
Figure IX-2. Comparison of lodge and control groups on employment for 40 months of follow-up. (Redrawn from Fairweather, Sanders, Maynard, & Cressler, 1969.)

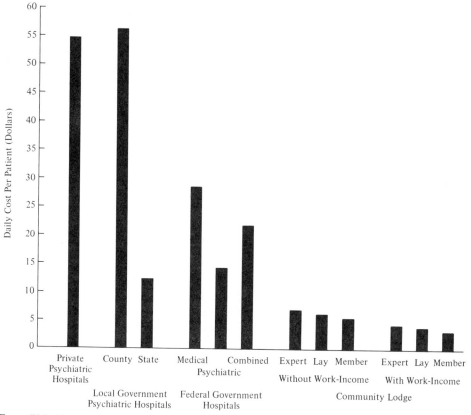

Figure IX-3. Mean daily cost per person for alternative treatment settings in California Bay Area, 1964 to 1966. (Redrawn from Fairweather, Sanders, Maynard, & Cressler, 1969.)

tal is available it tends to be used, at least some of the time. The lodge serves two primary functions. It increases freedom and decreases stigma. It does not "cure" mental illness. If hospitals were not available it is likely that many patients would still require an ongoing supportive lodge-like living arrangement. In this sense, it must be emphasized that the community lodge is suggested as a viable alternative setting of less cost to society and of increased freedom for those members of society who are now fully dependent on institutional care.

The above constitute the major criteria used for outcome evaluation in Fairweather's work, but they by no means tell the whole story. In terms of both the self-report of patients and of significant others in their life, few differences in psychosocial adjustment between the experimental and control groups were found. The major effect of the lodge was on length of stay and productivity in the community. The major implication seems to be that the social systems in which individuals find themselves may be a much more potent factor for community adjustment than "psychological well-being." Other findings include the demonstration that the lodge was a successful living arrangement even for long-term patients who are unable to adjust to other community programs. In addition, patients who did not volunteer for the lodge experiment adjusted to the community just as well as those who did volunteer.

An equally important finding is based on the analysis of returning-patient reasons for failure to adjust to community life. In the control group the most frequently (41 percent) reported reason for returning to the hospital was pressure from significant others. This reason was almost nonexistent among lodge residents. The lodge members either tolerated each other or controlled their members' bizarre behavior. Justification for turning our thinking about care for chronic patients away from intrapsychic variables and toward work with significant others and the creation of settings is very strong.

Although the lodge setting has been cited and reviewed by many in terms of its clinical outcomes, like those who have reviewed Goldenberg's work (see Chapter VI, p. 186), few have focused attention on its broader value implications for the helping professions. Yet for Fairweather these implications are the crux of his work. He suggests several "principles" consistent with many of the values offered for community psychology in this book. As such, they are of interest even beyond the mental health system. The "principles" suggested by Fairweather *et al.* (1969) are summarized below as *necessary ingredients* in creating a social system which provides for its members an opportunity to upgrade their social status in the sense suggested by Sarbin in Chapter IV and in Table IX-2.

1. Participants must have a stake in the system. They need to be decision makers who can take pride in the success of the system of which they are a part.
2. Autonomy of each member, consistent with his or her own abilities and performance, is essential.
3. Although Fairweather favors a vertical organization, whereas Goldenberg suggests a horizontal organization, they agree in the more important sense of an ethic of mobility with regard to key roles and decision making in the setting. That is, each member should be offered the opportunity to perform in whatever roles he or she is capable and willing to assume.
4. The creation of a new social subsystem must be compatible with the larger society. In this regard Fairweather is particularly fond of a system oriented around an independent business because it fits so nicely with the work ethic of the larger society.
5. Subsystems need to establish internal norms tolerant of the deviant behavior normative for that particular population. For chronic mental patients this "tolerance for deviance" is particularly important because when occasional unusual or bizarre behavior is ignored, the person seems quite able to maintain himself most of the time without need for confinement.
6. Open lines of communication within the system are essential.
7. Mobile entry and exit from the system must be possible without penalty.
8. Persons should perform as a group whenever possible.
9. New systems need to be established that are not dependent on the good will of others, but have an independent existence.
10. Systems should be small enough so that close interpersonal and supportive relationships can be developed.
11. Systems should be structured so that members can substitute roles for each other.
12. For the chronic mental patient both rehabilitation and work norms are necessary.
13. For the chronic patient the system must also establish a means for administering adequate medication.

Although not all of these principles are applicable to all autonomous settings, the spirit of autonomy, self-control, and within-group communication is clearly applicable to other groups of people who deviate from mainstream society. Fairweather goes on to suggest that the basic notion of independent autonomous settings is a viable strategy for the creation of social change more generally (see also Chapter VI). Nevertheless, he is also aware of the difficulty in implementing such change.

It is possible that this kind of focus on social-problem solution will turn attention . . . to the creation of social systems which are fitted to human needs, rather than the fitting of human beings with their diverse needs into already-established social statuses in ongoing and unchanging social institutions. Historically, such institutions are beginning to show themselves inadequately prepared, because of their size, complexity, and rigidity, to take account of those needs in a flexible and responsive fashion. Only cooperative effort can create a social atmosphere in these institutions that will benefit all concerned. It may be, however, that this society cannot mount a cooperative effort to change its social institutions. Issues of power and control may so preoccupy its decision-making members that improving the social position of its marginal members will continue to be given a low priority. If such is the case, no research, however valid, can change those aspects of the society that are inhumane and unjust (Fairweather *et al.*, 1969, p. 343).

Releasing the Unreleasable: The Mendota Program

Although there is now little question that programs such as a community lodge are more effective than most in-hospital programs for helping chronic patients to live in their community, most such programs have focused on providing services only *after* discharge or when an identified patient is presumably "ready." A different approach has been taken by researchers at the Mendota State Hospital in Madison, Wisconsin (Marx, Test, & Stein, 1973). Rather than waiting for patients to reach some hypothetical level of readiness for release, these researchers have assumed that, given proper environmental resources and supports, almost any identified patient could learn to live in the world rather than in a hospital unit. They have viewed the tendency of other community programs to "fall back" on hospitalization as unfortunate and unnecessary. Rather than develop permanent sheltered enclaves of expatients, they have emphasized independent roles and independent living.

Like Paul's (see above) description of the social breakdown syndrome, Marx *et al.* suggest that regardless of psychiatric diagnosis, the patient who has a difficult time with community adjustment tends to have three characteristics:

1. A limited repertoire of instrumental and problem-solving behaviors to deal with stress, work, social activities, and leisure time;

2. a strong "dependency" on family and others;
3. demonstration of extreme behavior when under stress.

They emphasize that not only does the hospital contribute to "social regression," but that its very presence reinforces the patient's symptom expression by its availability, and thereby reduces the need for learning new problem-solving behaviors. This observation is quite compatible with a number of other researchers who find that the hospital itself comes to serve as a means for escape from the pressures of life (Braginsky, Braginsky, & Ring, 1969). Unfortunately, the only way to escape, particularly for those who cannot afford the expense of vacations and country retreats, is to "act crazy" and thus be removed from the daily stress of life.

With the above in mind, Marx and his colleagues developed a program for chronic hospitalized patients, under the following guidlines:

1. Treatment emphasized the teaching of coping skills for living in the community and took place in the community.
2. They refused to use the hospital as a backup for difficulty in community adjustment.
3. They emphasized work with family and/or significant others.
4. They emphasized the identified patient as a responsible person expected to "make it" in the community once they mobilize the natural reinforcements and contingencies that are a consequence of adequate coping behavior.
5. The staff emphasized a close relationship to all sorts of community agencies and people, in essentially a *problem solving-environmental resource and advocacy approach.*

To begin, the research team identified inpatients at the Mendota State Hospital who were clearly high risk for continued rehospitalization. These were identified by the hospital staff as "*not currently capable of sustained community living.*" In short, discharge was "unfeasible." The patients were hospitalized for three to fifteen months, and had spent about 50 percent of their time in the hospital during the recent past. They were between the ages of 20 and 45, and included all psychiatric diagnoses other than retardation, severe physical disability, or alcoholism. It should be noted that this population is quite representative of a large segment of the hospital population which would need to be discharged were the "five-year plan" proposed above implemented.

Current hospital inpatients who met the above criteria were randomly assigned to one of three treatment conditions. One group was immediately started on *total treatment in the community*. A second group was allowed to remain on their hospital unit to be prepared, in the usual way, by the usual staff, for discharge and future community living. A third group was transferred to a special research unit of the hospital and treated by the same staff that was working with the community treatment group. This latter "control group," while not accounting for possible differences in staff enthusiasm, was used to account for staff/patient ratio, and staff personality differences.

Patients in all three groups were quite similar at the onset of the project. Most were single or with a history of failed marital relationships. They had spent, since an early age, a good deal of time in psychiatric hospitals. Most were diagnosed as schizophrenic and all patients were about equally rated on measures of psychiatric symptoms and behaviors.

The community treatment group, "unprepared" as they were, were immediately placed in various independent living situations, such as apartments, boarding houses, hotels, YMCA, YWCA. Placement depended on individual patient resources and needs. Treatment consisted of participation in a schedule of daily real-life activities and, where appropriate, included the use of pharmacotherapy. The staff served as advocates, teachers, resource finders, and were available at first on a day and night basis, even hour by hour. They later phased themselves out. The staff helped find jobs or sheltered workshops; they were available for assistance in such mundane daily living activities as shopping, cooking, grooming, and using transportation. They prodded and supported recreational and social activity. The role of the staff was similar to that assumed by the homemakers in the program developed by Katkin *et al.* (see above). The

staff advocated for and represented the patients in contacts with the various community agencies controlling resources and encouraged these agencies to view the patients as responsible citizens. Families and other significant others were either supported or told that a "constructive separation" was necessary, but staff also made themselves available for consultation to concerned family members. In essence, these staff did everything they could think of to keep the patients independent of the usual mental health system and to help them obtain environmental resources.

The patients who were transferred to the special in-hospital research unit were given equal time and attention, but the focus was on "preparation" for release by means of group therapy, ward work details, medication, and instruction in problem solving and daily activity skills. Finally, when "ready" the patients were placed in a gradual transition program such as sheltered workshops and employment, day or night hospital care. All treatment efforts by the staff, however, took place *in the hospital*. The third group was left to the care of the regular hospital staff. All patients were treated for five months; thereafter any need for treatment was provided by other facilities.

Program evaluation involved assessment of each patient's psychiatric status and behavior as well as various intrapsychic measures. More importantly, measures of autonomy and quality of living and employment were also taken.

Results are presented for two phases of the study: during the five months of treatment and at the conclusion of the treatment phase. Table IX-3 presents the mean number of days in various kinds of living units spent by each group. From this table we see that almost all of the treatment time was spent by the community treatment group in independent or semi-independent living. The 6.33 days of psychiatric institutionalization were a function of a base line period used just prior to onset of the community program. All designated community treatment patients left the hospital within eight days, and only one returned to the hospital (for two days) and was then returned to the community. When patients got into legal difficulty they were not "rescued" to a hospital but spent time in jail,

TABLE IX–3.   Living situations of the patients during the five-
month treatment phase.*

Type of Facility	Mean No. Days		
	Community Treatment	Hospital Research Unit	Regular Hospital Unit
Psychiatric institutions	6.33	103.05	98.55
Penal institutions	6.48	0.16	0.25
Family (parental)	5.33	1.58	7.25
Family (nonparental)	0.05	19.00	8.50
Family care	0.00	4.47	10.10
Semi-sheltered (halfway house or boarding house)	34.90	16.00	9.00
Room	61.76	9.89	7.30
Apartment	34.57	0.00	7.10
Other	2.10	2.89	0.00

*From Marx, Test, & Stein, 1973.

like any other citizen (an average of 6.48 days for minor offenses). Interestingly, the researchers note that the patients were not rejected by the community as too troublesome, and even received favorable newspaper coverage. This can be contrasted with the experience of those who have interpreted "community care" to be dumping of patients without resources onto an unsuspecting community (see Chapter II, p. 45). Rather, the staff of this project were actively involved in an environmental resources, problem-solving, and social advocacy role. When "crises" occurred they were available *in the community* for support and consultation.

Tables IX-4 and IX-5 present the results of the study with regard to living situation and employment status at the conclusion of the treatment phase. The data in these tables were statistically compared and demonstrate that the community treatment patients had attained significantly more autonomy of living situation and had significantly better employment status. Interestingly, as with Fairweather's study reported above, there were *no differences* among the groups in psychiatric symptomatology or intrapsychic well-being. The researchers emphasize that "the learning of skills for good hospital adjustment has little value for good community adjustment." They argue against the dumping of "ready to release" patients into the city streets, in favor of a reorientation of the mental

health systems' resources toward provision of community resources.[8]

There are several issues that need reemphasis with regard to a plan for closing the custodial mental hospitals. It is clear that it will require work at *multiple levels*. At the institutional level, a social policy that eschews hospitalization is basic. So long as mental hospitals are available they will be used. At the organizational level the roles and relationships between mental health personnel and identified deviants must be reoriented. For those who are currently totally withdrawn as a function of their years of isolation, social learning and milieu units may be necessary as a temporary means of resocialization. No new residents should be admitted.[9] For many others an immediate move to placements in the community is clearly both feasible and desirable. At the individual level, the

---

[8]At the time of this writing the authors had not reported on a follow-up of their program. They did report data similar to those presented here on a larger number of patients (60 experimentals and 60 controls), and expect to conduct longer-term follow-up research (Stein, Test, & Marx, 1975). Even if it should turn out that more contact is needed, there is no reason to assume that if the mental health system were reoriented to community care, hospitalization would be required.

[9]As noted earlier, hospitalization may be necessary for those with severe physical damage who require nursing care. Such units should be run with an eye toward the maximum possible care, independent living, and the smallest possible size.

TABLE IX–4. Living situation at end of treatment program.*

Category (in Order of Increasing Autonomy)	Community Treatment N = 21	Hospital Research Unit N = 19**	Regular Hospital Unit N = 20
Institution Client spends overnight in an institution (psychiatric or penal) where supervision in all aspects of life is available.	1	4	9
Sheltered Client lives in the community but in a situation where psychosocial support is atuomatically available. That is, either guidance or direct services are provided in areas of daily living functions (meal preparation, laundry, upkeep, etc.).	3	9	8
High Shelter Client is not only given guidance but many things are done for him (e.g., family care settings).	(2)	(3)	(5)
Moderate Shelter Client satisfactorily performs in many areas of life with some guidance, but nothing is done for him (e.g., halfway house).	(1)	(6)	(3)
Independent Client lives in the community in a setting where there is no "built-in" psychosocial support. Thus the client either performs daily living functions autonomously and/or takes initiative in obtaining needed services.	17	6	3
Moderate Independence Client meets some of own needs and sees that additional needs are met.	(10)	(5)	(2)
Optimal Independence Client meets most of own needs and may even have partial "responsibility" for others (e.g., roommate).	(7)	(1)	(1)

*From Marx, Test, & Stein, 1973.
**Data are unavailable on one Hospital Research Unit patient, who left the program and whose whereabouts remain unknown.

money now used to hire staff and support mental hospitals must be redirected to hire and train staff to work as social advocates and locators of community resources. Similarly, the educational functions of employment and living skills need to be emphasized. For those who are in acute stress and need a temporary withdrawal, general hospitals may serve a useful function on a short-run basis (usually a matter of days). Chemotherapy may also be useful as an adjunct treatment for many patients. This should always be quickly followed by return to community living with an appropriate social advocate and/or teacher of skills as is necessary on an individual basis, as in the model established by the Mendota group. Community volunteers, such as

TABLE IX–5. Employment situations at end of treatment program.*

Category (in Order of Increasing Autonomy)	Community Treatment N = 21	Hospital Research Unit N = 19	Regular Hospital Unit N = 20
Unemployed	8	6	15
Sheltered			
Client attends a sheltered workshop or other similar structured and supervised facility in the community.	4	10	2
Competitive			
Client is employed in the competitive job market in the community.	9	3	2
Minimal—client works 10–24 hr/wk	(4)	(1)	(1)
Moderate—client works 25–32 hr/wk	(3)	(0)	(0)
Full time—client works over 32 hr/wk	(2)	(2)	(2)

*From Marx, Test, & Stein, 1973.

homemakers, college students, and others, can also serve in these social advocate roles (Katkin, Ginsburg, Rifkin, & Scott, 1971; McGee, 1974; Seidman & Rappaport, 1974b). The development of appropriate environmental niches such as communal patient living and working arrangements in the manner of Fairweather's lodge may be also necessary for those who cannot go it alone. For those individuals who choose not to work, for whatever reason, or not to face the stress of independent living, there is no reason why they cannot live in a semi-autonomous community residence without loss of individual freedom and consequent social stigma (see, for example, the suggestions of Braginsky, Braginsky, & Ring, 1969). In sum, there is now no reason to support the current mental hospital system. Instead, the rules of the game need to be reevaluated and the social thermostat set with an eye toward the provision of environmental resources.

Crisis Intervention in the Community

The above suggestions have focused on the mental health system as it pertains to those already deeply embedded in its procedures—the current chronic hospitalized or "revolving door" pa-tients. Next we focus on those who are in acute stress situations and therefore run the risk of being drawn into the mental health network. It will be suggested below that a system be developed to provide on-the-spot "crisis intervention" to those experiencing acute disturbance.

It has already been suggested that for some very small number of people relative to the total now hospitalized—those who are currently experiencing an extreme psychotic episode and cannot be calmed down with drugs and immediate interpersonal attention from family, friends, or a community intervention specialist—it may be necessary to provide a temporary (not more than a few days) emergency placement in a general hospital. This should be thought of as an extreme action, only taken as a last resort. The general hospital should have a definite upper limit on stay (three to five days is suggested) and be operated by a medical staff, with no pretense to psychiatric rehabilitation. Such units of a general hospital will need a *community intervention team* to plan with the person and his or her significant others for an immediate return to the community.[10]

---

[10]The team, to be described below, need not, and perhaps should not, be made up of traditional mental-health-oriented professionals.

For many who have a stable work and living arrangement, removal to a general hospital and return to family will prove sufficient to solve the immediate crisis. Some may desire chemical treatment or longer term counseling or psychotherapy; they could be referred as outpatients to the local mental health center, to an individual physician, or to a psychotherapist. For others who have less stable interpersonal living situations and lack significant others, or employment, the same kind of in-the-community support provided by the Mendota group (see above) for currently chronic patients may be necessary. For those who are new to the system (i.e., they have not been previously hospitalized) it is likely that the supports could be less total and begin at higher levels of expectation. The point is that such support would be real-world-oriented, with the goals of living, working, and being independent taken as legitimate in and of themselves. Abstract ideas about personality and intrapsychic adjustment would be secondary to keeping the individuals living in the community by teaching social roles, problem solving, and coping skills. This is much more a resource-for-living-in-the-world enterprise than a "mental health" program. Genuine and important human hurts, such as anxiety, unhappiness, and so on, could be dealt with in the context of their relationship to an ability to live in the real world, or could be referred to practicing psychotherapists.

It would not be expected that psychotherapists would solve practical problems in living. Rather, they would serve much more realistically in the solution of problems such as self-acceptance, awareness, and self-actualization (see, for example, Sarbin's distinctions in Table IV-4). Nor would therapists have the right or the responsibility to confine and/or control so-called mental patients. Persons with problems in living would not be forced to "fit in" or be confined. Rather, the ability of some to "fit in" to existing community roles, or to create new ones, would be dealt with through a mutual agreement concerning personal goals between a community intervention team and the person in difficulty. The person would suggest what goals are desirable and the team would help consider what resources are needed and

how to get them. The community interventionist would serve in the role of teacher-advocate and work within a model for obtaining environmental resources, such as the one described by Davidson and Rapp (see Chapter VI). They may require certain interpersonal, teaching, and social learning skills as well as an intimate knowledge of the community and its resources. Basic to this model is an agreement between the person and the advocate. It must be understood that the person always has a right to reject such assistance and that mental hospitals are *not* available to either the patients or the mental health system.[11]

The above plan would require a new set of rules for dealing with those who experience problems in living. Everyone would be regarded as a responsible citizen, with legal rights and strengths, but some may require assistance in mobilizing potential environmental resources. The current mental health system of psychotherapy and drug treatment would be an important *resource*, which for many people could be usefully mobilized. However, this system would not be central to decision making about the person's life. Rather, the person would retain that right. Added to this system is a set of crisis intervention workers who would be available not only to the general hospital, but on call to anyone, at anytime, in the community. Is such a system feasible? There are many experiences to indicate that it is, given the willingness to implement it.

The theoretical ideas behind crisis intervention, developed by Gerald Caplan, have already been described in some detail in Chapter III. It will be recalled that the basic notion of such an approach lies in the belief that everyone experiences two kinds of crises in his or her normal life span: (1) *developmental crises* which occur at predictable transitional periods in the life cycle (e.g., birth of a child, entry to school, menopause); (2) *accidental crises* which appear at unpredictable times and are a function of any number and kind of the stresses of life. Common

---

[11]The only exceptions to this freedom would be legal, in which a court could necessarily retain the ultimate power to control deviance. But this would be a legal, not a mental health, action.

events include loss of loved ones, loss of job, physical illness, and almost any event that has a characteristic of needing problem resolution. Such events will differ from person to person depending on his or her particular experiences, strengths, and weaknesses. Depending on how a crisis is handled one may learn to deal with future crises better or worse.

The earliest widespread application of crisis theory was in the realm of suicide prevention, developed at the Los Angeles Suicide Prevention Center (Schneidman & Farberow, 1965). It was in this context that many of the methods of crisis intervention were developed. They used a publicized telephone number that would put a caller in contact with a help agent (Litman *et al.*, 1965). The mobilization of significant others (Farberow, 1967) and the involvement of non-professional volunteers as effective crisis workers were also pioneered in the context of suicide prevention. McGee (1974) has recently described in some detail the contribution of this work to the broad development of methods for intervention in *any* crisis situation. The development of programs for crisis intervention is now quite widespread and has been demonstrated to be clearly feasible. As of 1972 there were almost 200 known centers.

As McGee points out, the expansion of such programs has been accelerated by the legal requirement that community mental health centers provide a 24-hour emergency service (see Chapter III, p. 55). However, McGee suggests that the most viable way for crisis intervention centers to relate to community mental health centers is to provide contractual services, rather than for such centers to be a part of the existing mental health system. This has the advantage of both satisfying the mental health centers' legal obligation and maintaining the crisis centers' independence from medical conceptions and style of delivery. Because many crises are irrelevant to medical care (e.g., they often involve financial, educational, employment, and interpersonal problems in living) McGee views such independence as crucial.

A model description of how a crisis intervention program can be implemented in a community, including what services can be delivered,

how to deliver them, who should deliver them, how people can be trained, and the outcomes evaluated, has been presented by McGee (1974). In this context he has reviewed the history, mistakes, and positive experiences of several past and present centers, as well as the development of an experimental program in Gainesville, Florida. McGee has detailed a clear course by which a community psychology dedicated to intervention in the mental health system can operate under the paradigm of an environmental resources model, quite similar in strategies and tactics to those emphasized in Chapter VI. Its conceptions are consistent with those of a community psychology developed in Chapter V.

McGee's Program for Crisis Intervention in the Community

Basic to McGee's suggestions, developed from an analysis of the actual experiences of ten early programs founded in the 1960s, is what he calls a "community orientation." Although the unique characteristics and requirements of a given locale must be understood prior to intervention, there are certain processes that remain consistent with its implementation regardless of local differences. McGee details the steps to be taken by a program innovater in establishing a crisis center. These steps revolve around seven "essential phases": (1) convergence of ideas or interest among community members, (2) initiation of activity, (3) legitimization and sponsorship, (4) development of a plan, (5) development of an organization, (6) implementation, and (7) evaluation (McGee, p. 23). These phases, each discussed in the specific context of crisis centers, are quite similar to the general strategies and tactics of social intervention described by Fairweather, by Gurin and Perlman, by Rothman, and others in Chapter VI. McGee has formalized them in a series of guidelines for the development and implementation of crisis centers per se. The specifics need not be repeated here other than to note that such strategies and tactics of community change, aimed at developing crisis centers, have also been found to involve political maneuvering, problem solving, and persistence emphasized earlier. The simple demonstration of a useful service is not sufficient to create a new program.

Given that establishment of a crisis center will require many of the strategies and tactics already discussed in Chapter VI of this volume (emphasizing change at the *institutional* and the *organizational* levels), we can turn more specifically in this chapter to the content of services to be provided within what amounts to a social advocacy and environmental resources conception applied to the mental health system. Basic to an effective service, McGee suggests six characteristics: the use of nonprofessional personnel; the use of professionals as consultants; an emphasis on prevention rather than treatment; avoidance of a pathology model; membership in a network of agencies; and commitment to evaluation research. In an analysis of the ten original crisis center programs McGee finds that when these characteristics have been applied, the programs have tended to be successful, at least as measured by a continued existence in their community.

Early programs for crisis intervention were oriented around a telephone answering service. The telephone number was publicized and people in crisis were encouraged to call for assistance. As a result of a survey of these early programs McGee began to suspect that telephone services alone were not only insufficient but ineffective unless operated under carefully controlled conditions. He and his colleagues investigated this further by means of a research project (McGee, Richard, & Bercun, 1972). They placed four calls, distributed in time over weekday office hours, early evening hours, middle of the night and weekend, to each of nine different crisis centers. They found that when a center had volunteers on duty who answered the phone directly, it took less than 20 seconds to complete a call. If answering services were used it took as much as three minutes. However, when a system was used where an answering service called the interventionist who then returned the call, it took as long as 49 minutes (average time was 15 minutes). When calls were taken by another social agency which was to

relay the call to a crisis worker, calls were not even completed two out of three times. They concluded that the only certain way to get quick 24-hour emergency services is to have a crisis worker directly receiving calls at all times. This is one very important part of a good crisis intervention service, and requires the use of more personnel than the limited numbers of professional mental health workers normally available.

In his examination of the early crisis programs McGee identified several other necessary services, often lacking in these early centers. One involves a willingness to follow-up callers, months or even as much as one year later, to find out how they are functioning. A related policy involves the need to be sure that the person actually gets to some other agency or service when referred. The largest single lack in early programs was due to an unwillingness to provide face-to-face contact. This reluctance McGee suggests was a function of the early control by medical and mental health professionals who discouraged crisis workers, generally nonprofessionals, from involving themselves in the lives of callers.

Other services that were sometimes, but not often provided, include follow-up for suicide attempters, even if they do not call directly, and follow-up with the survivors of suicide victims. Additional necessary components of a crisis intervention center include the need to provide immediate shelter, to provide transportation, and to plan follow-up actions. In short, the center staff must be well integrated into its community and have a viable relationship with all the potential providers of resources. They must also be willing to work with any and all requests for service. In addition, the need for careful record keeping and systematic feedback is stressed by McGee. Although some of these services were provided by some of the early centers, most were simply telephone answering services. According to McGee, all of these services and more must now be included in future programs. He argues that they can be provided largely by relying on nonprofessional manpower. Of the almost 200 programs now in existence, over 80 percent of the staff are volunteer community people without professional mental health training.

The real professional crisis worker has emerged in the form of the volunteer, whose availability has only begun to be tapped and whose devotion and dedication to the needs of fellow human beings are not constrained by time-honored roles and artificial status distinctions. The manpower issues in crisis intervention programs are now the easiest problems to solve when a new program is organized (McGee, 1974, p. 112).

With the above orientation in mind, McGee presents, by way of example, his development of the Suicide and Crisis Intervention Service (SCIS) in Gainesville, Florida. This center began with the hypothesis that face-to-face contact between trained volunteers and people in crisis, at the scene, rather than by telephone and office contact, was of utmost utility. The volunteer in this program is a "professional crisis worker," regardless of formal degree or salary. The operational policy of SCIS is stated simply and without ambivalence as:

The policy of this center is merely to respond to every request to participate in the solution of any human problem whenever and wherever it occurs. It is impossible to imagine a problem which falls outside the scope of appropriate involvement by the crisis center (McGee, 1974, p. 181, italics in original).

This policy means that there are no eligibility requirements, and no one with any problem is turned away. Obviously, it does not mean that they can solve every problem, but that they will try. The role of the crisis staff is as "ombudsman" on the behalf of people. They may go to court and tell the judge that they are trying to help the person find a job; they may try to reestablish contact between a juvenile and his or her parents. They may intervene, on request, in family disputes. They may try to find food, clothing, or shelter for someone. They will deal with suicide threats, as well as employment or housing problems. If there are resources or services available they help to find them. If not they help to provide them. The attitude toward people is expressed in the following philosophy:

1. People in crisis are not sick. Crisis intervention is not necessarily a medical service, nor even a health-related service.

2. People in crisis are not mentally ill. Crisis intervention is not necessarily a mental health service.
3. People in crisis need immediate, active, aggressive intervention.
4. People in crisis are the responsibility of the local community. Crisis intervention service is as much a rightful expectation of every citizen as the availability of public education, public health, police and fire protection, and public utilities (McGee, 1974, p. 182).

Rather than rely on a mental health service which teaches one to talk abstractly about problems, the crisis intervention center focuses on concrete solutions to problems of daily living. Professionalism and social distance are avoided. Even the special case of the person who has developed a life style of dependency can be dealt with in realistic fashion by incorporating that person into the goal-setting process and by emphasizing real-world rather than abstract solutions. The heart of the crisis center is the *crisis intervention team* which will provide on-the-spot assistance, including 24-hour response, to requests for help from the police, the only other service that will provide 24-hour assistance. Many times services for which police are called can better be handled by a crisis intervention-problem-solving agency.

For McGee, the crisis center represents the practice of community psychology which avoids the "old wine in new bottles" approach of the community mental health center. It is a place where the concepts of community control, by involvement of local volunteers, indigenous to a neighborhood, can assist their peers in problem solving. Its services can be based on an environmental resources model rather than on an intrapsychic model. In developing the program at Gainesville, McGee used an initial federal research grant with the program being phased, over three years, to local sources of funding as it demonstrated its utility.

Gainesville is a community of about 100,000 people, including some 20,000 students. Within the first three months of its existence the SCIS handled over 2100 calls from or about clients and averaged active involvement in

60 new cases per month. After the first year the number of cases per month doubled. They found that within one year 80 percent of a random sample of telephone subscribers listed in the local directory knew about SCIS, and 62 percent said they might call for themselves, while 85 percent said they would call for a friend or relative, if they were experiencing depression and/or suicidal ideas. Contrast these figures with the 3 percent who said they would use the community mental health center in a recent NIMH evaluation study (see Chapter III, p. 77). Of the cases actually handled, 72 percent neither threatened nor attempted suicide. Other problems presented included marriage, finance, parent-child relationship, pregnancy, physical-medical, personal inadequacy, and many others.

Given that the need for and use of the service is demonstrated, what does the crisis team actually do with its clients? The key to the service is described by McGee as active intervention on the spot and at follow-up. The orientation is to "act in every case so that the difference between that which is done and that which might be done is kept as small as possible." The actions are governed by what McGee terms a *four-phase model*, which is viewed as a process, rather than a set of single events.

Phase I—The Opening of a Case

This involves establishing communication, assessing the client's condition, and developing an action plan. The emphasis is on establishing early rapport, determining if the client is suicidal (they find this is usually not the case, but that it is frequent enough to be a major concern), and listening to determine the nature of the crisis. No label is attached, no "diagnosis" needed; rather, one looks for concrete resources required as well as existing strengths, and how to help the client to mobilize them. To accomplish this the center staff must maintain relationships with many of the resources and other agencies of the community, and sometimes referral to them will be sufficient. But follow-up to be sure they get there and are helped may also be be necessary. This may involve serving as an advocate for the client with the other agency. In other cases the crisis center worker himself may be able to pro-

vide the best service. They may need to contact and work with significant others, and all of the activities of the problem-solving and resource development model described in Chapter VI would be appropriate.

Phase II—The Management of the Case

Once a case is taken on by the crisis team the first step is to initiate a contract which details the expectations of the client and the worker. The emphasis is on confronting reality and finding resources to accomplish agreed-upon realistic goals. Guidelines include a heavy emphasis on avoiding dependency, and *never deny the person the use of whatever resources he or she already has*. Similarly, the process is viewed as a joint effort, through which client and worker move together, as rapidly as possible. The client is given clear expectations with regard to his role. The worker never manages the case alone. Rather, he or she helps the client to make use of all available resources, including actual and potential significant others. The emphasis is always to encourage a person to use his or her own resources and to avoid a bureaucratic agency where at all possible.

Phase III—The Closing of the Case

The closing of the case is done explicitly and initiated by the case worker who tells the client where he thinks things stand, and that follow-up will be provided. Similar contact is made with significant others and all agencies who have become involved.

Phase IV—The Follow-up

Clients must be recontacted to be sure the plan is working and to provide feedback to the program itself, so that it can change and improve. The SCIS program calls each client between six and eight weeks after closing a case. They find out (1) how the client is feeling in relation to the crisis that initiated contact; (2) what effect the crisis workers have had, from the client's view; (3) what other agencies' resources have been helpful; (4) how the client currently regards the crisis. Obviously special information will be required depending on the nature of the problem. In the SCIS experience almost all people appreciate the follow-up call that comes within two months of termination.

The heart of the SCIS program is what McGee calls the "CARE Team." This is usually two experienced volunteers who have begun as telephone workers. One is often more experienced and is training the other to be a team leader. The job is to go directly to the scene of a crisis and to provide direct and immediate assistance. The kinds of problems handled by the team are tabulated in Table IX-6. It can be seen that the services are wide ranging, but the aim is not to be imperialistic with regard to other agencies so much as useful and pertinent. This attitude is best expressed in McGee's words:

Every crisis center will find itself called upon to provide services which other agencies could provide better if they would. Where the other agencies in fact meet their responsibilities, the CARE Team role is to provide the contact between the client and the other service. Where there are no agencies to fill the need, the crisis center and the CARE Team are called upon to be imaginative, creative, and supportive. In the end, it is this first-hand, personal contact with the people in need which identifies the directions for the community to move in developing new services and restructuring existing ones (McGee, 1974, p. 253).

Although McGee discusses the importance of program evaluation in some detail and provides many suggestions about how to do it, as well as pointing out both the importance and the difficulty involved in knowing how effective a crisis center and each of its workers actually are, he provides, in his 1974 volume, little "outcome" data. At this point in time it might be agreed that the crisis center is clearly a feasible (implementable) alternative to the current mental health care system for acute problems in living. Although it may be more of a promise than a proven effective strategy, it is consistent with

TABLE IX-6.   **Examples of problems encountered by a crisis intervention team.***

Type of Problem Encountered	Frequency of problem occurrence in 250 sample cases	Percent
Marital problem	71	29.5
Other family problem	52	21.6
Chronic alcoholic	31	12.9
Drug abuse case	15	6.2
Welfare, basic support case	12	5.0
Need immediate food, lodging	12	5.0
Juvenile runaway	6	2.5
Legal, criminal problem	19	7.9
Transportation	11	4.6
Vocational problem	13	5.4
Student, school adjustment	8	3.3
Homosexual problem	2	0.8
Acute psychotic	17	7.1
Personal loneliness, alienation	84	34.9
Milirary, draft problem	3	1.2
Medical attention needed	29	12.0
Other	46	19.1
Total number of different problems among the 250 cases	431	**

*Adapted from McGee, 1974
**Percentages total greater than 100 because in most cases multiple problems are encountered in each contact.

the environmental resources conception of community psychology presented in this volume, and in that sense it provides a specific example of new directions in the mental health system. Bloom (1973) has recently suggested that the efficiency of such an approach (as compared to the amount of time spent in waiting for help, in long-term therapy, and for the large numbers of professionals required for psychotherapy) combined with research demonstrating that brief treatment is at least *no worse* than traditional psychotherapy, suggests that it is a viable direction for the future. Pittman, DeYoung, & Kalman (1966) have reported on the use of crisis intervention in family treatment with professional rather than nonprofessional crisis intervention workers and found that they were able to keep people out of the psychiatric hospital; while a control group (every other call) who requested but were not treated by the on-the-spot crisis approach averaged 26.1 days in the hospital. Huessy (1972) has argued that in his experience of crisis consultation to physicians in rural areas many of the acute cases "disappeared overnight," even when they were expected to require long-term care.

A recent report by Delaney, Seidman, and Willis (1977) also provides important evidence for the effectiveness of crisis intervention as a method for keeping people out of the custodial state hospital known to be detrimental to their future well-being. These authors describe a program, evaluated over a period of several years, which is considerably more modest than the one described by McGee, but which demonstrates how a change at the level of social policy may have wide-ranging effects on many people, while actually saving, rather than spending scarce resources.

Working in a geographical area of some 200,000 people, a crisis team consisting of two people (neither with an advanced degree in a mental health profession) established relationships with the major local sources of referral to the state mental health system. They made themselves available within 24 hours to visit, at the site of the problem (e.g., in a jail, in the home of an isolated person, in a bar, or any-

where else) all persons for whom hospitalization was being considered. They attempted to help the person and the family, if one was involved, to deal with the immediate crisis, or to refer to some other appropriate community resource. In all cases they attempted to use state hospitalization only as a last resort. They were aided in this by the willingness of a local general hospital to accept acutely distrubed patients for several days, during which time they could formulate plans for the future. In many cases they found that no mental health agency was required to solve the problem.

By comparing the number of state hospital admissions in their geographical area for a period of one and one-half years prior to the onset of the activity of the crisis intervention team with an equal amount of time following onset, they found a statistically significant decrease in the use of state hospitalization.

Because the state in which they work (Illinois) also has a series of residential hospitals that provides treatment for each geographical area independent of the state hospital, the authors also evaluated the use of the residential hospital in their area during the same time span to check for the possibility that they had simply shifted patients to other hospitals. They found no such increase in the use of this other hospital, despite the reduction in the use of the state hospital. In addition, they examined the number of state hospital admissions in a demographically comparable geographical area near their own and found no reduction during the same time period. It seems safe to conclude from this research that the wise use of a small number of people can help to redirect the tendency of our mental health system to confine those with problems in living. Finally, the authors also present data indicating that the state actually saved money by its reduced use of hospitalization.

Before concluding this section it must be recalled that what is suggested here is more than the application of "crisis theory" to the treatment of individuals, or the use of nonmedical experts in problem solving and developing human resources. These suggestions for change at the individual and organizational level are viewed as only part of a larger reorientation of the entire mental health system at the institutional level. The important innovations must come from changes at the institutional level so as to view problems in living from an entirely new perspective. Further implications of the perspective are developed below.

The Community Mental Health Center versus the Human Resources Center: Putting Mental Health in Perspective

It should be clear at this point that the role suggested for the community mental health center is one of reduced, rather than increased, responsibility. It is perhaps ironic that the community psychology movement may bring us full circle to the conclusion that the community members themselves, rather than the mental health professionals, are responsible for the well-being of their fellows. In this sense, the community mental health center may have a legitimate role to play as *one resource* for a local community, but not necessarily as a decision maker and/or organizer of that community. It serves the same function as any community resource—to be mobilized at the request of the clients; not to be monolithic, as in the therapeutic state. The idea of mental health needs to be put back into perspective as only one telescope through which to view people.

Such a perspective has several implications for the community mental health movement. The most apparent is one that is likely to be well received by the many traditional professionals who staff such centers. The message is: "You are *not* responsible for all the elements of life and well-being necessary to your clients. Indeed, you are only relevant when requested, and for limited functions at that." At first this may sound like a step backward to the days of elite services and "benign neglect." However, the implications of this position go much further when it is understood in the context of an environmental resources and social advocacy program.

Decreased responsibility also means limited utility, limited resources, and redistribution of them. It requires a social policy for the allocation of financial resources to all community services on the basis of their evaluation by the local community, defined as the residents of a given geographical area. The nature of such services must not be imposed upon them. Although for some communities traditional mental health services may be viewed as quite useful, for others such services may be low on their priority list. It is somewhat ironic that a poor minority community, suffering from unemployment, poor housing, and poor schools, can often only justify funds for "services" if they are administered by the welfare or mental health systems through one of the existing centers and sets of professionals. This tendency to provide imposed services, rather than access to environmental resources for enhancement of existing community strengths, may in part be a function of the lack of alternative structures to deliver resources, not because the welfare or the mental health systems are appropriate. Instead of expecting each community to have a community mental health center, it might make more sense to have each community provided with funds for an *environmental resources center*. Such centers (which need not necessarily be buildings so much as people, money, and local control) could be entirely different from place to place, depending on the nature of the community and the desires of its membership.

Funds from the current mental health system budget should not be considered as inviolate. Instead of allowing the mental health system (this holds for the welfare and education systems too) to hold private monopoly on use of available human and financial resources, it is suggested that the state legislatures and the federal government adopt a human resources budget, on a per capita basis, with a geographic breakdown of their state at the neighborhood level. Each neighborhood would then be allocated a human services budget, free to determine the nature of its own use of resources. Some might wish psychotherapy to be the major service; others might prefer to keep psychotherapy as a small enterprise and put the bulk of their funds into crisis intervention teams as described above; others might prefer employment programs or a corporation to help neighborhood economic development. Each service proposed would be directly accountable to the neighborhood and in competition for what is always a limited pie.

This competition is currently the case, but its outcome is now determined by mental health and social welfare professionals who provide services they happen to like or be trained for. An alternative is to let the content of services be determined by the local people themselves. Consistent with the value position described in Chapter I, this view would provide resources but not control.

Denner and Price (1973) have recently made a similar analysis and proposal. They have argued that a community mental health center may have various "ideologies" ranging on a continuum from individual freedom to social control, and suggest that there are potentially many community governing bodies with varying positions on the continuum. How a given community mental health center will interact with its local residents will depend in part on its ideology. Current social policy allows the selection of the center's orientation to be totally determined by the professionals who operate the center. Although "community control" is verbalized, in fact it is rarely a reality (see Chapter III, p. 78). There is an implicit assumption that professionals have expertise, skills, and useful services. Only they can determine what should be provided. Administratively, money goes to the mental health professionals and administrators who determine what will be done on the basis of their professional authority. As Denner and Price put it:

Difficulties arise in those areas of the country where, because of a variety of social factors, local people do not share the values . . . . Yet it was the unmet needs of these people that were used to justify launching an expensive and elaborate mental health program. . . . Did middle-class researchers stimulate interest in mental health by documenting the high rates of mental illness in the deteriorated communities only to obtain federal funds to better the lot of the middle class? . . . *The current community mental health program may benefit only the middle-class client because the model upon which this program is based introduces ethnic and cultural differences as an afterthought. Alternative models for community intervention that would be acceptable to different peoples need to be explored* (1973, p. 357, italics added).

Denner and Price have proposed, as examples rather than as the only alternatives, four

different kinds of community mental health centers that are not necessarily mutually exclusive.

1. *The traditional center.* Here concern is with intrapsychic problems. People voluntarily come for therapy because they are unhappy with their personal adjustment. Children, acute psychotics, and criminals may be referred by others. Services are diagnostic and therapeutic, with some consultation to schools. Policy is set by the professional staff and citizens are "advisory."

2. *The environmentally oriented center.* Individuals come here for help with personal problems, but are not diagnosed or given traditional psychotherapy. The emphasis is on crisis intervention. The center staff may serve as advocates for individuals. Policy is determined by professionals, but with a "strong" advisory board of community leaders.

3. *The social action center.* Emphasis is on social problems such as drug addition, crime, poverty, and racism. Staff may come into conflict with authority and established agencies of social control, when necessary. Policy is set by a local citizens' group who may even hire the staff. The first such program to function as such a community mental health center was the Lincoln Hospital Center in the South Bronx. It organized tenant councils, voter registration, storefront services, and developed the first extensive program using indigenous nonprofessionals (Reissman, 1967; Roman, 1973, see also below).

4. *The growth center.* Emphasis is on communication and small-group experiences. Citizens may serve as a vehicle for various community groups to interact and openly talk. Public education, improvement of self, and community understanding are emphasized.

These four alternatives are only a few of the large number possible, and any community may be able to use multiple models, depending on its priorities. The point is that each community would determine its own use of resources. Although this idea is consistent with what is proposed here, Denner and Price do not discuss the kind of *institutional change* or social policy implications necessary to implement the plan. They suggest that these multiple kinds of centers would be community mental health centers. Clearly, given the existing legal sanction for such centers this is a feasible social policy. However, so long as such centers are considered to be primarily concerned with "mental health" and administered by the professional mental health establishment, it is unlikely that they will effectively respond to the diversity of multiple communities. Rather, such a policy may only be workable when the centers are considered *environmental resource centers* whose nature is to be determined by local neighborhood residents. They must be directly given the funds and the power to hire and set local policy. They may choose to hire nonprofessionals, community organizers, urban planners, lawyers, physicians, social workers, or whomever they determine can help them to accomplish the best use of their resources. *As long as such centers are placed under the control of a given profession, rather than a community, they will serve more to advance the well-being of that profession than of that community.*

Some objections to this plan can be anticipated. Is the plan proposed as a panacea for all human needs? What would stop a community from "unwisely" spending its money and not fulfilling its genuine human needs? How could it be administered? To begin, it must be understood that the human resources center is *not* expected to be a panacea. The plan is proposed as an alternative to the current system in which all program decisions are made by professional care-givers. Currently, as is clear from the preceding chapters of this book, the system of professional care-givers fails to serve equitably. This plan is offered not as one which would solve all problems, but as one in which the *relative equity* of the system would be increased.

At the core of a preference for the existing rules of the game, or these newly proposed rules, lies the question, "Who do you trust—the professionals or the people?" To answer "the people" does not mean that expertise in particular skills is to be denied. It does mean that the people themselves may be the appropriate judge of what skills they are willing to pay for. Such a

system would be founded on two basic American priciples: democratic neighborhood control and competition. By allocating to neighborhoods, on a per capita basis, funds for human resources, each neighborhood would have equal access to resources. Next, those who would offer services or plans for use of the resources would need to publicly present their ideas to that neighborhood; by means of the election process each neighborhood could determine the nature of its use of monies. If a service is not provided in one's neighborhood, but one feels a need for it, everyone would have the right to go to the neighborhood where it is offered. However, that neighborhood would, the next year, be granted some or all of that person's per capita share of money. If enough people in a neighborhood used services outside their locality, the neighborhood would lose its own funds. For a given neighborhood to maintain its programs it must appeal to a sufficient number of people. In essence, programs would be in competition for useful services as defined by the local people.

What would constitute a legitimate use of human resources funds? This would be determined by the vote of the local people. Some communities may decide to use the funds for social action programs, others for psychotherapy, others for recreation centers, still others for crisis centers. Some neighborhoods might collaborate with others for increased diversity. Over time, competition for useful services would distribute funds on the basis of their utility as measured by use. Perhaps every four years, people could vote to retain or change existing services or uses for their human resources budget. It might be possible either to vote for representatives who would serve as policy makers on a board, or to actually take a direct vote on preferred services.[12] New plans would need to compete

---

[12]It is recognized that true neighborhood control may be inefficient in the sense of possible duplication of services. However, such duplication could be resolved as programs develop and neighborhoods learn to cooperate and support one another. Early duplication and inefficiency may be the price to pay for true representation. This strategy is essentially the autonomous alternative settings model, based on the strengths and decision making of local communities (see Chapters V and VI).

with existing ones, but in an open appeal to those whom the plan is supposed to benefit, not to the professionals. Professionals, or others, would be hired by the community to provide the services the people elected to have.

The "Failure" of Past Efforts at Community Control

Unlike what has been proposed above, the efforts at community control of mental health centers have heretofore largely been interpreted to mean control by people in lower socioeconomic communities of the services provided by the local mental health center. Generally, it is assumed that the middle-class residents already have a say in, and are satisfied with, their local services. This may be more myth than reality, and the suggestions for community control described in this chapter have been intended to apply to *all* neighborhoods. However, almost all of our current experience with local control of mental health centers comes from observing efforts to involve the poor. Consequently, we focus here on what can be learned from this (somewhat limited) experience.[13]

The earliest program that tried to deal with the issue of community control was established at the Lincoln Hospital Community Mental Health Center, in New York City (Riessman, 1967; Roman, 1973). It was also one of the first to experience the disruption, confusion, and misunderstanding inevitable in treading new ground. Such experiences must be risked if we are to learn new ways, rather than to retreat to old ways for fear of failure. In this respect the Lincoln Hospital program deserves credit as well as criticism. Roman (1973) has presented a candid analysis of the problems that developed

---

[13]Although some states (e.g., Illinois) have used a plan which has a local board make some allocation of funds decisions, these boards tend to be dominated and selected by existing professional interests, and the boards are usually not directly accountable to the citizens. In addition, the boards tend to represent (well or poorly) very large geographical areas, such as an entire county, rather than more homogenous neighborhoods. Finally, the only alternatives permitted are those of a "mental health" nature. What has been proposed here is a wider choice of human services.

at Lincoln Hospital. Although the program initially established a reputation for community service by hiring large numbers of indigenous nonprofessional Black and Puerto Rican residents as direct service deliverers, it is clear from Roman's description that it never established a base of consumer support and consensus in its community. Rather, the nonprofessionals were expected to serve in two roles—as both expert staff and as "representatives" of their community. At the same time, although "community control" was talked about, all decisions were actually under the authority of middle-class professionals who administered the program. The conflicts that eventually led to the demise of this program were oriented around the role of the nonprofessional staff in the program's decision-making process. They were not a function of the failure of community control to lead to viable programs because such community control never existed. Indeed, alienation of the local community was one source of its failure.

Rather than being based on true community control, select indigenous nonprofessional community workers were hired, supposedly because they were experts on their community's needs and how to serve them. They actually "represented" no one but themselves. The Lincoln Hospital program was based on a "community control" model which emphasized supposed technical expertise of the indigenous nonprofessionals because they supposedly possessed the skills to work effectively and directly with people in their own communities. This may be a useful clinical technique, but there was no attempt at *institutional change* in the sense of a change in the source of legitimacy for decision making. This legitimacy was retained by the professionals and administrators. Community residents had no say in determining the goals of the programs offered.

What followed is instructive. The nonprofessional staff, after several years of being told about their value to the center, combined with their lack of say with regard to administrative decision making and program policies, and the absence of sufficient space and money to meet their own personal and professional aims, ultimately revolted. Since they were removed from financial decision making and program planning, they, not surprisingly, developed feelings of resentment. The nonprofessionals' resentment, combined with resentment among the other community residents who were not part of the system at all, other than as consumers with no where else to go, led to strikes, building takeovers, and the ultimate demise of the program. Too late attempts to establish a community advisory board were followed by its decisions being vetoed by the program's higher administrators. In essence, they "initiated the program without organized and coherent community support and sponsorship" (Roman, 1973).

Zax and Specter (1974) have provided an excellent summary of the problems at Lincoln Hospital as well as several other reports of community control efforts (Salber, 1970; Tischler, 1971). Among the analyses they review is Panzetta's (1971), developed out of his experience with the Temple University Community Mental Health Center in Philadelphia. In Panzetta's view community representatives will always necessarily represent a special interest group rather than "the community." This view of community representatives seems to stem in part from a belief that those who are community leaders tend to be "pathological" or "paranoid" when they disagree with professionals (cf. Hersch, 1972), or from a failure of professionals to believe that democracy can work. "Communities rarely develop representatives who can speak authoritatively for the group as a whole" (Zax & Specter, 1974). The same, of course, could be said about our elected government officials, but what we try to do in that realm, given our traditions, is to improve representation, not withdraw it as unworkable. In mental health programs our traditions have been authoritatian rather than democratic. The "representatives" to "community advisory boards" have usually been self-selected or appointed by the mental health professionals, not elected. They are then criticized for being unrepresentative. In fact, there has never been any real attempt to make such boards representative. In Philadelphia (Panzetta, 1971; Kellman, Branch, Agrawal, & Grabill, 1972), the attempt at an

electoral process has led to domination by the existing political machine, small voter turnout, and loss of true neighborhood control. Such problems, however, are not solvable by giving up on democracy. They require true institutional reforms that might even serve as models for the larger political sphere. However, such difficulties have instead been met by withdrawal. In part, this is because if they really were elected by neighborhoods, the board's power over professional employees would be considerable. More subtle, but also more important, the source of authority would be legitimized from the people rather than from the professionals, and this would be genuine institutional change (cf. Walton's analysis, Chapter VI, p. 179).

Panzetta has suggested that rather than as a representative, the role of the community resident should be as a consumer. He argues, and Zax and Specter seem to agree, that a mental health center should define for itself its goals and aims, within a realistic analysis of the skills of its workers. They should only offer what they know how to do and feel comfortable doing. This should be followed by the offer of their services to the consumers, and if they use the service, then that is considered justification for its programs. Nonprofessionals should be used as workers, and not as community representatives. Although such suggestions are sensible, they unfortunately go only halfway. Certainly consumer use is a valid criterion by which to evaluate a service (see the preceding section). However, it is only a valid criterion if there is also consumer *choice*. If the mental health center get its funds directly, and is not forced to compete with other services, then the community has no choice but to take whatever it can get. Consumer use is not a valid criterion in a monopolistic system. To argue that it is would be similar to telling people that because they now use the present telephone system it must be the best one possible. Currently the programs proposed for a community are always sanctioned by the professional mental health establishment, rather than by the consumers. When new programs replace older ones it is on the basis of professional, not consumer, choice. In this way a monopoly is effectively maintained. (See Graziano's [1969] report, and Chapter II, p. 34.)[14]

There have been some reports of positive experience with community control. One example is the Woodlawn Community Mental Health Center, located in an urban Black neighborhood on the South Side of Chicago. Although the Woodlawn experience is not a perfect model, there are some clear differences in the way its leaders interpreted community control and the way it was interpreted at Lincoln Hospital. The differences have been well described by Schiff (1970) and the accomplishments of the program with particular regard to parent involvement in the schools and preparation of young children for first grade have also been described (Kellam, Branch, Agrawal, & Grabill, 1972; Schiff, 1972). The effectiveness of the center as a service agency appears to be no worse, and probably better than that of most community mental health centers in similar neighborhoods. Its community control orientation has not led to the demise of the programs; rather it has helped to spread them throughout the community. Schiff attributes this to three characteristics: (1) clearly defined mutual responsibility between professionals and community representatives, (2) the nature of the professionals' institutional base, and (3) the clear role of the professional and the nonprofessional.

From the outset the Woodlawn center developed a community advisory board of 25 citizens selcted from the leadership of existing community organizations. Although not an electoral process, this procedure, in this case, did seem to generate considerable community support, in part because the center worked closely with the other organizations and because the board members each already had a large, well-organized constituency whom they represented. The area represented included some 81,000 people and is far too large a group to be considered an instance of neighborhood control. Nor did the board have the option of considering other than mental health services. Nevertheless, the relationship between the center professionals

and this advisory board did capture the essence of true community control.

Although this board was only advisory, from the outset the professionals agreed that the board would have to provide community sanction and play a central role in all programs planned for the use of its community's resources. Later a constitution was framed giving the community board formal powers to advise and consent. The difference between this and the Lincoln Hospital program is clear. At Lincoln Hospital the nonprofessional worker was in an ambiguous role, with no power, yet he was supposed to "represent" his community. Equally important, the Woodlawn center made a "deliberate decision" to be funded by the local public health system, rather than by outside grants. Later, all grants sought were for specific programs requested by the community board. The board also had the right to review all work that would be published. Equally important differences between Lincoln Hospital and Woodlawn include the fact that nonprofessional skills at Woodlawn were placed in a perspective of mutual collaboration and expertise, rather than oversold and later rejected. In essence, the strengths of both professionals and nonprofessionals were emphasized. The nonprofessionals at Woodlawn were not expected to represent anyone. Rather, they were hired as staff.

Community Control and Errors of Logical Typing: Accountability versus Technical Skills

From the previous section it should be clear that the community mental health movement has had some, although very limited, experience with community control. Nowhere has it been instituted in the total sense suggested here, and for the foreseeable future it is unlikely to come about if left to the discretion of the mental health establishment. So long as tax monies are provided by states and the federal government to the professionals who are allowed to determine which services they choose to provide, they are unlikely to yield to genuine community control. The problem is reminiscent of leaving schools in

[14]See also Karno and Schwartz (1974) for a discussion of some of these issues.

the hands of the educational establishment rather than the local consumers of their services. Although community control in the sense described here (as a change at the institutional level) has not been attempted, there have been some limited attempts at organizational change in individual mental health centers. The results of such efforts have at best been "mixed," and a great number of problems have been confronted. Unfortunately, in each of these programs the underlying *institutional rules of the game had not been changed*, so that when "pushed to the wall" the real power still was vested in the professionals and the programs were still "mental health" rather than human resources more broadly conceived. In some measure this predoomed such programs to failure. It is only when true control (of money and decision making) is given to local people who are the consumers that a fair test of community control can be obtained. What has happened thus far has been a halfway measure. Some individual centers, on the basis of their own decision to include community residents, have "allowed" some of them to participate. This is referred power, not true power. It exists only at the pleasure of the professionals. What really may be needed is the reverse. Professionals should have control only at the pleasure of the community. Nevertheless, some things can be learned even from these halfway attempts to allow community input.

First, it is important to distinguish between control in the sense of *accountability*, which requires an institutional change, and control in the sense of *technical expertise*, which requires an organizational and individual level of analysis. The failure to keep these very different levels of analysis separate has led to much confusion and misunderstanding.

The need for community control derived from an institutional analysis, and operationalized as accountability, has been described best by Schiff (1970). It means that local citizen-consumers are the judge of what services should be offered, toward what ends, and ultimately of how effective they are. It does *not* mean that services are administered by people who are untrained or lack the necessary skills

but are given control simply because they live in the community or are the right race or ethnic background. For example, if services for employment training are seen as necessary, then people who have the technical skills should be hired. Likewise, if services to assist children in adapting to school are given priority by the local citizens, then they should hire people, professional and nonprofessional, who have the technical skills to provide such services. Usefulness of the program would be judged by its effects as viewed by the consumers. Community control as accountability does not necessarily infer that local people run the service, but that experts are employees of the local people who are the consumers. They may decide to hire local residents for some jobs (e.g., as community organizers or as crisis problem solvers) and professionals for others (e.g., to help evaluate the services, to do psychotherapy, or to train local people in problem-solving skills). The management of the programs likewise would be turned over to employees who have such skills. However, the consumers would judge effectiveness and decide on continuation of the service, expansion, or reorientation of the policy and programs. One does not need to know how to help others resolve a crisis to be able to decide that that is a worthwhile service and to later evaluate if it has been helpful to one's community. Voters do not need to run the government themselves in order to vote for the kind of leadership and policies they want established. This is community control as accountability. It has never been fully tested.

Because the changes called community control have been at the organizational, rather than at the institutional level, and confined to "mental health," the sources of the problems with programs of so-called community control have been organizational ones. The usual procedure has been either to hire community residents, or to establish a community (usually "advisory") board of directors, or both. Who should serve on the board, how they should be selected, and what power they should have have been the major preoccupations. This has led to a great deal of concern about program administration and very little attention as to whether the institutional problem was really solved. Careful analysis reveals that the attempts have been to solve an institutional problem by means of an organizational intervention. This *error of logical typing* has led to more problems than solutions.

The institutional problem is that services controlled by the mental health establishment are inequitably distributed and often irrelevant to poor and minority neighborhoods. This is because the bias of the system is toward a middle-class professional ideology which suggests that experts are not only technically competent, but also have the right, by virtue of their technical skills, to select the values and goals appropriate for their clients, and to decide on the basis of their own desires, what services to offer to whom. To solve this problem, *the institutional bias must be changed*, such that the goals, priorities, services, and resources offered are those requested by the consumers in a given neighborhood and are continually evaluated by them.

The problem of technical expertise, or how the goal gets accomplished, is a totally separate issue, not to be confused with priorities. One democratic way to solve the institutional problem is to provide each neighborhood with decision-making authority by means of a neighborhood electoral process in which everyone of age in that specific neighborhood has a vote. Proposals could be offered and voted on directly or representatives to a decision-making body, akin to a city government but at the neighborhood level, could be elected by the consumers. They would then represent the community as a decision-making body and would, in turn, hire professionals and non-professionals to provide the services and technical expertise their community desires. They would not run the program so much as to be sure that it remained oriented in the desired direction and provided the expected services. Such a plan was described above.

Whether or not one agrees that this is a good *strategy* for institutional change, it is imperative to keep in mind that the problem itself is basically an institutional one. To date, programs that have voiced community control have only applied organizational level solutions. Some of these solutions look, *on the surface*, to be similar to the one proposed here, but with rare exceptions, this is *not* the case. Rather, they turn out to be organizational solutions which mask the fact that the institutional bias remains unchanged. In short, they are apparent innovation without change, or first-order rather than second-order change, in the sense discussed in Chapter V.

If the problem is more equitable distribution of resources that are deemed *differentially relevant* by diverse communities, then the solution cannot be found by creating "new" programs *selected by professionals,* however apparently responsive they are to what the people desire. Rather, the task is to really let the people consider and vote on alternatives. It clearly requires an institutional bias that expresses a faith in the ultimate authority of the people rather than the professionals, and a faith in the strengths and abilities of people to be self-determined. If people who are offered a chance to make such decisions do not vote, or make "unwise" choices, then the problem is how to provide them with a system that they can believe is really responsive to them, not how to better run a benign dictatorship. It is apparent from the review of expectation, alienation, learned helplessness, and locus of control studies (Chapter IV) that people will not respond to a democratic system until they have reason to believe that they do have control over its outcomes. The development of such beliefs, based on real changes in our social institutions, can start in the health, education, and welfare domain only if professionals are willing to attempt true second-order changes. This is not an area where social scientists can retreat to the plea that they have no control over the system. Rather, they have almost total control, and could, if they were willing to forego vested interests, elitism, and the aggrandizement of knowledge in favor of democratic development of community strengths, help to create tremendous social change. Both those involved in Lincoln Hospital and Woodlawn seem to understand this:

The difficulties encountered at Lincoln are to be anticipated in all similarly innovative community based programs. The central point is that *community control is both the problem and the answer*. Power to the people translated into workable and effective models of control can and must be developed . . . they often involve entrenched institutions unwilling to relinquish power . . . nevertheless transfer of power is essential (Roman, 1973, pp. 283–284, italics in original).

There have been a number of reports describing the failure of community action programs. Some have revealed a disturbing pessimism about the ability of poor communities to effectively alter their own condition. Few of these reports address themselves to sources of failure other than the community citizens. Culpability for these failures must also be assessed in light of the problems presented by local government, agency professionals, and in the private sector, the role of the university and the large foundations (Schiff, 1970, p. 212).

The Community Psychologist as Consultant: Notes on Mental Health Consultation and "Mr. Everyman"

The community psychologist as consultant may engage in a wide variety of activities. Following the logic of this volume, with its emphasis on development of community strengths, environmental resources, advocacy and ecological conceptions, it would be reasonable to suggest that *many different kinds of consultation to various community groups is the major role of the community psychologist*. Rather than view consultation as a special set of techniques with a delimited content, most of the strategies and tactics discussed in this book, involving the professional as a resource for various constituencies, could be reconceptualized as methods of consultation. In this sense, the exact nature of consultation might be viewed as dictated by a pragmatic approach in which the consultant uses whatever social skills, ideas, problem-solving ability, knowledge, or experience he or she has to assist in achieving the pragmatic aims of the consultee. This view does not limit consultation to any identifiable set of specific principles or methods (Raine, 1975). The closest this view comes to specifying "technique" is the multiple strategy-environmental resources and problem-

solving approach to advocacy as discussed in Chapter VI. Who is consulted, the level of intervention, what is done, the goals and outcomes, and the criteria for success or failure, are all a function of a given community psychologist's use of whatever skills can be mustered to deal with a particular set of circumstances. Viewed in this way the strategies and tactics of community intervention discussed in Chapter VI may all be variants of consultation.

However, *mental health* consultation per se has taken on a rather specific and delimited meaning in the jargon of the mental health system. Consultation is much more narrowly conceived; there are a number of views that have specified its meaning.

Bloom (1973) has suggested that mental health consultation should be differentiated from other professional mental health activities. He describes it as different from supervision, in that the consultant may be from a different profession than the consultee, and usually has no direct organizational power nor administrative responsibility for the work. Consultation is often irregular in character, not continuous. He distinguishes it from formal education because the consultee has freedom to accept or reject the consultant's ideas; there is usually no specific curriculum, and no evaluative grading. The goal of consultation is improved work rather than improved personal adjustment, as in psychotherapy, and the relationship is more of a peer than a confidant. Finally, Bloom suggests that consultation is different from collaboration because there is no implication that the consultant will participate in the implementation of plans. Consistent with this reasoning is the definition adopted by the U.S. Department of Health, Education, and Welfare:

Mental health consultation is the provision of technical assistance by an expert to individual and agency caregivers related to the mental health dimensions of their work. Such assistance is directed to specific work-related problems, is advisory in nature, and the consultant has no direct responsibility for its acceptance and implementation. Consultation is offered by a mental health specialist either to other mental health workers less knowledgeable in some aspect of mental health, or to specialists in other fields who need assistance in the management of mental health and human relations problems (MacLennan, Quinn, & Schroeder, 1971, p. 3).

Papers and monographs about mental health consultation are legion. The most recent reference guide published by the Department of Health, Education, and Welfare (Mannino & Robinson, 1975) includes over 1100 references classified by profession, setting, form, role, process, planning, training, and evaluation. It includes papers, books, films, and tapes. Most of these references are other than research evaluations. However, Mannino and Shore (1975), who have been periodic chroniclers of consultation research, have most recently updated their review to include 35 outcome studies published between 1958 and 1972. Although they find that in 69 percent of the reports positive change in the consultee, client, or system is found, the studies are of variable quality, and the most frequent effects are on the consultee. Only two (of the four reviewed) report a measurable change at the systems level. Bloom has suggested that such consultee satisfaction may be more related to the process or style of consultation than to the outcome or competence of the consultant in accomplishing specific mental health goals. As he points out, evaluation of consultation is ultimately dependent on the objectives of the program. If mental health consultation is to be, as it was envisioned by the community mental health movement, a technique to prevent mental illness, then it must be demonstrated to do that. In this sense then, the effectiveness of (mental health) consultation has not yet been documented (Bloom, 1973).

Beyond distinguishing between individual and group consultation, perhaps the most popular view of mental health consultation is Gerald Caplan's (1970). Based on his notion of preventive psychiatry (see Chapter III), he has described four types of consultation by mental health professionals:

1. *Client-centered case consultation* is focused on assisting an individual client to cope with a current problem situation. This may involve helping the consultee to learn to deal with similar problems in the future, but that is a secondary goal. The focus is on a particular case and its resolution. For example, helping a teacher deal with a behavior problem child.

2. *Consultee-centered case consultation* is aimed at assisting the consultee to develop skills that will be useful for future cases. Here the consultant helps the consultee to acquire new abilities or overcome skill deficits that interfere with his or her work. For example, teaching a teacher how to reinforce positive and ignore disruptive behavior in the classroom.

3. *Program-centered administrative consultation.* Here the consultant helps to deal with the administration of a particular program. For example, if a school has a program for early detection of adjustment problems, the consultant may help to select the screening devices and plan treatment procedures.

4. *Consultee-centered administrative consultation.* In this form the consultant is trying to help the consultee become a better administrator. As with consultee-centered case consultation, the aim is to develop skills useful for the future. Techniques such as enhancing communication skills by means of T-groups and organization development tactics may be used.

Each of the above types of consultation is expressly aimed at enhancing the mental health of the consultee's clients, students, or employees. Emphasis is on individual and small-group behavior, and assistance to the agents of socialization. As Altrocchi has recently observed: "although consultants may push for change in certain ways, mental health consultation is usually oriented more toward conserving rather than changing the status quo of consultee's institutions and of society" (1972, p. 506). Nevertheless, if the role of consultation to individuals and small groups were combined with the organizational and institutional level aims and strategies suggested in this chapter, the consultant might benefit from a careful thinking through of the process of consultation. Altrocchi (1972) has described what he views as that process in the form of techniques and phases of consultation, and his analysis may be useful in this context. If consultation is a social influence process, the same techniques and phases may apply regardless of the goals. For example, a consultant to a nonprofessionally administered crisis center, or to any autonomous setting, might use many of the techniques and pass through the phases listed below. In this sense, Altrocchi's analysis could have been considered in Chapter VI as a set of tactics for social change at the individual and small-group level. Instead, it is presented here because the analysis and use of such techniques have most often been tied to more strictly mental health rather than social change aims.

A general principle of consultation emphasized in Altrocchi's (1972) review is that rather than "doing," the consultant should teach others to do. He suggests several *techniques* of mental health consultation:

1. Establishing and maintaining a consultation relationship
   a. Preparing the ground for consultation. This involves getting to know the consultees, their motives for working with you, and formulating a mutually agreed upon contract.
   b. Confidentiality is necessarily an important element, to be agreed upon early, especially when the consultant is working within an organization and runs the risk of being viewed as a "company spy."
   c. Establishing the relationship involves, in this view, a mutual learning atmosphere, respect for the consultees' competence, sensitivity to consultees' anxieties, acceptance of them as people, and warmth and openness. In short, the consultant needs to have excellent social as well as technical skills.
   d. Offering support for the problems of the consultees.
2. Defining the problem
   a. Gathering information. Here the use of questions that enable the consultant to better understand the situation is crucial.
   b. Listening carefully.

c. Asking the consultees to define or redefine the problem.
3. Searching for alternative actions
   a. Reviewing previous actions.
   b. Formulating alternative actions.
   c. Facilitating communication between consultees.
   d. Reducing and sharing anxiety.
   e. Focusing on group process. For many consultants, understanding group process and dynamics is the key to improving communication and problem solving of the members.
4. Dealing with affect in the consultees

Altrocchi discusses several psychotherapeutically derived techniques for dealing with the anger, anxiety, guilt, and other expected emotional involvements in consultation to individuals and groups. In this view, the consultant who deals with people, regardless of the goals of consultation, needs to be interpersonally sensitive and trained in clinical techniques.

He also posits the notion that all consultation will pass through both within-session and between-session phases. These phases are described as:

1. *The entry or preparatory phase.* This phase will involve different problems depending on whether the consultant is invited by the group, self-invited, or asked in by a supervisor. In any case, the clarification of a contractual relationship is crucial.
2. *The beginning or warming-up phase.* Here the techniques of establishing a working relationship are emphasized, together with the problem definition techniques (see above).
3. *The alternative actions phase.* This is viewed as the "heart of consultation." The key is to help the consultees arrive at well thought-out solutions using both your skills and knowledge as well as theirs, and to teach a problem-solving process useful in the future.
4. *Termination.* This should involve mutual agreement that consultation is no longer needed, or that a new contract should be negotiated if the previous aims have been met.

Rather than *limit* the role of the community psychologist to the use of a special list of techniques or mental health consultation, it is suggested here that by relying on the conceptions, strategies, and tactics detailed in Chapters V and VI, the community psychologist may be most useful as a social advocate, problem solver, and developer of environmental resources. Although he or she *may* use the techniques suggested above as a behavioral scientist, rather than as a mental health worker, one can make one's self available to many different groups who would potentially benefit from collaboration in accomplishing social change, whether regarded as "mental health" or not. As suggested earlier, the activities of such a consultant would only be limited by his or her imagination, social skills, knowledge, and problem-solving ability. In this sense the position of Seymour Sarason, presented to a recent conference on training in community psychology, and later published in *The American Psychologist* is very close to the one suggested here:

In concluding this paper I would like to deal with a criticism directed at my position by a student. Paraphrasing his remarks: "The way you describe a community psychologist he is remarkably similar to a lot of people in the community. Policemen, organized criminal syndicates, politicians, businessmen, fund raisers, and Mr. Joe Blow himself—all of them would say that what you are describing is a person with common sense who has lived in the real world and has tried to get something done. They will all tell you that you have to get to the right people, you have to learn who the right people are, and that you have to know the territory like the guy in The Music Man said. They would also agree with your critisism of professionals who screw things up when they want to do good in the community. What, they would say, do these professional do-gooders and bleeding hearts know about life in the real world? I would not be surprised if they looked on what you have said as another glimpse of the obvious described by another academic who does not know the difference between common and uncommon sense." The remarks bothered me because there was a part of me that was ready to agree with my critic, and yet, if I agreed, if only in part, I felt that the strength of my position would be considerably weakened. Besides, even if I was convinced he was wrong, I was not convinced by my reply to him, and, of course, neither was he. Reflection, if not candor,

forced me later to realize that what bothered me was the illness of professional preciousness. I wanted a community psychologist to be a distinctive and, perhaps, unique kind of person and, therefore, I was not going to look kindly at a criticism which said that far from being distinctive the community psychologist was like a lot of other people. That thought forced me to go back and read Carl Becker's 1931 presidential address to the American Historical Association. The title of his address was: *Every Man His Own Historian*. In his paper—which I would make mandatory for anyone pretending to seek a liberal (liberating) education—Becker shows the communalities between Mr. Everyman (today it would be Mr. Everyperson) and the professional historian. I cannot present here Becker's arguments—it defies brief summary. But this quotation will give you the aroma if not the taste of the intellectual dish he serves.

"If the essence of history is the memory of things said and done, then it is obvious that every normal person, Mr. Everyman, knows some history. Of course we do what we can to conceal this invidious truth. Assuming a professional manner, we say that so and so knows no history, when we mean no more than that he failed to pass the examinations set for a higher degree; and simple-minded persons, undergraduates and others, taken in by academic classifications of knowledge, think they know no history because they have never taken a course in history in college, or have never read Gibbon's *Decline and Fall of the Roman Empire*. No doubt the academic convention has its uses, but it is one of the superficial accretions that must be stripped off if we would understand history reduced to its lowest terms. Mr. Everyman, as well as you and I, remembers things said and done, and must do so at every waking moment." (pp. 235–236)

Toward the end of his paper Becker reassures the professional historian that he has both a common and uncommon role to play:

". . . the historian, like Mr. Everyman, like the bards and storytellers of an earlier time, will be conditioned by the specious present in which alone he can be aware of his world. Being neither omniscient nor omnipresent, the historian is not the same person always and everywhere; and for him, as for Mr. Everyman, the form and significance of remembered events, like the extension and velocity of physical objects, will vary with the time and place of the observer. After fifty years we can clearly see that it was not history which spoke through Fustel, but Fustel who spoke through history. We see less clearly perhaps that the voice of Fustel was the voice, amplified and freed from static as one may say, of Mr. Everyman; what the admiring students applauded on that famous occasion was neither history nor Fustel, but a deftly colored pattern of selected events which Fustel fashioned, all the more skillfully for not being aware of doing so, in the service of Mr. Everyman's emotional needs—the emotional satisfaction, so essential to Frenchmen at that time, of perceiving that French institutions were not of German origin. And so it must always be. Played upon by all the diverse, unnoted influences of his own time, the historian will elicit history out of documents by the same principle, however more consciously and expertly applied, that Mr. Everyman employs to breed legends out of remembered episodes and oral tradition." (pp. 251–252)

"More consciously and expertly applied"—that is the kernel of the answer I wish I had given my student critic. We are similar to and different from Mr. Everyman and that should be a powerful reassurance for the community psychologist. And if we forget that bond we have lost our roots and, as Becker says, "our proper function." (Sarason, 1976, pp. 327–328.)

Mental Health and the Schools: From Prevention to Problem Solving

It is commonly recognized that in addition to a monopoly on academic and vocational preparation, schools hold a powerful socialization influence over a literally captive population of young children from every strata of society. The young are emotionally as well as cognitively malleable, and it is not surprising that professional activity in the public elementary schools is popular and logically compelling for advocates of community mental health.

In both the mental health and the educational systems it has already been suggested that community control as accountability may be the crucial ingredient of institutional reform. Although such institutional changes may reduce the overall negative impact on a total community, some children will still experience difficulty which may require organizational and individual intervention. Nevertheless, these programs must not be viewed as isolated "solutions" so much as part of an overall plan for intervention at multiple levels. *If individual and organizational level programs are imposed in the absence of institutional change they are likely to be another instance of first-order change.* Specific programs

must be viewed as potential resources available to children and their families in the larger context of child advocacy, rather than as "mental health." The aim must be to assist children in obtaining the maximum of environmental resources. Within this orientation the advocate works by means of the style and conceptions of an environmental resources and social advocacy model as suggested by Davidson and Rapp (see Chapter VI, p. 200), rather than within the assumptions of an intrapsychic mental health model. This caution must be kept in mind as we proceed with the remainder of this chapter. We will not review the hundreds of studies concerned with mental health in the schools. However, in this section we will critique some methods and highlight others as promising directions consistent with the kind of community psychology proposed in this volume.

Zax and Specter (1974) have classified and described several school mental health programs as either primary or secondary prevention. In the former category they include work which emphasizes development of a total school atmosphere, such as the Bank Street projects based on the "child-centered" philosophy described by Shapiro and Biber in Chapter VII of this volume (see Figure VII-2 and p. 231). Programs of organization development such as the one conducted by Schmuck, Runkel, and Langmeyer described in Chapter VI (p. 174) might also be included. Zax and Specter also list as primary prevention consultation programs designed to help teachers feel more comfortable with themselves and the children, and presumably to do a better job of teaching. As a third example of primary prevention they consider programs that seek to modify teaching techniques, such as training teachers in effective use of behavior modification technology for classroom management. This orientation and some of its assets and liabilities have been reviewed in Chapter IV (pp. 81–92). In many ways the above programs suffer from the problems of community mental health and individual psychology discussed in detail in Chapters III and IV. They tend to emphasize the "be still, be quiet, be docile" aspects of socialization (Winett and Winkler, 1972) and and the single standard of "adjustment." A fourth type of primary preventive school mental health program is that which is aimed at curriculum improvement. This kind of program has a number of advantages and is described in some detail below.

In the category of secondary prevention Zax and Specter (1974) include programs that attempt to identify early, children likely to suffer school maladjustment and to find solutions to alleviate their difficulty. Such programs have a wide variation in how the children "at risk" are identified and what is done once they are so identified. Methods used often include tests, parent interviews, teacher reports, or some combination of these. There appears to be evidence that if a child is found to have difficulty in the first grade he or she may continue to have difficulty in later grades (e.g., Zax, Cowen, Rappaport, Beach, & Laird, 1968). It is not clear *why* this is the case. It could be a function of negative expectations on the part of school personnel, deficits on the part of the children, an inability of the school to match the needs and provide the resources necessary to a particular child, or a number of other possible causes. Early identification programs, however, have emphasized teacher, parent, or child training.

Regardless of whom they focus on, all such programs share in the implicit assumption that some children need assistance in adapting to the school environment, either academically, interpersonally, or both. They tend to emphasize discovery of weaknesses in children viewed as requiring correction. Efforts at correction are often handled by means of parent groups or through case consultation to school personnel (e.g., Glidewell, Gildea, & Kaufman, 1973). Others have favored the development of a more efficient mental health delivery system within the school itself. Perhaps the best described and most carefully conducted program is the one developed by Cowen and his associates in Rochester, New York (Cowen, Trost, Lorion, Dorr, Izzo, & Isaacson, 1975).

The Primary Mental Health Project

Begun in 1957, the development and evolution of the Rochester Primary Mental Health Project (PMHP) in many ways reflects the changing ideology of school-based mental health programs during the last 20 years. The impetus for this program was an early recognition among its founders of the threefold problem that stimulated the community mental health movement: ineffective means for amelioration of entrenched problems in living, an insufficient supply of professional mental health workers, and an inability to reach large numbers of people in need of services. Consequently, the PMHP from its onset was based on the notion that: (1) early detection of school maladjustment, presumed to lead to later difficulty, is a better strategy than waiting until the problems become entrenched, and (2) nonprofessional *child aides*, supervised by professionals, can be mobilized to provide the child with necessary assistance.

Beginning with a small number of experimental and control schools the PMHP has evolved first to district-wide and later multiple school district programs in the Rochester area, encompassing some 17 schools, and more recently to a national dissemination of the program's procedures. The model involves the use of minimally paid volunteer homemakers called *child aides* who are supervised by school mental health professionals. The key aspect is a system which makes available services to children other than those already in serious trouble. When school mental health programs rely on a small number of mental health professionals (often a half-time person or less in a given school) there is obviously very little they can do for most children. However, by mobilizing nonprofessional helping agents, who are recruited from the local community, the school can inexpensively offer assistance to more of its students. This plan may also simultaneously serve as a stimulus for involvement of local residents in the program and policies of the school.

In the PMHP the students of a school are provided with the special attention of a "committed adult" by means of individual out-of-class meetings from one to several times per week. Exactly what they do with the child has varied from individual to individual and is potentially open to the ingenuity, technical, and problem-solving skills of the nonprofessionals and their supervisors. Those students offered this service are selected on the basis of mass screening devices for primary grade youngsters, which identify children thought likely to have future problems of adjustment. By adoption of the mass screening and nonprofessional child aide procedures, Cowen *et al.* report that for a 40 percent increase in cost the schools have been provided with a 1000 percent increase in services. Direct contact has been provided for about 11 percent of the total number of primary-grade children in schools where the program has been located.

As the PMHP has evolved over the years it has continually maintained an important research, program evaluation, and feedback element which serves as a model for other interventionists. At present the research is most heavily concentrated in four schools within the Rochester community. These serve as pilot-testing schools for new procedures and program improvements. The information is then fed to the other participating schools in the Rochester area and to those in the developing national network. Much information is diffused by means of workshops, visiting internships for people from other schools districts, and on-site consultation by the innovators. Specific procedures for the development of such programs have now been well described in a recent book (Cowen *et al.*, 1975).

The PMHP has produced a wealth of published research over its almost 20 years of existence, and much of it has been summarized in the 1975 volume. Cowen and his colleagues are quite candid in discussing both the findings and the limitations of their research. They have carefully pointed out many of the methodological difficulties of large-scale research in public school settings. These include the problem of finding an adequate population of control subjects in a primarily service-oriented program and the difficulty of selecting criteria for outcome assessments that go beyond the reports of deeply involved teachers, child aides, and parents. Despite their awareness of such problems, they feel that the strategy of continual evaluation, program feedback, and change permits several conclusions from their over 40 empirical studies.

Some of the research has emphasized test development, including measures for the early detection of school adjustment problems. Some

of these measures are teacher completion of behavior checklists and devices such as the AML, which describe problems of classroom adjustment (see Chapter III, p. 65). They have recently begun to develop tests to evaluate the strengths and abilities as well as problem areas of young children. These tests now include measures that look for sociability, learning orientation, tolerance for frustration, ability to follow rules, and other such positive skills. Over the years the PMHP has also evaluated reactions of teachers to the programs, and finds them to be highly favorable. They have also carefully described the characteristics of their nonprofessional child aides, how they differ from other kinds of volunteers, what they do with the children they see, and how professionals in the schools have viewed the aides.

Basic studies of "outcome" have also evolved over the years and many such reports are now available. One early study found that treated as opposed to untreated children were later viewed by teachers as having more rather than less difficulty in school, a result that may be attributed to increased sensitivity of teachers in experimental as opposed to control schools (Cowen *et al.*, 1963; Levine & Graziano, 1972). However, a second study, of an improved program (Cowen *et al.*, 1966), found that when all teachers were oriented to the use of the scales the treated children were rated as superior to the controls. They also scored better on measures such as number of referrals to the nurse, achievement test scores, achievement-aptitude discrepancy scores, and self-reported anxiety.

Other early studies found that children identified as high risk and left untreated continued to perform poorly in school in the third and also in the seventh grade. A later study found that many of these same children also appeared in a psychiatric case register of clients requiring mental health services, and that the best predictor of later psychiatric problems was peer ratings collected when the children were nine years of age. Although this may mean a number of things (e.g., that peers are sensitive to the problems of their fellows, or that once they are perceived negatively by peers they are regarded negatively and continue to deteriorate), the finding itself is obviously important for those concerned with early detection and amelioration.

Later outcome studies have found that children seen by child aides (homemakers) were judged by teachers to have improved more than children seen by college student volunteers, who in turn were more improved on teachers' ratings than control children. A long-term study using follow-up interviews with parents of children who had been seen by the child aides several years earlier, found mothers and interviewers agreeing that the children had benefited from the program. Such evaluations, as noted by the authors, are less than ideal in that they rely on reports of those who are deeply involved in the program and lack adequate control subjects, problems that the authors are quick to point out have not been solved in their most recent work. Nevertheless, several studies find that the judgments of teachers and aides do agree in the conclusion that treated children improve in their rated classroom behavior and in developing areas of competence. If such outcomes create more positive expectations for children (although this has not been directly tested) they may not be trivial.

Other work also finds that children who were considered no longer in need of the service continued to be seen as improved in later years. Also, the number of times a child is seen by the aide each week (once, twice, or three times) may not be related to outcome. Cowen *et al.* also have found that the child aide was most effective with shy-anxious youngsters, and those who were younger, or came from higher socioeconomic backgrounds. Such results suggest several logical program modifications and illustrate the importance of program feedback and continual change.

In addition to positive results these researchers have not ignored negative findings. They mention a recent unpublished study which found that some PMHP children did not improve more than control children. In fact, on some criteria controls actually did better than experimentals. Regardless of the fact that the PMHP model is far from a panacea for all children, there is abundant evidence that many more children whose teachers feel that they require assistance in school actually receive such assistance when a program of nonprofessional aides is introduced into a school system; the professionals become supervisors, administrators, and program evaluators.

The PMHP may be most important as a stimulus for programs mobilizing nonprofessional volunteers to work with children in their local community, rather than as a "solution" to the problems of school adjustment per se. This program and others like it, even for severely troubled youngsters (cf. several programs reported in Cowen, Gardner, & Zax, 1967), have helped to demonstrate that children with school adjustment problems do not necessarily require isolation and professional treatment. Rather, just as McGee's experience with the Gainesville Crisis Center, the PMHP experience indicates that the mobilization of local community human resources may be a feasible style of delivery for "mental health" services. In this regard, Cowen (1967) has suggested that the role of the professional might best be what he calls a "mental health quarterback," who helps to organize and evaluate community resources rather than to perform traditional testing and psychotherapy.

On the other hand, an emphasis on early detection of problem children may not necessarily be, as was once believed, the best way to deliver the mobilized community resources. Identification of some children as requiring special attention could even be detrimental in the "label and stigmatization" sense. Such an orientation tends to focus on weaknesses and deficits as perceived in the identified child. It is quite possible, and probably desirable, to combine the local community volunteer model with a child advocacy model that emphasizes the right of *all children* to have an advocate who pays special attention to their strengths and needed resources. In short, instead of identifying "problem" children, the PMHP model could be applied to all children. The need for early identification of problem children was actually predicated on the fact of scarce professional resources, and the need to apply them to those viewed as most vulnerable. However, the experience of programs such as the PMHP, the Gainesville Crisis Center (McGee, 1974), and many others that have mobilized nonprofessionals (e.g., Guerney, 1969), finds that rather than scarce, the human resources of local nonprofessional people are large in number. Quite often such programs turn away many willing workers.

Given the above considerations it may make sense in the future to capitalize on the PMHP child-aide model for delivery of services—giving up the weakness and pathology oriented early identification of problem children in favor of advocacy programs for all children.[15] This does not mean that all children are viewed as the same, or even that some children do not require special attention. The specific things done with each child will of course vary with his or her particular abilities and characteristics. The point is that *all* children may be expected to benefit from the individualized attention of a committed adult. Although different children will require the mobilization of different resources, it may be most reasonable to provide this for everyone, instead of isolating and identifying it as useful only to those who are viewed as "failing." The emphasis of such an advocacy approach would be on developing the strengths of each child to cope with his or her particular developmental tasks and would require a close association between community resources and school programs.

Cowen and his co-workers have also recognized the desirability of moving beyond the PMHP model in favor of the development of all children. As they put it:

Thus, without demeaning our own effort we end up with the Avis-like conclusion that PMHP, conceptually, is only second best. Though the approach is realistic, responsive to present realities, and preferable to established, rutted, school mental health practices, it does not come to grips with the heart of the problem. Although it establishes a utilitarian new role for school mental health professionals (the mental health "quarterback"), that takes an important preventive stride,

the role nevertheless maintains a major repair component. Nor does this new role begin seriously to explore the important, sorely needed functions of the social system analyst and modifier required as core elements in an ideal, future, school mental health role . . . . Schools will, and must pay heed to today's problems. But we also hope that this need is not so overwhelmingly indulged that it blocks progress toward establishing school environments that promote healthy development, rich in learning, for all children and thus obviate the future need for restoration (Cowen *et al.*, 1975, pp. 360–361).

Other Approaches to School Intervention

Perhaps the best single critical review of intervention programs in elementary schools has been provided by Levine and Graziano (1972). They identify several logical groupings of programs. Among those already noted in this volume they include the traditional clinical methods of treatment for identified problem students (diagnosis and psychotherapy), mental health consultation to school personnel, early case finding and secondary prevention, and employment of nonprofessionals. In addition, they cite several other approaches including the use of special classes for the emotionally disturbed child, non-promotion as a remedial policy, and curriculum development.

Although the use of special classes has been shown to be effective when focused on highly structured and carefully defined short-term aims, they find no data to indicate long-term positive outcomes and are uncomfortable with the possible negative effects from the stigma of isolation. Sarason (1974) has more specifically attacked such programs as typical of both the mental health and educational institutions' tendency to deal with differences by isolating and removing opportunities for development. He suggests that retention of such children in the regular classrooms might benefit them in that they will have an opportunity to learn from other children. Equally important, Sarason suggests that the classroom which deals with children of differing cognitive and emotional statuses together may be a prime environment in which to teach tolerance for differences and humane at-

---

[15]Although there is no research which directly demonstrates that early identification necessarily has negative effects, the indirect research on teacher expectations (see Chapter VII), as well as the logic of abandoning an intrapsychic and deficit approach in favor of providing advocacy and resources for all children, is compelling within an ecological-environmental resources paradigm as described throughout this volume.

titudes toward one another. One wonders why young children, for example, would not benefit from the experience of having retarded or physically handicapped children in their own classroom. Such a classroom, which also used nonprofessionals as advocates for all children, need not deprive the retarded child of the special attention and structure needed and may be a more desirable social policy than teaching our youth that isolation is the best way to "solve" the special problems faced by those who have a slower than average rate of development or a physical problem.

With regard to the use of nonpromotion as a remedial policy, Levine and Graziano (1972) offer an abundance of evidence as to its failure, despite the fact that in the lower grades it may be used for as many as 20 percent of the children. The practice seems to rest on three major assumptions: (1) that failure is academic in nature, (2) that it is due to a deficit in the child's competence, and (3) that nonpromotion will result in greater subsequent achievement. They demonstrate that none of these assumptions appears to hold up under scrutiny. One review of studies over a 20-year period (Lafferty, 1948) and more recent reviews (Clark, 1959; Humphreys, 1965) find that vague and arbitrary criteria are often employed, including laziness, poor motivation, family problems, and physical defects. In addition, nonpromotion is predictable on the basis of demographic variables—race, sex, and parental marital status—which suggests that it is a social rather than an intellectual decision. Perhaps more crucial, they also find that studies as far back as 1911, and as recently as 1967 (Dobbs & Neville), suggest that promoted and retained children of the same mental age show no difference in later academic achievement; by the seventh and eighth grade 80 percent of the repeaters were not doing improved academic work, and nonpromotion was actually a disadvantage to achievement. Although Levine and Graziano point out that the definitive study (a random assignment of half the students eligible for retention to the next grade and half retained) had not been conducted, the weight of evidence demonstrates no positive academic gains and considerable *negative social consequences,*

so as to make the practice of nonpromotion suspect.

Toward the Teaching of Problem Solving

The kind of intervention in the schools that Levine and Graziano suggest as most highly promising is the development of a problem-solving school curriculum. This approach to mental health in the schools is closest to genuine primary prevention in that it is aimed at all children in the school, and seeks to maximize individual development by means of teaching children how to think systematically. It does not isolate "special" or "deficited" children because the curriculum is expected to be useful to everyone. Such an approach is not content specific as to the "correct" solutions so much as process-oriented toward training in the steps of problem solving. Such a curriculum is value-based only in that it teaches that events have causes and consequences; when presented with a problem situation one may solve it by applying what amounts to a logical consideration of alternative actions and anticipation of consequences. Ideally there is no attempt to suggest that a particular solution to a given problem is better than any other, so much as that one should make choices about one's actions based on a consideration of probable outcomes.

This is exactly the opposite of the passive, rote memory and conformity to "correct" answers approach found in many traditional school curricula. Actually, several variants have appeared in the literature. One, the most limited, provides a behavioral science content curriculum in the elementary school classroom (Roen, 1967). A second (Ojemann, 1960) is an attempt to introduce "causal thinking" into the regular elementary school curriculum. A third (Spivack & Shure, 1974) attempts to directly teach the steps of logical problem solving to young chilren in an interpersonal, rather than an academic context.

Roen (1967) has argued that the behavioral sciences are now sufficiently well steeped in information and a part of our culture so as to require teaching in the elementary school along with traditional subject matter. He suggests that from a teaching of knowledge point of view such information may help to bridge the gap between the humanities and the sciences as well as to recruit youngsters to an interest in behavioral science. He also suggests that by teaching behavioral science content to young children the schools may actually serve to prevent emotional disorder by providing a language for expression of emotion, helping children to anticipate their own developmental crises, to understand the educational process, and perhaps feel more comfortable in school. Finally, Roen argues that such curriculum may be a positive influence on teachers and administrators.

He has developed a core curriculum covering topics such as: behavior and environment, what is a person, heredity, motivation, stages of development, self-concept, learning, insight, emotions, anxiety, IQ, social structure, institutions, personality, and several others. The curriculum was taught to a fourth-grade classroom once per week in 40-minute sessions over an entire school year, using various instructional techniques. At the end of the year the students were given an examination also taken by undergraduates in an introductory psychology course and by graduate students. The elementary-school students compared favorably to both groups (actually they scored higher than the graduate students) and Roen argues that at least the content of the course was learned.

Rappaport and Sorenson (1971) have similarly reported satisfactory acquisition of similar content among a class of low-income high school students enrolled in a summer program. They suggest that teaching behavioral science content may be a legitimate entry point for school psychologists and social workers into the culture of the school classroom. However, there is no evidence in either report for improved "mental health" or changed behavior beyond paper and pencil tests.

Roen has also reported an unpublished doctoral dissertation by Spano (1965). He compared an experimental class from two different socioeconomic neighborhoods, each matched on IQ, achievement, and chronological age, with a control class in the same school. The experimental classes were provided with twenty, 50-minute lessons over a five-month period. Spano found that they were significantly better at the end of the school year on tests of "causal thinking" (see below) and democratic behavior. When IQ was controlled, he found that there was a significant relationship between causal thinking and teachers' ratings of social adjustment.

A second approach to curriculum development is offered by Ojemann and is designed to produce "causal thinking" by means of a method of teaching the regular content of the school curriculum. Basic to the approach is a redesign of the curriculum and consultation to teachers. A training course for teachers, including didactic work, classroom observation, and group therapy has been developed. The basic concepts taught are that all behavior has complex causes and a history, and that actions should be taken in relationship to the causes as well as the probable furture consequences. He contrasts this approach with what he considers to be the traditional classroom and textbook teaching style in which children are expected to learn facts and are punished for questioning them.

In several reports (Ojemann et al., 1955; Ojemann, 1960; Ojemann & Snider, 1964; Bruce, 1958) it has been found that children provided with this teaching experience are less likely to respond punitively in hypothetical problem situations, show a greater understanding of teacher behavior, and have reduced anxiety and insecurity. One comparison of four classes taught by causally trained teachers with four others taught by untrained teachers (children in experimental and control classes were matched on IQ and teachers were matched on sex, age, experience, and education) found the experimental group to change significantly more than control children in the direction of a causal orientation from pre- to posttesting on a problem situation test. As Levine and Graziano (1972) and Zax and Specter (1974) note, there is no evidence beyond paper and pencil tests that the training is effective or that it prevents future academic, emotional, or behavioral problems. Nevertheless, there is sufficient indication that such curriculum is worth further exploration.

A third variant of curriculum development emphasizes the training of *interpersonal* rather than strictly academic problem-solving skills. A comprehensive set of training materials for preschoolers, in the form of game-like scripts to be used in brief daily lessons led by a teacher, has recently been presented by Spivack and Shure (1974). These authors have also reviewed their research with various other age and target groups, and presented an extensive rationale for the training program.

Spivack and Shure argue that although there has been a good deal of research on problem solving in nonpersonal situations (e.g., how to solve an abstract puzzle such as obtaining a given amount of water from a well when only specific size jars are available), the skills needed may be different in human relations problem situations (e.g., how to get a toy from another child). They have measured, with various tests, the ability to complete tasks such as filling in the middle of a story when provided with only a beginning and an end (the mean-ends test), spelling out the possible consequences of alternative actions in a given interpersonal situation, planning of future actions, and thinking of alternative solutions. They have compared various identified "problem" groups with "normals" and find that impulsive or inhibited adolescents, hospitalized adolescents, adult psychiatric patients, and disturbed ten- to twelve-year-olds each score less well than comparison groups on the tests of human problem solving. They also find that the skills of interpersonal problem solving are not necessarily related to traditional indices of intellectual ability or social class; they are related to measures of "social adjustment." For example, in one reported study normal fifth graders from both lower- and middle-class settings were compared on the ability to imagine alternative solutions to stories of problem situations. Youngsters who were rated by the teachers on a standardized rating scale as "able to adapt in the classroom" were best at the problem-solving task. This is reported to be true *regardless of social class or measured IQ*. Similar results are reported among a group of four-year-old Head Start children. Problem-solving skills (as measured by a "Preschool Interpersonal Problem-Solving Test," consisting of pictures and stories in which the child is asked to tell as many alternative ways to achieve a particular end as he or she can imagine) were best among those children rated as adjusted in their classroom behavior. Scores on a language IQ test appropriate for this age group (the Peabody Picture Vocabulary Test) did not relate to the results. The outcome of these and many similar studies led the authors to investigate the possibility that the process of interpersonal problem solving could be taught and if it is learned, it should influence the social adjustment of young children. In this context they have described, in detail, such a training program for preschoolers (Spivack & Shure, 1974).

The results of their attempt to test the above hypotheses are reported in their 1974 volume. All children studied were from an inner-city preschool program for children of low-income families. In one preliminary study three groups of children were compared: A treatment group received 50 sessions of training, ranging from five to twenty minutes each, conducted by college students, over a period of ten weeks. They were compared with an attention control group (taken out of class for games). The teachers did not know who was in each treatment nor the intention of the training. A third group was never taken out of class. Spivak and Shure report that significantly more children in the trained group than in either of the control groups increased their ability to give relevant solutions to real-life problems; these results were unrelated to intelligence. However, they only report the number of children showing any improvement, not how much they improved. It also should be noted that the outcome measure is a test of what the children were actually being taught. It is not an independent assessment of the generalization of the ability to a new situation.

They also compared teachers' behavior ratings for the three groups and found that 50 percent of those in the training group increased in their rated "ability to delay gratification." It's unclear how many other comparisons of behavior ratings were made; and although a smaller percentage of controls improved, the difference between groups is not statistically significant. Despite these shortcomings they did find that the trained group children who showed the greatest improvement in problem solving also showed greater teacher-rated behavior change. The researchers hypothesize that there may be a connection between the two.

A second study examined the effects of the training program conducted by preschool teachers themselves. Four teachers were trained to use the program, and each then taught it to half of the class. As in the earlier study a significantly greater number of trained than untrained children improved on the problem-solving tests. Again, those who improved most were also rated as showing the most improved behavior in class. This study demonstrated that the problem-solving training was feasible as a classroom activity which could be conducted by the teachers themselves.

The third study reported is a larger scale program evaluation. Twenty preschool classes were included from nine different inner-city Philadelphia schools. One hundred and thirteen children from ten classes were trained and 106 from ten other classes served as controls. Training lasted for twelve weeks and was conducted by teachers who were simultaneously trained in weekly three-hour sessions. Children's in-class behavior was rated by teachers prior to the onset of the program and at its conclusion; all children were pre- and posttested on the problem-solving measures. The trained children significantly improved their ability to conceptualize alternative solutions. This enhancement was greatest for those who had been rated earlier as impulsive or inhibited (as opposed to "adjusted"). The improvement was found to be unrelated to simple verbosity. Training also significantly increased the proportion of relevant solutions given, and decreased the use of coercing, commanding, or hitting as solutions. This was most apparent for the originally impulsive children who were trained, while the controls increased their use of such solutions. These results were found despite the fact that training emphasized finding as many solutions as possible, and did not specifically ask for any given type of solutions. Training also increased the ability to see the

consequences of a given solution and the inclination to see causal connections in interpersonal events. The results of the test measures are concisely summarized by the authors:

Thus data indicate that this training program has four major effects. First, it enhances alternative, consequential, and cause-and-effect thinking. Second, it decreases superfluous and irrelevant thinking. Third, it enhances problem-solving ability among those who need it most (those who are behaviorally aberrant). Fourth, it shifts the priority away from aggressive solutions and trains children to see nonforceful as well as forceful possibilities (Spivack & Shure, 1974, p. 98).

The above results are for test behavior. The researchers also evaluated classroom behavior as rated by the teachers. They found that before training 36 percent of the trained group were rated by their teachers as adjusted; at the conclusion of training 71 percent were viewed as adjusted. Among control children the number rated as adjusted at the outset was 47 percent and 54 percent at the conclusion. More important are the results which compared children initially rated as adjusted or maladjusted by their teachers. Table IX-7 reports these data separately for initially adjusted, impulsive, and inhibited children. Among those initially rated as adjusted, both the group that received problem-solving training and the one that did not (controls) were also rated as adjusted by their teacher at the end of the training period. Among the initially impulsive children significantly more who were trained in problem-solving skills (50 percent) than who were not (21 percent) were later rated as adjusted. Likewise, for initially inhibited children, those trained were significantly more likely than those not trained to be rated as adjusted at the program's conclusion (75 percent versus 35 percent).

The researchers also report a number of more specific changes, for example, trained children were viewed by teachers as showing increased initiative and autonomy. Initially inhibited children showed an increased concern for others, and girls (but not boys) who were rated as inhibited or impulsive and later trained were sought out more often by their peers. In addition, the authors report that among children

TABLE IX-7. Effects of the training program on different kinds of children.*

Post-training Social Adjustment	Pre-training Social Adjustment****					
	Adjusted (N = 91)		Impulsive (N = 83)		Inhibited (N = 45)	
	Training Group (N = 41)	Control Group (N = 50)	Training Group (N = 44)	Control Group (N = 39)	Training Group (N = 28)	Control Group (N = 17)
Adjusted	37(90%)	43(86%)	22(50%)	8(21%)	21(75%)	6(35%)
Impulsive**	4(10%)	6(12%)	22(50%)	31(79%)	2(7%)	2(12%)
Inhibited**	0(0%)	1(2%)	0(0%)	0(0%)	5(18%)	9(53%)
	$\chi^2 = 0.09$***		$\chi^2 = 6.56$**		$\chi^2 = 5.39$**	
	d.f. = 1		d.f. = 1		d.f. = 1	
	p = NS		$p < 0.02$		$p < 0.05$	

*From Spivack and Shure, 1974.
**These categories were combined in calculating.
***Yates' correction of continuity was applied to all chi squares.
****Percentages refer to number of children rated by their teachers as adjusted, impulsive, or inhibited at the conclusion of the training.

who were initially rated as maladjusted in their classroom behavior, those who were later rated as adjusted had better scores on the problem-solving test measure than those who were not later rated as adjusted. This seems to indicate a connection between learned problem-solving skills and improved social adjustment.

The above results are less than conclusive in demonstrating the utility of problem-solving training. The major criteria are tests of the very behaviors taught and ratings by the same teachers who participated in the training program. Results are reported as percentages of "improved" or "not improved" children, rather than in terms of degree of improvement. The criteria for classification as "improved" are not clear. In addition, the underlying rationale, which bases "adjustment" on the judgment of teachers can be questioned. Although most would agree that children seen as adjusted by their teachers may be better off than those rated as maladjusted, it is not clear what this means in terms of later success or failure outside the classroom or in the future. As such, the data are suggestive rather than conclusive. However, the researchers did go one crucial step further.

After the spring and summer following the preschool training in problem solving, children entered regular kindergarten classes. In the late fall their kindergarten teachers (who had not been part of the training program) also rated each child as impulsive, inhibited, or adjusted. Of the 36 children who had been rated as maladjusted prior to the training program but were seen as adjusted at the conclusion of training, 30 were now still rated as adjusted by their kindergarten teachers.[16] Of the children classified as adjusted at the end of training, regardless of their initial status, 86 percent were viewed as adjusted by their kindergarten teachers, but only 66 percent of the control children who were rated as adjusted at the end of the preschool program continued to be so viewed by kindergarten teachers. Of 27 trained children rated as adjusted at *both* pre- and posttraining 25 (93 percent) remained adjusted in kindergarten. Of 27 untrained children rated as adjusted at the

pre- and posttraining times only 18 (67 percent) remained adjusted in kindergarten. Although once again the data are in terms of percentages of children categorized by teachers as adjusted, these data are from independent raters six months after the training program concluded.

Overall, the Spivak and Shure research indicates that training young children in problem-solving skills is feasible in a classroom situation. Although it may have differing impact on children with differing initial status, it seems to be useful for all children. Even those who are "adjusted" initially seem to benefit six months later. Effects are unrelated to IQ and social class. One of the most promising aspects of this type of program is that it does not require isolation and stigmatization but rather makes sense as a general method of building skills for all children.

A recent extension of the problem-solving curriculum to third- and fourth-grade children from six classrooms in a rural Connecticut elementary school has been reported by Larcen and his colleagues (Larcen, Selinger, Lochman, Chinsky, & Allen, 1974).[17] The actual training program differed in several ways from the Spivak and Shure efforts, although the basic elements remain. In this research the training was focused on 109 children of both sexes and taught by trained teachers and aides in the regular public school classroom. Teachers and aides were provided with training workshops in 18 weekly one-hour sessions. They concurrently taught the problem-solving curriculum in 24 half-hour sessions to their entire classrooms. The sessions used videotaped models, discussion, and actual practice. There were also three control classrooms. Teachers of both experimental and control classrooms had volunteered for participation.

---

[16]There were not enough untrained control subjects who had improved to allow a statistical comparison.

[17]Their report of training in problem solving is in the context of a "multilevel preventive mental health program." It combined curriculum development with a companionship program using college students as helping agents for socially isolated children, and teacher training in the application of behavior modification techniques to the classroom. By joint application of all three approaches they have attempted to affect an entire school. Their report of this work (Allen, Chinsky, Larcen, Lochman, & Selinger, 1976) was in preparation at the time of this writing.

The problem-solving curriculum taught a six-step process: (1) a general orientation to independent and divergent thinking; (2) how to define a problem; (3) how to generate alternative solutions; (4) how to find potential obstacles and consequences of particular solutions; (5) elaborations of solutions in logical steps; and (6) integration and implementation of the above steps in actual problem situations.

Subjects from all six classrooms (both experimentals and controls) were randomly assigned to either a pre- and posttraining assessment group or a posttesting only group to account for the effects of repeated testing alone. The assessment included a modified problem-solving measure similar to the one used by Platt and his associates (Platt, Spivack, Altman, Altman, & Peizer, 1974). It was administered by an experimenter who did not know about the training procedures or the scoring criteria. Subjects' responses to problem stories were tape-recorded and scored for number of alternative solutions, elaborations (steps for each solution), and obstacles. In addition to the test measures of problem solving 26 students were randomly selected for evaluation in a more "real life" situation. As they approached the testing room they were told that it was occupied, but that the experimenter really wanted to play the story-telling games. The experimenter asked for help in solving the problem. A tape recording of their answers was later scored for number of solutions generated.

Results of this experiment found that experimental and control students and teachers were comparable at pretesting. At the conclusion of training, however, the experimental students scored significantly higher than untrained control students on both the number of alternatives and number of elaborations on the problem-solving test. Significantly more trained students generated at least one solution to all problems presented. In addition, significantly more trained children generated more than one solution to the "real life" problem situation. Further analysis found that the results were not a function of differential teacher effectiveness, sex of students, grade, age, verbal intelligence as measured by the Peabody Picture Vocabulary Test, or total amount of verbalization. Interestingly, those children who received training also became more "internal" on the locus of control test (see Chapter IV, p. 100 for a discussion of the significance of this assessment device).

The importance of the Larcen *et al.* study lies in its extension of training in problem solving to the regular public school classroom, its use for *all* children rather than some negatively identified group, and the fact that some generalization beyond the test measure of problem-solving ability per se was found. The fact that trained students did better than untrained students in a "real life" problem situation and showed enhancement on a measure of their sense of control over the outcomes of their own behavior appears to be promising. The burden for future researchers is to examine other real-world effects such as peer relationships, and to conduct long-term follow-up studies.

One worker (Berck, 1976) at the time of this writing was in the process of extending the basic ideas of interpersonal problem-solving training to yet another situation. Combining the training curriculum with the observation that people in transition from one developmental context to another may be most vulnerable and most open to learning new behaviors, Berck has offered training in problem solving to students in transition from elementary school to junior high school. He provided a summer program for those entering seventh grade in the fall. Over a period of several weeks students met in small groups led by college students. Berck went on to evaluate their learned problem-solving skills and progress in their new school by means of self, peer, and teacher assessments. Such programs, which focus on interpersonal problem solving during important developmental crisis periods and are offered to *all persons* in anticipation of the actual transition time, seem to make sense as a nonpathologically oriented, strengths-building method of school intervention. Such methods of individual training combined with organizational and institutional reforms in the mental health system are among the most promising of our potential techniques, and fit well within the value system and conceptions developed in this volume.

INTERVENTIONS IN THE CRIMINAL JUSTICE SYSTEM[1]

> Violence is vastly overpredicted whether simple behavioral indicators are used or sophisticated multivariate analyses are employed, and whether psychological tests are administered or thorough psychiatric examinations are performed . . . we are left with the central moral issue: How many false positives—how many harmless men and women—are we willing to sacrifice to protect ourselves from one violent individual?
>
> —*John Monahan*

> It cannot be statistically established that recidivism can be reduced by shorter terms, or even by "community treatment" of offenders outside prison walls. But most studies do strongly suggest that recidivism *is not increased* by programs that keep people out of prison or get them out sooner. If that is so, immense sums of money are being wasted on prisons, and a great many Americans are being made to suffer the harsh and brutalizing experience of prison without the streets being made safer thereby.
>
> —*Tom Wicker*

Criminal justice may well be the most perplexing system approached by a community psychologist who shares the values and orientation detailed in this volume. Implicit in the systems of mental health and education, difficult as they are to change, is a rationale supportive of social reform avowedly designed to benefit the identified deviant persons or groups. In both of these systems, despite the fact that society places high value on its own protection and emphasizes socialization, the idea of a "live and let live" philosophy and the aims of a pluralistic society do not create a sense of immediate threat. That the stability of society is threatened by deviance in the education and mental health systems is more an abstraction than a fear of direct physical harm to persons and/or property. Educational failures and people with emotional problems are viewed as more harmful to themselves than to others, and although they may be a burden or a nuisance, they are not generally viewed as a direct threat to one's self and one's possessions.

To suggest that the systems of centralized social control in education and mental health be broken down so that citizens can be permitted to control their own neighborhood school and other human resources, controversial as it is, usually does not evoke a sense of fear. This is not the case when most of us think about "law breakers." Rather, there is usually a much more immediate sense of personal threat conjured up by an image of the armed robber, mugger, murderer, or rapist which underlies our popular images of the "criminal." Here is a person who is viewed not only as different from us, but also as one who may be a direct and immediate threat to our physical well-being.[2] In part, such images are exaggerated by what makes "good news" and good political campaigns, such that the subjective probability of being attacked by a violent criminal is, for most people, considerably higher than the objective or true probability (cf. Gerbner & Gross, 1976). Most of us who are frightened by the images of "crime in the streets" are quite unlikely to actually become a

[1]I am grateful for access to the unpublished lecture notes of Ronald Roesch of Simon Fraser University, which were markedly helpful in preparing this chapter.

[2]One recent survey (U.S. Department of Justice, 1975) found that 40 percent of a national sample of respondants indicated a fear of walking alone at night.

victim of violent crime. In fact, most of us are far more likely to be victimized by "white collar crime" committed by employees against their employers or by large corporations against the public; yet subjectively we are more threatened by the individuals who commit street crime than by the silent white collar criminals who cause increases in the prices we pay for the products we buy, or who commit corporate violence in the form of pollution, defective automobiles, factory negligence, and so on (Monahan, Novaco, & Geis, 1977).

It is within the context of such public expectations that a community psychology must operate if it is to deal with the criminal justice system. Because psychology is viewed as a "helping profession," the demands on its involvement tend to emphasize diagnosis and treatment for legal offenders in a system which all too often confuses the aims of crime prevention with treatment for individual offenders, as well as with the need for punishment of those who are among the most feared elements of society. For this reason, as we consider the possible application of a community psychology to the criminal justice system, there is one caution that must be kept in mind. Although it will be stated several times in this chapter, it needs to be given prominence even before we begin. Perhaps the easiest trap for those "helping professionals" who would step into the criminal justice system is to assume that because what they do is called "treatment," it is necessarily better than "punishment." Often, there is a tendency to ignore the possibility that treatment, even so-called community-based treatment, may simply be the *substitution of one form of social control for another*. This is an issue that will crop up throughout this chapter. It is one to which the community psychologist must be particularly sensitive if he or she is to remain committed to the values expressed throughout this book.

Punishment, Treatment, and Decriminalization

According to Meehl (1970) the traditions of the criminal justice system have theoretically served at least four purposes:

1. Physical isolation (to directly prevent further offenses).
2. Reform, rehabilitation, or treatment.
3. General deterrence (by threat and example).
4. Retributive justice (making the offender "pay" for his crime).

He suggests that because any single method for dealing with convicted law breakers cannot serve all four purposes at the same time, the society must decide which purpose is to be given priority. In Meehl's view the only purpose we currently know we can accomplish is the first because while in physical isolation one cannot commit a crime against the larger society. If this were our only goal, we could isolate forever, with no possible reprieve, all convicted criminals. Alternately, if we simply want our criminal justice system to serve as a means for retributive justice, it would make sense to set a definite sentence for all crimes, and apply it for all people convicted, without recourse or probation. However, because we also expect the prison system to serve the purposes of rehabilitation, and because we know that prisons as currently operated do not serve this function[3] (there is a high recidivism rate), the problem is to develop alternatives that do.[4]

One of the major problems of the criminal justice system results from a confusion between the purposes of retribution, or punishment, and rehabilitation. We often act as if one method of dealing with convicted persons can accomplish both. However, we must face the harsh fact that we really must choose between the two because they may be contradictory to each other. Given explicit laws which make certain actions illegal, for some crimes or for some number and type of previous offenses a society may prefer retribution to rehabilitation; for others treatment may

---

[3]The effect of prison as a general deterrent to crime is difficult to assess, and current evidence is ambiguous at best (cf. Gibbs, 1975).

[4]The problem of "rehabilitation" is further confounded by its psychological meanings. If, rather than applying an intra-psychic definition, we apply one such as reduced probability of committing future crimes, the goal at least becomes clear. Because it is unlikely that any alternative can reduce the probability to zero, society needs to decide how much failure it is willing to tolerate, and to select alternatives to imprisonment on the basis of their cost (in social as well as monetary terms) and their outcome.

be offered. *The point is that punishment and treatment are not necessarily the same thing, and to assume that they are is to confuse ourselves.*

Prisons can legitimately serve as a means of retribution, even if they do not serve as a means to rehabilitation. The choice between the two is more a matter of social policy than of psychological, medical, or scientific concern. One is not "right" and the other "wrong" except within a given value system. If we confuse rehabilitation, punishment, and preventive aims, we are likely to commit an "error of logical typing" by applying inappropriate solutions to difficulties and therefore creating more problems. For example, to try to simultaneously rehabilitate and punish convicted criminals by sending them to be housed with other mistreated criminals and then sending them back to the same community from which they were removed is likely to make better and more hardened criminals. If the aim is treatment, in the sense of preparing a person for a useful role in society, then it will be necessary for treatment to be voluntary rather than forced, and to be carried out in more sensible places than prisons (e.g., in real work-training environments). On the other hand, if the aim is simply to punish by isolation, the prison can accomplish its aim.

Again, it must also be understood that "treatment" itself may not necessarily provide anything useful to its recipients. It is quite possible for treatment programs, like prison, to simply be a form of social control, and one must be careful to access exactly what *form* treatment takes. Involuntary treatment, for example, may have more negative effects than punishment, and every punishable act is not necessarily grounds for involuntary therapy (cf. Robinson, 1974).

If we assume that a proper role for community psychology lies not as an agency of punishment so much as a developer of human resources (this is a value judgment), then the role of the community psychologist must be to innovate and test as many alternative programs as possible, and to apply these in as many places in the legal system as society will permit. Such interventions may involve broad institutional

change which reduces the likelihood or need for crime. The community psychologist need not serve as an agent of punishment, nor need the agents of punishment (corrections departments) be expected to "cure" criminals.

In order to apply the above reasoning with justice, the society, through its laws, must decide which crimes are to be punished by imprisonment and for how long, *independent of rehabilitation*. At present, many people are given prison sentences with a range of minimum-maximum (e.g., one to ten years). In these cases, time of release is dependent on the authority's judgment that "rehabilitation" has taken place. Such judgments are not only inaccurate,[5] but also tend to be unfairly applied such that persons who have committed exactly the same crime can be punished by widely varying amounts of time in prison.

In this chapter[6] we suggest that society may properly decide that certain serious crimes against the person (e.g., murder or rape) may best be dealt with as acts to be "paid for" by imprisonment for a definite period of time regardless of previous record; whereas persons convicted of other less serious crimes (e.g., those against property) could be dealt with as a function of number of previous offenses. Treatment while in prison, as Norval Morris (1974) suggests in his recent book on the future of imprisonment, should be available to those who wish to have it on a voluntary basis; it should be offered without coercion. This requires the availability of treatment independent of contingencies about time of release from prison. If treatment is offered in lieu of prison, it too must be on a voluntary basis and made available to all persons. To limit prison to some and alternatives to others on the basis of personal characteristics is unjust. Likewise, to force one to participate in a treatment alternative if one chooses to "pay" for one's crime by a definite term in a prison, where one may be isolated but not mistreated, is blatantly repressive.

Because we confuse punishment with treat-

---

[5] See the section of this chapter on *Individual Level Intervention in the Courts.*
[6] See the section on *Sentencing.*

ment aims, most methods of treatment have traditionally taken place in prisons. Those who would help lower socioeconomic class youngsters by means of group therapy while they are mistreated in prison and then send them back to the same situation that nurtured them (e.g., lack of resources) are destined to fail. Just as we find that isolation of mental patients in hospitals does not prepare them for the world to which they must return, so too do we make the same mistake with prison "treatment" for law violators. The mistake is somewhat more hidden in the corrections system than in the mental health system because of the confusion between punishment and treatment. In mental health, confinement is viewed as a means to treat and if it does not, one can easily argue that alternatives need to be found. In corrections the very name of the system confuses punishment and treatment such that failure to rehabilitate by confinement cannot so easily lead to the conclusion that alternatives to prisons need to be found. The person is still getting the "deserved" punishment.

Interventions in the criminal justice system, especially those that are most promising—for example, those that provide a means to autonomy and access to environmental resources in the society at large so as to reduce the need for crime—will not often satisfy our desire to exercise punishment. We do not argue that punishment is necessarily wrong or unjust, but, again, that punishment and rehabilitation are not the same thing and cannot be accomplished at the same time and by the same methods. Judge David L. Bazelon of the United States Court of Appeals, Washington, D.C., seems to recognize this when he sees research money being wasted on treatments that have no connection with the real issue. He cites a penal institution that spends $13,000 per year on each inmate, and asks "Could (the problem) be better handled by letting the inmates out of the institution and just giving each one of them $13,000 per year?" (Bazelon, 1973, p. 153.) Such a social policy is unlikely to be supported by society, not because we are sure it will not work, but because we would find it "unjust" to reward rather than punish criminal behavior.

Many of our more promising means to reduce crime may likewise (although not usually so obviously) be based on reward or on the provision of resources rather than punishment. However, if they are confounded with the need to punish, they may be less than useful. To the extent that punishment and rehabilitation are confounded, psychology may have to conclude that its role in criminal justice can only be a limited one.

A different alternative, which may avoid both the problems of imprisonment and of coerced therapeutic social control, is to decriminalize certain "crimes without victims" (see that section of this chapter). Treatment, imprisonment, and decriminalization must each be viewed as separate methods for dealing with crime. In this way, prison reform could focus on humane custodial care of persons isolated from the larger society for a definite term, not contingent on rehabilitation. Voluntary rehabilitation programs would likewise be freed from the inconsistency and confusion of combining punishment aims with rehabilitation goals. Similarly, decriminalization may need to be applied to certain socially deviant acts that neither require nor are eliminated by punishment or treatment.

If social interventions in the criminal justice system are to be tested not for how much they punish, but for the goal of a reduced likelihood of further crimes, or even the limited goal of humane alternatives that are at least as effective as prison, the community psychologist is faced with the fact that traditional paradigms and practices are simply inadequate. Applying the conceptions, strategies, and tactics described in this book will require, as in the other content areas, consideration of multilevel interventions. Many of the programs described in this chapter will be more promising as directions for future work than as "solutions" to crime and delinquency. The important question for the community psychologist in the legal system is not how to eliminate crime, an impossible task, but how our work can help to reduce the need for crime, and how the system itself can be administered with relatively greater social justice. In order to deal with such questions we must first describe the general outlines of the criminal justice system.

Overview of the Criminal Justice System

The criminal justice system is a sometimes confusing maze of administrative, judicial, and social procedures. To determine potential points for intervention and possible contributions of community psychology, it is necessary to describe at least the broad outlines of the system itself. One such description has been provided for exactly this purpose by Shalem Shah (1972). His analysis is the basis for what is presented below in some detail.

Shah describes the criminal justice system as that part of our legal institution which is ". . . charged with the regulation, control, and sanctioning of behavior which violates norms of conduct established by the criminal law."[7] This system is of course not the only one society uses to regulate behavior and to accomplish social control. However, unlike other social systems (e.g., education as socialization, informal social norms, and the mental health system) this one admittedly has social control and sanctions for violation of codified social norms as its prime purpose. Such a straightforward statement of goals is in many ways advantageous because the values are clear and the rights of both individuals and society are specified. Sometimes the criminal justice system is expected to be more than an agent of social control and sanction; for example, its agents may be expected to predict who is dangerous and to reform convicted criminals. When this is the case, procedures and methods can become distorted and less rather than more "just" in the sense of equal treatment for all members of society. This is not to say that a criminal justice system limited to social control and imposition of sanctions per se would necessarily be free of biases that allow its rules

to be unevenly applied to some segments of society, or that methods of punishment per se are either effective or humane. Rather, the addition of such goals as psychological treatment and individual prediction of dangerousness does not necessarily improve the administration of justice. If such aims are not always handled with careful attention to legal rights of accused offenders they may even reduce rather than enhance justice. (See section below on *The Paradigm of Prediction*.)

As Shah points out, criminal laws require strict and precise definition or *specificity*. They are expected to be applied *uniformly* and with specified *penal sanctions*. For an act to be considered a crime it must result in some "visible consequences regarded as detrimental to social interests" and the act must be legally forbidden. The act must actually be performed with intention to do harm.

The three common ways in which crimes are classified are as treason, as felonies, and as misdemeanors. A felony, generally a more serious crime than a misdemeanor, is defined differently from state to state. This can create various inequities. In addition, because the legal system works by means of advocates for and against prosecution, and by human judgments, there is a great deal of potential bias in the system in favor of people who can afford legal fees, and who are generally in a better bargaining position. This is of course true of all social systems, and the legal system is no exception. Furthermore, as Shah observes, the class of crime called "white-collar" to which businessmen, politicians, and other professionals are most subject, often provides for administrative or financial rather than criminal penalties. There is an obvious bias then in both the prosecution of offenders and the nature of the penalties, despite the fact that "white-collar" crimes such as "price fixing" may cost the public far more than theft.[8]

---

[7]Criminal law is separate from civil law which is concerned with wrong against an individual. In civil law, usually the injured person begins the proceedings. In criminal law a violation is considered "an offense against the state" and the agent of authority both initiates and carries out actions against the offender (Shah, 1972).

[8]Shah cites the report of the President's Commission on Law Enforcement and Administration of Justice that electrical companies' price fixing policies several years ago may have cost more money than the amount stolen by burglars in an entire year. Similarly, grocery store shoplifting and employee thefts are estimated to be as high as grocery store profits.

In carrying out its purposes,[9] the criminal justice system is divided into three parts with distinct functions: (1) police and law enforcement agencies; (2) administration of justice agencies—courts and prosecutors; and (3) correctional agencies (Shah, 1972, p. 79). The functions of the police are to investigate crimes, apprehend persons, and provide emergency services to persons and property. There are many levels of police, ranging from municipal to county, state, and federal (including the FBI as well as various special agencies such as postal and narcotics agents). In the enforcement of law, the police have a great deal of *discretion* as to when to make an arrest, when to warn, or when to refer to some system other than criminal justice. This is one point where the community psychologist could have a wide influence if he or she is able to provide alternatives to the criminal justice system that are not simply the substitution of one form of social control for another.

The actual administration of justice, given that a person is referred by police or enforcement agents to the system, is in the hands of various courts. These courts are administered by cities (for misdemeanors), states (generally for felonies and for appeals of a lower court decision), and by the federal government in the case of alleged violation of federal laws. Federal courts also have "higher level" appeals courts that of course include the U.S. Supreme Court as final arbiter of constitutional rights and issues. The courts are administered by magistrates and judges who are elected or appointed, prosecutors or district attorneys who work for the government, and defense lawyers who may be hired by the accused or appointed if the person is indigent.

The prosecutors, like the police, have a wide range of what Shah calls *discretionary power* to reduce charges by means of bargaining with the accused to obtain a plea of guilty.[10] This "bar-

gain" saves the court the expense of a trial and the prosecutor the possibility of losing the case, while it reduces the seriousness of the charge and therefore the penalty to the offender. Judges also have wide discretionary power. For example, they usually have the power, before trial, to set a high or low money bail which can determine if an accused person is allowed to go free while waiting for trial. The judge can also "continue" or delay a trial. If an accused person is found guilty, the judge usually has the power to institutionalize, suspend a sentence, or give some form of probation which can have various contingencies attached to it. All of these decisions could be influenced by community psychology interventions, some of which will be described below. If a person is found guilty, the options include local jails, state and county prisons, reformatories, training schools, or probation and parole systems for revenge, restitution, or reform.[11]

In the case of probation, which is used in lieu of jail, the judge has *discretionary power* to establish various contingencies, but these are often limited by the kinds of options actually available in a given community. Probation often ranges from periodic visits with a probation officer to a requirement to participate in some available therapeutic program. For example, many convicted of possessing marijuana in California are sentenced to individual counseling. This is another key place in the system where the community psychologist may find that the development of alternatives for the courts would be well received. The possibility that such acts require neither treatment nor punishment, but greater tolerance for deviance, must

---

[9]Shah cites three such purposes other than punishment: removal, deterrance, and reform or rehabilitation, as those commonly assigned to the criminal justice system. See also Meehl (1970), above.

[10]Called plea bargaining, this method is used to enable the courts to settle, without going through the long trial process,

many accusations. The accused can, if both prosecution and defense are willing, agree to plead guilty to a less serious offense than the one he is accused of. This provides less risk to a defendant and speeds the process. The merits of such a system are debatable (cf. Kipnis, 1976) as other than an administrative convenience and have gained recent notoriety from the way in which certain government officials were treated by the courts following the recent "Watergate" scandal.

[11]In the juvenile justice system much of the usual process for determination of guilt is often bypassed, and various probation contingencies can be established by judicial decree.

be considered by those who would seek true institutional change.

Parole is limited by laws which allow eligibility after some period of time served in jail. Generally it is decided through periodic review by a citizen board which tries to determine if a person serving time in prison is now "reformed" and can be released before the maximum sentence is completed. A sentence to prison is often for some minimum time, which must be served prior to consideration for parole, and some maximum time not to be exceeded. Once in a prison, there is wide *informal discretion* held by guards and wardens with regard to

quality of living conditions and treatment of inmates. The functions, personnel, and discretionary points for each of the three sub-systems of the criminal justice system are summarized in Table X-1.

As an accused person passes through the criminal justice system, there are several identifiable phases or stages that are under the control of the above-named agencies. At various points in the process, roughly coincident with the *discretionary points* noted above and in Table X-1, community psychologists and other professionals may enter the process. As can be seen from Table X-1, police, court, and incar-

TABLE X–1   Administrative components and discretionary points of the criminal justice system*

System Components	Police and Law Enforcement	Administration of Justice	Correctional Agencies
Functions	Investigate crimes; apprehend persons; provide emergency services; protect persons and property.	Lower (municipal) courts for misdemeanors. State courts for trial and appellate review of felonies. Federal courts (district, appeals) for federal crimes, and U.S. Supreme Court to rule on constitutionality.	Maintain jails, prisons, reformatories, training schools, probation, and parole systems for revenge, restitution, and reform.
Personnel	Municipal, county, and state police; special forces such as tax, alcohol, and narcotics agents. Federal government agents such as FBI, postal inspectors, and narcotics agents.	Magistrate, judge (elected or appointed), prosecutor, district attorney, and defense attorney.	Administrators, guards, and parole and probation officers.
Discretionary points	Arrest and filing of complaint. Enforcement policy is made by police within general guidelines. Can warn and refer out of the criminal justice system as well as arrest. Local values, neighborhoods, and circumstances influence the decisions.	Prosecutor has wide discretionary power to file charges or not and to bargain for reduced charges. Before trial, the judge has power to set high or low money bail or to release without bail. Can "continue" to a future date. After trial judge has power to institutionalize, suspend sentence, or give probation (with varying specifications), limited by actual community resources.	Determination of parole and contingencies. Treatment of offenders in custody and procedures for administration of correctional settings.

*Adapted from Shah, 1972.

ceration agencies each have *decision-making powers* that can be influenced by the kind of suggestions and options made available to them by outside interventionists such as community psychologists. At each stage in the process, then, the orientation of professionals with whom the criminal justice system has contact can potentially influence much of the actual way in which the accused person is treated. The agents of criminal justice are not generally forced by law to use these potential contacts, but it is often viewed as advantageous for them to do so. Possible advantages often cited are that the police can facilitate their own work by referring persons to professional helpers so that they do not have to perform "social work" functions themselves; the courts, by referring cases to the helping professions can clear their agenda for other trials; and the corrections system can run more efficiently, or can get people out of the overcrowded prisons by reducing sentences for those declared "reformed."

Thus there are some clear motivations for agents of criminal justice to work with outside professionals. However, since exactly what these professionals suggest or make available to the criminal justice system is as much related to their particular social value orientation as it is to their expertise, it is important that the community psychologist be aware that there are a wide variety of options at any point in the process.

To make decisions about the role one wishes to fill and the options one wishes to suggest, questions such as whom the community psychologist should work for will need to be confronted systematically. One such confrontation for mental health professionals working in the legal system has been offered by Brodsky (1973), who distinguishes in four ways between the "system professional" and the "system challenger." Each way concerns the professional's sense of responsibility: to the offender, to the agency, to himself and his profession, and to society. Table X-2 depicts this analysis. It will be clear from Table X-2 that although the so-called professional and the challenger are endpoints of a continuum, these anchoring viewpoints do suggest some very different assumptions about the role of the psychologist in the

legal system. As with the other social systems examined in this book, *the hard value choices between an institutional level of analysis required by the system challenger and an individual, small-group or organizational level of analysis cannot be avoided.*

As in all systems, change will require intervention at multiple levels. The remainder of this chapter reviews directions for intervention at multiple levels of the legal system. It must be kept in mind that an essential proposition of this chapter is that community psychology, by value choice, should not be involved in the punishment aims of the legal system, nor should we simply substitute treatment as social control. Consequently, programs that reduce both the punishing aspects of, and the amount of contact with, the formal criminal justice system are emphasized as desirable.

Interventions in the Criminal Justice System

The conceptions, strategies, and tactics discussed in Chapters V and VI emphasize developing strengths of local communities by working with existing organizations or helping to create new ones that are relatively more autonomous than the established systems of social control. For the community psychologist with an interest in the legal system, instead of focusing on a need for punishment and rehabilitation, *the question of central concern is how to mobilize actual and potential environmental resources so as to reduce the involvement of persons in the apparatus of the criminal justice system.* The point that must be made explicit is that there remains for the community psychologist, who subscribes to a value orientation as suggested in this volume, an underlying sense that we should keep as many people as possible away from the cumbersome networks of the social control systems and their negative side effects. These side effects are produced by labels and inhumane treatment that are justified by the need for socialization of offenders.

In the criminal justice area, although it may not be possible to establish totally independent

TABLE X–2   Range of responsibilities assumed and kind of corrections programs supported by professionals with different viewpoints*

Area of Responsibility	System Professional**	System Challenger**
To the offender	Rehabilitation means changing the offender to develop self-control and become less "antisocial." Favors indeterminant sentences and rehabilitation.	Opposed to treatment by coercion. Services should be voluntary. Social injustice rather than individuals require change. Usually favors determinant sentences not contingent on rehabilitation.
To the agency	Favors clear specification of organizational goals and direct assistance to the organization (e.g., the prison) in accomplishing them.	Role is as an outside critic who challenges the goals, methods, values, and social institutions which support the status quo of the criminal justice system.
To self and profession	The aims of the professions are to be consistent with those of the larger society and to help offenders conform to accepted norms and standards. Value judgments denied.	Values are seen as basic to any professional activity. Recommendations for activity should be based on an analysis of values openly confronted.
To society	By virtue of law violation the offender has surrendered himself to the care of the system and society has a responsibility to protect itself. The professional is not a social critic but one who must adapt the offender to society.	Emphasis should be on diversion of people out of the criminal justice system, increased tolerance for deviance, and "getting the system off our backs."

*Adapted from Brodsky, 1973.
**These represent the end points of a continuum.

alternative systems, there is a fair degree of room for alternatives to the standard procedures. Much of the remainder of this chapter is concerned with such alternatives. The major intervention strategy suggested here is that of a data-based change agent who develops, evaluates, and disseminates such alternative programs. The strategies of organization development, creation of autonomous settings, and social policy analysis will often be intertwined in such interventions.

The levels of analysis suggested in Chapter VI by the schema for identifying potential intervention points (see Table VI-1) may serve here as an aid in locating possible places in the system where the community psychologist may become active. It will be recalled that the level of

analysis selected should be consistent with one's value/goals. For example, in the criminal justice system, interventions at the individual level tend to focus on adjusting persons to fit more neatly into the existing rules of the system. Intervention at the organizational level is more concerned with helping the components of the system (in this case the police and law enforcement agents, the courts, and the correctional agencies) to do a more efficient and humane job in accomplishing their aims. Interventions at the institutional level are those that attempt to create changes in the very goals of the components of the system, or to change the "rules of the game."

By combining the above considerations with the analysis of *discretionary points* in the crimi-

TABLE X–3   Selected examples of interventions at multiple levels (points of intervention) in the three components of the criminal justice system.

Level of Analysis and Possible Points of Intervention	*Component of the Criminal Justice System*		
	Corrections Agencies	Administration of Justice (Courts)	Police and Law Enforcement
Individual* and Small-Group	Socialization programs and various forms of psycho-therapy for inmates. Training in vocational skills	Assessment of competency to stand trial, dangerousness, etc.	Individual counseling for both law enforcement agents and people they refer for assistance. Communication skills training (e.g., police-community relations programs). Police selection procedures.
Organizational	Development of more "humane" prisons (e.g., behavior modification and organization development in prison settings).	Pretrial interventions (e.g., bail-bond reforms, adult treatment or "true" diversion programs, intensive probation for juveniles).	Diversion programs for juveniles prior to court referral. Consultation and police training programs (e.g., in crisis intervention skills).
Institutional	Probation and parole alter-natives; community-based treatment settings (e.g., behavior modification based, or autonomous alter-native settings). Liberal-ization of prison rules (e.g., work release programs).	Reform of laws and proce-dures (e.g., jury proce-dures, sentencing); decrimi-nalization of victimless crimes; elimination of juvenile status offenses.	Reform or redirection of police procedures such as neighborhood control and/or recruiting of local police-men. Educational and infor-mational exchanges on values, mores, and lifestyle of local neighborhoods. Prevention of violence by means of situa-tional or environmental changes. Enforcement of gun control, environmental, and safety laws. Radical non-intervention; removal of social control functions.

Note: Although interventions at this level are included for the sake of completeness, they are not recommended as a direction for community psychology.

nal justice system, as identified by Shah (1972) in the preceding section of this chapter, we can identify those specific places where an interven-tion is likely to have impact on selected value/ goals. Because each discretionary point is a place where there is some flexibility in the sys-tem, such points may serve as "escape hatches" from the system, or places where the community psychologist can develop alternatives to stan-dard procedures. Table X-3 presents three levels of analysis—the individual and small-group, the organizational, and the institutional—as they may be applied to the three components of the criminal justice system (corrections, administra-tion of justice, and enforcement). Each of the nine intersections in Table X-3, representing a level and component of the system, suggests a focus for intervention. The ways in which one might expect to influence the system by focusing at any of these nine intercepts are determined in part by the discretionary points which correspond to that place in the system. Table X-3 names examples of interventions that will be discussed in the remainder of this chapter. For convenience we will discuss interventions at each level of analysis by beginning with corrections (the place where most programs have focused), then move backward through the system to the courts, and finally to the law enforcement component.

Individual and Small-Group Intervention in Corrections

For the sake of completeness, the discussion begins with interventions aimed at the individual and/or the small group housed in correctional settings. As with other social systems reviewed in this volume, we shall find that programs limited to the individual level are both largely ineffective and avoid the basic questions to be addressed by a community psychology. In this section a brief review of exemplary findings is presented.

Psychologists and other professionals working with individuals and small groups have long been involved in prisons as psychotherapists for inmates and as administrators of various kinds of socialization programs to prepare inmates for release. Often, willingness to participate in such treatment has directly or indirectly influenced an inmate's chances for parole. Unfortunately, Brodsky's (1973) review of *Psychologists in the Criminal Justice System* suggests that available research indicates that psychotherapy programs in prisons are less than effective in preparing prisoners for release. He cites two important longitudinal studies. One study (Jacobson & Wirt, 1969) evaluated, over a period of eight years, the effects of group psychotherapy on 446 adult inmates of a state prison. They found that controls actually made a "better adjustment to parole," as measured by a psychological examination, than those who had participated in treatment. In a second, more important study, Kassenbaum, Ward, and Wilner (1971), using various recidivism criteria to evaluate 955 adult California inmates, found that those who had participated in counseling treatment were just as

likely to become repeated offenders as those who refused to participate or who had wanted to participate but were referred to a control condition.

Table X-4 presents the results of the Kassenbaum *et al.* study after 36 months of follow-up. This table of success or failure represents a composite of various criteria (return to prison, jailed for major trouble, jailed for minor trouble, number of arrests). The table compares outcome results for various counseling treatment and control groups and finds no differences. As these authors point out, they purposely selected inmates who were neither the least nor the most likely to succeed; they represent the "average" inmate in a correctional system. The inmates were housed in the most modern facilities, with the most adequate staff in the system. In addition, because they sought to maximize outcome, the counseling leaders were trained beyond that which the normal resources of the Department of Corrections (in California) could afford. Even under such relatively ideal conditions, treatment was not effective in reducing recidivism.

The above findings are also consistent with the review by Bailey (1971) of over 100 studies completed prior to 1966. Bailey concluded that evidence supporting the effectiveness of correctional treatment was of questionable validity. A more recent report is the outgrowth of a review of 231 studies published between 1945 and 1966 by a committee appointed to prepare corrections recommendations for New York State (Lipton, Martinson & Wilkes, 1975). Martinson (1974) reports that the findings were so negative that the state refused to publish them. The report was not available until it was subpoenaed as evidence in a court case. In general, this review found no reduction of recidivism rates for adult or juvenile prisoners who had participated in educational and vocational training, individual and group counseling, or medical treatments.

Such results as summarized above are not terribly surprising in light of the general failure of psychotherapy for lower socioeconomic class clients (see Chapters III and IV).[12] Although it

---

[12]In addition to the usual limitations of psychotherapy, special problems related to its conduct in the prison atmosphere of coercion and fear have been well described by Katkin (1972).

TABLE X–4 Parole outcome at 36 months by treatment status (in percent).*

Parole Outcome at 36 Months	Treatment Category					
	Mandatory Controls (N = 269)	Voluntary Controls (N = 173)	Mandatory Large-Group Counseling (N = 68)	Mandatory Small-Group Counseling (N = 171)	Voluntary Small-Group Counseling (N = 274)	Total (N = 955)
*Dichotomized***						
Success	42	34	30	43	40	39
Failure	58	66	70	57	60	61
Total	100	100	100	100	100	100
*Four-Way***						
No problems	24	23	15	22	21	22
Minor problems	18	11	15	21	19	17
Major problems	10	10	11	7	10	10
Return to prison	48	56	59	50	50	51
Total	100	100	100	100	100	100

*From Kassenbaum, Ward, & Wilner, 1971.
**χ^2 = 6.62
  d.f. = 4
  Not significant
***χ^2 = 11.68
  d.f. = 12
  Not significant

may be reasonable to make available to those inmates who desire it such individual and small-group services as psychotherapy, education, and counseling, there is no justification on the basis of outcome for making release or parole contingent on participation. The most sensible direction for programs of individual treatment in prisons is to make them totally voluntary and to separate participation from any consideration regarding release (cf. Morris, 1974). The entire issue of the ethics of prison treatment and of the right to refuse treatment is a very complicated one and deserves far more discussion than is provided here.[13]

Individual Level Intervention in the Courts

In part because society is so concerned with individual criminal violence, and in part because mental health professionals have offered such services, psychologists are often regarded as professionals who can predict and control dangerous behavior. Despite a lack of empirical evidence to support the usefulness of such activities, mental health professionals have often been given the responsibility of both treating legal offenders and of making individual predictions regarding their future conduct. Consequently, much of the involvement of psychology in the courts has been in those areas. In this section we will argue that our ability to be useful as predictors of violence and dangerousness has been overestimated. It has been overestimated because of our acceptance of the "paradigm of prediction" and of "we and they" thinking, and because of a tendency to confuse the "rule of law." These conceptual errors, discussed below, lead us to a number of explications for social policy and to the conclusion that the prediction of violence should now be of considerably lower priority than interventions which seek organizational and institutional changes in the criminal justice system itself.

The Paradigm of Prediction

It would be comforting to think that psychologists and other social scientists have a history of combatting the view that the individual criminal is somehow different from the rest of us and is not quite human; yet the history of involvement of social science in criminology is more one of inadvertently perpetuating such views. Although the history of involvement is long term, the relationship between psychology and the legal system is more of a casual friendship (some would say animosity) than a mutual dependency. There are some advantages in this, since the community psychologist is potentially free from a traditional set of roles. Their power and control are minimal such that legitimacy for intervention requires justification to society. Unfortunately, potential freedom from traditional roles leads to resolution of ambiguity on both sides by a retreat to roles learned elsewhere, and the social scientist often seems to accept the same myths about the "criminal" as everyone else.

Early involvement of behavioral scientists in the legal system was through criminal anthropology and attempts to identify the "criminal type." Later, the child guidance movement, through programs such as William Healey's Juvenile Psychopathic Institution in Chicago (see Chapter I), became involved in the treatment of delinquents, but psychology's traditional emphasis on testing, classification, and prediction of criminal behavior as a function of individual characteristics has continued to be a major preoccupation. Many sociological studies, such as the well-known reports of Glueck and Glueck (1951, 1971) have likewise focused on differences between groups of delinquents, and nondelinquents.[14] Such research,

---

[13]For a fairly straightforward presentation of the issues, see Stone (1975). See also the discussion of behavior modification in this chapter.

[14]The label delinquent has not always been consistently applied. The most simple way to use the term seems to reserve it for adjudicated youngsters. One problem with such a definition for those interested in psychological-sociological typologies is that it separates the categories "delinquent" and "nondelinquent" on the basis of differential success of the law enforcement agents, rather than on the basis of the youngster's behavior. In neighborhoods where law enforcement is most strict the same behaviors that may be ignored

which is intended to allow early detection and prevention, generally assumes that there is something wrong with or different about the offender, and that if he or she can be identified early, amelioration can take place and crime be reduced.

Problems with such research are both methodological and theoretical. Any two large groups of people differing on some characteristic are likely to also differ on other characteristics without a necessary cause-effect relationship. The assumption that all people who break the law are somehow more like one another than they are like everyone else, or that they constitute a special "type" who require some kind of treatment, or that such available treatments are effective, are all highly questionable (cf. Bazelon, 1973; Meehl, 1970). Such work is steeped in the philosophy of victim-blaming and hypothetical social pathology of cultural subgroups which has been criticized in various ways throughout this book. It ignores the need for basic economic and social reform in the rules of the game in favor of an ideology of individual treatment which infrequently allows for legitimate access to environmental resources.

We and They

The philosophy of the "criminal type" as it prevails in our society has been well described by Tom Wicker (1974) as the "we and they" or the belief that there are two kinds of people—the good and the bad. In this view the bad *are* violent while the good only *use* violence for "good causes." Wicker cites as paradigmatic, in a description of events during the 1971 revolt of inmates in Attica, a New York State prison, the remark of a prison guard's wife: "The inmates are not normal humans like you and I. We never committed murder." Willing to forget for the moment the fact that neither have most prison inmates committed murder, Wicker explores the

roots of the belief that prison inmates are "different" and that the violence of criminals is evil, but our own is good:

The ingrained American myth of violence rang in the words (of the prison guard's wife), the old Puritan notion that "we" don't commit crimes, only "they" do. Since their first effort to wrest the continent from the Indians, white Americans had seen only "the enemy" as violent, and themselves as peaceful, law-abiding, wanting only to be left alone to develop their civilization without hindrance . . . Puritan theology may be dead, but Puritanism lives in its tendency to divide everyone into two opposed camps, the saved and the damned, we and they, the forces of light and the forces of dark; and Puritanism shapes the myth of justified violence (Wicker, 1975, pp. 124–125).

Neither the legal system nor behavioral scientists are immune from "we and they" simplifications. Judge David C. Bazelon, who has been an advocate of close relationships between behavioral science and law for many years,[15] has nevertheless been highly critical of traditional methods of psychological treatment. He notes that such treatment is often applied to legal offenders on the assumption that they are more criminal than human. They are different from the rest of us such that the roots of crime lie in their individual deficits. They must therefore be diagnosed, taught, rehabilitated, or changed in some way which allows them to quietly accept their place in society (Bazelon, 1973).

Prediction of Behavior and Confusion of the Rule of Law

For the social scientist who works within the criminal justice system, even if she or he can overcome the we-they type of thinking, other, often ignored value issues must be resolved. There is a basic philosophical inconsistency between legal and psychological-sociological rationales for social control. The legal traditions of criminal law emphasize punishment for an actually committed unlawful behavior and pro-

---

elsewhere are likely to find a youngster in difficulty. For example, some studies report that many adolescents who have never been arrested admit to violations which would, if they were caught and adjudicated, classify them as delinquent (Williams & Gold, 1972).

[15] His decisions and arguments with regard to the issue of the "right to treatment" promise to have landmark effects on the mental health system (see Chapter IX, footnote 3, p. 274 and the *Georgetown Law Journal,* volume 57, March 1969).

vide for legal rights of the accused through "due process." The early detection and treatment paradigm of the social scientist, based on identification of potential deviants, necessarily makes predictions about the likelihood of hypothetical future actions. The procedures followed by such methods often allow suspension of "due process," for example, the right not to testify against one's self. In general, such thinking has tended to be most influential in the area of civil commitment (for mental incompetence or "dangerousness") rather than in criminal procedure, although it has also extended to pre- and posttrial judicial administrative decisions affecting bail, probation and parole, and is especially influential in the juvenile justice system.

When the psychological tradition of prediction and treatment enters the arena of legal social policy, it may inadvertently threaten constitutionally guaranteed freedoms (cf., Platt, 1969; Murphy, 1974; Kittrie, 1971). When turning over decision making with regard to parole, probation, civil commitment, and the like to the behavioral scientists, the judicial system runs the risk that, despite good intentions, such practices may lead to unjustified confinement of deviants who have not actually broken the law.[16] Sometimes such a philosophy leads to confinement of people beyond the amount of time they might be jailed in the absence of such consideration. On other occasions there is a reduction of sentence by means of parole as a function of what amounts to diagnosed "psychological improvement." In either case, the empirical validity of such predictions is questionable (see below), and therefore so is the method of tampering with justice.[17]

A recent example of the involvement of mental health professionals in such decision making has come to popular attention through criticism by the press and by some social scien-

tists of what is perhaps the most extreme example of the therapeutic state—the Patuxent Institution in Jessup, Maryland (Trotter, 1975). Patuxent has been in operation about 20 years and houses some 400 to 500 "defective delinquents." It is a maximum security prison, but is staffed by mental health workers and devoted to the care of persons who are first convicted and sentenced to the state penitentiary, but then referred for treatment. At the time of Trotter's report, of the over 2000 men referred for possible commitment to Patuxent, about 50 percent had been committed on the basis of psychological tests, medical examinations, and psychiatric interviews. Although legally sane, Maryland law states that a person who reveals ". . . persistent aggravated antisocial or criminal behavior . . . and who is found to have either such intellectual deficiency or emotional imbalance, or both, as to *clearly demonstrate an actual danger* to society" may be sent to Patuxent for an indeterminant length of time (Trotter, 1975, italics added). Release is functionally dependent on the authority's decision that the convicted is "cured." Each patient is reviewed once a year and evaluated as to progress in understanding his problems and developing "internal controls."

According to Trotter, in 18 years only 135 of 976 committed men had been released as "cured." Recidivism for this group is reported to be only 7 percent, however, this is hardly surprising given such low release rates! Many issues of both legal and mental health social policy are intertwined in the case of Patuxent, but one of the prime issues concerns what to do with the person who refuses to cooperate in such treatment programs. Oftentimes, if that person were sent to a regular correctional facility he would be released long before he is released, if ever, from Patuxent as "cured."

Monahan (1976), in reviewing the Patuxent figures points out that some patients originally committed to the institution were later released by the court against staff advice. This group constitutes an interesting "natural control group" to compare with those released with the consent of the staff. Recidivism rates for the group released against the staff recommendation ranged from 39 percent for those who were

---

[16]Although officially the decision is made by a judge, functionally the judge follows so-called expert recommendations much of the time.

[17]Meehl (1970) has suggested that because clinical judgment is rarely found to be more accurate in predicting future behavior than an actuarial table, a judge's reliance on "expert testimony" rather than on the offender's record may actually lower accurate decision making. The same would hold for decision making by a probation board.

given a "conditional release experience" to 46 percent for those who had been directly released from the hospital. These figures do show that there is some predictive validity in the staff's judgment. They show a higher recidivism rate (39–46 percent) than for those released through the hospital's conservative discharge policy (7 percent recidivism). However, the situation is more complicated than that. As Monahan points out, variables other than "psychiatric dangerousness" may account for this difference. For example, those who remained in the hospital longer (until "cured") may simply have become older and therefore less likely to commit crimes. More importantly, the recidivism rates indicate that 54–61 percent of those the hospital would not release because they believed them to be dangerous did not actually become recidivists. The question this raises for our society is a very serious one: How many innocent people are we willing to confine in order to control the potentially dangerous person?

Many of the questions involved in civil commitment, a procedure that allows a person to be confined in a mental institution involuntarily, have been well described by Monahan (1973). He favors laws that would restrict the powers of the mental health professionals. He points out that arguments in favor of dropping criminal charges and removing persons diagnosed as mentally ill from the criminal justice system have been based on the belief that it is in the best interest of the person. The mentally incompetent are supposedly better off in a mental health hospital than in a prison, where they are less likely to be given treatment and more likely to be stigmatized. Monahan argues that not only is stigmatization just as severe for mental patients as for criminals,[18] but mental health treatment methods applied to criminal behavior are not shown to be effective. Most successful research on behavior change is on middle-class volunteer patients rather than on those forced into treatment, and he argues that the mental health and the criminal justice system are both ineffective in treating criminal behavior.

Monahan sees an advantage in keeping the criminal justice system predominant over the mental health system because of "the rule of law," or the assumption that "behavior that society wishes to prohibit must be clearly and legally defined before it occurs, and that the state may intervene only after a citizen has been legally convicted of performing the prohibited behavior" (Monahan, 1973). Perhaps equally important, as he points out, is the fact that criminal justice system forces a society to confront its values; it forces society to consider, by public debate, the behavior it will permit. The mental health system tends to hide such issues behind the "need for hospitalization" which assumes that the judgment of a few professionals can determine freedom or confinement. Confinement in the mental health system is supposedly the humane treatment, punishment is not. Such a system finds no place for "due process." Although it may be that hospitals are relatively more humane than prisons, Monahan goes on to suggest that if this is the concern, then prison reform should be applied for all persons, not only to those diagnosed as ill.

The Prediction of Violence

The role of psychologists and psychiatrists in providing so-called expert testimony on fitness for trial, on sanity, on dangerousness to self and others, and on readiness for release from prison, is widespread, despite the apparent lack of success at such prediction (Livermore, Malmquist, & Meehl, 1968). As Livermore *et al.* point out, if we were to justify imprisonment in usual criminal procedures on the basis of *potential dangerousness* in the absence of guilt, we would find it hard to rationalize why some groups are confined, and others, equally dangerous are not (for example, potential speeding violators or drunk drivers who are actually far more "dangerous" than most mental patients). However, when we move away from criminal law to the area of civil commitment we often identify and confine those who are deemed "dangerous to themselves or others," or are viewed as in need of treatment. Often these decisions are made by considering testimony of an "expert witness" because it is expected that be-

---

[18]See also Farina *et al.* (1971); and Farina, Holland, and Ring (1966).

havioral scientists can accurately identify the truly dangerous person. In critiquing this assumption Livermore *et al.* have argued that because dangerous behavior is of very low incidence in society (e.g., the number of people who will actually kill, rape, and so on, is small relative to the number who will not), any test of dangerousness must be applied to a large number of people. To isolate those who are dangerous it is necessary to incarcerate many who are not. They provide the following example: Assume that 1 of 1000 persons is dangerous to self or others and that a test identifying these persons is 95 percent accurate (there are no psychological tests or other methods shown to be anything near this accurate). If 100,000 people were screened, 95 out of 100 who are dangerous would be identified, five would be missed, but of the 99,900 who are not dangerous, 4995 would be called dangerous when they are not.

If, in the criminal law, it is better that ten guilty men go free than that one innocent man suffer, how can we say in the civil commitment area that it is better that fifty-four harmless people be incarcerated lest one dangerous man be free? (Livermore, Malmquist, & Meehl, 1968, p. 84.)

They go on to argue that such decision making should be explicitly based on two things: how serious the so-called probable dangerous act is, and how likely it is that the person will be changed by treatment. For example, to the extent that confinement of persons is more because they are a nuisance than because they are liable to physically harm others, and that confinement is unlikely to change their nuisance value if later released, unless we are willing to admit to a social policy that is blatantly repressive of individual idiosyncrasies, we need to develop alternatives to incarceration.[19] They suggest that the following questions be asked in all instances of proposed commitment:

I. What social purpose will be served by commitment?
   A. If protection from potential danger, what dangerous acts are threatened? How likely are they to occur? How long will the individual have to be confined before time or treatment will eliminate or reduce the danger so that he may be released?
   B. If protection from nuisance, how onerous is the nuisance in fact? Ought that to justify loss of freedom? If it should, how long will confinement last before time or treatment will eliminate or reduce the risk of nuisance so that release may occur?
II. Can the social interest be served by means less restrictive than total confinement?
III. Whatever standard is applied, is it one that can comfortably be applied to all members of society, mentally ill or healthy?
IV. If confinement is justified only because it is believed that it will be of short term for treatment, is the illness in fact treatable? If it is, will appropriate treatment in fact be given?

If these questions are asked—and we view it as the duty of the attorney for the potential patient to insure that they are—then more intelligent commitment practices may follow (Livermore, Malmquist, & Meehl, 1968, pp. 95–96).

The Monahan Review and Suggestions for Social Policy

In a review of the literature on prevention of violence Monahan (1976) has concluded that its occurrence turns out to be vastly overpredicted such that large numbers of persons who would not actually commit violent acts in the future are confined in prison. Table X-5 summarizes six recent studies reviewed by Monahan. Three of the studies are reported by Wenk, Robison, and Smith (1972). The first was an attempt to develop a "violence prediction scale" to aid in parole decision making. They report that 86 percent of those identified as violent by the scale

---

[19]That is not to say that actuarial prediction of probability of a future offense cannot be made. It is to say, however, that predictions, whether clinical or actuarial, are nowhere near so accurate as to be 100 percent correct. Error will be substantial, and the direction and kind of error to be tolerated should be recognized as questions of social values vis-à-vis criminal behavior, rather than masked in scientific-medical terms. In this sense, alternatives between incarceration and total freedom may be both sensible and needed.

TABLE X–5   Six recent studies predicting violence.*

Study	Percent of True Positives	Percent of False Positives	Follow-up Years
Wenk et al. (1972); Study 1	14.0	86.0	?
Wenk et al. (1972); Study 2	0.3	99.7	1
Wenk et al. (1972); Study 3	6.2	93.8	1
Steadman (1973) (in Monahan, 1976, "Baxtrom Cases")	20.0	80.0	4
Kozol et al. (1972)	34.7	65.3	5
State of Maryland (1973), Patuxent	46.0	54.0	3
Thornberry & Jacoby (in Monahan, 1976)	14.0	86.0	4

*Adapted from Monahan, 1976.

did not, in fact, commit a violent act while on parole. The second study, predicting on the basis of 7712 offender histories and psychiatric reports, found that only 3.1 per thousand of the "potentially aggressive" group were involved in violence one year after prediction, as opposed to 2.8 per thousand of the "less aggressive" group. As Monahan notes, for every correct identification there were 326 incorrect ones. The third study, of 4146 California youth authority wards, retrospectively examined 100 variables in order to *postdict* violent acts. No hypothetical combination of variables, using sophisticated statistical proceedures, did better than an eight false positives to one true positive ratio. The authors concluded that use of a history of violence on the part of the offender as the sole predictor would lead to 19 false positives out of every 20 predictions!

Kozol, Boucher, and Garafalo (1972), studying 592 males convicted of violent sex crimes developed predictions on the basis of two independent psychiatric examinations and data from two psychologists and a social worker who took a meticulous life history for each offender. After a five-year follow-up, only 8 percent of those not viewed as dangerous were found to be repeaters, as opposed to 34.7 percent of those labeled as dangerous. Like the Patuxent case discussed above, the prediction of future vio-

lence was not entirely invalid, yet over 65 percent of those called dangerous were not found to be so five years later. As Monahan (1976, p. 18) puts it: "Kozol et al. were wrong in two out of every three predictions of violence."

Several other studies reviewed by Monahan revolve around a 1966 U.S. Supreme Court decision in the case of *Baxtrom* v. *Herold*. The Court held that Baxtrom was denied his legal rights when he was transferred from prison to a mental hospital and held beyond the maximum prison sentence without benefit of a new hearing. As a consequence, nearly 1000 persons who had been confined to mental hospitals for the criminally insane in New York State were released or transferred to regular hospitals. Monahan reviewed eight published reports of the outcome of this "natural experiment" and concluded that "all concur in the finding that the level of violence experienced was much less than had been feared . . . and only 20 percent . . . were assaultive to persons in the civil hospital or community at any time during a four-year follow-up of their transfer." (Monahan, 1976, p. 19.) He also reports that of 121 patients released into the community, only nine were convicted of a crime, and only one for a violent act, an average of 2½ years later. Finally, a similar release of patients in Pennsylvania reported by Thornberry and Jacoby (cited in Monahan,

1976) found that during a four-year follow-up of 438 patients released into the community, only 14 percent engaged in behavior injurious to another person.

It is clear from Monahan's review that the cost of our willingness to confine on the basis of predicted violence is high and that "we are left with the central moral issue: How many false positives—how many harmless men and women—are we willing to sacrifice to protect ourselves from one violent individual?" (Monahan, 1976, p. 21.) Functionally, it appears that we are quite willing to pay the high cost of overprediction, and Monahan goes on to explore the possible causes behind our tendency to overpredict violence. He suggests at least seven factors encouraging the predictors to see dangerousness where there is none:

1. Lack of corrective feedback. The predictor seldom learns about his or her errors; they simply exist quietly in confinement.
2. Differential consequences to the predictor. If the predictor underpredicts, he is likely to hear about it in newspaper headlines such as: "Former mental patient attacks five-year-old girl." If he overpredicts he is not likely to hear about it at all.
3. Differential consequences to the subject. Mental health professionals may use such predictions to substitute treatment for imprisonment because in their judgment it is "best" for the patient.
4. Illusory correlation, or systematic errors, in which variables that in fact have no relationship to the criterion continue to be used as predictors because of the preconceived beliefs of the person doing the predicting. For example, the false and persistent belief that those diagnosed mentally ill are more likely to commit a violent crime, despite the lack of any demonstrated empirical relationship, continues to be a basis for confinement of persons.
5. Unreliability of the criterion. Violence itself has many definitions and often its prediction may lead to a self-fulfilling prophecy (for example, by more closely watching someone who is expected to be violent).

6. Low base rate. Because the actual occurrence of violent acts is low, the very act of prediction leads to a high number of false positives (cf. Livermore et al., 1968, above).
7. Powerlessness of the subject. Those who suffer from overprediction of violence are the most powerless people in our society (prisoners and mental patients) and are therefore least able to resist.

Additional Social Policy Implications

Each of the above factors suggested by Monahan to account for the overprediction of "dangerousness," like Rosenhan's (1973) observations concerning the overidentification of "mental illness" (see Chapter IX), point toward a need to understand the social psychology of the predictive role that forces the predictor to err on the side of seeing more danger than may be present in order to protect one's self. To assume that a mental health professional placed in the role of authoritative seer is guided only by objective scientific information ignores the fact that the predictive devices themselves are less than perfect, and that social, political, and value biases are heavily influential.

If we add to Monahan's seven factors the question, "why does our society permit this apparently unjust procedure to take place?," there are two possible answers: either (1) we understand the cost in terms of innocent victims and we don't care because we believe that it is worth the price; or (2) we don't really understand the cost because it is not made public. If the first answer is true (we know and don't care) or if the second answer is true (the public does not know) the responsibility of the social scientist is the same. In either case, both the public and the courts need to be informed about the cost; then the social scientist needs to help society to face the implications squarely by pointing out the error rate involved in such prediction, or by refusing to make predictions at all. If society then chooses to pay the price (in terms of innocent victims) the social scientist will at least not have served as a rationalizer for such social policy. This would force our society to openly face the paradox involved in maintaining social control by means of a repressive social policy when the ideals of the system suggest justice for all.

At least in the ideal, the criminal justice system does seek justice for individuals as well as for society. Indeed, the very procedures that allow for the involvement of mental health professionals in the system as predictors of dangerousness were introduced as a means to make the system more, rather than less just for the individual offender. *What may need to be recognized is that the experiment is a failure.* Individual prediction is simply not accurate enough to be permitted, and it is the responsibility of mental health professionals and other social scientists to keep the public informed of this fact. We do not suggest that there is no place in the criminal justice system for the community psychologist, but there are other more justifiable roles that must be developed. Much of the remainder of this chapter explores those possibilities.

Many of the above arguments, which have been concerned with the prediction of violence and the formal act of civil commitment, are also applicable to the prediction and decision making involved in probation, parole, and other such dispositional decisions about convicted law violators. There is little reason to believe that psychological tests or clinical judgments about people are accurate predictors of their future behavior. Rather than to continue acting as if they are good predictors, behavioral scientists may find that they would be most useful to society by helping to point out that *decision making about punishment and release should properly be viewed as an aspect of social policy and social values concerning how to deal with deviants and law breakers. These are moral and legal questions, not answerable by scientific methodology or psychological principles based on the study of individual behavior.*

Individual Level Intervention in Law Enforcement Agencies

The effect of individual level interventions in the law enforcement component of the criminal justice system has in part been determined by the discretionary points available to individual policemen; for example, the choice to warn or to arrest in a given encounter, and the choice to interact with citizens in hostile or reasonable ways. An intervention at this level often involves psychologists in devising procedures for selection of police officers—by means of personality or situational performance tests (Murphy, 1972), by providing psychotherapy for police officers, or by training police officers in community relations. It is usually argued that increased understanding between individual police officers and community residents may reduce the need for arrest or at least "defuse" the potential for interactions between police officers and citizens leading to additional or more serious charges and violent confrontations.

There have been several programs in police-community relations described in the literature. An early example is the one developed in Houston by Sikes and Cleveland (1968). This program was based on the notion of "sensitivity training," and involved all of Houston's police officers in small group discussions with volunteer community residents, led by psychologists. Each group of citizens developed a list of their self-perceptions and their perceptions of police officers. The police officers completed the same task and they exchanged these views in their discussion groups. The authors measured attitude change from the beginning to the end of the program, but did not conduct any study of subsequent behavior on the part of participants. It is not possible to tell if the desired impact on interactions between police officers' and citizens' behavior actually took place. Ironically, although community attitudes toward police officers seem to have softened a bit, the attitudes expressed by police officers at the end of the training actually showed increased defensiveness and prejudice toward minority groups.

More recently, Cross and Renner (1974) have suggested that instead of expecting behavior to change as a function of attitudes, it may be more sensible to directly train both police officers and citizens in the behaviors necessary to cope with problematic police-community interactions. For example, they suggest that by studying what factors make a police-citizen interaction volatile, and designing training methods that simulate difficult interactions under controlled conditions, police-community relations training programs might be able to provide actual practice in dealing with difficult situations before they arise. In one example of such work, Danish and Brodsky (1970) have described the use of videotaped actors portraying various hostile and aggressive scenes that were presented to police trainees. They have suggested that providing practice in dealing with a wide variety of potentially dangerous and aggression-producing situations, so that law enforcement officers may become more aware of their own responses, may be a useful training device. Unfortunately, such programs as yet have not presented convincing empirical evidence of effect on the police officers' daily activities. Other suggestions for improving police-community relations, aimed at the organizational level, and at the police officer's institutional role, rather than at the individual police officer, are presented in later sections of this chapter.

In general, work in the criminal justice system at the individual and small-group level, whether it be in corrections, in courts, or with law enforcement agents, does not appear to be terribly promising. Moreover, such work tends to reify the notion that there is something different or wrong with the individuals rather than the social conditions which increase the likelihood that people will become law breakers. Given the general orientation of this volume, it seems reasonable for community psychologists to turn toward more programmatic efforts to create change at the organizational and institutional levels. The remainder of this chapter discusses examples of work in those realms.

Organizational Change Programs in Correctional Agencies

The Role-making Aspects of Prison

Corrections facilities constitute a wide range of types from maximum security prisons through minimum security residential settings. The population of inmates ranges from adult "lifers" through youngsters sent for short-term

rehabilitation. Despite this range of settings and populations, it appears that providing various kinds of in-prison psychological treatment does not change the postrelease behavior of most imprisoned law breakers. Nevertheless, such results should not be misconstrued to suggest that prison settings would not benefit from a good deal of reform, even if only to make them more humane detention facilities. This aim in itself is a difficult task if one considers the fact that such settings house literally thousands of human beings, and if one accepts the value that "cruel and unusual punishment" is to be avoided.

The task of making prison settings more humane as a minimal aim for prison reform is far easier to agree with as a desirable goal than to accomplish. Part of the reason why it is difficult may be understood through the work of Phillip Zimbardo (1973), which demonstrates some of the powerful effects of the social roles provided for those who participate in prison settings.

Zimbardo began his study by advertising in a local newspaper for volunteers to participate, for $15 per day, in a study of prison life. From more than 75 applicants, he selected 21 persons who appeared to be "normal-average" in clinical interviews and on personality tests. Participants were all college-age males living in the Stanford University area, and each agreed to participate for two weeks in a situation that would involve violation of his civil rights and personal harassment.

The experiment began when the local police department came without warning to each of ten volunteer "prisoners'" homes, arrested and processed them before taking them to a simulated prison in the basement of the psychology department at Stanford. Prisoners were blindfolded and did not know where they were taken. There they were confined by eleven volunteer "guards." Assignment of the 21 participants to a prisoner or a guard role had been randomly determined.

The prison was designed to create an oppressive atmosphere, including barred cells, a dark "hole" for isolation, no windows, and sets of arbitrary rules. Prisoners were assigned ID numbers and loose-fitting smocks to be worn with no underwear. They were frequently awakened by shrill whistles for a "count" during which they stated their ID numbers. They needed permission to go to the toilet, and after 10 P.M. they had to use a bucket in their cell. Guards were uniformed and provided with reflecting glasses to prevent eye contact and clubs to maintain order. In short, the situation created was quite similar to the "normal" prison environment, including 24-hour surveillance and limited visiting privileges from friends and relatives.

Guards were given freedom to improvise in controlling the inmates. Zimbardo collected data by use of observation, video and audio tape recordings, diaries, and interviews. He describes how, over the course of just six days (they had expected the experiment to last for two weeks, but its effects on the participants were too powerful to continue), the prisoners went through a period of resistance and rebellion, were controlled by increasingly abusive guards, only to become depressed, confused, and withdrawn to the point where several had to be let out. The guards, on the other hand, became increasingly aggressive and sadistic.

It is clear from reading Zimbardo's description that normal young men placed in such a situation fell quickly into the roles demanded and lost their sense of humanitarian concern for one another. Many expressed surprise and disbelief at their own behavior and at how they could "for a good cause" conduct themselves in such a manner.[20] To his own later dismay, when the experimenter heard rumors of a possible planned escape, he went to extremes of preoccupation to avoid it rather than continue to collect data and observe the process. The importance of Zimbardo's work is perhaps best described in his own words:

The potential social value of this study derives precisely from the fact that normal, healthy, educated young men could be so radically transformed under the institutional pressures of a "prison environment." If this could happen to the 'cream-of-the-crop of American youth,' then one can only shudder to imagine what society is doing both to the actual guards

and prisoners who are at this very moment participating in that unnatural "social experiment." (Zimbardo, 1973, p. 56.)

Zimbardo's study is a reminder that the prison situation itself may be more than punishment by confinement, and less a "corrections" setting, than a setting which creates dehumanizing, maladaptive, inhumane, and aggressive behavior that is dysfunctional after release. The kind of behavior observed by Zimbardo is strikingly similar to the observations of many in real prison settings. To assume that the problems in such settings are primarily due to the evil character of the individual prisoners or sadistic tendencies of the guards, or other such explanations, is to ignore the essential dehumanizing structure of the setting and the roles into which it forces its actors. To assume that psychological treatment can go on in such an environment borders on the absurd. Katkin (1972), for example, has described his experience in attempting psychological consultation to a maximum security prison in New York. He observed, after several months of trying to implement services, that the "role clash" between psychological rehabilitation and the needs of punishment and control made treatment in the prison situation quite impossible to be realistically provided.

Milieu Treatment

As is often suggested by advocates of organization development in schools or milieu treatment in mental hospitals, the notion of an intervention that focuses on an entire setting, rather than on a single person or a small group, is quite logical for the criminal justice system. In particular, because prisons are frequently administered in a harsh and punitive fashion, exactly the opposite of anyone's idea of a therapeutic environment, changing such settings to more humane total environments where people might prepare themselves for release seems to have face validity.[21] Milieu programs

---

[20]These results are reminiscent of those found in the now notorious Milgram experiments on willingness to administer severe shock under authoritarian command and for a "good cause" (Milgram, 1974).

[21]As Dean and Reppucci (1974) have pointed out, the very term "corrections" for an agency administering harsh, punitive settings of confinement creates a "deliberate confusion between appearance and substance, between words and deeds." It is hardly the sort of atmosphere one might expect to promote positive human behavior.

in prison have been based on procedures similar to those in mental health settings, and emphasize the creation of a humane and participatory total environment for inmates. Unfortunately as Anthony *et al.* (1972) conclude from their review of in-hospital mental health treatment programs (see Chapter IX), in-prison treatment, regardless of its nature, also appears to have little differential effect on community adjustment post-release.

In Martinson's (1974) summary of the published literature on treatment programs in prison settings, which found no evidence to support individual or group treatment (see above), he also concludes that milieu treatment in prison settings has no clear evidence of success in reducing recidivism rates. This conclusion seems to hold for both adult and juvenile prison milieu programs. Martinson points out several flaws in research that had heretofore been regarded as evidence for the effectiveness of such programs in reducing recidivism. For example, he cites the work at Highfields, reported by Freeman (1956), and by McCorkle *et al.* (1958) as a milieu program reputed to be successful for juveniles, but which on closer examination shows that follow-up evidence is inconclusive, the treatment and control groups were not comparable, and the project design increased the likelihood of finding positive results for the treatment group. Martinson found that such programs did no worse than regular institutions; they may actually cost less to operate as well as being more humane in the treatment of prisoners. His conclusion is that such programs for convicted persons might be encouraged . . . "not on grounds of rehabilitation but on grounds of cost-effectiveness" (Martinson, 1974, p. 35).

Perhaps the most optimistic way of viewing such findings is to underscore the point Wicker (1975) makes in the heading quote to this chapter. There is no reason to believe that methods of treating convicted persons that are more humane than the standard prison setting are any *less* effective in preventing crime than the prisons themselves, and, therefore, on humanitarian as well as cost-effectiveness grounds, alternatives do seem desirable.

Behavior Modification in Prison Settings

Although treatment programs for individuals and small groups of persons confined to prisons have not been found to prevent recidivism more than a prison sentence alone, nor is there any demonstration that imprisonment itself reduces crime, some have argued that it is necessary to have a more total treatment environment which would eliminate negative situational forces, such as those described by Zimbardo, and create a benign atmosphere. Unfortunately, such approaches as milieu treatment, aimed at creating a "therapeutic environment" in the prison organization, have not been particularly successful (see above). Some have suggested that this may be because such programs have not made use of systematic principles which emphasize reward for desirable behavior, as detailed in the behavior modification-token economy literature (see Chapter IV). However, those who have reviewed the outcome of such programs in prison settings (e.g., Craighead, Kazden, & Mahoney, 1976) also find them to be largely unsuccessful, precisely because the contradictions between treatment and punishment cannot be eliminated in a prison setting. In addition, such programs have often been applied with what many consider to be an unethical disregard for the rights of inmates who are often coerced into participation either directly or by subtle promises of early release (Redd & Slater, 1977; Martin, 1975).[22]

Available evidence does not support the claim that token economies in prison settings are particularly successful in reducing future crime (Kennedy, 1976). The reasons most often given by reviewers for this lack of success are that such programs have been poorly operated and

---

[22]Much of the concern has centered on individual methods such as aversive conditioning, a technique which attempts to associate induced negative physiological reactions with antisocial behavior. However, the use of an entire living unit that forces prisoners to "earn" simple reinforcers such as food, or which uses isolation or punishment (called "time out") in order to simply control the prisoner's behavior in prison, rather than to prepare him for release, have also been widely rejected, even by those who are supportive of behavioral technology in voluntary treatment (cf. Redd & Slater, 1977). The most notorious of such cases was project START, which the Director of the Federal Bureau of Prisons ordered closed in 1974 (cf. Kennedy, 1976).

often exist under conditions that have simply used the terminology of behavior modification without a real test of its procedures, or have been done in poorly designed experiments where prisoners were coerced into participation and submission (Kennedy, 1976). Such criticism is more on the basis of poor use of the procedures than on the notion that such procedures themselves are unethical or not likely to be successful even if properly administered.

Davidson and Seidman (1974) have recently surveyed research reports on the use of behavior modification with problems of juvenile delinquency and conclude that claims of success are largely unproven. They found that 82 percent of the studies did not use an equivalent no-treatment control group for comparison purposes and only 18 percent reported follow-up data on the long-term effects of behavioral treatment. This research problem is particularly acute for studies that have focused on application of behavior modification in institutional settings. Here, only 3 of 20 such studies reviewed collected follow-up data.

One of the relatively more successful programs for adults (cited by Kennedy, 1976) was administered by the Rehabilitation Research Foundation at Draper Correctional Center in Elmore, Alabama, under the direction of John McKee and his colleagues. They operated a carefully run unit according to token economy procedures, had generally acceptable ethical controls, and included a series of new and heretofore unavailable attractive reinforcers for prisoners (such as visits to a woman's prison, two hours of fishing, and an interview with a parole board member). According to Kennedy, they emphasized individual independence rather than submissiveness as desirable behavior and were able to increase the amount of time the inmates spent in self-management, education, and volunteer maintenance work. However, an 18-month follow-up after release revealed no differences in recidivism between the token economy group and a control group. This study is an excellent example of what might be expected from well-run token economies, for which the inmates volunteer, in a prison setting. The setting includes a more humane, efficient,

and cooperative confinement period, one in which certain individual prisoners might even learn some useful skills, but with no particular benefit in terms of rehabilitation or community adjustment for the group as a whole. The authors of the program conclude that *"the beneficial effects of token programs within a prison may be short-lived unless they are sustained by transitional and community-based follow-up programs"* (cited in Kennedy, 1976).

The above conclusion is reminiscent of the results of token programs in mental health settings (see Chapters IV and IX), which may be useful as preparation for release of chronic patients. Despite Kennedy's essentially pessimistic review of empirical outcomes, he does suggest some useful ways (which he thinks are consistent with social learning principles) as means by which prisons may be reformed. These include:

1. Greater allocation of resources to educational-vocational skills training. He argues that because many crimes are a function of the need for money, positive alternatives need to be provided. Unfortunately, Kennedy does not deal with the fact that availability of good paying jobs may be more important in this regard than in-prison educational programs.

2. Graduated release. Kennedy suggests that allowing the prisoners a transition from prison to community by extended furlough with minimal supervision might work better than abrupt, unassisted release.

3. Decreasing the powerlessness of inmates. Totally powerless inmates are less likely to participate in active, positive problem solving (cf., the review of learned helplessness, Chapter IV). He suggests the use of inmate self-government as one means to increase the sense of control felt by inmates.

4. Increase the use of community-based facilities such as halfway houses, especially for those convicted of "victimless" crimes, so a person can learn to "make it" in the community.

5. Specify desired behaviors, even to the point of making written contracts between prisoner and parole board.

6. Make available individual voluntary behavior therapy with no coercion or external reward for participation.
7. Make correctional personnel accountable by establishing contingency systems which reward them for the successful release and community adjustment of inmates.

Although all of these suggestions are sensible, none as yet has convincing support for the conclusion that they are likely to lead to decreased recidivism rates, although they might lead to increased humanitarian operation of our prisons, a reasonable goal in and of itself.

An Example of Humane Reform in a Juvenile Correctional Setting

The negative situational characteristics found in prisons are not limited to maximum security settings for adult offenders. Regardless of euphemistic names such as "training school," prison settings for adjudicated juveniles, of which there are over 300 in the United States, often create the same oppressive atmosphere and role expectations as their adult counterparts. Dean and Reppucci (1974) have reviewed and described the present status of such settings, and find them, by and large, to be costly, understaffed, and in need of coherent goals and directions. According to their review, although statistics and interpretations of specific studies vary, "there is general agreement that over half the persons released from juvenile training facilities will be reincarcerated" (Dean & Reppucci, 1974, p. 874).

Reppucci and his colleagues (Dean & Reppucci, 1974; Reppucci & Saunders, in press) have written extensively on the need for reform in the practices of juvenile correctional settings. They have emphasized the use of a combination of principles from organizational psychology (see Chapter VI, p. 176) as a guide for creating change in human service settings, and behavior modification or social learning principles as a guide for operating procedures in dealing with the juveniles. Reppucci's own case history description of a politically volatile atmosphere is exemplary of the problem. There was widespread awareness of the failure of a state training school in Connecticut to provide useful help for children, and of the general inability of the staff to even control, in humane fashion, the behavior of its charges (there were over 350 runaways from the school per year). It serves as a specific example of both what can be accomplished by humane reform of such settings and what the limitations of such reform are.

Accepting the notion that residential settings for delinquents cannot simply be eliminated overnight, Reppucci and his colleagues worked at the level of organizational change to assist a corrections setting to accomplish its own goals more efficiently, by returning children to the community and systematically reducing the size of the setting.[23] Reppucci describes how the community psychologist, in the role of affiliated change agent, may establish entry conditions that will foster the control necessary to encourage cooperation. He also describes how he and his colleagues worked to develop a new culture in a setting for delinquent boys so as to make it more consistent with its stated aim of helping children. The principles emphasized by these consultants included obtaining a clear mandate before entry, breaking the institution into small, relatively autonomous units, and obtaining direct input and decision making in program planning from all levels of staff who would have to implement the new program. The consultants did not attempt to remove existing staff but retrained and reinvolved them in an exciting treatment program of which they became a vital part. Such an approach to organizational change is both fair to current employees and realistic, because they are often civil service workers who cannot simply be dismissed.

From the outset of their intervention these change agents were open about their own attitudes and receptive to those of the existing staff. They moved from this base of organization development, using many of the group communication techniques suggested in Chapter VI, to introduce systematic individualized goals

---

[23]Such efforts are similar to those of Paul in mental health settings (see Chapter IX, p. 276).

for each resident, based on the principles of a token economy (see Chapter IV). They involved themselves in careful staff training at each step along the way. The use of behavior modification in the form of a token economy served primarily as a way to structure the rules of the institution in a clear and open way.

Over a period of several years they managed to completely turn around the atmosphere of the setting and to decrease both the number of residents and the staff. They report elimination of brutality, closing of "maximum security" sections, addition of an educational program, and reduction of the "runaway" problem (Dean & Reppucci, 1974). Success seems to have been largely a function of creating an "experimental atmosphere" in which staff at all levels became committed to the goals of an essentially positive system designed to be fair to the children and to return them to their community. Long-term follow-up of success, once the excitement of a new program dies down and the procedures become routine, is necessary before one can conclude that such positive program atmosphere can be maintained, and unfortunately no data on recidivism are as yet reported. What does seem to be demonstrated is that involvement of staff at all levels in program planning and implementation is desirable. Despite their success in making the corrections facility more humane these workers are less than sanguine about the widespread use of such settings as a solution to the problems of crime and delinquency. Although they favor the use of small autonomous living units such as halfway houses as substitutes for the large training schools they also note that:

. . . it is hard to imagine that this move will fully solve the problems of delinquency, recidivism, or rehabilitation. It, like most changes in correctional programs, seems without adequate theoretical definitions of the causes of delinquency or the development of logical strategies to deal with them, but it may be the preferred route to follow given the history of failure by juvenile correctional facilities (Dean & Reppucci, 1974, p. 891).

Later in this chapter, particularly when the work of Goldenberg (1971) is reviewed, we will consider the necessary characteristics that may make community-based, rather than state training school settings, more promising for adjudicated persons.

Organizational Change and the Courts

As already noted, the roles of psychologists in the court system have traditionally been confined to individual evaluations for "dangerousness" and "competency to stand trial," rather than to interventions at the organizational level that may influence court procedures per se.[24] Nevertheless, for those who are interested in attempting to establish and evaluate innovative programs in the courts there is some reason to believe that many in the judicial system are willing to cooperate. Such interventions do require collaborative efforts with local officials, such as district attorneys and judges and there have been many such efforts nationally. This section provides a brief description of some of them. Programs that have gained widespread attention as organizational innovations in the court system include pretrial interventions such as bail-bond reform and various programs which divert offenders from the courts. One of the clearest observations of any reviewer of this work is the need for better evaluation, and here the role of the data-based affiliated change agent seems most promising (cf. Roesch, 1976b).

Bail Reform

Pretrial changes in court procedures have a variety of justifications based on critiques of the inequitable distribution of justice in the current system. Following arrest, when a person is brought before a judge for a hearing the judge usually has an option to release or confine the person prior to trial. In many cases the judge is empowered to set bail to insure the person's return for a later trial. This procedure requires the accused person to deposit some amount of

---

[24]Some psychologists have also studied issues such as jury and judge decision making which may have direct implications for court procedures (see the section of this chapter on *Jury Procedures*).

money to be held by the court presumably to encourage return on the appointed date. Or, the judge may regard the individual charged with a crime to be a "good risk" and release him or her "on his or her own recognizance"—without money bail. Many critics of this system (e.g., Freed & Wald, 1964; Goldfarb, 1965; Foote, 1965) have pointed out that the procedure discriminates against the poor, punishes by confinement of unconvicted defendants before they have been proven guilty, and reduces the ability of the accused to prepare his or her case by having free access to legal and other resources. In addition, there is some empirical evidence indicating that a person held in jail before trial may have a greater chance of being sentenced and of receiving a longer prison term than one who was living in the community at the time of trial (Ares, Rankin, & Sturz, 1963; Brockett, 1970), although it is not clear that detention alone accounts for this relationship (Mullen, 1974). Finally, it has been argued that putting up money for bail may have less to do with assuring a later court appearance than fear of apprehension and one's roots in the community (Schaffer, 1970).

As early as 1961 the Manhattan Bail Project (Ares *et al.*, 1963) began to test a method for advising the court on whom to release prior to trial. Their procedures are based on a brief interview which assesses the likelihood of an accused person's return to court. This interview procedure enables one to assign point values to variables such as length of time in the local community, employment status, past record, local relatives and friends, and other indicants of a person's social stability that are believed related to likelihood of return.[25] Persons who accumulate the necessary "points" are recommended for release, although the judge is not compelled to follow the recommendation. Goldfarb (1965) reported that the rate of nonreturn of defendants for whom such prediction factors led to a release recommendation (3505

cases) without money bail was only 1.6 percent as opposed to 3 percent of those who did pay bail. As a result of the Manhattan Project it was demonstrated that many people who would not normally have been released on their own recognizance could be expected to return. Although initially the project did not include those accused of certain serious crimes, later its procedures were extended to all defendants without changing the results. These procedures have become increasingly accepted, and Wice and Simon (1970) report that there were over 100 similar projects at the time of their study. Mullen (1974) presented data from eight different projects and found that in none were the released defendants less likely to return to court than those who had been released through the normal bail procedure.

One of the more recent evaluations of such a project, which included felons as well as less serious offenders (Nietzel & Dade, 1973), found that the establishment of an interview procedure, conducted by trained volunteers who presented recommendations to the judge, not only significantly increased the number of persons who were released without bail but also decreased the rate of failure to return. The Nietzel and Dade program was designed as an experimental one and lasted for only a limited time period. Therefore, these authors were able to observe the local court's release on recognizance figures for a period following the termination of their intervention and found that its use returned to the relatively lower, pre-project levels once the experimental project terminated. This datum indicates that if the maximum number of people who can safely be allowed to await trial in the community is to be realized, some permanent organizational procedures are necessary.

The use of nonprofessional, volunteer interviewers who can collect the relatively simple information necessary and make recommendations to the judge seems like a desirable and inexpensive procedure for routine use by local communities. The National Clearinghouse for Criminal Justice Planning and Architecture (1975) has recently made a similar recommendation to the state of Oklahoma court systems. They suggest the use of community volunteer

---

[25]Obviously these criteria are related to middle-class standards of behavior and do not go as far as they might in increasing the number of lower socioeconomic status people who could safely be released on their own recognizance.

TABLE X–6 Pretrial recidivism.*

Project Location	Project Rate (Percent) of Recidivism while Awaiting Trial	Comparison Group Source	Comparison Rate (Percent) of Recidivism while Awaiting Trial
Santa Clara	5.6	eligible for OR**	6.5
Monroe County	36.0	ineligible for OR	38.0
Charlotte	7.8	All other releases	7.8
Dallas	3.6	All other releases	12.0

*From Mullen, 1974.
**OR = release on own recognizance.
Note: Projects are for differing lengths of time and differing client populations. Comparison of rates across projects is therefore meaningless.

and/or college students as a means to provide such services inexpensively. The training of such volunteers, as well as the monitoring of the outcome of such procedural changes on the defendant's future behavior, is one example of a role in which the community psychologist may facilitate change in court procedures. Such programs may also have the additional side effect of providing public education about the courts to local residents who volunteer to serve as interviewers.

There has been no adequate experimental evaluation of the effect of pretrial release programs on the rate of new crimes committed while a person is released and awaiting trial. However, there is some evidence using comparison groups which indicates that persons released through such program's recommendations are no more likely to commit a crime while awaiting trial than those released through the normal bail procedure. Table X-6 presents the data from four such projects. If these results continue to hold up, there would be no reason to continue to detain large numbers of accused persons before trial on the basis of their inability to afford bail, or the presumed risk that they will commit a new crime. Here is a good example of a social change we can document as having positive value to many people, but remains as a procedure used in only selected jurisdictions. Research on dissemination of such court reforms and how to generate their acceptance by local jurisdictions is an example of the kind of knowledge the community psychologist might wish to pursue. Research such as Fairweather, Sanders, and Tornatzky's (1974) on diffusion of innovations would be of interest in this social system.

Adult Pretrial Treatment or "True" Diversion Programs

A second arena of court reform has involved the use of so-called pretrial diversion programs in lieu of the normal adjudication process. In most such programs an accused person, usually a first or second offender charged with a less serious crime, but sometimes with a felony, is given the option of participating in some kind of counseling, training, or employment program rather than being prosecuted. There is rarely an option of diversion from prosecution without "treatment," although Mullen (1974) has pointed out that these are really two very different alternatives. She argues that "true" diversion would involve the selection of people whose offenses are relatively minor and who do not require either treatment or criminal punishment. By eliminating such persons, to whom a judge is likely to give a suspended sentence anyway, from the trial process, the courts would reduce their case load, and the person could save both money and entanglement in the legal system. According to Mullen (1974) there has been only one reported diversion program of this nature, and although re-arrest rates for persons participating are reported to be quite low (about 6 percent), there was no randomly selected control group observed, a flaw which makes conclusions impossible.

One rationale for diversion alternatives to the legal system is based on the notion that once a person is labeled a criminal, the label itself makes it more difficult to function in society; for example, employment often becomes problematic. Many diversion treatment programs offer the prospect of no criminal record if they are completed successfully. Unfortunately, there is no evidence that assignment to a "treatment" does not create the same kind of negative labeling effect. In fact, the whole question of violation of legal rights by forcing people into a treatment program, which avoids a formal trial and the negative effects of court entanglement but assumes guilt without due process, is highly questionable.

Two extensive reviews of such programs have recently appeared (Mullen, 1974; Roesch, 1977b). Both reviewers agree that given the very poorly designed evaluation of such pretrial treatment programs their utility in preventing future crime is an open question. The reviews of individual "treatment" in mental health and in the corrections system provided earlier in this volume also lead to the question, "Why should we expect traditional psychological treatment, such as counseling, psychotherapy, or employment training, to reduce crime when these methods have not been demonstrated to accomplish their goals in other contexts?" One logical reason would be that threat of punishment, if one fails to successfully complete the treatment, may serve as a sufficient motivator. If that were the case then diversion alone (without treatment) might have the same effects. An alternative possibility is that diversion plus good counseling are both necessary, but unfortunately there is as yet no evidence one way or the other.

Both Roesch (1977b) and Mullen (1974) suggest that the necessary research should involve the random assignment of offenders who qualify for diversion to a diversion alone, a diversion plus treatment, or a nondiversion (court procedures as usual) condition. Follow-up comparisons would then provide information on the above questions. They both also provide an interesting discussion of the reasons why in the past courts have resisted such careful evaluation.

Once again, the role of the community psychologist as researcher and implementer needs to be emphasized, not only in carrying out such research as is suggested by these reviewers, but also in evaluating how the social scientist might establish the preconditions that enable researchers to engender cooperation from the system's agents. In this regard, Roesch (1977a) argues persuasively for a social policy of careful evaluation to be included in any diversion program funded by the government. Unfortunately, although there are now many diversion programs in operation, such evaluation has not been the case. Roesch's conclusion that "millions of dollars have been poured into (adult) diversion programs yet we do not know much more than we did eight years ago" (before the programs became widespread) should serve as a challenge to the community psychologist interested in legal system reforms.

True Diversion versus Intensive Probation for Juveniles

The preceding discussion of diversion was limited to programs for adults. Davidson (1975) has recently reviewed a large number of so-called diversion programs for juveniles and concluded that the research evidence is largely inconclusive and suffers from many of the same problems found in the adult studies, a conclusion also supported by the Mullen (1974) review.

The idea of diversion from the juvenile justice system is ironic and serves to illustrate how solutions may create problems out of difficulties in the sense suggested by Watzlawick, Wakeland, and Fisch (1974; see Chapter V). The origins of the juvenile court system as separate from the usual legal process for adjudication of adult crime lie in the liberal reforms that were popular at the end of the nineteenth and early twentieth centuries. These reforms were intended to more fairly deal with youngsters viewed as needing "protection" from both the urban evils of big cities and "hardened" adult criminals (Platt, 1969). As one consequence of the work of reformers (who Anthony Platt calls *The Child Savers*) an entire set of uniquely juvenile crimes and an entire system and set of procedures for dealing with youthful crime by diverting children from the adult legal process were established. Today much of that system is under severe attack as one that may produce more injustice than the system from which it was designed to protect the child.[26]

The irony of a discussion of diversion for juveniles comes with the realization that when we talk of diversion from the juvenile justice system we are talking about "diversion from diversion" (Mullen, 1974). That is, diversion from the court procedures now well established for juveniles that were intended to divert them from the adult system in the first place! To truly divert youngsters from the current system it is necessary to remove them *before* they ever get to court or to officials in the court system, such as probation officers. Once they do get to court they are likely to be "treated" by professionals who already think they are diverting them from the usual process, and who serve as both officials in the legal system and as professional helpers, a role that intentionally confounds punishment and treatment aims. If true diversion is to be accomplished it probably needs to be done *prior to court involvement*. Law enforcement agencies, such as the local police, generally have a much wider range of discretionary authority for juveniles than they do for adults. By intervening at that point in the system one theoretically should be able to generate programs to prevent recidivism before it becomes chronic and before the adolescent offender becomes heavily involved in the mechanisms of the legal system.

The way in which the majority of juvenile court systems work allows police officers to use a high rate of what is termed "station adjustment" for minors who commit trivial or first offenses. A station adjustment simply means that the officer "warns and releases" the youngster. This is true especially when the child is involved in what are known as "status offenses;"[27] most local law enforcement agencies will allow several repeated offenses before making a formal referral to the prosecutor, or filing a "court petition" that asks the judicial system to

act on the case. At the point of petition the child enters the official mechanisms of the juvenile justice system. Although legally the child is entitled to "due process," the formal act of a trial is rare. Most often the child agrees to admit guilt, although the child is theoretically being diverted from the system by the juvenile court.[28] At that point, a judge will decide on a disposition such as probation, institutionalization, or some other alternative depending on services available in a given community. Although this is supposed to "protect" the child it officially entangles her or him in the system.

A logical time for intervention in this process would be just when the police are prepared to file a court petition or to turn a child over to court authorities. This would allow the "station adjustment" alternative (which might be thought of as "true" diversion because it avoids all further contact unless the person is caught committing a new offense) to be applied for many cases without imposing unnecessary "treatment programs" on youngsters who would not become chronic recidivists, as is the case for most first offenders.[29]

Although it may be undesirable to intervene too early, intervention just before a court petition would be filed by police in the absence of some alternative, rather than earlier, would stop

---

[26]A more extensive consideration of this problem is presented later in the section on institutional change.

[27]Status offenses are "crimes" that are unique to minors, such as running away from home, curfew violation, and truancy.

[28]Although the U.S. Supreme Court rulings have supported the right of the child to due process, much of the informality of the juvenile court system remains intact.

[29]Many local police departments report that most contacts with youngsters are dealt with as station adjustments, and that most children are not involved in repeated contacts. There is also evidence that many children who are not caught actually engage in activities similar to those children who are caught (see footnote 14). These facts, plus the problem of "labeling," which occurs in so-called early detection programs (see Chapter IX, pp. 309–312) suggest that the so-called youth service bureaus (which have become popular as a means to divert "predelinquent" youth) may be unnecessary at best, or actually create more problems than they solve. They entangle the youth in the social control mechanisms of the quasilegal mental health system. This argument is largely untested at this point, and is another example of a place where research and program evaluation are sorely needed (see Fo and O'Donnell, 1975, and p. 360 of this chapter). Davidson (1975) notes that a survey by the U.S. Department of Health, Education, and Welfare (1973) found such youth service bureaus to be providing primarily traditional therapeutic services, and to be largely unevaluated, despite the expenditure of millions of dollars and the involvement of thousands of youths.

the usual process just short of allowing "problem children" to be referred to court and thus to become adjudicated delinquents entangled in the mechanisms of criminal justice.[30] Many attempts at what has been called "diversion" for juveniles do not manage to avoid the court system altogether because they require confession of culpability and/or the use of close supervision by probation officers as treatment agents. Therefore, such programs are referred to here as *intensive probation*. Although they change somewhat the organization of services, by giving close attention to individual probationers, and are therefore included here as organizational change programs, they might also have been classified as individual or small-group interventions. Intensive probation programs are really examples of treatments that are providing services only after formal entry into the court system, for example, by use of so-called unofficial probation (Venezia, 1972), which avoids adjudication but is carried out by a probation officer. Other programs are limited to offenses deemed too minor to adjudicate (Baron & Feeney, 1973, abstracted in Mullen, 1974; Baron, Feeney, & Thornton, 1973), and most are simply not well evaluated.

One of the few examples of intensive probation that has been relatively well evaluated is the work conducted through the Scaramento County Probation Department in California (Baron, Feeney, & Thornton, 1973). The California law considers any person under the age of 18 who is truant, refuses to obey parents or school authorities, or who is "in danger of leading an idle, dissolute, lewd, or immoral life" to be within the jurisdiction of the court. Such children in Sacramento County are typically referred to the probation department where an officer decides whether or not to file a court petition. This procedure usually results in the child being assigned to a probation officer who spends one-half to one hour per month with the child. Large numbers of these children continue to have re-

peated offenses. Baron *et al.* report that in one sample over 65 percent had repeated offenses, and they note what they consider to be the "inappropriateness" of handling such cases through the legal system because the problem often involves a family crisis and lack of communication.

To deal with such cases, a collaborative project between the probation office and the University of California, Davis, was developed. The intent of the project is to provide short-term crisis intervention, keep the child out of court, and reduce recidivism. The rationale for such a service is similar to the arguments presented in Chapter IX for the use of a crisis intervention program prepared to provide immediate short-term assistance for a wide variety of problems in living. The staff of the Sacramento project normally see referral families a maximum of five times, for about two hours per session. Project staff are probation officers provided with one week of intensive training and weekly consultation from psychiatrists and a psychologist on the handling of crisis cases.

For research purposes, during a nine-month period the experimental project handled referred cases four days of the week. Regular procedures were carried out by the probation department three days per week, considered to be a "treatment as usual control group." Records for youths were collected for a period of seven months after referral, and 45.5 percent of the controls were found to be "rebooked" as opposed to 35 percent of the project cases. Repeat rate for criminal offenses was 23.4 percent for controls and 15.3 percent for project cases.

Mullen's (1974) review of this project suggests that generalizability of the results may be limited for several reasons. The project was most successful with females; the clients were largely White and from at least lower middle-class families. Mullen suggests that family counseling may be most appropriate for such a group, but not necessarily for others, and asks for research to determine exactly which of the aspects of service delivery are most important in creating positive outcome. In addition, one must wonder why it is necessary to handle such cases through the probation office in the first place, if

---

[30]For a review of a program which does avoid the courts and the probation office, see the section of this chapter on *Diversion of Juveniles from the Legal System through Work with Local Police*, below.

true diversion from the legal system is intended. Nevertheless, the Sacramento project does provide a useful alternative to the typical probation office procedures. The fact that outcomes are being carefully monitored so that procedures can be evaluated is in and of itself an important contribution to organizational change in the courts.

Organizational Interventions in Law Enforcement Agencies

Implementation of organizational change in law enforcement agencies may take various forms. Described here are but two examples of the sort of interventions that have been designed by psychologists. Both were developed to influence the legal system at the discretionary point of police contact. The first is aimed at reducing the flow of adolescent offenders to the courts so as to avoid the possible negative effects of becoming an identified "delinquent;" reducing the need for police officers, probation officers, and other officials to deal with large numbers of juvenile cases; and, most important, reducing recidivism among the target population. The second was designed to help policemen deal with the large number of family crisis situations to which they are called for assistance.

Diversion of Juveniles from the Legal System through Work with Local Police

As described above, the official involvement of juveniles in the court system may be thought to begin at the point when contact with law enforcement agents leads to a formal petition or referral to the probation office. One strategy for dealing with children is to try to prevent such involvement by using so-called youth service bureaus. This is an attempt to involve "high risk" or "predelinquent" youth in the social service network rather than in the courts. Youth service bureaus are largely unevaluated, traditional services. They run the risk of creating unnecessary entanglements for youngsters who might not actually require "treatment" or go on to engage in serious crime (see footnote 29, p. 349).

The police often have wide discretionary power and rather than referring to a social service agency, they may use a "warn and release" policy for many children. This policy gives the youth another chance without serious consequences, and does not unnecessarily involve in treatment or punishment those who have "learned their lesson." It is not clear, and there is undoubtedly wide variation from one setting to another, at what point and on what basis a police officer will decide to refer to a social service agency, to warn and release, or to file a petition for court action. One group of researchers working with local police departments in Champaign-Urbana, Illinois have intervened in this process at the point of police officer discretion, in an attempt to decrease the use of formal court procedures (Seidman, Rappaport, & Davidson, 1976; Davidson, 1975).

One aim of the Champaign-Urbana diversion project was to avoid too early a referral by encouraging police to use a station adjustment disposition rather than a social service or a court referral for youth with whom they have contact. The diversion project was developed to provide police officers with a viable alternative to court referral, one which would not involve those children for whom station adjustment had not worked in the past with official members of the legal system. The program also had several other emphases. One was to mobilize nonprofessional person power in the form of local college students to provide a no-cost service for local youth, and to train and evaluate the effectiveness of college students (see the section on the Educational Pyramid, Chapter XI, for a detailed description of this aspect of the project). Because the program was funded by the National Institute of Mental Health as a multi-year but time-limited research project through the University of Illinois, it was necessary to design it so that it would continue to provide assistance after the project's termination. An additional aim was to disseminate those aspects of the service shown to be useful to other local service agencies.

The diversion project passed through five phases and is a good example of the need for longitudinal research in community work. In phase 1 the researchers were engaged with several graduate students in laying the groundwork for entry conditions. They spent two years developing service skills by providing graduate student-supervised contact with college students for adolescents already deeply involved in the legal system. Later, graduate students began to talk with and get to know the local police officers charged with decision making for adolescent offenders. After getting to know the local system, phase 2 began with a feasibility pilot study. During that time, rather than waiting for referral from the probation office to the project, the local police agreed to refer youth for whom court process was being seriously considered, thus *by-passing probation and taking the children out of the legal system.* The undergraduates registered for a year-long course. During that time they were required to spend eight to ten hours per week working with a referred youth, and two hours in supervision with graduate students who were in turn supervised by university faculty. After finding that these undergraduates seemed to make good progress with the youngsters, the formal research (phase 3) began.

During phase 3, 37 youths were referred by police and then randomly assigned either to the college-student program or a control condition in which they were simply interviewed but provided with no services. The college students provided the experimental youths with a combination of help-oriented services emphasizing contracts (Stuart, 1971) for responsibilities and privileges negotiated between them and their parents and teachers, and ''advocacy service'' through which the students helped the youths to use community resources (see Chapter VI, p. 200 for a discussion on this latter strategy). At the end of a three- to five-month period all cases carried by the students were terminated, and police contact record data were evaluated.

The approximately 100 police officers on the street did not know who had been randomly assigned to the program, or even who were referred. Police officers other than juvenile officers did not even know the program was in operation. Because the juvenile officers are only called into a case after a contact with a youth is made, that means that police contacts are a relatively unbiased estimate of continued involvement in the legal system. Figure X-1 reports the data for the first year of formal evaluation. As can be seen in this figure, randomly assigned control and experimental youths were comparable with regard to number of police contacts, average seriousness of contact (the range of seriousness was from status offenses through felonies), number of times a petition had been filed with the court, and seriousness of the charges, all covering a period of one year prior to the project. Both during and one year after termination of the project the control group was significantly worse on all of these criteria. When the researchers looked at individual cases they found that from the point of referral to one year after the end of the project only nine of 25 experimentals had further contact with the police, whereas 12 of 12 controls had one or more contacts. Two years after termination the differences in recidivism were still maintained and experimentals continued to have significantly less contact with police than controls, both as a group and for most of the individual cases.

Phase 4 of this research involved a replication of phase 3 in which 36 new youngsters were referred and the same procedures applied. This time, however, the experimental group was randomly assigned either to a behavioral contracting or an advocacy condition to examine each of these procedures independently. As in phase 3, phase 4 research found that the experimental youngsters were involved in significantly less recidivism than the control youth through a one-year follow-up. Both advocacy and contracting seemed to be effective.

During phase 4 Davidson (1975) also systematically collected data on differences in the lives of those children for whom the project was successful and those for whom it failed. He found, by conducting interviews with parents, supervisors, and referred youths and by closely following each child, those who were successful tended to become involved relatively more often with family and school (although neither ''success'' nor ''failure'' children in terms of recidivism changed on intrapsychic measures, and neither group became regular attenders in

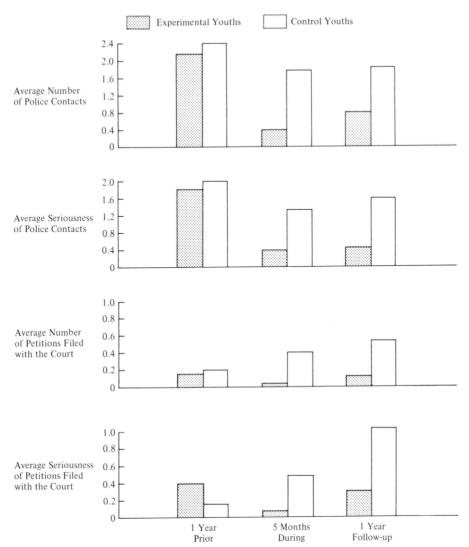

Figure X-1. Differences between experimental and control youth for police and court records during the prior year, program duration, and one-year follow-up ($N_E = 25$, $N_C = 12$). (Redrawn from Seidman, Rappaport, & Davidson, 1976.)

school). That is, those youths who did not have further contact with police did not become sudden success stories in other ways, although they did spend more time, relative to controls, in school and with family.

Interestingly, Davidson (1975) also found that those children who were recidivists tended to get involved with the police almost immedi-

ately after referral, and they and their college-student helpers become entangled in the legal system, rather than in work with school and family. If a child remained out of contact with the law during the first month or so after referral, apparently allowing the college student time in which to initiate new contacts in the school and family rather than with law enforcement agents and court personnel, the chances of nonrecidivism were greatest. Although these data must be viewed cautiously as they are based on a relatively small number of cases, they do provide some evidence for the notion of diversion from the court by direct work with the police so as to avoid official entanglement in the legal system. College students were clearly not viewed as law enforcement agents or as probation officers either by themselves or by the youth, and they were most successful when they stayed away from that system entirely. It should also be emphasized that students were all closely supervised in techniques for contracting and advocacy, and the authors view this supervision as essential to success.

Phase 5 of the Champaign-Urbana diversion project has involved its dissemination to local agencies. The researchers involved a local professional together with a graduate student in the supervision of college students during phase 4, and trained that person to take over the supervision the following year. In addition, those in a local program had agreed to continue to maintain data on success rates. As this last phase continues, cooperation has now developed between police and the new program administrators such that the local community has a viable alternative to court actions on youthful offenders, accomplished largely as a function of working directly with the local police and avoiding probation.

Police and Family Crisis Intervention

A second example of organizational intervention by means of work with local police is provided by the pioneering activities of Morton Bard in New York City (Bard, 1969, 1970, 1971; Bard & Berkowitz, 1967). Bard brought to law enforcement agencies many of the ideas of community mental health, including the involvement of nonprofessionals as providers of psychological services through use of the already existing network of community caregivers. He recognized that the police are frequently called to deal with interpersonal and especially family-oriented crisis situations. Not only are they the first to be called, especially in

lower socioeconomic neighborhoods, during an obvious psychiatric emergency (Liberman, 1969), but they are often the only 24-hour service available in an emergency, and actually spend a large portion of their time in family-crisis situations and other "social work" functions rather than in "crime fighting."[31]

Despite the large amount of time police officers spend dealing with family crises, training in how to handle such difficult situations is rare. Police departments typically want to play down this role and to emphasize their detection-of-criminals image. However, the FBI has reported that in one national study 22 percent of the police officers killed and 40 percent of the injuries sustained in the line of duty occurred during family disturbances (Bard, 1971). Given that police officers are called to perform such services, Bard set out to develop an organizational intervention in the New York City police department which would help them to more ably and safely perform their role.

Bard takes the view that police training should include careful attention to how to intervene in interpersonal crisis situations, and that this should be a regular part of training for all police officers rather than for some special force that only deals with family crises. To test the feasibility of such training for regular police officers who would continue performing all their usual duties, 18 officers (nine Whites and nine Blacks from a volunteer group of 42) from one precinct in New York City were selected. They each experienced formal lectures as well as participation in role playing of crisis situations, and group discussion of how to handle crises. Following training, these officers were called whenever there was a family crisis in their precinct. Each officer was provided with an advanced clinical psychology graduate student consultant with whom the officer met weekly for regular consultation. The officer also continued

---

[31]Wilson (1969) distinguishes between order maintenance (disputes between citizens) and law enforcement (helping to find and prove the guilt of a person who victimizes another). Estimates are that police spend 80–90 percent of their daily activity in order maintenance (Cumming, Cumming, & Edel, 1965; Epstein, 1962; Wilson, 1969).

to meet in a small group with other officers for discussion of their experiences.

For evaluation purposes a neighboring precinct was compared to the experimental precinct, but for various methodological reasons most of the reported statistical comparisons cannot be said to be a function of this project. Nevertheless, Bard did find that during the project there were no injuries to any of the 18 officers who were trained and intervened in a large number of family crises. However, two officers in the same precinct but not in the training program, and one in the control precinct, were injured during family disputes. By emphasizing the finding that police officers may be safer as a function of training, Bard has been able to have a great deal of influence in disseminating the program to other police departments. How he has managed this dissemination, as well as his descriptions of work in preparing the entry conditions to the police force in the first place, are important contributions to the thinking of community psychologists who wish to work with police departments.

Bard's study, although interesting and important in that it demonstrated the feasibility of training police officers in such roles, did not provide a great deal of research evidence with regard to the effects of such training. There is no evidence provided concerning the effect of the crisis intervention of patrol officers on the callers. The work has stimulated a number of other projects, most of which are supported on face validity rather than with research evidence (e.g., Blanton, 1976; Tesse & VanWormer, 1975); but one recent program evaluation study has been reported by a group of researchers working with the police in Louisville, Kentucky (Driscoll, Meyer, & Schanie, 1973).

The Louisville group adopted many of Bard's training techniques but emphasized training in exchange theory (Thibaut & Kelley, 1959)[32] and behavior modification. Police supervisors recruited 12 volunteers for this project. Each volunteer spent five to seven hours in

training each day for five weeks, using lectures, films, and reading material. In addition, they participated in small-group discussions and role played the handling of simulated crises. Feedback to the trainees was given by observing videotapes of their role playing, as well as actual observation of their performance in the field.

The research focused on effectiveness of the intervention in accomplishing its purpose, that is, dealing with the immediate crisis per se. A brief structured telephone questionnaire was administered to a sample of people who had called for help. Twenty-nine families who had received assistance from the specially trained officers, and 26 who had their call answered by untrained officers, were interviewed. Significantly more favorable evaluations of the interventions were given on four of six questions by those who had a trained police officer arrive at the scene (see Table X-7). There is no reason to believe that respondents would be likely to be biased in favor of trained or untrained police officers unless they saw a real difference. They could not have known who was whom or even that there were differentially trained officers, although from the report of this research it is not clear if the interviewer was "blind" with regard to which group the person interviewed was in. Presuming that the interviewer did not know which group the interviewee was in, and although this research does not demonstrate long-term effects on clients, it does seem to indicate that there was at least some immediate satisfaction on the part of the recipients of the service.[33] In addition, the police officers themselves report that they found the training to be valuable, especially in providing alternatives to the use of force.

---

[32]For an explanation of some of the principles of exchange theory, see Chapter IV, pp. 106–109.

[33]Although Bard's study was in an area largely populated by minority groups, the Louisville project was in a 90 percent White community (average income was about $7000 per year). It is not clear if the same satisfaction would be found in Bard's study, although anecdotal evidence of satisfaction is provided. In this regard, an interesting research question concerning the match in values, life style, and culture between police and local residents arises. It is reasonable, for example, to hypothesize that a police officer indigenous to a given neighborhood may be better able to cope with its interpersonal crises, as well as other problems that confront police officers each day, than one who is an "outsider." This suggestion is discussed more fully later in this chapter.

TABLE X–7   **Frequencies of choice of response categories on the client telephone questionnaire.***

Question	Trained (N = 29)			Untrained (N = 26)			Sig.**
	Neg.	Neut.	Pos.	Neg.	Neut.	Pos.	
1. Rapport	1	17	11	8	17	1	$p < 0.01$
2. Involvement	1	5	23	3	11	12	$p < 0.05$
3. Perceived success	5	6	18	3	10	13	n.s.
4. Satisfaction	1	5	23	3	14	9	$p < 0.01$
5. Regard		19	10		25	1	$p < 0.02$
6. Acceptance	3	11	15		14	12	n.s.

*From Driscoll, Meyer, & Schanie, 1973.
**By chi-square analysis. Low-frequency categories collapsed where necessary and possible.

Institutional Change

As with the other social systems discussed in this volume, the need for new paradigms in the criminal justice system and a change in the very "rules of the game" by which it operates is acute. Work at the organizational level can help to accomplish certain humane reforms by assisting the agents of law enforcement, administration of justice, and corrections to accomplish their stated mission. However, institutional change is required if we are to have more than a haphazard "bandaid" approach to crime and delinquency. Perhaps the most important issue to recognize is that value/goals must be faced squarely. What do we want the system to accomplish and how can these goals be realistically approximated?

In this chapter (pp. 321–324) it has already been suggested that community psychology separate itself from the punishment aspects of the criminal justice system. The argument is not that punishment is necessarily a bad or unnecessary aspect of criminal justice, but simply that it should not be misconstrued as being useful through association with the "helping professions." As some have suggested (e.g., Gibbs, 1975; Martinson, 1974), punishment may indeed be a deterrent to crime for some people; we do not really know and it at least satisfies our sense of justice for some crimes. On the other hand, although punishment *may* be both a deterrent and a legitimate form of justice, there is no reason to believe that it rehabilitates, in the positive sense, those who already have been convicted of a crime.

One legitimate focus for community psychology is to experiment with and evaluate *alternatives* to prison that might reduce recidivism. A second focus may be to develop and evaluate court and law enforcement procedures that enhance the equitable distribution of justice. A third, even more difficult, focus is to help society develop and test the preconditions that may reduce the need for crime, or to reevaluate social policy that makes certain deviant, but not necessarily harmful, acts crimes.

The conceptions, strategies, and tactics emphasized throughout this volume have been based on a value system supportive of diversity and the strengths and competencies of individuals; an ecological perspective fostering the development of local community resources; and strategies of social advocacy, community organization, and data-based experimental social innovation. Applied to the three foci for community psychology in the criminal justice system suggested above, where does this way of viewing the world lead? What new paradigms are suggested?

Institutional Changes in Corrections

Local Community-based Settings as an Alternative to Prison

In corrections programs for convicted persons our emphasis must turn away from isolated prison settings and how to reform them. Instead we must look for community-based alternatives.[34] These efforts de-emphasize punishment and removal from society and re-emphasize learning to live in the community.[35] Evidence for the utility of in-community alternatives is relatively rather than absolutely convincing. Such alternatives seem to do *no worse* than prisons in preventing future crime, and they are often less costly in terms of both money and human suffering (Klapmuts, 1973). If one believes that persons convicted of a crime should suffer degrading living conditions then prisons can be supported; if not, there is no reason to continue to use such settings for most offenders because they are no more effective at preventing recidivism than community-based programs. These programs may at least allow the motivated prisoner to learn to live in the society, rather than to simply exist in confinement. Even if one believes that some persons require prison as punishment, the use of confinement is generally admitted to be overdone and unfairly determined. Some (e.g., Klapmuts, 1973) have suggested that at least 50 percent of the people entering prison are no more serious offenders than those placed on probation. Even such organizations as the National Council on Crime and Delinquency (1975) have argued that the "nondangerous" offender should be kept out of prison.

In a recent review of *Community Alternatives for Prison*, Nora Klapmuts (1973) has listed many of the ways in which prison populations can be reduced without increasing risk to the community:

Some of the ways in which institutional populations can be or have been reduced include the expanded use of probation, diversion to "intensive" or specialized probation or other non-residential treatment programs, immediate release to special parole services, referral

to a halfway house, group-home, or other residential programs, and where such centers are a real alternative to prison, placement in a community-based correctional center (Klapmuts, 1973, p. 310).

The Klapmuts review covers many of the same programs that Martinson (1974; see above, p. 342) reviews. Klapmuts is more optimistic than is Martinson about the outcome of such work as the "guided group interaction" programs which focus on peer group pressure and involvement of offenders in decision making. Nevertheless, both agree that although the research does not show that community-based treatment programs are more effective in preventing recidivism than prison, they do at least no worse, and thus do not increase the danger to the community. Klapmuts suggests a social policy that would encourage development of a diverse set of programs, operated by local communities, and subsidized by the state, as an alternative to large state-run prisons. This diversity of programs makes a good deal of sense—it is not reasonable to assume that all who commit crime are the same, nor that what works well in one community will necessarily be useful for another, entirely different community. It is also reasonable to expect that locally developed small experimental units may, by means of the excitement of an innovation over which there is direct control, provide an atmosphere in which success is more likely than in a large prison setting.

Martinson (1972) has even suggested the use of a voucher system wherein convicted persons may participate in the selection of an alternative that they themselves prefer. That suggestion is, of course, quite consistent with the general viewpoint of this entire volume, which favors a diversity of options provided at the local level and the maximum possible individual choice. If such programs were to include systematic and ongoing evaluation and feedback, together with a willingness to change program procedures as a function of that feedback, we would move a long way toward institutional changes. These changes would emphasize some new rules of the game, that is, local responsibility for decision making.

We present below only a few selected examples of community-based treatment programs

---

[34]In a cautionary paper Greenberg (1975) has argued that the entire notion of "community corrections" is both oversold and poorly conceived. He suggests that its overemphasis may actually lead to worse rather than better conditions in prison settings, as well as to an increased tendency to use therapeutic programs as a substitute means of social control.

[35]Martinson, in a series of articles appearing in a popular magazine (*The New Republic*, 1972), argues that prison simply serves to interrupt the occupational life cycle, and therefore makes it more rather than less difficult for a person to adapt to the community after release.

that have some potential as alternatives to prison. They are presented as examples rather than as prescriptions for universal adoption. Although the need for in-community alternatives for both juvenile and adult offenders is seen by many as desirable, community intervention programs have not often been used for adult prison candidates (Greenberg, 1975; Klapmuts, 1973). However, Klapmuts does report some promising preliminary work in Michigan, using intensive community supervision with an emphasis on local resources in lieu of prison for adult recidivists. The idea of the "halfway house" as a transitional facility for prisoners as they return to the community is also often suggested. Unfortunately, research on the outcome of such settings for adults is largely negative or inconclusive (Doleschel & Geis, 1971; Roesch, 1976a). Many of the suggestions made by Kennedy (1976; see the section of this chapter on *Behavior Modification in Prison Settings*) are compatable with community-based programming for adult offenders and might be incorporated into such halfway houses rather than into traditional prison settings, but to date there is little such work with adults.[36] For more youthful offenders there has been both a greater willingness to try community-based alternatives to prison and somewhat better research. Consequently, most of the programs presented in this section focus on youth.

True institutional change in correctional settings is difficult to accomplish. In many ways the very existence of such settings is part of the problem. To assume that they can both exist and operate by different rules of the game may be naive. For this reason, some have gone so far as to suggest that, at least for adolescents, such settings as prisons called "training schools" are unnecessary (Massachusetts Department of Youth Services, 1972). Most agree, however, that for at least a small number of "hard-core" delinquent youths or neglected children, some form of residential program may be desirable. Exactly what the nature of such programs should be is still an open question; however, there is now some reason to believe that such settings should be both small and well-integrated with the local community. The aim is to ease transition to community life by allowing residents to continue living there. Many such settings now involve local nonprofessional people in daily living contact with the youth.[37]

Examples of such programs, based on a number of different assumptions about what community-based human service organizations should be like and how they should be operated, are presented below. The first involves the use of behavior modification technology as an organizing principle in a community based living situation. The assumptions about human behavior and learning as a means to behavior change are essentially those discussed in detail in Chapter IV. In this context it is assumed that by teaching and rewarding prosocial behaviors, the residents will learn new ways to deal with the problems they face, and consequently not become involved in illegal behavior.

Behavior Modification in Residential and Nonresidential Community Settings

There have been a large number of research reports and individual case studies using behavioral procedures as a means to treat juvenile delinquency. Davidson and Seidman (1975)

---

[36]Two programs for adult offenders recently described in the literature are worth noting as exemplary. One, known as St. Leonard's House (Durham, 1974) attempts to provide a community-based "anti-criminal" culture, for recently released offenders, by means of a program largely staffed by ex-offenders and well integrated with the local community. A second, Ellsworth House (Lamb & Goertzel, 1975), is a residential setting based on behavior modification technology. Ellsworth House accepts residents in lieu of incarceration following conviction for serious (felony) offenses. Outcome results of this latter program are typical in finding that it did not lead to increased recidivism compared to a control group who had gone to jail. Its supporters suggest that if recidivism is not increased, such programs are desirable in that they help to realistically integrate offenders in their local communities.

[37]The placement of such programs in this section, as representative of institutional change, may be somewhat arbitrary in that they can be viewed as attempts to change individual persons rather than systems, a problem for all "corrections" programs. Nevertheless, they are placed here because of their common emphasis on serving as *community-based alternatives to prisons* in the corrections component of the criminal justice system.

have reviewed over 60 separate reports with goals ranging from teaching self-care to reduction of delinquent behavior per se. The studies have used various kinds of research designs, ranging from the study of a single person to experimental and control group comparisons. Unfortunately, the authors of this review conclude that most studies have serious methodological problems, and taken as a whole, the positive results found when reinforcing some specific behavior while a person is in a treatment program have not been shown to generalize or to reduce later delinquent behavior.

One of the more well-known programs combining in-community treatment with a behavioral program is the work at Achievement Place conducted by researchers from the University of Kansas. (Phillips, 1968; Phillips, Phillips, Fixsen, & Wolf, 1971; Fixsen, Phillips, & Wolf, 1972, 1973; Wolf, Phillips, & Fixsen, 1972.) Recently Hoefler & Bornstein (1975) have presented an evaluative review of this work which summarizes both its accomplishments and directions for future study.

The Achievement Place program was designed to provide a family-like, small-group living arrangement for court-referred young boys, all from low income families, and all who had committed minor offenses including theft, fighting, and truancy. Usually these children are referred because they are considered neglected by their parents and are thought to be "predelinquent." The Achievement Place research has focused largely on teaching very specific kinds of prosocial behavior such as cleaning one's room, studying, learning to save money, being on time for dinner, and speaking in a proper fashion. Most of this research has focused on demonstrations of how specific contingencies are functionally related to obtaining the desired behaviors. Although the program began with a token-economy point system and continues to use that as a basic organizing principle, over the years "social reinforcement" aspects have gained prominence. Three such key elements of the program now emphasize the house parents as teacher-models, peers as a social influence mechanism, and a formal self-government system. Although there are a number of specific

questions which remain to be answered about how the behaviors are learned within the program, these issues are relatively esoteric compared to the more basic question of generalizability and effect on recidivism.

In one attempt to deal with the issue of recidivism, Phillips, Phillips, Fixsen, & Wolf (1973) report that, in a comparison of children released for at least one year, only 19 percent from Achievement Place had committed a delinquent act for which they were readjudicated and placed in a state institution, whereas over 50 percent of a group of boys either released from a Kansas correction facility or who had been on probation, suffered this fate. Unfortunately, as the authors themselves point out, this was not an experimental study, since children were not randomly assigned to these three treatment conditions. The need remains for long-term follow-up studies experimentally comparing different treatments with programs similar to Achievement Place.[38]

Another example of the use of behavior modification techniques in community treatment is the work of Tharp and Wetzel (1969). It deals with children and avoids residential care altogether. They used nonprofessional "behavior analysts" as persons who were specifically trained and worked with 89 delinquent children referred by the local schools, parents, social agencies, and the courts. The range of problems included theft, runaways, property destruction, and disruptive classroom behavior. Children continued to live at home, and the behavior analysts worked with persons who these researchers refer to as "mediators," or those who are influential in controlling the natural contingencies in a child's life. Examples of mediators are parents, teachers, and employers, who the behavior analysts could teach to use reinforcement techniques with the target children. In a series of individual case reports and by use of three follow-up assessments over a period of 18 months, Tharp and Wetzel show decline in legal

---

[38]Cohen & Filipczak (1971) have shown some positive effects of a token program when contrasted to a standard training school. They found recidivism rates to be lower for the experimental group after 2 years of follow-up but equal to the training school group after 3 years.

offenses and improvement in school performance and behavioral ratings from significant others.

In an extension of this sort of program, Fo and O'Donnell (1974) used graduate students as behavior analysts who supervised nonprofessionals serving as "buddies" for referred children. They found that they were successful in reducing problem behaviors such as truancy, fighting, and school attendance, but not grades. More recently they have extended this research to a study of 264 referred youngsters who were randomly assigned to the buddy program or to a no-treatment control group (Fo & O'Donnell, 1975). Although they found that the buddy program was successful in significantly reducing the number of serious offenses for youths who had committed such offenses in the year prior to the project, they also discovered that for youths who had no "major offenses" prior to project referral, those who participated in the buddy system committed significantly *more* offenses than control youngsters. These authors raise the question which others such as Schur (1973) have also raised: Can such programs, by overidentification and involvement of youths in the legal or treatment mechanisms, actually increase their delinquent behavior? Such questions merit serious consideration by those who would emphasize early identification and prevention (see the section on *Radical Nonintervention,* below).

The California Community Treatment Program

Perhaps the best known of the programs that have attempted to avoid the use of prison for young, already adjudicated offenders, is the longitudinal study begun in 1961 under the direction of the California Youth Authority. The major results of this work have been presented in two papers corresponding to phases of the research covering the periods 1961–1969 and 1969–1974 (Palmer, 1971, 1974). For the first portion of the work the question addressed was "could (the) CYA (California Youth Authority) parole agents work effectively with some of these individuals (juvenile offenders) *without first locking them up for several months* in a

large sized, state institution?'' (Palmer, 1974, p. 3, italics in original.)

In the 1961–1969 phase over 1000 children between the ages of 13 and 19, from the Sacramento, Stockton, and San Francisco areas were included, representing the population typical for the state as a whole. They had been in trouble with the law an average of 5.8 times by the time the court sent them to the Youth Authority, California's juvenile corrections agency. All eligible youths were first sent to a reception center for four to six weeks where they were routinely "processed" and then randomly assigned to the community treatment program or to a control program. Controls were sent to a prison setting for several months and then returned to their community under the usual supervision of parole agents. Strictly speaking, then, the control group was a treatment as usual condition. The community treatment program youths were not sent to an institution and were assigned to a parole officer who carried no more than 12 cases. In addition, the youths were classified as to "level of maturity" or "personality patterns" (most were labeled passive-conformist, power-oriented, or neurotic) and each parole officer was matched with the type of youths with whom he or she was thought to be effective.

Strategies of treatment used by the parole officers included planning where the youth would live, being available for emergencies, even on a daily basis, and "extensive surveillance" including evenings and weekends. Available resources included group and foster homes, a community center school, tutoring, and recreational activities. In short, this was an intensive intervention by parole officers in the lives of the youths.[39]

Results are reported for the group as a whole and by sex and "personality type." The most successful group, when compared to controls, were so-called male neurotics, who Palmer re-

---

[39]Such a program could be classified as an organizational intervention in the courts by means of intensive probation. It is included here because it *follows* adjudication, and because it was intended to serve as a model for correctional system change in California.

ports now also comprise about 70–75 percent of the Youth Authority population. Controls were arrested 2.7 times more often than these experimentals during the time of their involvement in the program. Results for the other types were less promising. "Power-oriented" youths, for example, did worse than the control youths. Nonetheless, the group of all boys, regardless of type, were still significantly less likely to be arrested than the control group during the time of involvement with the Youth Authority. Unfortunately, after the youths left the control of the Youth Authority, they were actually more likely to be arrested and convicted than the control group, although the "neurotic" boys alone did better than their controls. Girls tended to do about equally well regardless of program participation.

Although Palmer (1974) seems to argue that these results indicate a successful program, if one reads carefully the footnotes to the data analysis, the picture at best becomes clouded. The above results are for youths who were discharged from the California Youth Authority with a "favorable" report: 77 percent of the Es and 40 percent of the Cs at five years after their initial parole. If all boys in the study are included they found that 50 percent of both the experimentals and the controls who were given an unfavorable discharge were sent to a state or federal prison. Consequently, the research reporting reduced recidivism rates excludes a large number of failures.

Others (Robison & Takagi, 1971) have also suggested that the California Youth Authority recidivism findings may have been influenced by the decision-making process. Lerman (1968), for example, suggests that experimentals may have been treated with more leniency than controls. Nevertheless, as Klapmuts (1973) has pointed out, the California Youth Authority program does seem to have demonstrated that for most youths a noninstitutional program is both feasible and at least no less effective than prison and parole.

Finally, it should be noted that in recent years the Youth Authority has investigated the use of a small residential facility staffed by counselors and parole officers for a subset of youths found not to benefit from immediate community release, or to be the most difficult to handle. They suggest that this kind of facility, together with a community release program, provides a necessary range of choice for dealing with the various youths encountered.

The Residential Youth Center: An Autonomous Alternative Setting

Perhaps the best example of a residential setting designed for "hard-core" youths which managed to operate in innovative as opposed to prison-like ways is the Residential Youth Center developed by Ira Goldenberg (1971). Its basic orientation is very different from the programs discussed above.

Some of the significance of the Residential Youth Center has already been noted in other contexts in this volume. As a strategy for social change it typifies the autonomous alternative setting. The program was independent of the department of corrections. It was voluntary and operated so as to maximize control and participation for all members of the setting. The program dealt with youths on whom all the existing social service agencies agreed they had "given up." Ideologically, Goldenberg emphasized the *horizontal structure* of a true collaborative venture with residents and staff and, regardless of their specific job, all were deeply involved in program decision making. The setting may have actually succeeded in changing relationships between "treater" and "treated" and among staff members themselves, so as to include everyone in the process of running the setting. Goldenberg argues that this is an essential element in such a setting. He describes in great detail the entry conditions, the prehistory, and the procedures that often make staff and residents of such settings enemies and that alienate lower and upper level staff from one another, thereby robbing the setting of its vitality and its hope to be useful to its clients. His book, *Build Me a Mountain*, is an excellent concrete example of what Sarason calls the creation of settings.

Among Goldenberg's first premises was the belief that innovation would require change in the change agents themselves rather than in the targets per se. In essence, the goal was to create an "organizational vehicle" that would be a "growth" setting for staff as well as clients. All persons, regardless of their official job, performed all roles in the setting. They all lived in and they all made treatment decisions. The aim was interchangeability of people in a communal organization, and Goldenberg himself planned and carried out his own exit from the program so that a new leader would develop from within. The full-time staff were nonprofessionals who, now in their late twenties, knew the inner city and were often themselves viewed as trouble makers and complainers. Included also were part-time workers who were students at Yale; they also shared all duties.

The youths in the program were the "worst of the worst." They were selected from a cross-referenced list of the 178 youngsters most often mentioned by local agencies as impossible to help. They ranged in age from 16 to 21 and were irregularly employed. Seventy percent had been arrested (an average of 2.9 times). Almost all had been in an institution of one kind or another. Most came from welfare families and lived in fatherless or foster families. They were labeled by everyone as "hard-core" or "chronically disadvantaged."

The center aimed at developing a program where individual staff, residents, and families could work together. They began with an original group of 20 youngsters, and sought to help them become regularly employed and to return to independent living. Beyond that, the goals for staff and residents were viewed as similar: to develop collective growth in a shared living arrangement.

At no time was the program to be allowed to become or to resemble an institution: there were no visiting hours, parents were encouraged to come at any time of the day or night, the residents paid rent, and the boys were free to go home any time they wanted. The program, both formally and informally, was to consist of a house in which people—not "patients" or "inmates"—could work and live with one another, could grow and begin to perceive themselves as no longer powerless to alter and influence their lives, and, perhaps more than anything else, could begin to make some sense out of the paradoxical and often times contradictory world we all share (Goldenberg, 1971, p. 151).

For research purposes the 20 young men first admitted to the center were those mentioned by the most number of agencies as "hard core." The next most mentioned 20 became a control group, and the behavior and attitudes of both groups were observed over time.

Goldenberg found that work attendance records for the center youths went from about 66 percent prior to the program to 97 percent after 36 weeks of involvement, whereas the control youth deteriorated in work attendance records from 86 to 56 percent over the same period of time. There were parallel changes in both vocational status and amount of income. Although the two groups did not differ in their measured attitudes at the start of the study, six months later the center youths were expressing significantly less alienation as well as a number of other more positive attitudes than the controls. Table X-8 presents the arrest rate and the rate of time spent in jail for each group, six months before and six months after the beginning of the Residential Youth Center program. As can be seen from the table, the center youths were in-

TABLE X–8 Mean number of arrests and number of days in jail for RYC and control youths.***

	Six Months Prior to RYC Program		Six Months After the Onset of RYC	
	Number of Arrests	Days in Jail	Number of Arrests	Days in Jail
RYC Youths	1.87	153	0.96	70
Control Youths	1.70	140	2.08	258

*Adapted from Goldenberg, 1971.
**Residential Youth Center.
Note: Groups are not significantly different at the prepoint, but they are at post ($p < .01$).

volved in significantly fewer arrests and spent significantly less time in jail.

It is apparent that the youths involved in this program benefited from it in comparison to control youths. As Goldenberg is acutely aware, it is not possible to definitively argue that the reason for this relative success is some specific procedure in the program. He therefore talks of the ''RYC experience'' as a whole. It may even be that the improvement is simply due to the excitement of a new program, but given the history of these youths and the failure of other programs for similar youths, the kind of autonomous setting Goldenberg describes must be viewed as one worthy of future research and development by a community psychology seeking new methods for building on the strengths of young people, with a history of legal difficulty. It would also be of interest to extend this type of program to adult offenders, and to test the effectiveness of an autonomous alternative setting with that population.[40]

Other Reforms in Correctional Settings

Before leaving the issue of institutional change in correctional agencies, there are several ideas that deserve mention as possibly useful reforms. Because it is unlikely that prisons will ever be eliminated altogether, especially for adults, even if there is a wider use of community-based treatment several reforms that are different from those based on treatment models per se should be mentioned here. Many of these have recently been suggested by Tom Railsback, a member of the U.S. House of Representatives Judiciary Committee (Railsback, 1975). He has supported, for example, genuine attempts to provide gainful employment for prisoners, and cites such programs in Sweden, Holland, and Denmark which allow prisoners to work during the day and return to prison at night. As he points out, current employment opportunities in prison do not provide training in marketable skills, do not pay prisoners a fair

wage, and because of opposition from labor unions, prisoners have not been allowed to enter competition with free enterprise. His suggestion is to pass legislation that would encourage the business community to directly employ prisoners. He further argues that prisons should not be ''isolated fortresses,'' and that there should be curbs on their discretionary powers, minimal standards of treatment, freedom from personal abuse and from censorship, as well as an ombudsman for complaints. Finally, Railsback suggests that parole is currently handled in what appears to be an arbitrary and capricious manner. A prisoner should have less uncertainty about the length of his or her sentence and the law should be more equal for both rich and poor. Many of these suggestions are very general, but have the possibility of becoming both specific and functional through legislative changes which people in Congress such as Railsback may support. Obviously, one way to generate such support is to organize popular movements for legal reform and to back candidates who favor it. This brings us directly to a discussion of institutional change in the administration of justice and law enforcement.

Institutional Change in the Courts and Law Enforcement Agencies

Although the most heated debates about social policy in corrections concern the battle over in-prison or in-community treatment, with small-group residential settings discovered as a compromise, there are other alternatives to correctional programs that have not been well studied and that would constitute a more clear change in the ''rules of the game.'' These are changes that would require new paradigmatic ways to look at the problem of crime and the way in which it is handled by the courts and the law enforcement agencies. What would happen, for example, if we were to adopt a model that rejects *both* punishment and treatment, in favor of institutional rule changes that reduce the need for either one? Obviously there will be limits to this—for some crimes punishment may be legitimately regarded as ''just'' and for some persons, voluntary treatment may be useful. For example, we would probably all agree that mur-

---

[40]It should be noted in this regard that the program participants may not have been remarkably different from adults. These youths ranged up to 21 years of age, and all were out of school.

der deserves punishment, and regardless of whether or not it deters murderers, it does satisfy our sense of justice. On the other hand, a youthful high-school drop-out who is arrested for theft is far more likely to be a recidivist, regardless of treatment or punishment; hence he is in fact a greater "threat" to society. At the same time, to satisfy our sense of justice we seem to be willing, under some circumstances, not to punish the youth. Generally, when we have not punished we have treated (although these are not always distinguishable).

If society is willing to forego punishment under some circumstances and if treatment is not generally effective, why not try something else? One answer may be because we cannot think of anything else; or if we think of something else, some new ideas (paradigms or ways of viewing the world) are slow to take hold and literally require a kind of Kunnian revolution, as discussed in Chapter I. Those innovations that are often slowest to take hold are the ones that require change in role relationships (cf. Fairweather, 1972; Sarbin, 1970). This may be exactly what we require in the legal system.

If we take the position that the reasons for crime are not totally a function of the person but have some relationship to the situations in which persons reside, *as well as the way in which the legal system itself operates;* and if we combine this with a perspective which looks for strengths and resources in people and communities, as well as a social value system tolerant of differences and protective of society without requiring all people to match some ideal standard of middle-class behavior, we are led to some interesting possibilities that could result in a drastic reduction of crime rates.

Crimes without Victims

Several authors have questioned the usefulness of laws which consider as criminal offenses acts between consenting adults, or those which harm no one other than, perhaps, one's self (Geis, 1972; Schur, 1965). Those crimes most often considered to be without victims include drunkenness, disorderly conduct, violation of liquor laws, juvenile runaways, vagrancy, curfew and loitering, suspicion, gambling, and prostitution. Doleschel (1971), using the FBI's uniform crime reports for 1969, found that together these categories accounted for 51 percent of all arrests! A recent survey (U.S. Department of Justice, 1974) of inmates in local jails found many of those confined were actually serving time for one of these victimless crimes. Obviously, such crimes take up a great deal of the time spent by law enforcement agents and courts. Public drunkenness, for example (excluding drunk driving) accounted for just under 25 percent of all arrests in 1969, a rate higher than for those crimes the FBI calls "Index" or serious: homicide, rape, robbery, aggravated assault, burglary, larceny, and automobile theft (Roesch, 1976a). The prosecution of such crimes, in at least a substantial portion of cases, may be based on an archaic attempt to legislate personal morality.

Prostitution and homosexuality are examples of crimes often thought to require criminal sanctions in order to show public disapproval; yet this reasoning may be faulty. Social approval or disapproval for such behavior is already expressed as a natural consequence of public opinion. More to the point, to add formal criminal punishment does not rehabilitate, nor does it change behavior, except perhaps to teach people to be more discreet. The price we pay for our inability to tolerate deviance that does not harm others and is engaged in by consenting adults may be an unfair infringement on individual freedom. This infringement does not match the logic of a society which presumably prides itself on such freedom. It is not necessary to approve of such behavior in order to remove it from the concern of the law inforcement agencies and the courts. The issue of victimless crimes, in fact, presents many of the same problems that were discussed in the review of Szasz (1970), presented in Chapter II. In a more recent work, Szasz (1974) has extended his analysis of society's inability to tolerate deviance, and its ritual persecution by application of the illness paradigm to those accused of drug abuse and addiction.

In any discussion of crimes without victims it is important to be aware that in our society systems of social control are intimately interrelated. Usually when people have been diverted from the legal system, or when discussions of decriminalization are presented, the justification is in terms of mental health or medical treatment for people who are now viewed as sick rather than as criminals. We seem to insist either on legislating "normal" behavior and punishing those who deviate by calling them criminals, or treating the disapproved behavior as "sick." We often seem unwilling to allow people the right to be different, to use their own bodies as they please, to choose same sexed partners, or to ingest drugs that are arbitrarily made illegal. Yet as Szasz makes clear, the use of the legal system (or the mental health system) as a means to control such deviance is a solution which creates a problem in exactly the sense suggested by Watzlawick, Wakeland, and Fisch (1974; see Chapter V):

. . . the verbal shaping of the problem itself constitutes much or even all of the ensuing problem. We (seem) to have learned little or nothing from the fact that we had no problem with drugs until we quite literally talked ourselves into having one: we declared first this and then that drug "bad" and "dangerous"; gave them nasty names like "dope" and "narcotics"; and passed laws prohibiting their use. The result: our present "problem of drug abuse and drug addiction" (Szasz, 1974, p. 11).

The issue here is not the positive or negative effects of drugs on people. Many drugs are illegal, and others (often the same ones) are legal under "medical care."[41] This allows the rich to have access to greater individual freedom than the poor because they can more easily afford "medical care" and receive amphetamines and other drugs that are denied the poor. Unjust as that may be, in this context the real issue is that making the use of drugs illegal may be *creating* crime, not just because people violate the drug laws, but because they often need to engage in crime in order to obtain the money to get an overpriced illegal product (often more dangerous because of unknown additives put in the drugs to increase their volume). The lesson we

might have learned from our experience with prohibition of alcohol seems not to have been learned.

The problem is similar for gambling, in which the same act is legal if sanctioned by a state (e.g., in lotteries or at race tracks), but illegal if people "play the numbers." At the same time, the wealthy who can gamble in private clubs are allowed a pleasure which the more visible poor are denied.

Although he suggests the use of criminal restrictions on the "unlawful manufacture of addictive or other dangerous substances," as well as their sale, Nicholas N. Kittrie (1971) in his comprehensive volume, *The Right To Be Different,* suggests that:

We must reconsider the utility and justification of criminal or even of therapeutic sanctions with regard to the lesser offenses of drug possession and use by addicts . . . possession should be exempted from sanctions . . . It needs to be recognized that the desire for artificial euphoria must be controlled *on a different level* than in the past . . . by public education, by the removal of urban poverty and racial ghettos which lead to a sense of inadequacy and worthlessness, and by building a society better equipped to provide its members with a sense of individual well-being derived from an honorable and useful social role (pp. 259–260, italics added).

In like fashion Kittrie goes on to suggest that a similar problem comes from our treatment of drunkenness as a crime:

A realistic and pluralistic society must recognize, furthermore, that unless it is willing to pay the price for total conformity, it must learn to tolerate its deviants. This is particularly true with regard to those deviants who pose no immediate and direct threat to the public safety. Burdening the criminal process with two million public intoxication cases a year is not only an overextension of the police function but is also wasteful, economically as well as socially (p. 295).

And again, with regard to juvenile offenses:

By default of the modern family, church, school, and community, the role of principal guardian of social order and conformity depends increasingly on the police and the courts . . . The concept of "delinquency" has been stretched too far . . . Its business, usually, should be limited to juveniles whose conduct would constitute a violation of the law if committed by an adult. It should not be the province of the juvenile

---

[41] An example of this hypocrisy is the use of methadone as a substitute for heroine. In this treatment the addict simply substitutes one drug for another that is under the control of the state. Szasz is particularly concerned with this as another example of control of the medical profession over the rights of individual freedom.

court to serve as a family and child welfare agency or to rehabilitate children who run away from home, smoke, drink, who are truants, and who are otherwise "incorrigible" . . . major efforts must be made within the community itself . . . the problem of delinquency as a whole is not likely to be answered by severer penalties, nor by kindly treatment, or individual psychotherapy (pp. 165–168).

It is these latter cases of so-called status offenses or "crimes" by youths, not illegal for an adult, that have also stimulated the suggestions for institutional change made by Schur (1973, see below). The views of these two authors are quite consistent with the viewpoint expressed throughout this volume. If one were to take the "strengths perspective" suggested by Berck (1976b), and the environmental resources strategy of Davidson and Rapp (1976; see Chapters V and VI), people who commit socially deviant acts would be assumed to possess a variety of strengths and would be able to profit from access to environmental resources in developing these strengths, rather than being jailed as criminals or treated as sick. Berck's example (p. 127) of how the perspective would treat school truants is directly relevant here. (See also Wenk, 1974.)

To posit a different example, consider the case of prostitution. Making prostitution legal would enable it to come under the auspices of the department of public health, thereby reducing the spread of venereal disease and removing at least some of organized crime's control of such activities, both effects that are likely to have more benefit for society than putting prostitutes in prison. From the point of view of the person, prostitution might be viewed as a legitimate business, enabling one to earn a living, pay taxes, and become an above- rather than an "underground" member of society. Social disapproval of prostitution is not questioned here. One may disapprove of such activities without requiring that people go to jail for engaging in them, especially when the "victims" are willing participants.

Similarily, to continue to call people who engage in homosexual activities by mutual consent either sick or criminals is much less sensible for society than to allow its members to live otherwise normal and productive lives without interference (cf. Davison, 1976). It makes no more sense to call homosexuals criminals than to call married people who have children criminals or sick because they are contributing to the population explosion.

Perhaps the major point to be stressed here is the one Schur (1973) cites from the Wolfenden Report issued in 1957 by a British governmental committee which examined laws on homosexuality and prostitution:

Unless a deliberate attempt is to be made by society, acting through the agency of the law, to equate the sphere of crime with that of sin, there must remain a realm of private morality and immorality which is, in brief and crude terms, not the law's business. To say this is not to condone or encourage private immorality (cited in Schur, 1973, p. 143).

Radical Nonintervention

Edwin M. Schur (1973) has presented a persuasive case for what he calls radical nonintervention, or "leaving the kids alone whenever possible." He is particularily concerned with those specifically juvenile offenses such as truancy, curfew violation, running away from home, "incorrigibility," and other such instances of "status offenses" or official misconduct, but his analysis is also relevant to delinquent behavior more generally. As Schur notes, although delinquency is not always the same as victimless crime, there are a number of similarities. The behaviors are vaguely defined and wide ranging, often causing no direct harm to another person. In many instances a complaint is lodged "in the best interests of the child," and involves the imposition of rules by a powerful group of adults on powerless youths. Due process is often violated because guilt is simply assumed. Often the child is stereotyped by case descriptions which justify taking action on the basis of stereotypes about life style. For example, two children who commit the same act, say shoplifting, but who are from different family backgrounds often will be dealt with on the basis of their backgrounds rather than their illegal act. The middle-class child with a "good family" is far more likely to be returned to the custody of one's parents while the lower-class child from a "broken home" ends up under the supervision of a probation officer.

Schur's analysis is based in part on the notions of labeling theory which suggest, in this context, that calling a person a "criminal" begins a process in which the person is treated like a criminal by social agents. The person even begins to regard himself or herself in that way. The process, once begun, leads to a kind of self-fulfilling prophesy. Schur, like those who have emphasized these processes in explanations of "mental illness," suggests that a crucial step in the making of a delinquent involves the *response of others* to deviance. Once labeled "juvenile delinquent" the child is placed in a relationship to society that can serve as a kind of social trap. The child now has what Sarbin (1970, see Chapter IV) refers to as *ascribed status,* or a social position that cannot be understood by studying only the child, but requires analysis of those who make the rules and who react to the child:

In our society, lower-class children more than middle-class ones, black children more than white ones, and boys more than girls, face high probabilities (i.e., run a special "categorical risk" in the actuarial sense) not only of engaging in rule-violations in the first place, but also of becoming enmeshed in official negative labeling processes. By the same token, *their social positions offer them fewer resources with which to withstand the degrading consequences of such labeling* . . . The labeling approach, then, does not assert that the stigmatizing process is simple, direct, or unvarying. It has, however, alerted us to the strong possibility that various kinds of intervention in the lives of children have these effects; indeed that such *intervention often may do more harm than good* (Schur, 1973, p. 126, italics added).

This viewpoint is consistent with the logical arguments and research data (see, for example, Fo & O'Donnell, 1975, p. 360) presented throughout this volume that are critical of a victim-blaming, weakness-oriented approach to social problems. Schur reviews and criticizes the traditional means of controlling deviance based on a need for individual treatment or on liberal reform. By liberal reform he means the same paradigmatic views and methods that are criticized in this volume as the early-experience environmental approach (see especially Chapters VII and VIII), and as community mental health (see Chapter III). He rejects the view that a simple causal explanation for delinquency is sufficient (e.g., the person is different, delinquency prone, has a criminal personality, or that the environment is bad and therefore causes delinquency). Instead, Schur suggests that the problem must be viewed in what he calls "contingent and situational terms" which, translated into the terminology of this volume, emphasize that behavior is in part a function of resources available.

The discussion in Chapter VI of a *multiple strategy-environmental resources model* for social intervention (Davidson & Rapp, 1976) is based on a similar viewpoint which rejects the paradigms of individual or environmental deficit in favor of one based on analysis of the strengths of persons, the potential resources available in local communities, and an advocacy rather than an adversary approach to youth. In thinking about social interventions in the juvenile justice system this strategy may be directly applicable as an alternative to traditional approaches; indeed it was designed by Davidson and Rapp specifically for that purpose. This strategy also has the advantage of a multilevel view which recognizes the need for change in the responses of all the actors in the system, not simply the individual "delinquent." The model is thus consistent with labeling theory which asserts that the organizations of social control, by their very response to youth, may exacerbate rather than alleviate problems, and that advocating institutional change in the rules of the system is a legitimate strategy. This is exactly what Schur means by "radical nonintervention."

. . . the primary target for delinquency policy should be neither the individual nor the local community setting, but rather the delinquency-defining processes themselves . . . radical nonintervention implies policies that accommodate society to the widest possible diversity of behaviors and attitudes, rather than forcing as many individuals as possible to "adjust" to supposedly common standards. This does not mean that anything goes, that all behavior is socially acceptable. But traditional delinquency policy has proscribed youthful behavior well beyond what is required to maintain a smooth running society or to protect others from youthful depredation. (Schur, 1973, p. 154).

Finally, it should be noted that Schur is aware that radical nonintervention cannot solve all of the problems and he supports a variety of other approaches to be *combined* with his general social policy. He is most optimistic about those which use a community focus that avoids stigmatization, employs indigenous nonprofessionals, including older youths who have themselves been in legal difficulty, and noninstitutional, voluntary programs. But he cautions that these cannot get at the heart of the problem unless they are part of a more general social policy which respects the rights of youths to select a variety of life styles, stops viewing them as necessarily sick or vicious and avoids a "paternalistic, patronizing, or even hostile philosophy" (Schur, 1973, p. 168).

There are many who believe that beyond the problems of juvenile justice the entire criminal justice system is in need of drastic reform (cf. President's Commission on Law Enforcement and Criminal Justice, 1967). It would take several volumes to consider all the many suggestions that have been made. Here at least some of the issues not already made explicit should be mentioned.

Jury Procedures[42]

One area for possible study and reform involves increasing the fairness of jury procedures. These have usually been regarded as sacrosanct, although issues such as a jury's ability to understand the judge and how juries are selected have been studied (Kalven, 1957). Some have suggested that verdicts are to a large extent predictable from the proportion of jurors initially favoring conviction, and that concensus

increases with deliberation (Davis, 1973). If this is the case, obviously the implications for justice are profound, and careful assessment of the pretrial attitudes of potential jurors may be crucial to a fair trial.

Another issue of concern has been how jury size affects outcome; some jurisdictions allow six- rather than twelve-member juries. Valenti and Downing (1975), in a recent simulated jury study, found that, as predicted from small-group laboratory research, jury size had no effect on conviction if "apparent guilt" was low, but it did if apparent guilt was high. In the latter case six-person juries were more likely than twelve-person juries to convict. This finding is exactly the opposite to a ruling by the Supreme Court (Williams v. Florida, 1972) which held that in their opinion, size of the jury was irrelevant. Again, the implications of this sort of research for insuring fair jury procedures are obvious, and the researchers make several suggestions for future work useful to those who would like to base reform on well-controlled empirical laboratory studies.

Applying a different research strategy, Nagel and Weitzman (1972) reviewed data from actual jury decisions (rather than from simulated laboratory studies of college student "jurors") to determine whether or not the fact that few women serve on juries and as judges might affect the outcome of trials. They report data on a large number of civil cases which show that the predominant sex of the jury did not affect the findings of culpability in liability suits, but that it did affect the amount of damages awarded. Male-dominated juries gave larger awards to male plaintiffs, while female-dominated juries reversed the favoritism in favor of females. They suggest the need for a social policy that encourages women to attend law school so that they can become judges and laws that require more equal or balanced representation of the sexes on juries.

Sentencing

Another area of legal reform currently receiving widespread discussion involves questions concerning length of sentence and if a sentence should be definite or open-ended (i.e.,

---

[42]There is fast developing a fair amount of research in this realm, both in and outside of psychology. Although the details are beyond the scope of this chapter, the potential for useful findings being translated into reform is great. Those who wish to pursue this topic might begin with the following general references which approach the topic from various perspectives: Cunningham, 1974; Davis, Bray, & Holt, 1976; Gerbasi, Zuckerman, & Reis, in press; Kalven & Zeisel, 1966; and Simon, 1975.

with a minimum and a maximum term allowing actual time spent in jail to be determined by a parole board). Related questions concern the amount of discretion allowed the judge in setting a sentence, and whether the judge should be able to consider each case individually or have tight restrictions by means of mandatory sentences set by the state. This issue was touched on briefly early in this chapter with regard to cases involving civil commitment to "therapeutic" institutions such as Patuxent, but the arguments have also been extended to all sentencing procedures.

Dershowitz (1975) has written on the complicated issues of justice involved in the sentencing debate, and he suggests that the days of the indeterminate sentence are dawning. There is increasing agreement from "law and order" conservatives who feel such sentences pamper criminals, and from liberal "reformers" and prisoners themselves who feel that indeterminate sentences provide unfair power to parole boards as well as unfair variation in the treatment of people convicted of the same crime. There is also mounting evidence (some of which is detailed by Dershowitz) that sentences are often more a function of the judge or the demographic characteristics of the defendant than of the crime.

The option of replacing judicial discretion with legislatively determined fixed sentences is now being seriously considered. These debates are in part a function of realizing that the whole idea of regarding prison as treatment or rehabilitation has failed, and that to make release contingent upon rehabilitation is therefore absurd. Other arguments in favor of change include the desire to end the special privileges afforded white-collar criminals who some judges tend to treat with more leniency than street criminals. Most observers seem to agree that the best system would be to provide greater certainty of confinement for some definite length of time. Various possible practical combinations of judicial discretion and definite sentences are discussed by Dershowitz (1975).[43]

One detailed set of practical proposals has been offered by Judge Constance Baker Motley of the U.S. District Court for the Southern District of New York (1973). She has proposed that:

1. No first offender should be sentenced to prison except for "the most blameworthy offenses, such as premeditated murder."
2. Judges should be limited to sentences set by the legislature.
3. Suspended sentences should be rare and subject to review.
4. Length of sentence should be determined only by number of convictions and seriousness.
5. Following a second conviction the sentence should be short (she suggests six months to one year depending on the crime) and sentences should be increased in length for each additional time a person is convicted of a crime.[44]
6. Victimless crimes should be removed from the criminal justice system.

Judge Motley's overall point of view is best expressed in her own words:

> To say that a judge through the exercise of his presently uncharted discretion can in every case fashion punishment to fit not only the crime, but the individual, is to say that the judge is not only ordained by God but that he is God (Motley, 1973, p. 268).

Prevention of Violence and Crime by Change in Police and Law Enforcement Practices

As Monahan (1976, p. 27) points out, our failure to predict violence "may lie with the theoretical paradigms and research strategies which have constricted the psychological and psychiatric fields until very recently." He cites the work of behaviorists such as Mischel and

---

[43] One of the political issues hidden in this debate is the fear among "liberals" that the legislature might set sentences that are too severe, while "conservatives" have the opposite concern. What must be recognized is that a perfect system is impossible, but one which allows for public debate by elected officials is probably more desirable than private determination by a single judge. Public debate forces us to openly consider our values and our sense of justice.

[44] A similiar proposal for graduated sentencing severity has been offered by a National Advisory Commission appointed in 1971 by the Law Enforcement Assistance Administration.

Bandura (see Chapter IV) and environmental researchers such as Craik and Moos (see Chapter V) which indicates that behavior must be assumed to be a function of both the person and the situation. He goes on to suggest that we need to spend more time identifying and modifying the situations that lead to violence rather than predicting which people are "violence prone."[45] For example, modifying environmental characteristics such as lighting in urban areas, or training police officers to cope with family crisis situations (cf. Bard, 1969, and above) wherein they suffer a large number of injuries, may be more productive than treating potential criminals. He also suggests that increased public transportation and public education to advise women about the dangers of hitchhiking situations (and/or to provide courses in self-defense) may do more to decrease rape than treatment programs for sex offenders. Other suggestions include better gun control laws and limiting the availability of weapons, as well as increased penalties for drunk driving (which actually accounts for more deaths each year than the entire Vietnam war did in ten years). Finally, Monahan suggests that increased attention paid to corporate violence through enactment and strict enforcement of safety and environmental standards may save more lives than police campaigns against street corner crime.

A "system-centered" approach rather than a "person-centered" one . . . is less likely to result in "blaming the victim". . . . It shifts the emphasis from early case identification . . . to the modification of those factors which give rise to violence . . . (Monahan, 1976, p. 29).

If we turn our attention to institutional change in law enforcement agencies we begin to realize that many of the reforms in laws such as decriminalization of victimless crimes and status offenses for juveniles would necessarily change the role of police officers away from their being

agents of social control. Radical nonintervention would mean that they would "leave the kids alone"—they would no longer be "social workers," truant officers, or responsible for runaways. Removal of such functions would have the dual effect of not turning children in trouble into criminals, and at the same time freeing the police for more serious crime prevention and detection. Similarly, although the training of police officers as family crisis intervention experts makes sense because they are now expected to perform that role, there is no reason why it needs to be carried out by a uniformed armed officer of the law. Perhaps a better plan would be to develop the kind of crisis intervention centers suggested by McGee (1974, see Chapter IX) and to use local professional and nonprofessional people who are not associated with the criminal justice system. As discussed in Chapter IX, these settings need not be associated with the formal mental health system either, and could be under the control of local citizen groups, a plan consistent with the general orientation of this volume, favoring local citizens' control of their own neighborhood services.

There is at least one additional kind of institutional reform that is rarely considered, but may be quite consistent with the general arguments presented in this book. Most city police departments are centrally administered, and although in the larger cities they may have relative autonomy of administration at the precinct level, selection, training, policy, and so on are largely out of the hands of the people who live in the patrolled neighborhoods. Often this creates mutual confusion and disrespect between citizens and police. Instead, suppose each neighborhood were to have its officers and policies selected and determined by a neighborhood group. Remember (see *Overview of the Criminal Justice System* and Table X-1), there is a great deal of discretion in the way in which law enforcement agencies function, and in the decisions they make about arrests, warnings, and order maintenance. At present the police frequently represent a life style and set of values that differ from the style and values of many neighborhoods. They often function in an adver-

---

[45]Related work which has emphasized "defensible space" (Newman, 1973) should also be noted. Newman suggests that the kind of living units in which people reside (hi-rise or low-rise) as well as the availability of recreation areas affect crime rates.

sary relationship not only with criminals, but with law-abiding citizens as well. What would happen if the policies of law enforcement were set at the local neighborhood level in exactly the way proposed for the education and mental health systems in preceding chapters? These local groups could select the kind of police officers that may be best equipped to understand and respect local residents, and vice versa. Often people indigenous to the neighborhood might be selected. Although such a plan would need to be carefully worked out, there is no reason to assume that most residents in any neighborhood would not gladly cooperate with police officers they helped to select and whose enforcement policies (within the constraints of the law) they helped to determine. Such a plan could potentially change the relationship between police and citizens in such a way as to be a true second-order change.

Many of the suggestions in this chapter have been concerned with legal reform. Some of them require legislation at the federal, state, and local levels; others require administrative change within the components of the criminal justice system. One role for the community psychologist concerned with such reform is to serve as a social policy analyst. Through data collection, writing, teaching, and public education activities, the community psychologist can help to influence public policy. Although such a role is not to be discounted, it is unlikely, in itself, to gain the direct political power necessary to implement reform. What this suggests is that implementation requires the creation and support of community organizations which share the value/goals on which reforms are based. It is imperative for the community psychologist to operate in the world of action as well as the world of ideas. In this realm, the strategies and tactics of community organization and social advocacy are essential, and must be given top priority on the agenda of a community

psychology. Exactly which specific actions are likely to work best in a given locale cannot be determined ahead of time, but there are now sufficient experiences with such work to make it clear that a longitudinal time perspective is required and that the process must be on-going rather than time-limited. There are many examples of styles and methods that may be applied, and a number of them have been reviewed in Chapter VI.

The point to be made here is that it is not enough for a community psychology to see the problems; rather, we must be willing to spend the time and effort in the "nitty-gritty" work of day-to-day organization. It is all too easy to adopt the viewpoint that the problems of social reform, however desirable, are too large, and the locus of control too distant, to be handled by our own efforts at the local level. The antidote for such pessimism and alienation is action. Local groups must be formed, organized, and focused on local and specific issues. It is a mistake to assume that reforms can only come from centralized authority. Local school principals, police chiefs, judges, city council members, and citizens hold a great deal of informal as well as formal power, and they, as well as legislators, can be responsive to well-organized citizen groups. One model worth noting here as exemplary was developed by a group known as the Massachusetts Task Force (Edelman, 1973). By emphasizing investigation of local settings and problems, systematic data collection and report writing, combined with the development of a community organization with representatives of both the powerful and the powerless, this group has been quite influential in their own state. As they put it, "Here, then, is rule number one for citizen advocacy: Someone must identify the problem and set the process for action in motion." (Edelman, 1973, p. 641). Why not the community psychologist?

XI

TRAINING FOR A COMMUNITY PSYCHOLOGY: Professional and Nonprofessional

Always waiting untold in the souls of the armies of common people, is stuff better than anything that can possibly appear in the leadership of the same.

—Walt Whitman

For many years, serving as a Washington bureaucrat, I helped support universities in research training, while faced all too often with their inability to meet the needs of the society. How futile it was to ask for help from universities on major social programs; how distant from policy issues, and how unreal was their reaction to social change and the needs of new students.

—Leonard J. Duhl

The Distinction between Nonprofessional Citizen-Participants and Nonprofessional Service Deliverers

The preceding chapters of this volume have stressed the failure of traditional paradigms to provide an adequate understanding for community psychology. New paradigms, role relationships, and value/goals have been suggested. Within the context of cultural relativity, diversity, and an ecological view of human behavior it has been argued that professional skills may be useful as a resource to various communities, but that such skills do not justify authority to determine what programs and goals are to be implemented. Local resident control of decision making and resources has been stressed. In this sense, the community psychology emphasized in this volume requires participation by many members of a local community in their own self-determination. Some residents will be more active than others, but all have the right to participate when they care to, even if only to select local leaders and/or to vote on continuation or change of proposed programs.

Most people who engage in this process would do so because of the direct effect of resulting decisions on their own lives. The parents of children in a given school or the residents of a neighborhood who want a particular use to be made of their human resources budget would participate not as employees but as citizens deciding on what they desire for themselves and their children. *In such a community one important role for the professional is to help provide conditions which foster community involvement, in order to move local control from a "romantic ideal" to a practical reality.*

Nonprofessional citizen-participants, who are the target of human service programs, who are not earning money for work in the health, education, and welfare systems, and who are not themselves providing direct human services, are the key to a meaningful community psychology. These target-citizens are the decision makers in the community psychology emphasized in this volume. Obviously, such local control is not now the case, but movement in that direction must be the goal of a psychology of the community, and its accomplishment will require institutional changes in the "rules of the game" for health, education, and welfare systems management.

Such institutional changes are of the sort Walton (1972; see Chapter VI, p. 179) suggests when he calls for institutional legitimacy to be returned to the people, and what Sarason (1974) means when he calls for a "psychological sense of community." We seem to have come as far as to allow various "nondegree" people to participate in the health, education, welfare, and legal systems as "workers." Although, unfortunately, the use of so-called nonprofessionals in such roles does not address the question of community control, it may be justified in its own right, and as such it is one facet of community psychology which remains to be discussed in this volume.

There is ample evidence that persons who do not hold specific degrees which label them psychiatrists, psychologists, social workers, or other "certified" human service professionals can be mobilized in the human services network. Some of these people have no professional training at all. Many are students, retired people, formerly unemployed people, homemakers, and others who might normally not be in the work force. It is also evident that professionals such as police officers, teachers, and physicians can serve in mental health roles for which they have not been granted an academic degree. For example, Bard's use of police officers as family crisis interventionists (see Chapter X), or the use of teachers and parents as behavioral change agents in home and classroom settings (see Chapter IV) can be thought of as the use of nonprofessionals to deliver direct services traditionally reserved for mental health specialists.

The first part of this chapter is an overview and evaluation of the ways in which nonprofessionals have been used to deliver direct services. It must be kept in mind that these nonprofessionals are viewed as employees of the community (paid or not), and ideally they should be servants of the decisions and policies of the target community, in exactly the same sense as professionals. They do not necessarily represent the community or speak for its members with regard to value/goals simply because they are not professionals, even in cases where they are indigenous to the community and/or have the same social background or skin color as the target group. To put this viewpoint in perspective the reader may wish to refer back to Chapter IX, p. 301, for a discussion of the differences between community control as accountability and the use of specific skills. In part, it was confusion between these two elements that led to the Lincoln Hospital fiasco (p. 299) and the general misunderstanding of "community control."

Here we are concerned with the use of nonprofessionals' specific skills, some of which they may possess simply because they are human beings, some of which they may have acquired through experiences specific to their neighborhood or life style, or through special training and supervision. There has already been a widespread acceptance of nonprofessionals as service deliverers (Sobey, 1970) in the mental health network. Such workers have been granted legitimacy, largely as a result of the community mental health movement. Indeed, a dual emphasis on reduction of mental hospital populations and on mobilization of new kinds of personpower in the form of nonprofessionals may be the major contribution of the community mental health movement.

Nonprofessionals in direct service roles may be paid for their services, or they may be volunteers. They may be indigenous to the target community, or they may be an outside source of person-power, bought in to assist in accomplishing the aims of a given program. Exactly who they are and what they do will vary from place to place, and although precise description of each kind of nonprofessional must be generated for research purposes (cf. Karlsruher, 1974) precision of definition is not necessary in this general context. Here we are simply calling "nonprofessionals" those people who provide direct human services, but who do not hold an academic degree in the professional field in which they are working. Volunteers and paid employees both fit this definition. Although many nonprofessionals in mental health and social service agencies may work in other than direct human service roles (Grosser, 1969), here we are concerned only with those who are in that role; that is, those who are providing direct service as therapeutic or behavioral change agents.[1]

The Rationale for Nonprofessionals as Agents of Direct Service

Much of the rationale for the use of nonprofessionals in direct service delivery has already been given in earlier chapters. The failure of traditional mental health professionals to meet the needs of large numbers of target groups, for example, the poor, the chronic hospitalized patient, rural dwellers, public school children, potential and actual delinquents, the aged, has been well documented (see Chapters I and III; and Cowen, Gardner, & Zax, 1967). These failures have been seen to be the result of at least four general problems:

1. Inadequate professional person-power (Albee, 1959; Arnhoff, Rubinstein, & Spiesman, 1969).
2. The clinical ineffectiveness of traditional treatment approaches (Cowen, Gardner, & Zax, 1967).
3. Conceptual errors in our approach to problems in living, on both theoretical (Albee, 1968b; Ullmann & Krasner, 1969), and style of delivery grounds (Rappaport & Chinsky, 1974; Reiff, 1968).
4. The inability to make contact with large numbers of potential target groups (Ryan, 1969; Reissman, Cohen, & Pearl, 1964).

---

[1]There is some confusion raised here because increasing numbers of people are being trained with a Master's, Bachelor's, or Associate degree in one of the helping professions. Obviously, when they take a job they may be thought of as professionals. Often, however, they are discussed in the literature as nonprofessionals. In this chapter, we can regard them as professionals differing from those with a doctoral degree only to the extent of their academic training. The term "mental health professional" could be reserved for doctoral level psychologists and trained psychiatrists. Social workers, however, would be a special case because many with M.A. or B.A. degrees have traditionally been thought of as professionals. Similarly, teachers, nurses, probation officers, and other professional human service groups are largely composed of other than doctoral level persons. Although this is all somewhat confusing in the general case, it simply points to the need to state precisely the characteristics of the group being discussed, rather than to rely on the imprecise term "nonprofessional."

The nonprofessional movement is based on the assumption that the above constitute sound reasons to shift the roles of professionals away from direct service and toward seeking new ways to deliver services to reach more people. What Cowen has called the "mental health quarterback role" (cf. Cowen, 1973; Cowen, Chinsky, & Rappaport, 1970), in which a small number of professionals supervise larger numbers of nonprofessionals as "front-line" workers, is suggested as at least one solution to the problems of inadequate person-power, reach, and effectiveness.

Following Albee's (1959) clear assessment of our inability to ever train enough professional people to meet the demand for human services, the use of nonprofessionals became justified with the parallel realization that there are many more such people potentially available than there are professionals. As Zax and Specter (1974) have pointed out, the greatest benefit to society accrues when such persons are drawn from the segments of society that would not otherwise be a part of the economy. By bringing college and high school students, homemakers, retired people, parents, indigenous target neighborhood residents, and other such groups of people (including former recipients of direct services themselves) into the helping systems as the helpers, they become contributors to their community. This has been suggested as both a strategy to improve delivery of services per se, and as a means to change the helping systems, by inclusion of new viewpoints.

Reissman (1965) has suggested that the helpers often gain as much from helping others as do those they help. He has termed this the "helper therapy principle," and it has been found to operate in programs such as Alcoholics Anonymous and Synanon (a program entirely run by and for former drug addicts). Both of these programs use self-help groups that intentionally exclude professionals. Others (e.g., Peck, Kaplan, & Roman, 1966) have suggested that the involvement of indigenous neighborhood workers in social action programs may serve to enhance the "mental health" of the workers themselves by increasing their sense of control over their own lives. Zurcher (1970) has provided some empirical evidence for this claim.

Depending on who they are and with whom they are working, nonprofessionals have been suggested to have certain advantages over professionals. For example, college students have been described as effective because of a "naive enthusiasm" when working with chronic hospitalized patients on whom others have "given up" (Poser, 1966). Neighborhood workers indigenous to a poor community have been said to have a special understanding of the viewpoints, life style, language, and problems of their own community (Reiff & Reissman, 1965). Rioch (1966) and Cowen (1967) have suggested that the perception of nonprofessionals by some target people as closer to themselves in the social hierarchy may lead to an increased willingness to identify and model after the helper. There is general evidence that the characteristics of a model do influence his or her effectiveness as a change agent (Bandura, 1969), and some specific evidence that at least among chronic hospitalized patients nonprofessionals are viewed as more similar to themselves than are professional helpers (Chinsky & Rappaport, 1970).

Although there is now relatively widespread use of such nonprofessional workers, based on the rationale presented above, and many programs are amply described in the literature, some analysts (Allerhand & Lake, 1972; Zax & Specter, 1974) have questioned if this reflects a genuine change within the helping professions. Even though many programs can be cited these may actually be exceptions to the rule for delivery of service. By and large professionals continue to be unwilling to give up the direct delivery of service role, despite its inefficiency. There are many reasons for this reluctance; some are rational, others have to do with protection of status and economic concerns.

Overview of the Scope and Effectiveness of Nonprofessionals

One of the overriding rational objections to the use of nonprofessionals is said to be based on a lack of convincing evidence for effectiveness.

However, although it is true that "hard-nosed" empirical data are relatively scarce, the same is also true for evaluation of the effectiveness of the professionals. Most service delivery programs, be they professional or nonprofessional, traditional or innovative, are simply not well evaluated. They are usually not evaluated at all. It is often simpy *assumed* that professional services are useful, while the utility of nonprofessional services must be proven. The tenuous assumption that professional services are effective simply because they are delivered by a professional must be kept in mind whenever we evaluate nonprofessionals. It is likely that what is actually done in a given program is more important then who is doing it. The baseline for comparison of nonprofessional services must be selected by asking "What would happen to these target people in the absence of this program?" In some cases the appropriate comparison will be to a no-treatment or "treatment as usual" control group because many times the nonprofessional services are offered not as a substitute for professional care but as a substitute for no attention at all. Even in those cases where a professional service is offered, the burden of proof for effectiveness must rest on the professionals, because such services will generally cost more and be less available. If nonprofessionals do *no worse* than professionals then their use may be justified. For example, in the case of organizing grass-roots self-help groups there is often no comparison group of professionals dealing with the target population. If the local community nonprofessional does not do it, no one will. Similarly, in the case of programs such as McGee's (see Chapter IX) for crisis intervention, although professional services are theoretically available, it often turns out that the professionals are inaccessable and do not reach many people who have problems in living. In such cases the base line for comparison is appropriately this service versus nothing.

The exact nature of what nonprofessionals have done in the human services field is so varied that it would have made some sense to discuss the movement separately within each of the last four chapters on education, mental health, and the legal system. Many programs using nonprofessionals in direct service delivery roles, and the issues they raise, have already been mentioned in other contexts in this volume. Table XI-1 presents a listing of some of them. A scanning of the table will quickly reveal the variety of persons used, the target groups, types of services, and roles and responsibilities that have been assumed. To discuss community psychology at all has required, even without intending to emphasize it, the use of nonprofessionals.

Cowen (1973), in his recent review of social and community interventions, has emphasized the diversity of such programs and their widespread proliferation. He suggests that this rapid expansion is more a function of "social readiness" than of single influential programs or scientific breakthroughs, a theme consistent with the more general historical view presented in Chapter II of this volume. In that chapter it is argued that the history of the helping professions might best be understood as a reaction to social forces rather than to scientific advances.

The current mobilization of large numbers of nonprofessional helpers is directly traceable from two lines of work, the first of which derives from the pioneering study by Margaret Rioch and her colleagues at NIMH (Rioch, Elkes, Flint, Usdansky, Newman, & Silber, 1963). Their research led to a then startling break from the belief that one must be a traditionally trained psychotherapist in order to have "therapeutic" effects. In retrospect, although we hardly find it surprising that Rioch's training of college graduate women with backgrounds very similar to professionals, for two years prior to employing them as psychotherapists, led to their doing as good a job as professionals, at the time it helped to create an atmosphere suggestive of more daring programs. Others, such as Reiff and Reissman (1965) and Reissman (1967) went further in proposing and demonstrating the use of indigenous nonprofessionals from within the ranks of the poor, as did those at Howard University (e.g., Fishman, Klein, MacLennan, Mitchell, Pearl, & Walker, 1965; Fishman, Denham, Levins, & Schatz, 1969; Klein, 1967; MacLennan et al., 1966). Following the original Rioch study others have used homemakers who had only a few weeks, rather than years, of training. Typical is Cowen's (Cowen et al., 1975) work with homemakers and elementary-school children, and Katkin, Ginsburg, Rifkin, & Scott's (1971) use of homemakers to maintain "revolving door" psychiatric patients in the community (see Chapter IX). McGee's (1974) use of trained nonprofessionals in crisis intervention is another example. In addition, parents, retired persons, ex-patients, ex-drug addicts, and former delinquents have also served in a direct helping role (Cowen, 1973).

Guerney (1969), in an edited volume, has reviewed many early reports on nonprofessional workers, ranging from those trained in specific techniques such as behavior modification, to those asked to use only their "natural social skills." The nonprofessionals have ranged from parents, to teachers, to students, to neighborhood residents. They have worked in homes, schools, hospitals, and in the streets. Not only are such programs justified by manpower needs but also by claims of effectiveness and genuine contribution to the community mental health movement (Sobey, 1970).

A second front on which the use of nonprofessionals has developed appears in the literature as far back as the 1950s when the Harvard-Radcliffe group began to use college students as mental health "helpers" with hospitalized patients. Aside from a monograph report of an experiential nature (Umbarger, Dalsimer, Morrison, & Breggin, 1962), and a few minor evaluation studies (e.g., Beck, Kantor, & Gelineau, 1963), little sophisticated research was produced. Yet the idea of using college students in a mental hospital was a powerful one, and the Connecticut Valley State Hospital and Wesleyan University group, led by Jules Holzberg, made a number of significant attempts at extensions of the model. Before the beginning of this decade a number of research reports (Holzberg, 1963; Holzberg & Gewirtz, 1964; Holzberg & Knapp, 1965; Holzberg, Knapp, & Turner, 1966, 1967; Holzberg, Whiting, & Lowy, 1964) had documented the usefulness of college-student voluteer programs *to the students themselves*. Others (Hersch, Kulik, & Scheibe, 1969) found similar results in the development of the Connecticut Service Corps,

TABLE XI–1 A partial listing of nonprofessional programs and issues cited in other chapters.

Chapter Where Program or Issue Is Mentioned	Reference to Program Description, Conception, or Analysis	Type of Nonprofessionals Used	Target Group	Type of Direct Service Offered	Type of Evaluation
Chapter I	Clark & Hopkins (1969); Moynihan (1969)	Indigenous community workers in the "war on poverty"	Residents of low-income neighborhoods	Community organization and self-help programs	Rational and critical analysis
Chapter III	Joint Commission (1961); Hobbs (1964); Caplan (1964); Bloom (1973); Rappaport & Chinsky (1974)	Other professionals not trained in mental health	Various target groups	Mental health consultation to other professionals who have direct contact with the target group	Rational argument concerning the logic and efficiency of consultation
Chapter IV	Patterson (1974); O'Connor (1969, 1972)	Parents and teachers	Nursery and elementary school-age children	Behavior modification techniques and modeling films	Comparison of treated and untreated problem children and nonproblem children
Chapter IV	Goldstein (1973)	Various socialization agents	Adults	Structured learning therapy	Rational argument and empirical outcome data
Chapter VI	Alinsky (1971)	Grass-roots community self-help groups	Adults from powerless communities	Community organization	Rational argument, face validity, and achievement of stated goals
Chapters VI, IX	Fairweather et al. (1969. 1972)	Members of the target population	Chronic patients	Development of autonomous settings and self-help groups	Comparison of participants and those receiving treatment as usual
Chapter VI	Guttentag (1970); Kanter (1972); Mowrer & Vattano (1975)	Local community organizations and self-selected participants in self-help groups; total communities	Self-help and autonomous groups	Independent, self-directed organization, without professional interference	Rational analysis, review of historical outcomes of "natural" experiments, and laboratory empirical outcomes

TABLE XI-1 (continued)

Chapter Where Program or Issue Is Mentioned	Reference to Program Description, Conception, or Analysis	Type of Nonprofessionals Used	Target Group	Type of Direct Service Offered	Type of Evaluation
Chapters VII, VIII	Bereiter (1968); Bereiter & Englemann (1966); Englemann (1969, 1970)	Teachers	Preschool children	Behavior modification	Comparison of treated and untreated children
Chapter VII	Cundick, Gottfreidson, & Wilson (1974)	Foster parents	Elementary school-age children	Family socialization	School progress
Chapter VII	Gray & Klaus (1965, 1970); Klaus & Gray (1968); Karnes et al. (1970); Levenstein (1969); Plant & Southern (1972); Shaefer & Aaronson (1970)	Preschool teachers; parents from various "disadvantaged" populations; students	Preschool children from low-income families	Early academic experiences	Comparison to self and other nontreated children in school performance and achievements
Chapter IX	Allen et al. (1976); Spivack & Shure (1974)	Teachers, and college students	Elementary school-age children, preschoolers	Curriculum development	Comparison of treated and control group on problem-solving skills
Chapter IX	Cowen et al. (1975)	Homemakers, college students	Elementary school-age children	Therapeutic companionship and tutoring services	Comparison to self and control groups on academic and behavioral measures
Chapter IX	Delaney, Seidman, & Willis (1977)	R.N. and M.A. people in nonmental health fields	People in a crisis and in danger of referral to a mental institution	Crisis intervention	Evaluation of effectiveness in keeping people out of institutions
Chapter IX	Ellsworth (1968); Sanders et al. (1967)	Ward attendants and B.A. level mental health workers	Chronic hospitalized patients	Hospital ward mileu treatment	Comparison of treatment and control patients

Chapter	Reference	Personnel	Target population	Intervention	Evaluation
Chapter IX	Katkin et al. (1971)	Homemakers	Adult mental patients	Advocacy, problem solving, and supportive services	Comparison to base rate for return to hospital
Chapter IX	Marx, Test, & Stein (1973)	Former hospital workers	Chronic patients	Development of autonomous community settings	Comparison to treatment as usual and in-hospital control groups
Chapter IX	McGee (1974)	Community volunteers	Anyone in "crisis"	Immediate crisis intervention	Various program evaluation statistics provided
Chapter X	Roman (1969); Schiff (1970)	Indigenous nonprofessionals	A community mental health center "catchment area"	Various broadly defined mental health services	Primarily descriptive, some program evaluation
Chapter X	Baron, Feeney, & Thornton (1973); Palmer (1974)	Probation officers	Adolescents in legal difficulty	Short-term family-oriented crisis intervention; intensive casework	Comparison of treated and processed as usual adolescents
Chapter X	Goldenberg (1971)	Indigenous community workers	"Hard-core" youths	Autonomous community settings	Comparison to similar youths
Chapter X	Bard (1967); Driscoll, Meyer, & Schanie (1973)	Police officers	Families in conflict	Crisis intervention	Comparison between demonstration and control precincts; trained and untrained police officers
Chapter X	Tharp & Wetzel (1969)	Various young people with no previous experience	Behaviorally disordered children	Behavior modification techniques	Within treated group change measures
Chapter X	Seidman, Rappaport, & Davidson (1976); Davidson (1975)	College students	Adolescents in legal difficulty	Behavioral contracting and advocacy	Comparison of experimental and control groups

as did Cowen, Zax, and Laird (1966) when they used students in an elementary-school setting. Still others (Goodman, 1967) found similar results when students worked with troubled youngsters in the community rather than with chronic patients in a hospital.

As Cowen (1973) notes, undergraduates are not the only student group to become involved in human service. He has reviewed work performed by high-school students for preadolescents (Fellows & Wolpin, 1966) and for primary-grade youngsters (McWilliams & Finkel, 1973). Neale and Mussell (1968) have reported over 600 such "tutoring" programs and Gartner, Kohler, and Riessman (1971) cite the use of elementary-school-age children in similar helping roles for other children.

Despite the above-noted work, with few exceptions, little outcome data based on *objective* measures of the *target* populations have appeared in the literature (Gruver, 1971). One of the few studies during the 1960s which did provide evaluation of the target population in a mental hospital (Poser, 1966) presented a tantalising result. Poser found undergraduate females to be *more* effective than professionals (psychiatrists, psychologists, and social workers) in fostering patient improvement with groups of chronic hospitalized males. Although this study has not gone unchallenged (Rosenbaum, 1966) nor undefended (Rioch, 1966), it remained until recently the most careful evaluation of the outcome of college students working with chronic hospitalized patients. More recently, some of Poser's findings have been replicated and extended in a comprehensive report of a college-student program for 320 chronic hospitalized patients (Rappaport, Chinsky, & Cowen, 1971). One of the interesting findings of this report was that the sex match of student and patient was a key variable in outcome for this target population. Such results argue against any generalized conclusions with regard to the effectiveness of nonprofessionals, and suggest that like other areas of research, questions concerning the effectiveness of nonprofessionals will not have simple yes or no answers.

Gruver (1971), in his early review of college-student programs, divided them into three major areas: in addition to the use of students in hospital settings, he cited programs with children, and nonhospital programs in areas related to mental health. Among the studies with children his general conclusion was that the college students benefited from the programs (Goodman, 1967) and could easily learn behavior change principles (Davison, 1965) or client-centered therapy techniques (Stollak, 1969). However, data concerned with impact on the *target children* were found to be either inconclusive or impressionistic. More recently, Alden, Rappaport, and Seidman (1975) found that both the nature of the intervention (tutoring versus companionship) and the age of the children affected outcome, a finding that again argues against drawing single generalized conclusions with regard to the effectiveness of nonprofessionals.

Among the studies in settings other than traditional mental health institutions, Cowen, Zax, and their colleagues at the University of Rochester (Cowen, 1968, 1969; Cowen, Izzo, Miles, Telschow, Trost, & Zax, 1963; Cowen, Zax, Izzo, & Trost, 1966; Cowen, Zax, & Laird, 1966; Zax & Cowen, 1967) have been the most systematic. Working in an elementary-school setting within a secondary prevention model, they have used students, homemakers, elderly people, and others as therapeutic agents. These investigators have found positive effects on college students, similar to those found when students work in mental hospitals. They have also noted some improvements among the target children, although the results are suggestive at best (Cowen *et al.*, 1975; see Chapter IX). Many others who have used college students have either reported impressionistic data, or presented no research evaluations at all.

Although Gruver's (1971) review cites over 90 college-student programs, conclusions beyond a general positive effect on the students themselves are difficult to draw. Regardless of where students have been used Gruver concludes that it is impossible to draw firm conclusions about the relative effectiveness of college students as therapeutic agents" . . . less than 25 percent (of the studies) boasted a control group . . . only 5 used pre- and posttesting and only 5 (studies) . . . used objective measures." (Gruver, 1971, p. 123.) Even those studies that did investigate the impact on one target group fairly carefully (chronic patients) have not broached the question of social systems change in any systematic manner. Nor have they dealt with effectiveness with noninstitutional populations, nor with training and selection issues.

The above-cited programs and reviews have contributed directly to the rising "zeitgeist" in the use of college students as therapeutic agents. A number of other isolated reports have appeared in the literature (e.g., Buckey, Muench, & Sjoberg, 1970; Hunt, 1969; Levine, 1966; Vernis, 1969; Zunker & Brown, 1966) and point to the growning use of such person-power in ad hoc fashion. One National Institute of Mental Health report (1968) estimated that during the academic years 1955–1966, 8000 students from more than 300 schools served as volunteers in programs for mental hospital patients alone. Cowen (1973) has reported that there are now over 500 such programs.

A more recent review presenting a critical assessment of the effectiveness of nonprofessionals including but not limited to college students (Karlsruher, 1974) has suggested that empirical evidence for effectiveness with adult-hospitalized impatients is well established, but that similar evidence for success with outpatients and disturbed adolescents and children does not exist. Table XI-2 clearly shows the reason for Karlsruher's conclusions. Studies with adult inpatients he reviewed had most often included a comparable control group, and most found that the treatment group improved relative to the controls. However, it is important to keep in mind the context in which this conclusion is drawn. Research within institutional mental health settings has tended to use psychological test measures as criteria for improvement. Such measures may not have much relevance to non-test behavior. In addition, most studies demonstrate only improvement of in-the-hospital functioning. Perhaps the best conclusion would be that nonprofessionals of various types have

been shown to be able to stimulate the withdrawn hospitalized patient, and that together with programs such as behavior modification and milieu treatment, there is no reason why hospital wards with chronic isolated patients need exist. There is enough person-power and technological knowledge to eliminate them. The use of nonprofessionals in the hospital setting can be viewed as one additional resource to help clear out the mental hospitals by preparing residents to leave (see Chapter IX, p. 273).

There may be some reason to be somewhat more optimistic than Karlsruher about the use of nonprofessionals as therapeutic agents in other settings as well, as is concluded by Kelly, Snowden, and Muñoz (1977) in their chapter for the *Annual Review of Psychology*. The most promising directions for such programming include use of nonprofessionals as resources for all children in public school settings, not only for "disturbed" children (cf. the review of Cowen et al., 1975; Chapter IX, p. 309). In addition, homemakers have been successfully used to reduce the rate of return to mental hospitals (Katkin et al., 1971; see Chapter IX, p. 277). There is no reason why nonprofessionals cannot perform the sorts of roles described by Marx et al. (1973) in keeping chronic patients living in the community (see Chapter IX, p. 284). There is also some empirical evidence that nonprofessionals can serve useful roles in providing crisis intervention services (McGee, 1974; Chapter IX; Getz, Fujita, & Allen, 1975) and in preventing delinquency (Seidman, Rappaport, & Davidson, 1976; Davidson 1975; see Chapter X), if they are carefully supervised.

Despite the above-noted optimistic findings, such empirical studies are few and far between, and Cowen's (1973, p. 449) observation that ". . . for the moment our chips are placed on *exploring* an exciting, challenging, new world of usages rather than on hard-nosed evaluation" remains largely true. For that reason, Karlsruher's general caution that "lack of adequate empirical studies makes it impossible to determine the effectiveness of nonprofessionals with disturbed adolescents and outpatient adults and children" seems warranted, if not conclusive.

TABLE XI-2   Effectiveness of nonprofessionals, by patient category.

Reference	Type of Nonprofessional	Results
Inpatient Adults		
Anker & Walsh (1961)	Psychiatric aides	$NP > P$
Appelby (1963)	Psychiatric aides	$NP > C$
Beck, Kantor, & Gelineau (1963)	College students	$NP >$ No Control
Buckley, Muench, & Sjoberg (1970)	College students	$NP > C$
Carkhuff & Truax (1965)	Psychiatric aides	$NP > C$
Gelineau & Evans (1970)	College students	$NP >$ No Control
Greenblatt & Kantor (1962)	College students	$NP >$ No Control
Hartlage (1970)	Student nurses	$NP >$ No Control
Holzberg, Knapp, & Turner (1967)	College students	$NP > C$
Poser (1966)	College students	$NP > C, P$
Rappaport, Chinsky, & Cowen (1971)	College students	$NP > C$
Sines, Silver, & Lucero (1961)	Psychiatric aides	$NP = C$
Verinis (1970)	College students	$NP > C$
Outpatient Adults		
Albronda, Dean, & Starkweather (1964)		$NP >$ No Control
Berzon & Solomon (1966)	Community adults	$NP = P$
Denker (1946)	Physicians	$NP >$ No Control
Magoon, Golann, & Freeman (1969)	Community adults	$NP >$ No Control
Mendel & Rappaport (1963)	Psychiatric aides	$NP = P$
Rioch, Elkes, Flint, Usdansky, Newman, & Silber (1963)	Community adults	$NP >$ No Control
Outpatient Adolescents		
Brown (1965)	College students	$NP > C$
Magoon, Golann, & Freeman (1969)	Community adults	$NP >$ No Control
Rioch et al. (1963)	Community adults	$NP >$ No Control
Zunker & Brown (1966)	College students	$NP > P$
Outpatient Children		
Cowen, Dorr, Trost, & Izzo (1972)	Community adults	$NP >$ No Control
Dorr & Cowen (1973)	Community adults	$NP >$ No Control
Goodman (1972)	College students	?
Tolor (1968)	Community adults	$Np >$ No Control

Note: NP is the group treated by nonprofessional therapists; P is the group treated by professional therapists; C is the no-treatment or minimal-treatment-control group. No Control means the study did not employ a control group, and $>$ means improved significantly more than.

*For location of these references see Karlsruher (1974) from whom this table is adopted.

However, we must add that the same conclusion could be drawn from a review of professionals as therapeutic agents with similar populations.

The Educational Pyramid

In addition to the above-noted scarcity of well-controlled studies generating empirical data on effectiveness, Seidman and Rappaport (1974b) have pointed out that there has also been little evaluation of either professionals or nonprofessionals in terms of impact on the social systems in which they serve. In part, this is viewed as due to the ad hoc nature in which programs have developed and the failure to pay attention to conceptual and training issues. They point out the fact that a significant portion of the content of community psychology is concerned with training issues (Iscoe & Spielberger, 1970; Iscoe, Bloom, & Spielberger, 1976) and the efficient use of person-power in the mental health delivery system (Cowen, 1973; Bloom, 1973), which makes the need for systematic training and research paradigms acute.

Seidman and Rappaport have suggested one such paradigm, the *educational pyramid*, which uses professionals, graduate students, and undergraduate nonprofessionals in a cooperative support system. In this system a small number of professionals train and supervise a larger number of graduate students, who in turn supervise yet larger numbers of undergraduate nonprofessionals, who serve as therapeutic agents for various target populations. Although their focus is on the undergraduate and on university-based programs, the paradigm applies to work with any of a wide variety of nonprofessionals and settings. Likewise, although they talk of graduate-student supervisors, any variety of experienced subprofessional mental health worker could serve in the supervisory role.

As clinical and community psychology develop over the next decade, we are likely to find both a decrease in the number of doctoral-level psychologists and an increase in the number with B.A.- and master's-level training. At the same time, the role of the doctoral-level psychologist seems to be shifting away from direct intervention. Many psychologists spend the largest portion of their professional time either in research or in professional activities involving the supervision of others. Programs that anticipate these functions while students are still in school must be developed. At the University of Illinois, for example, this is now formalized into separate Doctor of Philosophy (Ph.D.) research and Doctor of Psychology (Psy.D.) professional degree programs, anticipating the division of labor to which many psychologists will subscribe in their later professional lives. This introduction of a professional degree program is beginning to take hold in other places as well, including New Jersey, Texas, and the California Professional School. Even where the formalization of professional service interests into a specific degree program has not taken place, most students in clinical and community psychology are interested in either the professional or the research role. Although the Boulder model of the "scientist-professional" is

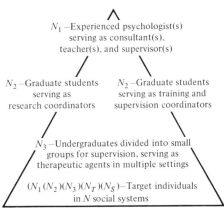

Figure XI-1. The educational pyramid applied to a university setting. *Note:* The pyramid diagrammed represents one social system where N_1 refers to the number of experienced psychologists; N_2 refers to the number of graduate student pairs supervised by each psychologist; N_3 refers to the number of undergraduate therapeutic agents supervised by each graduate-student pair; N_T refers to the number of target individuals per therapeutic agent. In this particular case it is assumed that the above terms are constant across N_S, where N_S refers to the number of social systems. Thus, $(N_1) (N_2) (N_3) (N_T) (N_S)$ equals the total number of people served by N_1 experienced psychologists. In the more general case when the above terms are not constant across N_S, the appropriate formula calls for an addition across N_S or $\sum_{i=N_s} (N_1 \cdot N_2 \cdot N_3 \cdot N_T)$. (Redrawn from Seidman & Rappaport, 1974b.)

widely accepted as a *program* goal, usually, *individuals* within programs specialize in one or the other aspect of the ideal "super-psychologist."

Taking into account the realities of this division of labor, the educational pyramid (see Figure XI-1) serves as a model for training in applied psychology at multiple levels, with efficient division of labor. The graduate student is trained to assume a role as either research director or clinical director of services, depending on his or her interest in a predominately research or a predominately professional career.

It may be observed from Figure XI-1 that the educational pyramid provides a geometrically expanding formula for the utilization of person-power in the mental health delivery system. N_1 refers to number of experienced psychologists; N_2 refers to number of graduate-student pairs; N_3 refers to number of undergraduate therapeutic agents; N_T is the number of target individuals per therapeutic agent; N_S is the number of social systems. Thus, (N_1) (N_2) (N_3) (N_T) (N_S) equals the total number of people served by N_1 experienced psychologists participating in the educational pyramid.

The use of graduate-student pairs as research and supervision coordinators allows the experienced psychologist to serve as teacher and consultant. The triangular model enables a small number of professionals to design and implement research and program evaluation while training doctoral-level students in research and professional supervision activities. The model may be replicated any number of times over any number of social systems in which college students or other nonprofessionals are used as therapeutic agents. The professional psychologists supervise, train, and consult with graduate students or perhaps other subprofessionals, each of whom is responsible for research or for training and supervision of undergraduate or other nonprofessional therapeutic agents. Each of the subprofessionals responsible for supervision handles several small groups of therapeutic agents. Each therapeutic agent is linked with one or several target persons. Thus, the impact of a small number of psychologists is expanded by each supervisor times a few small groups of therapeutic agents times between one and several target persons times some number of social systems. In addition, each program has a graduate student or perhaps a subprofessional research coordinator who is responsible for supervising a team of research assistants (e.g., undergraduates) in program evaluation.

The evaluation and training model proposed by Seidman and Rappaport (1974) has not been totally implemented in a systematic way, although at the time of this writing these researchers were themselves in the process of using it to evaluate nonprofessional service programs for children, adolescents, mental patients, and the elderly. The program for adolescents was described in Chapter X, p. 351 (Seidman, Rappaport, & Davidson, 1976; Davidson, 1975).

The nature of the questions raised by this model has been spelled out in detail, and such questions remain both unanswered and crucial to a comprehensive evaluation of nonprofessional programs:

1. Outcome at the individual level
   A. What is the measurable impact of nonprofessional interventions on *various target populations?*
   B. What are the changes that take place in therapeutic agents who participate in helping roles?
2. Selection and training of therapeutic agents
   A. Who is an effective therapeutic agent?
   B. Is it possible to match therapeutic agents and target persons in order to maximize impact?
   C. What training methods and procedures are most appropriate and efficient for such programming?
3. Outcome at the systems level
   A. What is the impact on the *social system* in which the various target populations reside (e.g., what changes are observable in the hospitals, schools, and court systems)?
   B. How do therapeutic agent interventions affect the *preventive potential* of mental health and related institutions?

Psychologists frequently limit their research questions to the individual level or to the same level at which they intervene. Perhaps the most significant aspect of the educational pyramid as a paradigm for research, quite apart from its efficiency in training and person-power utilization, is its emphasis on impact at other than the individual level. The model calls for programs in N social systems and thus implies research with regard to those systems. Such questions have almost never been directly asked in the form of research; however, they might reasonably be expected to constitute the basis of a genuine community psychology interested in prevention of problems in living.

At the present time, those questions posed by Seidman and Rappaport (1974b) outline the issues that must be answered through systematic research if the nonprofessional movement is to fulfill its promise.

Selection of Nonprofessionals

As research proceeds with the investigation of new ways to use college students and other non-professionals in direct service roles, there are some pressing practical questions of concern to those interested in adding this component to their treatment armamentarium. The most common question from professionals in applied settings is "How do I select from among the large number of college students and other volunteers?" At this point there are some promising, although not definitve directions.

To be useful a selection device must be relatively efficient, inexpensive, reliable, and predictive of success. Personality tests, although efficient and inexpensive, often lack predictive utility. Rappaport *et al.* (1971), for example, found that personality tests did not predict success in their large-scale investigation of college students working in a mental hospital. Individual interviews, although probably better than personality measures, have also not been shown to be either reliable or good enough predictors to make them worth the relatively high cost of professional time. Chinsky and Rappaport (1971) found that an actual behavioral measure of student volunteers was the most promising predictor of success when college students worked with chronic patients. This technique, developed by Gerald Goodman (Goodman, 1972a), is known as the Group Assessment of Interpersonal Traits (GAIT).

The GAIT is a small-group situation in which five to eight volunteers may participate at one time in a session lasting approximately one hour. Each group member is asked to tell the group something about his or her personal life. One person is asked to reveal an interpersonal problem, and one other person is asked to try to understand that problem, during a four-minute interaction. After the first interaction the next person presents his or her problem to a different understander, and so on until everyone in the group has performed both tasks once. Observation of performance on these tasks yields a behavioral measure of each nonprofessional's social skills in a therapeutic-like situation, and ratings of performance can be used as a selection device.

Chinsky and Rappaport (1971) asked their student therapeutic agents to participate with one another in a series of GAIT sessions, just prior to their introduction to work with chronic hospitalized patients, and found that the technique could be used reliably. Also, there was a moderate relationship between observers' global ratings of the college students' understanding and warmth, and patient change as measured by independent rating scales of patients taken six months later. At the same time they were finding the GAIT to be the only successful predictor in a broad-band battery of assessment techniques, Goodman (1972b) was also finding the technique to be useful in the prediction of success for college students working with fifth- and sixth-grade problem youngsters.

It is widely believed that social skills such as those measured by the GAIT are one factor of importance in selecting and training nonprofessionals. Given a method to reliably measure these skills, Rappaport, Gross, and Lepper (1973) investigated the relative efficacy of sensitivity training, modeling, and simple instructions in enhancing the social skills of college-student volunteers for human service projects. It was the authors' hypothesis that many college-student volunteers are likely to have a sufficient social skills repertoire such that acquisition of such skills may not be necessary for them to be effective as mental health workers. They hypothesized that the provision of clear instructions would prove to be the simplest and most efficient way of enhancing the social skills needed for a therapeutic interaction.

They randomly selected 60 college students taken from a pool of 120 volunteers and assigned each to one of three training conditions: *modeling*, in which they were exposed to a 20-minute videotape of actors being self-disclosing and understanding; *sensitivity training,* in which they spent 14 hours over a period of seven weeks in small group discussions; and a *no-training control* group. Following training the students were scheduled for a GAIT session that was tape recorded and later transcribed. The GAITs were conducted under one of two conditions: general instructions or specific instructions. The general instructions simply told the

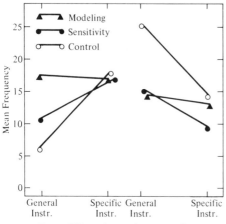

Figure XI-2. Mean frequency of personal and impersonal discussion statements, by the discloser, as a function of training and instructions. (Redrawn from Rappaport, Gross, & Lepper, 1973.)

students what to do; the specific instructions gave examples and suggestions about how to do it.

The results of this study are graphically presented in Figure XI-2. As can be seen, given general instructions, modeling-trained volunteers and sensitivity-trained volunteers present more personal discussion than untrained volunteers, with modeling being significantly superior to either of the other two. Again, under general instructions the modeling-trained group presented less impersonal discussion. However, given specific instructions both the sensitivity-trained students and the no-training control group significantly improved their performance so as to be essentially equal to the modeling-trained group. These results hold for both the analysis of specific behavioral data and for global qualitative ratings of understanding and psychological meaningfulness.

Each of the training methods investigated by Rappaport *et al.* appears to lead to the desired performance. If this is so, then the question of training becomes one of efficiency. It appears from this study that college student volunteers may be largely self-selected with regard to social skills, and further training of this nature, beyond simple instructions, may not be necessary. The study thus lends some support to those

who have argued that the success of nonprofessionals has much to do with their "natural" social skills (Cowen, 1967; Poser, 1966; Rioch, 1966). However, because there are undoubtedly individual differences, even among a self-selected population, it has been recommended that users of college-student volunteers adopt a behavioral selection procedure such as the GAIT. Administered under specific instructions, this procedure would allow selection of those volunteers who are most capable of performing in the desired fashion. Thus professionals would have more time to focus on training nonprofessionals in other skills such as behavior change techniques, problem solving, and advocacy. Recent work by D'Augelli and Chinsky (1974) has supported this suggestion.

Lindquist and Rappaport (1973) have further examined the GAIT technique as a selection device. They have reasoned that given the nature of college-student programs, in which the pool of applicants is large, and in which brief training and a few months of actual work is typical, the selection problem requires elimination of false positives (i.e., those who are selected but turn out to be good therapeutic agents). They present data which suggest that the GAIT is such a conservative selection device, and that the technique probably deserves further exploration as one that may be more efficient than individual interviews. More detailed analysis of this procedure and recommendations for its use can be found in Dooley (1975) and in Goodman (1972a). If the GAIT does turn out to have predictive utility with regard to social skills, training programs for nonprofessionals that use it as a selection device would be free to focus on specific techniques necessary to carry out the particular program goals instead of spending a great deal of time on general social skills training.

Methods of selection based on evaluation of college-students volunteers, such as the one described above, may not be generalizable to the selection of other kinds of community volunteers. Allerhand and Lake (1972) have suggested that in reviewing the results of many person-power and training programs for people indigenous to an economically poor community, "self-selection" is the critical variable. They suggest that drop-outs from the original pool of nonprofessionals recruited should be viewed as a necessary part of this self-selection process. Others (McGee, 1974) have described selection for nonprofessionals to work in crisis intervention centers as a series of "hurdles." Following an initial application, interview, and a series of psychological tests, applicants for McGee's program begin vigorous training in which they are required to attend every session, or to make up material missed. They are phased into actual work only after completing each prior step. Table XI-3 presents the drop-out results from this procedure. As can been seen in the table, over 50 percent drop out before they actually begin to work. Partly for research purposes McGee has not eliminated most applicants other than by this self-selection, unless they were very obviously poorly suited for the role.

At the present time the entire question of who should be chosen for human service work, beyond those with basic social skills and those who self-select by completing requirements, is as confusing in the nonprofessional movement as it is for selection of professionals. Most professional human service workers have been granted admission to a program, and later a degree, on the basis of academic, rather than therapeutic skills. Even in those cases of professional training where therapeutic skill is carefully judged by supervisors, there is little empirical research to support the validity of the supervisors' judgements. The selection of nonprofessionals is largely the same. Change agent effectiveness among professionals as well as nonprofessionals is far more complicated than the simple question "who is effective" seems to imply. As is already well understood in

psychotherapy research, the question must be put something like, "who works best with whom, using what techniques, and what criteria?" (cf., Kiesler, 1971; Paul, 1969a). It is likely that if such questions are to be answered in the future they will require extensive research programs using a variety of prediction devices and multivariate statistical procedures which combine a series of predictors and relate them to some complicated set of outcome criteria (Kramer, Rappaport, & Seidman, 1975).

Supervision and Training of Nonprofessionals

Beyond questions of how to select the nonprofessionals who will deliver direct human services, the nature of specific supervision procedures for monitoring their work is an important issue. Although the details of such supervision are beyond the scope of this volume, others have reviewed the issues raised and the techniques devised. The early monograph by Reiff and Riessman (1965) on training for indigenous nonprofessionals from low-income neighborhoods provides many insights and suggestions. They, and many since them, have emphasized "on the job" rather than didactic training. Issues of training are complicated by the wide range of nonprofessionals employed. There is a great deal of difference between the training needed for those who spend a few hours per week volunteering and those who literally are developing a "new career" (Pearl & Riessman, 1965; Riessman & Popper, 1968). The former tend to be middle-class students and homemakers; the latter tend to be residents of low-income neighborhoods.

TABLE XI–3   Results of screening applicants for the Gainesville crisis center.*

	No. Completing This Step	Percent of Total Applicants
1. Request application	404	100.0
2. Return application	401	99.2
3. Initial interview	305	75.5
4. Psychological tests	263	65.1
5. Begin training	225	55.7
6. Complete training	211	52.2
7. Begin service	195	48.3

*From McGee, 1974.

Obviously, training must also vary depending on what the nonprofessional is supposed to do and whom he or she is supposed to serve. Allerhand and Lake (1972) have discussed many of the issues with regard to training for new careers, and suggest several general components necessary for programs which use nonprofessionals in the welfare, health, school, and research systems. McGee (1974) has also spelled out a careful training program for nonprofessional crisis intervention workers. He includes an emphasis on experiential rather than didactic work, especially early in training, as well as self-awareness training, continuous in-service training and supervision, and a continual reevaluation of the relationship between volunteers and paid staff. This latter point is crucial in any program which uses nonprofessionals in any capacity.

Conter *et al.* (1977) have compared the experiences of college-student volunteers assigned to work with adolescents through a local mental health agency and those students who participated in a similar program for course credit in a university setting. In the former program the college students were provided with a brief orientation and only a periodic supervision and contact with the agency staff, once they had been assigned to a client. They were expected to maintain a ''supportive relationship'' with the client. In the later case, each student was enrolled in an academic course and was required to spend 8–10 hours per week with the target person. In addition, they were required to participate in a weekly supervision group during which every target person was discussed in detail, problems aired, and plans made.

Conter *et al.* (1977) found that not only were volunteer drop-out rates significantly higher in the mental health agency program, but even those students who stayed with the program rated their own experience, learning, and effectiveness significantly lower than those who were in the more closely supervised academic course experience. Interestingly, the agency group of volunteers liked their supervisors as well as the adacemic group, and seemed to blame themselves for their relative dissatisfaction.

Although there is not much literature on the matter, the above data may indicate that a sys-

tematic and careful plan for supervision, to which volunteers are committed before they are allowed to participate, is a necessary component of a successful volunteer program. That is, agencies wishing to use the nonprofessional in productive ways must be willing, as McGee (1974) also suggests, to spend the necessary time and attention to close monitoring of their activities, and to provide ongoing support in sometimes difficult situations. Within the university-based program evaluated by Conter (although they had not done so at the time of the report cited here) the researchers later even went so far as to use detailed manuals describing how to provide the necessary services. They also instructed the students in procedures for goal setting with the target persons. Although that program was quite effective both from the students' point of view as demonstrated by Conter's data, and from analyses of the effects on the target population (Seidman, Rappaport, & Davidson, 1976; Davidson, 1975), it underscores the fact that generalization to other programs without similar close supervision and volunteer commitment may not be warranted.

Given the rapid evolution of community psychology its adherents must not only deal with questions raised by the use of nonprofessionals, but with those of professional training as well. Unlike most professions, community psychology is almost defined by its continual role changes. As the profession seeks new paradigms so too does it seek new roles. It is these issues of professional training to which we now turn.

Professional Education for Community Psychology

Community Psychology as a Social Movement

Social movements have been variously defined by sociologists. Recently, McLoughlin (1969, p. 4), attempting to bring such definitions together, has cited the work of Killian (1964) as representative of the most salient characteristics found in the literature. The characteristics he notes include ''. . . a shared value system, a sense of community, norms for action, and an organizational structure. . . . the movement usually seeks to influence the social order and is oriented toward definite goals (although the ends and purposes of the individual members may vary considerably)."

To a reasonable extent the sort of community psychology described in this volume fits the above characteristics. The emerging value system is one which emphasizes cultural relativity, diversity, and ecology (person-environment fit). Conceptualizations that "blame" either persons or environments for "deficits" are explicitly rejected. Since 1966 there has been a division of Community Psychology within the American Psychological Association, concerned both with norms for action and development of an organizational structure. The division elects officers and representatives to the A.P.A. governing body, and has an executive committee and various subcommittees concerned with issues such as education and training. The division sponsors a journal as well as conferences and meetings. There is little question that the "ends and purposes of the individual members vary considerably," and there is also little question that there are definite, if multiple, goals. The movement seeks to influence the social order both within the profession of psychology and in the larger society. In short, community psychology may be thought of as a social movement.

In the context of professional education it is useful to regard community psychology as a social movement rather than as simply a new professional specialization because it helps to highlight some of the unique problems intrinsic to the field. In Chapter I, the answer to the question "What is community psychology?" led us to note that three, frequently conflicting sets of activities are emphasized: development of human resources, political activity, and the practice of science. For community psychology to be a social movement each of these activities is necessary, and the combination of roles required creates a unique set of socialization problems for training programs.

The need for access to a variety of realistic strategies and tactics for social change, appropriate to participants in a social movement, requires that the roles for which training in community psychology prepare people be flexible

rather than static. This means more for community psychology than it does in professions where change in knowledge leads to new techniques within the same role. For example, a psychotherapist who switches from psychoanalysis to behavior therapy applies a new understanding to essentially the same role. The community psychologist must be able to make entire role switches (for example, from researcher to grass-roots advocate, to consultant to a school system, to political activist), often within a very brief time frame. This is in part because he or she is participating in a social movement as well as in a profession, and must relate to, and identify with, various community as well as professional people.

We need to underscore the following: Throughout this book, although there have been many suggestions for programs, roles, and functions potentially useful for a community psychology, persons engaged in this profession require flexibility, willingness to change and to react to feedback, and continual reevaluation. To create a profession with static roles, techniques, programs, and methods would be simply that: it would create a new profession. Training programs must resist reification of roles which necessitate a "protection of turf," in favor of fostering problem-solving skills among active agents of social change.

Social change is a continuous process, not an end product, and those who would participate in the process will need to continue to change themselves as well. This means that unlike most professions, licensing of practitioners is undesirable. Such licensing of community psychology practitioners who complete a "certified" training program would only create another vested-interest profession rather than develop agents of social change. Those who seek structure and flee ambiguity should not be able to find comfort in community psychology. Job descriptions will change, be created and dissolve, as the community psychologist learns his or her trade and pursues an evolving career. If there is a "technology" for the profession, it is a research and program evaluation methodology, with skills in problem solving, social policy, and value analysis, and with the ability to listen to and represent diverse community groups. The skills are political as well as academic, social as well as psychological. *Such skills will require a great deal of practicum experience in diverse settings, combined with research experience in such settings, while the trainee is still in school.* In addition, the developing community psychologist will require a broad background and understanding of historical and political issues, as well as philosophy of science and human values, so that she or he can participate in applied science with an awareness of its political and value-based implications.

Just as conceptions from individual psychology and community mental health have supplemented this volume, the content of traditional psychology must supplement, but not dominate, the training of future community psychologists. Field research, program evaluation, direct participation in real communities, and in assisting others to accomplish their own goals will be paramount, together with what in earlier times was thought of as a "liberal education." Related skills, such as grant writing and writing for public as well as professional consumption, will also be central to a social movement concerned with resource development and social change. Taken together, the qualities of the ideal community psychologist are somewhat unique relative to traditional professionals.

Preparing Professionals Who Are Also Participants

In his presidential address to the division of community psychology, James G. Kelly (1970), with a paper aptly titled "Antidotes for Arrogance," detailed many of the qualities required of the professional community psychologist. Kelly began with the assumption that the community psychologist will attempt to be both innovative and change producing, and will work both inside and outside traditional social institutions; this shifting of reference groups will necessarily produce "strain" on the person.

George W. Fairweather has expressed similar ideas. Fairweather suggests that the professional as social innovator needs to straddle two worlds. He or she needs to keep one foot in a traditional setting which provides legitimacy and sanction, and the other foot in the community of concern. One needs to be able, on multiple occasions, to turn completely inside an institutional setting, such as a university, a school, a mental health organization, or a legal setting, and work with its members as a colleague. On other occasions the same person must be able to entirely shift reference groups and identify with the target community. In a sense, this will leave the person in an often ill-defined, "unsafe" role, not quite at home in either place. This is at least part of what Kelly takes for granted when he talks about "strain in being innovative and change producing." He suggests that psychologists need to become *participants in their local communities* and to alter their time perspective[2] so that they can help to build a psychology of the community. Producing this kind of a professional is the socialization problem for training programs. How does one create a program in which participation and continual change are paramount objectives?

What I advocate is a redefinition of the psychologist's job and I propose a new set of criteria for the hallmarks of this profession. To put it directly, you can't be a community psychologist just by being a good psychologist. For me, community psychology is a sufficiently different activity that *I don't think we can achieve valid training or able professional role models by accommodating to the heritages, assumptions and styles of previous guidelines for training.* Developing competencies in the community is a distinctly different task and requires new political alliances, and new criteria for personal and joint accountability.

. . . The spirit of the community psychologist is the spirit of a naturalist who dotes on his environment; of the journalist, who bird dogs his story; and of the conservationist who glows when he finds a new way to describe man's interdependence with his environment. *The recommended prevention for an extinct professional role is participation in the local community; the preferred antidote for arrogance is an ecological view of man.* (Kelly, 1970, p. 524.)

---

[2]In part, the question of time perspective suggests that observable changes as a function of our interventions and activities cannot be expected to be completed in the short "turnaround time" of laboratory work, but may require years of involvement.

Kelly is concerned with the arrogance of professional social scientists who analyze and plan, intrude, but rarely stay in their local communities. His solution is in part what he calls a "love of community." Rather than the academic, detached experimental role model, he suggests the need for us to develop in ourselves and our students the psychological sense of community that can only come from involvement in it. The community psychologist is a participant who uses his or her own skills and resources in conjunction with those of fellow residents to whom she or he is directly accountable. The reference group becomes the local community as well as the professional one. Influence on the larger professional-scientific community is an aim to be satisfied only *after* the local environment is understood and answered to. Such a role for the community psychologist requires both patience and a longitudinal perspective. One must be willing to wait, to plan, and to help communities to evolve over a period of years.

Kelly goes on to provide several concrete examples that emphasize not a new curriculum, but a new aim of socialization for professional training conducted in university settings. He suggests that future community psychologists not be selected solely on the basis of standardized admission tests of academic skills, but by also seeking people who have experienced a variety of settings in the real world. He goes so far as to suggest that we need to establish field training sites in high schools where students can be given the opportunity to experience the role of participant in their local community. Such a suggestion, if implemented, could lead to the collaboration of high schools, colleges, and local communities to create a kind of socialization process that would provide young people with a wide variety of practical experience at the local level, in addition to academic skills. Many students might then self-select in and out of such experiences along the way; however, by the time they reached a decision to devote a lifetime of work to community psychology they would have a great deal of experience in what it means. Interestingly, such a suggestion would serve as more than a training ground and recruitment de-

vice for the future professional; it would also allow local communities to provide useful activities for their teenage members who are now all too often simply held in waiting rather than given the opportunity to use their tremendous energies for the benefit of their community, and their own development as citizens. Obviously, such a mechanism is feasible through many of the nonprofessional programs discussed earlier in this chapter.

Postman (1975) has suggested a similar plan in another context. Reacting to the problems of New York City and many of its expensive human service and ecological concerns, he has suggested that the thousands of students in public schools might be mobilized to participate as problem solvers and workers in their city, rather than keeping them locked away for most of the day. The potential benefit to the city, its adolescents, and to the future of professions and citizens knowledgeable about their local community seems to be not only prospectively worthwhile, but is a vast area for research, program evaluation, and human service. The nonprofessional movement in the human service fields, discussed earlier in this chapter, has not yet realized the full potential of such programs. For example, what would happen, asks Postman, if our students began to follow Thoreau's advice in *Walden*:

Students should not play life, or study it merely, while the community supports them at this expensive game, but earnestly live it from the beginning to end. How could youths better learn to live than by at once trying the experiment of living?

Postman goes on to describe what he thinks could happen if this were taken seriously in New York City, where about one-third of the students enrolled in school are absent on any given day, and where millions of dollars per year are spent on replacing broken school windows. He suggests that the curriculum for children from seventh through twelfth grade include cleaning litter and graffiti from neighborhoods, planting trees and flowers, and tending public buildings. He suggests that older high-school students direct traffic and free the police for other duties; that students maintain day-care centers so that young mothers are free to seek employment; that students meet twice each week with elementary-school students to teach them to read, write, and do arithmetic; that they substitute on the job one day per week for adults who want to attend school. Many students could be assigned to publish neighborhood newspapers all over the city, or to provide information of use to local citizens. Students could organize science fairs and block parties and hold "olympics." College students in turn could operate buses, be parking and litter monitors empowered to give tickets, organize film festivals, operate a local television station, give seminars on drug addiciton and legal rights. Postman does not suggest that all the city's probelms would be solved, but that a renewed excitement might develop between the city and its students. Students with such experiences are the kind Kelly suggests might be later recruited to community psychology programs, should they want to become professionals who would use their skills after professional training in ways which are, as Seymour Sarason has put it, "more consciously and expertly applied." (See Chapter IX p. 308.)

Professional Socialization

As already suggested, training and professionalism in community psychology raise a number of two-sided issues for a social movement. On the one hand, for any social movement to survive, it must evoke institutional norms and create organizational structures that perpetuate its existence. In so doing, questions of the certification and qualifications of members often become paramount. Legitimizing membership in a professional group requires assessment of the technical competence of its members. This is especially true for those groups selling their services to the public, and requires indicating what the specific skills should be. It suggests a standard to which new members can be compared. The obvious problem with such standards is that they tend to reify and rigidify the status quo. Professional organizations, like other social organizations, tend to exist for the perpetuation of the organization and the benefit of its membership. Their primary aim

is not to protect the public, although that is often one aim. Those organizations which profess that their *raison d'être* is to serve others are not different in this regard. Although the aims of the organization may be stated in terms such as "advancement of knowledge" and "betterment of human welfare," the actual operations of the organization are perhaps better understood as a special kind of labor union, whose members control entrance, training, certification, and so on, in order to maintain control over their own profession. For the profession of community psychology this creates a special problem. If an avowed aim of community psychology is to participate in social change, then the very development of a profession, with its necessary structures, hierarchies, sanctioned methods, and so on, could serve to reify a status quo, rather than to foster change. Before (or simultaneous with) community psychologists' efforts to change other social institutions, they must deal with their own professional community and settings, and their institutional assumptions, organizations, and role relationships.

Where do community psychologists work? At present they can most often be found in government agencies, community mental health centers, and university settings. Training for community psychology is largely conducted in the university setting; this is where the profession must face many of the issues of professionalism, competence, and values. It is well understood that professional training is in large part a socialization process. It can only be through the educational settings which certify practicing professionals that the resocialization to new roles can begin. If community psychology is to be an effective social movement, the universities must send out a new kind of professional to the social systems of concern in health, education, welfare, and the legal system.

Some of these issues have been well discussed by Ira Goldenberg (1974), who suggests that the university and the larger society are now more similar than different in values, life style, and systems of reward and punishment. If university-based programs are to help create social changes of the sort suggested in this volume attention must first be given to their own "moral credibility,'' before (or while) they seek to change things ''out there.'' They must, argues Goldenberg, foster alternative models, rather than those which simply rely on the past covered by a rhetoric that makes us feel better. In Thomas Kuhn's terms, Goldenberg's message is that the old paradigms are failing, and if we are not serious about searching for new ones in our own training programs, community psychology will fail along with them.

A similar theme has been suggested by Leonard Duhl (1974) who argues that universities must search for new options and encourage diversity. In Duhl's words, ''a shift towards education rather than training would recognize our inability to predict the future.'' This plea for university training to be educational as well as technological, and to avoid rigidly predetermined criteria for ''certification,'' is consistent with the roles emphasized in this volume. The implications from both Goldenberg and Duhl are that the modeled values, roles, and ''rules of the game'' presented by university faculty to their students determine the nature of the future professionals at least as much as the actual skills in which they are trained.

With some of the above implications in mind Frank J. Corbett and Murray Levine (1974) have recently written on the problems of a university involvement in its local community. As they note, universities have a very limited tradition in community service and social change. The image of the ''ivory tower'' is perhaps well deserved.[3] Despite its medical schools, schools of social work and education, and graduate programs in psychology which place students in community facilities for the purpose of training, there has been little emphasis on creating changes in such agencies or in the local community, and almost no effort to assist grass-roots groups.

Most often the students are expected to ''fit in'' to an existing agency and to learn to be exactly like the professionals now working there. This is currently an important problem for many of the community psychology training programs. Because student financial support and income for the program are important to its functioning, many programs find it beneficial to place their students as part-time workers in local agencies. Although such experience is undoubtedly beneficial in that the student can meet, head on, the problems faced in the ''real world,'' and he or she can also meet and interact with the professional, nonacademic community, when students are hired by agencies they are necessarily constrained to act as employees, rather than as change agents. An alternate relationship, rare but not totally impossible, is to place students in settings without cost to the agency. This tends to make them less accountable to the agency and less vulnerable to the pressures of fitting in.

Although no one is going to be permitted to develop a relationship in an agency unless he or she can be somewhat accommodating to its culture, sensitive to its needs, and helpful, a relationship in which the student and his or her program is not dependent on the agency for financial well-being increases the likelihood that the student and his or her professors can feel less constrained about providing proposals for change in the rules of the game, and straightforward evaluations of the agency. Similarly, independence from funding sources frees the training program to place students in grass-roots organizations that cannot afford to pay for consultation, but might benefit from it while providing a unique experience for the student. Such placements open up the possibility of a student learning the skills and roles of working with the poor and the powerless rather than only with the current controllers of human services, from whom most of a student's education will be received anyway. In this sense, the possibilities of stimulating and assisting groups interested in social change are increased by placement outside established agencies.

---

[3]Some exceptions have been agricultural schools with an avowed mission of bringing technological assistance to the farming communities, and university-based psychological clinics with the aim of providing service to troubled individuals. In the latter case services have been oriented toward training needs of students; target populations have usually been screened to provide specific kinds of cases rather than to provide service to the local community as a primary objective. Although agricultural extensions have been more service-oriented, these have necessarily been technologically rather than social-change-oriented, and limited to the farming community.

There are many possible examples of the difference between working with the current agents of control and with the grass-roots groups in a community. If a student were interested in the educational system much could be learned by sanctioned consultation with teachers and administrators; however, this would be a different sort of experience from working directly with parents from the local community, outside the sanction of the school. Although one could work with parents because the school sanctions and refers "problem families" of children who do not fit into the school, an entirely different perspective would be obtained by going directly to community groups and individuals who wish to influence their local school, and assisting them in planning changes, advocating for their children, and starting new programs. Such groups cannot often afford to pay for these services; nevertheless the educational benefits to the student and his or her academic supervisors, as well as the potential for stimulating community development, may offset the financial losses.

For such a university-based training program to function it is probably necessary to have some other form of student financial support, be it fellowships from government agencies or private foundations, or teaching and research assistantships provided by the university. It is possible, for example, for a university to grant teaching assistantships to graduate students in such a role, who would supervise and train undergraduates in practicum course activities for which they would receive academic credit (Cowen, Chinsky, & Rappaport, 1970; Seidman & Rappaport, 1974b). Obviously, for such support to materialize, university academic departments need to support the notion that practicum supervision in social change techniques, field research, and work with grass-roots groups is as much a part of the education of social scientists and undergraduates as traditional classroom activities; it is therefore deserving of financial support in the form of graduate teaching assistantships. Alternately, the students might perform such duties for course credit rather than for salary. Such work need not be anti-intellectual and could, indeed must, be combined with appropriate reading, scholarly activities, program evaluation, and related academic preparation which is the keynote of university training. It is exactly this combination of experiences that makes university-based programs valuable to the society as a source of training as well as a means for development of new knowledge about our society.

The Culture of the University Academic Department

Corbett and Levine (1974) provide an excellent and realistic description of the culture of university academic departments. As they note, the values are operationalized by promotion policies for faculty, which reify the institutional aim of building and maintaining a national reputation for its faculty. Although such a view of the culture is more crass than university people typically like to admit, and normally the aims of the university are described in terms of contributions to knowledge, it is indisputable that functionally, the university's policies (at least most major universities engaged in graduate education) require its faculty to be primarily concerned with (1) publishing, (2) research grants, (3) participation in national and international meetings, and (4) invitations to give colloquia at other universities (Corbett & Levine, 1974).

Relatively light teaching loads and freedom to use one's time as one wishes (to accomplish the ends noted above) combined with a tenure system in which one typically has a certain amount of time (usually six to ten years) to become "known" help to foster competition between faculty rather than cooperation. Publication is easiest when writing papers that fit into existing paradigms. Teaching and research, but not community service, are also important. This culture tends to make community service activities "unprofitable" for faculty; and by implication for their students. Even in the area of publication, technical writing for a limited audience of scholars is more highly valued than writing for public consumption, and experimental "rigor" is valued over field research or program evaluation.

As already discussed in Chapter II, when comparing so-called basic and applied research, applied work is almost always in a "one-down" position. In this context, the implications for graduate education in community psychology are of interest. Not only do graduate students see short-term well-controlled laboratory studies "pay off" for their professors, but they also have requirements for their own research. Master's and Ph.D. theses that are laboratory studies are not only easier to accomplish and contain less risk of failure than field studies, but they typically take less time and are more well received in most departments. The longitudinal, high-risk program evaluation and field studies required of a community psychologist also require financial support. On the faculty side the problem of competition for scare resources makes the life of those interested in community service, even as a research area, expensive and difficult. It requires long-term commitment with high probability of low "payoff" vis-à-vis professional norms. It is the rare untenured professor who can afford the risk, and the rare tenured professor who is able to reject the model of work which led to his or her initial recognition and academic success. The current system is well designed to perpetuate itself through its students and its allocation of resources. It is a system that stores energy for its own maintenance.

It is reasonable to question whether or not such an environment can hope to foster the kind of social-change-oriented community psychology argued for in this volume. A recent national conference on training for community psychology (see p. 405), attended by some 80 invited psychologists mostly from academic settings, was most noteworthy to many of its participants for the sense of comradery that they found there. Most attendants expressed to one another the satisfaction of finding a reference group of people who in their "home settings" were largely isolated or members of a very small group of colleagues. It may be that the kind of borderline existence required of professional community psychologists can only be fostered by a reference group of national scope, and that large enclaves of community psychologists cannot develop in individual departments because they cannot be tolerated by the culture of the university. With regard to training, this may mean that involvement of students in the loose network of community psychologists nationally may be a key to continued development of the field. The sense of belonging to a very small group locally, but with national ties and colleagues, can be a positive force enabling one to ignore unpopularity in one's own department. Indeed, this situation may even have the advantages of an "undermanned" setting (see Barker & Gump (1964); Chapter V, p. 143).

The above picture is not intended to be bleak, so much as realistic. In most community psychology training programs few individual faculty members are primarily identified with community psychology. Often they develop allies in related areas of psychology or other disciplines, and small numbers of students. It may be that this is desirable because as a professional career community psychology, at least of the sort described in this volume, may require the kind of temperament that tolerates no clear and well-defined place in the social system. The ability to identify with various groups on an ad hoc basis, and to work primarily without institutional commitments, but with commitments to an ideal, a value base, and a community of concern, may be necessary. This description is not intended to be heroic so much as realistic. Advocates for social change within one's own university setting and in one's local community cannot expect to be welcomed with open arms by the very people and organizations one wants to change! This is especially true during times of decreasing budgets for educational innovations, as is likely to be the case in the foreseeable future.

University-Based Service Centers

Corbett and Levine (1974) note that one way in which some universities have responded to the call for community services has been to set up new settings or service centers, unrestrained by traditional academic departments. Unfortunately, the very strength of such settings has also been their weakness. Unhampered by the academic tradition, they must create their own; and unless the traditions created support training for students and the search for new knowledge, they will not be successful in a university. To turn such settings to complete community control, which makes sense for service delivery organizations, human resources centers, and public schools, may not be sensible for university-based centers whose unique mission is lost unless there is an explicit training and research function. As Corbett and Levine suggest, what may be required of a university-based service center is that it maintain its own values and goals but adapt to the local community for mutual benefit. Collaboration between university and local leadership, on an equal basis, is required.

In the context of orienting such centers to serve both the purposes of the community *and* training for students, Corbett and Levine have suggested that prior to student involvement it is necessary that the staff help to establish specific preconditions:

1. They must identify precise skills which they and their students have that may be helpful in the setting.
2. They must adapt the skills to the needs of the particular neighborhood.
3. They must prepare students in the "how to or implemental level of problem solving." They suggest that it is imperative that in such settings the faculty and students provide concrete services and skills not heretofore accessible to the neighborhood.
4. Programs of this nature require a clear, in-depth plan, worked out together with the local residents, including program evaluation.
5. Programs must make clear the values and goals of the university people as well as the local residents.
6. There must be sufficient freedom to complete commitments to local residents. This requires an ongoing, not a time-limited involvement. Change as a function of feedback is required, but data collection followed by leaving the setting cannot be allowed.
7. Staff and students must have a sound understanding of the ecology and history of the neighborhood.
8. Motivation must *not* be built on guilt, romantic idealism, or ill-defined ideas about citizen participation.
9. Although community participation is important, local people must not be led to believe that they can exercise policy and budget control, if they in fact cannot.
10. Educational goals must be co-equal with community goals.

Perhaps one of the best ways to arrange for such training and service settings is to develop them within an academic department, thereby combining the best elements of the university culture of research, evaluation, and teaching, and the aims of community development. The psycho-educational clinic established at Yale in the mid-1960s was one such setting (Sarason *et al.*, 1966), and more recently the Community Psychology Action Center at the University of Illinois has provided a similar model (Rappaport *et al.*, 1975). The more recent program at Illinois has taken a number of steps which may be illustrative. Key elements involve a clear contract with local leadership working in the setting. The have the right to control and direct the center's activities and programs, in exchange for agreeing to work, together with university faculty, to provide for the educational needs of students to whom the university is responsible. In addition, the university has made clear its ongoing commitment to a setting for continued exploration of mutual and collaborative ventures between university persons and local community residents, each providing resources and each giving respect to one another.

An important aspect of this setting is the agreement that community interventions, even when they involve students and academic psychologists, not be based on the short-term research grant model. Although research grants are certainly desirable to support specific evaluations of subprograms, the basic commitment of university/local community collaboration is to an ongoing involvement. In general, the setting has emphasized the idea that a university-based community psychologist needs to develop institutional support for activities in training and service which the psychologist, the students, and the community can count on as lasting rather than time-limited via a federal research grant. The model is not entirely new to the university setting, and it recalls the psychological clinic, designed to serve White middle-class persons requesting psychotherapy while training clinical psychology graduate students. Similarly, the agricultural extension model adopted by state universities to serve the rural farming community while pursuing new knowledge and training is comparable. Just as we have supported psychological clinics and agricultural extension services we must now support new settings as legitimate training and service sites in urban communities.

The application of this idea at the Community Psychology Action Center of the University of Illinois (Rappaport *et al.*, 1975) includes a number of components within the basic framework of establishing mini-social systems and training community psychologists to work in the Black community. A facility located in the local Black neighborhood houses the various programs. Concern with ongoing funding was met by seeking support from the university to establish a program whose existence would be a regular and continued part of the university, free to experiment and learn from an ongoing system, and free of outside research support and control. Although research grants are maintained, the program coordinators resisted seeking outside support as the basis of the training program. The particular service projects around which training is oriented are of less importance than how they were chosen and how they are implemented.

The first step was to contact identified Black community representatives. Six months of meetings were held in which it became clear that the needs of the community were such that to try to "solve" specific problems would be of no consequence. Therefore the program developers began to search for residents who had their own positive ideas which started from a position of strength; and they set out to accomplish the residents' aims while serving the needs of a training program.

One of the service projects that developed is an infant day-care center for one-parent families. The center is unusual because it provides services for children from six weeks to two years of age; children for whom the poor find it virtually impossible to obtain other than babysitting care, if they can afford that. The day-care operation itself is not viewed as simply providing an enriched environment for "disadvantaged" children. Rather, single parents need day-care so they can pursue their own education or employment. Resources are also used to help coordinate organized services for such parents. Finally, the center also serves as a natural child development laboratory for the training of students.

As a second example, the Community Psychology Action Center also houses a communications and information center. The director is a graphic artist who grew up and left the local community. His return was to specifically set up this program, and he brought to it a set of viable skills and leadership qualities. Such opportunities for local talented people, which encourage them to stay in their community, have been lacking to date. The operation of a printing press and a public information service provides a basis for training young Black residents in relevant job skills while distributing news related to issues of interest to the local Black community. A periodically published journal serves as an open forum for notices, discussions, and investigative reporting on topics of local concern. Many organizations in the local Black community have no access to the usual routes of media communication. The journal provides a vehicle to unite them with university students who can write about, research, and investigate issues of concern. For example, a course in investigative reporting and public education which can accomplish some of the tasks of information gathering is offered by the center. This setting may be an example of an ideal relationship between a university and a community, combining concerns of the community with the communication, publishing, and research skills of the university, and providing services as well as training. One of the key elements in this relationship, which inhibits the tendency of programs to ridigify, is the continual input from newly contacted community groups and individuals.

The Importance of Minority Students and Faculty in Community Psychology Training Programs

It is no secret that there are currently few social scientists from certain racial and ethnic minority groups.[4] This is, in part, because few relative to their number in the general population have been admitted to undergraduate programs, and even fewer to graduate and professional schools. A recent report by Moore (1977) cites Mommsen's (1974) estimate that there are only between 3000 and 3500 living Black Ph.D's. At the time of the Mommsen report, only 1.7 percent of *all* Arts and Sciences graduate students were Black, and Mommsen projected that this number would add only 200 new Black Ph.D's in the near future. One survey (Epps & Howze, 1971) found only 166 living Black Ph.D's in psychology. Padilla, Boxley, and Wagner (1973) found that 7.3 percent (348) of the total population of students in doctoral-level clinical psychology graduate programs in 1972 were members of a minority group, and only 3.3 percent (41) of the clinical psychology faculty members were Black. Obviously, if we are to have Black faculty, we must first have Black graduate students. For community psychology such students, both Blacks and members of other minority groups, who will become faculty as well as work in applied jobs, are crucial.[5]

Efforts to increase the proportion of underrepresented minorities in graduate and professional schools are obviously needed on the basis of simple social justice for both the potential students and their peers in the communities they will serve. It is also important as a means to enhance the scope, understanding, and quality of the professions. Such efforts will require both strenuous recruiting to increase the total applicant pool, and attention to the special strengths, experiences, interests, and abilities of such students vis-à-vis the particular academic discipline. In graduate school the quality of the students is of great importance to the faculty. The more competent the students the more likely the research of both students and faculty will be well done. Faculty usually must rely on research assistants selected from among their graduate students to carry out important functions in a research project. Of course, the same is true for graduate teaching assistants. In addition, the students' ideas, questions, interests, and abilities will influence the nature and quality of advanced graduate seminars taught by the faculty; and their theses and independent research projects will help faculty to keep abreast of their own research areas, and to learn new information.

Moore (1977) has pointed out that "minority students offer more to a program than just their presence. By virtue of life experiences minority students bring a different perspective to the research and applied sciences." Such students (and faculty) offer new ideas, perspectives, and skills. Their cultural biases will interact with the existing predominant ones in exactly the ways that such biases must affect social science (see Chapter II). They will surely help to change the discipline. The point is not that such students will make social science less biased, but rather that they may counter-balance existing biases by representing another cultural perspective.

The above viewpoint can only be denied if one assumes that social science is truly objective and not affected by personal experiences and cultural predispositions, an argument with which this entire volume takes issue. The point is not *only* that recruitment of minority students is a direction consistent with social justice, but that, *in addition*, the *impact of their presence on the graduate programs that they enter will be important in its own right*.

Although there have been repeated calls from a small number of Black psychologists for the development of a "Black Perspective" in

---

[4]Although this discussion is focused on the problem for Blacks, the problem is similar for native Americans, Spanish surname Americans, and Orientals. Priorities for attention to such groups might best be resolved depending on geographical area. For example, a graduate program in the southwestern United States might focus its efforts on Mexican-American students rather than Blacks.

[5]There is some danger in taking this position specifically for community psychology if it clouds the fact that simple social justice requires universities to open their doors to more minority group members in *every* discipline. We suggest here that this obligation is highlighted for the social sciences in general, and for those who would seek social change in particular.

psychology (Clark, 1973), as well as similar requests from other minority groups, there has been little appreciation among most academic departments of the fact that admitting minority students is not simply worthwhile in its own right, but that Black, native American, Mexican-American, Spanish surname, and Oriental students will benefit the university departments themselves by broadening their cultural perspectives and experiences, and over time making their work more representative of the world of concern. This is really a question of understanding that in the long run, social science may be getting more than it is giving; it is not clear who is doing whom a favor when minority students enter a heretofore White middle-class-dominated profession.

If a psychology department is to have a graduate program in community psychology of the sort described in this volume, it is essential that the faculty "practice what they preach." The recruitment and admission of minority students must be a top priority. Because social change and redistribution of resources to local disenfranchised communities are of concern to a community psychology program, evidence of qualifications for students in that program may be different from or additional to those in traditional psychology programs (but see also footnote 4). Although a high level of academic performance and experience is clearly required for any Ph.D. program, perhaps of equal importance are a student's interpersonal skills, ability to relate to community residents, and desire to engage in difficult independent work "in the field." A desire to combine research and social intervention skills is also important. Just as many clinical programs look for relevant experiences and interpersonal abilities increasing the likelihood that their students will be good practicing psychologists, so too community psychology students need to be selected so as to increase the likelihood that they will have the requisite characteristics to engage in the strategies and tactics of community psychology.

Given the advent of computer technology and programmed statistical data analysis techniques, which often make data analysis *per se* a routine task, it may very well be that social skills are now of at least equal importance to ability in advanced mathematics. It will be important for students to learn statistics and research design and to understand when to use what kind of data analysis and so on; but the ability to interact with and understand the viewpoint of diverse community groups must also be given a high priority. Yet today scores on the graduate record examination's "quantitative aptitude test" are given more weight in admission decisions than other skills by many graduate training programs. In part, this is because such information is readily available on a nationally standardized basis, and it is easier to compare students on their "percentile score" than it is to pay attention to their more difficult to define social skills.

Current admission criteria to graduate school in psychology tend to overweigh academic credentials and underweigh other characteristics. Many good programs have so many qualified applicants that the faculty will readily admit that admission of students only on the basis of grades and graduate record examinations is a strategy they use for efficiency, and one which eliminates many students who would probably "make it" academically. The scores may not even discriminate with regard to academic ability, beyond some level of performance.

A community psychology training program also needs to find minority students, as well as White middle-class students, who are competent in the nonacademic skills, which are more difficult to assess than mathematics ability. One way to do this is to strongly weigh admission criteria relevant to experiences in social action and community involvement, as well as social skills. *This does not argue for "lowering the standard," but for broadening the standards.* For example, a community psychology training program might legitimately use, in addition to information about an applicant's experience in the "real world," some form of problem-solving interview to assess the potential student's ability to put together a plan for intervention in a community problem situation. Although it is true that such performances are difficult to evaluate, this is hardly a reason not to try, to research the outcomes, and to improve the methods. Indeed it seems inconsistent with the values of research and evaluation *not* to develop and test new admissions procedures.

It must be acknowledged that one of the important areas for social change that cannot be ignored by a community psychology program is representation of minority groups. Every community psychologist must ask him or herself what is being done in his or her department to encourage minority student enrollment and faculty hiring.[6]

The entire issue is even more complicated. The real social change does not occur when minority students are enrolled in graduate programs. It is at that point that the social change process has a chance to begin. Minority students must not be expected simply to be socialized to prevailing graduate school norms. If second-order change and the creation of new programs and perspectives are to be the aim, the "rules of the game" require changing. If we expect Black and other minority students only to "fit in," we may have slightly more black, brown, and yellow faces in the classroom, but we will not have created a new understanding which benefits the society or the profession, beyond these individual people. Second-order change will require changes in the institutional structures of graduate education, changes which allow for the expression of new ideas that legitimize new settings for practice, such as those discussed in the preceding section of this chapter. Other ideas and settings, which are yet to be developed by minority students who are permitted the opportunity to enter the profession *and* to maintain their own interests and background, would also be desirable.

Examples of Specific Graduate Level Training Programs

With the exception of some examples drawn from the author's own experiences at the University of Illinois, specific training programs now in existence have not been described in this chapter. For those interested in the details of such programs the report of a recent national training conference (Iscoe, Bloom, & Spielberger, 1977) will provide information current to the time of its publication. An earlier volume, edited by Iscoe and Spielberger (1970), also describes a number of specific programs, many of which are reviewed by Zax and Specter (1974). Both of these latter volumes, but particularly the Iscoe and Spielberger book, provide a good deal of general information with regard to training issues as viewed by a variety of people, as does the *Handbook of Community Mental Health,* edited by Golann and Eisdorfer (1972). However, these program descriptions may be already out of date with regard to concrete examples of what a student is likely to experience.

Table XI-4 provides an incomplete list of schools that have indicated, either by answering a survey questionnaire (Golann, 1970), or by completing a program description for a national training conference held in the spring of 1975, that they offer some form of training in community psychology. Because the characteristics of almost all community psychology programs are closely tied to a small number of faculty members who are geographically mobile and constantly learning and rethinking their professional roles, methodological issues, and specific community work, training programs are in a constant flux. Consequently, it is important that a prospective student obtain current information about a given program directly from individual faculty and students now in the setting.

Despite the ongoing changes, it is useful for this general discussion to point out, as examples, a few specific programs that are particularly interesting because of some special characteristics.[7] No attempt has been made to fully

---

[6]The same is true with regard to hiring of women. Although this discussion has not stressed the issue, women are very much under-represented on many psychology department faculties.

[7]In many university settings there are now excellent examples of community psychology and community mental health, and even more commonly an individual faculty member or two who are developing innovative activities. Excellent training can be received by working with one or more such faculty who may be embedded in a more traditional psychology department structure. The emphasis here, however, is on programs that are relatively more independent as total programs, or relatively more toward the community psychology rather than the community mental health end of the continuum.

TABLE XI–4   An incomplete list of schools that have reported some form of graduate training in community psychology.

Adelphi University	University of Massachusetts
University of Arizona	University of Miami
University of Arkansas	University of Michigan
Boston College	Michigan State University
Boston University	University of Minnesota
California School of	University of Mississippi
Professional Psychology	University of Missouri
University of California	University of Nebraska
at Berkeley	City College of City
University of California	University of New York
at Irvine (Social Ecology)	New York University
University of California	State University of New York at Buffalo
at Los Angeles	University of North Carolina
Catholic University of	Northwestern University
America	Ohio State University
University of Chicago	Ohio University
University of Cincinnati	University of Oregon
University of Colorado	George Peabody College
Columbia Teachers College	Pennsylvania State University
University of Connecticut	University of Pittsburgh
Denver University	University of Portland
De Paul University	Purdue University
Duke University	Richmond College of CUNY
Emory University	University of Rochester
Federal City College	St. Louis University
University of Florida	University of Texas
Florida State University	University of Utah
Fordham University	University of Virginia
University of Georgia	Vanderbilt University
University of Houston	West Virginia University
University of Illinois at	Washington University at
Urbana-Champaign	St. Louis
Southern Illinois University	Wayne State University
Indiana University	Western Reserve University
University of Kansas	Wheaton College
University of Louisville	University of Wisconsin
Loyola University	at Green Bay
University of Maryland	Yale University

describe these programs; rather, the intention is to note how they have concretized some of the specific training issues in interesting ways. For example, we have already pointed out how the program at the University of Illinois provides a community-based setting where students and residents can experience a mutual involvement in programs oriented toward "strength building," based on the ability and skills of the local residents.

Recently, community, clinical, and personality psychologists at the University of Illinois have formed a training program in personality and social ecology that provides a number of unique practicum experiences. These experiences provide an arena for social change research and program evaluation, that are combined with basic research methods, sophisticated research design courses, and person-environment research perspectives ranging from study of the person-institutional environment, through the person-social environment and the person-physical environment. The faculty include community-action-oriented psychologists, personality and social psychology researchers, and those with expertise in physiological, social, and interpersonal psychology.

One of the earliest attempts to put the concepts of community mental health into action was initiated at the University of Rochester in the 1960s. In that program the model of the "mental health quarterback" (Cowen, 1973) with graduate students serving as supervisors for college students, retired people, high-school students, and a variety of other nonprofessionals, was introduced as a practicum course. Students have engaged in a variety of specific service delivery projects, and much of this work has been summarized by Cowen (1971). That training model has been expanded recently by Seidman and Rappaport (1974b) in what they have called the "Educational Pyramid" (see the section on nonprofessionals, above). It is clear that such practicum courses, when they are carefully supervised and monitored, can provide meaningful learning experiences for undergraduates (Conter *et al.*, 1977) as well as graduate students who are given the opportunity to experience an innovative role in the human service systems of their local community.

Price (1975b) has recently described the training program at the University of Michigan, where, beginning in 1971, community psychology became a separate, self-contained area of specialization, with its own full-time students. The program goals at the University of Michigan are to promote action research, training in methodologies appropriate for such research, and to disseminate findings and developments to community groups as well as to fellow professionals. In the typical four-year program of study, a student will combine methodological and content courses in community psychology with courses in other areas of psychology as well as those selected from outside the department. Field and practicum work is extensive. The program's stated value/goals are consistent with many of the directions suggested in this book. According to Price:

Our program is based on the assumption that community psychologists should be engaged in a systematic effort to transform social knowledge into social action and to evaluate social action for the purpose of contributing to scientific knowledge. We intend to train psychologists who do not see themselves as exclusively researchers or exclusively practitioners. Consequently, our program emphasizes training in problem oriented, value directed, action research. We are devoted to the idea that rigorous, well conceived action research is the most practical thing that a community psychologist could be doing. In this approach to research, (a) problem formation is stimulated by community needs, (b) research is seen as a tool for social action and social decision making, (c) value issues are made explicit, (d) and research products are designed to be used by community groups, agencies, and human service systems (1975b).

Partly as a consequence of the concern with value clarification and consistency between actions and value/goals, the Michigan program has instituted what is called "reflexivity" into its operation. A joint student-faculty evaluation group is formed each year to provide continual feedback and reanalysis so as to be sure that they "practice what they preach," and to provide internal and ongoing program evaluation. It is exactly this kind of self-conscious appraisal that is necessary for creating an environment wherein social change is recognized as an ongoing process, rather than an end-state; and where the setting continually reevaluates itself with regard to its stated mission. Perhaps one of the major important elements in the Michigan program is its avowed attempt to take seriously George Miller's (1969) plea for psychology to "give itself away."

Speaking in a presidential address to A.P.A. about the "relevance" of psychology to society, Miller observed that the public tends to get its social science "facts" from an outdated understanding, and largely by accident and selective journalism. He suggested that rather than to aggrandize our current understandings, a top priority for a "releveant" psychology would be an open and shared communication with the general public. It is somewhat ironic that the social scientists' views of human behavior often appear in the "common sense" of the society only after they have been discarded by the social scientists. Freudian psychology is probably the most currently influential conception of many in our modern society, yet it is in disrepute within the scientific community. The point here is simply that as Gergin (1973) and Cronbach (1975) (see Chapter II) have suggested, much of psychology may be viewed as a means to understand *contemporary* human events, rather than universal explanations. If this is so, then a shared relationship with local community residents co-involved with professionals is necessary in order to gather meaningful data, and to make its outcomes and insights accessible in the short as well as the long run. This means sharing our understanding with people in our *local community*, not only with other professionals and established agencies of social control. Such a psychology requires training programs where students are thrust, as a part of their learning experience, directly into contact with community residents who are asking for useful suggestions about how to deal with a here and now world. This includes grass-roots as well as established groups at all levels of the social structure.

The above is what community psychology needs to be about: The application of social science methodology and conceptions to contemporary social problems in a carefully evaluated format, wherein all information is directly shared with the community of concern and where research becomes a partnership. Graduate training for community psychology must be the place where these skills are learned, not where the student is shunted off to an isolated experimental room so that she or he may complete a "well-controled" thesis and will please a committee composed of people who value only laboratory research. This is not a plea for doing poor research nor for doing away with laboratory research; rather, it is a plea for doing field-collaborative research on contemporary human concerns as a top priority for graduate training in community psychology. There is little advantage in telling a student that the laboratory is where to go in order to do a thesis simply because it will be easier to conduct an acceptable project. All that advice does is reinforce the tendency to view laboratory research as both the best and easiest to do, neither of which is neces-

sarily true. Much laboratory research is difficult to do, and often it is done poorly. For some questions (most of those community psychology asks) field research and program evaluation may be *required*. Students need the freedom to try new methods and new research techniques. Students cannot be expected to be engaged in ten-year longitudinal research or to arrive at definitive answers in order to get a degree, but they can be required to engage in field research to learn how to do it, if they are to be community psychologists.

What is needed is a change in our conception of what a Ph.D. student is required to accomplish. Traditionally, he or she is expected to make the thesis "an independent contribution to knowledge." It is an open secret that this is a myth. A very small portion of theses contribute to our knowledge base; most are never read outside the university in which they are conducted, and often doing the work is made so distasteful and "unreal" to those interested in contemporary society that the student regards it as an experience necessary to get a "union card," but as one that has little bearing on his or her activities once club membership is attained. Instead of regarding graduate student research as necessarily leading to a "product" (defined as the discovery of some new "fact"), it may be more sensible to regard it as a *process*. Here the student, while still in the relatively protected environment of the University where she or he can afford to try new and high-risk research, must demonstrate the ability to take on the complexities of the real world by doing research which engages that world in some meaningful way, or engages community people in the give and take of collaboration. Rather than regard the student's thesis as a definitive piece of research, it may be more sensible to regard it as an opportunity for the student to take a risk that may be low "payoff" in the sense of outcome and statistical significance, but high payoff in the stimulation of new ideas. This may lead to both further social science questions for the students and useful information for the local community.

A training program in ecological psychology, which requires exactly the sort of experience described above, has been functioning for several years at Michigan State University (Tornatzky, Fairweather, & O'Kelly, 1970). The ecological psychology program is based on George Fairweather's notions of experimental social innovation, described in detail in Chapter VI. Basic to this program is the value that our concepts must be tested in the community. The program seeks to train students in evaluation and research skills applied in socially responsible ways. The faculty of the program see themselves as involved in:

". . . two general areas of social change: (a) the development of alternative social models or subsystems to replace contemporary systems that have been demonstrated to be ineffective or harmful; and (b) creating the conditions for adoption by the general population of such demonstrably successful models by experimental means." (Tornatzky, Fairweather, & O'Kelly, 1970, p. 886.)

The six key elements in this training include: (1) learning how to engage in *problem definition* by means of reviewing published literature, naturalistic observation, and generating feedback from the target population itself; (2) *designing innovative subsystems* that are acceptable to the intended users; (3) applying *experimental comparisons* between the newly developed and the traditional subsystems; (4) *carefully evaluating* over an extended period of time; (5) *assuming responsibility* for the lives and well-being of the participants; (6) *implementing* those subsystems that are shown to best serve the needs of the target population. All elements are intended to train persons whose careers "will be centered about producing and experimentally evaluating social change that enhances the general welfare" (Tornatzky *et al.*, 1970).

Early in the students' careers they are required to select a problem area of direct relevance to the well-being of society and amenable to longitudinal research. While learning methodology and academic material (including multidisciplinary work), the student begins to immediately engage the local community and to take the risks involved. The goal is to improve the quality of life, not the length of one's publication list, and the student is expected to remain deeply involved in community contact throughout his or her career.

Tornatzky (1976) has recently reported on the progress of the Ecological Psychology Training Program, and suggests that despite financial problems they have been able to turn out students with a commitment to experimental field research on urgent social problems. Many of their students have taken jobs in nonacademic settings at the state and local level. However, they often find that few agencies want to conduct true program evaluation, and suggest the need for the development of independent research centers that would support such activity.

Another recent innovation in training has developed on the University of California's Irvine campus, and is known as the Program in Social Ecology (Binder, 1972). Independent of any traditional academic department, this program houses faculty members whose own training is in one or more fields such as Community Psychology, Urban Planning, Environmental Psychology, Law, Human Develpment, Public Health, Criminology, and Human Ecology. The program is obviously multidisciplinary and provides the student with courses oriented toward urban problems as viewed from many different perspectives. Emphasis is on "social participation" as well as empirical work (Monahan, 1974). Begun as an undergraduate program and later expanded to provide master's level training, the program has only recently admitted Ph.D. students, and it is too early to tell what their products will be. Nevertheless, the willingness to engage in a new kind of degree program centered around the study of social problems is a step which is both courageous and potentially a contribution to many academic fields of study. Community psychology in particular will need to keep a close watch on this approach because its training and research aims are highly relevant to the areas of concern. In many ways this program has put into action the search for new paradigms by bringing together multiple viewpoints in close working relationship. The students produced could be unique among their colleagues.[8]

---

[8]Several other programs that have developed outside of psychology departments have recently been described in a symposium entitled *Careers in Public Affairs in Psychology* (1976). The programs at the Wright Institute in California, at the College of Human Development at Penn State, and at

From Boulder, to Vail, to Austin: Recent Directions

The Boulder Conference model (1949) of a "scientist-professional" who combines research and application to human problems set the ideal for professional clinical psychology training programs in the past generation. In 1965, the Boston Conference, attended by many clinical psychologists who were already working on issues of community mental health, adopted a similar model: the "participant-conceptualizer" (Bennett *et al.*, 1966). The difference from clinical psychology was a broadened view of legitimate problem areas, intervention strategies and tactics, and an emphasis on "environmental" rather than intrapsychic concerns. Community psychology became the name of the game for the psychologist with social change concerns and a willingness to engage in a mixture of politically and socially active interventions from a base of professional skills. As we have already seen in Chapters I and III, this expansion resulted in confusion, failure, upheaval, and disillusionment, all of which interacted with the general social upheaval in America in the 1960s and early 1970s to result in a search for new paradigms. The upheaval hit much of applied psychology, as is evidenced by the 1973 National Conference on Levels and Patterns of Training in Professional Psychology, held at Vail, Colorado.

A major motivation for the Vail Conference appears to have been formal sanctioning of a professional service degree, the Doctor of Psychology. The conferees, invited by the American Psychological Association, included university professionals, mental health center professionals, students, and government agency workers. They were predominantly representatives of clinical, community, counseling, school, and industrial-organizational psychology. Minorities and women were consciously invited and represented among the 133 attendees. The recommendations endorsed by this group (Korman, 1973) were far-reaching in the

sense of an expressed concern with many of the issues of racism, sexism, minority, and consumer representation in psychology's service activities. The conferees strongly endorsed professional training for delivery of service at all degree levels. They supported doctoral, masters, and bachelors as well as associate degree programs in service delivery, with an emphasis on part-time training and continuing education available to all professionals, theoretically giving everyone access to advancement in the profession. Beyond this, the most consistent tenor of the recommendations was a call for reform in the admissions practices of professional psychology training programs, with a movement toward greater inclusion of minority groups and women on the faculty and in the student body. About half of the recommendations concern these issues either directly or indirectly.

It is perhaps indicative of the tenor of university psychology departments that the Vail Conference recommendations have been largely ignored. Perhaps they were simply unrealistic and not representative of the views in most academic settings. It is unfortunate that this particular conference has been identified with issues of minority opportunity in psychology. The emphasis on training professional service delivery agents, as opposed to research training, runs counter to all the traditions of academic psychology and has almost predoomed the conference's potential for impact, other than to justify a few new programs. Its effect on established programs is likely to be small, especially because the economic picture for new support to graduate education is bleak. It might have been better to separate minority recruitment and admissions issues from the questions raised by a conference which focused on acceptance of new professional degrees. In any case, it is clear that the Vail Conference is more an indication of unrest among significant numbers of socially concerned psychologists than it is a carefully charted or likely to be widely accepted set of procedures for change in the practices of university-based training programs.

In 1975, marking the tenth anniversary of the Boston Conference, a national training conference in community psychology was held at the University of Texas, Austin, under the spon-

---

Claremont Graduate School, each present a viable alternative to training within a traditional psychology department.

sorship of the A.P.A.'s Division of Community Psychology. Although recognizing the importance of community psychology's possible contribution to issues of racism and sexism, the conference focused on more general conceptual and methodological issues (Iscoe, 1975). Nevertheless, the conference did provide an opportunity for input from Blacks, women, Chicanos, and Hispanic-Americans, and developed some mechanisms for involvement of ethnic minorities in the Division's governing structures (cf. Cowen, 1975).

About half of the attendees were professionally young (doctoral degrees held less than 5 years, or still graduate students); others included were more established academic and professional psychologists from universities, government agencies, and community mental health centers. The emphasis of the conference was on the nature of training in academic departments and field settings. The meetings were organized largely around discussions of six different "training models": community mental health, community development and systems, intervention and prevention models, social change models, social ecology and environmental models, and applied urban and social psychology. Each of these "model groups" has led to an explication of a set of conceptions, methodologies, problems, issues, and training suggestions, which, together with a number of other topical papers and descriptions of individual training programs, now comprises an important volume on *Community Psychology in Transition* (Iscoe, Bloom, & Spielberger, 1977).

The editors of the Austin volume have also compiled a set of specific program descriptions written by a national sample of community psychologists currently engaged in active training programs, primarily at the graduate level. Each respondent has described at least seven different aspects of the program in which she or he is involved, including its ideology and value base, its goals and objectives, the unit of study (i.e., level of intervention), its knowledge and research base, technology and skills required, content areas of prime interest, format or program organization and place in the departmental and/or university structure, as well as any other important aspects of the program. The book fairly well represents available formal training in community psychology at the time of its publication.

Analysis of the many program descriptions and models for community psychology presented in the Austin Conference report must lead to the conclusion that the specific value/goals and methods of one community psychologist are not necessarily those of another. The field cannot be thought of as building a monolithic discipline-based panacea for all problems in living. To understand community psychology we must recognize that its varieties are based on many different values and goals that cannot be hidden by the language of social science. We must actively pursue clarification of value differences, not as truths, but what they really are: different beliefs about the kind of society one wishes to work toward (Rappaport, 1977). The variety of models and training programs presented at the Austin Conference underscores that viewpoint, which has also been emphasized throughout this book.

If one is to avoid an "error of logical typing," such considerations as the above must be kept constantly in mind. For professional training programs this means that both students and faculty need to be well grounded in an explicitly open and ongoing reconsideration of their own social values. One cannot know if one's level of analysis is appropriate unless one steps back and examines the values and goals that motivate it. Honest self-appraisal is necessary and requires the skills of value analysis, only possible when a training program is soundly based in an historical, philosophical, and sociological understanding of itself and its community. Every intervention project must be continually reviewed for consistency in light of the values it verbalizes, questioned as to whether or not the strategies and tactics of social intervention are consistent with those verbalized values, and must continually include the view of the very people at whom it is aimed. *Such considerations must be made co-equal with technological, research design, and content skills and knowledge if community psychology is to be more than a first-order change within professional psychology.*

Current Themes Expressed at Austin

Despite the differing values of the various models and specific training programs discussed at Austin, there were a number of common concerns for the field as a whole. One overarching conceptual problem for community psychology appears to be how to deal with the question "What is a system?" Many at Austin suggested that the answer is to be found in interdisciplinary contacts that will help to transcend our traditional preoccupation with individuals. In some ways there is almost a naive faith in interdisciplinary contact, and sometimes one must wonder if it is not based on our ignorance of other fields. We may well be disappointed; although interdisciplinary work is desirable, it is not likely to answer all our questions.

A more specific variant of the concern with "systems" revolves around the question "How can environment be defined and understood?" Community psychology seems to be seeking conceptions of enviroments that are not so micro as the "discriminant stimuli" of behaviorists, nor so global as the "social forces" of historians. Community psychologists are looking for a set of referents that come between the person and the environment: "How do history, social forces, systems, and environments impinge on individuals?"

The above concerns led many at Austin to the common theme of "person-environment fit," as described throughout this volume. The idea means different things to different people. It is expressed in terms such as strength building, new behavioral repertoires, alternatives for coping, and enhancement of skills. The idea of strength building as expressed at Austin had at least three different meanings. One is skills training, a second is enhancement of development, and a third, which is very different, involves not training so much as discovering existing strengths in a person or a community, and supporting those strengths by means of access to resources. It implies that differences among people and communities may be desirable, and that the resources of a society should not be allocated on the basis of a single standard of competence. Although many at Austin did not

focus on this latter orientation, it is the one emphasized in this volume.

Chinsky (1977) has noted several additional "themes" which ran through the Austin Conference. Each of these, posed in the form of questions to be addressed, may be viewed to suggest specific kinds of courses and experiences required of our training programs. It is only by inclusion of such experiences in the training of community psychologists that the faculty as well as the students can begin to answer the questions raised. Table XI-5 lists several of these "themes."

A reading of the table will indicate a kind of "renaissance-person" as the ideal output from our professional training programs. It is reasonable to expect that not all students will experience all the possible courses and varieties of practicum experience suggested by Table XI-5, but that the ideal program will encourage individual students to use the resources of both their university setting and their local communitity. The aim is not to make all students come out looking exactly alike, but rather to train a set of professionals with a variety of competencies. Taken together the discipline must deal with a broader set of responsibilities and skills than will be found in any one person. The constant threads of any single program, and of the field as a whole, must lie in an emphasis on description and evaluation of social interventions. *It is the unique combination of collaborative social intervention and value analysis, together with careful description and evaluation, which may be the special province of a community psychology.* This model for training comes closest to what Fairweather has termed "experimental social innovation" (see Chapter VI), and emphasizes what Price (1975b) calls "transfer of competencies to members of the host community."

One of the most important, if intangible, outcomes of the Austin Conference is difficult to capture on paper. Many who attended have reported an increasing sense of comradery, a "sense of community," and of mutual excitement. Many who had never met one another began to talk of excitement in communication with each other. This was very much unlike a

TABLE XI-5 Themes from Austin and implied curriculum needs for professional training programs.

Some Themes* from the Austin Conference which Require Attention in Our Professional Training Programs	Implied Curriculum Needs for Professional Training Programs
1. What is "change?" How can change be induced and evaluated at multiple levels? What are the effects of various kinds of social change, both intended and unintended? What methodologies (statistical and research design) are appropriate to community psychology?	1. Conceptual courses in change, viewed from multiple perspectives, levels, and disciplines (including but not limited to psychology).
2. What is power? How can power be understood from a psychological, economic and political perspective.	2. Experience with a variety of established and grass-roots organizations and people at multiple levels in the existing power hierarchy. Student placement in government, health, education, legal and welfare agencies, as well as local grass-roots and informal organizations.
3. What is the proper relationship between professionals and the multiple communities of society; and what strategies and tactics of social intervention does this imply?	3. Courses in value analysis, philosophy, sociology, law, urban planning, and ethics.
4. How can we turn our experiences in communities and our expressed values inward to create changes in our own settings? To whom shall we communicate and be responsible—other professionals or the lay community?	4. Program evaluation-methodological courses tied to action programs.
5. How can settings be understood as multidimensional sets of interrelationships, rather than in simple linear terms? What are the implications of a person-environment fit (ecological model of man) instead of one based on the ideal or single standard of competence?	5. Courses in multivariate statistical procedures for data analysis and research designs which provide models for longitudinal research in the natural environment.
6. How can we use the concepts of historical and cultural development to understand the ties between the present, the future, and the past in terms of social forces, both local and national?	6. Courses in applying anthropological analysis and concepts of cultural relatively, social ecology, and social systems analysis. Training in the application of historical analysis to an understanding of current social forces at the societal as well as the local level, including the social history of specific settings, agencies, and neighborhoods.
7. How can data be translated into actions and results? How can understanding from current research be shared with local communities rather than aggrandized in jargon?	7. A variety of practicum courses exploring different strategies and tactics of social intervention, including data-based strategies, diffusion of innovations, and public education.

*Adapted from Chinsky (1977).

typical professional convention or conference. There seemed to be a different quality of communication among the participants. For many this was the first face-to-face meeting with members of a "reference group."

Community psychology in most university settings is represented by only a few individuals, rarely more than two or three in a large academic department, and often only one faculty member who is a part of some other program, usually in clinical or social psychology. This is not unusual for may subdisciplines of psychology because psychology itself is a very wide-ranging field. People specializing in perception or quantitative methods, for example, are often also relatively alone in their special interests, especially in departments which attempt to represent on their faculty the broad spectrum of psychology. Community psychologists, however, are somewhat unique in that they have few traditions of their own to rely on for identification and support. The area itself has only existed for little more than a decade. Moreover, the very subject matter of community psychology requires active involvement with other people, necessitating large amounts of human, if not material resources, and high risk of "failure," in the usual academic sense. Retreat to the lonely laboratory, where one can, despite colleagues, pursue one's interests, is hardly possible in an area whose domain is the community.

In addition, in many ways community psychology is a kind of social conscience for the discipline as a whole, and as such it is often viewed as an annoying stimulus for self-examination. For such a field, especially to the extent that it goes against traditional role models and values, a reference group of like-minded colleagues is essential, even for the most independent of scientists. This may turn out to be what was most beneficial from the Austin Conference. It became clear to many that despite their own relative isolation from the other professionals in their individual academic departments, a national reference group of people who are starting from at least some of the same assumptions, and who share some common value/goals may exist. There is, in the words of Seymour Sarason, a "network" of people who have begun to establish lines of professional and personal communication. This network is of importance to the future of community psychology as a social movement. It is with these lines of communication, both formal and informal, as well as with the type of training and intervention programs in which the members engage, that the future of community psychology rests.

REFERENCES

REFERENCES

Abram, R. E., & Rosinger, G. Behavioral science applications in environmental quality. *The Journal of Environmental Education*, 1972, *4*, 1–6.

Albee, G. W. *Mental health manpower trends*. New York: Basic Books, 1959.

Albee, G. W. Needed—A revolution in caring for the retarded. *Trans-Action*, January/February, 37–42, 1968(a).

Albee, G. W. Conceptual models and manpower requirements in psychology. *American Psychologist, 23*, 317–320, 1968(b).

Albee, G. W. The relation of conceptual models of disturbed behavior to institutional and manpower requirements. In F. N. Arnhoff, E. A. Rubinstein, & J. C. Speisman (Eds.), *Manpower for mental health*. Chicago: Aldine, 1969.

Alden, L. Psychiatric atmosphere and patient behavior change. Unpublished doctoral dissertation. University of Illinois at Urbana-Champaign, 1975.

Alden, L., Rappaport, J., & Seidman, E. College students as interventionists for primary-grade children: A comparison of structured academic and companionship programs for children from low-income families. *American Journal of Community Psychology*, 1975, *3*, 261–271.

Alinsky, S. D. *Rules for radicals*. New York: Random House, 1971.

Allen, G. J., Chinsky, J. M., Larcen, S. W., Lochman, J. E., & Sellinger, H. E. *Community psychology and the schools: A behaviorally oriented multi-level preventive approach*. Potomac, Md.: Erlbaum, 1976.

Allerhand, M. E., & Lake, G. New careerists in community psychology and mental health. In S. E. Golann & C. Eisdorfer (Eds.), *Handbook of community mental health*. New York: Appleton-Century-Crofts, 1972.

Altrocchi, J. Mental health consultation. In S. E. Golann & C. Eisdorfer (Eds.), *Handbook of community mental health*. New York: Appleton-Century-Crofts, 1972.

Amir, Y. Contact hypothesis in ethnic relations. *Psychological Bulletin*, 1969, *71*, 319–342.

Anderson, C. H. *The political economy of social class*. Englewood Cliffs, N.J.: Prentice Hall, 1974.

Anthony, W. A., Buell, G. J., Sharratt, S., & Althoff, M. E. Efficacy of psychiatric rehabilitation. *Psychological Bulletin*, 1972, *78*, 447–456.

Ares, C., Rankin, A., & Sturz, H. The Manhattan bail project: An interim report on the use of pre-trial parole. *New York University Law Review*, 1963, *38*, 67–95.

Arnhoff, F. N., Rubinstein, E. H., & Speisman, J. C. *Manpower for mental health*. Chicago: Aldine, 1969.

Atthowe, J. M., & Krasner, L. Preliminary report on the application of contingent reinforcement procedures (token economy) on a "chronic" psychiatric ward. *Journal of Abnormal Psychology*, 1968, *73*, 37–43.

Ayllon, T., & Azrin, N. *The token economy: A motivational system for therapy and rehabilitation*. New York: Appleton-Century-Crofts, 1968.

Bailey, W. C. An evaluation of one hundred reports. In L. Radzinowicz & M. E. Wolfgang (Eds.), *The criminal in confinement* (Vol. III). New York: Basic Books, 1971.

Bandura, A. Influence of models' reinforcement contingencies on the acquisition of imitative responses. *Journal of Personality and Social Psychology*, 1965, *1*, 589–595.

Bandura, A. Behavioral psychotherapy. *Scientific American*, 1967, *216*, 78–86.

Bandura, A. A social learning interpretation of psychological disfunctions. In P. London, & D. Rosenhan, *Foundations of abnormal psychology*. New York: Holt, Rinehart and Winston, 1968.

Bandura, A. *Principles of behavior modification*. New York: Holt, Rinehart and Winston, 1969.

Bandura, A. Psychotherapy based upon modeling principles. In A Bergin & S. Garfield (Eds.), *Handbook of psychotherapy and behavior change*. New York: Wiley, 1971.

Bandura, A., & Walters, R. H. *Social learning and personality development*. New York: Holt, Rinehart and Winston, 1963.

Banfield, E. C. *The unheavenly city: The nature and future of our urban crisis*. Boston: Little, Brown & Co., 1968.

Baratz, J. C. A bi-dialectal task for determining language proficiency in economically disadvantaged Negro children. *Child Development, 40*, 889–901, 1969(a).

Baratz, J. C. Teaching reading in an urban Negro school system. In J. C. Baratz & R. W. Shuy (Eds.), *Teaching black children to read*. Washington, D.C.: Center for Applied Linguistics, 1969(b).

Baratz, J. C., & Shuy, R. W. (Eds.) *Teaching black children to read*. Washington D.C.: Center for Applied Linguistics, 1969.

Baratz, S., & Baratz, J. C. Early childhood intervention: The social science base of institutional racism. *Harvard Educational Review*, 1970, *40*, 29–50.

Barber, T. X., & Silver, M. J. Fact, fiction and the experimenter bias effect. *Psychological Bulletin Monograph*, 1968, *70*, Part 2.

Bard, M. Extending psychology's impact through existing community institutions. *American Psychologist*, 1969, *24*, 610–612.

Bard, M. *Training police as specialists in family crisis intervention*. Washington, D.C.: National Institute of Law Enforcement and Criminal Justice, U.S. Government Printing Office, 1970.

Bard, M. The role of law enforcement in the helping system. *Community Mental Health Journal*, 1971, *7*, 151–160.

Bard, M., & Berkowitz, B. Training police as specialists in family crisis intervention: A community psychology action program. *Community Mental Health Journal*, 1967, *3*, 315–317.

Barker, R. G. *Ecological psychology: Concepts and methods for studying the environment of human behavior*. Stanford, Calif.: Stanford University Press, 1964.

Barker, R. G., & Gump, P. V. *Big school, small school*. Stanford, Calif.: Stanford University Press, 1964.

Barker, R. G., & Schoggen, P. *Qualities of community life*. San Francisco: Jossey-Bass, 1973.

Baron, R., & Feeney, F. The Sacramento County Probation Department 602 Diversion Project (1973). Abstracted in J. Mullen, *Pre-trial services: An evaluation of policy related research*. Cambridge, Mass.: ABT Associates, 1974.

Baron, R., Feeney, F., & Thornton, W. Preventing delinquency through diversion: The Sacramento County 601 diversion project. *Federal Probation*, 1973, *37*, 13–18.

Bateson, G. *Steps to an ecology of mind*. New York: Chandler, 1972.

Bayley, N. On the growth of intelligence. *American Psychologist*, 1955, *10*, 805–818.

Bayley, N. Research in child development: A longitudinal perspective. *Merrill-Palmer Quarterly*, 1965, *11*, 183–208.

Bazelon, D. L. Psychologists in corrections—Are they doing good for the offender or well for themselves? In S. L. Brodsky (Ed.), *Psychologists in the criminal justice system*. Urbana, Ill.: University of Illinois Press, 1973.

Beck, J. C., Gelineau, V. A., & Kanter, D. Follow-up study of chronic patients "treated" by college case-aide volunteers. *American Journal of Psychiatry*, 1963, *120*, 269–271.

Becker, C. Everyman his own historian. *Essays on history and politics*. New York: Appleton-Century-Crofts, 1935.

Becker, H. S. *Outsiders*. New York: Free Press, 1963.

Becker, W. C. *Parents are teachers: A child management program*. Champaign, Ill.: Research Press, 1971.

Becker, W. C., Arnold, C. A., Madsen, C. H., & Thomas, D. R. The contingent use of teacher attention and praise in reducing classroom behavior problems. *Journal of Special Education,* 1967, *1,* 287–307.

Beckhard, R. *Organization development—strategies and models.* Cambridge, Mass.: Addison-Wesley, 1969.

Beers, C. W. *A mind that found itself.* New York: Doubleday, 1921. 5th ed. (Originally published in 1908.)

Bem, D., & Allen, A. On predicting some of the people some of the time: The search for cross-situational consistencies in behavior. *Psychological Review,* 1974, *81,* 506–520.

Bennett, C. C., Anderson, L. S., Cooper, S., Hassol, L., Klein, D. C., & Rosenblum, G. (Eds.) *Community psychology: A report of the Boston conference on the education of psychologists for community mental health.* Boston: Boston University Press, 1966.

Bennis, W. G. *Changing organizations.* New York: McGraw-Hill, 1966.

Berck, P. Preparing elementary school children for junior high: An inter-personal problem-solving intervention. Unpublished masters' thesis, University of Illinois at Urbana-Champaign, 1976(a).

Berck, P. Building community strengths: A model for conceptualizing and implementing social change. Unpublished manuscript, University of Illinois at Urbana-Champaign, 1976(b).

Bereiter, C. A nonpsychological approach to early compensatory education. In M. Deutsch, I. Katz, & A. R. Jensen (Eds.), *Social class, race and psychological development.* New York: Holt, Rinehart and Winston, 1968.

Bereiter, C. An academic preschool for disadvantaged children: Conclusions from evaluation studies. In J. Stanley (Ed.), *Preschool programs for the disadvantaged: Five experimental approaches to early childhood education.* Baltimore: Johns Hopkins University Press, 1972(a).

Bereiter, C. Schools without education. *Harvard Educational Review, 42,* 390–413, 1972(b).

Bereiter, C. *Must we educate?* Englewood Cliffs, N.J.: Prentice Hall, 1973.

Bereiter, C., & Englemann, S. *Teaching disadvantaged children in the preschool.* Englewood Cliffs, N.J.: Prentice Hall, 1966.

Bergin, A. E. Some implications of psychotherapy research for therapeutic practice. *Journal of Abnormal Psychology,* 1966, *71,* 235–246.

Bergin, A. E., & Garfield, S. L. (Eds.) *Handbook of psychotherapy and behavior change: An empirical analysis.* New York: Wiley, 1971.

Berlyne, D. *Conflict, arousal and curiosity.* New York: McGraw-Hill, 1960.

Bernard, J. *The sociology of community.* Glenview, Ill.: Scott, Foresman, 1973.

Bernstein, B. Social class and linguistic development: A theory of social learning. In A. H. Halsey, J. Floud, & C. A. Anderson (Eds.), *Education, economy and society.* New York: Free Press, 1961.

Bertalanffy, L. V. *Organismic psychology and systems theory.* Worcester, Mass.: Clark University Press, 1968.

Biddle, W. W., & Biddle, L. J. *Encouraging community development: A training guide for local workers.* New York: Holt, Rinehart and Winston, 1968.

Bijou, S. W. A functional analysis of retarded development. In N. R. Ellis (Ed.), *International review of research in mental retardation* (Vol. I). New York: Academic Press, 1966.

Bijou, S. W. *Child development: The basic stage of early childhood.* Englewood Cliffs, N.J.: Prentice Hall, 1976.

Binder, A. A new context for psychology: Social ecology. *American Psychologist,* 1972, *27,* 903–908.

Bindman, A. J., & Spiegel, A. D. (Eds.), *Perspectives in community mental health.* Chicago: Aldine, 1969.

Blake, R. R., & Mouton, J. S. *The managerial grid.* Houston, Texas: Gulf, 1964.

Blake, R. R., & Mouton, J. S. *Corporate excellence through grid organization development.* Houston, Texas: Gulf, 1968.

Blanton, J. Self-study of family crisis intervention in a police unit. *Professional Psychology,* 1976, *7,* 61–67.

Blau, P., & Scott, W. R. *Formal organizations.* San Francisco: Chandler, 1962.

Bloom, B. *Community mental health: A historical and critical analysis.* Morristown, N.J.: General Learning Press, 1973.

Bloom, B. S., & Broder, B. *The problem-solving processes of college students.* Chicago: University of Chicago Press, 1950.

Boring, E. G. *A history of experimental psychology.* New York: Appleton-Century-Crofts, 1950.

Bowers, K. S. Situationism in psychology: An analysis and a critique. *Psychological Review,* 1973, *80,* 307–336.

Braginsky, B. M., Braginsky, D. D., & Ring, K. *Methods of madness: The mental hospital as a last resort.* New York: Holt, Rinehart and Winston, 1969.

Brockett, W. A. Presumed guilty: The pre-trial detainee. *The Yale Review of Law and Social Action,* 1970, *1,* 10–27.

Broden, B., Mitchell, M., Carter, V., & Hall, R. V. Effects of teacher attention on attending behavior of two boys at adjacent desks. *Journal of Applied Behavior Analysis,* 1970, *3,* 199–203.

Brodsky, S. L. *Psychologists in the criminal justice system.* Urbana, Ill.: University of Illinois Press, 1973.

Bronfenbrenner, U. Early deprivation in mammals: A cross-species analysis. In G. Newton & S. Levine (Eds.), *Early experience and behavior. The psychobiology of development.* Springfield, Ill.: Charles C. Thomas, 1968.

Bruce, P. Relationship of self-acceptance to other variables with sixth-grade children oriented in self-understanding. *Journal of Educational Psychology,* 1958, *49,* 229–238.

Bruner, J. S., & Postman, L. On perception of incongruity: A paradigm. *Journal of Personality,* 1949, *28,* 206–223.

Buckley, H. M., Muench, G. A., & Sjoberg, B. M. Effects of a college student visitation program on a group of chronic schizophrenics. *Journal of Abnormal Psychology,* 1970, *75,* 242–244.

Cairns, R. B., & Nakelski, J. S. On fighting in mice: Ontogenetic and experiential determinants. *Journal of Comparative and Physiological Psychology,* 1971, *74,* 354–364.

Caldwell, B. M. The fourth dimension in early childhood education. In R. D. Hess & R. M. Baer (Eds.), *Early education: Current theory, research and action.* Chicago: Aldine, 1969.

Campbell, D. T. Reforms as experiments. *American Psychologist,* 1969, *24,* 409–428.

Campbell, D. T. Methods for the experimenting society. Unpublished manuscript. Northwestern University, 1971.

Campbell, D. T. Introduction. In M. J. Herskovits, *Cultural relativism: Perspectives in cultural pluralism.* New York: Random House, 1972.

Campbell, D. T., & Eriebacher, A. How regression artifacts in quasi-experimental evaluation can mistakenly make compensatory education look harmful. In J. Hellmuth (Ed.), *Compensatory education: A national debate* (Vol. III): *the disadvantaged child.* New York: Brunner/Mazel, 1970.

Campbell, D. T., & Fiske, D. W. Convergent and discriminant validation by the multitrait–multimethod matrix. *Psychological Bulletin,* 1959, *56,* 81–105.

Campbell, D. T., Herskovits, M. J., & Segall, M. H. *The influence of culture on visual perception.* New York: Bobbs-Merrill, 1966.

Campbell, D. T., & Stanley, J. C. *Experimental and quasi-experimental design for research.* Chicago: Rand McNally, 1966.

Campbell, J. P., & Dunnette, M. D. Effectiveness of T-group experiences in managerial training and development. *Psychological Bulletin,* 1968, *70,* 73–104.

Campbell, J. P., Dunnette, M. D., Lawler, E. E., & Weick, K. E. *Managerial behavior, performance and effectiveness.* New York: McGraw-Hill, 1970.

Caplan, G. *Principles of preventive psychiatry.* New York: Basic Books, 1964.

Caplan, G. *The theory and practice of mental health consultation.* New York: Basic Books, 1970.

Caplan, R. B. *Psychiatry and the community in nineteenth-century America.* New York: Basic Books, 1969.

Careers in public affairs in psychology. Series of papers appearing in *American Psychologist,* 1976, *31,* 181–205.

Carr, E. H. *What is history?* New York: Random House, 1961.

Carson, R. C. *Interaction concepts of personality.* Chicago: Aldine, 1969.

Casler, L. Perceptual deprivation in institutional settings. In G. Newton & S. Levine (Eds.), *Early experience and behavior: The psychobiology of development.* Springfield, Ill.: Charles C. Thomas, 1968.

Chinsky, J. M. Nine coalescing themes at the Austin conference. In I. Iscoe, B. Bloom, & C. D. Spielberger. *Community psychology in transition.* Washington, D.C.: Hemisphere, 1977.

Chinsky, J. M., & Rappaport, J. Attitude change among college students and chronic patients: A dual perspective. *Journal of Consulting and Clinical Psychology,* 1970, *35,* 388–394.

Chinsky, J. M., & Rappaport, J. Evaluation of a technique for the behavioral assessment of nonprofessionals. *Journal of Clinical Psychology,* 1971, *27,* 400–402.

Chu, F. D., & Trotter, S. *The madness establishment: Ralph Nader's study group report on the National Institute of Mental Health.* New York: Grossman, 1974.

Cicirelli, V. G., Evans, J. W., & Schiller, J. S. The impact of Head Start: A reply to the report analysis. *Harvard Educational Review,* 1970, *40,* 105–131.

Clark (X), C. (Ed.) The white researcher in Black society. *Journal of Social Issues,* 1973, *29* (Whole No. 1).

Clark, W. Emotional problems: A major factor in retention. *Southeastern Louisiana State College Bulletin,* January, 1959, 16–17.

Clark, K. B., & Hopkins, J. *A relevant war against poverty: A study of community action programs and observable social change.* New York: Harper & Row, 1969.

Cloward, R., & Ohlin, L. *Delinquency and opportunity: A theory of delinquent gangs.* Glencoe, Ill.: Free Press, 1960.

Cohen, E. Environmental orientations: A multidimensional approach to social ecology. *Current Anthropology,* 1976, *17,* 49–61.

Cohen, H. L., & Filipczak, J. *A new learning environment.* San Francisco: Jossey-Bass, 1971.

Cohen, L. B. A two-process model of infant visual attention. *Merrill-Palmer Quarterly,* 1973, *19,* 158–180.

Cole, M., & Bruner, J. S. Cultural differences and inferences about psychological processes. *American Psychologist,* 1971, *26,* 867–876.

Coleman, J. S. *Equality of educational opportunity.* Washington, D.C.: U.S. Office of Education, 1966.

Conter, K., Seidman, E. S., Rappaport, J., Kniskern, D., & Desaulniers, G. A comparative evaluation of two college student volunteer programs by the volunteers themselves: The importance of commitment and supervision. Unpublished manuscript, University of Illinois, 1977.

Cook, P. E. (Ed.) *Community psychology and community mental health.* San Francisco: Holden-Day, 1970.

Cooke, A. *America.* New York: Knopf, 1973.

Corbett, F. J., & Levine, M. University involvement in the community. In H. Mitchell (Ed.), *The university and the urban crisis.* New York: Behavioral Publications, 1974.

Cowen, E. L. An overview and directions for future work. In E. L. Cowen, E. A. Gardner, & M. Zax (Eds.), *Emergent approaches to mental health problems.* New York: Appleton-Century-Crofts, 1967.

Cowen, E. L. The effectiveness of secondary prevention programs using nonprofessionals in the school setting. *Proceedings of the 76th Annual Convention of the American Psychological Association,* 1968, *2,* 705–706.

Cowen, E. L. Mothers in the classroom. *Psychology Today,* 1969, *2,* 36–39.

Cowen, E. L. Broadening community mental health practicum training. *Professional Psychology,* 1971, *2,* 159–168.

Cowen, E. L. Social and community interventions. *Annual Review of Psychology,* 1973, *24,* 423–472.

Cowen, E. L. President's message. *Division of Community Psychology Newsletter,* 1975, *9,* 1–2.

Cowen, E. L., Chinsky, J. M., & Rappaport, J. An undergraduate practicum in community mental health. *Community Mental Health Journal,* 1970, *6,* 91–100.

Cowen, E. L., Gardner, E. A., & Zax, M. (Eds.) *Emergent approaches to mental health problems.* New York: Appleton-Century-Crofts, 1967.

Cowen, E. L., Izzo, L. D., Miles, H., Telschow, E. F., Trost, M. A., & Zax, M. A preventive mental health program in the school setting: Description and evaluation. *Journal of Psychology,* 1963, *56,* 307–356.

Cowen, E. L., Trost, M. A., Lorion, R. P., Dorr, D., Izzo, L. D., & Isaacson, R. V. *New ways in school mental health: Early detection and prevention of school maladaption.* New York: Human Sciences, 1975.

Cowen, E. L., Zax, M., Izzo, L. D., & Trost, M. A. Prevention of emotional disorders in the school setting: A further investigation. *Journal of Consulting Psychology,* 1966, *30,* 381–387.

Cowen, E. L., Laird, J. D., & Zax, M. A college student volunteer program in the elementary school setting. *Community Mental Health Journal,* 1966, *2,* 319–328.

Cowen, E. L., Dorr, D., Clarfield, S., Kreling, B., McWilliams, S. A., Pokracki, D., Pratt, M., Terrell, D., & Wilson, A. The AML: A quick screening device for early identification of school maladaption. *American Journal of Community Psychology,* 1973, *1,* 12–35.

Craighead, W. E., Kazdin, A. E., & Mahoney, M. J. *Behavior modification: Principles, issues and applications.* Boston: Houghton Mifflin, 1976.

Craik, K. H. Environmental psychology. *Annual Review of Psychology,* 1973, *24,* 403–422.

Crandall, V. C., Katkovsky, W., & Crandall, V. J. Children's beliefs in their own control of reinforcement in intellectual-academic achievement situations. *Child Development,* 1965, *36,* 91–109.

Cronbach, L. J. The two disciplines of scientific psychology. *American Psychologist,* 1957, *12,* 671–684.

Cronbach, L. J. *Essentials of psychological testing.* (3rd ed.) New York: Harper & Row, 1970.

Cronbach, L. J. Beyond the two disciplines of scientific psychology. *American Psychologist,* 1975, *30,* 116–127.

Cronbach, L. J., & Meehl, P. E. Construct validity in psychological tests. *Psychological Bulletin,* 1955, *52,* 281–302.

Cross, S., & Renner, E. An interaction analysis of police–black relations. *Journal of Police Science and Administration,* 1974, *2,* 54–61.

Cumming, J., & Cumming, E. *Closed ranks.* Cambridge: Harvard University Press, 1957.

Cumming, E., Cumming, I., & Edel, L. Policeman as philosopher, guide and friend. *Social Problems,* 1965, *17,* 276–286.

Cundick, B. P., Gottfredson, D. K., & Willson, L. Changes in scholastic achievement and intelligence of Indian children enrolled in a foster placement program. *Developmental Psychology,* 1974, *10,* 815–820.

Cunningham, C. The trial of the Gainesville Eight: The legal lessons of a political trial. *Criminal Law Bulletin,* 1974, *10,* 215–227.

Danish, S. J., & Brodsky, S. L. Training of policemen in emotional control and awareness. *American Psychologist,* 1970, *25,* 368–369.

D'Augelli, A. R., & Chinsky, J. M. Interpersonal skills: An analogue study on the effects of members' interpersonal skills on peer ratings and group cohesiveness. *Journal of Consulting and Clinical Psychology,* 1974, *42,* 65–72.

Davidson, W. S. The diversion of juvenile delinquents: An examination of the processes and relative efficacy of child advocacy and behavioral contracting. Unpublished doctoral dissertation, University of Illinois at Urbana-Champaign, 1975.

Davidson, W. S., & Rapp, C. Child advocacy in the justice system. *Social Work,* 1976, *21,* 225–232.

Davidson, W. S., & Seidman, E. Studies of behavior modification and juvenile delinquency: A review, methodological critique and social perspective. *Psychological Bulletin,* 1974, *81,* 998–1011.

Davis, J. H. Group decision and social interaction: A theory of social decision schemes. *Psychological Review,* 1973, *80,* 97–125.

Davis, J. H., Bray, R. M., & Holt, R. W. The empirical study of social decision processes in juries. In J. Tapp & F. Levine (Eds.), *Law, justice, and the individual in society: Psychological and legal issues.* New York: Holt, Rinehart and Winston, 1976.

Davison, G. C. The training of undergraduates as social reinforcers for autistic children. In L. P. Ullmann & L. Krasner (Eds.), *Case studies in behavior modification.* New York: Holt, Rinehart and Winston, 1965.

Davison, G. C. Homosexuality: The ethical challenge. *Journal of Consulting and Clinical Psychology,* 1976, *44,* 157–162.

Dean, C. W., & Reppucci, N. D. Juvenile correctional institutions. In D. Glaser (Ed.), *Handbook of criminology.* New York: Rand McNally, 1974.

Delaney, J. A., Seidman, E., & Willis, G. Crisis intervention and the prevention of institutionalization: An interrupted time series analysis. *American Journal of Community Psychology,* 1977, *5,* in press.

Denner, B., & Price, R. H. (Eds.), *Community mental health: Social action and reaction.* New York: Holt, Rinehart and Winston, 1973.

Dennis, W. Causes of retardation among institutional children. *Journal of Genetic Psychology,* 1960, *96,* 47–59.

Dennis, W. *Children of the Créche.* New York: Appleton-Century-Crofts, 1973.

Dennis, W., & Najarian, P. Infant development under environmental handicap. *Psychological Monographs,* 1957, *71* (Whole No. 436).

Dershowitz, A. Let the punishment fit the crime. *New York Times Magazine,* December 28, 1975, p. 7.

Deutsch, C. P. Auditory discrimination and learning: Social factors. *Merrill-Palmer Quarterly,* 1964, *10,* 277–296.

Deutsch, M. The role of social class in language development and cognition. *American Journal of Orthopsychiatry,* 1965, *35,* 78–88.

Dobbs, V., & Neville, D. The effect of non-promotion on the achievement of groups matched from retained first-graders and promoted second-graders. *Journal of Educational Research,* 1967, *60,* 472–477.

Doleschel, E. Victimless crimes. *Crime and Delinquency Literature,* 1971, *3,* 254–269.

Doleschel, E., & Geis, G. *Graduated release.* Washington, D.C.: U.S. Government Printing Office, 1971.

Dollard, J., & Miller, N. E. *Personality and psychotherapy.* New York: McGraw-Hill, 1950.

Dooley, D. Selecting nonprofessional counselor trainees with the Group Assessment of Interpersonal Traits (GAIT). *American Journal of Community Psychology,* 1975, *3,* 371–383.

Driscoll, J. M., Meyer, R. G., & Schanie, C. F. Training in family crisis intervention. *Journal of Applied Behavioral Science,* 1973, *9,* 62–82.

Dubos, R. *Mirage of health: Utopias, progress and biological change.* Garden City, N.Y.: Doubleday, 1959.

Dubos, R. Recycling social man. *Saturday Review/World,* August 24, p. 8, 1974(a).

Dubos, R. *Beast or angel?* New York: Charles Scribner's Sons, 1974(b).

Duhl, L. J. A social psychiatrist's point of view. In H. E. Mitchell (Ed.), *The university and the urban crisis.* New York: Behavioral Publications, 1974.

Durant, W. *The story of civilization. Vol. I: Our oriental heritage.* New York: Simon & Schuster, 1954.

Durham, E. L. St. Leonard's house: A model in the use of ex-offenders in the administration of correction. *Crime and Delinquency,* 1974, *20,* 269–280.

Ecklein, J. L., & Lauffer, A. A. *Community organizers and social planners.* New York: Wiley, 1972.

Edelman, P. B. The Massachusetts task force reports: Advocacy for children. *Harvard Educational Review,* 1973, *43,* 639–652.

Ellsworth, R. B. *Nonprofessionals in psychiatric rehabilitation.* New York: Appleton-Century-Crofts, 1968.

Englemann, S. *Preventing failure in the primary grades.* Chicago: Science Research Associates, 1969.

Englemann, S. The effectiveness of direct instruction on IQ performance and achievement in reading and arithmetic. In J. Hellmuth (Ed.), *Compensatory education: A national debate.* (Vol. III: *The Disadvantaged child.* New York: Brunner/Mazel, 1970.

Ennis, B., & Siegel, L. *The rights of mental patients.* New York: Avon, 1973.

Epps, E. G., & Howze, G. R. *Survey of black social scientists.* New York: Russell Sage, 1971.

Epstein, C. *Intergroup relations for police officers.* Baltimore, Md.: Williams & Wilkins, 1962.

Erikson, E. H. *Childhood and society.* New York: Norton, 1950.

Etzioni, A. *Modern organizations.* New York: Prentice Hall, 1964.

Fainstein, N. I., & Fainstein, S. S. *Urban political movements: The search for power by minority groups in American cities.* Englewood Cliffs, N.J.: Prentice Hall, 1974.

Fairweather, G. W. (Ed.) *Social psychology in treating mental illness: An experimental approach.* New York: Wiley, 1964.

Fairweather, G. W. *Methods for experimental social innovation.* New York: Wiley, 1967.

Fairweather, G. W. *Social change: The challenge to survival.* Morristown, N.J.: General Learning Press, 1972.

Fairweather, G. W., Sanders, D. H., Cressler, D. L., & Maynard, H. *Community life for the mentally ill: An alternative to institutional care.* Chicago: Aldine, 1969.

Fairweather, G. W., Sanders, D. H., & Tornatzky, L. G. *Creating change in mental health organizations.* New York: Pergamon, 1974.

Fantz, R. Visual experience in infants: Decreased attention to familiar patterns relative to novel ones. *Science,* 1964, *146,* 668–670.

Farberow, N. L. Crisis, disaster, and suicide: Theory and therapy. In E. S. Schneidman (Ed.), *Essays in self-destruction.* New York: Science House. 1967.

Farina, A., Gliha, D., Boudreau, L. A., Allen, G. J., & Sherman, M. Mental illness and the impact of believing others know about it. *Journal of Abnormal Psychology,* 1971, *77,* 1–6.

Farina, A., Holland, C. H., & Ring, K. The role of stigma and set in inter-personal interaction. *Journal of Abnormal Psychology,* 1966, *71,* 421–428.

Faris, R. E. L., & Dunham, H. W. *Mental disorders in urban areas: An ecological study of schizophrenia and other psychoses.* Chicago: University of Chicago Press, 1939.

Fellows, L., & Wolpin, M. High school trainees in a mental hospital. *The use of nonprofessional personnel as a partial solution to the manpower shortage.* Camarillo, Calif.: Camarillo State Hospital, 1966.

Ferster, C. B. A functional analysis of depression. *American Psychologist,* 1973, *28,* 857–870.

Feuer, L. S. (Ed.) *Marx and Engles.* New York: Doubleday, 1959.

Fiedler, F. E. *A theory of leadership effectiveness.* New York: McGraw-Hill, 1967.

Fishbein, M., & Ajzen, I. *Belief, attitude, intention, and behavior: An introduction to theory and research.* Reading, Mass.: Addison-Wesley, 1975.

Fishman, J. R., Klein, W. L., MacLennan, B. W., Mitchell, L., Pearl, A., & Walker, W. *Training for new careers.* Washington, D.C.: President's Committee on Juvenile Delinquency and Youth Crime, 1965.

Fishman, J. R., Denham, W. H., Levine, M., & Shatz, E. O. *New careers for the disadvantaged in human service: Report of a social experiment.* Washington, D.C.: Howard University Institute for Youth Studies, 1969.

Fixsen, D. L., Phillips, E. L., & Wolf, M. M. Achievement place: The reliability of self-reporting and peer reporting and their affects on behavior. *Journal of Applied Behavior Analysis,* 1972, *5,* 19–30.

Fixsen, D. L., Phillips, E. L., & Wolf, M. M. Achievement place: Experiments in self government with pre-delinquents. *Journal of Applied Behavior Analysis,* 1973, *6,* 31–47.

Flanders, J. P. A review of research on imitative behavior. *Psychological Bulletin,* 1968, *69,* 316–337.

Flavell, J. H. *The developmental psychology of Jean Piaget.* Princeton, N.J.: D. Van Nostrand, 1963.

Fo, W. S. O., & O'Donnell, C. R. The buddy system: Relationship and contingency conditions in a community intervention program for youth with nonprofessionals as behavior change agents. *Journal of Consulting and Clinical Psychology,* 1974, *42,* 163–169.

Fo, W. S. O., & O'Donnell, C. R. The buddy system: Effect of community intervention on delinquent offenses. *Behavior Therapy,* 1975, *6,* 522–524.

Foote, C. The coming constitutional crisis in bail. *University of Pennsylvania Law Review,* 1965, *113,* 959–999.

Foucault, M. *Madness and civilization.* New York: Random House, 1965.

Frank, L. K. Projective methods for the study of personality. *The Journal of Psychology,* 1939, *8,* 389–413.

Freed, D., & Wald, P. *Bail in the United States: 1964,* U.S. Department of Justice, Washington, D.C.: U.S. Government Printing Office, 1964.

Freeman, H. E., & Weeks, H. A. Analysis of a program of treatment of delinquent boys. *American Journal of Sociology,* 1956, *62,* 56–61.

Gartner, A., Kohler, M. C., & Riessman, F. *Children teaching children.* New York: Harper & Row, 1971.

Gatchel, R. J., & Proctor, J. D. Physiological correlates of learned helplessness in man. *Journal of Abnormal Psychology,* 1976, *85,* 27–34.

Geis, G. *Not the law's business?* Washington, D.C.: U.S. Government Printing Office, 1972.

Gerbasi, K. C., Zuckerman, M., & Reis, H. T. Justice needs a new blindfold: A review of mock jury research. *Psychological Bulletin,* in press.

Gerbner, G., & Gross, L. The scary world of TV's heavy viewer. *Psychology Today,* April 1976, p. 41.

Gergin, K. J. Social psychology as history. *Journal of Personality and Social Psychology,* 1973, *26,* 309–320.

Getz, W. L., Fujita, B. N., & Allen, D. The use of paraprofessionals in crisis intervention: Evaluation of an innovative program. *American Journal of Community Psychology,* 1975, *3,* 135–144.

Gibbs, J. P. *Crime, punishment and deterrence.* New York: Elsevier, 1975.

Ginsburg, H. *The myth of the deprived child: Poor children's intellect and education.* Englewood Cliffs, N.J.: Prentice Hall, 1972.

Glaser, D. Architectural factors in isolation promotion in prisons. In J. F. Wohlwill & D. H. Carson, *Environment and the social sciences: Perspectives and applications.* Washington, D.C.: American Psychological Association, 1972.

Glaser, N., & Moynihan, D. P. *Beyond the melting pot.* Cambridge, Mass.: MIT Press, 1963.

Glidewell, J. C. Priorities for psychologists in community mental health. In G. Rosenblum (Ed.), *Issues in community psychology and preventive mental health.* New York: Behavioral Publications, 1971.

Glidewell, J. C., Gildea, C. L., & Kaufman, M. K. The preventive and therapeutic effects of two school mental health programs. *American Journal of Community Psychology,* 1973, *1,* 295–329.

Glueck, S., & Glueck, E. *Unraveling juvenile delinquency.* Cambridge, Mass.: Harvard University Press, 1951.

Glueck, S., & Glueck, E. *Toward a typology of juvenile offenders.* New York: Grunne and Stratton, 1971.

Goffman, E. *Asylums.* Garden City, N.Y.: Doubleday, 1961.

Golann, S. E. (Ed.) *Coordinate index reference guide to community mental health.* New York: Behavioral Publications, 1969.

Golann, S. E. Community psychology and mental health: An analysis of strategies and a survey of training. In I. Iscoe & C. D. Spielberger (Eds.), *Community psychology: Perspectives in training and research.* New York: Appleton-Century-Crofts, 1970.

Golann, S. E., & Eisdorfer, C. (Eds.) *Handbook of community mental health.* New York: Appleton-Century-Crofts, 1972.

Goldenberg, I. I. *Build me a mountain: Youth, poverty and the creation of new settings.* Cambridge, Mass.: MIT Press, 1971.

Goldenberg, I. I. The relationship of the university for the community: Implications for community mental health programs. In H. E. Mitchell (Ed.), *The university and the urban crisis.* New York: Behavioral Publications, 1974.

Goldfarb, R. *Ransom: A critique of the American bail system.* New York: Harper & Row, 1965.

Goldstein, A. P. *Structured learning therapy: Toward a psychotherapy for the poor.* New York: Academic Press, 1973.

Goldstein, A. P., & Sorcher, M. Changing managerial behavior by applied learning techniques. *Training and Development Journal,* 1973, *27,* 36–39.

Goldston, S. E. (Ed.) *Concepts of community psychiatry: A framework for training.* Bethesda, Md.: U.S. Department of Health, Education and Welfare, Public Health Service Publication No. 1319, 1965.

Goodman, G. An experiment with companionship therapy: College students and troubled boys—assumptions, selection and design. *American Journal of Public Health,* 1967, *57,* 1772–1777.

Goodman, G. Systematic selection of therapeutic talent: The group assessment of interpersonal traits. In S. E. Golann & C. Eisdorfer (Eds.), *Handbook of Community Mental Health.* New York: Appleton-Century-Crofts, 1972(a).

Goodman, G. *Companionship therapy: Studies of structural intimacy.* San Francisco: Jossey-Bass, 1972(b).

Goodman, K. S. Dialect barriers to reading comprehension. In J. C. Baratz & R. W. Shuy (Eds.), *Teaching black children to read.* Washington, D.C.: Center for Applied Linguistics, 1969.

Goodnow, J. J. A test of milieu effects with some of Piaget's tasks. *Psychological Monographs,* 1962, *76* (No. 555), 1–22.

Gordon, D. M. Recession is capitalism as usual. *New York Times Magazine,* April 27, 1975, p. 18.

Graziano, A. M. Clinical innovation and the mental health power structure: A social case history. *American Psychologist,* 1969, *24,* 10–18.

Gray, S. W., & Klaus, R. A. An experimental preschool program for culturally deprived children. *Child Development,* 1965, *36,* 887–898.

Gray, S. W., & Klaus, R. A. The early training project: A seventh year report. *Child Development,* 1970, *41,* 909–924.

Gray, S. W., Klaus, R. A., Miller, J. O., & Forrester, B. J. *Before first grade.* New York: Teachers College Press, Columbia University, 1966.

Greely, A. M. The rediscovery of diversity. *The Antioch Review,* 1971, *31* (Whole No. 3).

Greenberg, D. F. Problems in community corrections. *Issues in Criminology,* 1975, *10,* 1–33.

Greenfield, P. M. On culture and conservation. In J. S. Bruner, R. Olver, & P. M. Greenfield (Eds.), *Studies in cognitive growth.* New York: Wiley, 1966.

Greenough, W. T. Enduring brain effects of differential experience and training. In M. R. Rosenzweig & E. L. Bennet (Eds.), *Neural mechanisms of learning and memory.* Cambridge, Mass.: MIT University Press, 1976.

Greir, C. *The solution as part of the problem*. New York: Harper and Row, 1973.

Grobb, G. N. *Mental institutions in America: Social policy to 1875*. New York: Free Press, 1973.

Gross, T. R. Understanding adolesence and doing youth work: Program ideas. Unpublished Doctor of Psychology Professional Report. University of Illinois at Urbana-Champaign, 1975.

Grosser, C. Manpower development programs. In C. Grosser, W. E. Henry, & J. G. Kelly (Eds.), *Nonprofessionals in the human services*. San Francisco: Jossey-Bass, 1969.

Gruenberg, E. M. The social breakdown syndrome—some origins. *American Journal of Psychiatry*, 1967, *123*, 12–20.

Gruver, G. G. College students as therapeutic agents. *Psychological Bulletin*, 1971, *76*, 111–127.

Guerney, B. G. (Ed.) *Psychotherapeutic agents: New roles for nonprofessionals, parents and teachers*. New York: Holt, Rinehart and Winston, 1969.

Gump, P. V. Big schools, small schools. In R. H. Moos & P. M. Insel (Eds.), *Issues in social ecology*. Palo Alto, Calif.: National Press Books, 1974.

Gurin, G., & Gurin, P. Expectancy theory in the study of poverty. *Journal of Social Issues*, 1970, *26*, 83–104.

Gurin, P., Gurin, G., Lao, R. C., & Beattie, M. Internal-external control in the motivational dynamics of Negro youth. *Journal of Social Issues*, 1969, *25*, 29–53.

Gutride, M. E., Goldstein, A. P., & Hunter, G. F. The use of modeling and role playing to increase social interaction among asocial psychiatric patients. *Journal of Consulting and Clinical Psychology*, 1973, *40*, 408–415.

Guttentag, M. Group cohesiveness, ethnic organization and poverty. *Journal of Social Issues*, 1970, *26*, 105–132.

Hall, W. S., & Freedle, R. O. A developmental investigation of standard and nonstandard English among black and white children. *Human Development*, 1973, *16*, 440–464.

Hall, W., Reder, S., & Cole, M. Story recall in young black and white children: Effects of racial group membership, race of experimenter, and dialect. *Developmental Psychology*, 1975, *11*, 628–634.

Halleck, S. L. *The politics of therapy*. New York: Science House, 1971.

Harrington, M. *The other America: Poverty in the United States*. New York: Penguin, 1962.

Harvard Educational Review, 1969, *39*, 273–356.

Hauserman, N., Walen, S. R., & Behling, M. Reinforced racial integration in the first grade: A study in generalization. *Journal of Applied Bahavior Analysis*, 1973, *6*, 193–200.

Hebb, D. O. *Organization of behavior*. New York: Wiley, 1949.

Hebb, D. O. What psychology is about. *American Psychologist*, 1974, *29*, 71–79.

Heine, R. W., & Trosman, H. Initial expectations of the doctor-patient interaction as a factor in continuance in psychotherapy. *Psychiatry*, 1960, *23*, 275–278.

Held, R., & Hein, A. Movement produced stimulation in the development of visually guided behavior. *Journal of Comparative and Physiological Psychology*, 1963, *56*, 872–876.

Heller, K. Untitled colloquium presented to the Department of Psychology, University of Illinois at Urbana-Champaign, 1970.

Hellmuth, J. (Ed.) *Compensatory education: A national debate* (Vol. III): *The disadvantaged child*. New York: Bruner/Mazel, 1970.

Herrnstein, R. J. *I.Q. in the meritocracy*. Boston: Little, Brown, 1973.

Hersch, C. From mental health to social action: Clinical psychology in historical perspective. *American Psychologist*, 1969, *24*, 909–916.

Hersch, C. Social history, mental health, and community control. *American Psychologist*, 1972, *27*, 749–754.

Hersch, P. D., Kulik, J. A., & Scheibe, K. Personal characteristics of college volunteers in mental hospitals. *Journal of Consulting and Clinical Psychology*, 1969, *33*, 30–33.

Hershenson, M. Form perception in the newborn. Paper read at Second Annual Symposium, Center for Visual Science, University of Rochester, 1965.

Hershenson, M., Munsinger, H., & Kessen, W. Preferences for shapes of intermediate variability in the newborn human. *Science*, 1965, *147*, 630–631.

Herskovits, M. J. *Cultural relativism: Perspectives in cultural pluralism*. New York: Random House, 1972.

Hess, R. D., & Baer, R. M. (Eds.) *Early education: Current theory, research and action.* Chicago: Aldine, 1969.

Hess, R. D., & Shipman, V. Early experience and socialization of cognitive modes in children. *Child Development,* 1965, *36,* 869–886.

Hirsch, J. Behavior-genetic analysis and its biosocial consequences. *Seminars in Psychiatry,* 1970, *2,* 89–105.

Hobbs, N. Mental health's third revolution. *American Journal of Orthopsychiatry,* 1964, *34,* 822–833.

Hobbs, N. Reeducation, reality and community responsibility. In J. W. Carter (Ed.), *Research contributions from psychology to community mental health.* New York: Behavioral Publications, 1968.

Hoefler, S. A., & Bornstein, P. H. Achievement place: An evaluative review. *Criminal Justice and Behavior,* 1975, *2,* 146–168.

Hollingshead, B. B., & Redlich, F. C. *Social class and mental illness: A community study.* New York: Wiley, 1958.

Holzberg, J. D. The companion program: Implementing the manpower recommendations of the joint commission on mental illness and health. *American Psychologist,* 1963, *18,* 224–226.

Holzberg, J. D., & Gewirtz, H. Changes in self-acceptance and moral judgment in college students as a function of companionship with hospitalized mental patients. *Journal of Consulting and Clinical Psychology,* 1964, *28,* 299–303.

Holzberg, J. D., & Knapp, R. H. Social interaction of college students and chronically ill mental patients. *American Journal of Orthopsychiatry,* 1965, *35,* 487–492.

Holzberg, J. D., Knapp, R. H., & Turner, J. L. Companionship with the mentally ill: Effects on the personalities of college volunteers. *Psychiatry,* 1966, *29,* 395–405.

Holzberg, J. D., Knapp, R. H., & Turner, J. L. College students as companions to the mentally ill. In E. L. Cowen, E. A. Gardner, & M. Zax (Eds.), *Emergent approaches to mental health problems.* New York: Appleton-Century-Crofts, 1967.

Holzberg, J. D., Whiting, H. S., & Lowy, D. G. Chronic patients and a college companion program. *Mental Hospital,* 1964, *15,* 152–158.

Hornstein, H. A., Bunker, B. B., Burke, W. W., Gindes, M., & Lewicki, R. J. (Eds.), *Social intervention: A behavioral science approach.* New York: Free Press, 1971.

Huessy, H. Tactics and targets in the rural setting. In S. E. Golann & C. Eisdorfer (Eds.), *Handbook of community mental health.* New York: Appleton-Century-Crofts, 1972.

Humphreys, P. The school's concern over non-promotion. *Theory into Practice,* 1965, *4,* 88–89.

Hunt, J. McV. *Intelligence and experience.* New York: Ronald Press, 1961.

Hunt, J. McV. *The challenge of incompetence and poverty.* Urbana, Ill.: University of Illinois Press, 1969.

Insel, P. M., & Moos, R. H. Psychological environments: Expanding the scope of human ecology. *American Psychologist,* 1974, *29,* 179–188.

Iscoe, I. National training conference in community psychology. *American Psychologist,* 1975, *30,* 1198–1194.

Iscoe, I., Bloom, B., & Spielberger, C. D. (Eds.) *Community psychology in transition.* Washington, D.C.: Hemisphere, 1977.

Iscoe, I., & Spielberger, C. D. (Eds.) *Community psychology: Perspectives in training and research.* New York: Appleton-Century-Crofts, 1970.

Itard, J. M. G. *The wild boy of Aveyron* (1801). Translated by G. Humphrey & H. Humphrey. New York: Appleton-Century-Crofts, 1962.

Ittelson, W. H., Proshansky, H. M., & Rivlin, L. G. The environmental psychology of the psychiatric ward. In H. M. Proshansky, W. H. Ittelson, & L. G. Rivlin (Eds.), *Environmental psychology: Man and his physical setting.* New York: Holt, Rinehart and Winston, 1970.

Ittelson, W. H., Proshansky, H. M., & Rivlin, L. G. Bedroom size and social interaction of the psychiatric ward. In J. F. Wohlwill & D. H. Carson (Eds.), *Environment and the social sciences: Perspectives and applications.* Washington, D.C.: American Psychological Association, 1972.

Jacobson, J. L., & Wirt, R. D. MMPI profiles associated with outcomes of group psychotherapy with prisoners. In J. N. Butcher (Ed.), *MMPI: Research developments and clinical applications.* New York: McGraw-Hill, 1969.

Jaensch, E. R. *Der Geqentypus*. Leipzig, E. Germany: Barth, 1938. Cited in K. Gergin, Social psychology as history. *Journal of Personality and Social Psychology,* 1973, *26,* 309–320.

Jeffery, W. E., & Cohen, L. B. Habituation in the human infant. *Advances in child development and behavior* (Vol. 6). New York: Academic Press, 1971.

Jensen, A. R. How much can we boost I.Q. and scholastic achievement? *Harvard Educational Review,* 1969, *39,* 1–123.

Jensen, A. R. *Educability and group differences*. New York: Harper & Row, 1973(a).

Jensen, A. R. *Educational differences*. London: Methuen, 1973(b).

Jensen, A. R. *Genetics and education*. New York: Harper & Row, 1973(c).

Joint commission on mental health and illness. *Action for mental health*. New York: Wiley, 1961.

Joint commission on mental health of children. *Crisis in child mental health: Challenge for the 1970's*. New York: Harper & Row, 1970.

Jones, L. *Blues people*. New York: Morrow, 1963.

Kagan, J., & Klein, R. E. Cross-cultural perspectives on early development. *American Psychologist,* 1973, *28,* 947–961.

Kalven, H. J. A report on the jury project at the University of Chicago law school. *Insurance Council Journal,* 1957, *24,* 368–381.

Kalven, J. H., & Zeisel, H. *The American jury*. Boston: Little, Brown, 1966.

Kamin, L. J. Heredity, intelligence, politics and psychology. Paper presented at the meeting of the Eastern Psychological Association, 1974(a).

Kamin, L. J. *The science and politics of I.Q.* Potomac, Md.: Erlbaum, 1974(b).

Kanter, R. M. *Commitment and community: Communes and utopias in sociological perspective*. Cambridge, Mass.: Harvard University Press, 1972.

Kaplan, M. The partial transformation of a state mental hospital into a comprehensive community mental health center: A case study of Worcester State Hospital. Unpublished Doctor of Psychology Professional Report, University of Illinois at Champaign-Urbana, 1975.

Karabel, J. Community colleges and social stratification. In E. L. Useem & M. Useem, *The education establishment*. Englewood Cliffs, N. J.: Prentice Hall, 1974.

Karlsruher, A. E. The nonprofessional as a psychotherapeutic agent: A review of the empirical evidence pertaining to his effectiveness. *American Journal of Community Psychology,* 1974, *2,* 61–77.

Karnes, M. B., Teska, J. A., & Hodgins, A. S. The effects of four programs of classroom intervention on the intellectual and language development of 4-year-old disadvantaged children. *American Journal of Orthopsychiatry,* 1970, *40,* 58–76.

Karnes, M. B., Teska, J. A., Hodgins, A. S., & Badger, I. D. Educational intervention at home by mothers of disadvantaged infants. *Child Development,* 1970, *41,* 925–935.

Karno, M., & Schwartz, D. A. *Community mental health: Reflections and explorations*. Flushing, N.Y.: Spectrum, 1974.

Kassenbaum, G., Ward, D., & Wilner, D. *Prison treatment and parole survival: An empirical assessment*. New York: Wiley, 1971.

Kaswan, J. Some modest proposals for the 1975 community psychology conference. *Pre-conference materials. National training conference in community psychology*. Austin, Texas, 1975.

Katkin, E. S. Psychological consultation in a maximum security prison: A case history and some comments. In S. E. Golann & C. Eisdorfer (Eds.), *Handbook of community mental health*. New York: Appleton-Century-Crofts, 1972.

Katkin, S., Ginsburg, M., Rifkin, M. J., & Scott, J. T. Effectiveness of female volunteers in the treatment of out-patients. *Journal of Counseling Psychology,* 1971, *18,* 97–100.

Katz, D., & Kahn, R. L. *The social psychology of organizations*. New York: Wiley, 1966.

Kazdin, A. The effect of vicarious reinforcement on attentive behavior in the classroom. *Journal of Applied Behavior Analysis,* 1973, *6,* 71–78.

Kellam, S. G., Branch, J. D., Agrawal, K. C., & Grabill, M. E. Woodlawn Mental Health Center: An evolving strategy for planning in community mental health. In S. E. Golann & C. Eisdorfer (Eds.), *Handbook of community mental health*. New York: Appleton-Century-Crofts, 1972.

Kelley, H. H. *Causal schemata and the attribution process*. Morristown, N.J.: General Learning Press, 1971.

Kelley, H. H., & Stahelski, A. J. Social interaction basis of cooperators' and competitors' beliefs about others. *Journal of Personality and Social Psychology,* 1970, *16,* 66–91.

Kelly, J. G. Ecological constraints on mental health services. *American Psychologist,* 1966, *21,* 535–539.

Kelly, J. G. Naturalistic observation in contrasting social environments. In E. P. Willems & H. L. Raush (Eds.), *Naturalistic viewpoints in psychological research.* New York: Holt, Rinehart and Winston, 1969.

Kelly, J. G. The quest for valid preventive interventions. In G. Rosenblum (Ed.), *Issues in community psychology and preventive mental health.* New York: Behavioral Publications, 1971.

Kelly, J. G. Antidotes for arrogance: Training for a community psychology. *American Psychologist,* 1970, *25,* 524–531.

Kelly, J. G., Snowden, L. R., & Muñoz, R. F. Social and community interventions. *Annual Review of Psychology,* 1977, *28,* in press.

Kelman, H. C. Compliance, identification, and externalization: Three processes of attitude change. In H. Proshansky & B. Seidenberg (Eds.), *Basic studies in social psychology.* New York: Holt, Rinehart and Winston, 1965.

Kennedy, R. E. Behavior modification in prisons. In W. E. Craighead, A. E. Kazden, & M. J. Mahoney (Eds.), *Behavior modification: Principles, issues and applications.* Boston: Houghton Mifflin, 1976.

Kesey, K. *One flew over the cuckoo's nest.* New York: Viking, 1962.

Kiesler, D. J. Some myths of psychotherapy and the search for a paradigm. *Psychological Bulletin,* 1966, *65,* 110–136.

Kiesler, D. J. Experimental designs in psychotherapy research. In A. E. Bergin & S. L. Garfield (Eds.), *Handbook of psychotherapy and behavior change: An empirical analysis.* New York: Wiley, 1971.

Killian, L. M. Social movements. In R. E. L. Faris (Ed.), *Handbook of modern sociology.* Chicago: Rand McNally, 1964.

Kipnis, K. Criminal justice and the negotiated plea. *Ethics: An International Journal of Social, Political and Legal Philosophy,* 1976, *86,* 93–106.

Kirshner Associates. *A national survey of the impacts of Head Start centers on community institutions.* Report prepared for U.S. Department of Health, Education and Welfare, 1970.

Kittrie, N. *The right to be different: Deviance and enforced therapy.* Baltimore: The Johns Hopkins Press, 1971.

Klapmuts, N. Community alternatives to prison. *Crime and Delinquency,* 1973, *5,* 305–337.

Klaus, R. A., & Gray, S. W. The early training project for disadvantaged children: A report after five years. *Monograph of the Society for Research in Child Development,* 1968, *33* (4, Serial No. 120).

Klein, W. L. The training of human service aides. In E. L. Cowen, E. A. Gardner, & M. Zax (Eds.), *Emergent approaches to mental health problems.* New York: Appleton-Century-Crofts, 1967.

Kochman, T. (Ed.) Rappn' and stylin' out. *Communication in urban black America.* Urbana, Ill.: University of Illinois Press, 1972.

Korman, M. National conference on levels and patterns of professional training in psychology: The major themes. *American Psychologist,* 1974, *29,* 441–449.

Kozol, H., Boucher, R., & Garofalo, R. The diagnosis and treatment of dangerousness. *Crime and Delinquency,* 1972, *18,* 371–392.

Kramer, J., Rappaport, J., & Seidman, E. The college student interventionist: Selection, training and outcome research. Paper presented at the annual meeting of the American Psychological Association, New Orleans, 1974.

Krasner, L., & Ullmann, L. P. *Behavior influence and personality: The social matrix of human action.* New York: Holt, Rinehart and Winston, 1973.

Krech, D., Rosenzweig, M., & Bennet, E. L. Relations between brain chemistry and problem solving among rats raised in enriched and impoverished environments. *Journal of Comparative and Physiological Psychology,* 1962, *55,* 801–807.

Kuhn, T. S. *The structure of scientific revolutions.* Chicago: University of Chicago Press (2d ed.), 1970.

L'Abate, L. (Ed.) *Models of clinical psychology.* Atlanta, Ga.: School of Arts & Sciences, Georgia State College, 1969.

Labov, W. Some sources of reading problems for Negro speakers of nonstandard English. In J. C. Baratz & R. W. Shuy (Eds.), *Teaching black children to read.* Washington, D.C.: Center for Applied Linguistics, 1969.

Labov, W. *Language in the inner city: Studies in the black English vernacular.* Philadelphia: University of Pennsylvania Press, 1974.

Labov, W., Cohen, P., Rubins, C., & Lewis, J. *A study of the non-standard English of Negro and Puerto Rican speakers in New York City.* Project No. 3288. New York: Columbia University Press, 1968.

Lafferty, H. M. Reasons for pupil failures: A progress report. *American School Board Journal,* 1948, *117,* 18–20.

Lamb, R. H., & Goertzel, V. A community alternative to county jail: The hopes and the realities. *Federal Probation,* 1975, *39,* 33–39.

Langmeyer, D., Schmuck, R. A., & Runkel, P. J. *Technology for organizational training in schools.* (Technical Report No. 2). Center for the Advanced Study of Educational Administration, University of Oregon, 1970.

Lao, R. C. Internal-external control and competent and innovative behavior among Negro college students. *Journal of Personality and Social Psychology,* 1970, *14,* 263–270.

Larcen, S. W., Selinger, H. V., Lochman, J. E., Chinsky, J. M., & Allen, G. J. Implementation and evaluation of a multilevel preventive mental health program in a school system. Invited address, Philip A. Goodwin Research Award, Meeting of the American Psychological Association, New Orleans, 1974.

Latané, B., & Darley, J. M. *The unresponsive bystander: Why doesn't he help?* New York: Appleton-Century-Crofts, 1970.

Lazarus, A. *Behavior therapy and beyond.* New York: McGraw-Hill, 1971.

Leary, T. *Interpersonal diagnosis of personality.* New York: Ronald Press, 1957.

Leask, J., Haber, R. N., & Haber, R. B. Eidetic imagery in children: II. Longitudinal and experimental results. *Psychonomic Monograph Supplements,* 1969, 3 (Whole No. 35).

Lefcourt, H. M. Internal versus external control of reinforcement: A review. *Psychological Bulletin,* 1966, *65,* 206–220.

Lefcourt, H. M. Internal versus external control of reinforcement revisited: Recent developments. In B. A. Maher (Ed.), *Progress in experimental research in personality.* (Vol. 6). New York: Academic Press, 1972.

Leifer, R. *In the name of mental health: The social functions of psychiatry.* New York: Science House, 1969.

Lerman, P. Evaluating the outcome of institutions for delinquents. *Social Work,* 1968, *13,* 55–64.

Levine, C. Impact of work with mental patients on student volunteers. *Journal of Human Relations,* 1966, *14,* 422–433.

Levine, M., & Graziano, A. M. Intervention programs in elementary schools. In S. E. Golann & C. Eisdorfer (Eds.), *Handbook of community mental health.* New York: Appleton-Century-Crofts, 1972.

Levine, M., & Levine, A. *A social history of helping services: Clinic, court, school and community.* New York: Appleton-Century-Crofts, 1970.

Levinstein, P. Cognitive growth in preschoolers through stimulation of verbal interaction with mothers. Paper presented at the annual meeting of the American Orthopsychiatric Association, New York, 1969.

Lewin, K. *Principles of topological psychology.* New York: McGraw-Hill, 1935.

Liberman, R. Police as a community mental health resource. *Community Mental Health Journal,* 1969, *5,* 111–120.

Liebow, E. *Tally's corner: A study of Negro street cornermen.* Boston: Little, Brown, 1967.

Likert, R. *New patterns of management.* New York: McGraw-Hill, 1961.

Lindemann, E. Symptomatology and management of acute grief. *American Journal of Psychiatry,* 1944, *101,* 141–418.

Lindquist, C. U., & Rappaport, J. Selection of college student therapeutic agents: Further analysis of the GAIT technique. *Journal of Consulting and Clinical Psychology,* 1973, *41,* 316.

Lippitt, G. L. *Organizational renewal.* New York: Appleton-Century-Crofts, 1969.

Lipton, D., Martinson, R., & Wilkes, J. *Effectiveness of correctional treatment: A survey of treatment evaluation studies.* New York: Praeger, 1975.

Litman, R. E., Farberow, N. L., Schneidman, E. S., Heilig, S. M., & Kramer, J. A. Suicide-prevention telephone service. *Journal of the American Medical Association,* 1965, *192,* 107–111.

Livermore, J. M., Malmquist, C. P., & Meehl, P. E. On the justifications for civil commitment. *University of Pennsylvania Law Review,* 1968, *117,* 75–96.

Loban, W. D. *The language of elementary school children.* Champaign, Ill.: National Council of Teachers of English, 1963.

Loban, W. D. *Problems in oral English.* Champaign, Ill.: National Council of Teachers of English, 1966.

Loevinger, J. Objective tests as instruments of psychological theory. *Psychological Reports,* 1957, *3,* 635–694.

London, P. *The modes and morals of psychotherapy.* New York: Holt, Rinehart and Winston, 1965.

London, P. *Behavior control.* New York: Harper & Row, 1969.

Lorion, R. P. Socioeconomic status and traditional treatment approaches reconsidered. *Psychological Bulletin,* 1973, *79,* 263–270.

Lorion, R. P. Patient and therapist variables in the treatment of low-income patients. *Psychological Bulletin,* 1974, *81,* 344–354.

Lundgren, E. F. *Organizational management: Systems and process.* San Francisco: Canfield, 1974.

MacLennan, B. W., Klein, W. L., Pearl, A., & Fishman, J. R. Training for new careers. *Community Mental Health Journal,* 1966, *2,* 135–141.

MacLennan, B. W., Quinn, R. D., & Schroeder, D. *The scope of community mental health consultation and education.* Washington, D.C.: U.S. Public Health Service, 1971.

Malpass, R. S., & Kravitz, J. Recognition for faces of own and other "race." *Journal of Personality and Social Psychology,* 1969, *13,* 330–335.

Mannino, F. V., & Robinson, S. E. A reference guide to the consultation literature. In F. V. Mannino, B. W. MacLennan, & M. F. Shore, *The practice of mental health consultation.* Washington, D.C.: Department of Health, Education and Welfare, 1975.

Mannino, F. V., & Shore, M. F. The effects of consultation: A review of empirical studies. *American Journal of Community Psychology,* 1975, *3,* 1–21.

March, J. G., & Simon, H. A. *Organizations.* New York: Wiley, 1958.

Martin, R. *Legal challenges to behavior modification.* Champaign, Ill.: Research Press, 1975.

Martinson, R. The paradox of prison reform (Parts I–IV). *New Republic,* 1972, *166,* issues No. 14–17.

Martinson, R. What works?—Questions and answers about prison reform. *The Public Interest,* 1974, *35,* 22–54.

Marx, A. J., Test, M. A., & Stein, L. I. Extrohospital management of severe mental illness. *Archives of General Psychiatry,* 1973, *29,* 505–511.

Massachusetts Department of Youth Services. *A strategy for youth in trouble.* Boston, 1972.

Mathews, L. Free or treat harmless mentally ill, court rules, *Los Angeles Times,* June 27, 1975, p. 1.

McAfee, O. An integrated approach to early childhood education. In J. C. Stanley (Ed.), *Preschool programs for the disadvantaged.* Baltimore, Md.: The Johns Hopkins Press, 1972.

McCall, R. B., Applebaum, M. I., & Hogarty, P. S. Developmental changes in mental performance. *Monographs of the Society for Research in Child Development,* 1973, *38* (Whole No. 3), 1–84.

McCorkle, L. W., Elias, E., & Bixby, F. L. *The Highfields story: An experimental treatment project for youthful offenders.* New York: Holt, Rinehart and Winston, 1958.

McDavid, R. I. Dialectology and the teaching of reading. In J. C. Baratz & R. W. Shuy (Eds.), *Teaching black children to read.* Washington, D.C.: Center for Applied Linguistics, 1969.

McGee, R. K. *Crisis intervention in the community.* Baltimore, Md.: University Park Press, 1974.

McGee, R. K., Richard, W. C., & Bercun, C. A survey of telephone answering services in suicide prevention and crisis intervention agencies. *Life-Threatening Behavior,* 1972, *2,* 42–47.

McGregor, D. *The professional manager.* New York: McGraw-Hill, 1967.

McLoughlin, B. (Ed.) *Studies in social movements: A social psychological perspective.* New York: Free Press, 1969.

McWilliams, S. A., & Finkel, N. J. High school students as mental health aides in the elementary school setting. *Journal of Consulting and Clinical Psychology,* 1973, *40,* 39–42.

Meehl, P. E. Psychology and the criminal law. *University of Richmond Law Review,* 1970, *5,* 1–30.

Meltzoff, J., & Kornreich, M. *Research in psychotherapy.* New York: Atherton, 1970.

Merton, R. K. *Social theory and social structure.* Glencoe, Ill.: Free Press, 1957.

Meyers, A. W., Craighead, W. E., & Meyers, H. H. A behavioral-preventive approach to community mental health. *American Journal of Community Psychology,* 1974, *2,* 275–285.

Meyers, J. K., & Bean, L. L. *A decade later: A follow-up of social class and mental illness.* New York: Wiley, 1967.

Milgram, S. *Obedience to authority: An experimental view.* New York: Harper & Row, 1974.

Miller, G. A. Psychology as a means of promoting human welfare. *American Psychologist,* 1969, *24,* 1063–1075.

Miller, G. A., Galanter, E., & Pribram, K. *Plans and the structure of behavior.* New York: Holt, Rinehart and Winston, 1960.

Millon, T. Reflections on Rosenhan's "On being sane in insane places". *Journal of Abnormal Psychology,* 1975, *84,* 456–461.

Mills, R. C., & Kelly, J. G. Cultural adaptation and ecological analogies: Analysis of three Mexican villages. In S. E. Golann & C. Eisdorfer (Eds.), *Handbook of community mental health.* New York: Appleton-Century-Crofts, 1972.

Mirels, H. L. Dimensions of internal versus external control. *Journal of Consulting and Clinical Psychology,* 1970, *34,* 226–228.

Mischel, W. *Personality and assessment.* New York: Wiley, 1968.

Mischel, W. Continuity and change in personality. *American Psychologist,* 1969, *24,* 1012–1018.

Mischel, W. Toward a cognitive social learning reconceptualization of personality. *Psychological Review,* 1973, *80,* 252–283.

Mischel, W., Zeiss, A, & Zeiss, R. Internal-external control and persistence: Validation of the Stanford Preschool Internal-External Scale. *Journal of Personality and Social Psychology,* 1974, *29,* 265–268.

Mommsen, K. G., Black Ph.D.s in the academic marketplace: Supply, demand and price. *Journal of Higher Education,* 1974, *45,* 253–267.

Monahan, J. The psychiatrization of criminal behavior. *Hospital and Community Psychiatry,* 1973, *24,* 105–107.

Monahan, J. Program in social ecology at the University of California, Irvine. Unpublished, 1974.

Monahan, J. The prevention of violence. In J. Monahan (Ed.), *Community mental health and the criminal justice system.* New York: Pergamon, 1976.

Monahan, J., Novaco, R. W., & Geis, G. Corporate violence: Research strategies for community psychology. In T. Sarbin (Ed.), *Community psychology and criminal justice.* New York: Human Sciences Press, 1977.

Moore, T. Social change and community psychology. In I. Iscoe, B. Bloom, & C. D. Spielberger (Eds.), *Community psychology in transition.* Washington, D. C.: Hemisphere Press, 1977.

Moos, R. H. Conceptualizations of human environments. *American Psychologist,* 1973, *28,* 652–665.

Moos, R. H. Systems for the assessment and classification of human environments: An overview. In R. H. Moos & P. M. Insel (Eds.), *Issues in social ecology.* Palo Alto: National Press Books, 1974(a).

Moos, R. H. *The social climate scales: An overview.* Palo Alto: Consulting Psychologists Press, 1974(b).

Moos, R. H., & Insel, P. M. (Eds.), *Issues in social ecology.* Palo Alto: National Press, 1974.

Moos, R. H., Petty, C., & Shelton R. Perceived word climate and treatment outcome. *Journal of Abnormal Psychology,* 1973, *82,* 291–298.

Mora, G. The relevance of history for the community mental health approach to children. *American Journal of Psychiatry,* 1972, *129,* 68–74.

Morris, N. *The future of imprisonment: Studies in crime and justice.* Chicago: University of Chicago Press, 1974.

Motley, C. B. "Law and order" and the criminal justice system. *Journal of Criminal Law and Criminology,* 1973, *64,* 259–269.

Mowrer, O. H. & Vattano, A. J. *Integrity groups: The loss and recovery of community.* Urbana, Ill.: Integrity Groups, 1975.

Moynihan, D. P. U.S. Department of Labor, Office of Policy Planning and Research. *The Negro family: The case for national action.* Washington, D.C.: U.S. Government Printing Office, 1965.

Moynihan, D. P. *Maximum feasible misunderstanding.* New York: Free Press, 1969.

Mullen, J. *Pre-trial services: An evaluation of policy related research.* Cambridge, Mass.: ABT Associates, Inc., 1974.

Murphy, J. J. Current practices in the use of psychological testing by police agencies. *Journal of Criminal Law, Criminology and Police Science,* 1972, *63,* 570–576.

Murphy, P. T. *Our kindly parent . . . the state.* New York: Viking, 1974.

Murrell, S. A. *Community psychology and social systems.* New York: Behavioral Publications, 1973.

Mussen, P., Conger, J. J., & Kagan, J. *Child development and personality.* New York: Harper & Row, 1963.

Nagel, S., & Weitzman, L. Sex and the unbiased jury. *Judicature,* 1972, *56,* 108–111.

National Clearinghouse for Criminal Justice Planning and Architecture. *Oklahoma corrections master plan.* Champaign, Ill., 1975.

National Council on Crime and Delinquency. The nondangerous offender should not be imprisoned. *Crime and Delinquency,* 1975, *21,* 315–322.

National Institute of Mental Health. Student volunteers at state mental hospitals. *Mental Health News Digest,* 1968, 28–29.

Neal, A. G. & Seeman, M. Organizations and powerlessness: A test of the mediation hypothesis. *American Sociological Review,* 1964, *29,* 216–226.

Neale, D. C., & Mussell, B. Effects of big brother relationships on the school-related attitudes of disadvantaged children. *Journal of Special Education,* 1968, *2,* 397–404.

Newman, O. *Defensible space: Crime prevention through urban design.* New York: Macmillan, 1973.

Newton, G., & Levine, S. (Eds.), *Early experience and behavior: The psychobiology of development.* Springfield, Ill.: Charles C Thomas, 1968.

Nichols, R. S. The influence of economic and administrative factors on the type and quality of care given to persons with psychological disease. *Working Papers in Community Mental Health,* 1963, *1,* 1–34.

Nietzel, M. T., & Dade, J. T. Bail reform as an example of a community psychology intervention in the criminal justice system. *American Journal of Community Psychology,* 1973, *1,* 238–247.

O'Connor, R. D. Modification of social withdrawal through symbolic modeling. *Journal of Applied Behavior Analysis,* 1969, *2,* 15–22.

O'Connor, R. D. Relative efficacy of modeling, shaping, and the combined procedures for modification of social withdrawal. *Journal of Abnormal Psychology,* 1972, *79,* 327–334.

O'Connor, R. D., & Rappaport, J. Application of social learning principles to the training of ghetto blacks. *American Psychologist,* 1970, *25,* 659–661.

Ojemann, R. H. Sources of infection revealed in preventive psychiatry research. *American Journal of Public Health,* 1960, *50,* 329–335.

Ojemann, R. H., Levitt, E. E., Lyle, W. H., & Whiteside, M. F. The effects of a "causal" teacher-training program and certain curricular changes on grade school children. *Journal of Experimental Education,* 1955, *24,* 95–114.

Ojemann, R. H., & Snider, B. Effects of a teacher training program in behavioral science on changes in causal behavior scores. *Journal of Educational Research,* 1964, *57,* 255–260.

O'Leary, K. D., & Becker, W. C. Behavior modification of an adjustment class: A token reinforcement program. *Exceptional Children,* 1967, *33,* 637–642.

O. M. Collective. *The organizer's manual.* New York: Bantam, 1971.

Opper, S. Intellectual development in Thai children. Unpublished doctoral dissertation. Cornell University, 1971.

Ortega, G. Discussion of Sanford's paper. Presented at the annual meeting of the Association of Governing Boards of Colleges and Universities. Washington, D.C., November 1969.

Overmier, J. B., & Seligman, M. E. P. Effects of inescapable shock upon subsequent escape and avoidance learning. *Journal of Comparative and Physiological Psychology,* 1967, *63,* 23–33.

Padilla, E. R., Boxley, R., & Wagner, N. N. The desegregation of clinical psychology training. *Professional Psychology,* 1973, *4,* 259–264.

Palmer, T. B. California's treatment program for delinquent adolescents. *Journal of Research in Crime and Delinquency,* 1971, *8,* 74–92.

Palmer, T. B. The youth authority's community treatment project. *Federal Probation,* 1974, *38,* 3–14.

Panzetta, A. F. *Community mental health: Myth and reality.* Philadelphia: Lea & Febiger, 1971.

Park, R. E., & Burgess, E. W. *Introduction to the science of sociology.* Chicago: University of Chicago Press, 1921.

Patterson, G. R. *Families: Applications of social learning to family life*. Champaign, Ill.: Research Press, 1971.

Patterson, G. R. Interventions for boys with adult problems: Multiple settings, treatments and criteria. *Journal of Consulting and Clinical Psychology*, 1974, *42*, 471–481.

Paul, G. L. *Insight vs. desensitization in psychotherapy: An experiment in auxiety reduction*. Stanford: Stanford University Press, 1966.

Paul, G. L. Behavior modification research: Design and tactics. In C. M. Franks (Ed.), *Behavior therapy: Appraisal and status*. New York: McGraw-Hill, 1969(a).

Paul, G. L. Chronic mental patient: Current status—future directions. *Psychological Bulletin*, 1969, *71*, 81–94(b).

Paul, G. L., & Bernstein, D. A. *Anxiety and clinical problems: Treatment by systematic desensitization and related techniques*. New York: General Learning Press, 1973.

Paul, G. L., & Lentz, R. J. *Psychosocial treatment of chronically institutionalized mental patients: A comparative study of milieu vs. social learning programs*. In preparation, 1976.

Paul, G. L., Tobias, L. T., & Holly, B. L. Maintenance of psychotropic drugs in the presence of active treatment programs: A "triple blind" withdrawal study with long term mental patients. *Archives of General Psychiatry*, 1972, *27*, 106–115.

Pearl, A., & Reissman, F. *New careers for the poor*. New York: Free Press, 1965.

Peck, H. S., Kaplan, S. R., & Roman, M. Prevention, treatment and social action: A strategy of intervention in a disadvantaged urban area. *American Journal of Orthopsychiatry*, 1966, *36*, 57–69.

Perlman, R. Alinsky starts a fight. In J. L. Ecklein & A. A. Lauffer. *Community organizers and social planners*. New York: Wiley, 1972.

Perlman, R., & Gurin, A. *Community organization and social planning*. New York: Wiley, 1972.

Peterson, D. R. The doctor of psychology program at the University of Illinois. *American Psychologist*, 1968, *23*, 511–516.

Peterson, D. R. *The clinical study of social behavior*. New York: Appleton-Century Crofts, 1968(b).

Phares, E. J. *Locus of control: A personality determinant of behavior*. Morristown, N.J.: General Learning Press, 1973.

Phillips, E. L. Achievement place: Token reinforcement procedures in a home style rehabilitation setting for pre-delinquent boys. *Journal of Applied Behavior Analysis*, 1968, *1*, 213–223.

Phillips, E. L., Fixsen, D. L., Phillips, E. A., & Wolf, M. M. Achievement place: Modification of the behavior of predelinquent boys with a token economy. *Journal of Applied Behavior Analysis*, 1971, *4*, 45–59.

Phillips, E. L., Fixsen, D. L., Phillips, E. A., & Wolf, M. M. Behavior shaping for delinquents. *Psychology Today*, 1973, *7*, 74–79.

Pittman, F. S., DeYoung, C., & Kalman, F. In J. Masserman (Ed.), *Current psychiatric therapies*. New York: Grune & Stratton, 1966.

Plant, W. T., & Southern, M. L. The intellectual and achievement effects of preschool cognitive stimulation of poverty Mexican-American children. *Genetic Psychology Monographs*, 1972, *86*, 141–173.

Platt, A. M. *The child savers: The invention of delinquency*. Chicago: University of Chicago Press, 1969.

Platt, J. J., Spivack, G., Altman, N., Altman, D., & Peizer, S. B. Adolescent problem-solving thinking. *Journal of Consulting and Clinical Psychology*, 1974, *42*, 787–793.

Porter, L. W., & Lawler, E. E. Properties of organization structure in relation to job attitudes and job behavior. *Psychological Bulletin*, 1965, *64*, 23–51.

Poser, E. G. The effect of therapist training on group therapeutic outcome. *Journal of Consulting Psychology*, 1966, *30*, 283–289.

Postman, N. A fable whose time has come. *New York Times Magazine*, October 12, 1975, p. 70.

President's Commission on Law Enforcement and Criminal Justice. *The challenge of crime in a free society*. Washington, D.C.: U.S. Government Printing Office, 1967.

Price, R. H. *Abnormal behavior: Perspectives in conflict*. New York: Holt, Rinehart and Winston, 1972.

Price, R. H. Program description: Training in community psychology at the University of Michigan. Unpublished, 1975.

Price, R. H., & Blashfield, R. K. Explorations in the taxonomy of behavior settings: Analysis of dimensions and classification of settings. *American Journal of Community Psychology*, 1975, *3*, 335–351.

Price-Williams, D. R. A study concerning concepts of conservation of qualities among primitive children. *Acta Psychologica,* 1961, *18,* 297–305.

Proshansky, H. M., Ittelson, W. H., & Rivlin, L. G. (Eds.), *Environmental psychology: Man and his physical setting.* New York: Holt, Rinehart and Winston, 1970.

Rabin, A. I. Behavior research in collective settlements in Israel: Infants and children under conditions of "intermittent" mothering in the kibbutz. *American Journal of Orthopsychiatry,* 1958, *28,* 577–586.

Rachman, S. Clinical applications of observational learning, imitation and modeling. *Behavior Therapy,* 1972, *3,* 379–397.

Railsback, T. Corrections: A long way to go. *Federal Probation,* 1975, *39,* 48–51.

Raine, B. Mental health consultation. Unpublished Masters Equivalency Report. University of Illinois at Urbana-Champaign, 1975.

Rainwater, L. The problem of lower-class culture and poverty-war strategy. In Moynihan, D. P. (Ed.), *On understanding poverty.* New York: Basic Books, 1968.

Rappaport, J. From Noah to Babel: Relationships between conceptions, values, analysis levels and social intervention strategies. In I. Iscoe, B. Bloom & C. D. Spielberger (Eds.), *Community psychology in transition.* New York: Hemisphere Press, 1977.

Rappaport, J., & Chinsky, J. M. Models for delivery of service from a historical and conceptual perspective. *Professional Psychology,* 1974, *5,* 42–50.

Rappaport, J., Chinsky, J. M., & Cowen, E. L. *Innovations in helping chronic patients: College students in a mental institution.* New York: Academic Press, 1971.

Rappaport, J., Davidson, W., Mitchell, A., & Wilson, M. N. Alternatives to blaming the victim or the environment: Our places to stand have not moved the earth. *American Psychologist,* 1975, *30,* 525–528.

Rappaport, J., Gross, T., & Lepper, C. Modeling, sensitivity training, and instruction: Implications for the training of college student volunteers and for outcome research. *Journal of Consulting and Clinical Psychology,* 1973, *40,* 99–107.

Rappaport, J., & O'Connor, R. D. Advocacy and accountability in consultation in the poor. *Mental Hygiene,* 1972, *56,* 39–47.

Rappaport, J., & Sorensen, J. Teaching psychology to "disadvantaged" youth: Enhancing the relevance of psychology through public education. *Journal of School Psychology,* 1971, *9,* 120–126.

Raush, H. L., & Raush, C. L. *The halfway house movement: A search for sanity.* New York: Appleton-Century-Crofts, 1968.

Redd, W. H., & Sleator, W. W. *Take charge: A personal guide to behavior modification.* New York: Random House, 1977.

Reiff, R. R. Socialization in an urban setting. Paper presented at the meeting of the American Orthopsychiatric Association, Washington, D.C., 1967.

Reiff, R. R. Social intervention and the problem of psychological analysis. *American Psychologist,* 1968, *23,* 524–530.

Reiff, R. R. Community psychology and public policy. In J. C. Glidewell & G. Rosenblum (Eds.), *Issues in community psychology and preventive mental health.* New York: Behavioral Publications, 1971(a).

Reiff, R. R. From swampcott to swamp. *Division of Community Psychology Newsletter,* 1971(b), *4,* 1–3.

Reiff, R. R., & Reissman, F. The indigenous non-professional: A strategy of change in community action and community mental health programs. *Community Mental Health Journal,* Monograph No. 1, 1965.

Reingold, H. L., Cooley, J. A., & Stanley, W. C. A method for studying exploratory behavior in infants. *Science,* 1962, *136,* 1054–1055.

Reisman, J. M. *The development of clinical psychology.* New York: Appleton-Century-Crofts, 1966.

Reitan, R. M. The neurological model. In L. L'Abate (Ed.), *Models of clinical psychology.* Atlanta, Ga.: School of Arts & Sciences, Georgia State College, 1969.

Reppucci, N. D. The social psychology of institutional change: General principles for intervention. *American Journal of Community Psychology,* 1973, *1,* 330–341.

Reppucci, N. D., & Reiss, S. Effects of operant treatment with disruptive and normal elementary school children. Paper presented at the meeting of the American Psychological Association, Miami, September, 1970.

Reppucci, N. D., & Saunders, T. J. Social psychology of behavior modification: Problems of implementation in natural settings. *American Psychologist,* 1974, *29,* 649–660.

Reppucci, N. D., & Saunders, T. J. Innovation and implementation in a state training school for adjudicated delinquents. In R. Nelson & D. Yates (Eds.), *Innovation and implementation in public organizations.* Lexington, Mass.: D.C. Heath, in press.

Ricciuti, H. N. Society's responsibilities to children and youth: Can we meet them? Review of two volumes from the Joint Commission on Mental Health of Children. *Contemporary Psychology,* 1974, *14,* 497–499.

Rice, A. K. *Productivity and social organization: The ahmedabad experiment.* London: Tavistock, 1958.

Richardson, K., Spears, D., & Richards, M. (Eds.), *Race and intelligence.* Baltimore, Md.: Penguin, 1972.

Riegel, K. F. Influence of economic and political ideologies on the development of developmental psychology. *Psychological Bulletin,* 1972, *78,* 129–141.

Riesen, A. H. (Ed.), *The developmental neuropsychology of sensory deprivation.* New York: Academic Press, 1975.

Riessman, F. The "helper" therapy principle. *Social Work,* 1965, *10,* 27–32.

Riessman, F. A neighborhood based mental health approach. In E. L. Cowen, E. H. Gardner & M. Zax (Eds.), *Emergent approaches to mental health problems.* New York: Appleton-Century-Crofts, 1967.

Riessman, F., Cohen, J., & Pearl, A. (Eds.), *Mental health of the poor.* New York: Free Press, 1964.

Riessman, F., & Popper, H. I. (Eds.), *Up from poverty.* New York: Harper & Row, 1968.

Rioch, M. J. Changing concepts in the training of therapists. *Journal of Consulting Psychology,* 1966, *30,* 290–292.

Rioch, M. J., Elkes, C., Flint, A. A., Newman, R. G., Silber, E., & Usdansky, B. S. NIMH pilot study in training mental health counselors. *American Journal of Orthopsychiatry,* 1963, *33,* 678–689.

Rist, R. C. Student social class and teacher expectations: The self-fulfilling prophecy in ghetto education. *Harvard Educational Review,* 1970, *40,* 411–451.

Robinson, D. N. Harm, offense and nuisance: Some first steps in the establishment of and ethics of treatment. *American Psychologist,* 1974, *29,* 233–238.

Robinson, W. P. The elaborated code in working class language. *Language and Speech,* 1965, *8,* 243–252.

Robison, J., & Takagi, P. Case decisions in a state parole system. California Department of Corrections, Research Division, 1968, Administrative Abstract Research Report No. 31.

Roen, S. R. Primary prevention in the classroom through a teaching program in the behavioral sciences. In E. L. Cowen, E. H. Gardner & M. Zax (Eds.), *Emergent approaches to mental health problems.* New York: Appleton-Century-Crofts, 1967.

Roesch, R. Unpublished lecture notes. Simon Fraser University, 1976(a).

Roesch, R. Predicting the effects of pre-trial intervention programs on jail populations: A method for planning and decision making. *Federal Probation,* 1976(b), *40,* in press.

Roesch, R. Pre-trial interventions in the criminal justice system. In T. Sarbin (Ed.), *Community psychology and criminal justice.* New York: Human Sciences Press, 1977(a).

Roesch, R. Does adult diversion work? The failure of research in criminal justice. *Crime and Delinquency,* 1977(b), *23,* in press.

Roman, M. Community control and the community mental health center: A view from the Lincoln Bridge. In B. Denner & R. Price (Eds.), *Community mental health: Social action and reaction.* New York: Holt, Rinehart and Winston, 1973.

Romano, J. Psychiatry, the university and the community. In E. L. Cowen, E. H. Gardner & M. Zax (Eds.), *Emergent approaches to mental health problems.* New York: Appleton-Century-Crofts, 1967.

Rose, J. B., & McLaughlin, M. H. *A portable medieval reader.* New York: Viking Press, 1949. Cited in P. H. Mussen, J. J. Conger & J. Kagan, *Child development and personality* (2nd ed.). New York: Harper & Row, 1963.

Rosen, G. Social stress and mental disease from the eighteenth century to the present: Some origins of social psychiatry. *Milbank Memorial Quarterly,* 1959, *37,* 5–32.

Rosenbaum, M. Some comments on the use of untrained therapists. *Journal of Consulting Psychology,* 1966, *30,* 292–294.

Rosenhan, D. On being sane in insane places. *Science,* 1973, *179,* 250–258.

Rosenthal, R. *Experimenter effects in behavioral research.* New York: Appleton-Century-Crofts, 1966.

Rosenthal, R., & Jacobson, L. *Pygmalion in the classroom: Teacher expectation and pupil's intellectual development.* New York: Holt, Rinehart, and Winston, 1968.

Rosenzweig, M. R. Environmental complexity, cerebral change, and behavior. *American Psychologist,* 1966, *21,* 321–331.

Ross, A. O. *The practice of clinical child psychology.* New York: Grune & Stratton, 1959.

Rothman, D. J. *The discovery of the asylum.* Boston: Little, Brown & Co., 1971.

Rothman, J. Three models of community organization practice. In National Conference on Social Welfare. *Social work practice.* New York: Columbia University Press, 1968.

Rothman, J. *Planning and organizing for social change: Action principles from social science research.* New York: Columbia University Press, 1974.

Rotter, G. S., & Rotter, N. Race, work performance, and merit rating: An experimental evaluation. Paper presented at the meeting of the Eastern Psychological Association, Philadelphia, 1969.

Rotter, J. B. *Social learning and clinical psychology.* Englewood, N.J.: Prentice Hall, 1954.

Rotter, J. B. Generalized expectances for internal versus external control of reinforcement. *Psychological Monographs,* 1966, *80* (1 Whole No. 609).

Rotter, J. B. Some implications of a social learning theory for the practice of psychotherapy. In D. J. Levis (Ed.), *Learning approaches to therapeutic behavior change.* Chicago: Aldine, 1970.

Rotter, J. B. Some problems and misconceptions related to the construct of internal versus external control of reinforcement. *Journal of Consulting and Clinical Psychology,* 1975, *43,* 56–57.

Rotter, J. B., Chance, J., & Phares, E. J. An introduction to social learning theory. In J. B. Rotter, J. Chance & E. J. Phares (Eds.), *Applications of a social learning theory of personality.* New York: Holt, Rinehart and Winston, 1972.

Rubovitz, P. C., & Maher, M. L. Pygmalion black and white. *Journal of Personality and Social Psychology,* 1973, *25,* 210–218.

Ryan, W. (Ed.), *Distress in the city: Essays on the design and administration of urban mental health services.* Cleveland: Case Western Reserve University Press, 1969.

Ryan, W. *Blaming the victim.* New York: Random House, 1971.

Salapatek, P. & Kessen, W. Visual scanning of triangles by the human newborn. *Journal of Experimental Child Psychology,* 1966, *3,* 155–167.

Salber, E. J. Community participation in neighborhood health centers. *New England Journal of Medicine,* 1970, *283,* 515–518.

Sampson, E. E. *Social psychology and contemporary psychology.* New York: Wiley, 1971.

Sanders, R., Smith, R. S., & Weinman, B. *Chronic psychosis and recovery: An experiment in socio-environmental therapy.* San Francisco: Jossey-Bass, 1967.

Sanford, N. Is the concept of prevention necessary or useful? In S. E. Golann & C. Eisdorfer(Eds.), *Handbook of Community Mental Health.* New York: Appleton-Century-Crofts, 1972.

Sarason, I. G., & Ganzer, V. Developing appropriate social behaviors of juvenile delinquents. In J. Krumboltz & C. Thoresen (Eds.), *Behavioral Counseling: Cases and techniques.* New York: Holt, Rinehart and Winston, 1969.

Sarason, S. B. *The creation of settings and the future societies.* San Francisco: Jossey-Bass, 1972.

Sarason, S. B. *The psychological sense of community: Prospects for the community psychology.* San Francisco: Jossey-Bass, 1974.

Sarason, S. B. Psychology "to the Finland Station" in "the heavenly city of the eighteenth century philosophers." *American Psychologist,* 1975, *30,* 1072–1080.

Sarason, S. B. Community psychology, networks, and Mr. Everyman. *American Psychologist,* 1976, *31,* 317–328.

Sarason, S. B., Levine, M., Goldenberg, I. I., Cherlin, D. L., & Bennett, E. M. *Psychology in community settings.* New York: Wiley, 1966.

Sarbin, T. R. A role theory perspective for community psychology: The structure of social identity. In D. Adelson & B. L. Kalis (Eds.), *Community psychology and mental health: Perspectives and challenges.* Scranton, Pa.: Chandler, 1970.

Sashkin, M., Morris, W. C., & Horst, L. A comparison of social and organizational change models: Information flow and data use processes. *Psychological Review,* 1973, *80,* 510–526.

Scarr, S., & Weinberg, R. A. IQ test performance of Black children adopted by White families. *American Psychologist,* 1976, *31,* 726–739.

Schaffer, A. S. *Bail and parole jumping in Manhattan in 1967.* New York: Vera Institute of Justice, 1970.

Schaefer, E. S., & Aronson, M. Infant education research project: Implementation and implications of a home tutoring program. Unpublished manuscript, 1970.

Scheff, T. J. *Being mentally ill.* Chicago: Aldine, 1966.

Scheff, T. J. (Ed.), *Mental illness and social processes.* New York: Harper & Row, 1967.

Schein, E. H. *Organizational psychology.* Englewood Cliffs, N.J.: Prentice Hall, 1970.

Schiff, S. K. Community accountability and mental health services. *Mental Hygiene,* 1970, *54,* 205–214.

Schiff, S. K. Free inquiry and the enduring commitment: The Woodlawn Mental Health Center, 1963–1970. In S. E. Golann & C. Eisdorfer (Eds.), *Handbook of community mental health.* New York: Appleton-Century-Crofts, 1972.

Schlenker, B. Social psychology and science. *Journal of Personality and Social Psychology,* 1974, *29,* 1–15.

Schlosman, S. L. G. Stanley Hall and the boys' club: Conservative applications of recapitulation theory. *Journal of the History of the Behavioral Sciences*, 1973, *9*, 140–147.

Schmuck, R. A., Runkel, P. J., & Langmeyer, D. Improving organizational problem-solving in a school faculty. *Applied Behavioral Science*, 1969, *5*, 455–482.

Schneidman, E. S., & Farberow, N. L. The Los Angeles suicide prevention center: A demonstration of public health feasibilities. *American Journal of Public Health*, 1965, *55*, 21–26.

Schofield, W. *Psychotherapy: The purchase of friendship*. Englewood Cliffs, N.J.: Prentice Hall, 1964.

Schur, E. M. *Crimes without victims: Deviant behavior and public policy*. Englewood Cliffs, N.J.: Prentice Hall, 1965.

Schur, E. M. *Radical non-intervention: Rethinking the delinquency problem*. Englewood Cliffs, N.J.: Prentice Hall, 1973.

Schwitzgebel, R. K., & Kolb, D. A. *Changing human behavior: Principles of planned intervention*. New York: McGraw-Hill, 1974.

Seaver, W. B. Effects of naturally induced teacher expectations. *Journal of Personality and Social Psychology*, 1973, *28*, 333–342.

Seeman, M. Alienation and social learning in a reformatory. *American Journal of Sociology*, 1963, *69*, 270–284.

Seeman, M. Social learning theory and the theory of mass society. In J. B. Rotter, J. Chance & E. J. Phares, *Applications of a social learning theory of personality*. New York: Holt, Rinehard and Winston, 1972.

Seeman, M., & Evans, J. W. Alienation and learning in a hospital setting. *American Sociological Review*, 1962, *27*, 772–783.

Seidman, E., & Rappaport, J. You have got to have a dream, but it's not enough. *American Psychologist*, 1974(a), *29*, 569–570.

Seidman, E., & Rappaport, J. The educational pyramid: A paradigm for research, training, and manpower utilization in community psychology. *American Journal of Community Psychology*, 1974(b), *2*, 119–130.

Seidman, E., Rappaport, J., & Davidson, W. S. Adolescents in legal jeopardy: Initial success and replication of an alternative to the criminal justice system. Invited address: 1976 National Psychological Consultants to Management Consulting Psychology Research Award. Meeting of the American Psychological Association, Washington, D.C., 1976.

Seligman, M. E. P. *Helplessness: On depression, development and death*. San Francisco: W. H. Freeman, 1975.

Seligman, M. E. P., & Maier, S. F. Failure to escape traumatic shock. *Journal of Experimental Psychology*, 1967, *74*, 1–9.

Seligman, M. E. P., Greer, J., & Maier, S. F. The alleviation of learned helplessness in the dog. *Journal of Abnormal and Social Psychology*, 1968, *73*, 256–262.

Shah, S. A. The criminal justice system. In S. E. Golann & C. Eisdorfer (Eds.), *Handbook of community mental health*. New York: Appleton-Century-Crofts, 1972.

Shapiro, E., & Biber, B. The education of young children: A developmental-interaction approach. *Teachers College Record*, 1972, *74*, 55–79.

Shils, E. Primordial, personal, sacred, and civil ties. *British Journal of Sociology*, June, 1957, 130–145.

Shulberg, H. C., Sheldon, A., & Baker, F. (Eds.) *Program evaluation in health fields*. New York: Behavioral Publications, 1969.

Shuy, R. W. A linguistic background for developing beginning reading materials for black children. In J. C. Baratz & R. W. Shuy (Eds.), *Teaching black children to read*. Washington, D.C.: Center for Applied Linguistics, 1969.

Sikes, M. P., & Cleveland, S. E. Human relations training for police and public policy. *American Psychologist*, 1968, *23*, 766–769.

Simon, R. J. (Ed.), *The jury system in America: A critical overview*. Beverly Hills, Calif.: Sage Publications, 1975.

Skeels, H. M. Some preliminary findings of three follow-up studies on the effects of adoption on children. *Children*, 1965, *12*, 33–34.

Skeels, H. M., & Dye, H. B. A study of the effects of differential stimulation on mentally retarded children. *Proceedings of the American Association of Mental Deficiency*, 1939, *44*, 114–136.

Skinner, B. F. *Walden two*. New York: Macmillan, 1948.

Skinner, B. F. *Beyond freedom and dignity*. New York: Knopf, 1971.

Smith, V. H. *Alternative schools: The development of options in public education*. Lincoln, Nebr.: Professional Educators Publications, 1974.

Smith, M. S., & Bissell, J. S. Report analysis: The impact of head start. *Harvard Educational Review*, 1970, *40*, 51–104.

Smith, M. B., & Hobbs, N. The community and the community mental health center. *American Psychologist*, 1966, *15*, 113–118.

Sobey, F. *The nonprofessional revolution in mental health*. New York: Columbia University Press, 1970.

Solomon, R. L., Kamin, L. J., & Wynne, L. C. Traumatic avoidance learning: The outcomes of several extinction procedures with dogs. *Journal of Abnormal and Social Psychology*, 1953, *48*, 291–302.

Spano, B. J. Causal thinking, adjustment and social perception as a function of behavioral science concepts in elementary school children. Unpublished doctoral dissertation. University of Florida, 1965.

Spencer, H. *The principles of psychology* (Vol. I). New York: Appleton, 1897.

Spitz, R. Hospitalism: An inquiry into the genesis of psychiatric conditions in early childhood. *Psychoanalytic Study of the Child*, 1945, *1*, 53–74.

Spitz, R. A. Anaclitic depression. *Psychoanalytic Study of the Child*, 1946, *2*, 313–342.

Spivack, G., & Schure, M. B. *Social adjustment of young children*. San Francisco: Jossey-Bass, 1974.

Star, S. A., & Hughes, H. M. Report on an education campaign: The Cincinnati plan for the United Nations. *American Journal of Sociology*, 1950, *55*, 389–400.

Steadman, H. Some evidence on the inadequacy of the concept and determination of dangerousness in law and psychiatry. *The Journal of Psychiatry and Law*, 1973, Winter, 909–426.

Stein, L. I., Test, M. A., & Marx, A. J. Alternative to the hospital: a controlled study. *American Journal of Psychiatry*, 1975, *132*, 517–522.

Stewart, W. On the use of Negro dialect in the teaching of reading. In J. C. Baratz & R. Shuy (Eds.), *Teaching black children to read*. Washington, D.C.: Center for Applied Linguistics, 1969.

Stollack, G. E. The experimental effects of training college students as play therapists. In B. G. Guerney (Ed.), *Psychotherapeutic agents: New roles for nonprofessionals, parents, and teachers*. New York: Holt, Rinehart and Winston, 1969.

Stone, A. A. *Mental health and law: A system in transition*. Washington, D.C.: Department of Health, Education and Welfare, 1975.

Struening, E. L., & Guttentag, M. (Eds.), *Handbook of evaluation research*. Beverly Hills, Calif.: Sage Publications, 1975.

Stuart, R. B. Behavioral contracting within the families of delinquents. *Journal of Behavior Therapy and Experimental Psychiatry*, 1971, *2*, 1–11.

Sue, S., McKinney, H., Allen, D., & Hall, J. Delivery of community mental health services to black and white clients. *Journal of Consulting and Clinical Psychology*, 1974, *42*, 794–801.

Sullivan, H. S. *The interpersonal theory of psychiatry*. New York: Norton, 1953.

Suomi, S. J., & Harlow, H. F. Social rehabilitation of isolate reared monkeys. *Developmental Psychology*, 1972, *6*, 487–496.

Susser, M. *Community psychiatry: Epidemiologic and social themes*. New York: Random House, 1968.

Swan, J. Public response to air pollution. In J. F. Wohlwill & D. H. Carson (Eds.), *Environment and the social sciences: Perspectives and applications*. Washington, D.C. American Psychological Association, 1972.

Szasz, T. S. *The manufacture of madness: A comparative study of the inquisition and the mental health movement*. New York: Harper & Row, 1970.

Szasz, T. S. *Ceremonial chemistry*. Garden City, New York: Anchor Press, 1974.

Tapp, R. B., & Tapp, J. L. Religious systems as sources of control and support. In S. E. Golann & C. Eisdorfer (Eds.), *Handbook of Community Mental Health*. New York: Appleton-Century-Crofts, 1972.

Templin, M. C. *Certain language skills in children: Their development and inter-relationships*. Minneapolis: University of Minnesota Press, 1975.

Tesse, C. F., & Van Wormer, J. Mental health training and consultation with suburban police. *Community Mental Health Journal*, 1975, *11*, 115–121.

Tharp, R. G., & Wetzel, R. J. *Behavior modification in the natural environment.* New York: Academic Press, 1969.

Thibaut, J., & Kelley, H. H. *The social psychology of groups.* New York: Wiley, 1959.

Thomas, A., & Sillen, S. *Racism and psychiatry.* New York: Bruner/Mazel, 1972.

Throop, W. F., & MacDonald, A. P. Internal-external locus of control: A bibliography. *Psychological Reports,* 1971, *28,* 175–190.

Time Magazine. Behavior mod behind the walls. March 11, 1974, 74–75.

Tischler, G. L. The effects of consumer control on the delivery of services. *American Journal of Orthopsychiatry,* 1971, *41,* 501–505.

Tornatzky, L. G. How a Ph.D. program aimed at survival issues survived. *American Psychologist,* 1976, *31,* 189–192.

Tornatzky, L. G., Fairweather, G. W., & O'Kelly, L. I. A Ph.D. program aimed at survival. *American Psychologist,* 1970, *25,* 884–888.

Trickett, E. J., Kelly, J. G., & Todd, D. M. The social environment of the high school: Guidelines for individual change and organizational redevelopment. In S. E. Golann, & C. Eisdorfer (Eds.), *Handbook of community mental health.* New York: Appleton-Century-Crofts, 1972.

Trickett, E., & Moos, R. Personal correlates of contracting environments: Student satisfaction in high school classrooms. *American Journal of Community Psychology,* 1974, *21,* 1–12.

Trimble, J. E. Say goodbye to the Hollywood Indian: Results of a nationwide survey of the self-image of the American Indian. Paper presented at the meeting of the American Psychological Association, New Orleans, 1974.

Trotter, S. Patuxent: "Therapeutic" prison faces test. *A.P.A. Monitor,* 1975, *6,* p. 1.

Turner, R. J., & Cumming, J. Theoretical malaise and community mental health. In E. L. Cowen, E. A. Gardner & M. Zax (Eds.), *Emergent approaches to mental health problems.* New York: Appleton-Century-Crofts, 1967.

Ullmann, L. P., & Krasner, L. (Eds.). *Case studies in behavior modification.* New York: Holt, Rinehart and Winston, 1965.

Ullmann, L. P., & Krasner, L. *A psychological approach to abnormal behavior.* New York: Holt, Rinehart and Winston, 1969.

Umbarger, C. C., Dalsimer, J. S., Morrison, A. P., & Breggin, P. R. *College students in a mental hospital.* New York: Grune & Stratton, 1962.

United States Department of Health, Education and Welfare. *The challenge of youth service bureaus.* Washington, D.C.: ERIC #ED083526, 1973.

United States Department of Justice. *Survey of inmates of local jails: Advance report.* Washington, D.C.: Law Enforcement Assistance Administration, 1974.

United States Department of Justice. *Public opinion regarding crime: Criminal justice and related topics.* Washington, D.C.: U.S. Government Printing Office, 1975.

U.S. Supreme Court. Baxtrom vs. Herold. *U. S. Reports,* 1966, *383,* 107.

U.S. Supreme Court. Williams vs. Florida. *Supreme Court Reporter,* 1972, *92,* 1628–1653.

Useem, E. L., & Useem, M. (Eds.), *The education establishment.* Englewood Cliffs, N.J.: Prentice Hall, 1974.

Valenti, A. C., & Downing, L. L. Differential effects of jury size on verdicts following deliberation as a function of the apparent guilt of a defendant. *Journal of Personality and Social Psychology,* 1975, *32,* 655–663.

Venezia, P. S. Unofficial probation. An evaluation of its effectiveness. *Journal of Research in Crime and Delinquency,* 1972, *9,* 149–170.

Verinis, F. S. Therapeutic effectiveness of untrained volunteers. *Journal of Consulting and Clinical Psychology,* 1970, *34,* 152–155.

Vernon, P. E. Environmental handicaps and intellectual development: Part I. *British Journal of Educational Psychology,* 1965(a), *35,* 9–20.

Vernon, P. E. Environmental handicaps and intellectual development: Part II. *British Journal of Educational Psychology,* 1965(b), *35,* 117–126.

Wachtel, P. L. Psychodynamic, behavior therapy, and the implacable experiments: An inquiry into the consistency of personality. *Journal of Abnormal Psychology,* 1973, *82,* 324–334.

Wahler, R. G., Winkel, G. H., Peterson, R. F., & Morrison, D.C. Mothers as behavior therapists for their own children. *Behavior Research and Therapy,* 1965, *3,* 113–124.

Walker, H., & Buckley, N. Programming generalization and maintenance of treatment effects across time and across settings. *Journal of Applied Behavior Analysis,* 1972, 5, 209–224.

Walton, R. E. Frontiers beckoning the organizational psychologist. *Journal of Applied Behavioral Science,* 1972, *8,* 601–629.

Watson, D. Reinforcement theory of personality and social system: Dominance and position in a group power structure. *Journal of Personality and Social Psychology,* 1971, *20,* 180–185.

Watson, R. I. A brief history of clinical psychology, *Psychological Bulletin,* 1953, *50,* 321–346.

Watson, R. I. The experimental tradition in clinical psychology. In A. J. Bachrach (Ed.), *Experimental foundations of clinical psychology.* New York: Basic Books, 1962.

Watzlawick, P., Weakland, J. H., & Fisch, R. *Change: Principles of problem formation and problem resolution.* New York: Norton, 1974.

Weick, K. E. *The social psychology of organizing.* Reading, Mass.: Addison-Wesley, 1969.

Weikart, D. P. Preschool programs: Preliminary findings. *Journal of Special Education,* 1967, *1,* 163–181.

Weikart, D. P. Relationship of curriculum, teaching, and learning in preschool education. In J. C. Stanley (Ed.), *Preschool for the disadvantaged.* Baltimore, Md.: The Johns Hopkins University, 1972.

Weikart, D. P., Rogers, L., Adcock, C., & McClelland, D. *The cognitively oriented curriculum.* Urbana, Ill.: ERIC-NAEYC.

Weiss, C. H. *Evaluation research: Methods of assessing program effectiveness.* Englewood Cliffs, N.J.: Prentice Hall, 1972.

Wenk, E. A. Schools and delinquency prevention. *Crime and Delinquency Literature,* 1974, *6,* 236–258.

Wenk, E. A., Robison, J., & Smith, G., Can violence be predicted? *Crime and Delinquency,* 1972, *18,* 393–402.

Westinghouse Learning Corporation/Ohio University. *The impact of head start: An evaluation of the effects of head start on children's cognitive and affective development* (Vols. I & II). Springfield, Va.: U. S. Department of Commerce (No. PB 184329), 1969.

Whimbey, A. Something better than Binet? *Saturday Review/World,* June 1, 1974, 50–53.

White, R. W. Motivation reconsidered: The concept of competence. *Psychological Review,* 1959, *66,* 297–333.

White, S. H. Society's responsibilities to children and youth: Can we meet them? Review of two volumes from the Joint Commission on Mental Health of Children. *Contemporary Psychology,* 1974, *14,* 499–500.

Wice, R., & Simon, R. Pre-trial release, a survey of alternative practices. *Federal Probation,* 1970, *34,* 60–63.

Wicker, A. W. Attitudes versus action: The relationship of verbal and overt behavioral responses to attitude objects. *Journal of Social Issues,* 1969(a), *25,* 41–78.

Wicker, A. W. Size of church membership and members' support of church behavior settings. *Journal of Personality and Social Psychology,* 1969(b), *13,* 278–288.

Wicker, T. *A time to die.* New York: Quadrangle, 1975.

Wiggins, J. S. *Personality and prediction: Principles of personality assessment.* Reading, Mass.: Addison-Wesley, 1973.

Wiggins, J. S., Renner, K. E., Clore, G., & Rose, R. The psychology of personality. Reading, Mass.: Addison-Wesley, 1971.

Wiggins, N., Jones, L. E., & Wasserman, R. Racial differences in the perception of faces. Unpublished study. University of Illinois at Urbana-Champaign, 1975.

Wilkinson, L. An assessment of the dimensionality of Moos' social climate scales. *American Journal of Community Psychology,* 1973, *1,* 342–350.

Willems, E. P., & Raush, H. L. (Eds.), *Naturalistic viewpoints in psychological research.* New York: Holt, Rinehart and Winston, 1969.

Williams, J. R., & Gold, M. From delinquent behavior to official delinquency. *Social Problems,* 1972, *20,* 209–229.

Wilson, J. Q. What makes a better policeman? *Atlantic Monthly,* March 1969, 129–135.

Windle, C., Bass, R. D., & Taube, C. A. PR aside: Initial results from NIMH's service program evaluation studies. *American Journal of Community Psychology,* 1974, *2,* 311–327.

Winett, R. A. Behavior modification and social change. *Professional Psychology,* 1974, *5,* 244–250.

Winett, R. A., & Winkler, R. C. Current behavior modification in the classroom: Be still, be quiet, be docile. *Journal of Applied Behavior Analysis,* 1972, *5,* 499–504.

Wohwill, J. F., & Carson, D. H. (Eds.), *Environment and the social sciences: Perspectives and applications.* Washington, D.C.: American Psychological Association, 1972.

Wolf, M. M., Phillips, E. L., & Fixsen, D. L. The teaching family: A new model for the treatment of deviant child behavior in the community. In S. Bijou & E. Ribes-Inesta (Eds.), *Behavior modification.* New York: Academic Press, 1972.

Wolfred, T. R. The crisis care center: Institutional treatment for adolescents. Doctor of Psychology Professional Report, University of Illinois at Urbana-Champaign, 1974.

Wolfred, T. R., & Davidson, W. S. Evaluation of a community based program for the prevention of delinquency: The failure of success. *Community Mental Health Journal,* 1977, in press.

Yates, A. J. Psychologists are people, too. Review of L. Krasner and L. P. Ullmann, *Behavior influence and personality. Contemporary Psychology,* 1974, *19,* 436–437.

Yates, A. J. *Behavior therapy.* New York: Wiley, 1970.

Zax, M., & Cowen, E. L. Early identification and prevention of emotional disturbance in a public school. In E. L. Cowen, E. A. Gardner & M. Zax (Eds.), *Emergent approaches to mental health problems.* New York: Appleton-Century-Crofts, 1967.

Zax, M., & Cowen, E. L. Research on early detection and prevention of emotional dysfunction in young school children. In C. D. Spielberger (Ed.), *Current topics in clinical and community psychology* (Vol. I). New York: Academic Press, 1969.

Zax, M., Cowen, E. L., Rappaport, J., Beach, D. R., & Laird, J. D. A follow-up study of children identified early as emotionally disturbed. *Journal of Consulting and Clinical Psychology,* 1968, *32,* 359–374.

Zax, M., & Specter, G. A. *An introduction to community psychology.* New York: Wiley, 1974.

Zilboorg, G. A history of medical psychology. New York: Norton, 1941.

Zimbardo, P. G. The mind is a formidable jailer: A Pirandellian prison. *New York Times Magazine,* April 8, 1973, p. 38.

Zuñiga, R. B. The experimenting society and radical social reform: The role of the social scientist in Chile's Unidad popular experience. *American Psychologist,* 1975, *30,* 99–115.

Zunker, V. G., & Brown, W. F. Comparative effectiveness of student and professional counselors. *Personnel and Guidance Journal,* 1966, *44,* 738–743.

Zurcher, L. A. The poverty board: Some consequences of "maximum feasible participation." *Journal of Social Issues,* 1970, *26,* 85–107.

Zusman, J. Some explanations of the changing appearance of psychotic patients. In E. M. Gruenberg (Ed.), *Evaluating the effectiveness of community mental health services.* New York: Milbank, 1966.

NAME INDEX

SUBJECT INDEX